ISLAM AND THE MUSLIM WORLD

No. 5

General Editor: JOHN RALPH WILLIS
Centre of West African Studies, University of Birmingham

THE DARVISHES

OR

ORIENTAL SPIRITUALISM

THE DARVISHES

OR

ORIENTAL SPIRITUALISM

BY

JOHN P. BROWN

Edited with an Introduction and Notes
by
H. A. ROSE

FRANK CASS & CO. LTD.
1968

Published by
FRANK CASS AND COMPANY LIMITED
67 Great Russell Street, London WC1
by arrangement with Oxford University Press

First edition	1868
Second edition	1927
New impression	1968

Printed in Holland by
N. V. Grafische Industrie Haarlem

AUTHOR'S PREFACE

THE object of this volume is to afford information in regard to the Belief and Principles of the Darvishes, as well as to describe their various modes of worshipping the Creator.

That the Spiritual Principles of the Darvish Orders existed in Arabia previous to the time of the great and talented Islam Prophet cannot be doubted. The historical portions of the Old and New Testaments were also well known among the Arabs, differing traditionally, however, in many respects from the narratives of the Sacred Writings; and if a conjecture may be made as to the starting-point of Islamism, we would say that it originated in the act of perfect submission of Abraham to the will of the Almighty, when he determined to offer up his son Isaac in obedience to the Divine command.

The spiritualism of the Darvishes differing in many respects from Islamism, and having its origin in the religious conceptions of India and Greece, perhaps the information I have been enabled to collect together on the subject may not be without interest to the reader. Much of this is original; and having been extracted from Oriental works, and from Turkish, Arabic, and Persian MSS., may be relied upon as strictly accurate. In procuring materials from original sources, valuable assistance has been rendered me by personal friends, members of various Darvish Orders in this capital, to whom I would here express my thanks. Notwithstanding the unfavourable opinion entertained by many—principally in the Christian world—against their religious principles, I must, in strict justice, add that I have found these persons liberal and intelligent, sincere, and most faithful friends.

In the extracts from the works of other authors, some of

whom are too well known to the public to require more than to be named by me—D'Ohsson, Sir William Jones, Malcolm, Lane, Ubicini, and De Gobineau—some differences will be perceived, mostly with regard to the estimate placed by each of these upon the character and influence of " The Darvishes " in the Mussulman world. To these eminent authors I am under great obligations, and take the present opportunity of acknowledging them.

To the kindness of Dr. Rost, the Secretary of the Royal Asiatic Society, in getting my little work through the press, I am more deeply indebted than I can here properly express.

As a book of reference, I trust that this imperfect work will prove of use ; and travellers in the East will perhaps be enabled to learn from it much that would be otherwise obscure and hidden from their knowledge. Much more could have been added to it, especially with regard to the Darvish Orders in the more distant parts of Asia, India, and Africa ; but I hope that some one more competent than myself will collect the information which was beyond my reach.

THE AUTHOR.

CONSTANTINOPLE, *October* 1867.

BARĀQ, THE ANIMAL ON WHICH THE PROPHET VISITED HEAVEN.

CONTENTS

CHAPTER V

CHAPTER VI

CHAPTER VII

CHAPTER VIII

CHAPTER IX

CHAPTER X

CHAPTER XI

CHAPTER XII

CHAPTER XII., Extracts from Lane's Modern Egyptians, is not reprinted.

CHAPTER XIII

CHAPTER XIV

CHAPTER XV

CHAPTER XVI

CHAPTER XVII

APPENDICES

A MAULAVĪ DARVISH OF DAMASCUS

LIST OF ILLUSTRATIONS

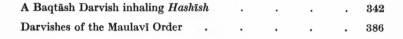

A QĀDIRĪ DARVISH.

EDITOR'S INTRODUCTION

. . . "*The Darvishes*", says Dr. F. Giese, "contains many valuable items of information, but must be read with extreme caution." The Editor's great object has been to make the information with which the work is packed more accessible to the student of religions in general and to the student of mysticism in particular. He has been scrupulous in correcting Brown's text, only venturing to put right a few obvious misprints, but he has, he trusts, made the work easier to use by standardising the spelling of the Arabic, Persian, and Turkish words contained in it. The system of transliteration adopted in the text is that accepted by the Royal Asiatic Society without diacritical points, but these have been more freely used in the footnotes added by the Editor.[1] To the general reader a rigidly scientific system of transliteration is merely confusing, while for the specialist it is unnecessary. In the case of Turkish words the system has been adhered to as far as words borrowed from Arabic or Persian are concerned, but in the purely Turkish terms Redhouse's transcriptions have been retained, in the main, as being closer to the actual pronunciation. As usual in the phraseology of popular religions, the investigator will come across words which are not to be found in the standard dictionaries. The footnotes to Brown's original text have been retained with their reference signs. Those added by the Editor are referred to by numbers, so that the reader can see at a glance who is responsible for each note. For the extent of the notes the Editor has no apology to offer. As Dr. Giese observes: "There is

[1] Absolute conformity is, however, not practicable, especially in quotations, wherein the writer's own spelling is respected. The editor's dislike of the hard breathing to represent the guttural '*ain* has led him to prefer, *e.g.* 'Ali to ʿAli.

as yet no systematic account of Islam in Turkey ", and though the Editor owes a heavy debt to *The Encyclopædia of Islam,* he ventures to think that in Brown's work will be found a supplement to it which will be indispensable when such an account comes to be written. All that the Editor has been able to do in the way of research has but served to confirm the scholarly accuracy of Brown's work.[1] As a book it suffers from defects of arrangement, inevitable when a writer reprints his contributions to periodical literature without the opportunity of recasting them in a condensed and ordered form. Brown was also unfortunate in his choice of the scholar who saw his book through the press. With ordinary diligence and care in the correction of the proofs many palpable but perplexing errors might have been avoided and the value of the work vastly increased.[2] Brown seems, moreover, to have been hampered by lack of access to a good library of works on Oriental literature, as he does not refer to several translators who would have rendered him invaluable aid. But this very deprivation had its advantages. Brown's work is clearly based on information gleaned by laborious inquiries at first-hand. It is not a compilation from orthodox literature, but the fruit of intimate acquaintance with the actualities of belief and practice among a people who have often evinced a noteworthy individuality in their religious thought.

If Turkey can be said to have had any constitutional history, its principal chapter would be concerned with the restraints which religion was able at times to impose on the worst excesses of despotism. In theory the Sultān was controlled by the Shaikh al-Islām in many important respects, but in practice that office seems to have been filled by men who could be trusted to support the administration in any step it chose to take. Nevertheless the Shaikh al-Islām was sometimes able to assert the authority of the religious law against purely arbitrary measures, and he doubtless found in the religious Orders much moral support on occasion. Their influence was, however, generally weakened by the fact that they were looked upon as unorthodox by the legally constituted ecclesiastical authorities. In the absence of anything

[1] In *E.R.E.* (*Encyclopædia of Religion and Ethics*), 8, p. 907.

[2] Such as 'condition' for 'audition' on p. 47; 'ten' for 'two' on p. 377; 'Nashihat' for 'Rashihat' on p. 212; misspelling of the names of well-known Orientalists; and a few others.

approaching an authentic record of the part really played by the Orders in the revolt headed by Jalandarūghlū in Anatolia in the sixteenth century, and of the relations of the Orders, other than the Baqtāsh, to the Janissaries, it is impossible to say what their political ideals were. Count Leon Ostrorog writes of "the stubborn and blind bigotry of the *hodjas* (*khojas*), and of their coalition with the Janissaries when they had lost all discipline and become the masters of the State". But the only Order which seems to have supported the unruly soldiery was that of the Baqtāsh, and on that account ostensibly it owed its expulsion from Constantinople and its virtual suppression throughout Turkey. The only other Order which was suppressed was the Malāmatī, but the reasons for its persecution are obscure. The truth may be that any Order which displayed political activities was suppressed, while those which survived were made to understand that their existence would only be tolerated on condition that their members indulged in harmless mystic practices and refrained from independent speculation, and, above all, from any overt act or teaching savouring of reform. This would explain why, as Count Ostrorog says, the most important privilege of primitive Muhammadanism, the right of examination and personal interpretation of the sacred texts, has long since disappeared from Turkish Islām. Yet, as he admits, the *khojas* were once, in the time of Sultān Salīm (in the middle of the sixteenth century, when the Sultanate was at the zenith of its power), able to offer such a strong moral resistance to that ruler's policy of extermination for all Jews and Christians as would not accept Islam that even that iron will had to give way, and Eastern Christendom was thus saved by the religious law of Islam. That was no small achievement in an age when the Sultān was under no other restraining influences whatsoever.

Another functionary who, at least in modern times, exercised an important power was the Fatwā-Amīna, who alone could issue a *fatwā* for the deposition of a reigning Ṣultān. This, though a religious act, could not originate from the Shaikh al-Islām,[1] though the *fatwā* had to be countersigned by him. Moreover,

[1] See the note on p. 254 *infra*. In his translation of the *Mesnevi* of Jalāl-ud-Dīn Redhouse explains the term to mean 'local vice-chancellor', p. 15. This would make the title as old as the thirteenth century, but it throws no light on the history and functions of the office.

the Fatwā-Amīna is not called upon to give any decision on the merits of the case for deposition, but merely his opinion on the point of law : whether a Sultān who has been guilty of certain acts is liable to be deposed (W. M. Ramsay, *The Revolution in Constantinople and Turkey*, 1909, p. 112).

H. N. Brailsford well describes Turkey " in its original fabric as a theocratic Power with a military basis ".[1] This description is, however, hardly complete, as it does not take into account the economic factors in the Osmānlī system. In Constantinople, at any rate, the Sultāns created or tolerated an elaborate system of trade-guilds, attaining in number the conventional figure 1001, borrowed from other countries, or possibly a revival of more ancient organisations. The *Siyyāh-nāma*[2] of Evliya Effendi gives an exhaustive enumeration of these guilds, but picturesque as it is, it affords few facts upon which a scientific history of them could be reconstructed. Evliya describes what corresponded to the Lord Mayor's Show in the Turkish capital of the seventeenth century, and dwells on the religious affinities of the guilds. Each had its patron-saint, though a saint might be patron of more than one guild. The saints of the crafts were peculiarly affected by the Qādirīs, as in India, where a great saint of that Order is known as the Pīr Dastgīr, 'The Helpful Saint', and may be regarded as the protector of industry in general, while some of his descendants are patrons of specific crafts. But this was not an exelusively Qādirī function, as other Orders also took some avocations and arts under their patronage. Hence we shall find in the list of the convents at Constantinople[3] that many are called after the guilds, while the position of others in a particular quarter or street occupied by workers in a trade probably indicates some connexion with its guild.

But if Brailsford's description of the social fabric in Turkey unduly diminishes the importance of its industrial guilds, it must be admitted that they were closely interwoven with the military system, just as they were linked up with the religious organisation of the empire. From Evliya's account, imperfect as it is, it will be seen that many crafts formed corps more or less organised as

[1] *Macedonia*, p. 21.

[2] Translated by Ritter J. von Hammer, 1846; cited as Evliya in the notes.

[3] App. III., p. 459 *infra*.

train-bands for war. Thus the miners, employed on cleansing roads in times of peace, were available as sappers in war. They were "for the most part Armenians from Qaisaria, a bad-smelling set of men, but necessary in sieges".[1] The axe-men and stone-cutters were similarly employed as pioneers, though there seems to have been also a regular body of pioneers (*Salahoran*) who had a different patron-saint. In all, says Evliya, there were nine corps of such auxiliaries who were reckoned to form part of the infantry of the camp, though one of them at least, that of the pages, could hardly have been actually employed on a campaign. The horse-jobbers, biscuit-bakers, water-carriers, and apothecaries were all similarly employed in war.

It is certain that these guilds were not confined to Constantinople, but how far their organisation was developed in other parts of the Turkish empire does not appear. The Takhtajīs, or workers in wood, for instance, form a strong sectarian community in Asia Minor, but they do not seem to constitute a true guild. However this may be, the guild system is still a force in Turkey owing to its vitality in the capital, though the disappearance of many once flourishing industries has diminished the number of the guilds. Evliya's picture of its history is certainly inaccurate, but it is curious that the guild traditions derived many of their patron-saints from lands which never formed part of the Turkish empire, and were not even dominated by Islām until some centuries had elapsed after its foundation. The significance of these legends is obscure, but they may express a feeling, more or less conscious, that industry was not a matter of race or creed, but dependent on international comity and religious tolerance. This suggestion is supported by the fact that some guilds admit both Christians and Muhammadans to membership. Another beneficent feature of Turkish life, at least in the towns, is the strict specialisation of each particular branch of industry or commerce, and the absence of the middleman in the generality of transactions connected with supplying the necessaries of existence. In this respect the Turkish system seems to have been economically more suited to the conditions of a backward community than the caste system of India, though it failed to provide any means of financing industry or agriculture independent of the middleman, alien in creed or in caste to the toiling masses of the country.

[1] Evliya, i. Part ii. pp. 107, 109, 125, and 123.

Herein it displayed no advantage over the Indian system. The religious Orders, especially the Qādirīs or developments of that Order, seem to have stood originally for a notable advance in the economic organisation of the East, but they were looked at askance as politically heterodox, and appear to have been unable to do more than establish industrial guilds on mediæval models at a time when the rest of Europe was finally discarding that system for a more effective commercial organisation. As in India, again, local self-government never made any headway in Turkey, but within the guild, as in the industrial caste, there was and is a considerable measure of self-administration, some possessing a *qānūn* or written constitution in addition to the traditional laws and practices. In many respects the organisation is very similar to that of the religious Orders.[1]

But did any of the Turkish guilds actually originate in religious fraternities, as happened in mediæval Germany and elsewhere? In the present state of our knowledge no definite answer can be given to this question. In the Nearer East systems of trade-guilds are of great antiquity, and just as the Christian Orders played a great part in the economic reconstruction of Europe after the barbaric invasions, so in the Moslem East the religious Orders must at an early period have taken industry under their patronage, even if their fundamental principles forbade them to found industries of their own. Among the earlier Ṣūfīs the doctrine of *tawakkul*, 'dependence upon God', was carried to excess, yet among the more sober thinkers, even in that community, it was vehemently opposed, and in its stead was inculcated the duty or practice of *kasb*, 'the gaining of daily bread by labour'. It was seemingly in accord with this teaching that many of the earlier Ṣūfīs were well content to be called by occupational surnames, such as al-Ḥallāj, 'the carder'.[2]

On the other hand, the artisan, the merchant, and even the professions may well have found it politic to place their vocational interests under the protection of religion during an epoch when the law was almost powerless to safeguard them, and all lay organisations were apt to be regarded with suspicion by authority. If this was so, the position in the Muhammadan world was

[1] See *The Turkish People*, by Miss L. M. J. Garnett, pp. 15-20, for an account of the modern guild system.

[2] D. B. Macdonald, *Muslim Theology*, p. 179.

strikingly like that in mediæval Christendom. That position is admirably summed up in these words: "We know how in earlier days the London journeymen and apprentices conspired 'under a feigned colour of sanctity' to gain more independence; and how the merchant adventurers of London were charged with having mounted to authority, 'so by colour of such feigned holiness as the name of St. Thomas conferred'; and it is not impossible that traces of a lost chapter of history may be preserved in some of the numerous religious guilds of which the records have been preserved".[1]

Popular tradition makes a saint, Shaikh Mehmed Gilani, a companion of Sultan Muḥammad II., who wished to give him all the sea-front 'twixt the Akhor Gate and the Seven Towers. The saint, however, was content to take a site for a retreat near the Wazir Iskele-si, where later on was built the Arpa-ji Mosque (the Mosque of the Barley-seller). The saint erected there a takia and prayer-house, not far from the Baghcha Gate, and close by he and his brother Arslan 'Ali were buried. But in course of time all traces of these structures disappeared. Not until the reign of Sultan Mehmed II. (*sic*) was the memory of the two saints revived. The Shaikh Gilani appeared to the Sultan in a dream, and bade him dig in a certain place. There the bodies of the two saints were found still wrapped in their shrouds. They were laid in a (new ?) turba, and both are honoured under the one name of Salamat Baba. Their function is to aid those who are in irremediable difficulties. The title Gilani suggests that this two-fold saint is the 'Helpful' Pir of the Qādirīs, a conjecture perhaps supported by his association with the Arpa-ji Mosque.[2]

The stories of Bābā or Shaikh Iliās illustrate the power of the *religieux* before the rise of the Ottoman Turks. The last of the Saljūqs to wield any real power, Ghiyās-ud-Dīn II. (1236–1259), ordered a general massacre of the Ṣūfīs, in fear, it is said, of a *darvish* revolt. Bābā Iliās al-Khurāsānī, who is however described as dwelling at Amasia, was probably a refugee from the inroads of Jengiz Khān, but he was able to make many disciples in Rūm. Nevertheless, when he fell into the hands of the Saljūqian troops he was beheaded, 'and his succession cut off'. This must mean

[1] Mrs. J. R. Green in a review of *Two Thousand Years of Gild Life*, by the Rev. J. Malet Lambert, *Eng. Hist. Review*, viii. (1893), p. 339.

[2] Fried. Schrader, *Konstantinopel*, pp. 85-7.

that he left no spiritual heirs, for his son Shaikh Mukhlis was raised to power over Yunān (Ionia) by the people, and especially by his own disciples, for he, too, was a mystic teacher. But after a rule of six months he resigned his power to Qaramān, son of Nūr-ud-Dīn, a Ṣūfī of Bābā Iliās. If we had not been told that the latter's succession had been cut off, we should here suspect that a contest of the usual kind had arisen between the Bābā's spiritual and physical heirs, in which the former prevailed. Another version is given in von Hammer, *GdOR*. ii. p. 58, but it leaves the main outline of the tale as it stands above. That the downfall of the Saljūqs was largely due to religious dissensions is also indicated in the *Mesnevi*, Redhouse's trans., p. 55. Who the Shaikh Bābā of that work may be, or what connexion he had with the earlier Nūr Ṣūfī, the Armenian, the Nūr-ud-Dīn whose son founded the principality of Qaramānia, does not appear (Gibb, *Hist. of Ott. Poetry*, i. pp. 176 ff.). A Shaikh Bābā of Marand is mentioned once in *Les Saints des Dervishes tourneurs* (i. pp. 113-14), where it is related the dynasty of the Saljūqs came to be overthrown. The Sulṭān Rukn-ud-Dīn became the disciple of our Master, Jalāl-ud-Dīn Rūmī, and he convened a great assembly at which he held *une séance d'intronisation sans pareille*, presumably to enthrone Jalāl-ud-Dīn. But Shaikh Bābā, an ascetic by repute (*mutarassim*), and his friends, a gang of demons in human form, won over the Sulṭān by flattery, and he informed Jalāl-ud-Dīn that he accepted the Shaikh as his father. Whereupon the supplanted mystic declared that he would take another son. He refused to aid the Sulṭān by his influence against the Mongols, and the luckless ruler was strangled at Āq-Sarāī.

The history of the relations of the religious Orders to the secular rulers of the Turkish provinces is a long one, but our information concerning them is very imperfect. To begin with the events of the reign of the last Saljūqian Sulṭān, Ghiyās-ud-Dīn (1236–59), we find Bābā Iliās of Amasia, surnamed al-Khurāsānī, exciting a *darvish* revolt, of which the accounts differ. According to one, the Bābā was killed in a general massacre of the Ṣūfīs, and 'his succession was cut off'. This phrase prepares us for a story of a disputed succession to the headship of his movement. According to another version, the Bābā, despite his rebellion, which was suppressed, was received into such favour by the Sulṭān Ghiyās-ud-Dīn that the Maulāna Jalāl-ud-Dīn and the Maulavīs, his followers, left the Saljūqian Court in dudgeon. This tale carries little conviction, the more so in that the same historian states that the Bābā was eventually killed in an attempt to raise the people of Amasia.

The Bābā left a son, Shaikh al-Mukhlis, and, as usual, many disciples. Al-Mukhlis in turn left a son, 'Alī, known as Shaikh Pasha al-'Āshiq, or 'Āshiq-pasha. The last-named wrote a history of his family, though he was professedly a mystic, and had as a poet assumed the style of al-'Āshiq, ' the lover '. His history, which is merely a preface to his poems, must clearly be received with caution. In it he says that al-Mukhlis was invited to become ruler of Ionia (Qaramania) by its inhabitants, and that he actually ruled it for six months, but then resigned it to Qaramān, son of Nūr-ud-Dīn, a ' Ṣūfī ', or disciple, of Bābā Iliās. This being interpreted means that al-Mukhlis set up a claim to succeed his father by physical descent and failed in his purpose. The truth seems to be that Nūr-ud-Dīn, who was by birth an Armenian, one of the most fanatical disciples of Iliās, and also known as Nūr Ṣūfī, had even in the reign of Sultān 'Alā-ud-Dīn (1219–36) made his position secure by seizing the Byzantine fortress of Selefke, and securing the daughter of 'Alā-ud-Dīn as a wife for his son Qaramān. Thus he must be regarded as the real founder of the kingdom of Qaramānia.

But the descendants of Iliās having lost temporal power retained considerable spiritual influence. 'Āshiq himself wrote a long *masnawī* called the *Gharīb-nāma,* otherwise known as the *Ma'ārif-nāma,* or ' Book of the Sciences '. It is usually but incorrectly called his *Dīwān.* On his death in 1332, at the age of sixty-one, he was buried at Qīr-shahr, and his shrine became a place of pilgrimage. His son 'Ulwān, also a mystic poet, had a similar shrine at Amasia.

'Āshiq has also another claim to notice in that towards the close of his life he settled in Qīr-shahr, where he became a companion of Ḥājī Bektāsh, then living in its neighbourhood. This association is said to have begun after the accession of Orkhān in 1326, and as the *Gharīb-nāma* was finished in 1329–30 it can hardly have owed much to the influence of Bektāsh, but it is conceivable that the latter was in debt to the poem. It is, however, nowhere stated that the Ḥājī was a successor of Bājā Iliās or his school. On the contrary, his immediate teacher is sometimes given as Luqmān, also styled al-Khurāsānī (M. Hartmann, *Der islamische Orient,* vi.-x. p. 209).

In the fifteenth century we have the Ardabilī risings, described on p. 86.

We now come to the sixteenth century. In 1520 the Persians openly incited the revolt of the Mahdi, Jalālī, so that Jalālī came to mean 'rebel'! (Fr. Babinger in *Der Islam,* xi. p. 14).

In 1527 ensued the rising headed by Qalandar-ūghlū, who claimed to be a descendant of Ḥājī Bektāsh, in Qaramān. It is plainly stated that his following included many *darvishes, 'abdāls,* and Qalandars (von Hammer, *GdOR.* ii. p. 58). But Evliya, who visited Asia Minor in the next century, speaks of " the Anatolian rebels, Qarā Yazījī, Qalandar-ughlī, Delī Ḥasān, and Jannat-ughlī ", as if they were joint leaders of this rising. If anything, he suggests that it was headed by Qarā Yazījī, just as the one about to be described was led by one Qarā Sa'īd, rather than by the later Qalandar-ughlī (*Travels,* ii. pp. 5 and 98).

In the military revolt of 1632 one of the most influential of the rebel leaders was Delī Ilāhī, ' the Narrengott ', a nephew of the Dāghlar-delī-sī or ' Bergnarr '.[1]

The seventeenth century opened with still graver rebellions, and another Qalandar-ughlū rebelled and burnt Brūsa. But it does not appear that his followers were under any religious influences.[2]

We now come to a new phase in the attitude of the Turkish Sultanate towards the Darvish Orders. Henceforward their leaders do not appear to have countenanced insurrection. Possibly an exception must be made as regards the Bektāsh, but every other Order may be regarded as averse to violence, whatever its aims may have been. In 1656, however, the great minister, Muḥammad Kuprīlī, began his term of office under difficulties. The strictly orthodox party threatened not only the Ṣūfīs and Darvishes with violence, but also demanded the suppression of luxury in attire, the prohibition of tobacco, opium, and coffee, and the destruction of all superfluous minarets in the mosques, as they considered that a single minaret for each was sufficient, and therefore lawful. This agitation Muḥammad Kuprīlī put down by firm but merciful measures. The hostility of the

[1] *V. GdOR.* iii. p. 111. [2] *GdOR.* ii. pp. 704-12.

reformers was confined apparently to the Orders specified on p. 342 *infra*.

But during the *wizārat* of the younger Kuprīlī, Aḥmad, the preacher Vānī Effendi acquired great influence, and from about 1664 great efforts were made to suppress the Ṣūfī mystics and the *darvish* Orders. He was able to secure the banishment of the Khalwati Shaikh Miṣrī Effendi, the Niāzī Effendi of p. 204. The Maulavīs also were persecuted in his time (*v.* note on p. 182). The descriptions given of him are unflattering. A repulsive old hunchback with one eye smaller than the other, he was depicted as a casuistical hypocrite. But not dissimilar charges had been made against the orthodox reformers of 1656, and G. F. Abbott's view is that the Shaikh's zeal for religious purity was the counterpart of Kuprīlī's in the cause of political morality (*Under the Turk at Constantinople*, pp. 153-7 ; *GdOR*. iii. pp. 467 ff. and 549). There was undoubtedly a strong Puritan movement in Turkey at this time. It was opposed to superstitious practices (though the accusations of Kabalistic reckonings and astrological predictions may not always have been true, *ib.* p. 520), and the *darvish* Orders had dabbled in many such. It was also believed that the dancing, flute-playing, and mystical exercises generally were enervating in their effects.

" For nearly 1400 years," says a recent writer, " about as long as there have been English in England, Asia Minor was European in language and culture ; and since the Roman conquest in the second century B.C. it had been politically European as well. Its culture was, it is true, tinged by the phantasies of the East, but it remained essentially European." [1]

[1] A. W. Gomme, *Mr. Wells as Historian*, p. 38.

THE MAULAVĪ SHAIKH OF PERA, CONSTANTINOPLE

THE DARVISHES

CHAPTER I

INTRODUCTION — ABRAHAM AND MUHAMMAD — THE SACRIFICE OF ISMĀĪL — THE DECEASE OF IBRĀHĪM — THE ĀTMBODHA, OR KNOWLEDGE OF THE SPIRIT.

THE earliest form, or principle, of Religion is connected with an intuitive conviction in the mind of man of the possession of a soul or spirit, independent of his body, or corporeal existence. The soul is believed to survive the body, and refers to a superior Spirit, creative and providential in its character. A more perfect knowledge and communion with this greater Spirit, or God, is the object of man's continuous aspirations. The senses (or faculties) of man are possessed in common with other animals. These are all intimately connected with his intellectual faculty, so much so that, when they do not exist, as in childhood and advanced age, or are enfeebled by accidental causes, as in idiocy, it is seriously affected. The reasoning faculty, and that of speech, seem to be those which distinguish man from ordinary animal nature, and yet both of these are possessed, in a greater and less degree, by most animals. It is supposed that the brain is the seat of the 'intellectual faculty', and its operations are explained by its connexion with the nervous system and the other senses, such as hearing, seeing, and the touch. The size of the brain does not increase the reasoning faculty, nor that of the body the other ordinary faculties.

Man, thus, in his most degraded and least intellectual condition, in his most barbarous state, seems to have an 'intuitive conviction' of the possession of a *soul*, and of a future existence after the death of his body. It seems not to be dependent upon mental culture, nor upon a knowledge of the greatness of this God, and the magnitude of His power and works. Does this perception extend to any other of His creatures, vegetable or animal, or is it restricted entirely to man? * I believe that the idea is always limited to the fact that there is *a* God, and that the belief in a plurality of Gods is a matter of pure imagination, dependent upon the varied convictions and wants of man in the several parts of the world.

Just as the soul of man thus leads him to believe in the existence of God, so does it likewise impress him with a conviction of the greatness of the Deity, and, in his helplessness, to supplicate Him in the hour of need, of suffering, and of danger. This, therefore, is the original means of communicating with the Creator on the part of the creature. Divine providences are not restricted to man only, but are experienced throughout all creation. The same laws of nature which affect him in this life extend also to all living beings, and the question may be again repeated, whether inanimate as well as animate creation, the vegetable as well as animal, have any perception of this fact?

Leaving the idea of the unity of the Deity, it is found that man has endeavoured to give to this simple conviction a place and a form. On the former there seems to be a belief in common among all men, that the Creator of all things exists far beyond the conceptions of the senses, and invisible to the ordinary senses; whilst the imagination ascribes to Him innumerable forms, all dependent upon the imagination and the fancied wants of ordinary life. With some He is all benevolence, with others avenging; whilst some believe that all His providences are unchangeable, and therefore constitute what is called destiny and fate, others regard them as merciful, and adapted to the needs of those who implore His compassion. Whilst He is considered omnipotent in all things, it is held that He may, and does, alter His laws of nature, and so permit of occurrences which are called miracles. They even go still further, and hold that He grants this power to those who invoke Him, so that they may effect equally surprising supernatural acts.

Besides this communion with God by spiritual means only, and a direct intercourse between the Spirit of the Creator and

* *Vide* Psalm cl. 6, and others.

the soul of man, many—particularly in the East, the birth-place of humanity, according to the earliest history—believe it possible for him to *approach near to God.* This is effected by a devout adoration of Him, a frequent calling upon His Name ; and the method of doing so has been established in a regular system. As this is peculiar to the East, the following account of the Darvishes will serve in some manner to explain it.

For most of the religious creeds of the Moslems I believe the source, or at least parallels, may be found in the Bible, and the history of Christian saints. The same thoughts give rise to a similarity of impulses and of acts ; and this fact, with many, leads the mind to believe in their truthfulness.

A closer application to the contemplation of the Deity as the one Supreme Spirit, Creator of all things, and omnipotent Sovereign of the universe, and of the immortality of the soul of man, leads the mind to a disregard of the history of the human race as a Divine revelation. It places the *forms* of worship—sanctified in our estimation only by the assumption of their founder, that he possessed a position of devout communion with the Deity not possessed by his fellow-creatures generally—in a secondary, if not, indeed, in an unessential, point of view. They are valued only as the creation of the mind of one who commands our respect by his evident intention to benefit his fellow-beings, by elevating them from a meaningless idolatry to an adoration of the One only true Deity, and by wise moral laws and regulations to guide their ignorant and feeble intellects in a 'pathway' leading from earth to heaven. Although we may be disposed to accept the idea that man has an 'intuitive conviction' of the existence of God, this same intuition gives us no insight into the condition of the soul in its future existence. It nevertheless strongly suggests the fact of a right and a wrong, of good and evil acts, and of a future reward for the one, and a punishment for the other. The insignificancy of the historical part of the Bible, in comparison with that which relates to man's spirituality, becomes the more apparent as we pursue the latter. It is, in almost every instance, only the narrative of temporary human weaknesses,—of the empire of the passions, and of the feebleness of the soul, when unsupported by the Spirit of the Deity ; often offering some of the worst deeds which darken and degrade mankind in his short career in this existence. These cannot be attributed to Divine inspiration, though the narrator may have been inspired to record them for a wise and useful purpose. The spiritual history of man only demands our deepest attention. In this we are led to regard with complacency, as non-essential to his future existence, the forms and particular rules of worship, established in modern as well as in ancient times, by the various individuals who fully considered the frailties of human nature, the necessity of external appearances, and the strength of whatever is mysterious upon the mind of men generally. How many men and women have believed themselves as especially called upon to assume the character of prophets and prophetesses, and to appeal to their fellow-beings in the language of Divine inspiration! We are struck by the strange mixture of good and evil which appears in the history of their own lives, and by the termination of their careers. We are lost in the vain endeavour to seize upon one fact calculated to procure a self-conviction of the truthfulness of their assumption. With some, we find youth and manhood devoted to mental instruction, in a religious point of view, and we are, therefore, led to give them our respect. And yet such instruction as this seems to command no claim to Divine inspiration, for the most unlearned have effected the most salutary results, the deepest and most lasting. Others, by the apparent purity of their lives, and the purely spiritual character of their administrations, place them high in our estimation; so that we do not care to call into question either their intellectual attainments or the grounds of their assumption, satisfied, as we are, by the evident benevolence of their designs to their fellow-beings.

In the East there is another class, who assume to have attained, by their own efforts, to a superior degree of spirituality, and to powers which come from Divine inspiration. These recognise the prophets and prophetesses who have preceded them, and who, through the purity of their lives, have become saints in the spirit-world, there filling positions of varied eminence and influence, which their followers invoke in their own behalf. This may be said also of some of the branches of Christianity, in which the theory of patron-saints is so far extended as to obviate the necessity of the worship and adoration of the Deity.

Revealed religion requires an unlimited degree of faith, and prescribes the exercise of reason, the same faculty which, from its peculiar character, seems to have had a direct origin from the Creator, inasmuch as it places man above all other creatures. The simple religion of man, which is intuitive to his nature, is so perverted in modern times as no longer to inspire its principal feature, viz. that of universal benevolence ; and, in its varied forms, is antagonistic to the evident will of the Supreme Deity, which cannot have any other object than that of justice, peace, and affection between all mankind. Revealed religion also teaches the existence of celestial spirits, who are supposed to be near the Deity, where they have been from a period the length of which cannot be even imagined. Of their origin nothing whatever is known : yet they must have been created in a manner different from that of man and his progeny. These are called Archangels and Angels, some of whose names we even know, such as Michael, Gabriel,[1] etc. ; and, in more modern times, the abode of God has been peopled with saints, transformed from ordinary corporeal beings in this world to purely spiritual ones in heaven ; and we still give them there the same names which they bore on earth.

Revelation relieves the mind of man of much of what is dark and concealed. It sheds a light upon the mysterious and the unknown, and, when accepted as a pure matter of faith, gives calmness and repose to the believer. A firmly-seated conviction, be it whatever it may, right or wrong, renders its possessor tranquil ; and with it the Jew, the Christian, the Moslem, as well as even the idolater or the fire-worshipper, passes through his career in life, satisfied with his faith, and meets the hour of his departure with cheerful confidence. *Religion*, in its ordinary signification, means the outward expression of a belief, accompanied by various forms of worship and external ceremonies. *Spiritualism* rejects these as non-essentials, and is the simple communion of the human soul with the Divine Spirit, by means of prayer and contemplation. The heart's adoration of the Supreme Creator may be audible or silent, and each be equal to the other, in point of value, with Him to whom nothing is secret. The inutility of forms and ceremonies is, therefore, evident, and

[1] Gabriel plays an important part in the *Qurān* and his legend is highly developed among Moslems. His name is also used in charms and talismans (*E.I.* i. 990). He presented the Prophet with an apron of silk or a girdle, said to have been manufactured in Paradise, and he is thus credited with the invention of aprons (Spry, *Life on the Bosphorus*, 1895, p. 235).

at best may be regarded as human conceptions, or as symbols of mysteries having for object only an influence upon the mind and imagination of the worshipper. If these be considered as insignificant in the sight of the Almighty, they may also be regarded as innocent and harmless. These should not, however, tend to withdraw the worshipper from the Creator to the creature. It is impossible to suppose God unwilling to hear the supplications of any one who appeals to Him in a sincere and fervid spirit. It is equally impossible to believe that He has placed a barrier to this faculty, in the form of a multitude of intermediate creatures, or that He has given to any one a power to accept or refuse the salvation of another. The laws of God are equally over all and for all, and never can be otherwise than perfectly just. Any assertion to the contrary must, therefore, be attributed entirely to the imagination, the vanity, and the weakness of man. Some men have been good for their own sakes only; others have not only been themselves good, but have endeavoured to induce others to be equally good, so far as weak human nature and the power of the passions permit. Here, then, is an evident principle of benevolence, which alone renders its advocate superior to those who disregard it. That religion which is erected on this basis rests upon an eternal foundation, and possesses a Divine origin; whilst any other which inculcates strife and enmity, with all their attendant evils, must be held as antagonistic to the design of the Supreme Creator and Judge of the whole human race. The laws prescribed by the earliest legislatist of whom we have any knowledge, Moses, impressed upon the minds of those whom he designed to benefit, *first,* the unity of the Deity, to whom only man must address his adorations, and *next,* the principle of right and wrong towards each other—or, in other words, the necessity of mutual benevolence.

The subject of Spiritual Powers is the principal object of the writer in collecting the materials of the present little work. No one, so far as he can learn, has devoted a book to the Darvishes exclusively. Some accounts of them, especially of the external forms of their worship, are found in various writings; but few have gone further than these, or have given, at most, biographical sketches of their more prominent members.

The subject is not a new one. It can be traced in the Old and New Testament, as well as in the *Qurān*, and, I fully believe, is peculiar to the learned ranks of the people of India, from whence it entered into Arabia and Persia. It has its origin in the belief that man's spirit is a Divine emanation, and, under certain peculiar circumstances, is possessed of a Divine faculty disconnected with his corporeal part, and, therefore, to be attributed wholly to his spiritual. The unity of the Deity was the principle of the Greeks and the Hindus, and the other gods were supposed to be emanations from the One great Supreme Deity, called among the former Jove, and the latter Brahman. Among the Jews the unity was retained, and among the people of Arabia the same principle has not been forsaken, though that of emanations, or peculiar gifts of the Spirit of Allāh to those who devotedly invoke and adore Him, is sustained to its fullest extent. The Trinity of the Christian creed seems to have been the chief object of Muhammad's abhorrence. In chap. cxii. of the *Qurān* is found the whole basis of his doctrine: "God is one God; He begetteth not, neither is He begotten; and there is not any one like unto Him."

Whilst Moslems reject the divinity of Jesus Christ, they fully believe in His miraculous conception, and even call Him, *par excellence*, the 'Spirit of God' (*Rūh-Ullāh*); they reject the theory of His mission as a Redeemer and Saviour, and of the Baptism, and yet admit Him as one of the saints (*aulia*) whose intercession with God is beneficial to those who implore Divine mercy.

I cannot do better than here quote the remarks of M. Garcin de Tassy, in his preface to the admirable translation of the poem *Mantic Uttaïr*[1] (one of the most beautiful collections of ideas on the Spiritualism of the East), to demonstrate the subject before me:—

"The enigma of nature has been variously explained by philosophy. Great geniuses have arisen in different places and in different ages, and their varied suppositions on this subject have been reduced to systems and found millions of docile followers. However, an authentic explanation was needed for this great mystery which would satisfy the mind and the heart.

"Mussulmans have shown a remarkable subtlety in developing the mystery of nature. They have undertaken the most serious

[1] *Mantiq-ut-Tair*, 'The Speech of Birds,' by Farīd-ud-Dīn 'Attār. An abridged translation, *The Conference of the Birds*, by R. P. Masani, has been published by the Clarendon Press, 1924.

task of showing the alliance between philosophy and revelation. Placed between the Pantheism of the Indian Jogīs and the *Qurān*, which is sometimes an informal copy of the Bible, their philosophers, named the Sūfīs, have established a pantheistic school appropriate to Islām ideas—a sort of esoteric doctrine of Islamism, which must be distinguished from Indian Pantheism, though indeed it presents only the errors of the *Vedānta* and the *Sānkhya*. 'Pantheism, as a moral doctrine, leads to the same conclusions as materialism—the negation of human liberty, the indifference to actions, and the legitimacy of temporal enjoyments.' In this system *all is God, except God Himself*, for He thereby ceases to be God.

"The spiritualism of the Sūfī, though contrary to materialism, is, in reality, identical with it. But if their doctrine is not more reasonable, it is, at least, more elevated and poetical. Among their authors, there are some who have endeavoured to form a concord between Muhammadan dogmas and their own principles, so as to establish for them a character of orthodoxy.

"The doctrine of the Sūfī is ancient in Islamism, and is much spread, especially among the partisans of 'Alī (the fourth caliph). Out of it grew the belief in the infusion of the Divinity in 'Alī, and their allegorical explanation of all religious precepts and ceremonies. One Islām writer[1] says that the first person who took the name of Sūfī was 'Abū-Hāshim[2] of Kūfa, in the latter part of the 8th century [A.D.]; whilst another declares that the seeds of Sūfīsm were sown in the time of Adam, germed in that of Noah, budded in that of Abraham, and the fruit commenced to be developed in that of Moses. They reached their maturity in that of Christ; and in that of Muhammad produced pure wine. Those of its sectarians who loved this wine have so drunk of it as to lose all knowledge of themselves, and to exclaim, 'Praise be to me! Is there any greater than me?' or rather, 'I am the Truth (that is to say, God)! There is no other God than me!'

"It is well to remember that the word Sūfī does not come from the Greek word σοφὸς (*sage* or *wise*), as one might be tempted to

[1] Jāmī, in his *Nafahāt al-Uns*, ed. W. N. Lees, Calcutta, 1859, p. 34.

[2] 'Abū Hāshim, a contemporary of Sufyān ul-Thauri (*E.R.E.*, art. 'Sūfīs'). Abū Hāshim had a notable theological discussion with his father, al-Jubbā'ī, who died in 303 H., regarding the relation of God to His qualities (Macdonald, *Muslim Theology*, pp. 159-160).

suppose, but from the Arabic word *sūf* (wool), and signifies a *woollen dress*, which forms the costume of the Darvishes and *faqīrs*, 'contemplatifs and spiritualists'. From this name comes that of the Sūfīs, *mutasawwaf*, and signifies especially a *tālib*,[1] or novice, who desires to become a Sūfī. They generally give the name of *sālik* to the *tālib*, as 'one who walks in a spiritual path'. This name also simply signifies 'a man'. They call *'abūdiyat*,[2] 'slavery' or 'servitude', the service of God; and *'abd*, he who devotes himself to His service. *'Ārif*, or the 'knowing,' is the devout contemplator; and *ma'rifat*, the 'knowledge of God', is the object of the contemplation. He who has reached this knowledge is called a *wāli*,[3] or one who is brought near to God; an expression which, in the end, signifies a *saint*. *Jazb* is the Divine attraction; the ecstatic state, which is the result of contemplation, is called *hāl*, and its degrees, *maqām*; the union with God is *jam'a*;[4] the separation, *farq*, and the continuation with Him, *sukināt*.[5] They call the ignorant or worldly individual *jāhil*, and this expression signifies one who is not occupied with spiritual matters;[5] and a distinction in fervour is thus defined, viz.: love of God, *'ishq-Ullāh*, differs from 'affection'; friendship, *muhabbat*; *shauq*, 'desire'; *ishti'āq*,[6] 'ardour'; and *wajd*, 'ecstasy'.

[1] *Ṭālib*, literally a 'seeker'; the fuller term is *ṭālib-ul-'ilm*, 'a seeker after knowledge'.

[2] *'Ubūdiyyat*, 'servantship', *'ibādat* (or *'ubādiat*), 'service' (*Kashf-ul-Maḥjūb*, Nicholson, p. 79).

[3] *Wālī* is properly a prince or governor, one who rules over a *walāyat*. *Walī*, *walīy*, pl. *aulia*, is a saint; and saintship is *walīyat* or *walāyat*, both terms connoting 'lordship', just as *maulawī*, from the same root, means literally 'sovereign' or 'supreme'.

[4] *Jam'a*, the root of which means 'to be collected, gathered together', gives such derivatives as *jamā'at*, pp. 295 and 379 *infra*. *Jam'a* as a simple state in mysticism inclines to heretical atheism and disregard of outward observances. But a combination of the right eye of *jam'a* with the left eye of *tafrīqa* is most to be desired, and this degree is called the *jam'a al-jam'a* or *farq-uṣ-ṣānī*, and is the highest in mysticism (Nassau Lees, *Nafahāt al-Uns*, p. 9). *Farq-uṣ-ṣānī*, 'the second difference', appears to be the second or highest stage of *tafrīqa*, which is "the condition in which the votary retains his reason, but being subject to the material world his spirit is veiled from the Divine essence" (*ib.*).

[5] Probably *sakīnat*, 'tranquillity', the word used in *Qurān*, ii. v. 249, where, however, Palmer says *sakīna* is the Heb. *shechina* and is incorrectly translated 'repose'. The root connotes 'dwelling', and *sakināt* would mean 'habitations'.

[6] *Ishti'āq*, from the same root as *shauq*.

" These are the principal expressions used by Mussulman Spiritualists, though there are many others, which cannot here be given."

The following extract from a mystical poem on spiritualism, cited by the same author, will serve to develop the Darvish idea of God and man :—

" Man is the most perfect of God's creatures ; he is the king of nature, because he is the only one in the world who knows himself —knows, thus, the Creator, and possesses the intelligence of revelation. One may compare God to the sun reflected upon the waters ; this reflection of light is nothing other than the light itself. For this reason, religious men, intoxicated with the cup of Divine communion, exclaim, ' I am God '. In fact, man's attributes are of a Divine character—what do I say ?—his substance is that even of God. The only difference is, that he is a casual being, whilst God is the only necessary being." *

The following is a succinct account of the doctrine of the Sūfīs which is generally adopted in the Darvish Orders :—

1. God only exists,—He is in all things, and all things are in Him.

2. All visible and invisible beings are an emanation from Him (' *divinæ particula auræ* '), and are not, really, distinct from Him. Creation is only a pastime with God.

3. Paradise and Hell, and all the dogmas of positive religions, are only so many allegories, the spirit of which is only known to the Sūfī.

4. Religions are matters of indifference ; they, however, serve as a means of reaching to realities. Some, for this purpose, are more advantageous than others, among which is the Mussulman religion, of which the doctrine of the Sūfī is the philosophy.

(On this subject, Jalāl-ud-Dīn ur-Rumī, the author of the text-book of the Order of the Maulavīs, called the *Masnavī Sharīf*, remarks in one of his verses : " In whatever place we may set our foot, we are always, Lord, within Thy resort. In what-

* St. Paul says in Hebrews xi. 3 : " Through faith we understand that the worlds were framed by the word of God; so that things which are seen were not made of things which do appear." John of Parma, General of the Franciscans, the author of a celebrated Catholic work called the *Eternal Gospel*, and the author of the *Imitation*, proclaims that " To lose oneself in God is the only object towards which man should strive ".

ever place or corner we may entrench ourselves, we are always near to Thee. Perhaps, we say, there is a path which leads elsewhere, and yet, let our pathway be whatever it will, it invariably leads to Thee.")

5. There does not really exist any difference between good and evil, for all is reduced to unity, and God is the real author of the acts of mankind.

6. It is God who fixes the will of man, and he is therefore not free in his actions.

7. The soul existed before the body, and is confined within the latter as in a cage. Death, therefore, should be the object of the wishes of the Sūfī—for it is then that he returns to the bosom of the Divinity, from which he emanated, and he obtains what the Buddhists call the *nirvāna*, or, 'annihilation in God'.

8. It is by this metempsychosis that souls which have not fulfilled their destination here below are purified, and become worthy of reunion with God.

9. The principal occupation of the Sūfī is meditation on the Unity, and progressive advancement, so as to gradually attain to spiritual perfection, and to 'die in God', and whilst in this life to reach to a unification with God.

10. Without the grace of God, which they call *faiz-Ullāh*, no one can attain to this spiritual union ; but this they assert is practicable, for it is held by them that God does not refuse His aid to those that fervently ask it.

M. de Tassy adds, that these doctrines have had their partisans in Christian Europe ; for the Adamites teach that the human soul is an emanation of the Deity, imprisoned in bodily organs, from which it must be freed ; and that the acts of the body are matters of indifference, which have no influence on the soul. In the seventh century, some held that God was in all nature, and that His essence gave life to it. Others maintained that it was necessary to disengage the soul from the weight of the faculties, so as to arrive at an absolute fusion with the infallible One, and that was only by contemplation.

The religious or mystical poems of the people of the East are mostly upon this subject. They serve to show that the writers, though nominally Mussulmans, were, nevertheless, not held by the ties of ordinary religion, its forms, dogmas, and ceremonies, to all of which they attached but little importance, when compared with the vast idea of the greatness of the Creator and Providential God of the universe. With them, there is but one book worthy of their research—that of Nature; in every page of which they read the unity and power and perfection of the Deity. In the journey of this life, there are many paths, all of which meet at the same goal—the death of the body, the immortality of the soul, and its reunion with its First Great Cause. Many extracts and translations might be offered to explain the Darvish's idea of the Deity, but the following ode appears to me to convey it far more beautifully than anything else I have ever seen. It is also peculiarly Oriental in its character.

GOD

O Thou Eternal One! whose presence bright
All space doth occupy! all motion guide;
Unchanged through Time's all-devastating flight,
Thou only God! There is no God beside.
Being above all beings! Mighty One!
Whom none can comprehend, and none explore;
Who fill'st existence with Thyself alone;
Embracing all—supporting—ruling o'er—
Being whom we call God—and know no more!

In its sublime research, Philosophy
May measure out the ocean deep—may count
The sands, or the sun's rays; but, God! for Thee
There is no weight nor measure; none can mount
Up to Thy mysteries. Reason's brightest spark,
Though kindled by Thy light, in vain would try
To trace Thy counsels, infinite and dark;
And thought is lost ere thought can soar so high,
E'en like past moments in eternity.

Thou from primeval nothingness did'st call
First Chaos, then Existence. Lord, on Thee
Eternity hath its foundation; all
Sprung forth from Thee; of Light, Joy, Harmony,
Sole origin—all life, beauty, Thine.
Thy word created all and doth create:
Thy splendour fills all space with rays Divine.
Thou art, and wert, and shalt be glorious! great!
Life-giving, life-sustaining Potentate.

Thy chains the unmeasured universe surround,
Upheld by Thee, by Thee inspired with breath!
Thou the beginning with the end hast bound,
And beautifully mingled Life and Death!
As sparks mount upward from the fiery blaze,
So suns are born, so worlds spring forth from Thee!
And as the spangles in the sunny rays
Shine round the silver snow, the pageantry
Of Heaven's bright army glitters in Thy praise.

A million torches lighted by Thy hand
Wander unwearied through the blue abyss;
They own Thy power, accomplish Thy command,
All gay with life, all eloquent with bliss:
What shall we call them? Piles of crystal light?
A glorious company of golden streams?
Lamps of celestial ether burning bright?
Suns, lighting systems with their joyous beams?
But Thou, to those, art as the noon to night.

Yes! as a drop of water in the sea,
All this magnificence in Thee is lost:
What are a thousand worlds compared to Thee?
And what am I, when heaven's unnumbered host,
Though multiplied by myriads, and arrayed
In all the glory of sublimest thought,
Is but an atom in the balance, weighed
Against Thy greatness—is a cypher brought
Against Infinity? What am I, then? Nought.

Nought! but the effluence of Thy light Divine,
Pervading worlds, hath reached my bosom too;
Yes, in my spirit doth Thy Spirit shine,
As shines the sunbeam in a drop of dew.
Nought! but I live and on hope's pinions fly,
Eager towards Thy presence; for in Thee
I live, and breathe, and dwell; aspiring high,
E'en to the throne of Thy Divinity.
I am, O God, and surely Thou must be!

Thou art! directing, guiding all, Thou art!
Direct my understanding, then, to Thee;
Control my spirit, guide my wandering heart;
Though but an atom 'midst immensity,
Still I am something fashioned by Thy hand!

I hold a middle rank, 'twixt heaven and earth ;
On the last verge of mortal being stand,
Close to the realm where angels have their birth,
Just on the boundary of the spirit-land !

The chain of being is complete in me ;
In me is matter's last gradation lost,
And the next step is spirit—Deity !
I can command the lightning, and am dust !
A monarch, and a slave ; a worm, a God !
Whence came I here, and how ? so marvellously
Constructed and conceived, unknown ? This clod
Lives surely through some higher energy ;
For from itself alone it could not be.

Creator ! Yes ! Thy Wisdom and Thy Word
Created me ! Thou Source of Life and Good !
Thou Spirit of my spirit, and my Lord !
Thy Light, Thy Love, in their bright plenitude
Filled me with an immortal soul, to spring
O'er the abyss of death, and bade it wear
The garments of Eternal Day, and wing
Its heavenly flight beyond this little sphere,
Even in its Source, to Thee, its Author, Thee.

O thought ineffable ! O vision blest !
(Though worthless our conceptions all of Thee,)
Yet shall Thy shadowed image fill our breast,
And waft its homage to the Deity.
God ! thus alone my lowly thoughts can soar,
Thus seek Thy presence. Being wise and good !
'Midst Thy vast works, admire, obey, adore ;
And when the tongue is eloquent no more,
The soul shall speak in tears of gratitude.

Just as some of the Darvishes use internal incentives to religious fervour, such as the *hashīsh*, hereafter described, and believe that the imagination, excited by such physical means, obtains a glimpse of future spiritual felicity, so others enliven the mental faculty by corporeal excitements. In this view, they inspire each other with increased fervour by the agitation of the body and the continued exercise of the powers of speech, which they call invoking the Deity or the *zikr*. With some, such as the *maulavīs*, the sense of hearing is excited by the sound of a sweet or harmonious music. At least, such to themselves is the performance of their little orchestra, and it is used more as a calming or soothing element than as an exciting one. If, by certain means, the senses can be excited almost to a point of frenzy, by others they may be lulled into a condition almost of inertia. The power of the moral influence of the ‘ spiritual guide ’ (*shaikh* or *murshid*) is fully explained in the system of the Darvishes, and the submissive deportment of his *murīds*, or pupils, or disciples, is so visible to the observer that he is almost led to believe in the theory of the power of the superior will over the inferior and willing spirit, which is so important an element in their system. Nature and its laws are studied and understood, whilst life and the soul are inexplicable, as much so as is their great Author Himself. The latter may possess qualities yet unknown to the most learned in the sciences, yet of which some persons, often the least instructed, imagine they have glimpses, from which theories are formed totally at variance with natural science, and must, therefore, be qualified as ‘ spiritual ’.

The following extract from the Oriental work called *Fusūs*,[1] by Muhyī-ud-Dīn al ’Arabī, will serve to give the ideas of a Mussulman on the preceding :—

“ Man having been formed, by the hand of his Creator, out of the best of the soil of the earth, became composed of all of the varied natures which characterise the diversities of vegetable matter, which is the natural product of soil, and of all that partakes of the four distinct elements of nature, fire, air, earth, and water, and also possessing the three properties, animal, vegetable, and mineral ; he received the most noble of forms, and his human material was formed with the finest traits that adorn the living creature. God blessed His work with the gift of His own Holy Spirit, and endowed man with the powers of intellect and of speech ; so that he possessed the attributes of his own Creator. These precious gifts were bestowed upon him, so as to enable

[1] ‘ Gems ’. Its full title was *Fuṣūṣ al-Ḥikm*, in which “the author discourses upon the nature and significance of the divine revelations imparted to twenty-seven prophets ” from Adam to Muḥammad (*E.R.E.* 8, 907). Born at Murcia in 1165 A.D., Ibn al-’Arabī, as he is generally styled, travelled widely, through North Africa, in Babylonia, Asia Minor and Syria, dying at Damascus in 1240. For *ḥikm*, ‘wisdom,’ see art. Ḥikma in *E.I.* i. 305, and that on *al-Insān al-Kāmil*, ‘the Perfect Man,’ *ib.* 510. See also note on p. 84 *infra*.

him to comprehend the wondrous works of his Divine Originator and to speak His praises.

"Adam, thus blessed with Divine gifts, was permitted to speak to his own posterity in the language of prophecy, and to direct it to the worship of his Creator. The knowledge which he possessed of his creation and his Creator has been transmitted to us through his descendants. God also gave him power over the whole vast universe in which he was placed, and an intellectual capacity requisite for the acquisition of a knowledge of all that surrounded him.

"As to those more elevated beings who occupy the upper celestial abodes, God has given them that knowledge which it pleases Him for them to possess. They worshipped in Adam an intellectual capacity and power superior to their own, notwithstanding that they do possess a knowledge of the hidden and the veiled secrets of the Divinity which was not known to him. They are permitted to behold the attributes of the Most High, of which man only knows the names ; and, from their position near Him, are able to see the exercise of them over all His creation throughout the vast and interminable universe. Man was gifted with a mental capacity, because he possessed a knowledge of his own creation and of the exalted attributes of his Creator. Why it pleased the Almighty to create him, except it be to serve Him, is unknown to him, and it does not become him to seek to penetrate into the mysterious Will of Him who said, 'Be', and it was."

Among mankind differences of opinion have arisen with regard to the ways of God in this world, as well as respecting the hereafter, and the condition of those who exist in His heavenly abode. Whilst some believe that there is nothing in existence but what is visible to the sight, and to the ordinary organs of vision, others consider that there is much that is veiled from sight, and which can only be seen through a nearer approach to their Divine Creator ; and that this faculty is only to be obtained by a life of deep contemplation and adoration of Him, and a close spiritual communion with His eternal and all-pervading Spirit. They are, consequently, divided into two classes, viz. :
1. Those who attach themselves to whatever is clear and external.
2. Those who seek to penetrate into the veiled and mystical,—otherwise into what is purely 'Spiritual'.

Of these, the first explains all that is external, as well as what is secret, by means of the ordinary human intellect, or reason; they are called the *aṣḥāb-i-'ilm-i-zāhir*: and the second devote themselves to the ways of Mysticism, and to pointing out the *paths* by which a knowledge of the veiled and the hidden may be obtained; these are called the *aṣḥāb-i-'ilm-i-bātin*: and God, in His merciful compassion, teaches them, through the power of His names and attributes, in Divine and spiritual visions. The beginning of their hopes is based upon the verse of the *Qurān* which says, "Ye are of those who are near (to Me)", and their termination, "Ye are of those who are the inheritors of them who inherit Paradise, and remain there perpetually".

It would be interesting to trace the growth of the belief in saints and other human beings to whom man has assigned a position in the other life. The oldest record of history, the Bible, shows clearly that the earliest conviction of mankind—that which was doubtless handed down from Adam, to whom it no doubt was a Divine revelation, vouchsafed at the period of his creation,—was, strictly speaking, in the Unity of God, and in the existence of angelic beings, created previous to this world, or to the first progenitors of the human race. To this may be added a perfect knowledge of good and evil, and the consequent belief in rewards and punishments. A conviction, however, based upon the preceding, of a future condition of happiness or misery after this life, nowhere gives to any one a place superior to another. Each individual is held responsible by the Creator for his own acts, and the Omniscient and All-Just rewards or punishes them, according to their respective merits. To the truly repentant His mercy endures for ever. God alone is the Judge and Arbitrator, and His decisions are beyond appeal or intercession in the life to come. At a later period, the sinfulness of the human passions and the feebleness of the mind of man are apparent in the necessity of a Mediator between God and man, as shown in the symbolic sacrifices prescribed in the laws of Moses.

Among the Romans and Greeks, to whom revealed religion was unknown, the system of celestial hierarchy seems to have been a matter of poetical imagination, which supposes that each element must be under the especial direction of a titular deity. These from time to time becoming more and more numerous, some were placed in higher, and some in lower positions; and all connected, as emanations from a One Supreme Deity, who reigned over and commanded all of the others. To these, however, were ascribed human attributes and human passions ; so that the whole system is readily seen to be wholly inconsistent with the character and attributes of the One Divine Creator. Besides that, the existence of the greater part of these gods is due to human imagination, assemblies of men believed that they could confer honour upon individuals by deifying them, or, in other words, conferring upon them positions of eminence in the heavens. Such is the ruling principle of what we call Mythology. To these gods were ascribed various characteristics, and varied powers over certain elements. In the hour of danger men appealed to them for succour and safety ; and even consulted them when desirous of penetrating into the dark and hidden Future. The gods and goddesses became the patrons and patronesses of credulous mortals, and to each was assigned certain distinct forms, which have been handed down to our times in the masterly works of art now existing.

It would therefore appear that the system of modern saints and saintesses—so to speak—is totally different from the original faith of Adam and his descendants possessing revelation, and this is a continuation only of that of Mythology. The resemblance, at least, is so striking that it is impossible to attribute it to any other origin.

This modern system of ' saints ' varies among different people, and the degree to which it has attained among the Darvishes, and Mussulmans in general, is seen in the following chapters. Among these, prayers are offered to the saints for their intercession with the prophets ; and prayers are also presented to them in the view of increasing their influence over the Deity. As it is not generally supposed that the souls of mankind will remain for ever in a condition of wretchedness, far from the presence of a merciful God, prayers are offered up to Him in behalf of those who, it is supposed, are still expiating their sins in unhappiness, in the hope that the offering of supplications will be acceptable to the Almighty, and induce Him to pardon and forgive. Prayers for those still in life seem to be only for their worldly happiness and prosperity, without any reference to their future existence ; though they may be in the desire and hope that they lead lives of purity, so as to merit happiness hereafter. Revealed religion teaches, by examples, that the sincerely devout may pray for the living, in the full expectation that their prayers will be heard and accepted ; whilst I believe it does not admit of the efficacy of supplication for those who, having departed this life, have entered upon the responsibilities of their mortal career. This may, therefore, have given rise to the belief in the necessity of possessing patron saints and saintesses, already in heaven, and therefore near to the Deity, whose intercession may be invoked.

A study of the subject to which the following chapters relate has given rise to the preceding reflections, all of which are not, necessarily, those of the Darvishes. Perhaps I should apologise for thus expressing them, and for not having allowed the patient reader to form his own conclusions from the perusal of what I have collected.

In conclusion, these may be summed up in the idea that there is but One God, the Creator of all things. When God created man, He was pleased to give him faculties which He did not give to any other of His creatures ; these were given him in the perfect vigour of manhood, and not in infancy, to be developed and strengthened in after years, as is now the case ; they consisted of Reason and Speech. Man was created with a perfect knowledge of his own creation ; possessed the faculty of reasoning thereon, and of communicating that knowledge to his posterity, which he did, and it has in this manner come down to our time. God also was pleased to gift man with an existence which, we may suppose, He did not give to any other of His creatures. He gave him an existence like His own, which will not only live in the present life, but will continue to exist hereafter in another. It is said that he was created even superior to the angels, but in what respect we know not ; whether it refers to the power which he is enabled to exercise over other creatures of a secondary character, and even inanimate nature, in this world. This part of man's existence is called his *Spirit* or *Soul.* The peculiar character of this existence is such as to lead to the conviction that it is more than human, and must, therefore, be *Divine.* Oriental Spiritualism believes that its origin is due to a direct emanation from the Deity ; and differs from the ordinary breath of life, which all other animated nature received on its creation.

We next are led to ask the question which remains unanswered, Is the spirit of man cut off entirely from that of its

First Source and Origin, or has it still a connexion with it? When we sincerely and ardently pray to God, we feel that we approach Him—that we commune with Him; that He hears and answers our supplications; and that in this manner we re-unite our spirit to His. On the other hand, we feel that all evil acts—those which are the produce of our human passions—separate us from God, and destroy in us that pleasing conviction of the benefits to be derived from the influences of His Spirit, all of which are for good and wise purposes, such as tend to render man happy in his present life, and hold out for him a hope of continual happiness in that future life of which he knows almost nothing.

It is evident that the history of man's creation—such as has been written by Moses—is the only correct one, because it is that which the original man has handed down to his posterity. Why parts of it were veiled in allegory we scarcely dare to ask, and may only suppose that the knowledge was withheld from a good and wise cause. This history may be regarded more as a *revealed* than as an *inspired* one. We need not inquire in what manner God revealed or made known to man (Adam) a knowledge of his own creation. If God did not make it known to him, how did he learn it? To deny that God made it known to him is to deny the existence of God and His creation of man, and leaves the imagination to wander, without any guide, in search of a spontaneous creation, or a self-creating nature, which ultimately, nevertheless, terminates in the conviction of the absolute necessity of a 'Great First Cause', which is none other than the Almighty.

With this knowledge of our own creation, we are led also to believe that man originally possessed a profound conviction of evil and good, of right and wrong, unbiassed by the influences of the human passions. When these began to affect him, he lost much of the knowledge with which he was originally gifted. Just as these tend to withdraw him from God, so his spirit influences him to approach Him. To call upon His holy name, and to praise Him, is what renders man in this life similar to the angels in heaven. We need not ask why God was pleased to create him with two such adverse characteristics; for it is evident that they are inherent to knowledge and ignorance, to good and evil, to merit and demerit. Without them he would have been perfect in knowledge; have been perfectly good and pure; would have had no duty to perform towards his Divine Creator other than to praise Him; in fact, he would have been possessed of all the characteristics of God Himself, and have been entirely a *spirit* dwelling upon earth.

Inspiration is a subject upon which depends the whole theory of the prophets and of the saints, and consequently opens upon a vast field for the imagination. Independent of the influences which the Divine Spirit is believed to exercise upon that of man, Oriental Spiritualism fully teaches that good men do not only have an influence upon him whilst an occupant of this life, but that the former may and do exercise one upon those who invoke their spirits after their departure, by inspiring them for beneficial purposes. This is therefore a subject only considered secondary to that of the creation of man, and of his being gifted with an ever-existing soul.

To possess the gift of approaching God in prayer, and to entertain the conviction that He will and does hear as well as answer our prayers, does not necessarily imply that God *inspires* any one. The powers of the passions are allayed; and the purer impulses of the Spirit are unrestrained. A conviction of our own helplessness and insignificancy—of our impotence to help ourselves under circumstances of need or of peril—naturally leads us to seek for some one who is able to aid and protect us. That One we feel can only be God. We therefore call upon Him, not only for ourselves, but for those whom we desire to benefit or to succour, as the Creator and Dispenser of all providences. Is this impulse to be attributed to a direct influence of the Spirit of God, or, in other words, to His inspiration? In reply it may be said that revealed religion teaches us that the Spirit of God does even *strive* with man, evidently so as to induce him to withstand the temptations of the *flesh*, and obey Divine influences, all tending towards his present and future welfare. Do those who accept and obey these influences become thereby gifted with characteristics of a superhuman nature in this life, and are consequently peculiarly holy? If we analyse the history of the 'prophets', we find that, even if they were not always themselves pure and faultless, they endeavoured to benefit their fellow-men, and forasmuch received what is called inspiration. That God loves whatever is good, and abhors what is evil, cannot be doubted by any one who entertains a proper conception of His character ; but the whole history of man shows us, by innumerable examples, that the benefits to be derived from a submission to His influences are not of this life, but of the future. The most holy men have prospered but little in this world, and met with the most cruel and painful of deaths. If, therefore, men acquired superhuman powers through 'inspiration', it is natural to suppose that they would exercise them for their own preservation. In our entire ignorance of the future, we pray to God for our necessities and protection ; or, in other words, to bless our own labours and those of others who labour for us, and when we receive them we attribute the results as an answer to our prayers. When they are not granted, we must either suppose that God has not heard us, or not been pleased to grant our requests. We even believe in the efficacy of the prayers of others in our behalf. Are these more efficacious when the prayers are of a good than when of a bad person ? If the former, we are led to believe in the intermediation of those whom the world calls 'living saints' ; or of human beings who, on account of the purity of their lives in this world, possess a superior degree of influence with the Creator of all mankind. To deny this is to deny the many examples offered in support of it in revealed religion. Not only among the Darvishes, but other religions, holy persons are held to possess and exercise spiritual powers which appertain only to the Omnipotent Creator, and are worshipped accordingly by their followers, disregardful of the fact that, at the most, they are only the mediums of Divine providences. They are supposed to be able to perform what are called *miracles*. These superhuman powers are even attributed by many persons of great intellectual attainments to the bones of the departed, and these are believed to possess the power of changing and arresting the providences of God. Thus we see that 'inspiration' leads even to the belief in the power of the animal portion of man—that which belongs not only to dumb brutes, but to inanimate creation—over the spiritual, thus reversing the whole theory of spiritual religion.

The Darvishes hold the saints in exalted estimation. They fully believe that some holy individuals possess great 'spiritual powers', whilst yet in this life, and that those who follow in the 'paths' pointed out by them, all, however, bowing to the same universal Creator, may profit by their intercession with Him.

They believe that blessed spirits are ever around them, and, like that of the Omnipresent Deity, know no particular place of abode, and may therefore be invoked anywhere. They nevertheless venerate the places of their interment, as localities sanctified by the presence of their remains. They do not, however, attribute any miraculous powers to their bones. With them, 'inspiration' is the fruit of prayer and devotion, in connexion with holy lives; and that it is mostly during slumber, when the physical faculties are lulled in an incomprehensible manner, that the sleeper sees visions and receives Divine influences. It was at such times as these that the prophets were spoken to by God, and commanded to proclaim certain Divine truths which were necessary to the future welfare and happiness of mankind. These 'truths' are held to be incontrovertible, and are therefore declared in succinct terms, having the form of proverbs and maxims, and have therefore the force of commands.

ABRAHAM AND MUHAMMAD

In the course of the observations offered in the present work, allusion is sometimes made to certain principles contained in or deduced from the *Qurān*, which, not being either originally taken from the Old or New Testament, remain a matter of speculation. To a good Mussulmān, for whose mind the *Qurān* offers a distinct field of belief, these are naturally attributed wholly to inspiration. Some of these ideas are certainly very sublime. The prophet of Islāmism entertained the most elevated and exalted ideas of the Deity, akin to those so beautifully expressed in the Psalms of David. He called himself of the sect or faith of Abraham, thus forming a distinction between what he considered to be the religion of this patriarch and the Jews personally. In the second chapter [v. 130 f.] of the *Qurān*, it is stated: "Say, We believe in God, and in what has been sent to us from on high,—to Abraham, Ismail, Isaac, Jacob, and the twelve tribes. We believe in the books given to Moses and Jesus,—to those given to the prophets by the Lord. We make no difference between them, and we give ourselves up to God."

"Would you say that Abraham, Ismail, Isaac, Jacob, and the twelve tribes, were Jews or Christians? Tell then, Who is more knowing—God or you? And who is more culpable than he who conceals the truth confided to him by God? He is not indifferent to what you do."

"These generations have all gone by. They have received the fruits of their works, as you will of yours. No one will ask you an account of what they may have done."

And in the third chapter [v. 60 f.]: "Abraham was neither Jew nor Christian. He was pious, and given up entirely to God, and did not associate any other person than One in the Godhead."

"Those who hold to the Faith of Abraham are those who follow him; such is the Prophet of the True Believers, and God protects those who are faithful to him."

In the verse preceding this latter, the word Jew is Yahūd, and Christian Naṣrānī [1] or Nazarene; whilst that which expresses the idea that Abraham was pious and submissive to God is the Hanafī [2] Mussulman, or as by some translators, a Mussulman of the Hanafī (orthodox) rite.

The question thus arises, Was there a people in the prophet's time who were neither Jew, Christian, nor Idolater, and whose dogmas formed the basis of his peculiar principles? If so, what were those principles, and from what source derived?

Oriental traditions contain much more minute details about Ibrāhīm (Abraham) than the Bible. He is supposed to have lived in the reign of King Namrūd (Nimrod), one of whose confidential officers his father Āzar was. This king and all his people were idolaters. It was a tradition of those times that a child would be born, who would be the cause of the destruction of his kingdom. To prevent this, the king ordered, on a particular occasion, all of the men of his city of Babel to be removed outside of its walls, and the females to remain within; but, as Āzar was one of the king's officers, and was stationed inside one of the gates, his wife joined him there. The king's astrologers, however, having

[1] Fr. *naṣara*, 'helped'. In several of its forms the root connotes affinity to the Nazarenes or Christians (see Salmoné's *Arab. Dict.*, *s.v.*, p. 1069).

[2] Of the sect of the Ḥanīfites, as the allusion to Abraham shows. The Ḥanīfiya meant the religion of Abraham (*Encycl. of Islam*, ii. p. 258). For a full account see "The Words 'Ḥanīf' and 'Muslim'," by the late Sir Charles Lyall, in *J.R.A.S.*, 1903, p. 772: the term *ḥanīf* is nearly synonymous with Muslim in the *Qurān*, but generally refers to the religion of Abraham, or implies a return to it.

been able to learn this fact, communicated it to him ; and consequently, the child born to Āzar was concealed in a cave, until he reached the age of puberty.[1]

" On issuing from this confinement, he was struck with the grandeur of the world and the celestial bodies, and impressed with contempt for the absurdity of the worship of idols. He, therefore, refused, at all times, to worship them, and became the object of the anger of King Namrūd. Called before him, he boldly told the king that his idols were only the work of man's hands, whilst the Great Creator of the Universe was the only true God, and Author of man's own existence ; and, consequently, the proper object of his adoration. Finding an opportunity, he destroyed all of the idols, except one, the largest ; and, having placed the axe with which he had knocked off their heads in the mouth of this one, said that probably he had destroyed the others, which argument rather forcibly struck the worshippers. On another occasion he asked the king to afford him an exhibition of his power, saying that the God whom he adored not only brought man into existence in this world, but gave him another in the life to come. The king produced two criminals, and having put one to death, pardoned the other ; meaning thereby, that he could take away and bestow life. Abraham next asked him to cause the sun to rise and set, and the planets to appear, which were the daily works of his God ; and this the king being unable to effect, the king's anger became increased, and he determined to put Abraham to death. For this purpose he had an immense fire prepared, and cast him into it. God, however, did not forget His faithful servant, and sent His celestial messenger, the angel Jibrā'īl (Gabriel, signifying the ' power of God ') to his rescue. After the king and his people saw that Abraham was protected by a power hitherto unknown to them, many of the latter adopted his faith, and worshipped the only One true God.

" This fidelity of Abraham to the Creator, amidst a larger number of idolaters, acquired for him the title of the *khalīl*, ' the friend ' or ' sincere advocate of God ', by which he is still known among Mussulmans.*

" In the course of time he took Sāra or Sarah, a name

[1] For an account of Namrūd's massacre of children and pregnant women, owing to bad dreams, see *Encycl. of Islam*, ii. p. 431.

* James ii. 23.

signifying 'the pleasant', or 'agreeable', to wife; and as she proved to be barren, according to the Oriental custom, still in practice, she gave him her handmaiden Hājir, or Hagar,[1] from *hajara*, to fly from, or escape[2]; the same root from which is derived the well-known word, *Hijra* (Hegira), or 'Flight of the Prophet', and from which the Mussulman period is taken. Hājir having borne him a son named Ismā'īl or Ishmael, or the 'heard of God', from *sama'*, to hear, and *Alā*, God, she became the object of the envy of her mistress, and Abraham was compelled to remove her into a remote part of the country (Arabia). There God heard her voice, and protected her from death by thirst and starvation. The well, so much revered by Mussulmans, called *Zamzam*, at Makka, was erected for her especial benefit. Ibrahīm, when conveying Hājir and Ismā'īl from the Land of Shām [Syria], where he resided, to the spot on which Makka stands, was guided by the angel Jibrāīl, and directed to stop precisely where this celebrated well still exists. A tree sprang up at the time, to shelter them from the heat of the sun, and there he left them. Hājir implored him not to abandon her and her helpless child in so desolate a place; and, though he was much affected by her appeal, he told her that such was the will of God, conveyed to him during his sleep in a dream. She, on hearing this, resigned herself up to God's supreme will. He left her near to the *Bait-ul-harām*, and to the spot designed for the Ka'bah, neither of which were yet in existence. The first simply signifies the 'Holy House', and the latter 'The Cube'."

The destitute condition of Hājir and her child is one of the most touching narratives of the Orient; only surpassed by that of the intended sacrifice of Ismā'īl by Abraham, in obedience to the command of God.

"It is related that, having consumed all of the food left with her by Abraham, hunger and thirst caused her milk to dry up, and her child, as well as herself, was apparently doomed to die a most cruel death, far from those who might come to her relief. She ascended Mount Safā, and looked around her. No sign of

[1] This is the accepted derivation, though Renan (*Hist. of Israel*, i. 81 *n.*, Eng. trans.) connects the name with Ar. *ḥagar*, 'rock', Hagar thus personifying the tribes of Arabia Petræa, Hastings, *D.B.*, ii. p. 278.

[2] The term does not connote 'flight', but 'migration' (*Encyclopædia of Islam*, ii. p. 302).

cultivation or of water could be seen within the extent of her vision. Seated there, she wept, and in the anguish of her heart, at the sight of the starving child, cried out aloud for assistance. Descending from the mountain, she hurried across the intervening valley, and ascended Mount Meroeh,[1] which also offered a wide field to her vision. She still was unable to see any habitation, or any fountain of water. In her grief she went seven times to and fro between these mountains, on the spot where the pilgrims of our times still encamp. At each passage, she would stop to see her child, and guard him against the wild animals of the desert. At length, from Mount Meroeh she thought she heard a voice. It seemed so distant and vague that she was unable to ascertain whence it proceeded. At length she became aware that it was from the spot on which she had left her son. Hastening to the spot, she became delighted with the sight of a running stream of pure water. By some it is supposed that the water gushed out of the spot where the child lay; whilst by others it is said that the same angel which accompanied them in the flight still watched over them, and that God, in answer to the cries of the mother and her suffering boy, touched the earth, and let a spring of water gush up from the sources which it everywhere contains. After both had drunk of the refreshing stream, she designed to fill her jug for future use, but the same unseen voice forbade her, saying that the stream would for ever afterwards continue to flow. She also designed to erect a dam of earth, so as to raise up the stream ; but this was likewise forbidden to her, and she was told that Abraham would return and build a house there, which should become the Qibla, towards which millions of sovereigns and subjects would turn their faces in adoration of God. She was also told that her son should become a prophet, and guide men in the true path of religion.

" Hājir was not long left in this condition. A tribe of Arabs called the Bani Jarham,[2] whilst on their way from Yaman to Shām, attracted by the unexpected appearance of birds hovering around the stream, were delighted to find so useful a provision for themselves and their animals. These were distant relations of

[1] Safā and Marwā, the two mountains on which were anciently two idols (Sale's *Preliminary Discourse to the Koran*, Sir E. Denison Ross' ed., ii. p. 22).

[2] The Jorham of Sale's *Koran*, Preliminary Discourse, i. p. 15 f.

Abraham, but possessed no knowledge of his flight with Hājir and Ismā'īl, and much less of the well of Zamzam, on a spot where they had previously only found dry soil.

"Soon after this, and after hearing the history of Hājir and her son Ismā'īl, Jarham, with all his people and flocks, established themselves on the spot now known as Makka.[1] With them came the tribes called Katira and Mezamen bin-'Amru, the chief of which was Semedā bin-'Āmir, and thus formed the earliest residents of that city, among whom Ismā'īl grew up and found aid and sustenance. From them he learned the Arab tongue.

"Abraham was informed, through a visit of the angelic visitor, Jibrā'īl, of the prosperous condition of Hājir and Ismā'īl, and once a year paid them a visit, on a swift-footed animal called Barāq, from *barq*, or lightning." [2]

[1] Anas said: When God gave His Prophet the plunder of the property of the tribe Hawazen, his majesty gave to the men of the Quraish, who really became Mussulmans, a hundred camels each (Mathews, *Mishcat ul-Masabih*, ii. p. 797). Mezamen seems an error.

[2] The fullest account of Barāq or Burāq is that by E. Rehatsek in *Journal*, Bombay Branch, R. Asiatic Soc., 1881, xv. p. 25 f. "Burāq is the vehicle of obedience and the allegorical representation of prayer", according to Nūrbakhsh, founder of the Nūrbakhshī sect in Kashmīr, *ib.* p. 33, citing *Dabistān*, p. 481. Burāq was supposed to have a woman's head and a peacock's tail—cf. the illustration on p. vii *supra*, and *E.I.* i. p. 793. His colour was chestnut as in the verse: *Sawār-i-jahāngīr ikrān Buràq*, 'the earth-conquering horseman with his chestnut Burāq', *i.e.* Muhammad (Sa'di's *Scroll of Wisdom*, by Wollostan, in The Wisdom of the East Series, p. 32).

Burāq is the steed of all prophets, but more especially of Abraham. In the case of Muhammad his proper function is to carry him to Jerusalem, not to Heaven, but the Prophet will ride him again at the Last Day. It is at best doubtful if the name is really connected with *barq*, 'lightning', and it may be of Persian origin: *v.* the learned arts. by B. Schrieke and J. Horovitz in *Der Islam*, vi. and ix., where the problems of the history of the versions of Muhammad's ascension are discussed. That given in the text contains some additional incidents, notably the story of Ismā'īl's first wife, her dismissal, and Ismā'īl's second and monogamous union. The sacrifice of a son by Abraham was reproduced in the original version of the *mi'rāj* legend in the form of the incident of the Prophet's purification by the cutting open of his breast, but "when the Ascension was shifted from its original position and placed at a later period in his life, the cleansing was no longer an appropriate feature", and was omitted (Bevan, in *Studien zur semitischen Philologie und Religionsgeschichte J. Wellhausen . . . 1914 . . . gewidmet*, p. 58). In its later forms the *mi'rāj* was distinguished from the *'isra'*, or night-journey to Jerusalem. The encounter with the lion

This is the same name which the prophet gave to the animal on which he proceeded from earth to heaven in the night called the *mi'rāj*, or ascension. In the shortest imaginable space of time, he saw and heard much in the seven heavens through which he passed, and the whole affair is now supposed by the more intelligent Mussulmans to have been only a vision, like the revelation of St. John.

"On the fleet-footed Barāq, Abraham annually made a visit to Hājir and her son. The latter had reached the age of fifteen when his mother died, and, aided by the Bani Jarham, he laid her beloved remains in Makka, close by the black stone which is so much revered by all the faithful, and was deeply affected by the loss of so affectionate and devoted a mother. After this he planned the design of emigrating from that country, and to prevent this his friends married him to one of the most noble of the daughters of the afore-named tribe.

"It is a matter of tradition that Ismā'īl was an excellent cavalier and an adroit hunter. It happened that Abraham, according to his habit, that year made his annual visit to Makka, and during Ismā'īl's absence in search of game arrived at his door. Knocking at it, his son's wife made her appearance, and, not knowing the stranger, failed to offer him the usual tokens of respect and hospitality due to him, which, giving him offence, he departed, bidding her describe his appearance to her husband on his return, and that he recommended him to change the sill[1] of his door. Ismā'īl, on learning what had occurred, immediately recognised his father Abraham, and in the advice to change his sill a command to dismiss his wife, which he forthwith did. He next married another wife from among the maidens of the same tribe, and on the return of his father he was gratified by his dutiful obedience to his wishes. On the second occasion Ismā'īl's

---

('Alī's spiritual force) described on p. 422 *infra* must be an even later accretion.

It may be worth adding that Syed Ahmed Khan rejects the story of the Shakki-Sadar or 'Cutting open of the Breast' altogether, and only accepts that of the *mi'rāj* as a vision (*Essays on the Life of Mohammed*, Ess. on Shakki-Sadar and Meraj, p. 34).

[1] The threshold, symbolising the inviolability of the home or its mistress. The symbol may explain much of the folk-lore of the threshold collected in Sir James Frazer's *Folk-Lore of the Old Testament*, iii.

wife was most attentive to her guest—offered him hospitality, and pressed him to partake of a meal got ready for him. This latter Abraham, however, declined dismounting to partake of, and so had to dine seated on his animal. The cause of this was that he had formally promised Sarah, when he visited Hājir and Ismā'īl, not to dismount. After dining as aforesaid, his daughter-in-law brought water and washed his hands and feet, and combed his hair. Much as she begged him to descend from his animal, he persisted in his refusal, but so far gratified her as to rest one of his feet on a stone near her door, and the print of it remained upon it. On departing, Abraham bade her tell her husband, on his return from the chase, that the sill of his door was good, and he must be careful not to change it. On hearing what had occurred, Ismā'īl was extremely gratified, and informed his wife that the unknown stranger whom she had entertained was none other than his father Abraham. In conformity with his recommendation, he never during his lifetime married any other wife."

Connected with the history of Abraham, whose religion, the Islām prophet declares in the *Qurān*, was his own, mention may be made of the children borne to him by Sarah, viz. Isḥāq (Isaac) and Ya'qūb (Jacob). The same work from which the present Arabian tradition is derived (*Rauzat-as-Safā* [1]), adds that by the great favour of the Almighty, Hājir was made illustrious among women, and Sarah ardently also desired to have a son, so that the prophetship might be continued in her offspring.

" About this time the angel Jibrāīl, or Gabrāīl, was sent with several other celestial messengers to destroy the people of Lot [Sodom], called Lūt.[2] They became the guests of Abraham in the form of men, and he killed a fatted calf for their entertainment. They refused, however, to partake of it until they should be made acquainted with its price. Abraham, in reply, said that in the beginning its price was the benediction still used by all Mussulmans, especially by Darvishes, ' In the name of God, the

[1] *The Rauẓat-us-Ṣafā*, or '*Pleasaunce of Purity*', by Mirkhond (Mir Khwānd), who wrote in the reign of Ḥusain Mirza, king of Khurāsān, A.D. 1469–1506 : cf. note on p. 404 *infra*. The translation (incomplete) of this work by E. Rehatsek forms vol. i. (Parts I. and II.) of the Oriental Translation Fund New Series, 1892.

[2] Lūt is Sodom, and its people were called Lūṭīy. The modern Arab term for the Dead Sea is Baḥr Lūṭ (*E.I.* i. p. 582).

merciful and the clement', and in the end, 'Blessed be God' for His bounties. Notwithstanding this act of piety, which Jibrāīl greatly applauded, the angels persisted in not partaking of the food, much to the alarm of their host; for in those times, whenever a guest entertained hostile designs, he would refuse to eat with their object. Fully aware of Abraham's fears, they informed him who they were, and the object of their Divine mission. Gabrāīl also gave good news to him, that God, in His great mercy, would give him and Sarah a son. Now Sarah heard this from behind a curtain, and smiled, and this circumstance is alluded to in the *Qurān*: 'His wife was standing by, and laughed. We gave her the good news, that (she should bear) Isḥāq, and afterwards Ya'qūb.' By some it is said that she laughed on account of the utter improbability of her bearing children; and by others, because she knew they were angels, and was rejoiced that they were sent to destroy the sinful people of Lot. Be this as it may, the angels knew what was passing in her mind, for, addressing her, they observed, 'Do you not know how the Almighty created Adam without father or mother, and that from him all his race is descended?' Soon after this Sarah bore Isḥāq, in the hundredth year of her husband's age, and it is traditioned that on the night of his birth he beheld a thousand shooting stars pass before his sight in the firmament, and having asked of the angel Jibrāīl the meaning of so uncommon an occurrence, learned that from his son then born a thousand prophets would descend. Abraham praised God, and begged that his other son, Ismā'īl, should also be the object of His Divine favour. A voice was heard to reply, 'O Abraham, from Ismā'īl shall proceed one prophet, whose intercession mankind, to the end of time, will implore, and who will be the crown of all prophets'. Abraham blessed and thanked God for His mercies (*Qurān* xiv. 41): 'Praise be unto God, who hath given me in my old age Ismā'īl and Isḥāq, for my Lord hears supplications'. It is related that Abraham was ninety-nine years of age when he was directed by inspiration to circumcise himself, and that he circumcised Ismā'īl at thirteen and Isḥāq at one year of age; some say that the former was three years older than the latter, whilst others say fourteen. It was after the Divine intimation that through these the prophetship would be carried down, that he was directed to offer one of them up as a sacrifice."

THE SACRIFICE OF ISMĀ'ĪL

On this subject there exist conflicting statements regarding which of the two sons, Ismā'īl or Isḥāq, it was. Some of the *aṣḥābs* of the blessed Prophet, the commander of the faithful, 'Umar bin al-Khattāb, 'Alī bin Abū Tālib, and others [read 'some'] of the *tābi'īn*[1] (those who were their followers), Ka'b al-Ahbār,[2] Sa'id bin Jabīr,[3] Masrūq,[4] Abū'l-Zahīl,[5] Zahrī,[6] Sa'd,[7] and others narrate that it was Isḥāq. On the other hand, some of the *aṣḥāb* and *tābi'īn*, such as 'Abdullāh bin 'Abbās,[8] Abū Huraira,[9] 'Abdulla bin 'Umar,[10] 'Āas,[11] and Abū Tufail 'Āmir bin Vaileh[12] [*sic*], as

[1] Tābi'ūn is the better form. They were the successors of the companions of the Prophet, the *aṣḥāb-i-ṣuffa* or *ahl-i-ṣuffa*, and so were styled 'the followers', *tābi'ūn*. The second part of this passage is given in Rehatsek's translation of the *Rauzat-us-Safā* as follows: "But another galaxy of noble companions, such as 'Abdullāh, 'Abbās, Abū Hasiwa, O'mar, 'Aam, Abū'l-Fazīl, son of A'amar and Omm Solma . . . (she was one of the widows of Muhammad), and among the emams of guidance, Ja'fer, the son of Muhammad-ussadiq, Sa'id, the son of Masib, Yusuf, the son of Mahran, and Mujahed, asserted that it was the sacrifice of the lord Esma'il". Their successors again were the *tubba'*.

[2] Ka'b-ul-Aḥbār was an expositor of the sacred book at the court of the first caliph. Rehatsek gives his name as Ka'b-ul-Akhbār; but see *E.I.* ii. p. 311. Le Strange says Ka'b-ul-Aḥbār or al-Hibr was originally a Jew, a celebrated authority for traditions and a very learned man. He died in 32 H. (*J.R.A.S.* xix., Part II. p. 17). Aḥbār is thus probably correct. He was surnamed Abū Isḥāq ibn Māni' al-Ḥimyarī.

[3] Sa'īd bin-Jabīr is also given by Rehatsek, *op. cit.* p. 165. He is mentioned again on p. 426 *infra.*

[4] Masrūq = Abu'l-'Abbās Aḥmād bin Masrūq (Rehatsek, *ib.*, and Nicholson, *Kashf-ul-Maḥjūb*, p. 146).

[5] Abū'l Zahīl appears in Rehatsek as Ab-uzzib.

[6] Zahrī = Ibn Shihāb az-Zuhrī. (Cf. Nicholson, *op. cit.* p. 71.)

[7] Sa'd doubtless = Sa'd ibn Abī Waqqās, as to whom see p. 409 *infra.*

[8] 'Abdullāh bin 'Abbās, who appears as 'Abdullāh (and) 'Abbās in Rehatsek, one of the most learned of the companions and ancestor of the Abbasside sovereigns. (See p. 426 *infra.*)

[9] Abū Huraira, for which Abū Hasiwa is doubtless a misprint in Rehatsek, is the patron of the deliverers of tradition. (See p. 417 *infra.*)

[10] 'Abdullāh bin 'Umar (O'mar in Rehatsek) is doubtless 'Abdullāh, son of 'Umr ibn al-Khaṭṭāb. He also is mentioned on p. 412 *infra.*

[11] 'Āas appears as A'am in Rehatsek, but probably Malik ibn-Anas is intended.

[12] Abū Tufail 'Āmir bin Vaila appears in Rehatsek as Abū'l-Fazīl, son of A'amar.

well as one of the [most] eminent of the latter, Imām al-Hudā Ja'far bin Muhammad bin Sādiq [and] Sa'id bin al-Musīb,[1] Yūsuf bin Mihrān,[2] Mujāhid,[3] and Sha'bī,[4] all declare that it was Ismā'īl. Many proofs are brought to sustain the two statements. The composer of the present work says that after having examined them all with much care, he has concluded (though God only knows the truth) that the son to be offered up was Ismā'īl.

"It is narrated that Ibrāhīm had vowed that if the Most High should favour him with a son, he would offer up to God a sacrifice, and that after this both Ismā'īl and Isḥāq were born to him. He had, however, forgotten his vow; and one night, when sleeping at Makka, the 'Place of Sacrifices'[5], he had a dream, in which some one said to him that it was the command of God he should offer up his son as a sacrifice. Waking up, he collected his thoughts, and, after pondering over the occurrence, decided in his own mind that it was not obligatory upon him. On the following night, however, he had precisely the same dream, and the same again during the third, and at the same time he heard a voice asking him how he could permit Satan (Shaitān) to mislead him from his obedience to God. On awaking, he bade Sarah to wash Ismā'īl's head, and anoint it, and dress him neatly; and to Ismā'īl he spoke: 'My dear boy, take some cord and a sharp knife, and accompany me, for the purpose of collecting wood on the mountain'. After this they set out together, and on the way Iblīs (the 'Tempter'[6]) went to Ibrāhīm in the form of an aged man, an adviser, who inquired of him where he was going, and

[1] Sa'īd bin-al-Musīb = Sa'īd bin-al-Musayyib (Nicholson, *op. cit.* p. 87).

[2] Yūsuf bin-Mihrān (-Mahrān in Rehatsek).

[3] Mujāhid, Majāhid on p. 405, may be Abū 'Abdullāh b. Mujāhid, the Shaikh of the Mutakallims and of the Qāẓī Abū Bakr al-Bāqilānī (*ob.* 403 H.). But he is better identified with the Abū'l 'Abbās b. Mujāhid at-Tā'ī al-Baṣrī, who was an immediate pupil of al-Ash'arī. Al-Mujāhid was also the title of another Abū Bakr, al-Baghdādī, who died in 324 H. (*J.R.A.S.*, 1901, p. 204[3]).

[4] Sha'bī, Āmir b. Sharāḥīl ash-Sha'bī of Kūfa, d. 104 H. (A.D. 722-3) at the age of ninety-two. He was one of the *tābi'ūn* of Kūfa and esteemed for his learning (Mathews, *Mishcat*, ii. p. 405).

[5] Or, more precisely, 'at the Minā'.

[6] Iblīs does not mean 'the tempter', though he tempted Eve. It is the personal name of the devil—*al-shaiṭān*, which is not a proper name (*E.I.* ii. p. 351). Iblīs is supposed to be derived from the Gr. *diabolos*; but Dante may have equated him to Ephialtes, 'chained one hand in front and the other behind his back'.

the former replied that he was going to the foot of the mountain, where business called him. Iblīs remarked, 'O Ibrāhīm, Satan has tempted you, and induced you to offer up Ismā'īl as a sacrifice to no purpose, whilst the whole world will become filled with his race alive'. Notwithstanding these words, Ibrāhīm knew, through his own spiritual powers as a prophet, and by the aid of Divine Light, that the speaker was Satan in disguise, and he exclaimed, 'O enemy of God, depart from me, for I must obey the commands of the Most High'. Iblīs, both disappointed and scornful, departed, and having found Ismā'īl, he addressed him, 'Do you not know where your father is taking you? Under the pretence of cutting wood, he intends to sacrifice you, misled by Iblīs, who has induced him to believe that his slumbers were of the Merciful.' Ismā'īl to this replied, 'Can any father sacrifice his own son? Whatever God has commanded, and my father decided to execute, I shall most cheerfully conform to.'

"Thus Iblīs was unable to mislead either the father or the son, and he now returned to Hājir (Hagar), to whom he related how that Ibrāhīm, with the pretext of cutting wood on the mountain, had taken Ismā'īl there for the purpose of sacrificing him. Hājir replied, 'Can Ibrāhīm be so cruel as to kill his son, he who is so humane even to his enemies? But be this as it may, let your statement be false or true, it concerns himself, and my duty is to submit to his will.' On this Iblīs, desponding, left, and thus the Most High preserved Ibrāhīm and his family from the tempter.

"Now it is narrated that Ibrāhīm reached a place called Shāb,[1] and there he told Ismā'īl of his dream, in the following words:

[1] The 'place called Shāb' suggests 'the Sheb of Abū Tālib', to which Muḥammad and his followers were driven to retire five or six years before the Hijra when proscribed by the Quraish. (Cf. Sale's *Koran*, Wherry's recension, ii. p. 224.) The word *sheb* (*shab*) means simply 'quarter', and the *sheb* of Abū Tālib probably comprised the *sheb* of 'Alī. It was a defile of the mountains where the projecting rocks of Abu Cobeis pressed upon the eastern outskirts of the city (Muir, *The Life of Mahomet*, p. 91). But the text has Shāb, and the place meant may be identical with the spot now known as Shaab-i-'Alī, ''Alī's date', which adjoins the Suk-ul-Lail and where 'Alī is said to have been born (*The Story of a Pilgrimage to Hijaz*, by Sultan Jahan Begam (of Bhopal), p. 103). The writer also mentions the Jannat al-mualla, or 'lofty Paradise', the plain near Mecca in which lies a plot of land called the Makān-i-Sha'b-un-Nūr or 'the place of the Valley of Light'. In it are buried 70,000 saints who will rise from their graves on

'O my dear son, I saw in my dream that I should put you to death; reflect upon it, and tell me your opinion'. Ismā'īl answered, 'O my father, whatever you have been commanded to do let it be done'. 'How can you, my son, resign yourself thus to so dreadful an end?' asked Ibrāhīm; and Ismā'īl only replied, 'My father, God will enable me to bear it with patience', and added, 'Tie my hands and my feet, so that when I am struggling in death, my blood may not fall upon you; sharpen, also, well the knife, that I may soon be freed from life; turn my face downwards, that lest you, beholding my struggles, may be deterred from the Divine commands, through paternal pity, and so deviate from your duty. Console my aged and beloved mother, Hājir, for my death, with the assurance that I terminated my earthly career in the path of God!'

"On this, Ibrāhīm was greatly affected, and cried out aloud: 'O God, during all my life, the mention (*zikr*) of my petition and devotion to Thee has ascended up to Thy abode; in my old age, Thou hast given me a son; many months and years I have grieved for his absence; if this deed be according to Thy divine will, who am I, that I should oppose it? but if it be not, I will repent of so sinful a design'.

"All the angels and spirits upon earth, and in the heavens, beheld the submission (*islāmiat*) of Ibrāhīm and Ismā'īl, and heard the devotion of the parent; and they wept, and cried aloud. Ibrāhīm pressed his knife to the throat of his son, but it would not cut, and turned upon its side, and just then an unknown voice was heard, saying, 'Thou hast verified thy dream!' and another, bidding him look behind him, and directing him to sacrifice whatever appeared to his sight, in the place of his own child.

"Turning round, Ibrāhīm perceived a large ram descending the mountain. This ram, it is said, had pastured for forty years in the garden of Paradise (*Jannat*); while others state that it was the same animal that the martyr Hābīl (Abel, from *habala*, or any one taken away by death) had offered up in sacrifice, and which God had preserved for this occurrence. Ibrāhīm ran after the ram, and so performed the solemnity observed at the present

---

the Last Day. Many pilgrims dig graves here in the belief that, wherever they may die, their spirits will find them after death (*ib.* p. 97). This work gives many details concerning the modern usages during the *hajj* at Mecca.

time, called the *jamrah*, by the pilgrims to the Ka'ba, when they throw stones (at the devil), for he also cast stones at the animal as he pursued it. The *jamrah* of the people of Muhammad (the Prophet) has its origin in this occasion. There are, however, three *jamrahs*, called the first, second, and third.

"It is related that Ibrāhīm threw seven stones at the ram, and at the third *jamrah* he caught it. He then conveyed it to the spot of sacrifices at Makka, called Minā, and appeared to sacrifice it. The angel Gabriel now appeared, and freed the hands and feet of Ismā'īl, and said to him, 'Whatever you may desire to ask of God, ask it now, for this is a holy moment'; and so, raising up his hands, he prayed: 'O Lord of the universe, I implore that Thou wipest away from Thy registers the sins of any of Thy servants about to die who believe in Thee and in Thy unity'.

"When Ibrāhīm had finished his sacrifice, he came back to his son Ismā'īl, and beheld that the angel Jibrāīl had loosed his hands and feet, and learned that he had prayed in behalf of the believing; he was greatly rejoiced, and said to him: 'My son, thou art surely protected and aided by God', and at the same moment an unknown voice was heard to say: 'O Ibrāhīm, thou art the truthful of those who speak, and the best of those who are patient; thou art above all trial in temptation; thy devotion is perfect, and under all troubles thou showest submission. I have, therefore, prepared for thee an exalted place in Paradise, and made thy fidelity to be eminent in both worlds; this is the recompense which we give to those who do well' (this latter expression meaning 'devotion'), 'for God sees every one, whilst no one is able to see Him. Thou, Ibrāhīm, art my faithful one (*khalīl*) and my prophet (*paighambar*); I have clothed thee with a pre-eminence superior to that of all creation. And thou, Ismā'īl, thou art pure and my prophet (*rasūl*); I have made thee eminent above all the world's inhabitants for the purity of thy heart.' Both Ibrāhīm and Ismā'īl hereon offered up thanks and praises to the Most High for His great goodness, figurative and explicative in nature.

"The historian Tabarī states that when Ibrāhīm heard the voice declare, 'Thou hast verified thy dream', he was greatly frightened, and trembled, and so let the knife fall from his hand. Jibrāīl caught the ram by the ear and brought it with him from

Paradise, at the same time exclaiming, *Allāhu-akbar!* (God is the greatest of all gods), and Ibrāhīm hearing this repeated the *takbīr*; for on seeing the ram he cried out, *Lā ilāha illā Allāh*, and *Allāh-akbar* (there is no God but Allāh, and Allāh is the greatest). He then added to Ismā'īl: 'My dear son, raise up your head, for the Most High has gladdened our hearts', which he did, and they both beholding Jibrā'īl and the ram, exclaimed: *Allāhu-akbar wa ul-Hamd*, 'Allāh is the greatest of gods, and is the praised'. In the work entitled the *Manāhij-at-Tālibīn*,[1] it is narrated that Ja'far-us-Sādiq stated that God relieved Ibrāhīm from the sacrifice of his beloved son through that ram, as a great atonement. Khalīl was deeply afflicted by the Divine command, and God, by inspiration, said to him, 'O Ibrāhīm, the reason of my preserving Ismā'īl from being sacrificed is, because the Light of the prophetship of that seal of all prophets, Muhammad, was on the brow of that fortunate youth; that all of the prophets, from Adam down to that Seal (Muhammad), should be of his race'. Khalīl prayed to God, and a message was sent to him, by revelation, saying that all of the prophets which he beheld should surely spring from the loins of his son. Among these Ibrāhīm saw Muhammad 'Alī bin-Abī-Tālib, and the sons borne to him by the pure Fātima. Ibrāhīm inquired who it was that he saw near to Muhammad filling so eminent a position, and was informed that it was Husain, the son of 'Alī bin-Abī-Tālib, the prophet of the latter times and the light of all the prophets, the son of the daughter of Muhammad Mustafā. 'I have a greater affection', replied Ibrāhīm, 'for that figured soul than for Ismā'īl, though the son of my own loins'; and God thereon continued: 'I have accepted of Husain on account of the devotedness of Ismā'īl'.

"Thus, according to the statement of the Imām Ja'far, the great sacrifice was Husain bin-'Alī, and the ram was figurative of that sacrifice which was to come in after years; for, he remarks with much correctness, what could a simple ram be, that God should call it the Great Sacrifice in the Holy *Qurān*? The second application of this remarkable occurrence is that Adam was the original builder and founder of the Ka'ba, that after his death, Seth[2] (Shīth) repaired it, and all mankind performed the solemn

[1] The *Manāhij uṭ-Ṭālibīn*, or 'Roads of the Seekers', of Abū Zakāria an-Nawawī, the jurist.

[2] See note on p. 174 *infra*.

ceremony of the *tawāf* [1] (walking round) around it, just as the people of Muhammad do at the present time, on the occasion of their pilgrimage—a duty commanded by the Most High. When the deluge of Noah approached, by God's permission angels descended from heaven, and removed to the summit of the mountains both the Black Stone which Adam brought out of Paradise (Jannat), and the other stones which he collected for the Ka'ba in the mountains.

"It is related that when Adam became bent with the blows of his disobedience to God (*Qurān*, xx. v. 119) [2] he descended from the Blue Paradise to this world, and for a great length of time wept tears of regret; and in his affliction prayed: 'O Thou who hearest the cries of those who weep, under all circumstances: I no more hear the voices of the angels, and this affliction is greater than all others'. The voice of God was heard saying, 'O Adam! out of regard for thy posterity I have caused a house of joy to descend from heaven to earth, around which always make it your duty to perform the *tawāf* (or circuit), just as the angels in heaven make circular processions around the Great Arch (or Throne). It is, at this moment, thy duty—even obligatory—to go at once to that house; there let thy heart be free from all other imaginations than those of love and affection for me.' Adam immediately proceeded to the Ka'ba Allāh (verse in Persian): 'The pilgrim on the Ka'ba road seeks for a sight of the Divine countenance of Him who is the master of this house'.

"Filled with reflections as he went, he made no less than fifty

[1] Only women pilgrims walk in the *ṭawāf*, men performing it at a run, when it is performed between Safa, the eminence close to a corner of the Kaaba, and Marwa, a building on another eminence exactly opposite it. The stretch of ground between is called Milain and is 225 paces in length. Across it Hagar is said to have walked seven times in her search for water, leaving her son at the spot now marked by the well Zamzam so that she could keep him in view. The circumbulatory *ṭawāf* alluded to in the text is performed on the Matāf or Path of Circuit round the Kaaba, starting from the Black Stone. Each *ṭawāf* consists of seven *shut*, each a complete circuit. In the first three *shuts* men walk stiff and upright with the chest well thrown out, but in the last four they walk as usual. Women walk at their customary pace. There are, moreover, seven kinds of *ṭawāf*. The one specifically intended in the text is probably the second, the *ṭawāf-uz-ziārat* or *-ud-Dīn*, also called the *ṭawāf-i-ifāza*, *ṭawāf-ul-ḥajj*, *ṭawāf-ul-farz* or *ṭawāf-i-yaum-un-nahr* (Sultan Jahan Begam, *op. cit.* p. 112).

[2] Ch. xx. describes Adam's fall but does not allude to his descent from Paradise.

farsangs[1] between each of his steps, so that, in this way, he soon passed over a great distance, and, reaching the object of his desires, beheld a house constructed out of one red ruby, the two doors of which were of green emeralds, the one looking to the east, and the other to the west. By Divine command an angel appeared and taught Adam the ceremonies required at that holy spot. Whilst Adam was thus engaged, the angel showed himself to him, and said, 'O Adam! the Most High has been pleased with your conduct, your performance of the holy *Hajj*, or pilgrimage, and has forgiven your sins'.

"It is said that, on the occasion of the Deluge, the angels conveyed this house up to the heavens; and another narrative relates that after it had subsided a small mound of red earth pointed out its location, around which the people performed the *tawāf*, on which account the Great Judge of all necessities (God) answered their prayers, until the time when Khalīl (Ibrāhīm), by Divine command, reconstructed it. In the view of having this pious service remain in the family of Khalīl, God commanded the angel Jibrāīl to accompany him from Shām to Makka and employ Ismā'īl and his mother on that edifice. Thus both the father and the son, who are the very best of the human race, renewed the foundations of that House of Mercy, and invited all mankind to visit it.

"On Khalīl's arrival at Makka, he found Ismā'īl employed in making arrows, and having made known to him God's commands, he cheerfully accepted them. Ibrāhīm designed to reconstruct the house in its previous dimensions. He was aware of what these were at the time of Adam; but on this subject there are various accounts, each of which are given in the work called the *Rauzat-ul-Ahbāb*,[2] and from all of them it would seem that the angel Jibrāīl made them known to Ibrāhīm. Ismā'īl brought the earth and clay, and his father constructed the House of God;

[1] The Persian form of the Ar. *farsakh*, about 18,000 feet.

[2] The *Rauẓat-ul-Aḥbāb fī siyar al-Nabī wa'l-Al wa'l-Aṣḥāb* ('the Garden of Endeavour concerning the life of the Prophet, his family and companions') of 'Jamāl-ul-Ḥusainī', by which complimentary title the Persian historian 'Aṭā-Ullāh b. Faẓl Allāh al-Shirāzī is known. He wrote between A.D. 1484-95 and died in 1511 or 1520, but his work has only been translated into Turkish (*E.I.* i. p. 1008). Beale, who assigns his death to 917 H. (1511) says he was *wazīr* to Sultan Husain Mīrza of Herāt, and gives three versions of his names (*Or. Biogr. Dict.* p. 84).

and in this way it reached such lofty dimensions that the latter was no longer able to raise the stones as high as its walls. He therefore had to mount upon a stone for that purpose, and the print of his feet has still remained on it. The stone in question is, at the present time, called the *maqām-i-Ibrāhīm*[1] (' place of Abraham '). Upon reaching the elevation of the ' Black Stone ', which the angels had preserved from the effects of the Deluge by conveying it to the summit of the mountain called Abū Qubais,[2] they went and brought it thence, and, taking it from them, Ibrāhīm put it in its place. When this stone first came from Jannat, it was whiter than snow or milk, but it has been discoloured by contact with the hands and faces of the disobedient to the Almighty.*[3]

" Another tradition states that when the edifice had reached a certain elevation, Ibrāhīm bade Ismā'īl bring him a stone of an excellent and agreeable form, which should remain as a sign to the people, and that, though the latter brought one, his father did not like it, and was about departing for another, when he heard a voice saying, ' O Ibrāhīm! on Mount Abū Qubais there is one deposited '. So, proceeding to the spot, he found and brought away, himself, the Black Stone; and as Ismā'īl was absent at the moment, he only learned the facts from his father on his return. On the termination of their work they both prayed to God to bless and accept of their labours, which He was pleased to do. It was then that the angel Jibrāīl appeared and taught

[1] More correctly the Maqām-i-Ibrāhīm, or 'Abraham's Standing-place', is a small bungalow-shaped building, which pilgrims enter on one side, passing out on the other. The stone is known as Hajar-i-Ibrāhīm, and pilgrims fill the cavities of the foot-prints with Zamzam water (Sultan Jahan Begam, *op. cit.* p. 109).

[2] Abu Kebees in original; the Abu Kobeis of Sale's *Koran*, ch. xxii. (iii. p. 161 in Wherry's recension). The mountain was visited by Abraham, who thence proclaimed the duty of pilgrimage. It lies on the eastern frontier of Mecca, and was known in Pagan times as al-Amīn because the Black Stone was preserved there. It also held the Treasure Cave in which the progenitors of mankind dwelt (*E.I.* i. p. 97).

* Near the Āt Maidān, an ancient hippodrome of Constantinople, there is a small mosque, called 'Mehmed-Pāsha Jāmi-'sī', which was originally a Greek church. In this mosque is a fragment of the celebrated *Hajir-al-aswad*, or ' Black Stone ', brought from Makka, and placed here by its founder.

[3] Āt-Maidānī, 'hippodrome'. For much Turkish and Christian folklore on other stones see F. W. Hasluck in *Annual*, B.S.A. xxi. pp. 62 ff.

them the solemnities of the *tawāf*, of the *manāsik* [1] (sacrifices), of Mount 'Arafāt, the *ramī jamrah* [2] (casting of the stones), the *saī* [3] and the *shayī* (sacred symbols), all of which are *sunnat* (commanded by the Prophet) to the pilgrims of Muhammadan people, to the present time.

"Before Ibrāhīm departed from Makka for Shām, he appointed Ismā'īl to be his *khalīfa*, Caliph or successor, and it is said that he reached the age of 120 years."

THE DECEASE OF IBRĀHĪM

By some it is said that, after the death of Sarah, Ibrāhīm took another wife from the land of Canaan, by whom he had six sons. From these sprang so many individuals as to greatly increase the number of his children and grandchildren, as well as of the tribes. The prophetship, however, remained with Isḥāq and Ismā'īl. Ibrāhīm became excessively wealthy in flocks and herds. He is supposed to have been the first person whose beard became white with age, a circumstance so much to his surprise as to cause him to ask God, in prayer, the cause of so extraordinary an occurrence, and, in reply, heard that it was a sign of seriousness of mind, and respect. He thereon asked that the former might be increased.

Ibrāhīm is said also to have asked of God that he might not be required to leave this life before he himself requested it; and that his prayer was granted. Now when the time approached for his departure, the Angel of Death appeared to him, in the shape of an aged man; and when, according to his principles of hospitality, he had food placed before him, he remarked that the hands of his guest trembled very much, so that he was unable to partake of the provisions, and through feebleness, he raised them even to his nose and ears, in place of carrying them to his

[1] Lit. 'places of sacrifice'.

[2] Ramīat Jamrat, more correctly, 'casting (of stones) at the Jamras'. Al-jamra, originally a 'pebble', is particularly used of the heaps of stones in the valley of Minā. There are three such heaps (*E.I.* i. p. 1012). The Begam of Bhopal translates the term *jamrat* by 'devil', and says there is a place in Minā where three pillars have been built close to one another, and these are known as the Jamrat (*op. cit.* p. 123).

[3] Saī = sevenfold running. With the *ṭawāf* it concludes the *ḥajj* (*E.I.* ii. p. 199).

mouth. Ibrāhīm, surprised at such a spectacle of human weakness, inquired of the aged man its cause, and was told that it was the consequence of advanced age. He next asked him how old he was, and the old man replied that he calculated his years were even less than those of Ibrāhīm ; the latter thereon observed that there was not much difference between their ages, and he wondered whether or not he would be subject to the same degree of feebleness. "Yes, you will", said the guest ; and Ibrāhīm, after some moments of reflection, having prayed to God to relieve him of this life and its infirmities, the Angel of Death conveyed his soul to Paradise (or *Farādīs*—the plural of the Arabic noun Firdaus).

Another tradition is, that when the Angel of Death ('Azrāīl) appeared to Ibrāhīm, the latter asked him whether it was possible for one friend to wish to take away the soul or life of another friend ; and that this question having been, by the angel, conveyed to God, he was commanded to reply, "Is it not natural that a friend should ardently desire to see the face of his friend ?" On this, he consented freely to depart, and was buried in the fields of Khairūn,[1] by the side of Sarah.

"In those days, hospitality was much exercised, and not only were the guests treated with great generosity in the houses of their hosts, but were provisioned on their departure. It is narrated, that once Ibrāhīm entertained an aged individual, whom he conducted to his residence ; but, as he ascertained that his guest was an infidel (*kāfir*), he did not lay before him the choice providences of God, and drove him away. The Most High thereon addressing Ibrāhīm, said : 'O Ibrāhīm, this infidel has, for many years, enjoyed my bounties, and yet served idols ; and not for even one day have I deprived him of them. How much less, then, does it become you, as my friend and apostle, to cut him off from the use of my mercies ?' On hearing this, Ibrāhīm made haste to follow after the old man, and related to him what he had learnt. The aged infidel was greatly affected, and wept ; and having made the reflection that if a sovereign reproaches his own friend for his conduct to his foe, how great must be his goodness to his friends ! thereon became a true believer.*

"It is said that ten books were sent down from heaven to

[1] Or Khabrūn.

* This is evidently the origin of Franklin's celebrated story to the French of Paris.

Ibrāhīm, all filled with pious injunctions and wise commands. Of these, the following is one : ' O ye who are the rulers, judges, and sovereigns over the poor, be not misled by the temptations of worldly enjoyments, by those of the body, nor by Satan ; I did not select you from the others of my creatures for the purpose of depriving the public of their goods and stores ; perhaps you even think that I did so, that you might prevent the helpless from praying to me ? Know then that I do not reject the prayers of the poor and the helpless—even if these be infidels.'

" To Ibrāhīm, it is related, are attributed many of the *sunnats*, or religious observances of the present day " ; and the same author adds, that " the best of all is that the ' Pride of the Universe ' (Muhammad) was a subject of his nation, or community (one of it), and many of his *sunnats* are now practised in the Muhammadan religious laws ".

The preceding suffices to show the connexion which exists between the faith of Abraham and that of Muhammad. The essence of the latter (*Islām*) is, perfect submission to the will of the Almighty ; and of this, the most striking exemplification in the record of man's history is the obedience of Abraham, when he prepared to offer up his own son as a sacrifice to his Creator. This figures largely in the principles of the Baqtāshīs, as will be seen in the account given of them hereafter.

Regarding the term or expression *Hanīfīya*,[1] the celebrated *Histoire des Arabes*, of Caussin de Perceval, states that it simply signifies " Orthodoxy, or the religion of Abraham ". In the same work (vol. i. p. 323) there is the following : " 'Ubaidallāh, son of Jahsh, though established at Makka, was not a Quraishite ; but on his father's side descended from Asad, son of Khuzaima, and belonged to the Quraish tribe through his mother 'Umaima,[2] the daughter of 'Abd-ul-Muttalib. After fruitless efforts to reach the religion of Abraham, or orthodoxy (*al-Hanīfīya*), he remained in doubt and uncertainty, until Muhammad commenced preaching.

[1] Or, rarely, Ḥanafīya, the religion of Abraham, while *al-Ḥanīfīya al-samḥā*, the mild or liberal Hanīfism, is the religion of Muḥammad (*E.I.* ii. 258, *s.v.* Ḥanīf).

[2] Cf. A. Sprenger, *Das Leben und die Lehre des Mohammad*, i. p. 81. The point is that 'Umaima was an aunt of the Prophet and 'Ubaidullāh was his cousin ; Muḥammad was thus confronted by waverers even amongst his near kinsmen. (For the meaning of 'Abd-ul-Muṭṭalib's name see Robertson Smith's *Kinship and Marriage in Early Arabia*, p. 260.)

It was then that 'Ubaidallāh decided to recognise Islamism, as the true religion which he sought after. He therefore embraced it, but soon after abjured it, as will be seen elsewhere, to devote himself definitively to Christianity."

He was one of four persons who, on the occasion of the festival of the Arab idols, publicly denounced all participation in such a faith, saying, " Our countrymen walk in a false path, and are far from the religion of Abraham. What is this pretended divinity to which they immolate victims, and around which they make solemn processions ? A mute and insensible block of stone, incapable of doing good or evil. Let us seek the true faith of our father Abraham ; and to find it, let us, if it be necessary, even wander over foreign lands."

M. de Perceval adds, with regard to the new doctrine proclaimed by Muhammad : " This was not a new religion which he announced, but the ancient religion of Abraham restored to its primitive purity ".

Thus, the researches into the history of the Arabs, by this eminent writer, fully establish the fact that, in the traditional accounts possessed by them of the patriarch Abraham, Muhammad found the basis of his new faith; and that whatever is not clearly of this origin must be sought for in other traditions, drawn from India and Greece ; or, as he so repeatedly declares in the *Qurān*, in ' Divine Inspiration '.

THE *ATMBODHA*, OR ' KNOWLEDGE OF THE SPIRIT '

In the chapter on the Sūfīism of the Darvishes, as well as the others relating to them, the reader will find a strong analogy of doctrine with that of the people of India, as shown in the *vedānta*. An interesting article [' Atmabodha '] in the *Journal Asiatique*[1] of Paris, contains much on this subject, clearly showing that the peculiarities of the *tarīqats*[2] have their origin in the writings of the Sanskrit authors ; and it may not be amiss to quote some of the more striking of these parables.

[1] Série 6, t. vii., January 1866, p. 1. The article is an annotated version of the Vedantic poem of Shankara Acharya, by Félix Nève.

[2] From *ṭaraqa*, ' drank thick, muddy water '. The root idea suggests a string of camels following a difficult track to a well. Salmoné's *Arab. Dict. s.v.* (p. 499) shows the extended meanings given to the root.

Brahma, the chief divinity of the *Vedas*, or sacred writings of India, is the great spirit from which all the others are emanations. He is the source of all the pantheistic doctrines of the believers in him.

Mīmānsā is the desire to know, or the 'Divine science'; in other words, the contemplative and mystical theology of Brahma. The fundamental idea of the *vedānta* is that Brahma is the Absolute Spirit, and the Pure Being. It is also the doctrine which any one must know and deeply study who desires to aspire to the fourth degree of a religious life—or who wishes to become a Sannyāsī, or perfect ascetic. The religion of Brahma is too compendious and complicated to be explained in detail, and such is not the object of the present short notice. Indeed, there has been, of late years, so much written on the subject by the philologists of Europe, that it would be presumptuous to do more than refer the reader, for more minute information, to the many interesting works now existing in its various languages. Suffice it to say, that these point out the source and origin of whatever is pantheistic and mystical in the doctrines of the Darvish *tarīqats*, which are not strictly Mussulman; and that, after penetrating through Northern India into Persia, they have spread over Asia, wherever these sects have been established. It would even seem that the polytheism of India is the origin of all the fabled gods and goddesses of the people of northern Europe. The pantheism of the one becomes the mythology of the other, shaped into varied forms, dependent upon the climate, the character of the seasons, and the varied productions of nature of each of the degrees of latitude through which it passed. The influence of language over the human mind is greater than at first seems apparent. The Sanskrit, a dead language of India, is one particularly adapted for the expression of the most minute details of mystical ideas—quite without a parallel in the great family of idioms used by mankind. In it the human imagination found an able and willing servant, so capable of photographing—so to speak—the least tangible of its productions, that it in time became the sacred language of India—that of its books, and not that spoken by its people. India has rivalled Greece in her philosophers—each has had her teachers and her schools, both undirected by Divine Light, though the intuitive reflections of reason and intelligence seem to have penetrated into the remote and misty future which so deeply interests mankind. Their 'ancient wisdom' is still the object of the studies of the curious, even in modern times; and the human mind, still fettered and unfreed from the weight of long centuries of slavery in matters of religious faith, is unable to cast off the dogmas of a spiritual and mystical character, which, like the clouds, obscure the light of the One only true Divinity. Mankind deified at one period, is sanctified in another; and both in Vedantism and Sufīism, we find the idea carried so far as to declare that the spirit of man, when properly purified by contemplation, religious fervour, and ecstatic love, becomes even that of God, from whom it is declared it is an emanation. Even the most reasonable of the Darvish *tarīqats* hold that by means of a certain form of worship, differing with each one, the creature *approaches* his Creator, and that this is the object of his adorations. His spirit becomes even absorbed in that of the Divinity. The soul is a Divine emanation incorporated in a human form. It exists in five conditions, viz. it is awake, it dreams, it is plunged in slumber, it fills a state of half-death, and finally, even perfectly separated from the body. During the third state, it is reabsorbed already in the Divine Spirit. After death, it must pass through several new existences. Virtuous souls occupy spheres superior to that of this world, and enjoy the fruits of their good works, whilst the guilty ones are condemned to fill conditions inferior to that of humanity. The Darvish thus interprets the verse of the *Qurān* lxviii. 18: "My people in the eternal life will rise up in companies"; and holds that wicked people who have degraded humanity in this life will live again in the shape of animal existence, to which it has become debased. The final effort of man in the *vedānta* is his passage to the world of Brahma, when his soul will be delivered from all human ties, and return to its original source and be confounded with his principle. The Darvish, by a series of mental contemplations and fervid efforts, returns to the divine spirit of Allāh; and even, for example, the *maulavī*, as he whirls round, according to the *modus* prescribed by his founder or *pīr*, believes that he is spiritually drawn nearer to God; or the *Rifā'ī* as he howls the *zikr* supposes that he becomes holy, and is absorbed in the spirit of the Allāh whom he thus invokes. The *çravana*,[1]

[1] *Çravana* (Nève, *op. cit.* p. 74) is to listen, while *mānana* is to accept with obedience what is taught.

manana, and *nididhyāsana*[1] (audition, meditation, and contemplation), are nothing other than the *samā'*, *murāqaba*, *tawajjuh*[2] and the *zikr*, of the Darvish *tarīqat*. The *bodha*[3] of the Brahman is the *'ilm*, and the *jnāna* is the *ma'rifat* of the Darvish, without which it is not possible to emancipate and free the soul. The Baktāshīs believe that God is in all things, and that the soul, after its separation from the human frame, may enter into the body of an animal, for which reason they are unwilling to kill any living creature, lest it contain the soul or spirit of a late human being. This is the principle of the Supreme Master Brahma, who penetrates all things. The *manas* is the *'anāsīr arba'* of Sūfīism, viz. the four great elements of fire, air, earth, and water, which are supposed to compose the body, and constitute the internal faculty of comprehension; whilst the *upādhi*,[4] or subtle fluid, is the invigorating element of life, different from the *prānās*, or 'breath',[5] which is known to the Darvish as the *naffs*, or *nafs*, the original emanation from the Creator, and which, after a serious and impressional invocation of Him, becomes so holy. The *'ālam-i-misāl*, or 'world of fancy'—the *'ālam-i-khiyāl*, the 'world of illusion',—form an important part of the Brahmanic system.[6] All is said to be transitory in this world—illusory; and there is nothing true and real but Brahma, which word, with Sūfīism, is equivalent to Allāh. "Brahma has no resemblance with the world—nothing really exists but he; if anything else be produced other than he, it is vain and illusory, like the mirage in the desert." "The eye of science (spiritual) contemplates the Living Being (with the Darvish *Hay wa Qayyūm*, the 'Living

[1] *Nididhyāsā*, 'meditation', is placing Bhagavat before the mind's eye to the exclusion of everything else (*Vaishnavism, Shaivism, and Minor Religious Systems*, R. G. Bhandarkar (Grundriss der I.A.Ph. und Alt.), p. 61). Nève translates the term '*la contemplation*' (*op. cit.* p. 47). *Manas* is the interior faculty of comprehension (*op. cit.* p. 59); but it has also the meaning of 'feeling' in a lofty sense (p. 75). Samā', lit. 'hearing' or 'listening', came to be a Ṣūfī technical term for the devotional exercise of *darwīsh* (D. B. Macdonald in *J.R.A.S.*, 1901, p. 236 n.)

[2] For *murāqaba* and *tawajjuh*, *v.* note on p. 144 *infra*.

[3] *Bodha*, 'cognition' (Nève, *op. cit.* p. 69); *jñāna* is 'science' (p. 87).

[4] *Upādhi*, 'attribute' (*op. cit.* p. 58). Brown's account of the *Atmabodha* is not correct. There are three *upādhis* or 'attributes', one of which is subtile. And the elements are five in number, not four.

[5] *Prānās* is for *prāna*, 'breath' (*op. cit.* p. 59).

[6] Under the generic term *māyā*, or 'illusion'.

and the Eternal') ; but the eye of ignorance cannot contemplate Him, no more than a blind man can behold the sun." "He who undertakes the pilgrimage of the Spirit, which is in himself, penetrates all, without regard either to the state of the sky, the country, or time ; dissipating cold and warmth, securing to himself a perpetual happiness, free from all impurity ; frees himself completely from works, becomes omniscient, penetrates all, and is immortal." "He who, renouncing all labour, reaches the state or condition called *paramahansa*, or the ascetic of the last degree, frequents the *tīrtha* of the Spirit, knows all, in all things through the proper nature of the sovereign Spirit, becomes immortal, viz. absolutely free."

Such is the parallel between the principles of Brahmanism and Sūfīism, and which have evidently become engrafted on the ex-Mussulman systems of some, if not indeed all, of the modern Darvish sects. The *Mantiq-ut-Tair* of Farīd-ud-dīn 'Attār, and the *Masnawī Sharīf* of Jalāl-ud-dīn ur-Rūmī, furnish much to corroborate the conviction that these Mussulman authors drew their inspiration from the religious reveries of the Hindus. Even the mystical *ghazals* of Hāfiz are deeply imbued with the same.

CHAPTER II

ON THE ORIGIN OF THE DARVISH ORDERS—THE ORIGINAL ORDERS ; FORMS OF PRAYER ; CAPS, ETC.—TRADITIONS OF THE ORDERS

THE word *darwīsh* or *darvēsh* is from the Persian language, and is written درويش. It is composed of two syllables, *dar* and *vish.* The first, or *dar,* is the same as the English word ' door ', and has the same signification. *Vish* is probably from the Persian verb *vihtan,* to beg.

Various meanings are assigned to the two syllables taken together. Some say it means the ' sill of the door ' ; others, ' those who beg from door to door ' ; whilst there are many who declare that it signifies ' in thought ' or ' deep meditation ', using the *dar* as a Persian preposition *in,* and not as a substantive, and the *vish* as ' thought '.

I am inclined to give to the word the signification now almost universally accepted, which is, ' a poor fellow who goes from door to door for assistance '. This is evidently the one in use all over the East, in India, Bukhāra, Persia, Turkey, Syria, and Egypt—in fact, wherever this class of people are known ; though in those countries where the Arabic language is spoken, Darvishes are known as *faqīrs,* plural *fuqirā* ; and in Turkey the latter is often used, though of course erroneously, in the singular sense.

The Darvishes say that their original orders were twelve in number. They trace back their source as follows :—

Allāh (God).
Jibrāīl (Angel Gabriel).
Muhammad (the Prophet).
'Alī (the fourth Caliph).
Abū Bakr (the first Caliph).

From the Caliph 'Alī, they say, descended—

Hasan-al-Bahrī.
Marufi Kerhī [Ma'rūf Karkhī].[1]
Surayī Sakattī [Sarī Saqatī].[2]
Dāūdī Taī.[3]
Junaydī Bagdadī.[4]
Habībī 'Ajamī.[5]
Abū Bakr Shiblī.[6]

[1] Abū Maḥfūẓ Ma'rūf b. Fīrūz al-Karkhī is described as a spiritual descendant of Dā'ūd; but there is some uncertainty as to his place in the sequence of Ṣūfī teachers (Nicholson, *Kashf al-Maḥjūb*, p. 113). He died in 200 H., A.D. 816 (*J.R.A.S.*, 1906, p. 331). Born a Christian, he was converted to Islam (*ib.*, 1912, p. 566).

[2] Abū'l Ḥasan Sarī b. Mughallis al-Saqaṭī, 'the huckster', was a disciple of Ma'rūf Karkhī, but he had also seen Ḥabīb al-Rā'ī, a companion of Salmān Fārsī. Junaid was his sister's son (Nicholson, *Kashf al-Maḥjūb*, p. 110). Saqaṭī died in 257 H. (A.D. 871). He founded the Saqaṭī or Siqṭī Order, which, like the Karkhī Order, is now grouped in the Qādirī Order by Persian writers on Ṣūfī history.

[3] Abū Sulaimān Dā'ūd b. Nuṣair al-Ṭāī, sometimes described as a pupil of Abū Ḥanīfa, sometimes as a disciple or successor of Ḥabīb al-Rā'ī (cf. Nicholson, *Kashf al-Maḥjūb*, p. 109). He died in 165 H. (A.D. 782).

[4] Abū'l Qāsim al-Junaid b. Muḥammad b. al-Junaid al-Baghdādī, a follower of Thaurī, under whom he studied law, died in 297 H. (A.D. 910). 'Perhaps the greatest name in early Ṣufiism', no shadow of heresy has ever fallen on his memory. (See Macdonald, *Muslim Theology*, p. 176 ff., for a full account of his teaching; also Nicholson, *Kashf al-Maḥjūb*, p. 129.) His titles are variously given and he was also called the Saiyid al-Ṭā'ifa, 'lord of the sect', and Ṭā'ūs al-'ulamā, 'peacock of the learned' (*E.I.* i. p. 1063). Al-Junaid also studied under Abū 'Abdullāh al-Ḥāris b. Asad al-Muḥāsibī, who as a Shāfi'ite was so at variance with Ibn Ḥanbal that he led a retired life and was so unpopular that at his death only four persons ventured to say the funeral prayers for him. He was also a Ṣūfī, learned in the traditions and in scholasticism. He died in 243 H. (A.D. 858), and his writings are of cardinal importance on these subjects (Wüstenfeld, *Der Imam Schafi'i*, p. 59).

[5] Ḥabīb al-'Ajamī was a Persian and spoke Arabic imperfectly, so that Ḥasan of Baṣra, by whom his conversion was begun, refused to pray under his leadership, but was divinely rebuked for his failure to realise Ḥabīb's rightness of intention (Nicholson, *Kashf al-Maḥjūb*, p. 88). This Ḥabīb must not be confused with Ḥabīb al-Rā'ī, as to whom see note on p. 156-7 *infra*.

[6] Abū Bakr b. Dalaf b. Jaḥdar ash-Shiblī died in 334 H. (A.D. 946). He was a disciple of al-Junaid, but gave himself more completely to the ascetic and contemplative life. In his verses the vocabulary of the amorous intercourse with God is fully developed (Macdonald, *Muslim Theology*, p. 176).

Abū'l Mubārak Mahzumī.[1]

'Abd ul-Qādir Gilānī.

And from Abū Bakr, the first Caliph—

Salmān Fārsī.[2]

The twelve original orders are :—

1. The Rufā'ī . . . [*v*. Chap. VI. *infra*].
2. The Sa'dī . . . [*v*. App. II. *infra*].
3. The Suhravardī . . . [*v*. pp. 158-61 *infra*].
4. The Shibānī.[3]
5. The Maulavī . . . [*v*. Chap. X. *infra*].
6. The Qādirī . . . [*v*. pp. 99-116 *infra*, and Index].
7. The Naqshibandī . . . [*v*. App. I. *infra*].
8. The Uvaisī (which latter, they say, are ante-Muḥammad), *v*. App. II.
9. The Jalwatī, *v*. App. II.
10. The Khalwatī, *v*. App. II
11. The Badawī, *v*. App. II.
12. The Dasūqī.

The Darvish from whom I derived the preceding is a member of the Order of the Qādirīs; and as there is much *esprit de corps* and rivalry among the various Orders, he may have been biassed in favour of those whom he placed highest in the list.

[1] Abū'l Mubārik Mahzūmī, doubtless the *qāzī* Abū Sa'd Mubārak Mukharrimī, head of the school of Hanbalite law at Baghdād. He bestowed the *khirqa* of a Ṣūfī on 'Abd-ul-Qādir Gīlānī (*E.I.* i. p. 41). Malcolm, however, speaks of a Shaikh Abū Saiyid Makzūmī as investing 'Abd-ul-Qādir (*Hist. of Persia*, ii. p. 286 *n*.). Mukharrim is a place in Baghdād and from it Mubārak's name was clearly derived, though in several texts it is corrupted to Makhzūmī (D. S. Margoliouth, in *J.R.A.S.*, 1907, p. 289 *n*. 1). The mistake probably arose from confusion with Abū Khālid Muslim b. Khālid al-Quraishī al-Makhzūmī al-Zinjī, *mufti* of Makka and a teacher of theology and jurisprudence, whose authority in the lore of tradition is disputed. He died in 180 H. (A.D. 797) (Wüstenfeld, *Der Imam-el-Schafi'i*, p. 33). He is doubtless alluded to on p. 101 *infra*.

[2] Shalmān or Salmān al-Fārsī, 'the Persian', was named Sulaimān ibn-Būhaira al-Khodr (Khiẓr). Ibn-Būhaira means 'son of the lake', and doubtless recalls the legend of the source of life. In the Nuṣairī Trinity, Salmān, created by Muhammad, is the Bāb or 'Gate'. The letter *sin* (s) is his emblem, but its meaning is not clear. He is also called Salsal Salmān (cf. G. R. Dussaud, *Hist. et religion des Nosairis*, Paris, 1900, pp. 133, 62, and 163).

[3] The founder of the Sha'bānias, Shaikh Sha'bān Walī, is buried at Kastamūnī, where he died in 977 H. (A.D. 1569–70) (Jacob, *Beiträge*, p. 88). The Shaikh Shaban, at whose *takia* near Caesarea an imprint of his hand is shown, was apparently another saint (cf. Hasluck in *Annual*, B.S.A. xxi. p. 66).

'Abd-ul-Qādir Gīlānī was the founder of the sect to which my friend and assistant belongs, and I may here add, as a word of information regarding Arabic surnames such as the present, that '*abd* signifies the *servant; ul* is the Arabic article and preposition, *the* and *of the*; and *Qādir*, the *Powerful*, which is one of the Islam attributes of God; so that his name is the 'Servant of the Almighty'. *Gīlānī* shows that he was a native of the province of Gīlān, in Persia. The Islam names of Muhammad, Ahmad, Mahmūd, Mustafā, Ismā'īl, 'Alī, etc., have each a distinct signification, more or less connected with God, and most Mussulmans have properly two names, though neither are family names in our sense. The Prophet's names were Muhammad-al-Mustafā, or 'Muhammad the Chosen'.

Ahmad Sa'īd Rifā'ī was the founder of the Order of the Rifā'īs, generally known among European travellers as the 'Howling Darvishes', from their peculiar mode of worship. He was the nephew of 'Abd-ul-Qādir Gīlānī, and, therefore, also from the same part of Persia. His own followers considered him peculiarly holy; so much so, that they say he even declared regarding himself, "This foot of mine is over the necks of all the saints of Allāh".

Among the Qādirīs, the office of *shaikh*, or chief of a *takia* (convent), is hereditary, and descends from father to son; and in case the latter be a minor, the brethren select one of themselves to act for him until he becomes of the age of twenty.

Among the traditions of the Order of the Qādirīs I would quote the following, as it sustains the saying of his ['Abd-ul-Qādir's] nephew Rifā'ī:

"It is related that once the daughter of the Prophet of God, Fātima, saw in a dream, that a man came out of her father's apartment, holding a large candle in his hand, the light of which extended from the East to the West. She mentioned this to her father, in the presence of her husband 'Alī, who was the nephew of the Prophet. The latter interpreted it, that 'one would come after him ('Alī), whose sanctity would resemble the candle, and be the chief of all saints'. 'Alī exclaimed against this, on the ground that he himself was the chief. 'No,' said the Prophet; 'the one I allude to will have his foot on the neck of all the saints, and all will come under his rule; those who do not bear his feet on their shoulders, and bend before him, will bear bags on their shoulders.' 'Alī would not admit this, and declared that for one he would refuse to bear him. Just then, the Prophet miraculously created a child; and as there was some fruit on a high shelf of the room, he asked 'Alī to reach it down for the child. 'Alī attempted to do it, but was not high enough, and the Prophet placed the child on his ('Alī's) neck, so as to reach the fruit. 'Alī having submitted to this, 'See, see!' exclaimed the Prophet, 'you already bear the person I allude to on your neck.' This child was 'Abd-ul-Qādir himself."

If there be really but twelve original Orders, these have many branches. The principal branches are said to be descended from Hasan al-Basrī, and it is these which are prevalent now in the Ottoman empire. Some others are from Shalmān-i-Fārsi. The Maulavīs, the Naqshbandīs, and the Baqtāshīs are thus said to be descended from Abū-Bakr-us-Siddīq, the first Caliph. The Baqtāshīs are all deemed to be Saiyids, or descendants from the family of the Prophet. The *taslīm-tāsh* (a white stone), worn on their necks, has its origin from Abū-Bakr, who, they say, once having used language which gave offence to the Prophet, repented of it, and in memory of his fault fastened a small stone around his neck, and when he came to chapel put it, in the presence of the Prophet, into his mouth to prevent himself from speaking improperly. The Baqtāshīs are all 'Alīide (Darvishes).

The Khalwatīs wear leggings, called *somāk*,[1] in memory of those worn by the Prophet in the battles of Badr and Uhud,[2] and great care is taken by them not to soil them. They are in the form of boots, and made of black leather.

In the earlier times of the Darvishes, their Orders have names or titles different from those of the present. These were mere explications of their tenets or principles, and it was only at a later period that they took the names of their founders.

I will therefore mention a few of these titles[3], but refrain from digressing on a part of my subject foreign to the object in view.

[1] Somāk, apparently for *tomāq*, Turk., "a kind of short, heavy boot formerly worn by horsemen" (Redhouse, *Turk.-Eng. Lex.* p. 1262). Evliya's translator calls it a half-boot. In popular Turk. *sum* (Pers. = 'hoof') means '*sabot*', but Redhouse does not give this meaning. Turk. *sūmāq*: "a leather bottle for holding water" (Redhouse, *ib.* p. 1195).

[2] Not 'battle of Badr-i-Uhud', as in original.

[3] The list of 'Orders' which follows (given again on p. 323 *infra*) is taken from Malcolm's *Hist. of Persia*, ii. p. 271. The term 'Order' is not, strictly

1. The Hulūlīa[1]: or those who, by devout contemplation, became inspired by God.

---

speaking, applicable to these schools, but as Brown rightly points out, the practice of naming a school or sect from its principles was abandoned in favour of a system of designating it by its founder's name. Moreover, it is very doubtful whether these groups ever formed really distinct 'schools'. Judging from what Shahrastānī says (*v.* note on p. 377 *infra*) there was much overlapping, so that the sects and schools were cross-divided. This indicates that the period before the rise of Ṣufīism was one of considerable independence of thought. The transformation into 'personal' sects was probably aided by the Ṣūfī institution of *pirs* and *murīds*. However this may be, the Ṣūfīs were at an early stage of their history grouped on quite new principles as follows:

APPROVED (*maqbūl*) SECTS

1. Muḥāsibi.
2. Qassārī or Hamdūnī.
3. Ṭaifūrī, who inculcated rapture and intoxication.
4. Junaidī, whose doctrine was based on sobriety, in opposition to the Ṭaifūrī. Their 'path' was to keep watch over one's spiritual state.
5. Nūrī.
6. Sahlī.
7. Ḥakīmī; *v.* note on p. 412 *infra.*
8. Kharrāzī.
9. Khafīfī.
10. Sayyārī.

REJECTED (*mardūd*) SECTS

11. Ḥulūlī.
12. Ḥallājī, which had in turn two dissenting groups: (i.) the Fārisī, founded by Fāris, a professed follower of Ḥallāj, but disavowed by the sect; and (ii.) the Ibāḥatī or Ibāḥī who regarded everything as permissible: *Kashf al-Maḥjūb* of al-Rujwiri (d. about 1070), Nicholson, pp. 130-1 and 260.

In this classification all the 'approved' sects are named after their founders, as is also the Ḥallājī. In some cases it looks as if the 'personal' name was assumed retrospectively, *e.g.* in that of the followers of al-Junaid. As to the Ḥulūlīs, the term seems to have been applied to a number of sects, mostly personal, while others also held some of the Ḥulūlī tenets. That they ever formed a regularly organised sect is at best doubtful.

[1] Ḥulūlī is derived from *ḥulūl*, from *ḥalla*, to 'settle' in a place, *maḥall.* It is used in two distinct senses as meaning the subtantial union (i.) of body and soul, and (ii.) of a divine spirit with man. Almost all Muslim theologians reject these doctrines, even the second, and so they excommunicated the Ḥulūlī, who comprised a number of sects, such as the Ghulāt, or extreme Shī'a, the Druzes and the Ṣūfīs (*E.I.* ii. p. 333, *s.v.* Hulūl). "With a vague tradition," say the Indian authorities, "that the original Order was the

2. The Ittihādīa [1]: or those who deem God ever present, and

---

Sabātia, the ancient Sabians, the Ṣūfī were early divided into two Orders, or schools, the Ḥulūlīa, or 'inspired', which held that the divine spirit enters all who are devout, and the Ittiḥādia, or 'unionists', who held that the soul by union with God becomes God."

It is sometimes said that the Ḥulūlīs are also called Ḥulmānīa, from the teacher Abū Ḥulmān al-Fārisī al-Halabī, of Damascus (apparently distinct from the founder of the Fārisī: see *infra*). Abū Ḥulmān taught the doctrines of *ḥulūl*, 'incarnation', *imtizāj*, 'commixture' and *naskh-i-arwāḥ*, 'transmigration of spirits'.

He seems to have been a follower of Ibn Sālim of Baṣra who died in 297 H. (A.D. 909). However this may be, the Ḥulūlī are connected with the Sālimīs or Anthromorphists, who held Ḥallāj to be a true Ṣūfī. The Sālimis comprised most of the jurists and traditionists of Baṣra, but precise information regarding the sect is lacking. According to some authorities it was founded by one Abū 'Abdullah, son of (Abū'l) Ḥasan b. Muḥammad b. Aḥmad b. Ṣālim, who died in 350 H. (A.D. 971) or ten years later, and that it was Abū 'Abdullah who died in 297 H. But others make the latter the father of Ḥasan (*J.R.A.S.*, 1912, p. 573). Another sect of Anthropomorphists was the Mushabbiha, as to which see p. 377 *infra*. The truth is that at this period the Islamic sects were in a fluid state, and Shahrastānī who describes so many of them has much to say about the Ḥulūlīs and Mushabbihas, for instance, but nothing about the Sālimīs or even about al-Junaid. This writer died in 548 or 549 H. (A.D. 1153), having been born in A.D. 1086, more than a century after Junaid's death. Yet to judge from his silence concerning them, the Junaidi were not recognised as a distinct sect or order in his day. Similarly the Ḥulūlīa may not have been so recognised. Yet an earlier writer, the Shaikh Tāhir ibn Muḥammad al-Isfaraini (Imām Abū'l-Muzaffar), who died in 471 H., speaks of the Ḥulūlīa as a sect divided into at least six sub-sects, including the Ḥulmānīa, Hallājīa, Muqanna'īa and others, but not the Sālimīa. The last-named are also described as Mutakallimūn of Baṣra who belonged to the group of the Hashwīa and approved of Ḥallāj (Haarbrucker, *Religionsparteien und Philosophen-Schulen* (Trans. of Shahrastani), ii. p. 417).

As a sect the Ḥulūlīs have long been extinct, yet despite their condemnation as unorthodox we find the term curiously revived in one Ḥulūlī Dede, a saint whom popular tradition makes the Halwā-jī-bāshī of Sultān Sulaimān (I., the Legislator, 1520–26). The saint could make sweets out of nothing. He lies in a *turba* at the Shāhzāda Mosque, and is the helper of children who are slow in learning to walk, and of girls who do not find husbands (Fried. Schrader, *Konstantinopel*, pp. 87-8). Possibly there is a confusion between the words *halwā* and *hulūl.* Both the Gulshanīs and the Rifā'īs have saints named Halwī and Halwāī (*v.* pp. 460 and 478 *infra*).

[1] Like the Ḥulūlīa the Ittiḥādīa are excommunicate for their adherence to the second doctrine of *ḥulūl*. So, too, were the Janāhia, but while Tāhir al-Isfara'inī mentions the latter, neither he nor Shahrastānī allude to the Ittiḥādīa (cf. Haarbrucker, *op. cit.* ii. p. 486-7). It would seem that the doctrine of *'ittiḥād*, 'identification', was developed after his time.

fill the mind of His worshippers with no other idea than of Himself.

THE HULŪLĪA.

3. The Wasūlīa[1] [Wāsilīa]: or those who believe that by constant devout contemplation of God they become peculiarly connected with Ḥim, even in the present life.

4. The 'Ashiqīa[2] ['Ashāqia]: or those who keep their minds constantly filled with a devout love for God.

5. The Talqīnīa[3]: or those who reach God by prayer, and by the means of constant devotion.

[1] Waṣūlīa, from waṣūl, 'union', as opposed to *ḥulūl*, 'fusion', and to *ittiḥād*, 'identification', as Macdonald translates these terms (*Muslim Theology*, p. 228). But for Waṣūlīa Wilberforce Clarke has Wāṣilīa, and herein he seems to have followed the Indian tradition. The Wāṣilīa, however, owed their name to Wāṣil b. 'Aṭā, Abū Huẓaifa (cf. *J.R.A.S.*, 1902, p. 85). In the full account of his teaching given by Shahrastānī no mention of the doctrine of *waṣūl* occurs. Wāṣil b. 'Atā, born, according to Osborn, in the same year as the other founder of free-thought in Islam, Amr ibn 'Ubaid, *i.e.* in 80 H., was a pupil of Ḥasan of Baṣra, but broke away from his teaching and became famous as one of the founders of the Mu'tazilites. He died in 131 H. (A.D. 849), long before the Ṣūfīs began to debate the problems of union with the divine (Osborn, *Islam under the Khalifs of Baghdad*, p. 140, and Macdonald, *op. cit.* p. 129).

[2] 'Ashkieh in original, '*ashāqia* in Wilberforce Clarke (*Hafiz*, iii. p. 6).

[3] On p. 323 *infra* Talqīnīa is rendered 'learned', and more correctly so.

6. The Zurīqīa [Zāqīa][1]: or those who by constant contemplation of their founder, or their immediate *shaikh*, enter into his spirit, and dwell with it.

7. The Wahdatīa[2] [Wāhidīa]: or those who constantly contemplate the unity of God.

I have much endeavoured to find a sensible cause for the peculiar forms prescribed by the founders of the various Orders of prayers and costumes, but without success. Some wear caps of peculiar shapes, many made up of gores, or sections, called by the Darvishes *tark*[3], a word signifying *abandon*, varying in number in different Orders. For instance, whilst the Baqtāshīs wear five or seven *tarks*, the Naqshbandīs have eighteen. Some

---

Talqīn is teaching a novice to repeat the articles of the faith of Islam, or a prompting them to a deceased person so that he may have answer for the questioning angels (Redhouse, *Turk.-Eng. Dicty.* p. 588). Shahrastānī does not mention this sect, though he speaks of the Ta'līmīa, from *ta'līm*, 'learning', whom he identifies with the Mulāhida or 'heretics' of Khurāsān and the Bātinīa, etc., of 'Irāq, but no direct connexion between these sects can be traced. For various meanings of *talqīn*, *v.* pp. 192, 209, and 275 *infra*.

[1] On p. 323 *infra* Zurīqia (Zureekieh in original) is translated 'Penetrating': as if from *zuraqa*, 'pierced with a lance or javelin'. But the school seems also to have been known as the Zakīa, 'those who grow in divine grace', from the same root as *zakā*, 'righteousness', and *zakāt*, 'devotion', especially by setting aside a fortieth part of one's property as God's due; cf. too, az-Zaki, 'der Rechtschaffene', the second title of the 11th Imām (Haarbrucker, *op. cit.* i. p. 193). Wilberforce Clarke calls this school the Zāqīa, and renders it 'penetrated' (*Hafiz*, iii. p. 6). But that term would seem to mean 'people of discernment' or 'tested' (Salmoné, *Ar. Dy.* p. 254).

[2] Wahdatīa, from the same root as Wāhidīa, *wahada*, 'was alone, unique'. It must not, however, be positively assumed that the two terms apply to one and the same sect. Shahrastānī mentions the Wāhidīa as a sub-sect of the Qarrāmīa, who were founded by Abū 'Abdullah Muḥammad ibn Qarrām and whose tenets he describes. They laid little stress on the divine unity, holding that God was regardless of it. The divergences between the sub-sects are not detailed, and Tāhir al-Isfara'ainī omits them, only allotting three sub-sects to the Qarrāmīa as against Shahrastānī's twelve, though the latter says the Wāhidīa were one of the six which are of importance (Haarbrucker, *op. cit.* i. p. 119 and ii. p. 403). The Wāhidī apparently survived until Evliya's time, for he mentions them and says they trace their origin to 'Umr (*Travels*, ii. p. 29). Burton alludes to the sect founded by 'Wahid Muḥammad', who, he says, identified the Qibla and the sun; wherefore, he taught, the door of the Ka'aba fronts the East (*Pilgrimage*, iii. p. 202).

The above sects are not given in any chronological order.

[3] From the Ar. root *taraka*, 'forsook'. It has no connexion with *tarīq*.

of their caps bear inscriptions, mostly verses of the *Qurān*, and some are made in the shape of a rose. Others wear a turban of black, white, or green colour. The colour of their mantles also varies. They have a variety of prayers, though generally these are the same as those of all other Mussulmans, and are followed by one for the Prophet, his family, and friends, their founder, and the reigning sovereign. In fact, I have only been able to learn that they all owe their origin to the will of their founder, called by them the *pīr*, a Persian name signifying ‘ elder ’. To some of their customs and parts of their dresses also a miraculous origin is assigned, which, I do not doubt, is perfectly satisfactory to themselves.

Some of them stand upright when performing the *zikr*, or ‘ call upon the name of Allāh ’ ; others sit; some form a circle, and put their hands on the shoulders of their companions to the right and left, and shake their bodies forward and aft, to the right and to the left, their animation and excitement increasing as the ceremony proceeds. Some cry out the *zikr* with a loud voice, as also the Mussulman ‘ Confession of Faith ’ (*Lā ilāha illā Allāh wa Muhammad Rasul-Allāh*), ‘ There is no God but Allāh (*the God*), and Muhammad is *the* prophet of Allāh ’ ; whilst others, like the Maulavīs (called by travellers from Europe the Dancing or Turning Darvishes), move round in a *quasi*-mystic circle, in profound silence, mentally reciting the same. I have been told that the custom of these latter refers to the harmonious movement of the universe, and that the soft music of their order is symbolic of that of the spheres ; but I am inclined to doubt it.

These two distinctions of *vocative* and *contemplative* Darvishes are said to refer to the command of the Prophet to Abū-Bakr, the first caliph, whilst concealed together in a cave, ‘ to recite the *zikr* in silence ’, so as not to be heard by their pursuers ; and to ’Alī, the fourth caliph, when he inquired of him what he ought to do so as to receive Divine assistance—‘ to call loudly God’s name without ceasing ’.

All of these forms of worship are of Muhammadan origin, whilst many of the principles of the Orders date back to a much more remote period, and may be therefore designated as Sūfīism, of which more will be said hereafter.

As a general rule, no Darvish who has not been the *shaikh* (chief or master) of a *takia* can wear a turban folded round his cap. The turban is called *sāriq*, *imāma*,[1] and *dastār*. A *shaikh* may, however, name a large number of *khalīfas*, or 'deputies' (successors), all of whom can wear the turban around their caps. These are consequently considered as honorary *shaikhs*, or masters. The cap is called by most of the orders *kulāh*.[2]

The Rifā'īs wear twelve *tarks*, and the colour of the *shaikh's* turban is black. They perform the *zikr* standing upright. The hall in which they worship is called the *sarhīd-khāna*.[3]

MAULAVĪ.

The Maulavīs wear a tall white or yellowish cap, without any

[1] The *imāma* was worn by Aḥmad al-Badawī (p. 268 *infra*). It clearly denoted 'leadership'—*imāmat*. The *dastār* has a similar significance, being assumed in token of accession to a chiefship.

[2] Kulāh, Pers., a cap or cowl. In Turkish the word *kulāh* or *kulah* has the same meaning, but *kūlah*, a 'tower', is also applied to the head-dress worn by the Maulavī *darvish* (Hasluck, *Annual*, B.S.A. xxi. p. 123). The Ar. equivalent of the Pers. *kulah* is *qurmus*. It denotes the pointed head-dress of the *darvish*, and 'the royal tiara placed according to usage on the heads of those condemned to death' (Massignon, *Kitāb al-Ṭawāsīn*, p. 108).

[3] Serheed-khaneh in original (cf. Terheed-khaneh on p. 60 *infra*). These words seem to be derived from Ar. *ṣarīd*, which in Turkish takes the form *tarīd*, vulg. *tirīt*, 'a sop of bread soaked with gravy' (Redhouse, *Turk.-Eng. Lex.* p. 624 and p. 540). If so, *sarīd-khāna* would mean 'refectory', rather than 'the hall in which they worship'.

tarks, and the colour of the *shaikh's* turban is green, because these are generally Saiyids, or descendants of the Prophet. As aforestated, they perform their prayers standing upright, and in silence, turning round from east to west. On Sunday and Friday they perform a prayer called the *ism-i-jalāl,* seated in a circle, 1001 times. This prayer is simply the word Allāh. Their hall is called the *samā-khāna.*

MAULAVĪ.

The Qādirīs wear four *tarks* in their cap, embroidered. Their *shaikhs* have each seven *tarks,* and the colour of their cap is white if they be not Saiyids. They move round the hall standing upright, their hands placed on the shoulders of their neighbours. Their hall is called the *tarhīd-khāna.*

The Badawīs have twelve *tarks* in their cap ; the colour is red, and they perform their religious exercises like the Rifāʿīs. Their hall is also called the *tarhīd-khāna.*

The Dusūqīs have no *tarks* ; the colour is white, and they perform on foot.

The Sa'dīas have twelve *tarks* ; they wear turbans of a yellowish colour, and perform on foot.

The Khalwatīs have no *tarks* in their *kula,* or cap ; it is, however, divided into four angles ; the colour is white, yellow, green, or other, and they pray on foot.

The Naqshbandīs have four *tarks* ; colour generally white,

though they may wear any other: the cap is always embroidered, and originally contained a verse of the Qurān. They perform

NAQSHBANDĪ.

seated a prayer called the *ikhlās* 1001 times. One remarkable peculiarity of this Order is, that when they assemble to perform this prayer they divide among their number 1001 pebbles; and as each one recites an *ikhlās*, he lays down in the circle one of these as evidence of the fact, until all are recited.

The Jalwatīs wear twelve *tarks*: the colour of their cap is green, and all may wear turbans. They perform on their knees the *zikr* and the *ism-i-jalāl*.

The Hamzāwīs, otherwise called the Malāmīyūn,[1] have no distinction of costume, cap, nor belt. They all perform seated, and in silence, contemplating the Divine Spirit, and seeking for *nūr*, or 'Divine Light'.

The Bairāmīs,[2] [Dasūqi] Sha'bānīs, etc., all are like the Khalwatīs.

[1] *V*. Chap. VIII.

[2] Described in *E.I.* i. p. 595 as a branch of the Naqshbandīs with settlements in Stambūl, Aiyūb, Scutari and Qāsim Pāsha at Constantinople, the Bairāmī is probably more akin to the Baqtāsh order. *E.g.* Evliya assigns the *takia* of Ak-Bi'īk Sultān at Brūsa to it or to the Bairāmīs: Jacob, *Beiträge*, p. 13, citing *Travels*, vol. ii. pp. 8 and 26. (It would be more precise to say that Evliya calls Ak-Bi'īk Sultān first a Baqtāsh and then a Bairāmī darvish.) The Albanian Baqtāsh appear also to lay claim to Hājī Bairām, just as they do to Shams-ud-Dīn Tabrīzī and Nasr-ud-Dīn Khoja of Aqshahr

The Baqtāshīs have four and twelve *tarks*; their colour is white and green. They have no special form of prayer, nor position; but it is said that they perform like the Naqshbandīs.

Some say that there are as many as sixty different Orders of Darvishes, and others even a hundred, each bearing the name of its founder. It would scarcely repay one the trouble to endeavour to enumerate them, and their shades of difference. In the Order of the Baqtāshīs, there are branches from the original stock, some more pantheistic than the others, and I presume that the same may be said of some of the other Orders. A few have been prohibited at Constantinople, such as the Baqtāshīs, on account of

(Hasluck, *Annual*, B.S.A. xx. p. 99[3] and xxi. p. 94[5]. The Bairāmī are locally predominant in the Angora district (*ib.* xxi. p. 97).

On p. 269 *infra* the date of Hājī Bairām's death is given as A.D. 1471, but in *E.I.* i. it is assigned to 833 H. (A.D. 1429–30), and this date is accepted by Gibb (*Hist. of Ottoman Poetry*, i. p. 299). Born at a village near Angora (Evliya says "on the banks of the river Chepūl in the village of Solkoī"), he was the disciple of one Sh. Hāmed (Evliya, *Travels*, ii. p. 233). His tomb at Angora is still a place of pious visitation. His successors had a chequered history, in marked contrast to his own, which was only disturbed by traducers who caused Murād II. to summon him to Adrianople, where he won the Sultān's heart. His disciple the Sh. Bārdāqlī Bābā, who obtained a living by making cans (*bārdāq*), imitated his example of supplying his own needs by labour. He also had a miraculous power of supplying water to his disciples for ablutions which still subsists at his shrine (*ib.* p. 225). Other pupils of his were the poet Shaīkhī, Sinān, born at Kutahia, the capital of Germian, who studied under Ahmadī, but became a disciple of the Hājī and then settled at Kutahia, until he died (not later than 1451). Known also as Hakīm Sinān this follower was acquainted with Nesimi. Another was Sh. Salāh-ud-Dīn of Boli, the Scribe, and his two sons, the Yāzījī-oghlī (sons of the clerks), named Sh. Muḥammad and 'Aḥmad Be-jān (the 'lifeless', owing to frailty of a frame consumed by the fire of asceticism) continued this tradition. The former studied under Zain-ul-'Ārab and Haidarī Khāfī, dying in 1451 or 1453. He may be the Mehmed Āghā whose *takia* is in the mosque (aforesaid). Sh. Muḥammad built an oratory at Gallipoli, then an outpost of Islam, where he was joined by his brother. No trace of this foundation seems to exist, though legends have grown up round Sh. Muḥammad's name. The next poet-follower of Hājī Bairām was Kamāl-i-Khalwatī. Another Kamāl, Kamāl-i-Ummī, a darvish of Laranda, a companion of Nesimi and with him a guest of the famous mystic Sh. Shujā'-ud-Dīn of Qaramān, was hanged for blasphemy. If he, too, was a disciple of Hājī Bairām, as seems possible, his fate would go far to explain why the Bairāmī order, which had hitherto held a high position and contributed more poets to Turkish literature than any other order, now yielded place to the Maulavīs. (Gibb, *op. cit*, i. pp. 299, 390-2, 396, 401, 412, 421.)

their too intimate connexion with the Janissaries ; though, at the present time, they are not molested. They do not generally bear a good reputation, and are said to be quite atheistic, and not much attached to the principle of the *Qurān*, nor firm believers in the prophetic mission of Muhammad. They generally are warm 'Alīides, or followers of the Caliph 'Alī, and are therefore Sūfīists, or 'Islām Spiritualists ', which will be alluded to later in this work.

I am not aware that any one has written either a history or an account of the various Mussulman religious orders known under the title of Darvishes. The subject seems to be one of an original character, and interesting to the public, and especially to the travellers in the East, who have no means of acquiring any information regarding a class of individuals whose forms of worship strike their curiosity.

The difficulty which lies in the way of collecting facts respecting the Darvish Orders will be apparent to Oriental students, and indeed I feel that I have been presumptuous in venturing to assume so serious a task. To all things there is, however, a beginning, and, though my humble sketches may appear imperfect, nevertheless they will serve as a nucleus to the labours of those who succeed me.

I have endeavoured to obtain my information from the most authentic sources within my reach, both oral and written, as well as printed. To offer a criticism on the belief of my Mussulman friends (for among the Darvishes of Constantinople I have several estimable and valued friends), to draw comparisons between what may be called the religious superstitions of Muhammadanism and Christianity, forms no part of my plan. The enlightened reader is left to draw his own conclusions thereon, and to receive whatever impressions, favourable or unfavourable, which the recital may make upon his mind.

It has been thought by some persons that Freemasonry existed among the Mussulmans of Constantinople under another title, and consequently in other parts of the East. This I do not find to be the case, though, like in most secret fraternities, there may be points of resemblance accidentally. I have had an indirect intercourse with a Mussulman, who asserted that Freemasonry does exist there, and he gave even a list of the places in which lodges were held in various parts of the empire, adding that the Grand Lodge existed on the Lake of Tiberias, in Palestine, where it had been taken after the destruction of Jerusalem. It must, therefore, have existed, and does still exist, among the Jews. I regret to have to state that, notwithstanding all my researches to verify this declaration, I have not found any trace of the fact on which I could rely. My opportunities of inquiry here have been numerous, and my desire to meet with brethren amongst Mussulmans led me to use all proper zeal in the pursuit of this desirable object. Others may, perhaps, meet with more success. The title by which, it is said, Mussulman Freemasons are known is Malāmīyūn; and, when I come to speak of this Order of Mussulman Darvishes of the ’Alīide sect, the reader may judge how far the statement is incorrect.

I may here add that there are a few Mussulmans of my acquaintance, some of them in high official positions, who have become Masons in Europe, mostly in France. There are also others who belong to lodges in Constantinople and other cities of the Ottoman empire, and there are many lodges in India, to which Hindu [Indian] Mussulmans belong.

It is rather strange that the Darvishes of the Baqtāshī order consider themselves quite the same as the Freemasons, and are disposed to fraternise with them. The name of Freemasonry in the Turkish language is *farmāson*,[1] and is one of great reproach. It signifies atheism of the most condemnable character, and this may be said of the Baqtāshīs, who, from some reason or other not quite clear to me, are held in small repute among other Mussulmans, even those belonging to the other Darvish Orders. No one in Constantinople may consider himself at all complimented when he is called a ‘ Farmāson ’ or a ‘ Baqtāshī ’, no more than a Protestant is when called a Methodist by a devout Catholic, or a Voltairean by an ordinary Christian.

Inspired with the most laudable desire to withdraw his people of Arabia from the worship of idols, Muhammad proclaimed to them the adoration of an Universal Deity, the Creator of all things, and a perfect resignation to His Divine will.

[1] *Fārmāsūn* = freemason : *-lūq*, -ry, or atheism. For the possible connexion between ‘ freemason ’ and *φάρμακον*, see Morley Roberts and Miss Jane Harrison in *Folklore* xxvii. (1916), pp. 218 f. and 298. The word *farmaçion* has in the East the meanings ‘ outlaw ’, ‘ satanist ’, and ‘ devil-worshipper ’. Its descent seems to be from Aeolic *βερπύρ*, Lat. *verber*, ‘ whip ’, Turk. *vourmak*, ‘ to beat ’.

This Deity must have been already well known in Arabia, previous to the advent of Muhammad as a prophet, under the name of *Allāh* ; a word most probably derived from the Hebrew 'Elohīm'. It is composed of two Arabic words, *al*, the article *the*, and *lāh* or *alāh*, which together is now written *Allāh*. It is formed in Arabic of only four letters, *A*, *l*, *l*, *h*, called four mystical letters, marking in a peculiar manner the Divine Essence.

I need no more than remind the reader that the Arabic language is derived from the Hebrew, and that it is a Semitic tongue. It is therefore composed of radical letters, two, three, or four of which forming all the words of the language, under certain grammatical rules.

The definition which Muhammad gave to this Deity, when interrogated thereon by the Jews and Christians, the Magi, and other idolaters, is seen in one of the chapters [cxii.] of the *Qurān*—the book containing his inspirations—and called the *Ikhlās*[1] ['Sincerity'] or the 'most pure'. He there says: "It is that God, who is unique, self-existing, from whom all creatures receive their existence; who does not beget, nor was begotten; and who has no equal amongst all that exists".

The latter part of this definition shows that he understood the Christians of Syria and Arabia as believing in more than one God. Whether or not the nature of the Trinity was ever properly explained to him, cannot now be ascertained, but it is clearly seen that it was unsatisfactory to him; so much so, that during the whole of his career he condemned, in the strongest terms, the Trinity, as a system of false religion, as much to be avoided as the worship of fire and of idols. He denominates the Christians in the *Qurān* as *mushrikīn*, or those who associate others with God. The idolaters he calls *sanāim*,[2] or those who actually worship idols made by the hand of man.

This comprises all that he had in view to combat or refute in other religions, and it has thus been explained by an eminent writer on his faith:

"The God whom I adore, and who should be adored by all,

[1] In the language of religious ethics as developed especially by the Ṣūfīs, *ikhlās* particularly refers to the effort to come nearer to God, and means the keeping free of this ideal from all subsidiary thoughts. In this sense it is often opposed to *riyā*, the wish to be seen (*E.I.* ii. p. 458).

[2] From Ar. *ṣannama*, 'made himself idols'.

is a unique Deity, simple in His essence, and separated from all other beings by attributes peculiar to Himself. He is self-existing, and has no need of anything for His existence ; and all things exist by Him. He does not beget (this is against the opinion of the Jews, who believe that 'Uzair or Esdras[1] was the son of God) ; He was not begotten (which is against the Christians, who believe that Jesus Christ, born of the Virgin Mary, is the Son of God, and is God), and that He has no equal (which replies to the Magi of Persia, followers of Zoroaster and Manes, and believers in the two equal principles of power—Oromasdes [Ahura Mazda] and Ahriman—the Good and Evil Spirits and Deities ; as well as against the Arabian idolaters, who sustained that there were certain spirits called the Banū Hūsha,[2] which were the companions and associates of God)."

This God he declared to be without beginning or end, and so far superior to His creatures that no one could have any conception of His immensity. Though His power and essence pervades every part of His creation, He is wholly invisible to ordinary mortal eyes, and His power and magnitude can only be comprehended by witnessing His works. One eminent writer says, " All that the mind, the sense, and the imagination of man can fancy regarding Him, be it ever so solid, falls at once before His majesty ". Another declares, " Do not fatigue yourself with any ideal conceptions of Him, for it is all a useless labour ". A celebrated Mussulman writer says it is impossible to form any idea of God, because He is superior to all comparisons, and there are no terms of human language which can convey any idea of His magnitude. 'Alī, the fourth Caliph, who among the Arabs was a man of much education, and served as an amanuensis for the Prophet, whose daughter he married, is said to have observed that " he who knows himself knows God " ; and the same idea is confirmed in the words,—" Thy soul is a cunning proof, and an invincible argument, of the existence of God. By reflection thou knowest thyself, thou knowest that thy existence is the work, and that there must be a worker."

[1] 'Uzair, son of Shara'ya, is the same as Khizr (*v.* note in Palmer's *Qurān* S.B.E. vi. p. 45). But cf. R. Bell, *The Origin of Islam*, 1926, p. 159, and p. 175 *infra.*

[2] For Benau Hasha in original. Ḥūsh was a fabulous region, a land of genii.

Another states,—" The existence of God being the same as His essence, know then that thy being, which receives its existence from Him, is the proof of thy existence ".

The Founder of the Order of the Maulavīs, and the author of a celebrated mystical work called the *Masnawī Sharīf*, says: " To what purpose are all the efforts of the human mind to comprehend that Being who is above all combination, all distinction ? He is a tree without branches or body, or roots, to which the mind can be attached. He is an enigma for which no natural nor metaphysical meaning can be found ; nor of whom a satisfactory explanation can be given. Who has ever found in His existence any mystical, symbolical, or demonstrative comparison ? He is infinitely above the capacity of our understanding—of our imagination ; and we lose ourselves in vain conjectures whenever we seek to comprehend Him, or even to suspect what He is. It is, therefore, in vain for us to seek for words by which to discuss properly His being. All that we may do is to adore Him in respectful silence."

In the view of still further explaining what Muhammad understood by Allāh, I may be permitted to add that the unity of God is alluded to in the 89th chapter of the Qurān, where God is said to have sworn by the *pair* and *impair*; the first are His creatures, and the second Himself; and one of its verses says,—" We have created all things double; but we say that God is one and unique ".

A Persian writer states that no one should say ' I ', because that property belongs alone to God ; and a Turkish proverb adds that—" Whoever, other than God, says ' I ', is a Satan ; because he who says ' I ' must be a demon ; for none but God can use that word with truthfulness, as all things came from Him, all are in Him, and obey Him. He only is self-existent."

A pious Mussulman, and an author of celebrity, used to declare, —" When I say ' God ', I have said all things ; for all else is but folly, or the fancy of foolish desires ".

Another states,—" Since my heart is turned towards God, speak to me of nothing else than Him ".

Allāh is therefore defined as Omniscient and Omnipotent, and pervades all His creation. It is not held that He is in any particular place. I would, nevertheless, express my conviction that Muhammad was not pantheistic, in the modern sense, and much less that he believed in the modern metempsychosis. He, however, believed that the spirit of man was of a Divine origin, but made a wide distinction between the life which all creation enjoys, and the breath of life possessed by human beings. In this sense a writer tells us as a tradition, that Moses having asked of God where He was, he received the reply, " Know that when you seek for me you have already found me ".

It is related that an Arab of the desert, being asked how he knew there was a God, answered :—" By the same by which I know from the traces in the sand that a man or an animal has passed over it. Is not the heaven decked with its bright stars,

A DEVOUT MUSSULMAN AT PRAYER IN THE DESERT

the earth with its fertile fields, the sea with its numerous waves, sufficient proofs of the existence and the greatness of a Creator ? "

Another child of the desert, in reply to a similar question, said :—" Is there any kind of a torch to behold the brightness of the Aurora ? "

And, to a companion who had met with a serious misfortune against which his own cares were unavailable, he said :—" There is no other recourse or refuge from God than in Him ".

In the Ḍarvish acceptation of Allāh, He is their All in all. To think of Him at all times, to contemplate His majesty and power, and to call upon His name for aid and succour during their mortal existence ; to adore and worship Him in the most devout manner, and thereby increase their own sanctity and consequent spiritual power,—is the basis of all their belief. They consider it highly meritorious to pronounce audibly, or mentally, His holy name most frequently, and even go so far as to strive to do this in a short space of time. If any one can call upon the name of Allāh a hundred times in a minute, it is held to be still more meritorious to do so double that number of times in the same period of time. They believe that God, or Allāh, will, and does, manifest Himself to the devout worshipper in a special manner whilst so occupied, and that around the heart a Divine light, or *nūr*, is shed in answer to his frequent calls. Also that the word Allāh becomes distinctly impressed upon the heart in letters visible to the spiritual eyes of the devotee.

The faith or religion which Muhammad proclaimed to his brethren of Arabia he called the *Dīn-al-Islām*, or the obligation of perfect submission to the Divine will and decrees of Allāh. He considered the word *dīn* to be the only true and correct faith, the right path leading to eternal happiness.

The word *Islām* is fruitful in definitions, all derived from the same radical letters, *s*, *l*, *m*, *salama*, among which is *salām*, ' compliment ' or ' salutation ', and peace ; and *salāmat*, salutation or safety. From it also is framed the past participle, Muslim, and its plural, a noun of multitude, Musalmān, and the feminine noun, Muslima, all signifying those whose faith is a belief in Divine decrees, and humble submission to the will of Allāh.

The author of the *Masnawī Sharīf* afore-mentioned says :— " In whatever place we may be, we are, Lord, subject to Thy commands ; be we wherever we may, we are always with Thee. We say to ourselves, ' Perhaps we may find a path leading elsewhere '. How vain is this idea, for all paths lead ever to Thee."

The opening chapter of the *Qurān* commences :—" Lead us, O Lord, in the right path ", that is, in the true path of Islām ; and in the [6th] chapter [v. 153] called *An'ām* [Cattle], the Lord says :—" This is the true path, follow it, and seek none other, for they will mislead you ".

This mention of a *path* is evidently the origin and basis of the paths (*tarīqāt*) of the Darvishes. I mention them as Orders, or sects, but the proper and correct term is paths. All these are different pathways leading to the same *Allāh*, just as an Oriental poet says :—" Though we may each look out of different windows, we all see the same one great sun, source of light and warmth ".

In the [14th] chapter [v. 29 f.] of the *Qurān* called *Ibrāhīm*, there is the following :—" Religion is like unto a tree—like the palm-tree, the roots of which are in the depths of the ground, and its branches raised towards heaven, and which, by Divine order, gives fruit in its time. On the contrary, impiety is a wicked plant, like the coloquint, which is out of the ground, for it is easily pulled up on account of possessing no roots to sustain it." [1]

An Islām author says there are four kinds of persons who serve God :—" The wise through a spirit of obedience, the penitent through fear, the devout through desire, and the just from a sincere love for Him ".

In one of the chapters [the 16th, closing verses] of the *Qurān* it is forbidden to compel any one to abandon his own faith for that of Islām ; but in another [the 9th], produced at a later period of the Prophet's mission, it is ordered that war should be carried on against all those who did not believe in it—the Jews, Christians, Magi, and Sabeans,—either to compel them to embrace it, or pay him (Muhammad) tribute as a temporal sovereign.[2]

So intimately is an account of the Darvishes connected with the history of Muhammad, the prophet of the Arabs, and now of the whole Mussulman world, that some particular allusion to him seems to me here necessary. No one can peruse the *Qurān* without being impressed with a high estimate of his character as a religious reformer and a law-giver, especially when they remember him only as a *camel-driver* (the title of reproach generally given to him by Christian writers). How different his origin and early history when compared to that of Moses, who was brought up at the court of Pharaoh, among the learned and wise of Egypt ! All Mussulmans say that he could neither read nor write, and we have no knowledge of his early education in any religion whatever,

[1] The accepted text of the *Qurān* contrasts a good word with an evil word—not ' religion ' with impiety—and omits the comparisons with palm-tree and ' coloquint ' ; but the meaning is disputed (*v.* Sale in Wherry's reprint, iii. p. 7 ; Rodwell, p. 228 ; and Palmer, *S.B.E.* vi. p. 241). It may be suggested that the verses are intended to recall the Ṭūba or ' tree of happiness ', described in Sale's Prelim. Discourse, i. p. 154.

[2] It is at best doubtful if *Qurān* ix. v. 29 bears this interpretation (*v.* Sale's trans. in Wherry's reprint, ii. p. 287 ; Palmer's in *S.B.E.* vi. p. 176 ; or Rodwell, p. 473).

much less in the deeply spiritual principles which appear in the *Qurān*. Under these circumstances, it is but common justice to admit that he was certainly a very extraordinary *man* ; indeed one of the most remarkable that the world has upon its records. When arrived at an age when man can feel and judge for himself, he was fully impressed with the deeply-seated conviction that he was specially designed by the Creator of the Universe to reform his brethren the Arabs, and withdraw them from the most absurd belief in the power of idols, the work of human ingenuity, and lead them to the worship of one only God. This conviction he entertained to his last hour, and he never presumed to ascribe to himself any other character than a *rasūl*, or ' envoy ' of Allāh to call the misled into the true path. We call him a Prophet, signifying one inspired by God, and the question is open only as to his inspiration. With the convictions which he fully entertained of the errors of a Christian faith in a Trinity, and of the Arabs in the worship of their idols, his intentions were salutary, honest, and benevolent ; and we are led to ask whence he received these impressions, these impulsions, to do good, if not from the great Source of all good designs ? To plead for him a want of education, of a more intimate and correct acquaintance with the contents of the Old and New Testaments, is to admit the falsity of his inspiration, for it is proper to suppose that God would have supplied this deficiency in a prophet.

We must, therefore, take him as he was—an Arab, an uneducated man, a strong-minded human being, gifted with an extraordinary intellect, and of a strength of will and purpose which sustained him through an eventful career. Still the weaknesses of humanity were strong in him : he had many of the frailties of the flesh, and was filled with a strong ambition to carry out what he had designed to effect. He showed much ability in managing the various people upon whom he wished to exert an influence for their own spiritual good, and he stood perfectly alone in the opening of his career. That he succeeded in correcting their abuses, and withdrawing them from their idols, cannot be denied ; and his religious principles are still honoured by a vast portion of the human race in Asia, Africa, and Europe. There are reflections in the *Qurān* which would do honour to an educated theologian, and his followers are taught to expect only his intercession as a saint in heaven with the Allāh whom he himself adored and worshipped. Although many of the Arabs of his time possessed much mental ability—many of them were even poets—they possessed no literature, and had but small means of extending and perpetuating knowledge. Thrown at an early age upon his own resources, Muhammad evidently acted upon principles of honesty and uprightness, and it has never been shown that he deviated from them, or abused the confidence of his employer, who subsequently married him. He grew up to manhood, possessing the respect of all of his acquaintances and relatives, and it is only a matter of surprise that, knowing the value and utility of letters, he never applied himself to learn them. As a merchant he is said to have made several journeys into Syria. During these he became acquainted with the Christianity of the Greeks and the faith of the Jews. His unfavourable impressions of the former are seen from his continual condemnation of it in the *Qurān*. He probably visited their churches, and witnessed the reverence paid there to the images of the saints of the Greeks ; he there learned the doctrine of the Trinity, without, however, being able to comprehend it, and in his own conscience denounced both as unworthy of his respect.

There is no reason to believe that Muhammad received any religious instruction either from the Jews or the Christians. The Arabs doubtlessly possessed a knowledge of the Old and New Testaments, especially of the former, and many traditions regarding the earlier history of mankind, some of which differ widely from the accounts given in the Bible. Few copies of the New Testament must have existed among them, judging from the little allusion to any of its characters by the *Qurān*. Muhammad's innumerable mystical and philosophical reasonings are totally distinct from the writings of those who composed the Bible. The story that he procured the Biblical knowledge which is comprised in the *Qurān* from a Jew is too baseless for belief, and evidences its origin in the malice and hatred of the earlier denunciators of his faith. There is really no proof existing to show that the *Qurān* is due to any other source than his own inspiration ; and whatever it contains of good or evil must, therefore, be attributed to no one else than himself.

Muhammad does not reject either the Old Testament or the New. He believed in the Prophets who preceded him, and that those who were so directed left each his own book. Whatever in their books did not agree with the information possessed by him, he attributed to the perversion of more recent copyists. As to the New Testament of the Christians, it would seem that he believed these had perverted its original contents on important points, and so made Jesus Christ to say many things regarding Himself which are not true. This has led many Mussulmans to believe that there exists another New Testament, containing none of the changes introduced, they say, by modern Christians, and I do not doubt but that they really entertain this conviction.

Muhammad declared that Jesus Christ was of a miraculous origin—that he was born of a virgin, and that he was both a Prophet and the 'Spirit of God', *Rūh Allāh*, yet he denies in strong terms that He is God. He says, moreover, that Christ foretold his coming when He said:—"I will send a Comforter", etc. This appears in the [61st] chapter of the *Qurān* called *Saf* [the Ranks], when Christ says to the Jews:—"O children of Israel! I am He whom God has sent to verify and accomplish all that has been revealed before me in the law of Moses, and to announce another envoy who is to come after me, and who will bear the name of Ahmad".

Muhammad declares himself to be the *last* of the Prophets, and that his mission is the *seal* of all those who preceded him. In the third chapter of the *Qurān* it is said that the angel Gabriel was sent to Mary to announce to her, "God announces to you His *word* (*kalāmat*, or Word), whose name will be Christ, or Messiah Jesus, and who will be your Son, worthy of all respect in this world and in the other".

Again, it is stated therein, "O Mary, God has elevated, purified, and very particularly chosen you among all the women in the world. O Mary, submit to your Lord; prostrate yourself before Him, and worship Him with all those other creatures who adore Him. This is a great secret which I reveal to you."

In another chapter [iv. v. 165], called the *Nissā* [Women], are these words:—"The Messiah is Jesus, Son of Mary, the Envoy of God, His *word*, which He announced to Mary, and the same Jesus is the *Spirit* proceeding from Him".

By the word *Spirit* an eminent Oriental author says is meant, "He is endowed with a 'Spirit', which proceeded immediately from God, without the medium of any other cause".

In [v. 170] the chapter last alluded to there is the following statement, which shows that Muhammad considered the Messiah in the light only of one of God's creatures, and not as God Himself:—"The Messiah does not disdain to be and to call Himself the Servant of God, as do the angels, the nearest to Him".

Muhammad commenced proclaiming his mission in the fortieth year of his age. His inspirations were retained in his memory, and, long after they were forgotten by those to whom he delivered them orally, he not unfrequently renewed them, showing thereby the great strength of his memory. They were, however, written down by his son-in-law and nephew, 'Alī, and by 'Othmān, both of whom became caliphs, or vicars of his mission, after his death. Thus the *Qurān* was only completed in twenty-three years. The elegant construction of the *Qurān*, its perfect grammatical formation, and the almost poetical beauties which it contains, have always been the admiration of its readers; and though in prose, it is susceptible of an intonation which almost amounts to a rhythmical measure.

The word *Qurān* is from the Arabic radical *q*, *r*, *a*, to read, and, conformably with the grammar of that language, the object read is *Qurān*, or otherwise a 'book'. Muhammad declared that its contents, in the form of inspirations, commenced descending from heaven, under the charge of the angel Gabriel, during the moon or month of Ramazān, in the night called the *Lailat-al-Qadar*, or the 'Night of Power'.[1] It has always been the subject of discussion among pious Mussulmans, whether or not the *Qurān* was created, or emanated directly from God, and this especially during the times of the Abbāside caliphs. His own son-in-law, 'Alī, believed that it was created like any other of God's creations, and, having acted as the Prophet's amanuensis in writing it out, he ought to know best.

After Muhammad's death, the chapters and verses of the *Qurān* were much dispersed, and Abū-Bakr, the first caliph, had them collected in one volume, which he named the *Muṣḥaf*,[2] a title still used by many when alluding to it. There are seven original copies mentioned by its commentators—two made at Madīna, one at Makka, one at Kūfa, one at Basra, and one in

[1] Cf. the chapter (xcvii.) of the *Qurān* called the *Qadr*.

[2] The Ethiopic for 'book' (*E.R.E.* 10, p. 538).

Syria, and another called the Vulgate.[1] That made by Abū-Bakr is considered the primitive, and was referred to for corrections by others. The Caliph 'Othmān copied it out himself, and so did the Caliph 'Alī (the original), aided, however, by another friend of the Prophet.[2] Several chapters were abrogated, and these now form a volume into which they have been collected, called the *Mansūkhāt* (or ' the Abrogated '),[3] one of which, a Darvish friend assures me, is now in the library of the Royal Mosque of Sultān Bāyazīd of Constantinople. There are also other copies of it in existence,—one at Basra ; and it would be worthy of translation into one of the European languages.

Muhammad died without any male heir. It is uncertain whether he had any desire to form a dynasty. He was evidently warmly attached to his son-in-law and nephew, 'Alī, the fourth of the direct caliphs or vicars of his mission. The regular caliphs were Abū Bakr, 'Umar, 'Othmān, and 'Alī, called the *khulafā rāshidīn*, or the direct or regular caliphs. They were all elected by the Moslems of Madīna, and were men of great mental abilities, —of simple and frugal habits, and worthy to follow their illustrious Prophet, and carry out the principles which he had inculcated.

Oriental writers represent that 'Alī aspired to become the successor of his uncle, and there is no room to doubt but that such would have been satisfactory to his deceased relative, to whom he had rendered the most confidential and important

[1] Brown here is clearly misquoting Sale, *Koran*, Prelim. Discourse, i. p. 80, where seven principal editions of the *Qurān* are mentioned, the seventh being the common or *vulgar* edition. Goldziher, no doubt, speaks of the ' *Mawaṭṭa'-vulgate* ', but the *Mawaṭṭa'* was a collection of traditions (*Muhammadanische Studien*, ii. pp. 243, 213). With Brown's account may be compared that of Mingana in *E.R.E.* 10 pp. 547-8. The only recension at all analogous to the *Vulgate* would be one of the two official recensions of the *Qurān*.

[2] The Wahhābīs also claim to possess those parts of the *Qurān* which were suppressed by the Caliph 'Uṣmān, but they maintain that it is unlawful to disclose them to any who differ from them (*Imams and Seyyids of 'Oman*, Hakluyt Soc., p. 252). The Ishrāqīs seem to have had a somewhat similar claim (*v.* p. 457 in App. I.).

[3] *Mensuhat* in original. The *Qurān* itself (ch. xvi. v. 103) contains evidence that verses were abrogated by the Prophet himself. But no authentic manuscript of them is known to exist. The theory that several chapters, sufficient to form a volume, were abrogated goes far beyond anything put forward in the orthodox ' doctrine of abrogation ' ; as to which see Sale's Prelim. Discourse in Wherry's recension of his *Koran*, i. p. 110.

services, both with his pen and his sword. But republics are apt to forget the claims of their great men to their suffrages, and popular favour is often carried away by the current of events, and to be bestowed upon those who neither expect nor merit it. Eminent men are allowed by them to descend to their graves in disappointment, too often carrying with them even the memory of their great deeds, and, in the hour of peril and misfortune, these cry out, like the blood of Abel from the ground, to the hearts of their countrymen, who thus neglected them whilst living. So it was with 'Alī, and the wrong done to him still divides the Mussulman world into two distinct sections. Most of the Darvishes, however, are *'Alīides*, who, as will be shown hereafter, revere his memory, as well as deplore his fate.

The most influential members of the citizens of Madīna were the *ansārs*, or those who had been the faithful 'assistants' of the Prophet. The widow of the Prophet also still resided there, named 'Āyisha, and her influence was very great among the devoted followers of her late husband. This lady was the daughter of the second caliph, 'Umar.[1] It is worthy of remark that the Prophet, as well as his direct successors, had Christian and idolatrous servants in their service, and that it is nowhere mentioned that any violence was ever used to induce them to become Moslems.

The Darvishes declare that the Prophet designed 'Alī as his successor, and they attach a mystical signification to the intimate connexion which existed between them. They say that the Prophet on many occasions declared :—" I am the House, and 'Alī is my Door ". They ascribe to 'Alī all that is metaphysical in their faith,—that is, *mystical* and *spiritual*, and some go so far as to declare him superior in this respect even to the Prophet. The warmer devotees of Sūfīism call him *'Alī-al-Illāhī*, or ' 'Alī, the Divine '.

On the decease of 'Umar, the Moslems were again called upon to elect his successor, and their choice fell upon 'Othmān, though 'Alī still refused to waive what he considered to be his right. Seeing, however, the will of the people, he acquiesced in their decision, and paid homage to his more fortunate rival. His partisans were greatly disappointed, and, aided by the widow of

[1] 'Āyisha was the daughter of Abū Bakr.

the Prophet, fermented trouble to the new caliph. Now commenced the first dissensions amongst Moslems, which have had so direful an effect upon their political and religious career. It is not improbable that differences of interpretation had now also begun on passages of the *Qurān*, and that sectarianism had its origin at this early period.

On the final succession of 'Alī, the fourth caliph, he began his administration by removing from office all those who had been appointed by his predecessor, without any regard to their past eminent services, elevated characters, and distinguished qualifications. This he did, contrary to the advice of his friends and the wiser of the citizens of Madīna, who saw, in such a course, the seeds of future party strife, as well as disregard of the welfare of the whole community, by men ambitious only of attaining to power, so as to punish others for the wrongs done to themselves.

The sad fate of 'Alī is well known to most readers of Eastern history. He, and nearly all of his family, were put to death by an Arab general named Mu'āwia, who seized upon the caliphate without asking to be elected to it. This violence is the origin of the present two Islām sections, the Shī'as[1] and the Sunnīs, as well as their varied subdivisions—among which are the Darvish Orders.

It seems to me necessary to add a few remarks on the personal character of the Caliph 'Alī, with whose history is connected so much that is interesting in an account of the Darvish Orders. It is, however, desired to limit them, as much as possible, to his position as a seceder from the original principles of the Prophet. His biography is so made up by them of the marvellous and the incredible, that it rivals the position assumed by the Prophet himself, and strongly conflicts with his own remarks concerning him. If but a small portion of what they relate about him be correct, the Prophet would certainly have clearly stated his desire for him to succeed him, and even proclaimed him as such previous to his decease.

'Alī is my *beau idéal* of the most chivalrous of warriors in the times of the Prophet, who, in consequence of his valour, called him the 'Lion of God', and his sword, the gift of the Prophet, is revered throughout the Islām world under the name of *Zil farkain*.

[1] Shī'a: the full name would be *Shī'a 'ahl-ul-bait*, or 'followers of the Prophet's kindred'.

In the coat of arms of the Shāh of Persia, a lion is seen holding a sword in his paw, in memory of 'Alī. The Prophet is said to have, on one important occasion, wrapped his own mantle around himself and 'Alī, and declared that they were one spirit.

On another occasion he is said to have declared :—" 'Alī is for me, and I am for him ; he is to me what Aaron was to Moses ; I am the city in which all knowledge is contained, and 'Alī is its portal ".

It is from among the descendants of 'Alī that the more devout Moslems expect the Mahdī, who is to reappear on earth in company with the Prophet Elias, on the second coming of Christ. This belief is connected with the partisans of the metempsychosis, —among whom the most prominent of the Darvish Orders are the Baqtāshīs.

The Shī'a Moslems reject the caliphates of Abū-Bakr, 'Umar, and 'Othmān, and commence directly with that of 'Alī, whom they call the first *Imām*. After him are eleven others, completing the full number of twelve,—the last being the Mahdī aforementioned. The Druzes declare that the founder of their religion, [the Caliph] *al-Hākim bi Amr Allāh*,[1] was this same Mahdī, and that, having disappeared in a mysterious manner, he will reappear in some new form hereafter.

Not satisfied with the contents of the *Qurān*, his followers, soon after his decease, collected all of his sayings together, under the title of *hadīsāt*,[2] or traditions, which have now a value in their eyes almost equal to the verses of that book. They were collected, not only from the mouths of his immediate friends and companions, the *ansārs* and the *aṣḥābs*, but from others, who declare that they heard them maintain them as coming from the Prophet.

The friends of 'Alī have also collected his sayings, independent of the remarks made by the Prophet, and they hold them in high estimation. I cannot see in them anything peculiarly mystical, or even religious, so as to warrant him to be placed in the elevated position assigned to him by the 'Alīide Darvishes. The following are a few of his sayings :—' I am a servant of whoever has taught me one letter.' ' A secret known to ten persons is no longer a secret.' ' Benefit your offspring with the blessings of learning.'

[1] *V.* note on p. 121 *infra*.

[2] Hadīṣ, ' tradition ' (see art. in *E.I.* ii. pp. 189 f.). The traditions are of varying value (cf. note on p. 414 *infra*).

'Any service ever written is perpetuated.' 'When you are troubled by worldly affairs, remember the pleasure existing between ease and difficulty.'

In concluding the present chapter, I will add that the earlier commentators on the *Qurān* deduced from it the laws and precepts which still form the basis of Mussulman jurisprudence. They are comprised in a small work entitled the *Multaqā*.[1] These were—Hanefi [Abū Ḥanīfa [2]], born in Kūfa, 80 H., and died in prison at Baghdād in 150 H.; Shāfi'ī,[3] born at Ghaza, in Palestine,

[1] The *Multaqa'l-Abḥur* of al-Halabī (*v.* note on p. 181 *infra*).

[2] Abū Ḥanīfa, al-Numān ibn Sābit al-Kūfī, the famous jurist who founded the Hanafite school of Muslim law, born in A.D. 699, died in 767 (*E.I.* i. p. 90). The usual view that the Ḥanafīs represent more liberal principles than the other schools of Muhammadan law is contested by the writer of the art. in *E.I.* ii. pp. 256-7. The two companions of Abū Ḥanīfa, the Imāms Muḥammad (*d.* 189 H. = A.D. 805) and Abū Yūsuf, who died seven years earlier, were called the Ṣāḥibain. His friend was Muḥammad al-Shaibānī (Nassau Lees, *Nafaḥāt al-Uns*, p. 1).

[3] Shāfi'ī was essentially the law-giver of the poor, and his tenets are therefore observed by many backward and out-caste peoples throughout Islām. Hence the somewhat rigid distribution of the schools propounded on p. 379 *infra* requires a little modification. For example, in Asia Minor and the adjoining provinces Shāfi'ī doctrines were in Evliya's day freely professed by many sections of the people. Thus among those of Qarābāghlar in Nakshivān Evliya found quite a nest of curious heresies, and at Nakshivān itself the inhabitants pretended to be orthodox Shāfi'ites but were really Ja'aferite heretics. But at Ajān they were genuinely of that school though they kept their doctrines secret. At Ardabīl the Shāfi'ī tenets again were only professed, but between Tabrīz and Erivān the sect was numerous, though it had apparently been taxed, like the Sunnīs, for the privilege of letting its beards grow by the earlier Safawīs. The Kaitāks, an uncouth tribe of Mughal Turks on the frontiers of Dāghistān, also professed to be Shāfi'ites (*Travels*, ii. pp. 127, 145-6, 148-9, and 157). In India Aurangzeb adhered to the school except in matters of law wherein he was a Hanafī (Elliott and Dowson, *Hist. of India*, vii. p. 158). In the south of the Peninsula the Moplas and Labbais are Shāfi'ya by sect, and in the north tribes which eat unclean animals, like the semi-nomad Kehals of the Punjab, profess to follow the Imām Shāfī (Rose, *Gloss. of Punjab Tribes and Castes*, ii. p. 486). Similarly his followers are excused prayer as they must drink the water required for ablution, the giving of alms as they have to beg, fasting in Ramaẓān as they starve all the year, and pilgrimage as the world is the House of Allah (Burton, *Pilgrimage to El-Medinah and Meccah*, iii. p. 80). Burton cites many points of difference in the usages of the Shāfi'īs and the other schools (*ib.* i. 112, ii. pp. 67, 333, 309, iii. 228, 235, 239, 285, 385, and 309). In Arabia he found that almost all the Bedouin and many of the citizens of al-Madīna are Shāfi'ī, though the Ḥanafī hold the first

150 H. (A.D. 767), and died in Egypt, 204 H. (A.D. 820) ; Han Balī [Abū Hanbal [1]], born in 164 H. at Baghdād, and died there in 241 H. ; and Mālikī, born at Madīna, 95 H. (A.D. 713), and died at the same place 179 H. (A.D. 795).

Each has his advocates and followers, who differ from each other quite as much as do the Darvish Orders.

---

rank in that city (*ib.* ii. p. 262). Al-Madīna has or had only two *muftīs*, one Ḥanafī, the other Shāfi'ī (*ib.* p. 158). But according to one authority the Shāfi'ī have precedence in prayer at the Ka'aba (*ib.* iii. p. 170). In Indian usage the Shāfi'ī hold that ablutions are only lawful if performed in running water (Rose, *op. cit.* i. p. 498). It is not easy to say what are the distinctive features in the teaching of the various schools, but it may be pointed out that the pupils of Abū Ḥanīfa wrote important monographs on constitutional law, and that one of them, Abū Yūsuf (*d.* A.D. 795), recognised canon law in the government of the State (*E.I.* ii. p. 103). This suggests that the Ḥanafī school upheld the principle that the State was controlled by the principles of that law.

[1] Abū Ḥanbal, Aḥmad b. Muḥammad b. Ḥanbal, born in A.D. 780, died in 855, was a theologian as well as a jurist. He occupied himself more with the sources of the *hadīṣ* than with the derivation of the law. Nevertheless he founded the Hanbalite school of law, but it is now only sparsely represented in Islām, the predominance of the Ottomans having dealt it a very severe blow (*E.I.* i. p. 188). According to Burton, the Ḥanbalīs are nowhere common except in Najd and the lands eastward as far as al-Hasa (*Pilgrimage*, p. 158). They have no *muftī* at Madīna or Cairo ; and are supposed to have thrown out a bad off-shoot, the Wahhābīs. For the '5th rite' of the 'Ibādiya see note on p. 453-4 *infra* (in App. II.).

CHAPTER III

NAMES OF THE ORDERS OF DARVISHES—BRANCHES OF THE ORIGINAL ORDERS AT CONSTANTINOPLE—PECULIAR TITLES GIVEN TO FOUNDERS—THE SĀHIB-I-TASAWWUF OR 'SPIRITUAL OWNERS' OF THE DARVISHES

AN author of much celebrity for his Oriental studies (von Hammer) says, in reference to the Darvish Orders, that " the tombs of the Shaikhs and Darvishes who have acquired a certain celebrity by the foundation of an Order, or by the sanctity of their lives, are not less important in the Ottoman Empire than those of heroes and conquerors.

" During the reign of the Sultān 'Othmān, these Islām monks formed a community more powerful and redoubtable than that latterly of the *'ulamā*, or Doctors of Holy Law. ' No monks in Islāmism ', an expression of the Prophet which should have been sufficient to prevent all innovations and imitations of the monachism of the Hindus and the Greeks; but the natural disposition of the Arabs for a solitary and contemplative life caused them soon to forget this precept, and the other phrase of the *Qurān*, ' Poverty is my pride ', was the argument which, thirty years after the death of the Prophet, is that on which his sectarians based the origin of their numerous monasteries ; since the Order of *faqīrs* (poor) and of Darvishes (sills of the door) so multiplied in Arabia, Turkey, and Persia, that they reached the number of seventy-two, exclusive of an equal number of heretic sects."

The following are the names which this writer gives to the *tarīqs*, or orders existing previous to the foundation of the Ottoman empire :—

1. Uwaisī, *v.* App. II.
2. 'Ilwānī, *v.* App. II.
3. Adhamī, *v.* p. 82 *infra.*
4. Bustāmī, *v.* p. 156.
5. Saqatī, *v.* p. 50 *supra.*
6. Qādirī, *v.* pp. 99-116.

7. Rifā'ī, *v.* Ch. VI.
8. Nūrbakhshī, or Suharwardī, *v.* pp. 158-61.
9. Qubrāwī, *v.* p. 142.
10. Shāzilī, *v.* App. II.
11. Maulavī, *v.* Ch. X.
12. Badāwī, *v.* App. II.

After the foundation of the empire, there were the

13. Naqshbandī, *v.* App. I.
14. Sa'dī, *v.* App. II.
15. Baqtāshī, *v.* Ch. VIII.
16. Khalwatī, *v.* App. II.
17. Sainī [Zainī], *v.* App. II.
18. Bābāyī, *v.* p. 268.
19. Bairāmī, *v.* App. II.
20. Ashrafī, *v.* p. 99 ff.
21. Wafāyī, *v.* App. II.
22. Sunbulī, *v.* App. II.
23. Gulchannī [Gulshanī], *v.* App. II.
24. Yagitbāshī [Igithbāshī], *v.* p. 270.
25. Ummī Sinānī, *v.* p. 271.
26. Jalwatī, *v.* App. II.
27. 'Ushāqī, *v.* p. 271.
28. Shamsī, *v.* p. 271.
29. Sinān Ummī, *v.* p. 271.
30. Niyāzī, *v.* App. II.
31. Murādī, *v.* App. II.
32. Nūruddīnī, *v.* App. II.
33. Jamālī, *v.* App. II.
34. Ashrakī, *v.* App. II.
35. Ni'amatullāhī, *v.* App II.
36. Haidarī, *v.* App. II.

Of the thirty-six Orders, twelve are anterior to the foundation of the Ottoman empire ; the twenty-four others have been instituted since the commencement of the fourteenth century, down to the middle of the eighteenth. The first, viz. the Naqshbandīs,

KHALWATI

was founded by 'Othmān[1] in A.D. 1319, and the Jamālīs under Ahmad III. in A.D. 1750.

Thirty-seven years after the 'Flight', or 'Emigration' (*Hijrā*) of the Prophet, the Archangel Gabriel or Jibrāīl appeared to Uwais, a native of Karn, in Yaman, and commanded him in the name of the Lord to renounce the world, and to devote himself to a life of penitence. In honour of the Prophet, who had lost two teeth in the battle of Uhud, Uwais had all his teeth extracted, and required the same sacrifice of his disciples, from which it may be readily understood that he made few proselytes among the fanatics of Arabia. The Shaikhs 'Ilwan, Ibrāhīm [ibn] Adham,[2] Bāyazīd of Bustām, and Sarī Saqatī, followed the example of Uwais, and founded the Orders which took their names, giving

[1] Not by 'Othmān but by Bahā-ud-Dīn, *ob.* A.D. 1309.

[2] This famous saint, whose full name was Ībrahīm b. Adham b. Manṣūr b. Yazīd b. Jābir (Abū Iṣḥāq) al-Tamīmī al-'Ijlī, was a native of Balkh, who died between 160 and 166 H. (A.D. 776–783). The Ṣūfī legend concerning him is evidently modelled upon the story of Buddha, for in it he appears as a prince who, while hunting, was warned by an unseen voice that he was not created for such pursuits. Thereupon he abandoned the path of worldly pomp for the path of asceticism and piety. He became a quietist of a practical type, and did not carry the doctrine of *tawakkul* to the point of refusing to earn his livelihood; on the contrary, he supported himself by gardening and so on. He approved of begging in so far as it incites men to give alms and thereby increases their chance of salvation, but he condemned it as a means of livelihood. So he distinguished two kinds of begging. C. van Arendonk says that a trait far more characteristic of Indian and Syrian than of Moslem asceticism appears in the story that one of the three occasions on which Ībrahīm felt joy was when he looked at the fur garment that he was wearing, and could not distinguish the fur from the lice (*E.I.* ii. p. 432). But this story is poor evidence of Buddhist or Indian influence on Ībrahīm, because a very similar episode is told of the Breton saint, Le Petit St. Jean. A notable legend says that angels ministered to Ībrahīm on the banks of the Tigris after he had resigned his kingdom, bringing him ten dishes of food. This roused the envy of a *darvīsh* who had been a poor man before he assumed the habit of a beggar, and to whom only one plate was vouchsafed. The incident is a commonplace topic of Indo-Persian or Mughal painting (*J.R.A.S.*, 1909, p. 751, and 1910, p. 167).

There can, however, be no doubt that Ībrahīm was a great figure in his day, and his memory still survives in Islām as far as India. The tale that he married a princess is even more persistent than the tradition that he was of royal birth. Leigh Hunt bestowed on Ībrahīm bin Adham the title of 'Abou' in his well-known lines :—

"Abou spoke more low,
But cheerly still; and said, 'I pray thee then,
Write me as one that loves his fellow-men'."

them the several rules of discipline. The most celebrated of these religious persons is the *Pīr* of the Qādirīs, named 'Abd-ul-Qādir Gīlānī, who had been proposed as guardian of the tomb of the great Imām Abū-Hanīfa of Baghdād. After the decease of 'Abd-ul-Qādir his mausoleum was surrounded by those of the most renowned mystical Shaikhs. These tombs are those of Junaid, Shiblī, Hasan Karkhī, Husain Mansūr,[1] Sarī Saqatī, and others. Of the most celebrated followers of 'Abd-ul-Qādir are Junaid of Baghdād, Abū-Bakr Shiblī, and the great mystical writers Muhyī-ud-Dīn al-'Arabī [2] and Sadr-ud-Dīn of Qonia [3] in Asia Minor. These tombs have given rise to the name of the 'City of Saints', possessed by Baghdād, and, no doubt, to the religious fanaticism of its inhabitants. Baghdād has always been the object of the veneration of Mussulmans in general, and the various Darvishes in particular, and these often wander from Constantinople through Syria or Asia Minor, to pray over the tombs of the pious and holy men whose remains are there interred.

The Order of the Rifā'īs, named after the founder, Sa'īd Ahmad Rifā'ī, is the most generally known to the foreigners visiting Con-

[1] Ḥusain Manṣūr, Husain bin Manṣūr al-Ḥallāj, a wild antinomian pantheist, the Ṣūfī martyr, executed by the Caliph Muqtadir in A.D. 922 at Baghdād (Nicholson, *A Literary History of the Arabs*, pp. 399, 375). For accounts of his execution see Dozy, *Essai sur l'histoire de l'Islamisne*, p. 329 f., or L. M. J. Garnett, *Mysticism and Magic in Turkey*, pp. 12-14. But all these are now superseded by Louis Massignon's outstanding work, *Al-Hallaj, martyr mystique de l'Islam*, 2 vols., Paris, 1922.

Manṣūr also enjoyed the title of Abū'l Mughīs, 'the Intercessor'; and it is significant that he is said to have dabbled in alchemy and magic (*E.R.E.* 6 p. 480).

[2] A descendant of the poet-knight, Ḥātim al-Tā'ī, the Arab paragon of generosity, he was born in Spain in A.D. 1165, and was therefore styled al-Andalūsī. Having spent thirty years at Seville he visited the East, and died at Damascus in 1240. Nominally submitting to the Zāhirite doctrines, he, nevertheless, rejected *taqlīd*—'recognition of authority'—and passed for an esoteric, and was even denounced as a *zindīq*. Besides the *Fuṣūṣ-al-Ḥikam* he wrote the *Futuḥāt al-Makkīa* or 'Meccan Victories', and their contents involved him in charges of adherence to the doctrines of *ḥulūl* and *ittiḥād*. These charges were, however, refuted by a quotation from his last-named work (R. A. Nicholson in *J.R.A.S.*, 1906, p. 799, where a full account of his life and works is given). Or *E.R.E.* 8 p. 908, may be consulted.

[3] Ṣadr-ud-Dīn Muḥammad (or Abū'l-Ma'āli Mehmed) b. Isḥāq al-Qonawī, was a pupil and son-in-law of Muḥyī-ud-Dīn ibn 'Arabī and an intimate friend of Jalāl-ud-Dīn Rūmī. He died in 672 H. (A.D. 1274). Jāmī gives an account of his life in the *Nafaḥāt-ul-Uns*. His death is sometimes assigned to 671 H. (A.D. 1272-73). His grave is at Qonia.

stantinople. The members of this sect offer the spectacle of the most startling self-torture; they perform acts of jugglery, such as swallowing swords and fire, expose parts of their body to the flames, dance in the most grotesque positions, and frightfully contort their limbs. The lives of these recall the ancient Etruscan priests of the sun, mentioned in the eleventh book of the *Æneid*, line 28.

BRANCHES OF THE ORIGINAL ORDERS OF DARVISHES AT CONSTANTINOPLE

Of the twelve original Orders there are a number of branches called *furū'*,[1] at Constantinople, whose *pīrs* or Founders are buried there; among these are the Sunbullīs,[2] at Khoja Mustafā Pasha, and at Psamatia.

The Ardaballīs,[3] between the gates of the city, Top Qapū and Selivria Qapū-su, on the roadside.

[1] Ferru' in original. *Far'* (S.) means 'a branch'. As a term in Moslem jurisprudence *furū'al-fiqh*, 'the doctrine of the branches', is applied *fiqh* as opposed to *uṣūl al-fiqh*, 'the doctrine of the roots', *i.e.* the sources of the law. On p. 106 *infra* the term may be translated 'corollaries', implying the systematic elaboration of positive theology (not as usual of positive law) under its separate heads; but this meaning of the word is not given in *E.I.* i. p. 104.

[2] See note on p. 455. The list on pp. 480-1 ff. *infra* assigns some fourteen *takias* in Constantinople to the Sunbulīs, but does not mention one at Psamatia.

[3] Ardabīl was the headquarters of the Ṣafawīs. That Persian dynasty derived its descent from Shaikh Ṣafīyyu'd-Dīn, a contemporary of 'Alā'u'd-Daula Samnānī (p. 142 *infra*), who was born in 650 H. (A.D. 1252-53). The Ṣafawī were a saintly family which eventually acquired temporal power; and appears to have lost its spiritual position in this wise: Its founder Fīrūz Shāh-i-Zarrīn-kulāh ('gold-cap'—a title which may denote that he held high civil office) was appointed governor of Ardabīl by a 'King' of Persia who is said to have been one of the sons of Ibrāhīm Adham! He claimed descent from Ḥamza, son of Mūsā Kāẓim, the seventh Imām. Shaikh Ṣafīyyu'd-Dīn Abū'l Fatḥ Iṣḥāq, to give his full name, was directed to the Shaikh Zāhid of Gīlān at Ardabīl, whom he succeeded as head of the 'order'. He also married his daughter. Dying in 1334, Ṣafī was succeeded by his son, Ṣadr-ud-Dīn, one of whose pupils was the Saiyid-ul-'Ushshāq or Qāsim-ul-Anwār (the 'Lord of Lovers', or 'Apportioner of Lights'), the celebrated mystical poet whose disciples are taxed by Jāmī with communism and contempt for the law. In 1302 Ṣadr-ud-Dīn was succeeded by his son Khwāja 'Alī, and he in 1427 by his son Shaikh Shāh, whose daughter became superior of the female members of the order. In 1447-48 his son, Shaikh Junaid, became head of the order, and was eventually killed in battle. His grandson, Shāh Ismā'īl, then became king. Shāh 'Abbās the

The Ummī Sinān,[1] at the Mosque of Aiyūb, in the quarter of the Dukmajilar.

Great appointed Shaikh Abdāl, described as a descendant of Shaikh Zāhid, custodian of the shrine at Ardabīl in 1600. Thus, if the story told by the Zāhidī historian is correct, the shrine at Ardabīl reverted to the family which had founded the 'order' (*Manuscript Hist. of the Safawi Dynasty of Persia,* by Prof. E. G. Browne, in *J.R.A.S.*, 1921, pp. 395 ff. The analogies in this version to the Baqtāsh traditions are patent. Both assert a descent from Mūsā al-Kāẓim. Both allude to an organisation of the women of the 'order'. But very little trust can be placed in its chronicles. Its founder or *pīr* was certainly not buried at Constantinople, and it is difficult to believe that it was ever allowed to possess a shrine or a *takia* there. The Turkish writers throw some light on the fate of Shaikh Junaid. Banished from Ardabīl, he fled to Uzūn Ḥasan, chief of the Black Sheep, and was by him given the hand of his daughter by the Christian princess Despina Katon. Then he visited the shrine of Ṣadr-ud-Dīn Qonawī, but its incumbent, Shaikh 'Abd-ul-Laṭīf, denounced him as a heretic, and he sought refuge in the Jabal Arsūs, in the district of Aleppo, where he was able to collect a following which included a number of the adherents of Badr-ud-Dīn. He was killed, however, in 1456, and his son Sulṭān Ḥaidar met his fate also in battle in 1488. Yet the curious tolerance which permitted Badr-ud-Dīn's followers to erect his shrine at Seres may have allowed an Ardabīlī or Safawī convent to exist outside the walls of Constantinople (*v.* F. Babinger in *Der Islam*, xi. pp. 78 ff.). Khwāja 'Alī is said to be buried at Quds-i-Khalīl (? Jerusalem), where he is known as Saiyid 'Alī 'Ajam, Saiyid 'Alī the Persian (Browne, *op. cit.* p. 407). If this is true, the Ardabīlī movement may at one time have been very widespread.

Evliya's account is very misleading. According to him—

Shaikh Safr (? Safī)-ud-Dīn Abū Isḥāq (founder of the Safī dynasty).

Shaikh Ṣadr-ud-Dīn Mūsā.

Shaikh Khwāja 'Alī.

Shaikh Safi (?), who governed only in a spiritual sense.

Shaikh Ḥaidar.

Shaikh Ibrāhīm, who was the first who enjoyed rights of sovereignty. Yet he says from Sh. Safī to Shāh 'Abbās are five Shāhs who coined money. In reality Sh. Ibrāhīm, better known as Shaikh Shāh, was son and successor of Khwāja 'Alī, and all Ḥaidar's sons were put to death, excepting Shāh Ismā'īl. Evliya substitutes a second Safī for Junaid (*Travels*, ii. p. 147). If Evliya is to be trusted the Ardabīlīs were in close touch with the Baqtāsh, as Shaikh Safī, who came from Erdebīl to visit the convent of the Baqtāsh saint Pīr Marizāt near Shamākhī, spent treasures in building it. Evliya says it has its equal perhaps only in the town of Mashhad Mūsā Rizā. The convent is called also Pīr Mirza or Mirka, but its correct name is Marīzāt, meaning 'incurvated', because the saint's body is seated in a corner of the convent in an incurvated posture, his face turned towards the Qibla, his head recumbent on a rock. His body is light and white like cotton, without corruption (*ib.* p. 160). *V.* however Erratum, p. 483.

[1] An limmī Sinān *takia* is now held by the Khalwatīs ; *v.* p. 463.

The 'Ushshāqīs,[1] at Qāsim Pāsha, and the valley of Uzun Yolda.

The Hudāyīs,[2] or Jalvatīs,[3] at Scutari.

[1] 'Ushshāqīs. Doubtless the Khussām-ud-Dīn 'Ushshāqī *takia-sī* (p. 482). They seem to have none now at Uzun Yol, 'the long road' (cf. p. 455).

[2] Brown does not explain the name Hudāyī here given as another title of the order. It appears to be derived from *hudā*, 'guidance', 'the right road', and thus there is probably an allusion in it to the Ar. *hadī*, 'a bride when conducted home in public procession' (Redhouse, *Turk.-Eng. Lex.* p. 2160). The Jalwatīs are also said to wear the hair long (*E.I.* i. p. 1044); but they are not described as affecting feminine garments, like a few orders of Indian *faqīrs*. Hudāyī was the name in poetry of the great Shaikh Maḥmūd of Scutari, who played a leading rôle in the reign of Sulṭān Aḥmad I. A follower of the Pīr Uftāda, who founded the Jalwatīs (*v.* p. 271 *infra*), he saw visions and was gifted with second sight. Before his death in 1628 he had written many important works of his own, and collected those of his master. The latter included expositions of the ninety-nine names of God corresponding to the ninety-nine names of Muḥammad, and a *Silsilanāma*, or spiritual pedigree of the Pīr Uftāda, which is of interest as it differs from those generally given in some respects. Beginning as usual with Muḥammad, 'Alī, Ḥasan Basrī, Habīb 'Ajamī, Dāūd Tā'ī, Karkhī, Sarī Saqatī, and Junaid, it next specifies Māmī Shāh of Dināwar, Maḥmūd of Dinawār, Muḥammad Kubrā, Muḥyī-ud-Dīn the judge, Jamāl-ud-Dīn of Tabrīz, Rukn-ud-Dīn Sinjarī, Qutb-ud-Dīn al-Abhari, Najīb Suhrawardī, 'Umar al-Bakrī, Ibrāhīm Gīlānī, Safī-ud-Dīn of Ardabīl, Ṣadr-ud-Dīn of Ardabīl, Khoja 'Alī of Ardabīl, Hamīd-ud-Dīn of Āq-Sarāī, Hājī Bairām, founder of the Bairāmīs, and Shaikh Uftāda Effendi. He also left a collection of *ilāhiāt*, and converted the small mosque at his cell in Scutari into a cathedral mosque. The cloister of Azīz Maḥmūd Effendi there seems to be his foundation (*v.* Hammer-Purgstall, *GdOD*, iii. pp. 192-202, and Evliya, i., Part ii., p. 83). Gibb gives his name as Sh. Ḥalwājī-zāda, born at Sīvrī Ḥiṣṣār, and settled in Scutari in 1593. His cell there became a sanctuary for officials who had incurred the wrath of Sulṭān 'Uṣmān (*Hist. of Ott. Poetry*, iii. p. 218).

[3] Pīr Uftāda, to whom the foundation of the order is rightly ascribed on p. 271 *infra*, is described as a pupil of Ḥājī Bairām, and is buried in the mosque of the citadel at Brūsa near the mother-house of the order. In mystical parlance *jilwa* (lit. the 'ceremony of raising the bride's veil', when her husband sees her for the first time) is the state in which the mystic is on coming out of the *khalwa*: filled with the emanation of divine attributes, his own personality has disappeared and mingles with the being of God. One of the two sacred books of the Yazīdīs is called *Kitāb al-Jilwa* (*E.I.* i. p. 1044). It may be noted that in Turkish *jilwat* means 'charm', or as a verb 'to appear', 'to make oneself seen'. It thus appears to connote the opposite of *khalwat.* The Jalwatīs have four *takias* at Scutari (*v.* pp. 460-2, *infra*), besides many others in Constantinople.

The Qādirīs,[1] at Topkhāna, and the name of the Pīr was Ismā'il-ar-Rumī.

The Malāmiyūns have a *shaikh* at Psamatia now living. Once a year they go to the Oq Maidān above the Navy Yard, to the grave of Idrīsī Muhtafī,[2] where a *shaikh* meets them. They have also another at Scutari who, it is said, never goes out of his premises. They are now called Hamzāwīs.

They pray over the graves of the 'Holy Dead'. It may be here mentioned that Mussulmans in general pray at the tomb of those whom they repute Saints (*auliā*), and implore their intercession in their own behalf. If at an ordinary grave, it is for the benefit of the soul of the deceased, the place and actual condition of which is unknown to the prayer. If the deceased, however, be in Paradise, the prayer is conveyed as an offering to the happy soul from the prayers; if it be in hell, it aids it out of that place of punishment.

There is a *hadīth*, or traditional saying, of the Prophet to this effect: "If your hearts be oppressed with sorrow, go, seek consolation at the graves of the holy dead". Many of the *takias* of the Darvishes are erected at, or even over, the tombs of eminently pious shaikhs, or other holy men. Their remains offer additional attraction to the public. Great care is taken of them, and much respect evinced for them by the costly shawls and embroidered cloths spread over the tombs, wholly irrespective of the civil or official position which the deceased may have occupied. Lamps are kept burning before them, as an emblem of the spiritual light which they shed around them, and vows are offered up at them by passers-by or visitors, called *nazr*, in the view of procuring relief through their saintly intercession, from sickness, misfortune, sterility, etc. With each vow a common rag is tied on the iron

[1] The Qādirīs hold a larger number of the Constantinople *takias* than any other order (*v.* pp. 474-7). The one at the Topkhāna is not apparently dedicated to Ismā'īl ar-Rūmī.

[2] See Chap. VIII. *infra.* Idrīsī Mukhtāfī, the 'occult' or 'concealed', doubtless the Idrīsī 'Alī Effendi of p. 232 *infra.* Originally of Tirkhala, the ancient Tricca, in Thessaly, Idris Mukhtafī lived from time to time at Constantinople under the name of 'Ali beg. There he seems to have come under the influence of the Bairamia Malamias, especially two of their leaders, Sari 'Abdah Effendi and Sa'irkaji. On his death in 1024 H. (A.D. 1615) he was buried at the place described in the text. His works do not seem to have been yet printed (*O.M.* p. 32).

bars of the tomb, as an earnest of the vow. Miraculous results are declared to have occurred at these tombs, quite equal to those of the greater Christian saints. Lights are often seen to float over them, or to lead to them, and the living holy shaikhs, by means of their spiritual powers of vision, acquired by long meditation and prayer, often are enabled to discover the graves of deceased holy men, long after they have been lost to human knowledge.

PECULIAR TITLES GIVEN TO THE FOUNDERS OF SOME OF THE ORDERS OF DARVISHES

Qādirīs.—'Abd-ul-Qādir Gīlānī is called the *Sultān-al-Auliā*, or 'the Sovereign of the Saints'.

Maulavīs.[1]—Ahmad-ur-Rifā'ī is called *Abū-al-'Ālamain*, or 'the Parent of the Two Worlds', which alludes to the temporal and spiritual worlds.

Badāwīs.—Ahmad-al-Badāwī is called *Abu'l-'Ainain*, 'the Parent or Father of the Two Sources', in reference to his connexion with the two original Orders of 'Alī and Abū Bakr.

Sa'dīs, or *Jabāwīs.*—Sa'd-ud-Dīn al-Jabāwī is called *Abū-'l-Futūh*, or 'the Father of Victories'.[2]

Dasūqīs.—Ibrāhīm ad-Dasūqī is called the *Shaikh-ul-'Arab*, or 'the Shaikh of the Arabs'

THE SĀHIB-I-TASAWWUF, OR 'SPIRITUAL OWNERS' OF THE DARVISHES

"I left Madīna", so related to me one of my Darvish friends, "and went to the *Mashhad-i-Ullā*,[3] or the Holy Tomb of the fourth Caliph 'Alī; I remained there three days, visiting and performing my prayers over it. I had read in a work called the

[1] The Maulavīs were founded by Jalāl-ud-Dīn Rūmī, not by Aḥmad ar-Rifā'i.

[2] Not 'victims' as in original.

[3] Mashhad, lit. 'place of testimony or martyrdom'. Mashhad-i-'Alī or 'place of 'Alī's martyrdom'. 'Alī was interred at Kūfa, according to the usual tradition, close by the dike which protected the town against the inundations of the Euphrates, on the spot where afterwards the town of Najaf arose—the present Mashhad 'Alī (*E.R.E.* 1, p. 284). Mashhad in Persia is quite a different place.

Tabaqāt-i-Sharwālī[1] mention of those persons who are called the *sāhib-i-tasawwuf*,[2] and wished to learn something about them. I had heard that there was one of these, named *Jamāl-ud-Dīn Kūfī*, who frequented the tomb of 'Alī.

"On leaving Baghdād, I passed by Kūfa, where the Imām (Caliph) 'Alī was martyrised by Ibn Maljan.[3] I met Jamal-ud-Dīn, on his way out to the desert, and immediately got off my horse and approached him, for the purpose of kissing his hand. I was behind him, at the distance of a dozen paces ; he turning round, looked up at me, and cried out in a loud voice : *arruh-al-Allāh*, 'Go to God'. I was frightened and trembled from emotion, and stopped, so that I was unable to kiss his hand.

"He was a person, of middle stature, perfectly naked ; his beard was scanty, only a little hair on his chin, of a feeble frame, and of some forty to forty-five years of age. His hair was also scanty. I returned to Kūfa, so as to visit its *masjid*, or chapel, erected on the spot of 'Alī's martyrdom. I inquired, at the door, where the person slept whom I had seen, and he showed me a spot near to the tomb of the son of the brother of 'Alī, named Muslim ibn 'Uqail,[4] adding that he always slept there on a mat made of date palms, with a stem for a pillow. I next asked what he did, what he ate and drank, and he answered that he really did not know, for every evening he came in to sleep, and early in the

[1] Possibly the *Ṭabaqāt* of al-Sha'rāwī (al-Sha'rānī), who also wrote the *Nasb al-Khirqat*. The full title of his *Ṭabaqāt* appears to be *Lawā'iḥ al-Anwār fī Ṭabaqāt al-Ahjār* (*J.R.A.S.*, 1903, 159 ; 1906, 799).

[2] In its 'Contents' the original has *tesavvuf*; but here and in the heading above '*tesarruf*', which might mean mystic power. But *tasawwuf* is doubtless correct, and *ṣaḥib-i-taṣawwuf* would mean rather 'master of mysticism'. *Taṣawwuf*, formed from *ṣūfī*, means that actions should be done upon the Ṣūfī which are known to God only, and that he should always be with God in a way known to God only (R. A. Nicholson in *J.R.A.S.*, 1906, 331).

[3] Ibn Muljam, a Khārijite conspirator, assassinated 'Alī in the mosque at Kūfa in A.D. 661, after he had concluded peace with Mu'awīya (cf. R. A. Nicholson, *A Literary History of the Arabs*, p. 193). His full name was 'Abd-ur-Raḥmān b. Muljam al-Ṣārimī, and a full account of his deed and its motive will be found in *E.I.* i. p. 234.

[4] Muslim ibn 'Uqīl, cousin of Ḥusain, who was executed by 'Ubaidullāh, governor of 'Irāq, a few days before Ḥusain's own death at Karbalā in A.D. 680. Styled Abū Muslim on p. 176 *infra*, he is there described as the sword of Allāh. He is the patron saint of the Hāfiz, 'those who learn the *Qurān* by heart' (Evliya, i., Part 2, p. 112).

morning left again for the Desert, without ever speaking to any one. In 1260 H.[1] this person died, and in his place another, named Badr-ud-Dīn us-Sābir, filled his place. His native place is called Dār-us-Sūr, wa Hadd-ul-Ard, and he will live to 1280 H. [1864 A.D.]. After him another will come, named Husain-ud-Dīn Makkaī, who will then be the *khātam-i-auliā*, or *wallāya*, 'the last of the saints'."

My friend explained to me that these persons are considered as being the chief of the numerous *sāhib-i-tasawwufs*, who live in the world, and to whom is given a spiritual command over souls, similar to the temporal authority of sovereigns and other rulers over the bodies of mankind.

In connexion with this belief, he explained to me that the chief of all these individuals is called the *qutb*, centre or axis; he is unique of his kind; on his right and left are two persons called the *umanā*, plural of *amnī*, or *amīn*, the 'faithful'. When the one in the middle dies, the one on his left succeeds him, and the one on the right takes his place. The latter place is then filled up by a person called the *autād* (plural of *watd*).[2] These are four in number. There are also five others, called the *anwār* (plural of *nūr*, or light), who succeed to the *autād*, or *middle*. There are also seven *akhiār* (plural of *khair*, or 'the good'), who succeed to the *anwār*. There are forty others called the *shuhadā* (plural of *shahīd*, the 'martyrs'). By some they are called the *rijāl-i-ghaib*, or the 'absent ones'. These have a *dāïra*, or 'circle' divided into thirty parts, equal to the days of the month. The circle has a North, South, East, and West, and on each day they all together wander over the surface of the globe, which is the *dāïra*, in a certain direction of the compass, fixed for each day of the month, of which they all possess a perfect knowledge, through the *data* written in this circle.

The celebrated author, Muhyī-ed-Dīn al-'Arabī, has written a detailed account of these, and Mullā Jāmī, one of the most celebrated of the Persian poets, comments upon them in the book called the *Nafahāt-al-Uns*,[3] or the 'Breath of Man'.

Any one consulting the tables of the circle, so as to ascertain

[1] =1844 A.D.

[2] Lit. stake or peg.

[3] The *Nafaḥāt-ul-Uns*, or 'Perfumes of Politeness', was written in A.D. 1478. It was edited by W. N. Lees, Calcutta, 1859.

where the *rijāl-i-ghaib*[1] are proceeding, and thus look to them for spiritual aid, will, it is said, be sure to meet with success. My informant assures me that Darvishes believe firmly in their existence. Makka is their centre and point of departure, and to which place they return daily. All the transactions of mankind come under their jurisdiction, and are decided upon spiritually, previous to being carried into execution temporally by the rulers of the earth. They are the *nāibs*[2] and *vakīls*, or deputies of the prophets and saints who have left this world, and God makes known to them His supreme will, with regard to the actions of men. Even the designs of individuals depend upon their favour; for if they do not favour them, unexpected obstacles will arise to frustrate them.

Besides the preceding, there are other spiritual beings, called the Abdāls,[3] people whose intellects are supposed by the public to be weak, and that they are even maniacs of a harmless character. Many of these are in this world, where they often exercise a strong influence, though unknown in their true character. Their number is limited to seventy, and they succeed to the forty *rijāl-ul-ghaib*. There are also eighty others, called the *nuqabā* (plural of *naqīb*),

[1] Rijāl is translated 'men' (*Männer*) by Goldziher (*Muhammadanische Studien*, ii. p. 141); but on p. 144 he explains the discipline of the *ma'rifat al-rijāl* to mean 'the knowledge of the authority or sureties (*Gewährsmänner*)'. The term undoubtedly implies vigilance or watching, but it is sometimes rendered 'hidden wayfarers'. Al-Ghaib has come to mean 'the unseen spiritual world', the *'ālam al-ghaib* being opposed to the *'ālam al-shahāda* or 'the world as perceived by the senses', and the *rijāl al-ghaib* are the saintly hierarchy presided over by the Qutb (*E.I.* ii. p. 135). In the science of tradition *rijāl* means 'authorities' (*ib.* p. 190). *V.* p. 202 *infra.*

[2] *Vide* note on p. 202 *infra.*

[3] The Abdāls are also called Turkalū (apparently from *turkān*, 'importunate beggars': Redhouse, p. 536) in Turkey, and are there described as wearing no clothing. They held women in horror, but early in the nineteenth century they achieved such an evil reputation that they were almost exterminated. They were, however, still to be found in provincial towns of recent years (W. S. Monroe, *Turkey and the Turks*, 1908, pp. 280-81). Miss L. M. J. Garnett says: "In the mysterious Ṣūfī hierarchy the *abdāl*, 'substitutes', form a particular class". The *qutb* is the head of the hierarchy. The *abdāl* correspond to and were derived from the *nuqabā* of the Shī'as according to Ibn Khaldūn (R. A. Nicholson in *J.R.A.S.*, 1906, p. 322). They are also called Perishān (apparently *parēshān*, Pers., 'dishevelled', 'distracted or perplexed'). Miss Garnett also gives a detailed account of their doings and their immunity from control (*Mysticism and Magic in Turkey*, p 37 f.).

or magistrates, who succeed to the seventy, and are all taken from the most worthy of mankind.

There have been, and it is supposed still are, many persons bearing the title of Abdāls, though it is not known with any degree of certainty whether or not they belong to the seventy. These are sometimes to be seen in the public streets, wandering about in a state of nudity—or nearly so—and seem to be idiots.

ABDĀL.

Others possess all their faculties, and are very intelligent, but retire from the ordinary intercourse with mankind, and live on mountains, in caves, and other deserted places, cultivating intimacy with wild beasts, over which they exert a remarkable spiritual power, so as to render them perfectly harmless; and they are much revered for their sanctity. There were several celebrated Abdāls in Asia Minor during the earlier Ottoman Sultans.

WANDERING DARVISHES

The Darvishes whom one meets in Constantinople and throughout the East, generally dressed either peculiarly or shabbily, and wearing either a tiger or leopard's skin over their shoulders, and bearing a cup, called *kashkūl*, in their hand, are from India and

Bukhāra. They are not always Darvishes, but are simply *faqīrs*, or men who prefer to remain poor and miserable than to devote themselves to an honest calling. They are supposed to have abandoned the pleasures and attractions of the world, and to be totally divested of all human ambition, for the love of God. Sometimes, if questioned as to the object of their vagabond life, they represent that they are, in the fulfilment of a vow, visiting certain holy tombs, and spend much of their time in prayer and meditation. Many of them, however, belong to the orders of the Keshtīs [1] and Suharwardīs, and those from Bukhāra to the Naqshbandīs and Qādirīs. Beggary is forbidden in nearly all of the orders. Some of these pious Darvishes go as far as Hungary to visit the tomb of a santon, named Gūl Bābā.[2]

The Qalandars are not an Order. One of the Darvishes of the Qādirīs was named Shāhbāz-i-Qalandarī, as also another of the Maulavīs, called Shams-ud-Dīn Tabrīzī Qalandarī. Those who carry with them a crooked horn, called the *liffer*, and call out *Yā ! Wadūd*, belong to the Order of the Baqtāshīs.

There are still another class, supposed by many to be Darvishes, but who are not so. They are known in Constantinople by the name of *khavāsjīlar*. These may be seen sitting in small shops, often dressed somewhat like Darvishes, and wearing green turbans.

[1] By Keshtee Brown undoubtedly meant the Chishtī order, whose foundation is by some ascribed to Khwāja Ahmad Abdāl of Chisht, a disciple of Abū Isḥāq Shāmī, who was buried at Akka in Shām (Syria), and not in Chisht as often stated. But the generally accepted account is that the order was founded by Abū Isḥāq himself. He was ninth in descent from 'Alī, and migrating from Asia Minor settled at Chisht in Khurāsān. The order, or rather sect, is of importance in India (see *e.g.* Rose, *Glossary of Punjab Tribes and Castes*, i. p. 528, where Indian accounts are followed). Other authorities assign a later origin to the order, ascribing its foundation to Mu'īn-ud-Dīn Muḥammad Chishtī, the Aftāb-i-Mulk-i-Hind, or 'Sun of the Kingdom of India', who was born in 537 H. (A.D. 1142) in Sistān. At Baghdad he was acquainted with Najm-ud-Dīn Qubrā, Shihāb-ud-Dīn Suhrawardī, and other famous Ṣūfīs; but he went to Delhi in 1193 and died at Ajmīr in A.D. 1236, his tomb becoming one of the most popular places of Moslem pilgrimage in India (*E.I.* i. p. 862).

[2] Buried at Budapest. A native of Marsiwān in the Sīwās *wilāyat* of Asia Minor, he took part in several wars during the reigns of Muḥammad II., Bāyazīd II., Salīm I., and Sulaimān II., and fell during the siege of Buda (Ofen) in A.D. 1541. The last-named Sulṭān declared him *gözjüsü*, 'patron saint', of the city (*E.I.* ii. p. 181). Turk. *gyūzjū* = a 'watcher or sentinel' (Redhouse, *Turk.-Eng. Lex.* p. 1591). See also pp. 221 and 223.

They are diviners, and tell where lost objects may be found, how the affections of erring husbands may be restored to their wives, etc. The drawings on an open hand, stuck up in the windows, represent the hand of the Prophet, in which are written *āyats*, or verses of the *Qurān*. Their divinations are made by means of the science called *'ilm-i-ramal*, or of sand, and by cabalistic calculations, generally of the numerical value of the letters forming the name of the party interested. The four elements, *'anāsīr-i-arba'*,—viz. fire, air, earth, and water,—are also consulted, to ascertain which of them predominates in the person's system; this found, a *nuskha* [' copy '] or charm, is written out and delivered to the applicant. One of these four elements is supposed to be destroyed by the others, and the one which predominates in the system to its injury must be got rid of. The *nuskhas* are composed of verses from the *Qurān*, to which is connected a belief of peculiar power in especial cases, and are hung about the necks. When the verses are not from the *Qurān*, they are the original handwritings of certain holy men of high repute. One kind of such writings is called *istakhāra*,[1] and are placed under the pillow to influence the dreams of the sleeper. They even are supposed to be the cause of visits from benevolent spirits to the sufferer, or the troubled in mind, and to respond to the wishes of the applicant.

These persons are likewise often seen manipulating the faces, heads, shoulders, and arms of invalids, and, after praying over them, blow in their faces, or gently breathe upon the limbs affected. The invocation of the names of Allāh has, it is supposed in such cases, sanctified his breath, and enabled him to exercise a salutary effect upon the sufferer.

[1] *Istikhāra*, lit. ' seeking good ': Zwemer translates it ' to know what is best ', and says it is one of the forms of divination by means of the rosary. This form is attributed to one of the Prophet's wives, and in it the diviner, after repeating the *Fātiḥa*, breathes on the rosary in order to put the magic power of the chapter into the beads. Then he seizes a particular bead and counts towards the ' pointer ', saying " God, Muḥammad, Abū Jahal ", in turn. If the count ends with Abū Jahal's name the omen is bad. Others say ' Adam, Eve, the Devil '. If the count ends with Eve the omen is doubtful, since woman's judgement is fickle. This is said to be an almost universal practice in North Africa, including Egypt, among the common people (*Influence of Animism on Islam*, p. 33). It cannot, however, be said that such usages are unknown in Christendom.

CHAPTER IV

TRANSLATION OF A TRACT ON THE COSTUMES AND TENETS OF THE DARVISHES — THE HOLY MANTLE OF THE PROPHET — THE KULAHS, OR DARVISH CAPS—[THE QĀDIRĪS].

RESPECTING the costumes and tenets of the *tarīqs*, or Orders of the Darvishes, the earliest mention is found made by 'Abdullah Ansārī,[1] a faithful friend and companion of the blessed Prophet, on the occasion of his flight from Makka to Madīna.

[1] Who 'Abdullāh Anṣārī may be it is not easy to say. A 'companion of the Prophet' could hardly have witnessed events in the time of the fifth Imām. The author of the tract seems to have confused 'Abdullāh Anṣārī (Abū Ismā'īl 'Abdullāh b. Abū Manṣūr Muḥammad), "one of the oldest and most famous Persian mystics, usually called the Pīr-i-Anṣār", with Abū 'Abdullāh Jābir b. 'Abdullāh al-Anṣārī (Matthews, *Mishcāt-ul-Masābih*, i. p. 13), who is styled Jābur by Rehatsek (*Rauzat-us-Safā*, i. p. 34). The Pīr-i-Anṣār was born in 396 H. (A.D. 1006), and died in 481 H. (A.D. 1088), and was also called the Pīr-i-Hirī from Herāt, his birthplace (Browne, *Literary Hist. of Persia*, ii. p. 269, and *E.I.* i. p. 358). His principal work appears to have been the *Ṭabaqāt al-Ṣūfiyya*, of which Jāmī's *Nafaḥāt al-Uns* is an enlarged recension (Nicholson, *Kashf al-Maḥjūb*, pp. 21 and 26). Another 'Abdullāh Anṣārī, 'Abdullāh b. Amr b. al-'Āsī, author of a work called *al-Ṣadīqa*, is mentioned by Goldziher (*Muhammadanische Studien*, ii. p. 10). In the text the writer doubtless merely intended to explain the term Anṣārī and to indicate the Pīr-i-Anṣār, who claimed descent from Abū Ayyūb, a companion of the Prophet, but it is hardly correct to say that he was the first to mention the tenets of the orders. His *Ṭabaqāt* was only an enlarged edition of Sullamī's work; but he also wrote the *Manāzilu'l-Sā'irīn*, or Stages of the Pilgrims, the *Anwāru'l-Taḥqīq*, or 'Lights of Verification', the *Nasīhāt*, or 'Advice', the *Zādu'l-'Ārifīn*, or 'Gnostics' Provision', the *Kitāb-i-Asrār*, or 'Book of Mysteries', and an *Ilāhī-nāma*; besides his *Munajāt*, or 'Supplications', and *Rubā'iyyāt*, or Quatrains (Browne, *op. cit.* p. 270). Beale describes him as the founder of the sect called 'Anṣārīs in Herāt and Khurāsān, assigning his birth to 396 H. (A.D. 1006), and says he was pelted to death by boys while doing penance, when eighty-four lunar years of age. He is buried at Herāt (*Or. Biogr. Dict.* p. 7). His names and

By this person it is related that Muhammad Bāqir,[1] the fifth Imām, and a successor as well as a descendant of 'Alī, the fourth direct Caliph, gave the name of *irshād-i-kiswa*,[2] or 'robe of uprightness', to one of the garments worn at this period by pious and holy men; and that Ja'far Sādiq, the sixth Imām, also a lineal descendant of the same 'Alī, and son of Muhammad Bāqir, gave the name of *Arkān*[3]*-i-Auliā*, to those good men who wore that garment. For the correctness of this relation, however, we can only place our trust in Allāh.

The perfect *Murshids*, or Superiors, of Darvish *takias*, or convents, were bound to make this known to the *Arkān-i-Auliā*, or 'Columns of Saints'; and to their youthful disciples the *murīds*, they should point their appropriate places in the *takias*, and explain to them how to wear, and the meaning of, their *tāj*, or cap, and their *khirqa*, or mantle. They should only put them on after having been invested by the *Arkān-i-'Ain*,[4] or Elders of the *takia*,[5] so that the use of them would be legitimate. Should the latter be ignorant of this knowledge, the *murshid* must expose them as impostors; and, in that case, to intercede for them is a crime equal to blasphemy.

On being publicly selected as the *murshid* of a *takia*, the guide of a painful career, and the depositary of all the secrets and traditions of his Order, he must hold the following discourse :—

---

style are also given as Abū Ismā'īl 'Abdullāh b. Abil-Manṣūr al-Anṣārī al-Ḥarawī 'Shaikh ul-Islām' (but whether this was an official title or merely an honorific one does not appear), author of the *Manāzil al-Sā'irīn* (*Cat. of Pers. MSS. in B.M.* i. p. 35).

[1] Bāqir, 'the dealer in secrets' (Hammer's *Hist. of the Assassins*, Eng. trans., p. 20). Or the 'investigator' (lit. the 'splitter': *E.I.* i. p. 64).

[2] Irshād, 'rule', from the same root as *murshid.* Apparently the phrase should read *kiswat-* (or *kuswat*) *-i-arshād*, 'raiment of orthodoxy'. The *kiswa* is the covering of the Ka'ba. *Irshād-i-kiswa* is the title of a tract in Turkish on the Ḥurūfī doctrines (E. G. Browne in *J.R.A.S.*, 1907, p. 552).

[3] Arkān, pl. of *urk*, 'pillar', a word which can in a certain way signify the four elements (C. Huart, *Textes Houroufis*, Gibb Memorial Series, ix. p. 126).

[4] 'Ain here doubtless means fountain or source. It also means 'eye', 'influence of the evil eye', etc. (Salmoné, *s.v.* p. 624).

[5] Takia, lit. 'a place of repose', also 'a prop', in Persian. In Syro-Egyptian architecture the *takia* supplanted the *ribāṭ* and *khānqāh* after the Ottoman conquest, its arrangement, a hall with cupolas, being influenced by the school of Constantinople (*E.I.* i. p. 424).

"Brethren! Ye who are designed to become in eternal life the heads of the Assembly of the Believers in the blessed Prophet, and of the Water Carriers of the fountain of Kausar, the blessed martyr 'Ali—elevate the standard of your Order in every seat, and in the Council of Heaven. Be careful, above all things, to learn who are impostors, and who are genuine members of your Order, so that none but the latter be found amongst you."

He must inquire for his duties of the most eminent *Khalāfats*, or Vicars[1] of the Order, and so become fully acquainted with its chief secrets. In the eyes of the All-Just poverty is preferable to worldly advantage. He will cause him to drink of the waters of Salsabīl[2] and Kausar; put on him apparel made of the satin and silk of Paradise, and enjoy the delightful pleasures of the *hūrīs* and *ghulāms* of eternal Paradise—intoxicated with the delights of that exalted abode.

As to the *muqallids*,[3] or impostors, the Prophet of Allah has said: "They shall suffer anxious desires for this world and for eternity". Yet, through the grace of God, and by faith in the Prophet, they shall also be shown favour and spiritual direction. The impostor is one who is not known to the good *murshid*; this latter has never taken him by the hand, and he is one who does not follow the commands of the *Arkān-i-'Ain*, or superior officers of the Order, who do not die spiritually before their physical death, and who only wear the rags of indigence for personal gratification. Of such, it has been said, "They die before the close of their lives".

THE HOLY MANTLE OF THE PROPHET

It is said that the holy Prophet had a particular friend, named Uwais, to whom he commanded that his mantle should be given. This mantle is made of a coarse woollen material. It is a long robe, with a collar, and wide sleeves reaching low beneath the knees.

This person was much beloved of the Prophet; and when the latter had a tooth knocked out in a battle with the Arabs, Uwais had all of his, thirty-two in number, pulled out in token of

[1] ? Khalīfa. *Khilāfat* would = 'the office of a vicar'.

[2] Salsabīl, 'fresh milk', 'wine', 'a fountain' (Salmoné, *s.v.* p. 366).

[3] Muklid in original, apparently for *muqallid*; cf. *taqlīd*, 'blind acceptance' (Macdonald, *Muslim Theology*, p. 316); from *qalada*, 'twisted'.

sympathy for the loss sustained by the Prophet. He felt no pain from the operation. On this occasion God caused to grow in Arabia a fruit called *mūs*,[1] until then unknown, as a provision for Uwais.

The charge of this mantle has ever since remained in the family of Uwais, and a descendant of his, now a youth (A.D. 1860), and consequently a minor, has charge of it at Constantinople. Until he reaches the age of puberty, a *vakīl*, or deputy, appointed by the Sultān, as caliph, acts for him. Once a year it is carried in procession to the Old Seraglio, where it is exhibited to a few select Mussulmans, and, after receiving their adorations, is replaced in its particular building.

The mantles of the Darvish Orders are all symbols of that of the Prophet.

THE *KULAHS*, OR DARVISH 'CAPS'

Before the present world existed there is said to have been a spiritual world, called in the Arabic tongue *'Alim-i-Arwāh*,[2] or 'World of Spirits'. In the same belief a soul is considered as being a *Nūr*, or 'Light', without body or substance.

The soul of Muhammad, the blessed Prophet, is said to have already existed in that world of spirits, and the Creator there placed it in a vase also made of light, in the form adopted by the Darvishes, especially those of the Order of the Maulavīs, for their *kulah*, or cap. It therefore is held to be of a Divine origin. As aforestated, the *kulah* is made of a certain number of gores, called *tark*, each signifying a sin abandoned, and the last one is called the *tark-i-tark*[3], or the abandonment of all sins. The Qādirīs wear a rose in their cap, embroidered, to which they attach the following legendary history, translated from a Turkish MS. :—

"O ye who pursue the path of the Qādirīs ! O nightingale of the rose-garden of the path of the *ashrafīas*! Have ye made choice of the meaning of the rose of our Order, known throughout the land of Fārs (Persia) as the *gul*, a rose?

"Know ye that every *tarīq*, or path, has its particular sign,

[1] ? Maūz^{an}; *musa*, 'a fig-like fruit' (Freytag). In Turkish *mūz* = 'plantain'; Pers. *mauz* or *mūz*.

[2] Arwāḥ, pl. of *rūḥ*, 'soul'.

[3] *Tark-i-tark*. Possibly this should be *tark-i-ṭuruq*, 'abandonment of ways', *i.e.* abandonment of all religious methods or practices.

and that of the noble *Qādirī* is the rose, the origin and colours of which have thus been explained by the great Shaikhs and *'āshiqs* of our Order. May they be visited with the especial favour of Allāh!

"The present humble Darvish, Ibrāhīm al-Eshremī-al-Qādirī, was once in the service of the beloved Shaikh 'Alī-al-Wāhidī-al-Qādirī, the 'Axis of the Lord', the 'Centre of the Eternal', the 'Bestower of the Cup of Him who bestows light', the 'Splendour of Evidence', the 'Ka'ba (Caaba) of the glorious Eternal'. The Shaikh al-Sa'īd 'Abd-ul-Qādir Gīlānī was directed by Khizr [1]

[1] Khidr or Khiẓr means 'sea-green', and so this saint corresponds to Glaucus. His attributes are immortality and omnipresence, and he is the patron saint of travellers, especially by sea. He constantly meets them and at times reveals to them divine secrets. Cumont suggests Ahasuerus = Khiẓr. The story of Khiẓr is, however, apparently of Greek origin. In the pseudo-Callisthenes' tale of Andreas, the cook of Alexander the Great, he finds the elixir or Water of Life; and for obtaining immortality by drinking it he is hurled by the angry king into the sea, where he becomes Glaucus, husband of Scylla and Circe. Jewish influence contributed to the identification of Elijah with Khiẓr; and in Islām the view is generally accepted that Khidr was Iliās; and the Turks have merged the two names into one—Khidrlās. But the *Qurān's* mention of Elijah by name in his biblical character of severity and sternness gave rise apparently to Khidr's identification with Elisha, Elijah appearing as his inseparable companion. Elijah thus becomes guardian of wayfarers by land, while Elisha-Khidr is *mukallaf fi'l-baḥr*, 'guardian of the sea', patron of sailors, and one 'who traverses the waters'—*khāwad-al-buḥūr*. As such he is honoured from Northern Syria to Hindustān. [For example, he is said to lie buried in the heart of the Kūh-i-Khidr Zinda, or 'Mount of the Living Khizr', in Karmān (Major P. M. Sykes, *Ten Thousand Miles in Persia*, p. 141; for his portrait in a picture see p. 152, *ib.*).] Khidr is also the subject of orthodox Muslim speculation as a 'recurrent prophet', and as such is identified with Melchiżedek, Seth, Enoch, Lot, Jonah, Jeremiah, and the Messiah—the seven incarnations. As Khodr or Khadhir he is the god *par excellence* of the uninitiated among the Nusairīs; but the adepts among them call him 'Alī. On the other hand, in Syria Khidr has been identified with St. George, and its coast is studded with little shrines where sacrifices and the first-born are offered (F. W. Bussell in *Folk-Lore*, xxviii. pp. 280-85). But in Greek hagiology St. Elias, who is either Elijah or a Christian hermit of the fourth century A.D., has some affinities with Odysseus, the tale that he was once a sailor and was told to put his oar on his shoulder and travel until he reached a land where the people did not know what an oar was, being told of both (W. R. Halliday in *Folk-Lore*, xxv. p. 123 f.). It has been suggested (*ib.* p. 125) that St. Elias is Helios, the Sun; but this is not very likely. A more plausible equation would be Elias = Ulysses = Odysseus. The tale referred to above explains why St. Elias is placed, like St. Michael, on all the mountain

(Elias) to proceed to Baghdād. On his arrival there, the Shaikh sent him a cup filled with water, the meaning of which was that the city of Baghdād was full of holy people, and that it contained no place for him. This occurred during the winter season, and no flowers were in bloom. The Shaikh[1] ['Abd-ul-Qādir-Gīlānī] put a rose in the cup, signifying that Baghdād would afford a place for him. Seeing this, all present exclaimed, 'The Shaikh is our rose', and going to meet him they conducted him to the city, and showed him marked respect. This is the real origin of the rose of the Qādirīs.

"So far as I know, our Shaikh performed the following unusual acts through the power of the All-just. He descended from the family of the blessed Prophet, of whom it is related that he once called his two grandsons, Hasan and Husain, his 'two eyes' and his 'two roses', and it is to his connexion with the Prophet that we must ascribe his power to produce, miraculously, a rose. How great should, therefore, be the love and respect of his disciples! Sulaimān Effendi,[2] in his work on the *Maulād*, or birth of the blessed Prophet, has the following verse in relation to the Shaikh *Qādirī* :—

'Whenever he perspired, each drop became a rose,
Each drop, as it fell, was gathered as a treasure.'

---

tops. For his identification with Idrīs also see *E.I.* ii. p. 450, and with Djirdjīs (St. George), *ib.* i. p. 1047.

Covel declares that St. George is a great saint even among the Turks, and "their galleyes commonly set out on that day to the White Seas". He identifies Khiderleh or Khidreleh, "the best prospect about all Adrianople", with a former Greek church dedicated to St. George (*Early Voyages and Travels in the Levant*, p. 248).

[1] The Shaikh who politely intimated to Shaikh 'Abd-ul-Qādir Gīlānī that Baghdād had no need of him was presumably Abū 'l Mubārak Mukharrimī, who eventually invested him with the *khirqa*. Ashramī appears to be an error for Ashrafī, and an attempt is seemingly made to link up the Ashrafīs with the Qādirīs. The author says that 'Alī al-Wāḥidī al-Qādirī was not succeeded by himself, but by an Ashraf-zāda (p. 102) on his death. He describes this Ashrafzāda as a follower of 'Abd-ul-Qādir, then immediately speaks of the Ashrafīs as an order already existing, but endeavours to reconcile its doctrine with that of the Qādirīs. Then he goes on to claim Ismā'īl as a Qādirī also, with this addition that he too adopted the rose. The Ashrafīs were founded in 1493 (*v.* p. 269 *infra*).

[2] This title is derived from Mod. Greek ἀφέντης (class. αὐθέντης), meaning 'master'.

"The rose of the Shaikh is therefore a sign of the Prophet himself, like in the proverb, 'The son is the secret of his father'.

"On the death of my Shaikh 'Alī al-Wāhidī, his successor was Ashrafzāda,[1] a follower of 'Abd-ul-Qādir.[2] One night, whilst in my cell after sunset, employed in reciting the *zikr*, the rose of my Order came into my mind, and I reflected that there was a difference between the roses of Baghdād and Stambūl, and I tried to comprehend the cause. By divine favour it became clear to me. I thought why the *Ashrafīs* have no rose, and suddenly the form of one appeared before me. After terminating my prayers, I hastened to trace out its shape, and decided in my own mind that it should be their rose. I wrote out also some of its secrets, and drew the colours of various roses, and named my little work: *The Risāla of the Gulābād* (*Treatise of the Home of the Rose*).

'The rose on the head honours the wearer,
It points to the path of Qādir Gīlānī.'"

The word *gul*, or rose, is written in the Oriental characters with only two letters, named *kāf* and *lām*, or *k* and *l*. These are

[1] The poet Ashraf-oghlī Rūmī, commonly called Ashrafzāda, was buried at Iznīk (Nicaea), and in the seventeenth century his shrine was already a famous place of pilgrimage. He composed a mystical *Dīwān*, including verses in praise of 'Abd-ul-Qādir Gīlānī (Hammer-Purgstall, *GdOD.*, iv. p. 473.

'Abdulla, Ashraf Rumi, Ashraf-zada or Ashraf-oghlū, was a Qādirī who founded the Ashrafīas (*v.* p. 269 *infra*). His spiritual father was Hāji Bairām Walī, but he was also influenced by Husain Humwi, grandson (?) of the Jīlānī. He died in 874 H., according to the *O.M.* p. 17.

[2] The spiritual pedigree of the Qādirīs from 'Abd-ul-Qādir appears thus in the *sanad* granted to Burton on his initiation into the Order:—

'Abd-ul-Qādir of Jīlān.
'Abd-ul-Azīz.
'Muḥammad al-Hattak.
Shams-ud-Dīn, *v.* p. 286 *infra*.
Sharf-ud-Dīn.
Zain-ud-Dīn.
Walī-ud-Dīn.
Nūr-ud-Dīn.
Ḥusām-ud-Dīn.
Saiyid Darvīsh.
Nūr-ud-Dīn.
'Abd-ul-Wahhāb.
Ismā'īl. ? Rūmī, *v.* p. 104 *infra*.
Abū Bakr. *Pilgrimage*, App. III.

the first letters of the two lines of the verse of the *Qurān* (37th verse of the 39th chapter) :—" Is not God above all to protect His servant? The infidels will seek to alarm thee with the idols : but he whom God leads astray will never more find a guide to the true path. God is full of goodness towards His servants ; He gives food to whom He wishes ; He is strong and powerful."

The form of the rose of Baghdād is as follows :—It has two outside and two inside rings, and three circles, and is made of green cloth. The first circle signifies *shar'at*, or 'God's law as revealed by His Prophet' ; the second signifies the *tarīqat*, or 'Path' of the Order ; the third signifies the *ma'rifat*, or 'knowledge' of God. The three together are a sign that their acquisi-

---

Ismā'īl would appear to be the Shaikh Ismā'īl ar-Rūmī who founded forty-eight convents, and died in A.D. 1643 (Hammer-Hellert, *Hist. of the Ottoman Empire*, xviii. p. 77). Hence he could not possibly have become the *immediate khalīfa* of 'Abd-ul-Qādir Gīlānī, who died in the year A.D. 1166. A Qādirī *takia* at Constantinople is still named after him (*v.* pp. 116 and 476 *infra*). But doubtless many of his foundations perished during the persecutions of the Khoja of Vān, who banished the Qādirī Qarābāsh 'Alī of Scutari, as well as Niāzī Miṣrī (Hammer-Hellert, xii. p. 45).

Evliya in one of his most tantalising passages, which show how his work had to be expurgated to avoid giving umbrage to the government of his day, abruptly introduced the following passage under the heading *Pilgrimage to Rūmeli Hissār and Miracles of Shaikh Ismā'īl* :—

" The Emperor being at Kandillī when the Shaikh's and his disciples' bodies were thrown into the sea at Constantinople, at the stable-gate, he and his ten followers came floating before that place, dancing on the waves with their heads in their hands. The Emperor's suite seeing this miracle, represented to him that they had been unjustly executed. The Emperor began to weep as he watched them floating against the current to the opposite shore of Rūmelī Hissār, where they were buried at the foot of Dūrmish Dedeh, and where, during ten nights, light was seen pouring down on their graves. This Sh. Ismā'īl Chelebī was executed at the Hippodrome, near the fountain of Chokūr Chashma, with his ten followers ; he was called Qūrbān Ismā'īl at his birth (Ismā'īl, the victim), and really died a victim seventy years afterwards. On the spot where he fell a chapel has been erected by his friends, which is to be seen at the back of Dikilī-Tāsh (the burnt column), as a *masjid* with iron rails " (*Travels*, i. Part 2, p. 68).

He gives no hint of the date of this occurrence, and no explanation of the executions. The only other Ismā'īl he mentions was obviously *not* Shaikh Ismā'īl ar-Rūmi, or a Qādirī. A few pages earlier he had alluded to :—

" A Sh. Maulavī Ismā'īl Dedeh of Angora who died in 1041 H. (A.D. 1632), was buried at the Maulavī-khāna of Kullei Qāpū-sī (the tower of Galata). He wrote eleven books, besides a commentary on the *Mesnevi*. He was followed by Adelī 'Alī Adam Dedeh " (*ib.* p. 48).

tion has bestowed the *hāl*, or condition, known as the *haqīqat*, or 'Truth'. The holy word *Hay*, or 'The Living God,' manifested to one Shaikh, has for its colour *green*, and for this reason the rose is made on cloth of that colour. The circles are white, and the reason is that this same is a sign of perfect submission to the Shaikh, according to the traditional words of the Prophet, 'The Divine law is my word; the path is my acts (practices); the knowledge is the chief of all things; and the truth is my condition'. Whoever knows these secrets must assume the disposition of the moral laws of God, and the character of the Divine nature. The blessings which will accompany him in eternal life are those of everlasting felicity and never-ending aid.

"The axis of the Lord, the Shaikh Ismā'īl ur-Rūmī,—may God bless to him his secret!—was originally of the Khalwatīs. In a dream or vision, he became the *khalīfa* or successor of 'Abd-ul-Qādir Gīlānī. He adopted this rose as a sign of the seven Names of God, and their branches. The seven colours adopted by him are emblems of the *Anvārs*,* or Lights of these same seven Names; its eighteen *tarks*, or gores, are emblems of the eighteen numeral values of the two letters of the Arabic word [Hay] *H*, *y*, or the Living (God). The roses given to the Shaikhs of the Order have nineteen *tarks*, emblems of the letters of the *Bismillāh Sharīf* and *Jannat-ul-asmā*[1] (used as *nuskhas* or charms). In its centre is the *mühr-i-Sulaimān*[2] (Solomon's seal), the *belief of the unknown*, which has six letters, *s*, *l*, *y*, *m*, *a*, *n*, signifying that the holy Shaikhs are blessed with six peculiar qualifications, viz.—*s* means freedom from all defect; *l*, gentleness of disposition; *y*, the power of spiritual vision; *m*, familiarity with his companions; *a*, the pious character of praying at midnight; *n*, that his prayers and his rectitude all belong to God. This latter he calls the *Na'bidu nasta'īn*, a part of the 4th verse of the 1st chapter of the *Qurān*,—'Thee do we worship, and of Thee do we ask assistance'."

* Sing. *nūr*.

[1] Apparently 'the sublime or highest Paradise' (cf. *ḥaẓrat al-asmā* (God) on p. 147 *infra*).

[2] Sulaimān, probably not the historical Sulaimān bin Dāūd, but Sulaimān Jārad, fifth monarch of the world after Adam. His seal was the most famous talisman in the East, as it controlled not only the elements but also the demons and every created being (Beckford's *Vathek* (1849), p. 107, citing Richardson's *Dissertat.*, p. 272, and D'Herbelot, p. 820).

The same writer adds, on the subject of the mystical rose of the Order of the Qādirīs, that " He who reposes in the cradle of Divine pardon, the Sultān of Shaikhs, Ashrafzāda Rūmī,—may Allāh bless his secret !—states : ' The emblems of the Most High, comprised in said rose, are as follows : There are three series of leaves ; the first has five leaves ; *H*, *y*, *a*, *z*, refer to the five virtues, which he said belong to the followers of Islamism. The second series has six leaves, emblems of the six characteristics of Faith ; and the third series has seven leaves, referring to the holy crown—that mother of the *Qurān*—*i.e.* the seven verses of the *Fātiha*, or first verse [chapter] of the *Qurān*. The full number, eighteen, all allude to the circumstance that the blessed Prophet brought mercy to eighteen different worlds. It has four colours, yellow, white, red, and black, all chosen from other roses, signifying the same as aforesaid, holy law, the *tarīqāt* (paths), knowledge and truth. In the centre are the seven petals, all alluding to the seven names of Allāh. The entire rose must be embroidered on felt of camel's hair, in reference to the felt mantle (*khirqa*)[1] presented by the blessed Prophet to that Sultān of faithful lovers, wais-al-Karanī. The green cord surrounding the rose is an emblem of the one living God.' "

The description is followed by a prayer, of which this is a translation :—" Bless us, O Lord, with Thy blessings in both worlds. Amen. O Thou, who art the blessed of all the blest ; Thou best of all aiders—on whom be the Divine satisfaction !—our Lord and Master, Muhammad, who created the rose (*al-ward*) by his own knowledge,—on his family and companions, give peace to them on the Great Day of Judgment,—to all the prophets, those sent from God,—the saints,—the pure in heart,—the martyrs,—and those who follow in the right path ; and raise us up with them all, through Thy great mercy."

The copyist calls himself,—" The *faqīr*, the *haqīr*,[2] the *qitmīr* (or dog of the seven sleepers) of the gate of the Sultān of the saints who dwell by the rivulets of Paradise—a Qādirī Darvish."

The founder of the Order of the Qādirīs, the Shaikh 'Abd-ul-Qādir Gīlānī, represents the *atwār-i-sab'a*,[3] or seven paths, as the following :—

[1] *Hirkah* in original.

[2] ' Contemptible '.

[3] Sing. *ṭaur*, ' manner, way, method, limit or boundary ', but not ' path '.

"There are seven names of Allāh which the brethren pronounce when performing the *zikr*,—

"1. *Lā illāhi ill' Ullāh.* (There is no God but Allāh.) Its light is blue, and must be recited 100,000 times, and has its own peculiar prayer.

"2. Allāh, called the *Ism-i-Jalīl*, or 'beauteous name'. Its colour is yellow; it must be recited 78,586 times, and has its peculiar prayer. He says that after reciting it that number of times, he himself saw its Light.

"3. *Ism-i-Hū.* (His name.) Its light is red, and number 44,630, and has its peculiar prayer.

"4. *Ism-i-Hai.* (Name of the Eternal.) Its light is white, and number 20,092. [No. 63.][1]

"5. *Wāhid.* (The One God.) Its light is green, and number 93,420. [No. 67.]

"6. *'Azīz.* (The dear or precious God.) Its light is black, and number 74,644. [No. 9.]

"7. *Wadūd.* (The loving God.) It has no light, and its number is 30,202. [No. 48.]"

It formerly was the rule that no one should be made a Shaikh until he had recited these names of the Deity according to their numbers, but it is now disregarded. After becoming a Shaikh, he must recite the following branches, called *furū'*,[2] viz.:—

"*Haqq*, or the Just. [No. 52.]

"*Qāhhir*, or the Avenging.[3] [No. 16.]

"*Qayyām*, or the Everlasting. [No. 64.]

"*Wahhāb*, or the Giving. [No. 17.]

"*Mahāimin*,[4] or the Protecting. [No. 8.]

"*Bāsit*, or the Extending God." [No. 22.]

A young Mussulman friend informs me that when he desired to join the Order of the Qādirīs, he had already been in the habit of attending at one of their *takias*, or convents,—the same to which he now belongs. He was then twenty-two years of age. Any one, he explained, can be admitted at eighteen. The Shaikh

[1] The Nos. in square brackets refer to those in the list at pp. 130 f. *infra*. The translations are doubtless based on the interpretations favoured by the Qādirīs.

[2] Furū', 'corollaries', *v.* note on p. 85 *supra*.

[3] Or 'Subduer', from *qahara*, 'overcame'.

[4] Muhāmin in original.

of the convent had a *déddé* [dāda], or old man, his servant, also a Darvish. To this person he had made known his intention, and he had promised to mention it to the Shaikh. " One day the latter called me into his private room, and directed me to perform two *raka'āts* or genuflexions, and to recite the *istighfār*, or prayer of pardon, one hundred times, as also the *salāt-i-salām*, or prayer to the Prophet for his intercession, the same number of times, and then be attentive to what I should behold in my dreams. I did this that same night, and then lay down to sleep, when I dreamed that all the brethren of the *takia* had assembled in it, and were performing the *zikr*, I amongst them. They led an individual to the Shaikh, who put an *'arāqīa*, or felt cap, on his head; they next did the same to another person, and then led me to the Shaikh. I said to the person who conducted me, that I already had become a Darvish.[1] Not satisfied with my assertion, he persisted in leading me on, and the Shaikh having put the same cap on me, made me a Darvish.

" On the following morning, after performing my prayers, I went to the Shaikh, and told him my dream. He directed me to procure an *'arāqīa*, and having put it on my head, I truly became a Darvish, in the presence of the whole fraternity,—they all performing the *Takbīr*,[2] in which he joined.

" The Shaikh now presented me with a copy of the *aurād*, or litany of the *Pīr*, or founder of the Order, and directed me to read it. It was the one usually used by all of the fraternity,—especially during the ' holy nights '. I next performed the usual prayers, such as the *zikr*, etc., and used the *tasbīh*, or rosary; and, whenever I had a dream, told it to my Shaikh, who directed me to recite such or such prayers, indicated by the nature of the dreams.

" I remained thus for five years. The number is not fixed for the *murīd*, or neophyte, as this part of his career depends upon his ability, and the nature of his dreams. At the close of that time, the Shaikh gave me the *bai'at*,[3] or giving of the hand in a peculiar manner, viz. his right hand clasped in mine, with the

[1] Like the Tertiaries of the Dominicans and Franciscans there are lay *darvish* (Macdonald, *Aspects of Islam*, p. 158).

[2] Taqbīr: the first and sixth formulas of the orthodox Muhammadan *azān* or call to prayer, *Allāhu akbar*, ' God is great ' (*E.I.* i. p. 133).

[3] See note, p. 127.

two thumbs raised up against each other. He bade me also repeat after him the tenth verse of the forty-eighth chapter of the *Qurān*, as follows :—' Verily, they who give thee their hand, and take an oath of fidelity, swear it to God ; the hand of God is upon their hands ; and whoever violates such an oath, does it to his own hurt ; and unto him who keeps it faithfully will be given a magnificent recompense '.

" I truly believe," he added, " that I have frequently seen the *pīr* of my Order in my dreams. Spirits see each other, though not with the eyes ; we may see, in our dreams, persons whom we have never seen in our lives, and know them distinctly. I have never seen, once, the portrait of my *pīr*, and yet I would know his portrait among a thousand others, in consequence of having seen him so often in my visions. I fully believe in dreams ; they all have a meaning. For instance, if one dreams that he becomes rich in worldly stores, it means that his prayers will be accepted in the other life ; and if he dreams that he has fallen in filth, it signifies that he will eventually become wealthy. To dream that any one has received base and vile treatment from another, signifies that he will receive great benefits from the same person."

My friend related the following to me:—

" In the year of the Hijrā 1268 (A.D. 1851), I left Constantinople with a brother of my own Order for Egypt, by steamer, intending to visit the two Holy Cities (Makka and Madīna). This was done, on the recommendation of our Shaikh, in consequence of a dream which both of us had seen, in which we clearly and distinctly beheld the blessed Prophet of Islamism. I still retain a vivid impression of his appearance, dressed as an Arab, wearing a mantle over his shoulders, and of a thoughtful and deeply intelligent countenance. He looked at me with a stern, though pleasing gaze, and then gradullay disappeared from my sight.

" We took goods with us for sale, and from Alexandria and Cairo went to Suez, whence we sailed for Jedda. From this place we travelled to Makka, and performed the pilgrimage. We next went to Madīna, and remained there three years, opening a shop for the sale of our goods. We left Madīna for Baghdād, with Bin Rashī, an Arab Shaikh of the Jabal Shammar tribe. He was also the *amīr*, or commander of the *hājjīs*, or pilgrims, who had come from Baghdād, the most of whom were Persians on their way to the Holy Cities. Such pilgrims hire camels of the Shaikh to come and return; and he makes much money from such persons in the following manner. On reaching a spring of water in the desert, he encamps, and tells his pilgrims that he cannot proceed farther without purchasing the right of passage from a neighbouring tribe, which threatens to rob them unless a certain sum is made up by the company for it. We all expected this, and accordingly were prepared for it; the sum was collected, but the Shaikh kept it for his own use. We had with us food for ninety days. We finally reached the country of the Shaikh, called Najd, famous for its fine breed of horses. It is a fine, fruitful land, very cold in winter, and having an abundance of water. I reached Baghdād in some ninety days, and remained there three years, in the *takia* of my own Order, where is the tomb of our *pīr*, 'Abd-ul-Qādir Gīlānī. We did not engage in any business, but lived on the bounty of the *naqīb*, or *shaikh* of the *takia*, who is a lineal descendant of our *pīr*. From thence we returned to Constantinople, through Karkūt, Mosul, Diārbakr, Urfa,[1] Aleppo, and Iskandarūn, where we took ship for Stambūl.

"When I was at Karkūt, in the province of Shahrazor, near to Mosul, I visited a *takia* of the Qādirī Order, for the purpose of seeing a Shaikh of much repute and great spiritual powers. The Shaikh presided over the *takia* in question.

"When I reached the *takia*, a large number of *murīds*, or neophytes (disciples), were present, all appearing to be much excited by the power or the spell of the Shaikh; so much so as to rise and dance, sing or cry out involuntarily. On entering the hall where they were assembled in the presence of the Shaikh, I was also much affected by the spectacle, and, retiring to a corner, sat down and closed my eyes in devout meditation, mentally praying to the Shaikh to send away those persons, and to permit me to enjoy, alone, his society. The Shaikh was several paces distant from me, and, as I did not speak, could only have known what was passing in my mind by means of his wonderful spiritual powers, by which expression I mean the faculty which one spirit has of communing with another, and the power which a superior spirit has over the will of another spirit.

"On opening my eyes, I was amazed to hear the Shaikh address me in the following words: 'In a few minutes' time your prayer, young man, will be granted, and you will commune

[1] Urfa: the ancient Edessa.

with me alone'. To my surprise, in a few minutes, the Shaikh, without speaking a word to any one present, had dismissed all his disciples from the hall, and so I remained with him alone. One by one each had ceased to be affected by his spell, and withdrew. I then experienced an impulse beyond my power of refusal, to arise and approach him,—which I did. I threw myself, helpless, at his feet, and kissed the hand which he extended to me. We next sat down together, and I had a long and most instructive conversation with him."

The following is a translation of a small *risāla*, or treatise on the *mubāya'*,[1] or initiation of a Darvish of the Qādirī, which same was appointed by its *pīr*, the Shaikh Muhyī-ud-Dīn 'Abd-ul-Qādirī—on whom be the Divine satisfaction!

"In the name of Allāh, the Merciful, and the Clement,—Abūl 'Abbās ('Abd-ul-Qādir) taught me, Ahmad bin-Abū-'l-Fath Abū-'l-Hasan 'Alī al-Damashkī, the following from the rules established by the Shaikh al-Imām Jamāl al-Islām, the Qadwat-us-sālikin,[2] the Tāj-al-'ārifīn, Muhyī-ad-Dīn Abū-'l-Qādirī, ibn Abū-Sālih bin-'Abd-Ullāh al-Hasanī (from Hasan, son of 'Alī, and grandson of the Prophet), of Gīlān in Persia, of which he was a native—on whom be the Divine Satisfaction!

"When the *murīd*, or disciple desirous of becoming a Darvish, is seated with his hand in that of the Shaikh, and is desirous of expressing his repentance, and take upon himself the engagement (*'ahd*) from the Shaikh, it is necessary that the *faqīr* be of an active mind, brilliant in thought, of good repute, near in approach to God, of a good heart, of a meek demeanour among men, of serious deportment, easy to acquire knowledge, prepared to teach others who are ignorant, disposed to trouble no one, though they trouble him; to speak only of those things which belong to his faith; generous of his means; to avoid what is forbidden and wrong; to be careful in refraining from what is doubtful; to aid those who are strangers; to be a parent to the fatherless; to be of a pleasant countenance; to be gentle of heart, joyful of spirit; to be agreeable and happy even in poverty; not to expose his secrets to others, nor to destroy them; to be gentle in conduct, and of intercourse; to be bountiful of his benefits, kind in lan-

[1] From *bai'*, see note, p. 127.

[2] Qadwat-us-Sālikīn, 'model of ascetics'; Tāj-ul-'Ārifīn, 'crown of those who know'.

guage, few in his words ; to be patient with the ignorant, and to refrain from doing them any wrong ; to show respect tó great and small ; to be faithful to those who confide in him, and to keep aloof from all duplicity ; to be strict in his religious duties ; to refrain from sloth and slumber ; to speak ill of no one ; to be sedate and easily satisfied; thankful for benefits bestowed; much in prayer and fasting ; truthful of tongue ; permanent in abode ; to curse no one ; without calumny, hatred, or stupidity ; of a pure heart, and careful of the perfect performance of all the religious duties of his order; and to be as correct in thought as in deed.

" After uttering this advice to the *murīd*, the Shaikh should, holding his hand in his own, recite the *fātiha* once (1st chapter of the *Qurān*) ; the 10th chapter, entitled 'Assistance ' [Jonah] ; the first ten verses of the 48th chapter, called the ' Victory ' ; the 56th verse of the 33rd chapter, called the *ahzāb* [' confederates '] ; and the 180th, 181st, and 182nd verses of the 37th chapter of the *Qurān*.

" The Shaikh next offers the following prayer, called the *istighfār*, or for ' pardon ' :—' I beseech Thee, O Great God, to pardon me, Thou, like whom there is none other ; I repent of my sins to Him ; I ask of Him to pardon me, and accept of my repentance ; to lead me in the true path ; and to have mercy on all those who repent of their sins.'

" After this :—' Accept my oath of fealty, or the same oath which the Prophet of God administered to the *asḥābs* (companions) of his mission.'

" The Shaikh next resuming his instructions, bids the *murīd* : ' All Mussulmans are bound to offer up their devotions, to give alms, to give religious advice, not to believe in any association with God (Father, Son, and Holy Ghost), not to drink wine, not to waste their means, not to commit adultery, not to kill for food what God has forbidden, and not to calumniate any one. I command you now to observe these as implicitly as the dead body is submissive to the hands of the one who prepares it for interment. Rebel not against what you know has been commanded thee of God, nor commit what is forbidden. Make no innovations in your prayers, commit no sins, and distinguish between the wrong and the true path, and that which leads to salvation. Bear your Shaikh ever in mind, in this world and in the other. The Prophet is our prophet, and the Shaikh 'Abd-ul-Qādir Gīlānī is our *pīr* ; the oath of fealty is the oath of God ; this hand is the hand of the Shaikh 'Abd-ul-Qādir, and the Director of the True Path is in your hand.'

" The Shaikh adds :—' I am the Shaikh of 'Abd-ul-Qādir ; I accepted this hand from him, and now with it accept of you as one of his disciples.'

" The *murīd* rejoins :—' And I also accept of you as such.'

" The Shaikh responds :—' I therefore do now admit you.'

" The Shaikh next pronounces the *zikr*, which the *murīd* repeats after him three times. The Shaikh next bids him recite the *fātiha*, which he does with the Shaikh, together with a prayer for the Prophet, called the *salāt-i-salām*. The *murīd* kisses the hand of the Shaikh, which act is called the *musāfaha*, and does the same to all of the Darvishes present. The Shaikh now offers up a prayer (the *istighfār*) for the pardon of the sins of the new disciple, and, addressing the company, adds : ' The acceptance of this initiation by the *murīd* is a source of future advantage to him ; the Prayer which we have offered up for him is for the submission of his body to his Spiritual Will, just as when the Angels, before addressing the Creator, prostrate themselves humbly before Him. So, in like manner, has he, by his acceptance of this *bai'at*, submitted to my rule. Our Shaikh has said : It is not proper for the Shaikh to sit on the *pōst* [' skin '] of pillage, nor to gird on the sword of benevolence, until he becomes qualified by the following twelve qualities :—

' 1. The qualities of Allāh (each having two).

' 2. Those of the Prophet (each having two).

' 3. Those of Abū Bakr (Caliph) (each having two).

' 4. Those of the Caliph 'Umar (each having two).

' 5. Those of the Caliph 'Othmān (each having two).

' 6. Those of the Caliph 'Alī (each having two).

' The qualities of Allāh are to cover up and forgive.

' Those of the Prophet, to intercede and accompany.

' Those of Abū Bakr, truthfulness and benevolence.

' Those of 'Umar, to command and forbid.

' Those of 'Othmān, to feed the poor, and to pray when others sleep.

' Those of 'Alī, to be knowing and brave.

' If these qualities be not possessed by the Shaikh, he is unworthy of the submission of the *murīd*, and the public needs to have recognised them in him. You must follow under his banner when he does ; and if he does not, Satan has made him his friend, and he will not participate in the benefits of this life, or the one to come. It is related of the blessed Prophet, that when a Shaikh gives spiritual advice to one of his disciples, and he refuses to abide by it, God abandons him. The Shaikh 'Abd-ul-Qādir has also said, on the subject of the *istighfār* (prayer of pardon): When any of my disciples is oppressed with affliction, let him walk three steps to the eastward and recite these lines :—

'O Thou who art much desired ; Thou who art the aid of all things in the hour of trouble ;

'In the deepest of darkness, as in the dangers of the desert, Thou seest all things ;

'In the hour of shame and confusion, Thou only canst protect me ;

'When I am overcome with affliction,—in the hour of danger Thy supreme intelligence will support me ;

'O Thou who art ever present, I implore Thee to free me from my grief.' "

Among the Qādirīs this is a much-used prayer, and is generally addressed to their *pīr* ('Abd-ul-Qādir Gīlānī).

From another source I have obtained the following account of the affiliation of a *murīd* into the Order of the *Qādirīs*,—perhaps more of a modern character than the preceding.

Whenever any one desires to enter this *tarīq*, and feels an affection for the Shaikh of a *takia*, he seeks for a *murīd* already belonging to it, and expresses his wish to become a disciple of his Shaikh. In reply, the *murīd* enjoins upon him to continue frequenting the *takia*, and to wait upon its members and visitors. The service required of him is of a domestic character, and must, however, be performed by the pupil, whatever may be his social or official position. It lasts for several months, or a year, and serves to increase his love for the order of the Shaikh, and prevents his falling off, or joining any other *takia*. He is not, however, under any obligation to continue in it, and may leave it and join another if he so chooses.

At the expiration of this period the pupil, on the direction of his friend the *murīd*, brings with him an *'arāqīa*, or small felt cap, without any gores. When this is done the *murīd* carries it to the Shaikh, who consents to receive him, and orders the *murīd* to attach a *gul* or rose to it. This is a rose of eighteen points, called *tarks*, which are the number of the letters of the words *Bismillāh ur-Rahmān ur-Rahīm*, ' In the name of God, the Clement and the Merciful ', or the numerical value of the letters of the word *Hay* (Living God) : *h*, 8, and *y*, 10. In their centre is the figure of the *muhr-i-Sulaimān*, or Solomon's Seal, which is two triangles crossed, ✡. The rose to be attached to the cap or *kulah* is placed by the Shaikh in his bosom ; he takes it with him to a mosque, or to his *takia*, the day or night at which his disciples assemble to perform the *zikr*. Whilst seated on the *postakī*, or sheepskin mat, the *murīd* conducts the pupil before him ; the *murīd* kisses the hand of the Shaikh, the pupil does the same, kneeling before the former, who is also on his knees. The Shaikh now takes off the cap usually worn by the pupil, and, putting in its place the *'arāqīa*, recites the *Allāhu akbar* three times.

If the *tarīq* be the *Qādirī*, this is the customary form of investiture of a neophyte ; if the *Rifā'īa*, the Shaikh fills a coffee-cup with water from the sacred well, called Zamzam, at Makka, or in its place with any other water,—prays over it, and gives it to the pupil to drink ; if the Sa'dia, the Shaikh orders an *oke* [1] of dates to be brought to him, and places them on the *postākī* beside him. He next takes one of these dates in his hand, and after taking out its seed, breathes on it and recites a prayer, and puts the date into the mouth of the pupil. On each side of the latter is a *murīd*, balancing him and themselves from right to left, reciting the prayer, *La ilāhu illā Allāh*. The Shaikh also balances or rocks himself at the same time, and in the interval the pupil swallows the date.

They all now rise, and the pupil, having become a *murīd* or Darvish, kisses the hand of the Shaikh.

In all *takias* there are but three grades of Darvishes:

1. The Shaikh.
2. The *khalīfa* (vicar of the former).
3. The *murīds*.

There is no fee required for the initiation ; yet all the *murīds* are supposed to aid in the support of the Shaikh and the other expenses of the *takia*, and they seldom visit him without bringing him a present. There are no officers whatever to any *takia* except the Shaikh; he alone directs and commands absolutely, and must use all his influence for the interests and welfare of his *murīds*.

[1] The Arabian uqqa = 400 drachms.

There is no purser, or clerk, nor any sum for the public use or charitable purposes in or out of the *takia*. The *murīds* live in the world, and gain their livelihood as they please ; but the Shaikh has no other occupation than the service of his own *takia*, and trusts to Providence for a support,—as the Darvishes express it—*alà bāb Ullāh*, "on the door of Allāh".

I may here add that of the two hundred, or more, *takias* in Constantinople, some fifty only are possessed of sufficient wealth for their support. By far the greater number are poor. Their resources consist in *wuqūfs*, or real estate bequeathed to them by private individuals, or gifts from the sovereign. It has frequently happened that the reigning Sultān becomes an honorary member of an Order of Darvishes, and sometimes attends its religious exercises. They are more disposed to join the Maulavīs than any other Order, on account of the connexion of this Order with the earliest Sultāns of the Ottoman family.

The *bai'at*, or election of the *murīd*, by placing of hands on his head, or the hand of the Shaikh in his hand, in some cases, only takes place several years after his original admission to the Order. The period much depends upon the will of the Shaikh, and the degree of knowledge and spiritual acquirements of the *murīd*. The Shaikh or the *murīd* is held to see in a vision, either the Prophet 'Alī, or the *pīr* of the Order ; and this ceremonial is the only one of which the secret, if indeed one exists, has not been divulged to me. The *murīd*, at that time, takes an oath never to divulge it, and not to commit certain ordinary sins. I believe there is no secret sign of recognition by which one Darvish can tell another. The costume fully explains the Order to which the Darvish belongs; and the *kulh*, or cap, and the *khirqa* or mantle, as well as the *kamar*[1] or girdle, are the principal parts which designate him. Among the Baqtāshīs, an arm is left out of the sleeve on certain occasions, signifying, "I come to you in pure amity, and without any desire to seek profit".

Of the Qādirīs, the cap is called *tāj* or crown, and the belt, *kamar*. These may be of any colour ; green is, however, mostly used. The cap is also called *muzzān*.[2] At their devotions, after

[1] *Kewer* in original: but see below and on p. 204 *infra*. Kaur, Ar.= wound round; but Pers. *kamar*, 'girdle', is probably meant.

[2] Muzzān, Ar., 'dressed', 'adorned': possibly amice is derived from it, but see *N.E.D.*, *s.v.*

reciting the *fātiha*, the Darvishes take each other by the shoulder, and turn round in the hall of the *takia*, calling out, " *Hay Allāh !* " This ceremony is called the *dawān*,[1] or turning. Its originator was *Hazrat-i-Ismā'īl-i-Rūmī*,[2] who is interred in the *Qādirī Khāna*, or *takia* of Topkhāna. All Darvishes say grace at their meals, called the *gul bank*,[3] which differs in different Orders. That of the Qādirīs is the following prayer :—

" Praise be to God. May He increase His bounties. By the blessings of Khalīl (Abraham) ; by the Light of the Prophet,—

PENITENCE

the grace of 'Alī ; by the war-cry of Muhammad (Allāh ! Allāh !) ; the secret of the Sultān Muhyī-ud-Dīn 'Abd-ul-Qādir Gīlānī, we beseech Thee to be of good favour to our Lord (the *pīr* of the Order). O ! Allāh Hu ! "

Whilst the Shaikh is occupied, after the meal, in reciting the *takbīr* (*Allāhu-akbar*), or even in repeating this grace, his disciples simply exclaim, " Allāh ! Allāh ! " and at its conclusion all cry out, *Hū* ! " Him ", signifying God.

I am informed that nearly all the Orders use this form, the only difference being that each one uses the name of its own *pīr*.

[1] Redhouse has ' running ' simply. [2] Ismā'īl, see note on p. 103 *supra*.
[3] Or *gul-bāng*.

CHAPTER V

SACRED BOOKS AND THE CREATION OF MAN—THE AULIĀ OR SAINTS

There is much in the belief of the Darvishes which has its origin in the ordinary religion of Islamism. None venture to separate themselves from the tenets promulgated by the Prophet in the *Qurān*, but rather seek to spiritualise its language, and evoke hidden and concealed meanings from isolated verses, without consulting the sense of the entire chapter, or the occurrences which gave rise to it. They declare that most parts of the *Qurān* have a hidden, inner, or spiritual significance, called by them, *ma'āna-i-bātinī*, in addition to the ordinary conception, called *ma'āna-i-zāhirī*.

From a repeated and careful perusal of some of their mystical or spiritual writings, I conclude that their appreciation of the *Qurān*, and religion in general, is as follows. The *Qurān* and all other pious books, including, of course, the Bible and Testament, are divided into three, or even more divisions, viz. what is historical, biographical, and purely spiritual. Religion is considered to be the external parts of the worship of God, and is liable to change, according to the teachings of individual prophets or other pious men, such as the *pīrs* of their numerous *tarīqs* or Orders. These are conformed to, in consequence, more out of personal regard for those who established them, and whose good will in the spiritual world will be propitiated by their observance, than as a duty to God. The historical and biographical portions of these books may even comprise errors, omissions, and exaggerations, and even may have been more or less changed from time to time by copyists ; whilst that which is purely spiritual and essential to the soul of man commenced with his creation, has always existed unchanged, and will so continue to the end of time.

In various verses of the *Qurān* [1] it is clearly enunciated that

[1] *E.g.* chap. xvii. v. 87, may be alluded to.

the soul or spirit of man has a Divine origin, and emanated directly from the Great Spirit of God ; whilst the body of man was created from the earth on which he dwells. After God had created Adam, he breathed upon him the breath of life, and that differs widely from the life or existence of ordinary animal nature. The former is eternal, whilst the latter is temporary, and ceases with the flesh of which the body is composed. All bodies, therefore, come from the earth, of which they are made, and return to it after death ; whilst the spirit of man came from the Great Spirit of God, and returns to Him, after the decease of the body.

With regard to creation, their best writers state that there are four distinct ones :

1. The creation of Adam from the clay, or mud, of which the earth is composed.

2. The creation of Eve from a rib, or part of Adam.

3. The creation of the human species,—that is, the children of Adam and Eve, by natural propagation.

4. The creation of Jesus Christ by a special breath of God conveyed to a virgin—Mary—by the angel Gabrāil.

It is believed that the spirit of man communes directly with the Holy Spirit of God—and that the latter, also, communes with the former, not only in visions, but even in wakeful hours, always for good, and never for evil. Holy and pious men hold frequent intercourse with God, by contemplation, meditation, and prayer ; and there is no more sacred duty than the invocation or ‘ calling ’ upon His name, called the *zikr*, already frequently alluded to in preceding chapters. This frequent invocation renders the breath of man additionally holy, and gives to it a spiritual or superhuman power. By this intercourse with God, men reach a superior and more sublime character ; leading holy and, as it were, sinless lives, they become friends of God, and assume an intimate connexion with Him, even in the present life. A man fully impressed with the possibility of attaining to such a position naturally enough regards all that is connected with the transient existence of this world as insignificant, and unworthy of any serious consideration and regard. He becomes indifferent to the ordinary pleasures and gratifications of life ; his mind is supposed to be continuously absorbed in the one whole object of his life, and to revert at all times to the contemplation of God. The more destitute he is of worldly goods, the less his mind is connected with the ordinary cares of life, and he is left free to devote his entire existence to communion with the Creator and His Divine Spirit. He is proud of a destitute and impoverished condition, as it is a sure outward proof of his spiritual superiority and excellence. This is in strict accordance with a remark of the Prophet: " My poverty is my pride ", and is the origin of all those wandering Orders of Darvishes, or, more correctly, simple *faqīrs* of the East.

THE AULIĀ OR 'SAINTS'

The Darvish Orders put full faith in all the grades of spiritually superior men and angelic beings. The former compose what are ordinarily termed saints or friends of Allāh. These in the *Qurān* are designated as " the friends of God who fear nothing; they are not subject to any affliction, because they entertain the true faith; they have lived consistently with it, and in exact obedience with God, from whom they receive a reward in this life and in the other ". " They are those who among men are the nearest united to God, and who consequently enjoy His most intimate presence." " Those who, having been the enemies of themselves in this life, become the friends of God in the other." " They are the title of the book of the law of God; the demonstration of all the truths and mysteries of faith; their external appearance leads us to an observance of the laws of God, and their interior incites us to abandon and detach ourselves from all the pleasures of this world." " They commenced their career before the beginning of time, and labour only for eternity." " During their lives, they never left the portals of the sacred palace of the Divinity, and finally enter therein." " They discover and behold the spiritual secrets which God reveals to them, and maintain therein a religious silence."

It is held that holy men do not fear the evils of life, nor the terrors which surround death and the judgment. The calm which they possess in this life is only a foretaste of the happiness prepared for them hereafter, of which they are allowed a foresight. A part of their recompense in this life is the love and respect of their fellow-men, and the veneration shown to their memories after death. They are favoured with spiritual visions and apparitions, and frequent intercourse with angelic visitors, who appear to them in that semi-existence called a state of bodily slumber. In this world the saint hears the will of God, and in the other he understands it.

The Darvishes and ordinary Mussulmans possess many biographies of the saints (*auliā*), and the pure (*sālihīn*), from which much may be learned with regard to the spiritual visions and spiritual powers, attained by lives of great purity and constant meditation on the Divinity. These put the reader on his guard against impostors and hypocrites, who, for worldly purposes, pretend to a degree of piety and consequent purity of character which they do not possess.

These saints commence with the earliest period of the world's existence. Adam was superiorly a holy man, and on his creation the angels were commanded by God,—who had animated his earthly body with His own holy breath,—to worship him, which all did save one—Satan—and he was in consequence expelled from the presence of God, for his disobedience. Abraham was the 'friend of God' *par excellence*—and Jesus Christ owns His existence as a saint to the special breath of His Divine Creator—but is not, nevertheless, considered as being God. He is held to be only a Divine Emanation of the most sublime character.

It is also held by some that the spirits of some men return again to this world, and animate new human forms; and even that the spirits of others existed among celestial beings in the Divine presence, previous to their coming to this world. Muhammad is supposed to have been one of these; and the faithful admirers of 'Alī, the fourth Caliph, attribute to him a similar distinction. This is the origin of the metempsychosis—or the transmigration of souls—a point of doctrine which has been greatly abused, and changed from its original interpretation. Among the Baqtāshī Darvishes, a belief is generally entertained that those spirits which have during their existence in man never loved nor obeyed God, are degraded to continue in this world, in an animal form of existence, and, on the decease of their human form, enter the bodies of certain animals; but their condemnation to this kind of existence is not defined, and is hidden from mortal comprehension. God alone is said to fix and know the extent of its continuance. Man, thus, by a sinful and vicious life, actually debases himself to a brute; and, it is held, at the death of the body, or at the final day of judgment, rises up again in the form which he held in this world.

Muhammad called himself the *rasūl*, or 'sent of God'.[1] He is

[1] For the distinction between *nabī*, 'prophet', applied to Abraham,

also now called by his followers in Arabia, the *nabī*, or 'prophet', and in Persia and Turkey, the *paighāmbar*, or 'he who bears a message' from God to mankind. The Turkish language, as far as I know, has no other word sufficiently significant of his mission, and so has adopted that of the Persians. His mission was to call men from the errors of idolatry—the worship of fire, and the belief in the existence of Three Gods (Father, Son, and Holy Spirit)—to the adoration of One God only, Allāh. He declared that each of the others who preceded him with Divine messages, was sent for special purposes, and, having accomplished his mission, returned to God. Jesus Christ, he declared, was not killed by the Jews; that another person, resembling Him, was put to death in His stead, and that He will return again, at the Judgment Day. Of the family of 'Alī, the fourth direct Caliph, his followers, in particular, believe that the twelfth Imām, called the Mahdī, or 'Spiritual Director', will reappear for the benefit of the faithful. They say that he disappeared in a mysterious manner in a cave, and that he will come again into existence, together with Christ, for the purpose of overthrowing the Antichrist, and uniting Christianity and Islamism. It is this belief in the reappearance of holy personages which gave rise to the religion of the Druzes, whose founder [Al-Hākim] b. Amr Allāh, after having already existed in this life in another form, returned as the Caliph and Reformer of Egypt, and, having mysteriously disappeared, will reappear at a future period.[1]

As to the Prophet Muhammad, all Mussulmans and the Darvish Orders assert that he existed before the creation of this world, and that had it not been for him it would never have been created; that he was created out of light, or *nūr*, referring, I presume, only to his spirit. They declare that his coming was fully predicted by Christ, and the following is supposed to be an extract from the *Injīl*, or New Testament:

"In the latter times a child will be born, who will be a bearer

Isaac and Jacob, and *rasūl*, 'apostle', applied to Hūd, Sālih, Shu'aib, etc.; see Rodwell, p. 120. In Moses, Jesus and Muhammad are united the office and gift of both prophet and envoy. *Paighāmbar* simply means 'bearer of a message'.

[1] Ḥamza b. 'Alī b. Aḥmad was the founder of the theological system of the Druzes, who date the manifestation of the divine incarnation in the person of the Fātimid caliph al-Ḥākim bi Amr Allāh from 408 H. (A.D. 1017) (*E.I.* ii. p. 255; *v.* p. 325 *infra*).

of a message from God (*paighāmbar*), and never utter an untruth. His birthplace will be Makka, and he will emigrate to Madīna; his name will be Muhammad, and his character praisable. Those who incline to him, I believe, will go to the Paradise, or *Jannat*, of the faithful; he will be in this world an avenger and a conqueror. He will conquer the lands of the Qaiṣar-i-Rūm, or the Emperor of Constantinople."

A pious commentator on the preceding says that this extract, taken from the real and true Testament, has been copied and widely spread; that among the Jews and Christians some said that he had not yet come, and others that, though he had truly come, they did not put faith in him, and so blasphemed against the prediction of Christ.

Another extract from the real Testament is said to be the following: "A child will come into the world, of the Quraish family, who will be the Lord of the two worlds. Those whom he will call to the true faith will never enter the fires of hell (Jahannam).[1] He will be the messenger of the latter times, and his name be Muhammad, on whom will be the peace and satisfaction of the Most High God."

Both of these extracts were given to me by a Darvish friend, and in his note he added that a monk having perused them was convinced of their truthfulness, and embraced the true faith. What language they are in I am unable to say.

[1] Jahannum is purgatory, Laza blazing for Christians, al-Hatuma for Jews, Sa'īr for Sabæans, Saqar for the Magi, al-Jahīm for idolators, and Hāwia for hypocrites, according to the commentaries on the *Qurān* which only gives the seven names: Zwemer, *op. cit.* p. 54. According to Geiger Jahannum is of Biblical origin, from the vale of Ben Hinnom, which was dedicated to idolatry and where smoke issuing from between two palms marked the entrance to hell. But in the *Qurān* Jahannam is 'the prince of Gehinnom' (*Judaism and Islam*, pp. 49-50). The seven names for hell appear in the *Talmud*, and later on are construed as the seven hells.

Palmer gives the names of the second and third hells a little differently, as Laṣā and Huṭamah, 'the Raging Fire that splits everything to pieces'; and he translates all the names by fire in some form or other, excepting Hāwia, 'the Abyss', and Jahannum (*S.B.E.* vi. p. 70). As regards the doctrine of purgatory, it may be mentioned that it was at one time at least prominent in the teaching of the Eastern Church (Adrian Fortescue, *The Orthodox Eastern Church*, p. 105).

CHAPTER VI

THE RIFĀ'ĪA[1] (HOWLING[2] DARVISHES)—THE NAQSHBANDIS

THIS Order of Darvishes commence their devotions by reciting the *fātiha*, the [2nd] chapter of the *Qurān* called the *baqra* [of the

[1] The founder of the Rifā'īa, pl. of Rifā'ī, was Aḥmad Rifā'a al-Kabīr. Their banners and turbans are black; or the latter are of a very deep blue woollen stuff, or muslin of a very dark green. Lane classes the Sa'dīa as a sect of the Rifā'īs and the 'Ilwānīa as another sect (*Modern Egyptians*, p. 248). The Turkish pronunciation is Rufā'ī. Some Rifā'ī affect the saint Sī Dāūd al-'Azab (David the Bachelor) of Tafāhina in Lower Egypt. This saint had a calf which brought him water, etc., and so these Rifā'ī rear calves at his burial-place there and train them to walk upstairs, lie down at command, and so on. With these they go about the country begging. A calf so trained is called 'a calf of al-'Azab' and is believed to bring a blessing to every house it enters (*ib.* p. 252).

[2] It may be questioned whether 'Weeping' rather than 'Howling' would not be a better term to describe this Order. At Sarajevo these *darvishes* are known as 'those who weep'. Both they and the dancing fraternity perform at the Sinān *takia* in that town. The rite begins with an invocation, an aged *darvish* uttering a series of long, throbbing cries, to which at last comes an answering cry from the majority of the brotherhood, who have hitherto remained outside the *takia*. At first only nine form the circle, but eventually all join it and, after prayers, they sing the first chant, which is accompanied, in a manner common in the East, by a dance performed in a sitting posture. In this dance the *darvishes* rock their heads backwards and forwards fervently. This is followed by a second chant, with a different refrain to a different tune, but the dance appears to be the same. In the third and last chant great emphasis is laid on the first and third words, and on the first syllable of the last word in the formula *La he, la hey, Il-lah-lah*, the only words used. This is accompanied by a dance in which the heads are no longer rocked backwards and forwards, but are jerked in pairs, the head of one of each pair of *darvishes* to the right, and that of his partner to the left, with an inclination of their bodies towards each other so that the heads nearly meet; and then the same motion or figure with their partners on the other side of them. Individual performers also give their heads a rapid circular movement. Each chant ceases abruptly

'Heifer'[1]] (or *lām-alif*), the *aurād*, and the *tauhīd*. Those prayers for their *pīr* and the Sultān are simply *du'ā*, or supplications.

Their belt is called *alif-lām-and*. Their mantle is called the *ridālī khirqa*,[2] and may be of any colour ; its edging, however, is green. The latter colour has its origin in the circumstance that the angel Gabrāīl once brought some good news to the Prophet, who, from joy, turned round like the Maulavīs, and let fall his cloak. His disciples cut it in pieces, and sewed the strips around their own. Its colour was green.

The cap is called *tāj*, and is made of white cloth, with eight *tarks*, each signifying a carnal sin abandoned. Some are of twelve *tarks*. The turban is black, and is called *shamla*,[3] or *siāh-i-sharīf*.[4]

---

without any signal. The *séance* ends with an invocation of Allāh, alternately loud and soft, uttered from different parts of the circle. This is worked up into as great a frenzy as the third chant, and, when it ceases, after a pause there floats from one side of the circle a wail and then it comes from the next in line until the sound dies away. In this finale there is no movement of the heads. The dancing *darvishes* also begin their rite with a wailing chant, and their dances are accompanied too by chants. Each dance, and there are four or five, has its own steps as well as its own tune. To the last the only accompaniment is vocal, and in it sounds produced low down in the throat alternate with cries like the startled expulsion of a breath from an open mouth (Major Percy Henderson, *A British Officer in the Balkans*, pp. 108 f. and 256 f.). In the East grief is expressed rather by loud cries of lamentation than by tears, and the ritual of the Howling Darvishes may be a revival of that of the 'Weepers', one of the oldest sects at Mecca.

[1] Chap. ii., 'the heifer' (*baqar*), is not called Lām-alif, and no chapter of the *Qurān* is introduced by the letters L.A. or A.L., though chaps. ii., iii., vi., and others are prefaced by the letters A.L.M. (cf. Sale's *Koran* in Wherry's recension, i. p. 293). The meaning of these three letters has never been satisfactorily explained. In Moslem magic *lām-alif* represents the planet Venus, E. Rehatsek (*Journal*, Bombay Branch R. Asiatic Soc., 1879 [xiv.] p. 215. The Ḥurūfīs attribute much mystical significance to the letters *lām* and *alif* (C. Huart, *Textes Houroufis*, pp. 2 f.). The *alif-lām-ad* is also worn by the Baqtāsh (*v.* note on p. 196 *infra*).

[2] *Ridālī khirqa*, apparently the 'habit of humility or abasement', from *raḍālat*, 'baseness'; *ruḍāl*, 'vile'; though its green edging is hardly consistent with this derivation, green being the distinctive colour of the Prophet's descendants.

[3] Shamla, Ar. *shamlat*, 'mantle, cloak', or 'wrapper, kerchief, or small turban'. In Egypt it is translated 'amice', and is synonymous with *ṭailasān* in the Coptic ritual (Adrian Fortescue, *The Lesser Eastern Churches*, p. 272). In India *shamla* = the tail of a turban. It is tempting to think that *ṭailasān* means 'tying of the tongue (*lisān*)'; but Evliya says it is the Jewish *talas* (*v.* note on p. 126).

[4] Lit. 'sacred black'.

Most of these Shaikhs wear black garments: the mantle of the Prophet was green or black, and they follow his example. The black cloth thrown over their shoulders is called *shad*.[1]

[1] Shad, doubtless *shadd*, Ar., 'binding' or 'girding'; in Morocco, the head-covering worn by the higher classes. It will be noted that, like *shamla*, this word seems to be imported from Egypt. Evliya tells us a certain amount about the *shadd*, which he says means investiture, or religious tie, "to remind men continually of the contest with Satan". He also says that the taking of the *shadd*, or 'habit', has been exemplified by ten prophets, from Adam down to the first four Caliphs and Hamza and Khālid bin Walīd, who all wore aprons. The last six were declared by the Prophet heads of orders, and received from him the faculty of investing others (*Travels*, i., Part ii., pp. 91-92). That the investiture with the *shadd* was of much greater importance among the Rifā'īs than Brown realised must be conceded. Thorning quotes the following description of it: "The disciple faces the *mihrāb* and recites a *fātiḥa*, addressed to Muḥammad. Then the black *shadd* is laid on his shoulders with the recitation of a *fātiḥa* to 'Alī. Then the first knot is tied with a *fātiḥa* for Abraham, and two verses of the *Qurān*. The second knot is tied with a *fātiḥa* for Moses, . . . and the third for Jesus. Then the ends are hung on the left and right sides (of the *murīd*) with *fātiḥas* to Ḥasan and Ḥusain. Turning to the *mihrāb*, a *fātiḥa* is finally recited to Aḥmad ar-Rifā'ī, the founder of the Order. And after the knots have been untied all ends with a verse from the *Qurān*" (*Türk. Bib.* xvi. p. 124). But then *shadd*, or 'binding', seems to mark a second stage in an initiation. The *shadd* is assumed in Egypt as the token of promotion to the office of *naqīb* (P. Kahle, *Zur Organisation der Derwischorden in Egypten, Der Islam*, vi. p. 165). By this investiture the *murīd* becomes a *mashdūd* and his *khalīfa* his *abū'l mashdūd*, *i.e.* his spiritual father, as it were. This is at any rate the general rule among the orders in Egypt, *e.g.* the Aḥmadīa. The Rifā'īs may, however, have rules peculiar to themselves. Indeed this is the more likely because the account given by Kable does not mention the *alif-lām-and*, the *ridālī khirqa*, the earrings, etc., but specifies various insignia not alluded to by Brown. Thorning goes on to suggest that the *shadd* investiture is really referred to on p. 115 *supra*, and pp. 206 ff., and 275-76 *infra*. But this is surely doubtful. Common as the *shadd* is or was in the Guilds (and it is in connexion with them that Thorning gives so much information of value), it seems to have been confined to Egypt, and the Baqtāsh and Maulavī had neither the *shadd* nor any rite of investiture with it. It is also clear that Brown was right in describing the *shadd* as a cloth, though Evliya defines *shadd* as "taking the habit or religious tie, so called from tying up the handkerchief round the head (*imāma*, turban), and that round the loins (*pishtimāl*, apron)". The *pushtamāl* is not so much an 'apron' as a waist-cloth, and its use may be due to the idea held in Arabia that a firmly tied waistband supports the whole frame. Redhouse actually renders *pushtamāl* by 'waist-belt', but it is much more like a garment which could be unfolded so as to gird up the loins and yet leave a fold long enough to fall over the head. But it could hardly be draped down the *murīd's* sides, as Thorning translates; it is more probably hung over the lower part of the face and down both cheeks, as in the *lisān*.

Riā is a principle followed by them and all Darvishes in general, and signifies a retirement from the world, and abandonment of all the pleasures of life, entirely satisfied with Allāh alone. These abandonments are four in number, *riā* being the chief of all. They are *sharī'at*, *tarīqat*, *haqīqat*, and *ma'rifat*.

The *tāj* of their Shaikh has twelve *tarks*, four of which are called *kapū*, or doors. The twelve refer to the twelve Imāms, and the four to the *riās*.

The *murīd*, or neophyte, is held to bring with him to the *takia* a sheep or lamb for a sacrifice ; it is sacrificed at the sill of the door by one of its *murīds*, and its flesh is eaten in common by all the members of the *takia*. The wool is made into a belt, called *taiband*,[1] for the use of the neophyte.

Mangusay[2] is the name of the earrings of the new Darvish. If only one of his ears is drilled, he is called a Hasanī, from Hasan, one of the sons of 'Alī ; if both, he is called a Husainī, from his second son. This is left optional with him.

Qanā'at-tāshī[3] is the name of the stone which they wear in the

[1] The precise meaning and significance of *taiband* are obscure. *Tai*, Ar., means 'a fold'; and in Pers. *ṭai kardan* is 'to cross' or 'traverse'. At p. 191 *taiband* is equated to *dahband* and explained to mean a cord placed round the disciple's neck. (It was a common Eastern usage for suppliants to wear a halter in token of submission.) But *tah-band*, Pers., means a strip worn round the loins, and *dahband* appears to be a corruption of that word; *dahband* not being given in the lexicons, though *dih* may mean 'body' (for *dihi mairān*='the human body, Johnson's *Persian Dict.*, p. 589). Like *dōl-band*, Pers. (whence our 'turban'; *N.E.D.* x. p. 471), *dahband* may possibly mean both 'sash' and 'turban', or anything folded round any part of the body, and *taiband* may be a corruption of it, though the existence of *ṭailisān* in Coptic Arabic points to its formation from Ar. *ṭai* with the Pers. *-band*. Finally, according to the MSS. of the *Jāwidān*, *taiband* should be *tegh-band*, *tegh*, in Turkish *tīgh*, meaning a sword or anything pointed. Apparently *teghband* would thus mean 'sword-knot' (cf. Jacob, *Beiträge*, p. 52, n. 2). As to *tailīsān*, Evliya says it is the Jewish *talas* and a kind of handkerchief; when the Prophet blessed 'Alī he put on his head a black crown with two *tailesān* hanging from it (*Travels*, i., Part ii., p. 100). Burton describes the *taylasān* as a scarf thrown over the head, with one end brought round under the chin and passed over the left shoulder (*Pilgrimage*, iii. p. 315).

[2] The *man-gosh* of the Baqtāsh (pp. 179 and 197 *infra*).

[3] The *qanā'at-ṭāsh* is also worn by the Baqtāsh (p. 179 *infra*). *Qanā'at* is from the same root as Muqanna', 'veiled'. No hint is given as to the kind of stone worn to appease hunger. The Chelidonius was a guarantee of constancy, as well as a guard against temptations, incubus, witchcraft, etc.

centre of their belts. This is figurative of the means which poor Darvishes use to appease the cravings of their stomachs for food. In place of one stone, there may be as many as four in number, though it is supposed that before the Darvish is called upon by hunger to compress his stomach with so many, the one over the other, Providence will have procured him food.

The shape of the cap of the Rifā'ī previous to his making the *bai'at*,[1] or final initiation—when he accepts of Hazrat-i-Rifā'ī as

(Joan Evans, *Magical Jewels*, pp. 63, 52). One is tempted to think the agate was favoured, since Covel in his Diary (1674), after describing the playing of the '*tambur*' by the old supravisor of the dervises and their wearing of a "great 6 or 8 square agat" in the girdle, which stone foretold sickness by growing pale on the edges, and death by growing pale towards the hole in the middle, and which sweated against poison, continues: "I remember two Kalenderis aboard the Viner had each such a one; they had the caps of a wandering Dervise, but in all things else like the habit of the Kalenderi, in Mr. Ricaut, he makes them Santons, but in good earnest they are meer Tomes of Bedlam. One had a horne tyed about his shoulders (like a wild goates, but longer); he blew it like our sow gelders, high to low. He had a great hand jar, a terrible crab-tree truncheon, a leather kind of petticoat about his middle, naked above and beneath, . . . he had a course Arnout Jamurluck [an Albanian garment]" (*Early Voyages and Travels in the Levant*, Hakluyt Soc., p. 153).

One or two points in this passage merit brief comment. Incidentally Covel seems to say that the Kalenderi were not wandering Dervise. He is more precise about the behaviour of the agat, but does not expressly say that it was shaped like a ring, though it had a hole in the middle. Lastly, he does not tell us what spiritual properties, if any, the 'agat' was believed by the darvishes to possess. The power to reveal the presence of poison was long believed to attach to many stones, as in King John's case (Evans, *op. cit.* p. 114). It was not peculiar to the agate, though that stone certainly had it (*ib.* p. 225). That stone, too, could avert thirst, but not, apparently, hunger. That belief is as old as Pliny (*ib.* p. 17). But it was one of the comparatively few stones which possessed spiritual efficacy, as the following extract shows: "*Flos Solsequij cum flore pulegij* (the plants associated with the agate) *positus, etc., dat graciam apud deum et homines reddit hominem graciosum super spiritus Aeris* . . .". In this, however, it was not singular, the topaz, too, having much the same property (*ib.* pp. 248 and 249).

[1] Bai', lit. 'a sale', also means 'redemption'; but Evliya's translator rightly renders it by 'homage', and the idea underlying the term is self-surrender (*E.I.* i. p. 588). The observance consisted in placing the hand in the ruler's open hand. The present writer has been informed that when a woman is initiated into a religious order in India the end of her shawl is placed in the *pīr's* hand. The *bai'at* and the *khutba* form the most important part of the installation of a Muhammadan sovereign, or at least did so as long as the Caliphs reigned (Pīrzāda Muhammad Husain in *Journ. Punjab Hist. Soc.* i. p. 140).

his *pīr*, and the actual head of the *takia* as his *murshid* or Shaikh—is a perfect circle, or rather two circles, the one within the other, and between the two are the initial letters of the words composing his six *tarks*. Within these is another circle, much resembling a wheel with its spokes. After the initiation, a cap somewhat similar, differing only in form, is used.

Their prayers are as follow: " In the name of Allāh, the Merciful and the Clement. Say, Allāh is One; He is the Eternal God; He was never begotten, nor has He ever begotten; nor has He any one equal to Himself" (*Qurān*, cii.).[1]

" In the name of Allāh, the Merciful and the Clement. Say, I seek a refuge in God, from the break of day; against the wickedness of those beings whom He has created; against the evils of the dark night when it comes upon us; against the wickedness of sorcerers who breathe upon knots; against the evils of curious who envy us" (*Qurān*, ciii.).[1]

" In the name of Allāh, the Merciful and the Clement. Say, I seek a refuge in the God of mankind; the King of men; the God of all men; against the wickedness of him who suggests evil thoughts, and develops them; who breathes evil into the hearts of mankind; against the genii (evil spirits), and against men" (*Qurān*, civ.).[1]

" In the name of Allāh, the Merciful and the Clement. Praise be to God, the sovereign Master of the universe—the Clement and the Merciful; the Sovereign of the day of retribution. It is Thee whom we adore, and it is of Thee that we implore help. Direct us in the true path; in the path of those on whom Thou bestowest Thy blessings, and not those who have incurred Thy displeasure; nor those who have wandered away from Thee into darkness" (*Qurān*, i.).

" In the name of Allāh, the Merciful and the Clement. This is the book of which there is no doubt: it is the direction pointed out to those who fear the Lord; of those who put their faith in hidden things; who observe exactly their prayers, and give bountifully of the good things which have been bestowed upon them; of those who believe in the revelation which has been given to thee (Muhammad), and to those who have preceded thee (the other prophets); of those who believe in the truth of the life

[1] These references are all misleading. For cii. read vi. v. 107; for ciii., cxiii.; for civ., cxiv.; and compare Sale, Palmer, or Rodwell's renderings.

to come. They only will be led by their Lord (to heaven); they will be of the happy" (*Qurān*, ii. [vv. 1-5]).[1]

The 157[164[1]]th verse of the same chapter: "Your God is the unique Allāh; there is none other; He is the Clement and the Merciful."

The 256[255]th verse of the same:[2] "Allāh is the only God; there is no other God than Him; He is the living and the everlasting; He knows no drowsiness nor slumber; all that is in the heavens, or upon the earth, belongs to Him. Who can intercede near Him, without His permission? He knows who is before thee, and who is behind thee, and no man learns of His knowledge except that which He wishes him to learn; His throne extends throughout the heavens, and over the earth, and the charge of them gives Him no trouble whatever. He is the most high, and the most exalted."

The 286th verse [vv. 284-86][1] of the same: "All that is in the heavens and upon the earth, belongs to [is [3]] God; whether you expose your acts in the great day (of judgment), or whether you conceal them, He will surely call you to an account for them; He will pardon whom He pleases, and punish those whom He pleases. God is all-powerful. The prophet believes that the Lord has sent him; the faithful believe in God, His angels, books, and the prophets whom He has sent. They say, 'We have heard, and we obey—pardon our sins, O Lord, we will return to Thee'. God imposes upon each soul a burden according to its strength; that which it has done will be alleged against, or in favour of it. Lord, punish us not for the sins of forgetfulness, or of error. Lord, do not place upon us the burden which Thou hast imposed upon those who lived before our times. Lord, do not burden us beyond what we are able to support; blot out our sins—pardon us—have pity on us—have pity on us, and pardon us, Thou art our Lord, and give us victory over the infidels."

(I am) "That God, beyond whom there is none other" (*Qurān*, lix. part of v. 22).

Then follow the various titles of God, for which, *Qurān*, vii. 179 [181] is cited as authority.

[1] The references in square brackets are to the verses as numbered in Wherry's recension of Sale's *Qurān*.

[2] The famous *āyat-ul-kursī*, or 'verse of the throne', frequently inscribed in mosques, etc.

[3] Cf. Palmer's *Qurān* S.B.E. vi. p. 40.

ASMĀ-UL-HUSNĀ,[1] *or the 'Beautiful Names of God'; ninety-nine in number*

(Those with numbers in round brackets are not in the *Qurān*.)

1. Allāh	God.
2. Ar Rahmān . . .	The Merciful.
3. Ar Rahīm . . .	The Clement.
4. Al Malik . . .	The Possessor.
5. Al Quddūs . . .	The Holy.
6. As Salām . . .	The Saviour. [The Peace or Peace-man.]
7. Al Mumin . . .	The Giver of faith. [The Faithful.]
8. Al Muhai-min . .	The Giver of safety.

[1] The attributes of God are called *ismā-ul-sifat* by Moslems, and in the *Qurān* the *ismā-ul-husna*, or 'excellent names'. Lists are given in the *Mishkāt-ul-Misābih*, *Al-Mustatraf*, Nofel's *Sinajat-ul-Tarb*, Hughes' *Dict. of Islam*, and Arnold's *Pearls of the Faith*; Aḥmad bin-'Alī al-Būni's *Shams-ul-Mu'-ārif* is one of many books on the ninety-nine names of God. But perhaps the best commentary on them is J. W. Redhouse's paper in *J.R.A.S.*, 1880, pp. 1 f. Redhouse found instead of ninety-nine upwards of two hundred and fifty names, but of these some are compounds. Indeed in the *Qurān* itself he actually found more than five hundred, a number which he says might be extended even to a thousand. The names are divided into two grades, the *ismā-ul-jalālīa*, or 'terrible', and the *ismā-ul-jamālīa*, or 'glorious' attributes, the former being the more numerous. But another and more common division is into three classes, of wisdom, power, and goodness, each class containing thirty-three names. The rosary of ninety-nine beads is also divided into three corresponding sections.

2-3. According to Baidhāwī, ar-Raḥmān is a more exalted attribute than ar-Raḥīm, because it contains five letters as against four and expresses the universal mercy extended to all men, bad as well as good, unbelievers as well as believers.

4. Al-Malik would mean the King, al-Mālik, the possessor, a distinction overlooked by Zwemer (p. 36). He cites Sura 43. 77, where Malik is applied to the angel who presides over Hell. But according to Geiger (p. 44) *malak* means a messenger of God; and *malakūt*, 'government', also used for the 'realm of spirits', is a word of Rabbinical origin which is derived from *malak* by a false etymology. In the *Qurān* al-Malik occurs constantly as a name of God, alone or in compounds, but al-Malīk, 'Holder in possession', only twice, and al-Mālik never (Redhouse, *op. cit.* pp. 61-62).

6. As-Salām, the Peace-maker, according to Zamakhsharī; Baidhāwī defines it as meaning 'free from all loss and harm'. Redhouse translates 'the Safety' (p. 38).

9.	Al 'Azīz . . .	The Strong.
10.	Al Jabbār . . .	The Absolute. [The All-Compelling.]
11.	Al Mutakabbir . .	The Giver of greatness. [The Great.]
12.	Al Khāliq . . .	The Creator.
13.	Al Bārī' . . .	The Producer of souls.
14.	Al Musawwir . .	The Giver of forms.
15.	Al Ghaffār . . .	The Pardoner.
16.	Al Qahhār . . .	The Avenger. [The Dominant.]
17.	Al Waḥhāb . . .	The Bestower.
18.	Ar Razzāq . . .	The Provider.
19.	Al Fattāh . . .	The Opener (of His will).
20.	Al 'Alīm . . .	The Knowing One.
(21.)	Al Qābiz . . .	The Holder (of hearts). [The Restrainer.]
22.	Al Bāsit . . .	The Rejoicer (of hearts). [The Spreader.]
23.	Al Hāfiz . . .	The Restrainer. [The Guardian.]
24.	Ar Rāfi' . . .	The Elevator.
(25.)	Al Mu'izz . . .	The Honorer.

10. Al-Jabbār, whence the sect of the Jabarīa, who deny all free agency to man.

11. Al-Mutakabbir, a term which applied to a human being connotes pride; and Zamakhshari defines it as 'Supreme in pride and greatness, or the One who is haughty above the wickedness of his slaves', in Sura 59. 23. Redhouse translates 'the Proud One' (p. 56).

15-35. Al-Ghaffār and al-Ghafūr are both intensive, al-Ghāfar being also frequently used.

19. Al-Fattāḥ, the name inscribed over gates and doors, on the title-pages of books and as the first copy-book lesson for boys (Redhouse, p. 48).

21. Al-Qābiẓ, the Restrainer.

22. Al-Bāsit, the Spreader or Uncloser of the hand; in Sura 13. 15 it means He who dispenses riches; but it is not used as a divine title (Redhouse, p. 18).

23. Al-Ḥāfiz, the Abaser (?); but Redhouse, p. 21, translates 'the Preserver'; and it is used commonly in spells, etc., against dangers of every kind. Ḥāfiz is one who knows the whole *Qurān* by heart, and hence = 'a blind man'.

24. Or al-Rafia', but al-Rāfi' is the form in the *Qurān* (= Upraiser, Redhouse, p. 30).

25. Al-Muizz: the Strengthener from the idea expressed in Sura 3. 25. Redhouse has 'the Raiser to honour' (p. 59).

26.	Al Muzill . . .	The God who looks down upon all things.
27.	As Samī' . . .	The Hearer.
28.	Al Basīr . . .	The Seer.
29.	Al Hākim . . .	The God who judges.
(30.)	Al 'Adil ['Adl] . .	The Just. [Justice.]
31.	Al Latīf . . .	The Gracious. [The Subtle.]
32.	Al Khabīr . . .	The Knowing. [The Cognizant.]
33.	Al Halīm . . .	The Meek. [The Clement.]
34.	Al 'Azīm . . .	The Great.
35.	Al Ghafūr . . .	The Pitying (cf. 15).
36.	Ash Shakūr . . .	The Thankful.
37.	Al 'Alī	The High.
38.	Al Kabīr . . .	The Great.
39.	Al Hafīz . . .	The Protector.
40.	Al Muqīt . . .	The Supplier of wants.
41.	Al Hasīb . . .	The Esteemed. [The Reckoner.]
42.	Al Jalīl	The Beautiful. [The Majestic.]
43.	Al Karīm . . .	The Gracious. [The Generous.]
44.	Ar Raqīb . . .	The Envious. [Keeper.]
45.	Al Mujīb . . .	The Acceptor of prayers.
46.	Al Wasī' . . .	The Extensive. [The Capacious.]
47.	Al Hakīm . . .	The Decider.
48.	Al Wadūd . . .	The Loving.
49.	Al Majīd . . .	The Glorious.

26. Al-Muẓill: 'the One who leads astray'; 'the Abaser': Redhouse. But the term connotes imagination or mystery as in *wujud-ī-zillī* or *wujud-uz-zill*, 'body of the shadow'.

28. Al-Baṣīr, as God knows five secrets, the day of judgment, the times of rain, the child hid in the womb, the future, and the place of every man's death. Redhouse has 'the All-seeing' (p. 20).

30. Al-'Ādil from *'adl*, 'equity', used of God's words in Sura 5. 115. Redhouse has also al-'Adl as 'the Equitable One' (p. 42).

31. Al-Laṭīf: the Subtle or Aethereal, according to Zamakhshari; but Redhouse translates the Most-Pleasant (p. 53).

36. As-Shakūr: the Acknowledger of Thanksgiving—cf. Sura 35. 27—is a better rendering. Redhouse, however, has the 'All-thankful' (p. 41).

38. Al-Kabīr, the Possessor of Pride, according to Zamakshari: but Redhouse has the Very-Great (p. 53).

39. Al-Ḥafīẓ: the name often put over house doors. Redhouse has 'the Preserver', but the title is not used in the *Qurān*.

41. Al-Hasīb: the Reckoner.

44. Al-Raqīb: the Watchful.

50.	Al Bā'ith(s) . . .	The Sender. [The Raiser.]
51.	Ash Shāhid . . .	The Testifier.
52.	Al Haqq . . .	The Just. [The Truth.]
53.	Al Waqīl . . .	The Procurer. [The Guardian.]
54.	Al Qawwī . . .	The Strong.
55.	Al Mutīn . . .	The Solid.
56.	Al Walī . . .	The Friend. [The Helper.]
57.	Al Hamīd . . .	The Laudable.
58.	Al Muhsī . . .	The Calculator.
59.	Al Mubdī . . .	The Commencer.
60.	Al Mu'īd . . .	The Resuscitator.
61.	Al Muhayyī [Muhyī] .	The Reviver.
62.	Al Mumīt . . .	The Destroyer.
63.	Al Haī	The Eternal. [The Living.]
64.	Al Qayyūm . . .	The Everlasting.
(65.)	Al Wājid . . .	He who finds. [The Inventor, or Maker.]
66.	Al Mājid [Majīd] .	The Glorious.
67.	Al Wāhid . . .	The Unique. [The One.]
68.	As Samad . . .	The Everlasting.
69.	Al Qādir . . .	The Powerful.
70.	Al Muqtadir . .	The Giver of power.
(71.)	Al Muqaddim . .	The Preceder.
(72.)	Al Muākhir [-akhkhir]	The Follower. [The Deferrer.]
73.	Al Awwal . . .	The First. [The mothers of the attributes.]
74.	Al Ākhir . . .	The Last.
75.	Az Zāhir . . .	The Clear.
76.	Al Bātīn . . .	The Secret

50. Al-Bā'iṣ: the Awakener or Raiser—of the body at the Resurrection, a doctrine which Geiger claims was adopted from Jewish sources (*Judaism and Islam*, pp. 58-60); also Sender-forth (of apostles) (Redhouse, p. 18).

51. Ash-Shahīd (less correctly) would imply martyrdom rather than authoritative testimony. Ash-Shāhid is the Witness (Redhouse, p. 41).

52. Al-Ḥaqq: the Truth; next to Allāh the term most used by pious Moslems (Redhouse, p. 23).

53. Al-Vakīl: the Agent; the One in Charge (Redhouse, p. 67).

54. Al-Qawī, the Very Strong.

55. Al-Matīn: the Very Firm—in the sense of a fortress.

56. Al-Walī or Wālī, the Very-next Adjoining One (next of kin, next friend, patron) (Redhouse, p. 67).

61. Al-Muḥyī is correct: the Quickener, and

62. Al-Mumīt: the Slayer—in both the passages Suras 30. 49 and 41. 39 the quickening of soil after rain is cited as proof of the Resurrection.

77. Al Wāli . . .	The Governor.
78. Al Muta'āl . . .	The Most High.
79. Al Barr . . .	The Benign. [Righteousness.]
80. At Tawwāb . . .	The Cause of repentance.
81. Al Muntaqim . .	Who takes vengeance.
82. Al 'Afūw . . .	The Forgiving.
83. Ar Ra'ūf . . .	The Propitious. [The Indulgent.]
84. Mālik-ul-Mulk . .	The Possessor of possessions. [The Ruler of the Kingdom.]
85. Zū'l Jalālī wa'l Ikrām	The Possessor of greatness and honour.
(86.) Al Muqsit . . .	The Equitable.
87. Al Jāmi' . . .	The Assembler.
88. Al Ghanī . . .	The Rich. [The Independent.]
89. Al Mughannī [Mughnī]	The Bestower of wealth.
(90.) Al Mani . . .	The Preventer.
(91.) Ad Zarr . . .	The Harmer. [Darr.]
(92.) An Nāfi' . . .	The Benefiter.
93. An Nūr . . .	The Light.
94. Al Hadī . . .	The Guide.
95. Al Badī' . . .	The Commencer. [Incomparable.]
96. Al Bāqī . . .	The Ender. [Eternal.]
(97.) Al Wāris . . .	The Heir.
98. Ar Rashīd . . .	The Director.
99. As Sabūr . . .	The Patient.

These *Ism-ī-Jalāl*, or the 'Beautiful Names of God', are used as invocations, or as calls upon Him. They are ninety-nine in number, and figure on the *tasbīh*,[1] or rosary of all Mussulmans.[2]

[1] *Tasbihāt* (pl.) = 'doxologies', and the meaning 'rosaries' is secondary and not found in pure Arabic (Redhouse in *J.R.A.S.*, 1880, pp. 9 f).

[2] The Moslem rosary has ninety-nine beads and is divided into three equal parts by small oblong separators. Each bead recalls an attribute of the Divinity and the *kalima* is repeated at each separator; but most people are content to ejaculate 'Allāh' at each bead. A good deal of variety characterises Moslem rosaries. Thus *maulavīs* use one of *kahrubā*, 'amber', and the *sulaimānī* of various stones: but all *faqīrs* use these two as well as the *tasbīh* of variegated glass and the *sang-i-maqṣūd* or 'stone or purpose' of yellow stones (*Indian Notes and Queries*, iv. § 11, 146).

Zwemer, who has collected much information on the subject, says that in Egypt a rosary made of jet (*yusr*) or *kuk*, a special kind of wood from

There is still another list, reaching to as many as 1001. It is possible that I have not, in some few cases, given their exact interpretation, and some of them differ but slightly from the others in meaning.

The following is a common prayer of many of the Darvish Orders, and especially of the Rifā'īs :

" Thy attributes, O God ! are holy, without any doubt ; I abstain from comparing Thee to anything else ; I declare that Thou art our Lord,—that Thou art One, and all things prove it.

A RIFĀ'Ī DARVISH IN AN ECSTATIC STATE

Thou art One, and knowest no diminution ; Thou art subject to no disease ; Thou art known by Thy goodness and Thy knowledge ; to Thy knowledge there is no limit ; none can praise Thee too much ; Thou art the First—the Everlasting, and without any Beginning ; Thou art the Last, and the Benevolent, and without any end. Thou hast no genealogy,—no sons ; Thou canst never do wrong ; Thou revolvest with the cycles of time ; Thou never

Mecca, is used both by Copts and Moslems for the cure of a disorder in children. It is also used in divination (*v.* note on p. 95 *supra*). Citing Goldziher, he agrees that it was not imported into Islam until the third century of the Hijra (*The Influence of Animism on Islam*, p. 27 ff.). Its use was looked on by the orthodox with displeasure, but it was nevertheless widely adopted, and we are told that in India rosaries of 1000 beads (probably an error for 1001) are used in the *subha*, a rite observed on the night after a burial by *dervish*. Such practices are, however, exceptional.

weakenest with age ; all Thy creatures are submissive to Thy greatness and to Thy commands ; Thy *fiat* is the latters b and e, '*be*' ; the pure in heart behold Thy beauty by means of the *zikr* (the recital of His name), and bless Thee with the 'Thirties' (the rosary is divided into thirty-three parts, together making the full ninety-nine) ; Thy guidance directs them in the right path, through the same means ; they live in perfect love in Thy beneficent paradise ; Thy science is everlasting, and knows even the numbers of the breaths of Thy creatures ; Thou seest and hearest the movements of all Thy creatures : Thou hearest even the steps of the ant when in the dark night it walks on black stones ; even the birds of the air praise Thee in their nests ; the wild beasts of the desert adore Thee ; the most secret, as well as the most exposed thoughts of Thy servants, Thou knowest ; Thou art security for Thy faithful ones ; Thou strengthenest and givest to others victory, and rejoicest their hearts ; Thy *zikr* gives power, and overthrows concealed harms, and so do the *āyāt* (verses) of Thy book (when borne on the person as charms) ; Thy commands uphold the heavens, and support the earth ; and Thy science has circumvented the entire globe ; and Thou art merciful and beneficent to Thy sinning creatures.

"Like unto Thee, O God, never has anything existed ; Thou hearest and seest all things. O Lord, preserve us from evil (this is repeated three times). Thou canst allow even the occurrence of evil things—great and good God ! blessed be Thy holy councils. Have mercy upon us, O Lord, and give us victory, for there is no power or strength but in Thee. Blessings without number be upon Thee,—Thou who doest all that Thou deemest best. Thou art great, and great is Thy glory ; Thy power extends to all things ; Thy glory is manifested by Thy will. Living and inventing God, everlasting Lord, and merciful Creator of the heavens and the earth, none is worthy of adoration but Thee ; hear and accept of our prayers, O merciful God, for the sake of Thy blessed Prophet ; give us peace of soul, and freedom from all sin ; may Thy mercy rest, and its blessings be upon us, and in our families and friends—for Thou art the great, the glorious, and the clement God of all (*Qurān*, xxxiii. 33). 'God does not wish other than to deliver you all from the abomination, and to love his family, and to secure to you a perfect purity' (xxxiii. 56). 'God and the angels are precious to the Prophet. Believers ! address your prayers to the Lord, and pronounce (*zikr*) His name with salutation confidently.'

"O Allāh! give praise and peace to our Lord Muhammad and to his family, conformably with what Thou hast said of him, —in Abraham (Ibrāhīm) and his family, bless Muhammad and his offspring, as Thou didst Ibrāhīm, preserving him from fire in both worlds; for Thou art the glorious and the merciful! according to the numbers of Thy creatures and Thy holy will; be clement to the arch of Thy heavenly abode,—to each letter of Thy word; to the number of those who call Thy Name (*zikr*); according to the number of those who forget Thee, O Lord, praise with the choicest of Thy praises, the best of Thy creatures, our Lord Muhammad, his offspring and his companions (the *aṣḥābs*) according to the number of Thy science,—the number of Thy words, and of those who mention (*zikr*) Thy holy name, as well as those who forget Thee. O Allah! praise our Lord Muhammad, Thy secret, and Prophet and friend, and him whom Thou hast sent; he who was illiterate (the Darvishes say that none of the Prophets could read or write, and their knowledge therefore came directly from above), his family and friends, according to the number of Thy heavens and earths, and all things which are between them. Have mercy on our affairs, and upon all Mussulmans, O Lord of all worlds.

"O God, may Thy praises be upon our Lord Muhammad, and his family and friends, according to the number of years of this world's existence, and of those worlds which are to be, and of all that Thou knowest relative to this, Thy world. O God, may Thy praises be upon the soul of our Lord Muhammad, amongst all the other souls, in his body, among all the other bodies, and in his illuminated grave, and upon his name, amongat all other names.

"O God, may Thy praises be upon our Lord, the possessor of the sign of the Prophetship upon his back (a mole), and the cloud (which always accompanied and preserved him from the heat of the sun); on the intercessor and the pitying, and the embassy (the *Qurān*); on him who is more beauteous than the sun and the moon, according to the good deeds of Abū Bakr, 'Umr, 'Othman, and Haidar ('Alī); to the number of the plants of the earth and the leaves of the trees; on the good one—the possessor of the place in Paradise (*Maqām-i-Mahmūd*), and of the tongue of eloquence; he who comes with preaching and intelligence and pity, and upon his family and friends. May the best of Thy praises be upon him, according to the vast amount of Thy great knowledge,—to the number of the words which Thou hast written,—the mentions made of Thy name, and of those who make mention of Thee (*zikr*) ; of those who forget Thee ; of those who in assemblies bless Thee with innumerable breaths (*nafs*) ; upon Thy Prophet who enlightened the hearts of those who pointed out a path (*tarīq*) to each friend ; who came in tenth ; who was sent in mercy to the world, to intercede for sinners ; according to the merits of the blessed Prophets, and their greatness ; according to his (Muhammad's) influence with Thee, the all-powerful ; on him, the most blessed of all the prophets ; of those who are resigned to Thee ; on him, who is Thy Friend (such is the blessing of all Mussulmans) ; on his fathers ; on Ibrāhīm, the sincere friend of Allāh ; upon Mūsā (Moses), his brother, who spake with Thee ; and upon Israel (Jesus), the Faithful (*al-Amīn*) who was the Spirit of God (*ar-Rūh Allāh*) ; on Thy servant and prophet Sulīmān, and his father, David, and on all the other prophets and envoys, and all those who submit to Thee ; on all those who people the heavens and the earth ; those who call upon (*zikr*) Thy name, as well as those who forget Thee. Praises be upon the fountain of Thy mercy (the Prophet), the amount of Thy judgment day,—on the measure of Thy path (*tarīq*), on the ornament of the crown of Paradise,—the bride of the other world,—the sun of holy law,—whose words are deeds,—the intercessor for all mankind,—the Imām of all,—the Prophet of pity, our Lord Muhammad ; upon Adam and Noah ; on Ibrāhīm, the intimate friend of God,—his brother Moses, and the Spirit of God, Jesus ; on David and Sulīmān, Zukarīa, Yāhyā (Isaiah), and Sheb (Seth ?), and on all their offspring,—those who call upon Thee, as well as those who forget Thee.

" O our Eternal God of mercy, Thy praises be upon Thy people, who spread open their hands to glorify Thee,—Thou bestower of all good things ; Thou pardoner of all things, sins, and faults ; Thy praises be upon our Lord, who is the best of all those having good dispositions,—upon his offspring and friends, and the good men of this world ; pardon us who are now present. There is no God than Allāh, and Muhammad is the Prophet of Allāh, and Ibrāhīm is the intimate friend of Allāh.

" O our Lord ! O Prophet of God,—He whom we desire,—

who gives us from out of His abundance ; the Possessor of time ; Thou helper in the hour of need,—Thou purest of all prophets,—the Jewel of the Universe ; who elevates atoms into worlds ; Thou refuge of the poor (*fuqirā*) ; the Eye which beholds all the past ; Thou all-seeing, I have praised Thee, O Prophet of God ; I have believed in Thee, and in Thy sufficiency ; Thy goodness comes upon us kindly, and with Thy excellence it invites us to call upon Thee, approaches us to Thee.

"Thousands of prayers be upon Thee (three times repeated),—upon the 100th, 80th, and 1090th (this refers to the belief that in the 2280th year of the Hegira the world will end) ; praises be upon him who is the true light, Ahmad-al-Mustafā (Prophet),—the Lord of all prophets, his offspring and all his friends. O God, have mercy upon all the faithful. One thousand prayers, and one thousand salutations, be in the great secret of Thy Prophet. O Thou affectionate beneficent, lead us in our belief ; Thy praise be upon Thy perfect Son (the Prophet) in the judgment day,—during the length of days,—in the mode (sign or seal) of his prophetship,—on him who was shielded by a cloud, on Mustafā,—for the sake of Allāh,—Thy secret,—on his secrets ; bestow upon us thy favour, O Mustafā, bestow thy countenance upon us, for His sake, and thy own ; pity our weaknesses,—elevate us through thy peace (three times). O Prophet ! help us (three times) ; we believe in thee. O thou friend of God ! intercede for us,—we know that He will not reject thy intercession. Thou, O Lord, art Allāh,—favour us as Thou knowest best (three times). There is no God but Allāh, and Muhammad is the Prophet of Allāh."

The patient reader will have perceived much in this lengthy prayer peculiar to the belief of the Darvishes generally, though a great part of it is purely Mussulman.

THE NAQSHBANDĪS

The Order of the Naqshbandīs is one of the most extensive which exists in the East, and particularly in the Ottoman empire. They have a work in Turkish, called the ***Rashahāt 'Ain-al-Hayāt***,[1]

[1] A valuable account by H. Beveridge of a Persian MS. of this work will be found in *J.R.A.S.*, 1916, p. 59 ff. Its author was 'Alī s. Ḥusain al-Wā'iẓ al-Kāshifī al-Ṣāfī—to give his poetical cognomen—but his full name was Fakhr-ud-Dīn 'Alī. His father was a well-known writer (see p. 404 *infra*).

or *Drops from the Fountain of Life*, which is not only a perfect biography of their founder, Muhammad Bahā-ud-Dīn, but also a detailed account of his peculiar spiritual doctrines. M. d'Herbelot states that *Naqshband* was his surname ; that he was the author of a work entitled *Maqāmāt*, '*Stations*',[1] on various subjects connected with eloquence and academic studies ; and another called *Aurād-al-Bahiyāt*, 'Prayers of Bahā', taken from his own name, and that he died 791 H. [A.D. 1389–90].

In the addendum of the work called the *Shaqqāiq Numānia*,[2] the *silsila*, or succession of Naqshband, it is thus related, and the detail will serve as an example of the descent claimed by all of the Darvish Orders. "The Shaikh Bāyazīd Bustāmī has it from the Imām Ja'far Sādiq, who has it from the Imām Muhammad Bāqir, who has it from the Imām Zain-ul-'Abidīn, who has it from the Imām Husain, who has it from 'Alī (fourth Caliph), who has it from the Prophet of Allāh,—that Bāyazīd Bustāmī was born after the decease of the Imām Ja'far Sādiq, and, by the force of the will of the latter, received spiritual instruction from him. Imām Ja'far also spiritualised Qāsim bin-Muhammad bin-Abū-Bakr us-Sādiq [Siddīq].[3] He was one of the seven

---

The *Tricklings from the Fountain of Life*, as Beveridge translates the title of the MS., is an account of the Naqshbandī Khwājas of Central Asia, and especially of the saint Naṣīr-ud-Dīn 'Ubaid-Ullāh, commonly styled Ḥaẓrat Ishān or Khwāja Aḥrār of Samarqand, who was invested by Ya'qūb Charkhī, of Charkh in the Ghaznī district of Afghānistān. Ya'qūb bestowed his cap (*ṭāqiya*) on Ḥaẓrat Ishān and died in 851 H. (A.D. 1447-48). The *Rashahāt* was certainly not written by Bahā-ud-Dīn, as stated in *E.R.E.*, 8, p. 886. The death of 'Ubaid-Ullāh Aḥrār, 'one of the greatest theologians of his time', is assigned to the year A.D. 1489 at Kumaghiran near Samarqand (*ib.*) ; or to 895 H. (A.D. 1490) when nearly ninety years of age (Beveridge, *op. cit.*, p. 66 *n.*).

[1] Not *Sittings* as in original edition.

[2] Its correct title is the '*Shaqāiq-al-nu'māniya fī 'ulamā al-daula al-'Oṣmāniya*, 'Blood-red wild anemones touching learned of the Ottoman empire', by the Mullā Ṭāshköprüzāda, who died in A.D. 1560.

Evliya, or rather his translator, alludes to it as the '*Shakaiki-nāmeh*', by 'the great and virtuous Kamāl-ud-Dīn Muḥammad, son of Aḥmad', immortalised by the name of Ṭāsh Koprī-zāda, *i.e.* 'the son of Ṭāsh Koprī-zāda' (? Ṭāsh Koprī), at i. part ii., p. 22 of his *Travels*. He adds that he died at Yasī under Usmān.

[3] Qāsim b. Muḥammad b. Abū Bakr us-Ṣādiq, one of the seven *fuqahā*, 'learned in the *fiqh*', died in 106 H. (A.D. 725). The filiations of the Naqshbandīs are not consistently given, probably owing to divergent views.

doctors of Divine Law, and derived his spirituality through the mystic will of Salmān Fārsī. The latter enjoyed direct intercourse with the blessed Prophet of God, and beside this peculiar honour, received instruction (*tarbiyat*) from Abu-Bakr us-Sādiq [Siddīq] (second Caliph). When these were concealed together in the cave, and there conversed with the Prophet, they all performed the secret *zikr* (called upon God's name mentally), seated on their hips, with depressed eyes, repeating it three times.

"After the decease of Bāyazīd Bistāmī [in A.D. 877–78] Abū'l Ḥasan Khurqānī was born.[1]

"Shaikh Abū'l Qāsim Kerkiānī [Gurgānī] has connexion with both of these. According to this statement Abū'l Ḥasan Khurqānī was employed in their service.

"Shaikh Abū'l 'Uṣmān Maghribī received [instruction] from them,—Abū 'Alī Redūharī [?Rūdbārī] from them also; from them came the spiritual powers of Jụnaid Ḅaghdādī [*d.* in A.D. 911], from him to Sarī Saqatī, [and] from him to Ma'rūf Karkhī [*d.* in A.D. 816].

"The latter also had two sources of descent,—the one, Dā'ūd Ṭā'ī; from them came Habīb Sajamī ['Ajamī], from him Ḥasan Basrī, and these all received their spirituality from the Commander of the Faithful, 'Alī. Ma'rūf Karkhi drew [his spirituality] from 'Alī Rizā; he from the Imām Mūsā Kāzim,—he from Ja'far us-Sādiq.

"The continuation of the descent is as follows: Abū'l Qāsim Gurgānī left his powers to his pupil, Khoja 'Alī Fārmandī [Fārmadī]; his *khalīfa* (successor) was Khoja Yūsuf Hamadānī—that of the latter was his own servant 'Abd-ul-Khāliq Gajdivānī [Ghajdawānī]; after him Khoja 'Ārif Rivkarī [Reogari]; after him Muhammad Fagnawī; after him 'Alī Rametnī [Ramitanī]; after him Muhammad Bābā Sammāsī; after him the Amir Sa'īd Gulān (or Kalāl); after him the Khoja Bahā-ud-Dīn Naqshband[2];

Thus one scheme passes over 'Alī and derives the order from the Caliph Abū Bakr and his grandson Qāsim. This would indicate that the order is strictly orthodox. But there is also a Shī'a version, or one accepted by a Shī'a group within the order which omits Abū Bakr and includes 'Alī. The version in the text combines both versions.

[1] See Appendix A to this chapter.

[2] For the sequel of the Naqshbandī spiritual descent *v.* Appendix I. Brown next, after correctly describing the Nūrbakhshīs as an offshoot of

after him Alai-ud-Dīn al-'Attar; after him Nizām-ud-Dīn Khāmūsh; after him Sultān [Sa'īd]-ud-Dīn al-Kāshgarī; after him 'Ubaid-Ullāh Samarqandī; after him Shaikh 'Abdullāh al-Lāhī; after him Shaikh Sa'īd Ahmad al-Bukhārī; after him Shaikh Muhammad Chalabī, nephew of Azīz; after him Shaikh 'Abd-ul-Latīf, nephew of Muhammad Chalabī—may Allāh bless their secrets.

"From the Naqshbandī Order evidently sprang the Order of the Nūrbakhshīs; for the same author adds that the Amīr Sultān Shams-ud-Dīn derived from Sa'īd 'Alī, father of Muhammad bin-'Alī-al-Husainī al-Bukhārī; they derived from the Sa'īd Muhammad Nūrbakhshī. The *khalīfa* of Amīr Bukhārā, Hasan Khoja [of] Vān's *khalīfa* Walī Shams-ud-Dīn, are mentioned in the *Shaqqāiq*. These derived from Isḥāq Jalālī, he from Sa'īd 'Alī Hamadānī, he from Muḥammad Kharqānī, he from Alai-ud-Daulat Samnānī, he from 'Abd-ur-Rahmān Asfarānī, he from Ahmad Jūrqānī, he from 'Alī bin-Sa'īd Lālā, he from Najm-ud-Dīn Qubrā, he from 'Umar bin Yazīr Badlīsī, he from Abū'l Najīb Suharwardī,[1] and down through the whole succession."

The same author [on p. 8 of Ajdī's *Tarjuma*, as lithographed], in alluding to the Khwājas of the Naqshbandīs, says:

"This people (*tāifa*) polish the exterior of their minds and intellects with pictures, and being free from the rust and wiles of life are not of those who are captivated by the vain colourings of the world, as varied as those of the changeful chameleon; and as Naqshband drew incomparable pictures of the Divine Science, and painted figures of the Eternal Invention, which are not imperceptible, his followers are become celebrated by the title of the *Naqsh-bandīs*, 'The Painters'."

From the work before alluded to, called *Drops from the Fountain of Life*, it would appear that the originator of this order was 'Ubaid-ullāh, and that Bahā-ud-Dīn Naqshband was only a learned writer on its principles. The members of the order are

---

the Naqshbandīs, suddenly diverges into a spiritual pedigree of the Suhārwardīs, inverting the chronological order, and following in the main the text of 'Aṭāyī's *zail*, or supplement to the *Shaqā'iq* (*v.* lithographed ed., p. 62). But for Muḥmūd Chalabī, *dāmād*, 'son-in-law', he has Muḥammad Ch.; and for Isḥaq Jīlānī, Isḥāq Jalālī.

[1] For an account of the Suharwardis and their successors *v.* Appendix B to this chapter.

called *khojagiān*, or the teachers. The *khalīfas* (or successors) and the disciples of 'Ubaid-ullāh were *walīs*, and their holy tombs are scattered over various parts of the farther East, in Merv, Samarqand, Sind,[1] Bukhāra, and throughout Persia, where they are much visited for the purpose of seeking spiritual inspiration from the revered remains of the sainted men which they contain. Various members of the Order gave rise to varied points of belief, and one declared that the soul would, and does, return to this world in a new body. As this borders closely upon the theory of the metempsychosis, it is treated upon in various ways—all spiritually. Another teaches the necessity of the *khalwat*, or profound meditation on the Deity, which he says must be so perpetual and continuous as to absorb completely the mind; so much so, that when even in the midst of a crowd, the mediator can hear no voice or other sound. Every word spoken by others will then appear to him the *zikr*, and so will even his own words, when spoken on other subjects. But to attain to this the greatest attention and labour is necessary.

As advice to a *murīd*, or disciple, the following instructions are given by a member of the Order respecting the *zikr*, which he says is a union of the heart and the tongue in calling upon God's name. In the first place, the Shaikh, or teacher, must with his heart recite "There is no God but Allāh, and Muhammad is the Prophet of Allāh", whilst the *murīd* keeps his attention fixed by placing his heart opposite that of the Shaikh; he must close his eyes; keep his mouth firmly shut, and his tongue pressed against the roof of his mouth; his teeth tight against each other, and hold his breath; then, with great force, accompany the Shaikh in the *zikr*, which he must recite with his heart, and not with his tongue. He must retain his breath patiently, so that within one respiration he shall say the *zikr* three times, and by this means allow his heart to be impressed with the meditative *zikr*.

The heart, in this manner, is kept constantly occupied with the idea of the Most High God; it will be filled with awe, love, and respect for Him, and, if the practiser arrives at the power of continuing to effect this, when in the company of a crowd, the *zikr* is perfect. If he cannot do this, it is clear that he must

[1] Sind means not only the modern province of Sind but the whole country lying to the west of the Indus, or even the whole Indus valley, to the border of Khurāsān. It might be fairly rendered 'North-Western India'

continue his efforts. The heart is a subtle part of the human frame, and is apt to wander away after worldly concerns, so that the easier mode of arriving at the proceeding is to compress the breath, and keep the mouth firmly closed with the tongue forced against the lips. The heart is shaped like the cone of a fir-tree ; your meditations should be forced upon it, whilst you mentally recite the *zikr*. Let the ' *La* ' be upward, the ' *Illāhu* ' to the right, and the whole phrase ' *La Illāhu* ' (there is no God but Allāh) be formed upon the fir-cone, and through it to all the members of the whole frame, and they feel its warmth. By this means, the world and all its attractions disappear from your vision, and you are enabled to behold the excellence of the Most High. Nothing must be allowed to distract your attention from the *zikr*, and ultimately you retain, by its medium, a proper conception of the *tauhīd*, or ' Unity of God '.

The cone-shaped heart rests in the left breast, and contains the whole truth of man. Indeed it signifies the ' whole truth ', it comprises the whole of man's existence within itself, and is a compendium of man ; mankind, great and small, are but an extension of it, and it is of humanity what the seed is which contains within itself a whole tree ; in fine, the essence of the whole of God's book and of all His secrets is the heart of man. Whoever finds a way to the heart obtains his desire ; to find a way to the heart is by a heartful service, and the heart accepts of the services of the heart. It is only through the fatigues of water and ashes that the *murīd* reaches the conversation of the heart and the soul ; he will be then so drawn towards God that afterwards, without any difficulty, he may without trouble, in case of need, turn his face from all others toward Him. He will then know the real meaning of the *tark*, the *haqīqat*, the *hurrīt*,[1] and the *zikr*.

It is through the performance of the *zikr*, by *khalwat* (pious retirement for purposes of deep devotion), by the *tawajjuh*[2] (or

[1] Hurrīt, *hurreet* in original, doubtless for *ḥurrīyyat*, ' freedom ', ' liberty ', *Ḥurrīyyat 'āmah* = ' freedom from cupidity ' and *ḥurrīyyat khāṣa* = ' freedom from self-will ' in the language of the mystics (Redhouse, *Turk.-Eng. Lex.* p. 780). *Ḥairat* would mean ' continual amazement ', and so ' gnosis ' (Nicholson, *Kashf al-Maḥjūb*, p. 275).

[2] *Tawajjuh* will be found discussed, from one point of view, on pp. 336-9 *infra*. On p. 336 it is equated to *murāqaba*, a term which appeared early in Sufiism : originally it denoted the first of the mystical ' states ', following

turning the face or mind devoutly towards God in prayer), by the *murāqaba* (or fearful contemplation of God), the *tasarruf* (or self-abandonment to pious reflection and inspiration), and the *tasawwuf* (or mystical spiritualism), that the fervent Darvish reaches peculiar spiritual powers, called *quwwat-i-rūhī bātinī* (a mystical, internal, spiritual power). The life, or biography, of every eminent Shaikh, or *pīr*, details innumerable evidences of this power exercised in a strange and peculiar manner. This exercise is called the *quwwat*[1] *irādat*, or the 'Power of the Will', and, as a theory may be traced historically to the Divine Power—the soul of man being connected with the Divine Spirit—from which it emanates, and with which, through the means before mentioned, it commences. Some Shaikhs are more celebrated than others for their peculiar and strange powers, and it is to their superiority that their reputation and reverence in the Mussulman world in general, and among Darvishes in particular, is to be attributed. With the supposition that the details given of them by their biographers, disciples, or successors are not invented, or even exaggerated, their powers are certainly very remarkable. Whilst among them an implicit belief in them is firmly sustained, sultans and princes have evidently doubted them, and being alarmed with the influence the possessors acquired and sustained among the public generally, they have often shown a direful exercise of their own arbitrary will and power, which resulted in the untimely end of the unfortunate Shaikh. Many, on the other hand, have survived the frequent exercise of their 'spiritual powers', and either because they acquired a power and influence over the minds of their temporal rulers, or whether they used them for their own private purposes, so as to conciliate the more religious or fanatic, they succeeded in reaching advanced ages and a peaceful end of their remarkable careers. When the ruler of the

---

rizā, the last of the 'stations', and is rendered 'observation' (Nicholson, *Kitāb al-Luma'*, p. 16). But Gibb renders it 'spiritual communion' with the soul of the holy man to whose tomb the pilgrim betakes him. *Tawajjuh* he, too, equates with *murāqaba*, but the former word he translates 'saintly favour', meaning the spiritual assistance vouchsafed by a saint to a devotee or by a master to a disciple (*Hist. of Ott. Poetry*, i. p. 425). It is quite possible that both terms acquired a reciprocal meaning, the devout attention of the disciple on the one hand, and on the other the steadfast protection of the saint.

[1] For various other 'faculties', *quwwat*, *v.* Gibb, *op. cit.* i. pp. 49 f.

country has not cared to order the execution of the Shaikh who declared himself possessed of these 'spiritual powers', he has simply exiled him from his capital, or his territory, and permitted him freely to exercise his powers and renown in some less objectionable locality. These powers can only be acquired through the long instruction of a superior spiritual director, or *murshid*, or *asḥāb-i-yaqīn*, for whom the disciples ever retain a most grateful remembrance and attachment.

Among the practices of these powers is the faculty of foreseeing coming events—of predicting their occurrence—of preserving individuals from the harm and evil which would otherwise certainly result for them—of assuring to one person success over the machinations of another, so that he may freely attack him and prevail over him—of restoring harmony of sentiment between those who would otherwise be relentless enemies—of knowing when others have devised harm against themselves, and through certain spells of preserving themselves and causing harm to befall the evil-minded; and even of causing the death of any one against whom they wish to proceed. All this is done as well from a distance as when near.

In other parts of the world, and among other people, these attainments would have been attributed to sorcery and witchcraft; in modern times they would be ascribed to Spiritism, or magnetic influences, either of the spirit or of the body; but to the instructed Darvish they all derive their origin in the spirit of the holy Shaikh—the special gift of the great Spirit of God, which commences with the spirit of man from which it directly emanated. The condition or disposition necessary for these effects is called the *hāl* (state, or frame), and is much the same as that required by the magnetised, and the object of his operation. The powers of the body are enfeebled by fasting and mental fatigue in prayer, and the imagination kept in a fervid state, fully impressed with the conviction that such powers are really possessed by the Shaikh, and that he can readily exercise them over the willing mind and body of the disciple. How the Shaikh can produce such strange results on a distant and unconscious person is left to the admiration and imagination of the faithful disciple, as an incentive to exertions in the same true path as that of his Shaikh.

To exercise the power of the will, it is necessary to contract the thoughts suddenly upon the object designed to be effected, so perfectly as to leave no room for the mind to dwell, possibly, upon any other. The mind must not doubt, for an instant, of the success of this effort, nor the possibility of failure ; it must, in fact, be completely absorbed by the one sole idea of performing the determination strongly taken, and firmly relied upon. The person must, from time to time, practise this ; and as they proceed, they will be able to see how much propinquity exists between themselves and the *Hazrat-i-Asmā* [1] (God ?), and how much they are capable of exercising this power.

As an example, the author of the *Rashahāt* [3rd *maqṣad*, 1st *faṣl*], narrates the following :

" In my youth, I was ever with our Lord Maulānā Sa'īd-ud-Dīn Kāshgarī at Harīd.[2] It happened that we, one day, walked out together, and fell in with an assembly of the inhabitants of the place who were engaged in wrestling. To try our powers, we agreed to aid with our ' powers of the will ' one of the wrestlers, so that the other should be overcome by him ; and after doing so, to change our design in favour of the discomfited individual. So we stopped, and turning towards the parties, gave the full influence of our united wills to one, and immediately he was able to subdue his opponent. As the person we chose, each in turn, conquered the other. Whichever we willed to prevail became the most powerful of the two, and the power of our own wills was thus clearly manifested."

On another occasion, two other persons, possessed of these same powers, fell in with an assembly of people, at a place occupied by prize-fighters. " To prevent any of the crowd from passing between and separating us, we joined our hands together. Two persons were engaged fighting ; one was a powerful man, whilst the other was a spare and weak person. The former readily

[1] Ḥazrat (*ḥadra*), lit. ' presence ', a synonym of *ḥuẓūr*, meaning in the language of the mystics ' being in the presence (of Allāh) '. For developments of its doctrinal meaning see *E.I.* ii. p. 207, where D. B. Macdonald says its use as a title of respect belongs to the Lexicon. It may, however, be suggested that it connotes manifestation or presence of a sacred or divine nature when applied to a saint. In Egypt *ḥaẓrat* has the same meaning as *majlis* and *jama'*, *i.e.* ' reunion ', ' assembly ' (*Der Islam*, vi. p. 161). For *asmā* see note on p. 104.

[2] Hereed in original, for Harī, an old name of Herat, then the capital of Khurāsān (*Tārīkh-i-Rashīdī*, p. 193).

overcame the latter; and seeing this, I proposed to my companion, to aid the weak one by the power of our wills. So he bade me aid him in the project, whilst he concentrated his powers upon the weaker person. Immediately a wonderful occurrence took place; the thin, spare man seized upon his giant-like opponent, and threw him upon the ground with surprising force. The crowd cried out with astonishment, as he turned him over on his back, and held him down with much apparent ease. No one present, except ourselves, knew the cause. Seeing that my companion's eyes were much affected by the effort which he had made, I bade him remark how perfectly successful we had been, and adding that there was no longer any necessity for our remaining there, we walked away."

Just as it is impossible to conflict with the *Qurān*, so is it to conflict with an *'ārif*, or 'knowing person', possessed of the power of the will. His power conflicts with that of others, but there is no confliction in his designs; nor is it essential that the person to be assisted should be a believer; he may be, even, an infidel, for faith is not needed to the performance of the design of the willer. Just as is the influence of the pure heart, so is that of the breath of the wicked. Even the most powerful princes of this world do not prosper without assistance. The Shaikh once left for Samarqand, for the purpose of holding a conversation with the sovereign of that place, Mirza 'Abdullāh bin-Mirza Ibrāhīm bin-Mirza Shāhrukh.[1] "I," says the writer, "was then in his service, and went with him. On arriving, an officer of Mirza 'Abdullāh waited upon him, and the Shaikh explained to him the object of his visit, and added, that he did not doubt but much advantage would be derived from the interview.

"To this the officer impertinently replied, that his Mirza ['Abdullah] was a youth without any fear, and would excuse him from waiting upon him, and that he could well do without the demands of Darvishes. This language displeased the Shaikh so that he replied that he had an order to communicate with sovereigns, that he had not come of his own accord, and that if his Mirza was fearless, he could retire and give place to one who was fearful. The officer departed, and so soon as he had left, the Shaikh wrote his name upon the wall of the house wherein he was then dwelling, and a moment afterwards wiped it off with his

[1] A prince (mirza) of the house of Timur, whose fourth son was Shāhrukh.

own mouth, remarking that he could not receive hospitality from either the sovereign of the place, or from his officers. He, the same day, returned directly to Tāshkand. A week afterwards, the officer died, and within a month Abū Sa'īd Mirza Akza[1] appeared from Turkistān against Mirza 'Abdullāh, and killed him. From this occurrence, it is readily seen that Abū Sa'īd owed his success to the spiritual aid (*himmat*) of the holy Shaikh.

"On another occasion, the Shaikh was at a place called Farkat,[2] when he asked us to furnish him with pens and ink, with which he wrote several names upon a paper. Among these was the name of the Sultān, Abū Sa'īd Mirza, and he placed the paper in his turban. At that time no such person as this was anywhere known to exist. Some of those present asked the Shaikh why he was pleased to favour the names so greatly as to keep them in his revered turban. He replied, that they were the names of certain persons, whom he and we, and all of the people of Tāshkand, Samarqand, and Khurāsān, should respect. Very soon after this, Sultān Abū Sa'īd Mirza appeared from Turkistān. He had seen, in a dream, that our beloved Shaikh, together with the Khoja Ahmad Yasawī,[3] had recited the *fātiha* (first chapter of the *Qurān*), with especial reference to himself. He inquired of Khoja Ahmad the names of our Shaikh, and retained them in his memory, and made diligent search for him throughout the whole country. He soon learned that, of a truth, there was just such a person dwelling

[1] Mirza Akza: in MS. No. 625 (I.O.) the reading is: *Wa ba'd az ek māh Sultān Abū Sa'īd Mīrza az aqṣāī Turkīstān, etc.*, "and after one month Sulṭān Abū Sa'īd Mīrza came from the *aqṣā* of Turkīstān". *Aqṣā* has the meaning of 'very distant'—at least in Turkish—so the phrase may mean 'from the farthest confines of Turkīstān'. The writer seems to say that the Sulṭān did not make a direct attack on 'Abdullāh Mīrza, but suddenly invaded his territory from the north instead of from the direction of Herat.

[2] Farkat, a place some miles from Tāshkand.

[3] Aḥmad Yasawī (not Tessevvee, as in original) is the Kirghīz patron-saint of the twelfth century. He takes his title from Yasī, now Turkīstān or Ḥaẓrat-i-Yasī, a place far to the north of Tāshkand on the road to Orenburg. He wrote mystic poems, *ḥikmat* or *munājāt*, as well as a Dīwān, and founded a whole school of mystics, to which belonged *Hakīm Ata* in the fourth generation. Originally a disciple of one Bābā Arslān, he only became a pupil of Yūsuf Hamadhānī on the death of his first teacher. Dying in 1166 at the age of sixty-three, he was buried at Yasī, where Tīmūr erected a mausoleum over his tomb (Vambéry in *E.R.E.* 8, p. 887, and *E.I.* i. p. 204).

at Tāshkand; and he immediately set out to find him there. So soon as our Shaikh heard of his approach, he set out for Farkat. The Mirza came to Tāshkand, and, not finding the Shaikh there, proceeded to Farkat. As he approached the latter place, our Shaikh went out to meet him. When the Mirza saw the Shaikh, his countenance changed, and he exclaimed: 'By Allāh! you are certainly the same person whom I saw in my dream'. He threw himself at the Shaikh's feet, and with much anxiety implored the aid of his prayers. The Shaikh was extremely gracious to the Mirza, so that the latter became greatly attached to him.

"Later, when the Mirza desired to collect a force and march against Samarqand, he revisited our Shaikh, and begged his permission and assistance in favour of his campaign. The Shaikh asked him with what object he designed making it: 'If', he added, 'it is to enforce the law of God, and to act in a humane manner, you will be successful'. The Mirza declared that it was, and the Shaikh then bade him depart with his commendable intentions. By some it is related that the Shaikh told the Mirza: 'When you are opposite your opponents, do not attack them until you perceive a flight of crows coming up from your rear'. In consequence of this admonition, when the Mirza Abū Sa'īd was opposite the forces of Mirza 'Abdullāh, the latter ordered his cavalry to make an attack upon the troops of the latter; but Abū Sa'īd did not attempt to meet them, until a large flight of crows came up from behind them; and so soon as these appeared his troops' hearts became filled with joy and courage, and falling upon those of Mirza 'Abdullāh, completely overcame them. In the defeat, Mirza 'Abdullāh was thrown off his horse and taken captive, and his head cut off."

"From the preceding may be seen the spiritual powers of a holy man, who can by their aid commune with persons widely separated from him, predict coming events, and aid those in whose welfare and success he feels a pious interest for good.

"Hasan Bahādur was one of the chiefs of the country of Māman,[1] in Turkīstān, and the people of Maman formed a numerous tribe. He relates that 'When Sultān Abū Sa'īd marched with his forces from Tāshkand to Samarqand, I was with him;

[1] Mamen in original; may be Namangan in Farghāna. The Naiman tribe can hardly be meant as they were Uighurs, though many of them were settled in Mughalistān (*v. Tārīkh-i-Rashīdī*, pp. 73-4 of Introduction).

we met Mirza 'Abdullāh on the banks of the river Bulungūr,[1] drawn up in array: I was near to the Mirza, and our troops numbered some 7000 only, whilst those of the Mirza were well armed and in excellent condition. At this moment some of our men went over to the Mirza, which troubled greatly the Sultān, and alarmed him, so that he called out to me, "Ho! Hasan, what do you see?" and I replied that I saw the Khoja (the Shaikh) preceding us. The Sultān, on this, swore by Allāh that he likewise saw him. I bade him be of good cheer, for we would prevail over our enemies. At the same moment our troops made a charge against their opponents, and in half an hour all of the forces of Mirza 'Abdullāh were beaten, and he, falling into the hands of his enemies, was put to death. On that same day Samarqand was taken.' [2]

"The Shaikh himself states that, when Mirza 'Abdullāh was taken prisoner, 'I was on my way to Tāshkand, and saw a white bird fall from a height to the ground. This was caught and killed, from which circumstance I knew that Mirza 'Abdullāh had just met his fate.' The Khoja after this proceeded, on the request of Sultān Abū Sa'īd, to Samarqand.

"Mirza Bābur[3] bin-Mirza Baikar bin Mirza Shāhrukh came with 500,000 troops from Khurāsān against Samarqand. Sultān Abū Sa'īd went to the Shaikh, and told him: 'I have not sufficient troops with which to meet him,—what shall I do?' The Shaikh quieted his apprehensions. When Mirza Bābur crossed the Āb Amūī,[4] Sultān Abū Sa'īd Mirza sent a charge of troops to meet

[1] Bulungūr is not marked on the maps. It may be Bul (lit. 'bridge' or crossing) -Akar, also called Akar Kamar, near Khojand. It is not on the direct line between Tāshkand and Samarqand, but the route between those towns appears to have crossed the Jaxartes at Khojand or a little lower down at Akar (cf. *Tārīkh-i-Rashīdī*, pp. 29 and 32).

[2] All that the *Tārīkh-i-Rashīdī* says about this event is: "Sulṭān Abū Sa'īd Mīrza, son of Sulṭān Muḥammad Mīrza, son of Mīrānshāh Mīrza, son of Amīr Tīmūr, got the upper hand of his cousins and took Samarqand from 'Abdullāh Mīrza of Shirāz" (p. 83). Still more discreet is it in its allusion to the overthrow of Mīrza Bābur, as will be seen.

[3] Not Bābur, the conqueror of India, but Mīrza Bābar Qalandar (his real name was 'Abd-ul-Qāsim Bābur), son of Mīrza Baisanghar, son of M. Shāh Rukh, after whose death, says the *Tārīkh-i-Rashīdī* curtly, "there was no pādishāh in Khurāsān" (p. 83). That Bābur could raise 500,000 men is no doubt incredible, but it is clear that his attack on Samarqand was a formidable one. Why Bābur was surnamed Qalandar is not explained.

[4] Āb Amūī, 'the river Oxus'

him, and having repulsed him, the Mirza fled to Turkīstān, and fortified himself. In this view, he loaded his camels to depart, which becoming known to the Shaikh, he hastened to go to the drivers, and, in great anger, commanded them to put off their loads ; then going to the Mirza, he asked him where he was going. 'Do not go anywhere,' he said to the Mirza, 'for there is no need of such a proceeding ; your business is here, and I will be responsible for the result ; be of good cheer, for it is my business to overcome Bābur.' Abū Sa'īd's officers were much troubled by this language on the part of the Shaikh, and some of them, throwing their turbans on the ground, declared that they would all be sacrificed. The Mirza, however, had entire faith in the Shaikh, and would not listen to any one else ; he stopped his forces, and prepared to meet those of Bābur, whose officers, nevertheless, thought that Abū Sa'īd would certainly fly before him.

"The Sultān Abū Sa'īd conformed to the words of the Shaikh and commenced fortifying himself. Mirza Bābur came near to Samarqand, and sent forward Khalīl Hindū[1] with his ordnance as far as its gates. A few Persians came out of the city and fought them. Mirza Bābur had no men in armour, and Khalīl Hindū was taken prisoner, and whenever he sent men against the strong walls of Samarqand the inhabitants made sallies, and cut off the ears and noses of all the captives who fell into their hands, so that many of his people having returned to his camp in this mutilated condition, spread alarm among the others. In the course of a few days a disease broke out among his cavalry,[2] from which many died, and spread a malaria throughout the camp, greatly to the distress and annoyance of his own people, so that very shortly he sent the Maulānā Muhammad Mu'ammā (a Shaikh)

[1] Khalīl the Indian, not the Hindoo, Khalīl being a Muhammadan name.

[2] The murrain amongst Mīrza Bābur's horses was attributed to the saint 'Ubaid-Ullah. Similarly, when Sulṭān Maḥmūd, the younger son of Abū Sa'īd, besieged his brother Sulṭān Aḥmad in Samarqand the saint caused a typhoon which came from the Qipchāq Desert and compelled him to raise the siege. The version of the *Rashaḥāt* in the text suggests that the author is still speaking of Sa'īd-ud-Dīn Kāshgharī, but the murrain among the horses was the work of 'Ubaid-Ullah, the Khwāja Aḥrār, who survived Sulṭān Abū Sa'īd many years. That ruler died in 873 H. (A.D. 1469), and Khwāja Aḥrār lived till 1490 at least. In 1511 he appeared to the emperor Bābur in a dream and assured him that he would capture Samarqand from the Uzbegs (*J.R.A.S.* 1916, p. 69). That must have been after his death.

to our own Shaikh to treat for peace. Maulānā Muhammad, on meeting our Shaikh, greatly praised the Mirza Bābur, and said he was a prince of the most exalted sentiments ; and our Shaikh, in response, told him that the acts of his forefathers had done him much harm, and without this he might have effected great things ; that, in their time, he himself was a poor *faqīr* in Herāt, together with a great number of similar persons, all of whom suffered much from their persecutions. Finally, peace was made,[1] and Mirza Bābur made it a matter of stipulation that he should be permitted to concilate the goodwill and profit by the prayers of our pious Shaikh, from whose spiritual powers he had met with so much loss and discomfiture."

In the same work there are further statements regarding the spiritual powers of this celebrated Shaikh. He claimed to be able to affect the minds of the sovereigns in such a manner as to compel them to conform to his will, and even to leave their thrones and seek a refuge at his feet. This power is called *taskhīr*, or the 'subduing faculty'. The Shaikh says of himself: "Were I to live as a Shaikh, none other would have any *murīds* or disciples ; but my business is to preserve Mussulmans from the evils of oppression. On this account I am in conflict with sovereigns, and must therefore compel them to conform to my demands, and so promote the welfare and interests of the true believers. Through the especial favour of the Most High, a strength or power is given to me by which, should I desire it, the Sovereign of Khatai, who assumes to be a god, would obey a letter from me, and, leaving his kingdom, come barefooted after forsaking his kingdom, and seek the sill of my door. Although I possess so much power, I am wholly submissive to the will of the Most High ; and whenever it is a matter referring to the will, His command reaches me, and

[1] This reconciliation between Mīrza Bābur and Sulṭān Abū Sa'īd is not alluded to in the *Tārīkh-i-Rashīdī*, nor does it explain who the Maulāna Muḥammad Mu'amma was. *Mu'amma* means 'enigma', and Maulānā Sharaf-ud-Dīn Yazdī, author of the *Zafar-nāma*, had introduced a new kind of problem, apparently astronomical, before his death in 1454 (*Tārīkh-i-Rashīdī*, pp. 84-5). It was the fashion about this time for every Sulṭān to have one of Ḥazrat Maulāna's disciples for a spiritual guide, but who the guide of Mīrza Bābur was is not mentioned (*ib.* p. 213). Shahāb-ud-Dīn Mu'ammaī, 'the Punster', was a poet who also wrote a book of enigmas. He accompanied the Emperor Bābur to India, where he died in 942 H., A.D. 1535 (Beale, *Or. Biog. Dy.* p. 360).

it assumes a bodily form. For this, great moral sentiment is essential, and it is this which subdues my will to the superior one of the Most High, so that it is His will which ensures justice."

A person relates that he was once a spectator of a scene between the Shaikh and Sultān Ahmad Mirza, in the village of Mātrīd.[1] The latter had called to make a visit to the Shaikh, and they were both seated near to each other, the Shaikh composedly conversing with the Sultān, but the latter was so much under the influence of his 'subduing power' that great fear and alarm were clearly visible in his features, and large drops of perspiration flowed down his face, whilst his whole frame was singularly convulsed. This fact has been sustained by the testimony of witnesses, and its truthfulness is strongly corroborated. Then follows an account of the reunion of three princes through the powers of the Shaikh, and the subduing to peace of these and all their forces by a kind of spell.[2] The warlike spirits of these were wonderfully calmed, and kept in perfect subjection, until a formal document of pacification was drawn up by the Shaikh and signed by the princes.

On another occasion an employee of the Shaikh, whilst travelling in Khatai with a *karwān* (caravan) laden with goods, was attacked by Kalmucks, and through the wonderful powers of a sword belonging to the Shaikh, his pious master, he put the whole band of robbers to flight when all of his companions had given themselves up as lost. On his return, having related this surprising affair to the Shaikh, the latter explained it to him, by the fact that, having submitted his own feeble will to that of the Most High, a superhuman 'power of the will' was granted him, by which he overcame his enemies.

Many individuals who have seriously wronged and oppressed his friends received punishments through the powers of the Shaikh. Several instances are related wherein some such even fell sick and died, or were only restored to health by open declaration of repentance, and imploring his prayerful intercession with God. His spirit seems to have accompanied those in whose welfare he took an active interest, and enabled them to commune with him, though far distant from him. His power of hearing

[1] Mātrīd, Mātarīd, the quarter of Samarqand, which gave his title to Abū Manṣūr Mātarīdī of Samarqand (p. 379 *infra*).

[2] This is the incident fully described in Beveridge's article in *J.R.A.S.* 1916, pp. 70 ff.

them was well known to his friends, and several instances are cited to prove the fact. His power of affecting the health of those who injured him or his friends was greatly increased whilst he was excited by anger, and on such occasions his whole frame would be convulsed, and his beard move about as if moved by electricity. On learning details of cruelty done to innocent individuals, the Shaikh would be strangely affected, so much so that no one dared to address him until the paroxysm was passed; and on such occasions he never failed to commune spiritually with the sovereign or prince in such a mysterious manner, as to inspire him to deal justly with the guilty person, and secure his merited punishment.

Through his ' mystical powers ' many persons were impressed with the unrighteousness of their course, and having repented of the same, became good and pious and firm believers in his spiritual influences. These powers were always connected with his prayers, and it was during these that he was enabled to assure the parties interested of their salutary results, and the acceptation of their desires. It scarcely needs to be added that these prayers were in conformance with Islamism, and were offered up to Allah, whom he adored, and to whose supreme will he attributes his powers. He constantly performed the *zikr jihrī*, or ' audibly called God's name ', and the frequent repetition of this practice fitted him for such holy purposes. Sometimes he would affect the mind of the individual upon whom he exercised his powers, in such a manner as to throw him into a species of trance, after which he could remember nothing that he had previously known, and continued in this state until the Shaikh chose to restore him to the enjoyment of his ordinary faculties. Notwithstanding all of these eminent powers, this great Shaikh is reputed to have spent the latter days of his life at Herāt in extreme indigence, much slighted and neglected by those who had so admired him whilst in the vigour of his career. All fear of his mystical influences seems to have disappeared, and it is narrated that these greatly declined with his ordinary strength of mind and body.

APPENDICES TO CHAPTER VI

A. Precursors of the Naqshbandī and Allied Orders

A consideration of the known dates given in square brackets shows at once that this passage is a very inexact account of the sequence of the teachers mentioned in it. Khurqānī could hardly have been in the actual service of Bāyazīd, seeing that the latter must have been dead many years before he was born, as indeed the text itself admits.

To give the sequence in more exact order :

Abū Yazīd Ṭaifūr b. 'Isā al-Bisṭāmī, or b. 'Īsā b. Ādam b. Surūshān, died in 261 H. (A.D. 875), or two or three years later. His grandfather was a Magian, but little is known of him except that he led an ascetic life. Legend has deduced from his biography that he ascended to heaven (*mi'rāj*). He was clearly a convinced pantheist and probably the first to introduce the doctrine of *fanā'* (*nirvāna* in Buddhism) into Moslem thought. His followers are called Ṭaifūria or Bisṭāmīa (*E.I.* i. p. 686). His teacher was an Indian, one Abū 'Alī as-Sindī (R. Hartmann, *Der Islam*, vi. p. 43).

Abū 'Alī Muḥammad b. al-Qāsim al-Rudbārī died in 322 H. (A.D. 934). But he had a sister's son, Abū Abdullah Aḥmad b. 'Aṭā Rudbārī, who was also called Abū 'Alī al-Rudbārī and who may be meant. He lived at Sūr and died in 369 H. (A.D. 980) (Nicholson, *Kitāb al-Lumā'*, p. xviii and *n.* 1 on p. xix).

Abū 'Uṣmān Sa'īd b. Ismā'īl al-Maghribī died in 373 H. (A.D. 984). Some of his teaching was influenced by that of Manṣūr al-Hallāj (L. Massignon, *Kitāb al-Ṭawāsīn*, pp. 127, 161, 163-4, and 171).

Abū'l Ḥasan 'Alī b. Aḥmad al-Khurqānī, 'of Khurqān' (or Karraqān), successor of Abū Sa'īd, doubtless the Grand Shaikh Abū Sa'īd b. Abī'l-Khair Fazl-ullāh b. Muḥammad al-Maihanī, and like him one who looked upon Manṣūr al-Hallāj with favour (Nicholson, *Kashf al-Maḥjūb*, pp. 163 and 150). Abū'l Ḥasan died in 435 H. (A.D. 1034), or ten years earlier (M. Hartmann, *Der islamische Orient*, vi.-x. p. 308). An earlier Abū'l Ḥusain Kharqānī, author of the *Sharḥ-i-Makhzan al-Asrār* and *Mirāt al-Muhaqqiqīn*, containing explanations of the Ṣūfī rites of initiation and rules of the order, had died in 378 H. = A.D. 986 (Beale, *Or. Biogr. Dy.* 25).

Abū'l Qāsim 'Alī b. 'Abdullah al-Gurgānī died in 450 H. (A.D. 1058), or in 469 H. Nicholson regards the later date as the more probable (*Kashf al-Maḥjūb*, p. xix).

Here again we find discrepancies in the filiation, due possibly to doctrinal dissensions within the order. One authority omits this Abū'l Qāsim from the chain, but mentions him as a pupil of Khurqānī with the title of Ibn 'Abd-ul-Wāḥid. It also makes him affiliated to Junaid and through him to 'Alī (M. Hartmann, *op. cit.*, p. 308).

" From them," says the text, " came the spiritual powers of Junaid," etc. But this should read : To them came these powers from Junaid, d. A.D. 910, Saqaṭī, d. 871, Ma'rūf Karkhī, d. 816, and Dā'ūd Tā'ī, d. 782 (*v.* notes on p. 50 *supra*). Habīb Sajami can only be the Habīb 'Ajamī of p. 50, *n. supra* ; but as he is styled a teacher of Ḥasan of Baṣra it is more likely that

Habīb al-Rā'ī is meant. The latter was a companion of Salmān Fārsī, and his full name was Abū Halim Ḥabīb b. Sālim al-Rā'ī. He had flocks of sheep and his home was on the Euphrates. Unfortunately the only information we have about him is that he was miraculously supplied with milk and honey in the wilderness, while a wolf looked after his sheep (Nicholson, *Kashf al-Maḥjūb*, p. 90).

Ḥasan Baṣrī appears in the original as ' Hasan Basāree ', so it is not impossible that Ḥasan of Baṣra is not intended at all. If so, it is not easy to say whose identity is disguised under this name. One Abū'l-Ḥusain Baṣrī may be the Abū'l-Ḥasan al-Ḥuṣrī, a native of Baṣra who resided at Baghdād and died in 371 H. (A.D. 982), but he was a pupil of Shiblī, not of Ḥabīb (*v.* Nicholson, *Kitāb al-Luma'*, p. xvii). Baṣrī was also a title of ibn Sālim, the founder of the Sālimīs (*ib.* p. xix).

It is interesting to compare this ' apostolical succession ' with that of the communist Shaikh Badr-ud-Dīn Maḥmūd b. Isrā'īl b. 'Abd-ul-'Azīz, whose grave is at Seres in Macedonia, where he was hanged in A.D. 1416. It begins with Junaid, and Abū 'Alī Aḥmad, ar-Rudbārī is described as his successor under the curious variant, 'Alī Da'ūdbārī. After him come:

Abū 'Alī b. al-Kātib, who died post 340 H. (A.D. 951).
[Abū 'Oṣmān al-Maghribī, who died in A.D. 983.]
Abū'l Qāsim 'Alī al-Gurgānī.

Then the succession diverges from that of the Naqshbandīs and we have:

Abū Bakr Nassāj, ' the Weaver ', who died in 487 H. (A.D. 1094).
Aḥmad Ghazālī, who died in 517 H. (A.D. 1123).
Abū'l Faẓl Ibrāhīm of Baghdād.
Abū'l Barakāt of Baghdād.
Abū Sa'd of Andalusia.
Abū Madyan Shu'aib b. al-Ḥusain, also of Andalusia, who died in 594 H. (A.D. 1197).
Abū'l-Fatḥ as-Sa'īdī.
Ḥusain of Akhlāt.
Badr-ud-Dīn.

Although this Badr-ud-Dīn is not mentioned by Brown his activities are of cardinal importance in the history of Islam in Turkey. The succession given above is due to a modern writer (Meḥmed Ṭahir, author of the *'Osmānli Mu'ellifleri*) who does not indicate the sources whence it is taken. According to other authorities Badr-ud-Dīn was a descendant of the Saljūqian Sultāns. His father lived in Simāw, near Kutahia, and in spite of his descent was made *qāzī* of Simāw by Murād I. Badr-ud-Dīn received an excellent education and went as a youth to Egypt, where he studied under several well-known philosophers and jurists, chiefly of the Hanafite school. There, too, he may well have met Ḥusain of Akhlāt, a Ṣūfī of that Armenian town, whom he is said to have succeeded in the headship of the Ṣūfī order. This biography may not be devoid of historical fact, but it fails to bring out the probable truth that Badr-ud-Dīn was compelled to seek an asylum in Egypt from the Mughal inroads, just as Ḥusain certainly was. His subsequent career shows that he was employed as a Qāzī 'askarī, or judge of the forces, but eventually banished. In that office he acquired considerable influence in Rumelia, but he had, also in that capacity, a much more dangerous man in his employ. This was Muṣṭafā the Bürklüja, 'the small cap man ', who was his *kat-khudā* or *kiāya*, ' intendant ', and preached *ibāḥa*, the doctrine of communism with respect to all property save women. He also claimed the *wilāyat*, and his followers set him above the prophets. They abjured the wearing of the *zarkūla* or gold-embroidered cap, went bareheaded, and wore but a single garment. A leaning to, or at least a policy of union with, the Christians was undoubtedly part of their programme, but it is impossible to say how far it was based on genuine toleration and how far on the desire to obtain material support in their designs. What those were is equally obscure. The *zarkūla* or *uskūf*, as von Hammer calls it, became later on the headdress of the Janissary officers. It was prescribed by Murād I. as the head-covering of his courtiers (*Geschichte des osmanischen Reiches* (2), i. p. 156). It could hardly have been worn by the Anatolian peasantry or even by Bürklüja Muṣṭafā, himself an ordinary Turkish farmer. Its rejection looks like a protest against the Ottoman court, its luxury or extravagance. Possibly Muṣṭafā acquired his name by declining to wear a *zarkūla* even as an official. But all this is conjectural. All that seems certain is that Muṣṭafā raised a dangerous movement in Western Asia Minor, that though Badr-ud-Dīn took no active part in it he claimed Muṣṭafā as his servant, and escaping from his place of banishment (Isnīq) went to Rumelia to raise there also the standard of revolt. Badr-ud-Dīn was also in touch with another rebel, Ṭorlāq Hū Kamāl, or the Jew Ṭorlāq Kamāl, as he is called by some writers. Nothing certain is known about this sectary's names, aims, or principles, but Hans Löwenklau, the founder of Turkish studies in Europe, equates the Ṭorlāq-lar or followers of Ṭorlāq with the Dūrmish-lar, a body otherwise unknown. *Ṭorlāq* means ' untamed, untaught ', but it appears to have no connection with ṭūrmaq, from *ṭur-*, which may be connected with Durmish (*v.* note on p. 468 *infra*).

Where so much is obscure, the following points may be noted: Both Muṣṭafā and Ṭorlāq were put to death, but their graves are apparently forgotten. Their followers were exterminated and their tenets were never revived. Badr-ud-Dīn, on the contrary, was buried by his followers in a tomb built of stone, with a pyramid like the Saljūqian *gunbaz* or dome. But his cult is not popular.

B. The Suhrawardi Order and its Disciples

The first al-Suhrawardī was Abū'l Najīb 'Abd al-Qāhir b. 'Abdullah al-Suhrawardī, the well-known author of the *Ādāb al-Murīdīn*, ' Manners of the Disciples ', who died in 563 H. (A.D. 1167), leaving two sons, 'Abd al-Raḥīm and 'Abd al-Laṭīf, according to Nicholson, *Kitāb al-Luma'* (p. xl). He was also the author of a collection of anecdotes concerning Shāfi'ī (Wüstenfeld, *Der Imam Schafi'i*, p. 8).

Brown's authorities averred that Abū'l Najīb founded the Nūrbakhshīs, and that Shihāb-ud-Dīn Suhrawardī, who died at Baghdād in 1206, founded the Suhrawardīs. The latter statement is not based on the authority of Atāyi, who says that this Shihāb-ud-Dīn founded the Nūrbakhshīs, and places his death a year earlier, in 1205 = 602 H. (von Hammer,

GdOR., i. p. 139). It is usually held that the Nūrbakhshīs, Suhrawardīs, and Ishrāqīs were identical, and it is self-evident that they were closely akin; but Brown may be correct in drawing a distinction here, though on p. 82 he makes the Suhrawardīs the same as the Nūrbakhshīs. The Ishrāqīs apparently owed their foundation to another (?) Shihāb-ud-Dīn, surnamed Qatīl-ullah, Suhrawardī, of Aleppo, the Maqtūl, so known because he was executed at that city in A.D. 1191, at the age of thirty-eight. Belonging originally to the Shāfi'ī school, which was then regarded as of very doubtful orthodoxy, he studied jurisprudence at Maragha, but subsequently devoted himself to philosophy at Ispahān, Baghdād, and Aleppo. He set forth the tenets of his sect, the Ishrāqiūn or 'Illuminati', in his work, the *Ḥikmat al-Ishrāq*, 'the Philosophy of Enlightment'. He also wrote the *Kalimāt al-Taṣawwaf*, 'Precepts of Mysticism'. At Aleppo he found a powerful patron in the Viceroy Malik Zāhir, son of Saladin, but the influence of the orthodox party secured his condemnation. His grave is still pointed out at a spot outside the al-Faraj Gate close to the Christian quarter (A. von Kremer, *Gescht. der herrschenden Ideen des Islams*, p. 90, and Dr. F. Babinger in *Der Islam*, xi. p. 73; also L. Massignon, *Kitāb al-Ṭawāsīn*, p. xviii). After this event the scene changes to Baghdād, where in 632 H. (A.D. 1234–35) died Shihāb-ud-Dīn Suhrawardī or 'Umar al-Suhrawardī, the founder, according to one Indian tradition, of the Suhrawardīs. Another ascribes it to Sh. Ziā-ud-Dīn, a son of Abū'l Najīb, and yet a third to Abū'l Najīb himself. Probably Abu'l Najīb's unorthodox views and the condemnation of Shihāb-ud-Dīn (which we need not decide) rendered it dangerous to use the term Ishrāqī or to assign the foundation of the order to them, so it was content to be known by more colourless titles. In any case the real founder of the order or orders was doubtless Abū'l Najīb. One of his sons or immediate descendants carried his teaching into India, where the Nizām of Haidarābād claims descent from Shihāb-ud-Dīn.

There is considerable disagreement as to the chronology of the Suhrawardīs and their descent. Beale makes Shihāb-ud-Dīn I. a son of Abū'l Njaīb, and assigning his birth to 539 H. (A.D. 1145) extends his life to 632 H. (A.D. 1234), when he died at Baghdād in his ninety-third year. To him he ascribes the *Awārif al-Ma'ārif* and the *Awārif al-Haqā'iq*, adding that he is said to have written the *Ḥikmat al-Ishrāq* as well. The death of Shihāb-ud-Dīn II. he assigns to 585 H. (A.D. 1189) at Aleppo, and his condemnation to Saladin himself. He calls his Commentaries the *Sharah Hayākal* and the *Sharah Ayzāh*, adding that according to Hājī Khalfā he also wrote a work styled the *Aql Surkh* (*v. Oriental Biographical Dict.*, p. 360).

Massignon speaks of the school of Suhrawardī of Aleppo as 'émanatiste, *ishrāq*' (*La passion d'al-Hosayn-ibn-Mansour al-Hallaj*, ii. p. 561).

The *ishrāqiūn* made the Hellenistic invocation to Him Who causalises Beings, but is not Himself causalised, go back to Plato (Massignon, *La passion d'al-Hosayn-ibn-Mansour al-Hallaj*, ii. p. 641, citing Bahā 'Amilī, *Kashkūl*, 284, 330).

One ''Omar bin Yasserbedlissee', in original, Shaikh 'Umar Yazīr, founded a school or order to which belonged the mystic Ḥusām ud-Dīn. The latter's son, Maulāna Idrīs Ḥakīm ud-Dīn Bidlīsī (of Bitlīs in Turkish Armenia), served first in the chancellory of Ya'qūb, son of Uzun Ḥasan, Sulṭān of the

Turcomans of the White Sheep (died in 1490–91), but he was induced to enter the Ottoman service and attained fame as a soldier and historian, dying in 1520. Shaikh 'Umar Yazīr must thus have been earlier than the fifteenth century (cf. *E.I.* i. p. 715). As to Ḥusām-ud-Dīn, Evliya says he had a disciple, one Er Sultān, who was born at Angora, where he was also buried, and whose place of pilgrimage is Hīzr, on a high mountain east of Angora. When imprisoned at Angora he gave the order for his burial, and next morning was found washed and perfumed for it, a story which suggests that he was persecuted and secretly put to death. Suicide can hardly be hinted at (*Travels*, ii. p. 234). Evliya calls him "the leader of divine truth, the discoverer of mysteries". He also tells a story of a dream in which he was visited by a man with a yellow beard, honey-coloured cowl, and a turban of twelve folds, in whom we ought to have no difficulty in recognising Sārī ('yellow') Sāltik, 'the blond apostle', who is known at Angora as Er Sultān (*Travels*, ii. p. 232).

Najm-ud-Dīn Kubrā (or Qubrā according to some authorities) was Abū'l Jannab Aḥmad b. 'Umar al-Khiwaqi (of Khiva or Khwārazm), commonly known as Shaikh Najm-ud-Dīn Kubrā. Kubrā is said to be an abbreviation of his nickname at-Tammatu'l-Kubra, 'the supreme calamity', given to him on account of his great vigour in debate. The title of Abū'l-Jannab was given to him by the Prophet in a dream to denote that he was to sedulously avoid the world. He was also nicknamed Walī-tirāsh, 'the Saint-carver', because any one on whom his glance fell in moments of ecstasy was believed to attain to the degree of saintship; and this influence extended to the animal world. He wrote in Persian the *Sifatu'l-Adāb*, 'the Rules of Conduct', for Ṣūfī neophytes. On p. 268 *infra* his death is assigned to the year 1220, but it seems certain that he was massacred by the Mongols of Chingiz Khān at Khwārazm in the following year. He had many disciples, including Sh. Abū Sa'īd Majd-ud-Dīn, Sharaf b. al-Mu'ayyad b. Abi'l-Fatḥ al-Baghdādī (d. 1209 or 1219), Sh. Sa'd-ud-Dīn Hamawi of Hamat (d. 1253), Bābā Kamak of Jand, Sh. Raziyyu'd-Dīn 'Alī Lāla, Sh. Saif-ud-Dīn Bakharzī, Sh. Najm-ud-Dīn of Rāī, Sh. Jamāl-ud-Dīn of Gīlān, and, as some assert, Bahā-ud-Dīn Walad himself. On p. 268 *infra* Najm-ud-Dīn Kubrā is said to have founded an order of his own, the Kubrāwīs, but a tradition current in India makes him the founder of an order called Firdausi, a designation hard to explain. The 'Alī b. Sa'īd Lālā of the text is probably Raziyyu'd-Din 'Alī Lāla, and he may have continued the Nurbakhshī tradition (*v.* E. G. Browne, *A Literary Hist. of Persia*, ii. pp. 491 ff.).

A disciple of Najm-ud-Dīn was the poet and mystic Sh. Saif-ud-Dīn Bakharzī, of Bakharz in Khurāsān, who died in A.D. 1260 (Cl. Huart, *Les Saints des Derviches tourneurs*, p. 239).

'Amīr Sulṭān, Shams-ud-Dīn Muḥammad b. 'Alī al-Ḥusainī al-Bukhārī, also called Saiyid Muḥammad Bukhārī, Saiyid Amīr Sulṭān, and Amīr Saiyid, was born about 770 H. (A.D. 1369). Evliya says he was born at Bukhāra, and that on visiting Madīna he was refused recognition by the Sharīfs, but obtained it when a voice from the Prophet's tomb acknowledged him as a descendant of Muḥammad and bade him go to Rūm 'with the lamp'. He settled at Brūsa, where he made 400,000 disciples. He married Nilūfar Khānum, daughter of the Sulṭān Bāyazīd Ilderīm, and died at

Brūsa in 833 H., A.D. 1429 (*Travels*, ii. pp. 25-6). Such alliances between saints and daughters of ruling princes are a commonplace of religious tradition, but this union is said to be a historical fact (*E.I.* i. p. 900, *s.v.* Dāmād). The name of the princess is, however, given as Khūndī Sulṭān by other authorities (*ib.* ii. p. 26). It seems certain that he played an important part as a mediator in the invasion of Tīmūr. Tradition also says that when Bāyazīd I. (Ilderīm), the actual conqueror of Qaramania, had been recognised as Sulṭān of Rūm by the Caliph he granted the privilege of girding on his sword to his son-in-law 'Shaikh Bukhāra, surnamed Amīr Sultān'. That title was, however, bestowed in him on account of his learning, according to Miss L. M. J. Garnett (*Mysticism and Magic in Turkey*, pp. 167 and 33).

The Amīr Bukhāra of the text below (p. 142) is clearly another title of this Amīr Sulṭān. Three 'Amīr Bukhāra' *takias* at Constantinople are or were until recently held by the Naqshbandīs (*v.* pp. 470, 471, and 472 *infra*, and fourth in Stambūl, p. 470). But 'Amīr Sulṭān' is also said to be one of the titles of the Shaikh of the Maulavīs (Hasluck, *Annual*, B.S.A. xix. p. 210). The splendid mausoleum of the Amīr Sulṭān Shams-ud-Dīn at Brūsa is one of the most popular places of pilgrimage of Islam. He must not be confused with another 'Amīr Sulṭān', or 'Amīr Effendi' as he is generally called, Shaikh Uṣmān of Siwās, who was a Bairāmī and is buried at Kūlāksīz (*Evliya*, i. part 2, p. 48).

He must also be distinguished from Shams-ud-Dīn Bukhārī, so named from his Persian birth. He was the leading Shaikh of the reign of Muḥammad II. (1451–81), and is also claimed by the Naqshbandī as one of their principals, a disciple of Sh. Alahī. The convent of Sh. 'Bukhāra', still one of the most famed Naqshbandī cloisters at Constantinople, was called after him (Hammer-Purgstall, *GdOD.*, i. p. 211).

Ilahi brought Sh. Bukhārī (also known as Amīr Bukhārī) from Bukhāra to Constantinople, where he died in 922 H., A.D. 1516-17 (Gibb, *Hist. of Ott. Poetry*, ii. p. 374).

Muḥammad Bukhāra, as Sārī Sāltuk (or -ik) Dede was commonly called, was a disciple of Aḥmad Yasawī, who sent him with 700 men of Khurāsān to assist Ḥājī Baqtāsh on his mission to raise the Janissaries. Baqtāsh sent him into the Dobrūja with 70 men, and there he killed the dragon in the caves of Kilgra, and converted the king of the Dobrūja with 40,000 men. Sāltuk Muḥammad then went in disguise to Poland to kill the monk Sārī Sāltuk—whose name he took and dwelt in his cell. The new Sārī Sāltuk converted all the Lipka-Tatars to Islam, extended his conquests to Dantzig, and thence pushed his inroads towards Moscovy. He is now the patron saint of the makers of *buza* or beer, but Evliya disputes this saying that Sārī Sāltuk-Dedeh was a great saint (*Travels*, i. part 2, p. 245). Further on he extends the saint's itinerary from the Dobrūja to Wallachia, Moldavia, Poland, and Russia (ii. p. 21). This personage seems purely legendary.

CHAPTER VII

THE BAQTĀSHĪS [1]—THEIR COSTUME—THEIR TWELVE IMĀMS—THE INITIATION OF A BAQTĀSH

THE Darvishes bearing this denomination derived it from the name of the founder of the *tarīq*, or ' path '. He was a native of Bukhāra. It would seem that there were two persons of this name, Baqtāsh, the preceding one adding to his name *qūlī*, or 'servant' (of God), and was the author of a mystical work called *Būstān-al-Khiāl* (' *The Garden of Mental Reflection* '), in much repute among spiritual Mussulmans. The other is called Hājī Baqtāsh, and lived [2] in Asia Minor during the reign of the Ottoman

[1] The word Baqtāsh is so spelt by many good authorities, but it appears to be frequently pronounced Bagtāsh or Begtāsh. Its meaning is obscure. Its original form may have been Betesh or Petesh, but George of Hungary, writing in the middle of the fifteenth century, called the saint Hartschi Petesch, and his transliteration of the second word may have been as inaccurate as his transformation of Hājī into ' Hartschi '. Leake says the Bektāshlī are so called from a Cappadocian saint who wore a stone upon his navel, so the derivation from *geubek-tāsh*, lit. 'navel-stone', may be more than a false etymology, though Hasluck did not accept it (*Annual*, B.S.A. xx. p. 105). It may be noted that in the *Gulistān* Baktāsh appears as the name of a prudent man; it is also said to be the name of a king of Khwārazm; so it may be a proper name, connoting the power of foreknowledge. Redhouse defines *bek tāsh* (no *q*) as ' an equal in birth, station, or rank ; or rather an equal with a prince '. In Turkish -tāsh (dāsh) in compounds means ' companion ', as in *Khwāja-tāsh*, ' a fellow pupil '. A stone is *ṭash* (*Turk. and Eng. Lex.* pp. 395 and 477).

[2] The text here patently requires correction. 763 H. = A.D 1362. For ' lived ' should be read ' died '. But it is very doubtful if Baqtāsh lived into the reign of Murād I. According to a Turkish writer he died in 738 H. (A.D. 1337-38), and that is the traditional date of his death (*J.R.A.S.*, 1907, p. 535, and Hasluck in *B.S.A.* xx. p. 96). Evliya is quite explicit in his assertions that Ḥājī Baqtāsh was a historical personage. After 'Uṣmān

sovereign, Sultān Murād I. [1360–89] in 763 H. As this Order of Darvishes was intimately connected with the Ottoman militia [1] known as the Janissaries, now destroyed, some particular notice of him seems necessary, even in a work like the present.

Historians narrate that Hājī Baqtāsh or Bagtāsh blessed the newly instituted troops, and named them *Yanī Cherī*, or 'New Troops' (the signification of the word 'Janissaries'), whilst others dispute it. Von Hammer says they adopted for a head-dress the white felt cap of the Darvish Hājī Bagtāsh, the founder of an order spread over the Ottoman empire ; that the Sultān Orkhan, accompanied by the new renegades (of whom the Janissaries were composed), met him in the village of Sulijay Kenariyūn, near to Amasia, to implore his benediction, and the gifts of a standard and a flag for his new forces. The Shaikh put the sleeve of his mantle over the head of one of the soldiers in such a manner that it hung down behind his back, and then declared the following prophecy : "The militia which you have just created shall be called *Yanī Cherī*,—its figure shall be fair and shining, its arm redoubtable, its sword cutting, and its arrow steeled. It shall be victorious in all battles, and never return except triumphant." In commemoration of this benediction, the white felt cap of the Janissaries was increased by the addition of a piece of the same pendant on their backs, and ornamented with a wooden spoon. As most of the Janissaries were incorporated into the Order of the Baqtāshes, they formed a military fraternity, of which all the members were, at the same time, monks and soldiers, differing but little from the Knights of the Temple, the Hospital, and of Malta. It is possible that the approximity of the Knights of Rhodes, whose galleys aided the first crusaders to seize upon Smyrna during the reign of Sultān Orkhan, may have inspired this prince with the idea of uniting the renegade soldiers into a

had thrice laid siege to Brūsa without success, he sent his son Orkhān with Ḥājī Baqtāsh to renew the siege, and in 1322 it surrendered. Orkhān entered the city with the Ḥājī and there fixed his residence (*Travels*, ii. pp. 3-4). But Evliya adds that Ḥājī Begtāsh died in the reign of Orkhān and was buried in that ruler's presence in the capital of Crimea (surely Qaramānia), where his tomb was restored by one Shaitān Beg in the time of Sulṭān Sulaimān (*ib.* p. 21). Unfortunately, Evliya is not chronologically trustworthy, for he assigns Orkhān's death to 771 H. (A.D. 1369), whereas he died in 1360, or at all events ceased to reign in that year (cf. p. 19).

[1] See Appendix to this chapter.

monical-military corps, under the patronage of the Shaikh Hājī Baqtāsh. There was also this remarkable fact connected with his Order, that the Shaikh who directed it was at the same time Colonel of the 99th Regiment, and that eight of his Darvishes established in the barracks of the Janissaries offered up prayers there day and night for the prosperity of the empire and the success of the arms of their companions, who called themselves of the family of Hājī Baqtāsh.

The preceding is, however, denied in the Ottoman history of 'Āshiq Pāshā-Zāda,[1] of which the following extract has been furnished me by Dr. Mordtmann: "I have not included Hājī Baqtāsh among the list of the *'ulamā* and *fuqrā* of Rūm wilāyat, because, unlike the others, he had never any connection with the Ottoman Sultāns. Hājī Baqtāsh came from Khorāsān, with his brother Mantish,[2] and they established themselves at Siwās (in

[1] A MS. of his History is in the Vatican, and J. von Hammer published a study on him in *Journal Asiatique*, vol. iv. He wrote in the reign of Bāyazīd I., and his work is the nearest approach to an Ottoman source for the fourteenth century (H. A. Gibbons, *The Foundation of the Ottoman Empire*, pp. 327, 341).

[2] 'His brother Mentish'. No other allusion to any brother of Ḥājī Baqtāsh can be traced. The name also appears in the form Mintash (the all-powerful minister who dethroned Sulṭān Barqūq of Damascus, but was defeated in A.D. 1389, was so named: *E.I.* i. p. 908). One of the Turkish amirates of the fourteenth century, a modern *sanjāq*, was called Mentesh. Its founder, who gave his name to this amirate, was a contemporary of Orkhān, and during the latter part of his reign and that of Murād the '*amīr* of Menteshe' possessed great influence (H. A. Gibbons, *The Foundation of the Ottoman Empire*, p. 294). In later times the *dere beys* of Mentesh enjoyed a feudal jurisdiction under the Sulṭāns, and when it was broken up this "very ill-known Carian region" was rendered peculiarly uninviting by brigandage, and further exploration of it became difficult (D. G. Hogarth, *Ionia and the East*, p. 103).

The name Mentish may, however, be quite unconnected with the founder of Mentesh. Ḥājī Baqtāsh had a disciple called Khoja Aḥmad, by name Haidar, who travelled with him to Cæsarea and there took to wife a Christian named Mēnĕ. The whole village of the Hājī's burial-place claims descent from this pair, and Hasluck suggests that the Christian occupant (real or imaginary) of the site was S. Menas, who, on account of the popular derivation of his name from μηνύω, is looked on by the Orthodox as the revealer of things hidden (*Annual*, B.S.A. xx. p. 120). But the same writer mentions "the tribe of Mentish (which) eventually gave its name to the *qazā* of Mūghla in Caria, but can be traced by villages bearing its name right across Asia Minor from the Siwās district westward. In tradition Mentish figures as the brother of Hājī Bektāsh [Brown is cited as the authority], who was

Asia Minor), near to Bābā Iliās. At a later period they went to Kaisaria, from which place his brother returned to their own country by Siwās, and was killed on the way. Baqtāsh, whilst on his way from Kaisaria to the Kaza Ujuk,[1] died, and was interred there, where his holy tomb still exists.[2] The people of Rūm are divided into four classes of *musāfirs*[3] (guests),—one, *Ghāziyān-i-Rūm*, or the 'Heroes of Rūm'; one *Akhīān* [*Akhwān*]-*i-Rūm*,[4] or the 'Brothers of Rūm'; and the other, the *Abdālān-i-Rūm*, or the '*Abdāls* or ascetes of Rūm'.[5] There is also one more branch, called the *Ham-Bājiyān-i-Rūm*, or the 'Sisters of Rūm'.[6] Hājī Baqtāsh chose the *Bājiyān-i-Rūm* among the

---

himself probably before his usurpation by the Hurūfī sect no more than a tribal ancestor" ("Heterodox Tribes of Asia Minor", in *J. Anthrop. Inst.*, 1921, p. 319).

[1] 'The Kazā Ujuk' should be Suluja Qarā Uyuk or Yuk. This was the place which Aḥmad Yasawī bestowed saintship on the Ḥājī, and where the mother-convent of the Bektāsh was subsequently built.

[2] See Appendix to this chapter.

[3] *Musāfir*, itinerant, as opposed to *muqīm*, 'resident' (Nicholson, *Kashf ul-Maḥjūb*, p. 340).

[4] The Akhwān, a sect founded recently in Central Arabia, has revived the use of the white cap, claiming that it was the original Arab head-dress, and that the '*aqal* worn over the *kaffiyah* or usual woollen head-dress is of Persian origin and an invention of the Shī'a heretics. The *akh* or 'brother' practises extreme simplicity of life and costume, and says there is no difference between the *mudaiyin* or adherent of his sect and the Wahhābī (*Pioneer Mail*, June 4, 1920).

[5] The fourfold division is characteristic of many Oriental schemes of social and religious organisation (J. von Hammer, *GdOR.* (2), i. p. 583). The Ghāzī corresponds to the militant member of a Christian Order, and the *abdāl* probably to one who has taken the full vows. The position of the *akhī* is less easy to define. At the close of the fourteenth century the term was applied to the great landowners of Galatia, who had taken Angora, but were overthrown by Murād I. (J. von Hammer, *GdOR.* i. p. 144). The word then may here denote a lay brother, though in general it means or implies 'brother' in the spiritual sense.

[6] Rājī, 'sister', Turk. Hambājī is not given in Redhouse's *T.-E. Lex.*, but it appears to mean 'companion-sister'. Strictly speaking, *bājī* = 'elder sister', or even colloquially 'spouse'. The Bājī-lar were members of a women's sect in Asia Minor (Tschudi in *Türk. Bib.*, No. 17, p. 20).

For the Sisters of Rūm cf. L. M. J. Garnett, *Mysticism and Magic in Turkey*, pp. 175-6. Holy women have frequently been recognised in Islām, but the existence of regular 'societies of female devotees' may be doubted, although from time to time informal associations of pious women may have

Bulaurs,[1] and made over his principles of spiritual power to the Khātun Anādur (a lady of the latter name), and then died.

---

been more or less affiliated to Darvīsh Orders. The Ardabilis had some organisation of the women of their order (*v.* p. 86 *supra*).

Who was the Sybil who, according to Busbequius, made Sulaimān give up music and the chanting of young singers, and prohibit use of wine *c.* 1560? (Hubbard, *The Day of the Crescent*, p. 95).

[1] Bulaurs. The Tarikh-i-Rashidi describes Balur as an infidel country (Kafiristan), and defines it as bounded on the east by Kashghar and Yarkand, on the north by Badakhshan, on the west by Kabul and Lamghan, and on the south by the dependencies of Kashmir. The Kāfirs of this great knot of mountains retained their independence till quite recent times, and Hājī Baqtāsh had no sort of connection with any of the holy wars waged against them (*v. Tarikh-i-Rashidi*, by N. Elias and E. Denison Ross, pp. 384 ff. and the authorities there cited).

This country can, however, hardly be alluded to. The people meant are possibly the Bulghārs of the Caucasus, or the Buldur-göl district (*E.I.* i. p. 784).

It would, however, be more satisfactory to assume that Bulaurs is a misprint for *potūr*, 'a man converted to Islam from some other religion' (Redhouse, *T.-E. Dy.*, p. 456). Rycaut, indeed, calls the Potures 'a people of Bosna'. They are all, he says, "of the sect which strangely mixes Christianity and *Mahometanism* together, reading the Gospel in the *Sclavonian* tongue, with which they are supplied out of *Moravia* and the neighbouring city of *Ragusa*; besides which, they are curious to learn the Mysteries of the *Alchoran*, and the Law of the *Arabick* tongue, and not to be accounted rude and illiterate they affect the Courtly *Persian*. They drink wine in the month of Fast called the *Ramazan*, but to take off the scandal they refuse Cinnamon or other Spices in it and then call it *Hardali*, and passes current for lawful liquor. They have a Charity and Affection for Christians, and are ready to protect them from Injuries and Violences of the *Turks*. They believe yet that *Mahomet* was the Holy Ghost promised by Christ, and that the descending of the Holy Spirit on the day of Pentecost was a Figure and Type of *Mahomet*, interpreting in all places the word παράκλητος, to signifie their Prophet, in whose ear so often the White Dove revealed the Infallible directions to happiness. The *Potures* of *Bosna* are all of this Sect"; but, he says, it comprises "many of the Souldiers that live on the confines of *Hungary* and *Bosna*". If this conjecture is correct the allusion is to the spread of Bektashism in the Balkans, in Albania and Epirus (Hasluck in *Annual*, B.S.A. xxi., "The Geographical Distribution of the Bektāsh"). The Bektāsh influence in the Balkan Peninsula is, curiously enough, hardly touched upon by Brown. Yet, in spite of its origin in the eastern provinces, its main fields of activity were in the west of the empire, just in those lands which became the main recruiting grounds of the Janissaries (*v.* Rycaut, *The Present State of the Ottoman Empire*, p. 131). The derivation of Potūr is apparently uncertain, but the word also means 'a

Although it is stated by the Baqtāsh Darvishes that he gave the *tāj* (crown or cap) to the Janissaries, the assertion is certainly false. This white cap already existed in the time of Orkhān himself at Balejik. I do not wish to gainsay what I have already related in the preceding chapters, and persist in the assertion that the white felt cap of the Baqtāsh Darvishes was taken from the Janissaries. The impulsion for its adoption was given by a Shaikh of the Order of the Baqtāshīs named Abdāl-Mūsā, who, having formed the desire to make a campaign, joined the Janissaries, and one day begged from them an old felt cap, which one of them loaned him. This he put on his head, and after having made the campaign, returned to his own country, wearing it, so as to show that he wore the same head-dress as those who fight for the Faith. When he was interrogated as to its name, he said it was called *būkma-alif tāj*,[1] *i.e.* a cap which never bends, and is ever upright, and worn by those who fight for the true faith. This is the true origin of the cap of the Janissaries."

Near the city of Angora, in a village called Baqtāshkūī, is the tomb of Baqtāsh, much revered by all of his numerous followers scattered over the greater part of the Ottoman empire. Over it has been erected a pretty mausoleum and a *takia*, the object of veneration and visits from pious Mussulmans generally.

The Shaikh Hājī Baqtāsh received his spiritual education from Ahmad Yasavī Balkhī, a native of the city of Balkh. The lineal descent of the Order is as follows :—

Ahmad Yasavī from
Yūsuf Hamadānī, he from
[Khoja] Abū 'Alī al-Fārmadhī, he from
Abū'l-Qāsim Gurgānī, he from
Abū'l-Hasan Harrakianī [Khurqānī], he from

---

kind of full, plaited knee-breeches worn with tight leggings'. It seems to have no connection with Pomak, a word of equally unknown origin.

Possibly, however, the allusion is to the last-mentioned people, generally described as Bulgarian Moslems. They include Albanians and Slavs, according to Brailsford (*Macedonia*, pp. 88, 156, 331). The Pomacks "form a solid population in the almost purely Moslem belt between Drama and the Bulgarian frontier", but Hājī Baqtāsh had no special connection with this tract, though the story of Sārī Sāltik might be a greatly distorted account of its conversion.

[1] *Būkma alif tāj*, the 'unbending head-dress, straight as a line', of the Janissaries (Tschudi, in *Türk. Bib.*, No. 17, p. 8).

Abū-Yazīd Bastāmī, he from

Ja'far ibn-Muhammad Sādiq (who was of the race and family of the Imām Husain, one of the unfortunate sons of the fourth and last of the direct Caliphs, 'Alī), he from

Muhammad ibn-Abū-Bakr, he from

Salmān-i-Fārsī, he from the Shaikh of the two different *tarīqs*, viz.—the one of

Abū-Bakr-as-Siddīq (first Caliph), and the other of

'Alī (the assumptive fourth Caliph).

Abū-Bakr-as-Siddīq received his education direct from the holy Prophet.

This *tarīq* is therefore called the Siddīqīa (Faithful), from Abū-Bakr, and the 'Alīwīa ('Alīvide) from 'Alī.[1]

[1] The text is an attempt to vindicate the orthodoxy of the sects which style themselves 'Alīwīas. This name is affected by the Qizilbāsh, at least by those of Anatolia; and also by the Takhtajīs, at any rate by those of the province of Tekke (Lycia), in which the Qizilbāsh are generally known as Takhtaji, though they call themselves 'Alīwī. These Qizilbāsh are said to owe their conversion to Shaikhs of Qonia in the fourteenth century. But of the real religion of these Lycian Takhtajīs we have little exact information, though that little points to their close connection with the Qizilbāsh further east. The Takhtajīs of Cilicia are also reckoned by the Turks as Qizilbāsh, though some writers identify their religion with that of the Syrian Nusairī, apparently on insufficient grounds. It must be pointed out that the terms Qizilbāsh or 'red-cap', and Takhtajī or 'woodman', are very loosely used in Turkey. The former is a nickname applied to a widely distributed sect (or very possibly to a group of sects which really differ a good deal from one another in doctrine); while the latter term is essentially an occupational one, almost deserving to be regarded as that of an 'occupational caste' (though it, too, may have extended in practice to sectarians who are not Takhtajīs by occupation or connected in any way with them save that they hold some of the tenets followed by that lowly avocation). If we could accept the conjecture of G. Jacob that the name is a survival or a revival of the ancient *δενδροφόροι*—a term whose precise meaning has not yet been ascertained—we might surmise that the Takhtajī are an old guild, half industrial, half religious, very imperfectly Muhammadanised (*Der Islam,* ii. p. 233). Again, the term Qizilbāsh may never have been more than it now is, an offensive nickname. Its literal translation is 'red-head', but von Luschan states that the Qizilbāsh are not more red-haired than their neighbours, and that they are not conspicuous by the adoption of a red head-dress (*J. R. Anthropological Inst.*, 1911, p. 231). Crowfoot seems to confirm this, and adds that the term has now simply an obscene meaning (*ib.* 1900, p. 305). Seeing that among the Qizilbāsh 'the Virgin is regarded as the Mother of God and much venerated', one is tempted to conjecture that their enemies have distorted some name or

All of these persons are known as the Shaikhs, or 'Elders', and as the *murshid-i-kāmil*, or 'perfect spiritual instructors', who teach to others the 'true path' which leads mankind to Allāh. There are, however, said to be many such paths, for the holy Prophet said in a *hadīs*, or traditional assertion, collected and preserved by his earlier followers :—

"The paths leading to God are as numerous as the breaths of His creatures."

Hājī Baqtāsh, Jān-Nūsh, Shāhbāz-i-Qalandar,[1] Jalāl-i-Bukhārī,

---

doctrine connected with the Turkish word *kiz*, 'virgin', into the nickname. However this may be, it is certain that the Lycian Qizilbāsh are, or were, closely associated with the Bektāsh, both at their local centre at Almali and at the principal sanctuary at Qīrshahr, which latter lies at no great distance from the villages on the Halys where the Qizilbāsh actually hail one another as 'Bektāsh'. Indeed, Hasluck surmised that these Qizilbash may be affiliated to the Bektāsh as *muḥibb* or 'lay brethren' of the order; but the term *muḥibb* denotes one much more fully initiated than a layman could be. Still the fact remains that even the distant Qizilbāsh Kurds visit the Bektāsh shrine at Qīrshahr. The tenets of the Qizilbāsh centre round 'Alī, who is identified with Christ, but though the twelve Imāms are equated to the twelve Apostles no special reverence seems to be paid to Abū Bakr (*J. R. Anthropo. Inst.*, 1921, pp. 329 ff.), and so it is not clear why the *tarīq* is also called the *Ṣiddīqīa*.

Some account of the 'Alawīa Shi'as of Yeni (New) Apalak, Uran and other villages near Albistān is given in Mark Sykes' *Dar-ul-Islam.* Probably of Persian origin, they reverence 'Isā, Muḥammad, Moses, Abraham, and 'Alī, placing the last-named above Muḥammad, but not esteeming him divine. They have a private prayer, offered once a day, which is secret, but an 'Alawīa is bound to admit his faith on being asked directly. A man may marry three wives, and may kill an unfaithful wife, but divorce and temporary marriage are both disallowed. A *murshid* visits each village once a year to give definite readings and interpretations of the sacred books, and so on. These books appear to be the five collections of traditions. Jews and fire-worshippers are not recognised as *ahl-i-kitāb* (p. 122). These 'Alawīas have a fine physique and resemble the Druzes in their energetic methods of agriculture and in not veiling their women. They are distinct from the Afshars of Anatolia (p. 97).

[1] Shāhbāz, apparently Qalandar Yūsuf Andalūsī, 'of Andalusia'. Shāhbāz means 'falcon'. For the Qalandar see p. 94 *supra* and p. 299 *infra.* Assuming the Spanish origin of the Qalandar order it may be suggested that its name, which Brown translates 'pure gold', is derived from the Greek *chelidonion,* M. Lat. *chelidonia,* Sp. *celidonia* (see *N.E.D.*, s. vv. celidony and celandine). In alchemy the quintessence of celandine "changes the body and renovates it for the better" (*Hermetical and Alchemical Writings of Paracelsus,* A. E. Waite, ii. p. 27). It also "colours

Luqmān Qalandarī, were all disciples of Ahmad al-Yasavī. Of these, all were of the Order of the Naqshbandī, and at a later period founded each a separate Order.

Jān-Nūsh is buried at [in] Khorāsān; Jalāl Bukhārī and Shāhbāz-

---

just as though it were endowed with gold" (*ib.*, i. p. 54). The alchemists influenced religion in the East in other cases. Thus the Druzes took Hermes to be an incarnation of al-Ḥākim, their god, and the Ḥurūfī Baqtāshī attribute the doctrine of the microcosm to 'Alī (*Textes Houroufis*, p. 287). In India the Rasesvaras held that an immortal body could be developed by the use of mercury (J. N. Farquhar, *Outline of the Religious Literature of India*, p. 254).

It must, however, be confessed that the philological difficulties in the way of this suggestion are great, and if they are insuperable the choice lies between two others: (i.) fr. Pers. *kalāntar*, lit. 'a great head'—a chief man (especially for life) in a town (Johnson, *Pers.-Arab Dict.*, p. 1017), and (ii.) *kalantar*, 'an untrimmed stick', 'a rough, uncouth man' (*ib.*, p. 1019). Both these derivations seem equally unsatisfactory.

It may be that Qalandar represents the Gr. *kylindros*, 'roller', fr. *kylindein*, 'to roll', though the term never seems to have been used to describe a roving monk. The city of Kylindros appears to have been also called Kelenderis or Kilindria (W. M. Ramsay, *The Hist. Geography of Asia Minor*, pp. 367, 362, and 350).

The Qalandars were founded at Sāwa in Persia by Jamāl-ud-Dīn Sāwiji, who fell at Damietta on *jihād* in A.D. 1218. They appear to have been a militant order, or to have had a militant branch. But Najm-ud-Dīn ibn Isra'īl, a Qalandar poet of Damascus, in 1280 A.D., states that the term Qalandarīa means those who have attained the goal (*al-malhiqīn*). But in *E.I.* ii. pp. 676-7, Ch. Huart and Fr. Babinger express different views, stressing their nomad character.

Dr. F. Babinger thinks that the word is of Indian origin, but it has not an Indian sound, and no Indian term has been cited which at all resembles it. In Ibn Baṭuta it appears as Qarandarī. It has been thought that it is derived from *qarinda* or *qalandārī*, meaning apparently 'musical instruments', but the Qalandar never had any recorded predilection for music. The only Turkish word from which the name could be derived is *qāl*, which Babinger translates 'pure'; Redhouse gives its meaning as "the operation of smelting ores or refining metals" (*Turk.-Eng. Lex.*, p. 1419). Possibly Brown or his informant had this word in view when he explained Qalandar to mean 'pure gold'. (See "Schejch Bedr ed-Din, der Sohn des Richters von Simaw," in *Der Islam*, vol. xi. p. 94).

Whatever the origin of the name may be it connoted a servant of God, as in the quatrain of Abu Sa'īd b. Abū'l Khair:—

Tā madrass wa minãra wairān na-shavad.
Īn kār qalandarī bāsamān na-shavad.
Tā īmān kufr wa kufr īmān na-shavad.
Yak banda haqīqatan Musulmān na-shavad.

i-Qalandar at Simna, near Kurdistān and the Persian frontier. With the exception of Jalāl Bukhārī, they all wore the costume

---

"Till seminary and mosque fall into decay, God's work will not be fulfilled. Till belief becomes unbelief and unbelief belief, not one will be in truth a Moslem." The outward sign of this service was the removal of the hair, which was regarded as the visible token of the snare of the world.

According to the Rule of S. Benedict the girovagus was one "who spends all his life putting up at different cells throughout divers provinces for three or four days at a time" (*A New Medley of Memories*, by Sir David Hunter-Blair). What the equivalent term may have been in the Eastern Church does not appear, if, indeed, it had any wandering monks. Kolendhra in M. Gr. = a small cake in the shape of a ring. Hence (?) Kolendravet = Christmas (*Balkan Home-Life*, pp. 73-4).

Writing in 1548, Menavino mentions the Qalandars, who appear to have styled themselves *gazkīnjī* or "wanderers through the world", lit. "itinerant pedlars" (Redhouse, p. 1544). These Qalandars were generally celibate, wore iron rings in their ears, and read the works of the Ḥurūfī poet Nasīmī. They lived on alms. Jacob seems inclined to think that these were really Baqtāsh, though they are not so termed by Menavino. The identification is based on two facts: one, that the Baqtāsh sometimes wear earrings of iron, the other that a section of them observes celibacy. But the Baqtāsh earring may be of silver, and its shape is not that of a complete ring, but that of a horseshoe—as Luschan's description, quoted by Jacob, shows. The observance of celibacy was hardly an innovation of the Qalandars, nor do they seem to have strictly enforced it. No Islamic order has ever done so, though it has not infrequently been practised by individual saints and by their more ardent followers. In Islam the contest between the principle that sanctity follows natural descent and that of its devolution by spiritual adoption or otherwise is, after all, as old as 'Alī.

Gibb says that Yūsuf-i-Andalūsī required the Qalandars to travel through the Muslim world perpetually and to subsist on alms. The severest austerity was also inculcated in order to the attainment of heavenly favour, and more especially the state of ecstasy and illumination. Hence 'Qalandar' came to mean any *darvish* of any order who was distinguished above his fellows by works of supererogation, for divine revelations or marks of heavenly favour. Later still the name fell into disrepute for dissolute antinomianism, and the Qalandar was compared to a vulture which will eat carrion. But there was a Qalandar-khāna at Constantinople which gave its name to a College in the fifteenth century, a fact which suggests that the order did something for education (*Hist. of Ottoman Poetry*, i. p. 357, and ii. pp. 386 and 30). The parallel to the Malāmīs need hardly be pointed out.

In India the Qalandar are a kind of mystic mountebanks, but not much is really known about them. A tribe of nomads who make their living by conjuring and showing performing bears, etc., they live exclusively in tents. They have no dialect of their own, but use an *argot* intermixed with Persian words. A hitherto unrecorded peculiarity about them is that they have a distinctive gait by which they may be easily recognised. They walk very

of the Order of Hājī Baqtāsh; and the only difference is that Jān-Nūsh wore twelve *tarks* or gores in his cap, Jalāl Bukhārī one, Shāhbāz seven, and Luqmān Qalandarī four.

Regarding the principles of the Order of the Baqtāshes, the following will serve to give some explanation :—

There are six *ahkām*, or ' Commands '.

1. Liberality.	4. Holy Law.
2. Knowledge.	5. Submission.
3. Truth.	6. Contemplation.

There are six *arkān*, or ' Columns '.

1. Science.	4. Thankfulness.
2. Meekness.	5. Calling on God.
3. Contentment.	6. Retirement.

The Constructions are six (*binā*).

1. Repentance.	4. Increase of Spirituality.
2. Submission.	5. Contentment.
3. Fidelity.	6. Seclusion.

The Wisdoms are also six (*hukum*).

1. Knowledge.	4. Fidelity.
2. Liberality.	5. Reflection.
3. Approach to Divine Science.	6. Faith in God.

The evidences of the Order are six (*asbāt*).

1. Benevolence.	4. Abandonment of Passions.
2. God's Praise.	5. Fear of God.
3. Abandonment of Sin.	6. Cheerfulness of Spirit.

Regarding the cap, cloak, and girdle, called by the Baqtāshīs the three points, or principles, the following is legendary.

---

straight and rise on their toes as they move silently over the ground. In spite of their appearance of poverty they frequently possess large sums of money both in cash and in women's ornaments. They claim to be Jaṭṭs by caste and tell a story of the usual type about their origin—they slighted the request of a strange Saiyid, and were accordingly cursed by him and condemned to live a wandering life. They have a remarkable tribal council in which the proceedings are conducted with perfect order (Rev. T. Grahame Bailey, *Linguistic Studies from the Himalayas*, pp. 265 f.).

The angel Gabriel once visited the holy Prophet, during the war called the *Ghazā-i-Ahwat*,[1] and asked him what he was occupied in, and he replied in reciting the verses of the *Qurān*, shaving his beard and cutting his hair (*vide Qurān*, xlviii. v. 27). By Divine permission, the angel brought a razor from heaven, and cut the hair and shaved the beard of the prophet. He next put a cap on his head, a cloak over his shoulders, and a girdle around his waist. He had already done this to two other persons, viz. to Adam when he left the Garden of Eden, and to the patriarch Abraham when he dwelt in Makka, which was built by him. The Prophet next did for 'Alī what the angel of God had done for him ; 'Alī did the same, by the Prophet's permission, to Salmān-i-Fārsī,[2] and 'Umar Ummia Bilāl Habshī, and these did the same for twelve other persons.

One of these twelve, named Zu'nūn Misrī, was sent into Egypt, Salmān to Baghdād, Suhailī to Rūm (Asia Minor), Dāūd [3] Yamanī to Yaman (Arabia Felix), for the purpose of imparting instruction on these points. The people of Baghdād call the girdle the letter *alif*, *a*, of the alphabet; those of Rūm call it *lām alif*, *lā* ; and those of Egypt *barlām*.[4] The people of Yaman wear the girdle next to the skin, and not over the clothes.

On the girdle brought to the Prophet by the angel was written, " There is no God but Allāh, and Muhammad is His Prophet, and 'Alī is His friend ".

The Baqtāshīs relate that Adam was the first to wear the girdle used by them ; after him sixteen other prophets wore it

---

1 'War of the Blockade'; cf. Palmer's *Qurān* S.B.E. vi. p. xxxviii. In this chapter, called 'the Victory', Muhammad proclaimed that his vision had been fulfilled, and in that dream he saw that he and his companions entered Makka with their heads shaven (Wherry's recension of Sale's *Koran*, iv. p. 66). The text does not reproduce the accepted version of this chapter.

2 Salmān was a Persian, Bilāl an Abyssinian, and Suhaib (not Suhailī) b. Sinān, a Greek. The latter reached Mecca as a slave, but was converted, adopted an Arab pedigree and an Arab name, which alluded to his red or fair beard (cf. Goldziher, *Muh. Studien*, i. p. 136).

3 Dā'ud, but no Dū'ūd Yamanī is traceable in *E.I.* or in Goldziher, *loc. cit.*

4 *Barlām* may be an error for Ar. *baram*, 'a cord, rope, or twine' (cf. *barim*, 'girdle', as Dr. Fr. Babinger suggests).

in succession, viz. Seth,[1] Noah,[2] Idrīs,[3] Shu'aib,[4] Job,[5] Joseph, Abraham, Husha',[6] Yūsha',[7] Jarjīs,[8] Jonas, Sālih,[9] Zakarīa, Khizr, Iliās,[10]

[1] Seth appears correctly as Shīth (Shīs) on p. 37, and doubtfully as Sheb on p. 138. His name is not traceable in the *Qurān*, though he is reputed to have written a larger number—no less than 50—of the 104 sacred books ascribed to the prophets (Sale, i. p. 122).

[2] An old temple of Noah was converted into Mashhad 'Alī, according to Ker Porter (*Travels*, ii. p. 405).

[3] Enoch, surnamed Idrīs, the 'learned', from the Ar. root *drs*, which gives *madrasa*, 'college', etc. (cf. Sale's *Qurān*, ch. xix. v. 253). To Enoch the Muhammadans assigned 30 out of the 104 sacred books revealed to the prophets (*ib.* Prelim. Discourse, Sec. 4, p. 125, vol. i. of Wherry's recension). Rodwell points out that Enoch means initiated, and Arab writers, giving *darasa* its meaning to 'search out', say Idrīs was so named from his knowledge of the divine mysteries (p. 121). The *E.I.* lends no countenance to this derivation but accepts Nöldeke's theory that the name Idrīs conceals that of Andreas, and that this Andreas is Alexander's cook who obtained immortality, as conjectured by R. Hartmann. Like Enoch, Idrīs lived 365 years on earth, and God took him to himself.

[4] Shu'aib, the Jethro of the Bible (Palmer, *Qurān* S.B.E., vi. p. 149). His daughter married Moses.

[5] The traditions regarding Aiyūb come mainly from Jewish sources (*E.I.* i. p. 220).

[6] Husha', Hosea, not generally recognised by Muhammadans as a prophet (cf. Sale's *Koran*, Wherry's recension, i. p. 125).

[7] Joshua is recognised as one of the prophets, as are Adam, Seth, Lot, Ismā'īl, Nun and others (Sale, *Koran*, Prelim. Discourse, i. p. 125, Wherry's recension).

In *The Ansayrii* (*or Assassins*)—a sub-title which destroys confidence in the author's accuracy—Lt. the Hon. F. Walpole, R.N., describes the tomb of Joshua or 'Hosea' (Ousha) on Jebel Seth. Near it is that of Tubal, full 20 ft. long. The tomb of Joshua is shorter but covered with cotton (*The Ansayrii*, iii. pp. 309-10; London, Bentley, 1851). For an account of the newly discovered Samaritan book of Joshua, by M. Gaster, *v. J.R.A.S.*, 1908, pp. 795 f. At Hillah in Lower Mesopotamia the mosque called Mashhad-ush-Shams contains relics of Joshua in Arab (but not in Jewish) tradition (Ker Porter, *Travels*, ii. p. 325).

[8] Jirjīs is St. George, but Khizr is also identified with that saint (Salmoné, *s.v.*). Khizr again is identified with Iliās. Possibly for Iliās should be read Elisha. Otherwise the same prophet is mentioned thrice under different names, or if Khizr be identified with Idrīs, as is sometimes done, no less than four times. The equation Khizr = Iliās is generally accepted (see note on p. 100).

The Crusades gave an impetus to the worship of St. George. England, Aragon and Portugal assumed him as their patron saints, and so did most of the chivalrous orders founded at the date of these wars. In 1245 Frederic of Austria instituted an order of St. George, on his day. His standard was entrusted to the Swabian knights. In the early thirteenth

and Jesus.[1] God said of Moses in verse 65 of the 18th chapter of the *Qurān*: " May I follow thee, said Moses to Him, so that Thou mayest teach me what Thou knowest regarding the *true path* ? "

Moses learned the secrets of the 'True Path' from Khizr. Khizr, or Khazar, is a mythical character, who figures largely in Oriental Spiritualists.[2] Some say he lived in the earliest times,

century Genoa had a military order under his protection, and in 1201 an order was founded in Aragon, 'the Knights of St. George of Alfama'. The English order was founded in 1350. In 1415, Archbishop Chichely made St. George's day a major double feast, and ordered it to be observed like Christmas, and he received the title of spiritual patron of the English soldiery (Baring Gould, *Curious Myths of the Middle Ages*, pp. 314-15).

St. George is the subject of a legend curiously like that of Sari Saltik. God one day asked a poor man for food, and he set to work to cook his son; but the boy was found unscathed in the oven, and God bade his father sacrifice a lamb on St. George's day, which the Bulgarians still do. A folk-song sung on that day refers to Abraham (Garnett and Stuart-Glennie, *The Women of Turkey*, i. p. 332).

At Qonia is Araba-Yorgi, 'St. George of the Car'. On a mountain five hours north of Qonia St. George takes the place given in Greece to St. Elias. The festival of Araba-Yorgi is celebrated on 23rd April on a mountain above Ladik. At sunrise milk and water flow from a dry place. There is, moreover, a cult of St. George of old standing at Qonia, and churches of St. Elias and St. George at Sille (Ramsay, *Cities of St. Paul*, pp. 378-79 and 381).

These may, however, be St. George of Athos, the first apostle of Christianity in ancient Iberia (Riley, *Athos*, p. 141). But St. George only retranslated the Scriptures into Georgian (p. 135).

[9] Sālih lived between the time of Hud (Heber) and Abraham. Nabī Sālih, 'the righteous prophet', is held in great veneration by the Bedouins, and Palmer suggested his identity with Moses (*S.B.E.* vi. pp. 147-48 *n.*). See also Sale's *Koran*, Prel. Discourse, p. 7. Sālih is not the Selah of the O.T. Sālih's mission to convert the Thamūd, a godless tribe of cave-dwellers, failed, and they were destroyed by an earthquake, but the rock-sculptures of al-Hijr are still called Sālih's towns (*E.I.* ii. p. 301).

[10] In the Christian doctrine of the Two Advents Eliās was to be the Precursor of Christ (*v. e.g.* Rendel Harris, *Testimonies*, i. p. 107). Palmer seems to make 'Uzair (Esdras, Ezra) ibn Sar'yā identical with Eliās, al-Khizr (*S.B.E.*, vi. p. 41). Esdras seems to have left a book of prophecies now lost (Rendel Harris, *op. cit.*, p. 80 f.). But Ezra was surely historical: *v.* Rev. S. N. Sedgwick, *The Story of the Apocrypha*, pp. 71-3 and 36.

[1] 'Isā is one of the proper names not traceable in the Scriptures, though it is used as equivalent to Jesus; cf. Tālūt for Saul (*E.R.E.* 8, p. 874).

[2] For a good account of the Alexander Myth of the Persians, by E. Rehatsek, see *Journal*, Bombay Branch R. Asiatic Soc., 1881 (xv.), p. 37 f. Khizr appears as Alexander's guide, both in the *Shahnāma* and *Sikandar-nāma* (pp. 56-7).

and having drank of the fountain of life never has died; others that he was Elias, St. George (of the dragon), and an officer in the army of Alexander the Great. The place of Khizr is equally mythical. The *tarīqats*, or paths, are 'Alī's, and the *sharī'at*, or holy law, is the Prophet's. Khizr is called the chief of all of the *auliās*, or saints.

In the girdle of the Order is a stone called the *palank*;[1] it has seven corners, or points, called *tarks*, in token of the seven heavens and seven earths which God created, also the seven seas and the seven planets; for God has said, "We have created the seven heavens in seven folds, and seven earths in the same form, all out of light". He then commanded all of these to worship Him, which they do, continually revolving round His holy throne. The *palank* is very useful, and the Shaikh of the Order puts it on and off, each seven times, saying,—

1. "I tie up greediness, and unbind generosity.
2. "I tie up anger, and unbind meekness.
3. "I tie up avarice, and unbind piety.
4. "I tie up ignorance, and unbind the fear of God.
5. "I tie up passion, and unbind the love of God.
6. "I tie up hunger, and unbind (spiritual) contentment.
7. "I tie up Satanism, and unbind Divineness."

When putting it on a disciple, he says to him, "I now bind up thy waist in the path of God. O, holy name, possessed of all knowledge! Whoever knows His name will become the *nāib*, or successor of the Shaikh". He next offers up the following prayerful address: "There is no God but Allāh, Muhammad is the Prophet of Allāh: 'Alī is the *walī*, or friend of Allāh; Abū Muslim,[2] the nephew of 'Alī, is the sword of Allāh; Mahdī is the master of the *imāmat*, and the *amīn*, or confidant of Allāh. Moses is the Word of God, Jesus is the Spirit of God, and Noah is the sword of God. It is not to be opened by 'Alī excepting with the sword called *zūlfikār*. Our first *walī*, or founder, is Baqtāsh, the middle the Darvish Muhammad, and the last was Mustafā,[3] the owner of the *kitābat*, or writing. The knowledge of the world is

---

[1] Pelenk, a term which is thus explained by Evliya: there were, he says, certain idols on the Uk-Maidān or archery ground at Constantinople at which the Moslem heroes used to shoot, and one of these was called Pelenk, whence the term *pelenk* is derived (*Travels*, i. pt. 1, p. 46).

[2] *V.* note on p. 90, *supra*.

[3] Mustapha, in original.

to know the *sharī'at*, or holy law ; the *tarīqat*, or new path ; and the *ma'rifat*, or new science of spiritualism. These are the portals of our Order."

The Shaikh also adds as instruction: "There are 40[1] *maqāms*, or seats, 360 degrees, 28 *manzils* (places of rest), 12 spheres, 24 hours, 4 *fasls*, or chapters, 7 climes, 4 *qarārs*, 13,000 worlds, 7 *subul-i-masāwī*,[2] or *āyats* (verses), called the mother of the *Qurān*,[3] 7 letters, 7 *fātihas* (first chapters, or openings) of the *Qurān* ; all of these are called *hāl* (dispositions), and not *qāl* (sayings). There is but one light ; the truth is the moon, and these were given to Adam. He who has found the science of his own body, called the *'ilm-i-wujūd* (or the counterpart of himself in a spiritual sense), knows his Lord ; for the holy Prophet has said, 'To know thyself is to know the Lord'. In this is comprised a knowledge of thy own secret, and that of thy Creator."

The latter is a Mussulman idea that every one in this world possesses a *pīr* in the spiritual existence, called the *misāl*, or equal, who dies forty days previous to his temporal self. The

[1] The number 40 is characteristic of the Iranian Muslim folk-tales. In Balūchistān the volcano called Kūh-i-Taftān is known locally as the Kūh-i-Chihil-Tan or 'Mountain of the Forty Beings'. Another mountain in Karmān bears the same name, which indeed is common. Such mountains always have a shrine on the summit.

Near Bam in Karmān are the ruins of Chihil Kurra, 'Forty Colts', a garden so vast that a mare was not found in it until she had foaled forty colts (Major P. M. Sykes, *Ten Thousand Miles in Persia*, pp. 134, 219, 435). As pointed out by the author on p. 219 the number occurs in the tale of 'Alī Bābā and the Forty Thieves.

[2] *Subul-i-musāwī*, 'parallel paths', apparently the passages which contain parables, indexed in Wherry's recension of Sale's *Korān*, iv. p. 327, and in Rodwell, pp. 504-5. But which seven parables may be alluded to does not appear.

[3] The term *umm-ul-kitāb* occurs in the *Qurān*, ch. iii. v. 5, and various interpretations of it are given. The usual one is that it refers to the Fatiha ; others explain it as the fundamental parts of the *Qurān* ; others again as the Preserved Tablet on which is inscribed the original of that book (Gibb, *Hist. of Ottoman Poetry*, i. p. 339). The Fatiha itself was sometimes called the sab'-ul-masani, or 'the seven of the repetition', as in man the microcosm the face has seven signs, to wit the hair, two eyebrows and four lines of eyelashes. This term was frequently used by the Hurufis (cf. *ib.*, p. 374).

The term *ummahāt-ul-asmā*, or 'mothers of the names', *i.e.* the fundamental titles, is applied to the four divine names, the First, the Last, the External and the Internal (J. R. Redhouse in *J.R.A.S.*, 1880, p. 17).

misāl is supposed to know everything, and to teach the temporal body to which it belongs by visionary forewarnings. It is also believed (on a verse of the *Qurān*) that God does not make saints of the ignorant. He first has them taught by the *misāl*, and then makes them to be *auliā* (the plural of *wālī*, or saint). It therefore fills the place of a guardian spirit, or angel. The temporal body thus becomes, by its means, freed from all darkness, and moreover is transferred into a *nūr*, or light to others. It is then a complainer for the woes of mankind (*ahl-i-dard*) ; its pledge of faith finds its place, and is a " faithful one " in God.

THEIR COSTUME

The *haidarī*[1] is a vest without sleeves, and with a streak of a different colour, somewhat resembling in form a word, supposed to be that of the fourth Caliph 'Alī. It should also have twelve lines on it, signifying the twelve Imāms.

The *khirqa* is a cloak, or mantle, without a collar, and with the same streak as the vest.

The *taiband* is a girdle which is worn around the waist, and is made only of white woollen materials.

The *qambaria* is a cord, also worn around the waist, to which is attached a stone. This latter is round or oblong, mostly of crystal, called *najaf*.[2] The cord has three buttons or knots ; the first knot is called *al-bāghī*[3] (hand-tie), the second *dil-bāghī*[4] (tongue-tie), and the third *bal-bāghī*[5] (rein-tie). These serve to remind the wearer that he must neither steal, lie, nor commit fornication.

[1] Ḥaidarī, a word not given by Redhouse, is undoubtedly derived from Ar. *ḥaidar*, 'lion', a term applied to 'Alī (cf. p. 395 *infra*). But the (adjectival) form is here used of the sleeveless vest of the Baqtāsh, whereas it is more commonly applied to a head-dress. Thus the *tāj-i-ḥaidar* was the '*bonnet rouge*' adopted by Ḥaidar, son of Junaid, as the distinctive uniform of his followers. It was made of wool and dyed scarlet, and was eventually adopted by the Qizilbāsh or 'red caps', with the modification that it was made with twelve pleats—to signify the twelve Imāms. Similarly the Mevlevīs called their head-dress the *ḥaidarīa sharīf*, but according to Brown it is white or yellowish in colour and has no pleats (pp. 59-60 *supra*).

[2] *Najaf*, lit. a 'mound' or tumulus, is the name of 'Alī's burial-place. 'Crystal' is *zajāj*, lit. 'glass' ; *bilūr* is also crystal or beryl.

[3] *El*, Turk., 'band'. *Bāgh* is a 'knot', as well as a tie.

[4] *Dil*, or *dīl*, T., 'the tongue'.

[5] *Bal*, T., 'the loins'. *Qanbaria*, *v.* note on p. 187 *infra*.

The *mangosh* are earrings which are put in the ears of the new disciple. If only one ear is drilled it is called *Hasanī*, from one son of 'Alī; and if both are pierced they are called *Husainī*, from the other son of the same Caliph. It is optional with him.

The *tāj* is the name of the cap which all wear in common. It is made of white felt, and is in four parts. The first shows that the wearer has given up the world; the second, that he has abandoned all hopes of Paradise; the third, that he disdains all hypocrisy, and means that the Darvish cares not whether he is seen or not praying, and is wholly indifferent to public opinion;

A SHAIKH OF THE NAQSHBANDĪS SUBDUING A LION BY HIS SPIRITUAL POWERS.

the fourth is the total abandonment of all the pleasures of life, and that he belongs to and is fully satisfied with Allāh alone. Their names are *sharī'at*, *tarīqat*, *haqīqat*, and *ma'rifat*.

The Shaikhs all wear the *tāj*, with twelve *tarks*, which are of four *qapūs*,[1] or doors. These twelve allude to the twelve Imāms, and the four to the four preceding great principles of mystical spiritualism.

The *qanā'at-tāshī* ('stone of contentment') is the name of the stone worn in the belt or girdle, and is commemorative of the stones which poor Darvishes were wont to put in their girdles to appease or allay the pangs of hunger. They used to be three in number, the one worn inside the other; but it is supposed that

[1] *Qapū*, Turk., 'gate' or 'door'.

aid comes to their relief before the necessity arises of using the full number of three.

The *tarjumān* [dragoman], or interpreter, is the name of the secret word or phrase of the Baqtāshes. It varies according to the occasion.

When a *murīd*, or neophyte, is desirous of joining the Order, he goes to the *takia*, and at its sill a sheep is sacrificed by one of the fraternity. Its flesh is eaten by the members, and from its wool his *taiband* is made.

It is related that the Caliph 'Alī had a horse[1] called *Duldul*, on whose legs a rope was usually tied by his groom named *Qambarīa*. The latter, when accompanying his master, used to tie the rope around his waist. It had three knots, called as aforestated *al-bāghī*, *dil-bāghī*, and *bal-bāghī*.

Regarding the stone which was worn round the neck, the following tradition is given:[2] " Mūsā (the Prophet Moses) was

[1] A white mule (Lane, *Modern Egyptians*, p. 255). 'Alī's charger was named Maimūn or, according to others, Zū'l-Janāh, ' the winged ' (Burton, *Pilgrimage*, iii. p. 254). The same confusion occurs in India. According to the common Eastern practice the horse would be tethered by a rope fastened round each fetlock and attached to four pegs. By making these ropes taut the animal can be placed on a kind of rack and rendered so completely helpless that it can hardly swish the flies off its flanks with its tail. The four heel-ropes would of course have three knots when tied in one length and worn round the groom's waist on the march. No one who has seen the efficacy of this often cruel method of tethering can fail to realise the force of the symbol drawn from it.

[2] This tradition seems to be taken from Evliya, but his version is a little different. He is describing the methods of punishing novices, one of which consists in making the delinquent carry a heavy stone round his neck. Moses, it is said, never showed his body, on account of the continual emanation of divine light, and so he was said by his people to be leprous and afflicted with elephantiasis. One day, bathing in the Nile, he laid his dress on a stone, which straightway began to walk towards the capital (Memphis). Moses pursuing it, the people saw the brilliant whiteness and cleanness of his body, and thousands of disbelievers turned faithful. But Moses, angry at being seen naked, pierced the stone with his staff in twelve places. The stone protested that it had only obeyed a Divine command, whereon Moses craved its forgiveness, saying: " A Darvish, Darvishes forgive ". Hence the current saying, Darvishe darvishān, " a *darvish* is forgiven by *darvishes* ". The stone then bade Moses pass a rope through one of the holes and keep it as a collar of penitence. Both the stone usually worn and the stone-collar of punishment had their origin in this event and are named *sigil-ṭāshī* (*Travels*, i. pt. 2, p. 96). Then Evliya says *sigil*=' stone ', but it appears to mean ' weight ', Ar. *ṣiql*.

once bathing in the river Nile. He had laid his shirt on a stone, and the latter running away, followed by Moses, entered the city of Misr (Cairo). Moses reproached the stone for carrying off his clothes, but it told him that it did so by Divine command, and that he should ever after keep a stone suspended to his neck in memory of the occurrence. He called the stone *Darvish-darvishān* and it contained twelve holes. During all his travels, by means of this stone Moses performed miracles, among which was the producing of fountains of water, simply by striking it on the ground."

So much significancy is given to the *tāj*, or cap, worn by this Order of Darvishes, that I may add some further account of it.

They state that all the letters of the alphabet originated in the first one, called *alif*, or *a*. The original cap is said, in the same manner, to be of a similar source, and this is called the *alifī*, or cap of *a*. It is considered to be the sign of the *khilāfat*, or succession of the blessed Prophet, and when he appointed a Shaikh to succeed him, he made a cap of the form of the celebrated sword of 'Alī, named *Zūlfikār*. After this the cap assumed other forms, peculiar to the four chief *tarīqs*, or Orders; one was called the Malikī, one the Saifī,[1] one the Shurhī, and one the

[1] The *kulah-i-ṣaifī*, or sword-shaped helmet was also affected by the Maulavīs, together with the green shawl. The history of this order is too imperfectly known to permit of our saying what its real relations to the Baqtāsh were. Beginning with the story of Abaposh Sultan it was as follows:

Sultan Walad also left two daughters, one of whom, Mutahhara Khatun, espoused Sulaiman Shah, a prince of the house of Kermian. To him she bore two sons, regarding one of whom, Khizr Pasha, a miraculous tale is told. His son, Bali, believed his father's prediction that Sultan Yaqub of Kermian would be overthrown, and that the only power left to the descendants of Khizr Pasha and his brother, Ilias Pasha, in his kingdom, would be a mystical and spiritual one, so he assumed the cloak of a Maulavī and the title of 'Aba-posh, 'the 'aba-clothed', built a cloister at Qara-Hissar, and resigned its headship to his son Sima'i Diwani before his own death in 1485 (Hammer-Purgstall, *GdOD.*, i. p. 268). Gibb has pointed out the chronological difficulties in this account. Khizr Pasha is said to have died in 1349–50, and so 'Aba-posh must have been at least 140 years old if he died in 1485. But he is described as being only 120 years of age when he died. It is clear that a generation has dropped out in the pedigree-table (*v. Hist. of Ott. Poetry*, i. pp. 423-4). Others of this offshoot of Sultan Walad's family also wrote mystic poetry.

The poet 'Sulṭān Dīwānī' was son of the Shaikh Abaposh, who bestowed

Halawī.[1] The cap of Hājī Baqtāsh-i-walī is of twelve *tarks*. He made a second called the *Tāj-i-Jānnūsh* of nine *tarks*, and another

him on the Shaikh Fanāyī Dada. Initiated in his youth into all the esoteric learning of the Chihil Tan, or 'those who keep fasts of forty days', he travelled widely, and at Aleppo accepted the guidance of the Shaikh Abū Bakr al-Wafā. Thence he went to Qonia as principal of the Maulavīs and assumed the title of Dīwānī. He also visited Egypt to procure the release of the Gulshanī Shaikh from the prison into which he had been cast by the Sulṭān, Kansū Khawrī. Invited to Constantinople by Sulṭān Sulaimān, he was installed in the Maulavī convent at the Seven Towers, but died at his home in 1529. He is esteemed as one of the greatest poets of the Maulavīs (Hammer-Purgstall, *GdOD.* ii. pp. 12-13).

Sultan Diwani, doubtless the Simaii Diwani (or Sinaii) mentioned above, had a slave, Dervish Wasiq (died in 1529), who adopted the kulah-i-saif and green shawl as a Maulavī and became the master of Abū-Saīf Sultān. This Maulavī died like his master and many of his disciples in the year of the siege of Vienna, when the Maulavī order was persecuted (*ib.*, ii. p. 15). It had few cloisters in Constantinople prior to the time of Parwāna Dervish (died in 1543), so that Parwāna died in that of Shaikh Wafa', where his companion was Shamii, the translator of the Mesnevi (*ib.*, p. 228). It was not until the reign of Salim I. that the order obtained its great position, but it was then taken under the Sultan's protection owing to the prayers of its head, Khusrau Chelebi Effendi, which contributed to that ruler's victory over his brother Bayazid in the Qonia plain (*ib.*, p. 283). The succession to the headship of the order was, however, in dispute at a later period, apparently because the principle of physical devolution of the spiritual office asserted by Farrukh Chelebi (*d.* 1591) was denied by his opponents (*ib.*, iii. pp. 78-9). The fact that a similar contest occurred in the Baqtāsh order proves nothing, but the adoption of the saifi head-dress may indicate some connection between them and a branch of the earlier Maulavīs. The tale told of Sultan Diwani, that he went to Persia to rescue the Diwan of Jalal-ud-Din Rumi from the hands of Shah Isma'il, and that of one of his disciples, Dervish Sufī Khatayi, who instructed the princes of Shah Isma'il's family in spiritual mysteries, while Sultan Diwani himself performed miracles in the presence of Shah Isma'il, go to show that their connection with the Ardabilis was fairly close (cf. *ib.*, ii. p. 18). The poems of another disciple of Sultan Diwani, Shidayi, are still prized by Persian dervishes (*ib.*, p. 17). The title Sinayi or Sinnayi was derived from Sinna in Kurdistan.

The Maulavīs were exposed to persecution at times, notably in the time of 'Abd-ul-Halim, son of 'Abd-ur-Rahman, and a scion of the family of Jalal-ud-Din Rumi. Chief of the cloister at Qonia, he died in 1679. This was due to the preaching of Khoja Aḥmad of Van, who died six years later in 1685. After his death the Maulavīs seem to have regained their influence, for the sons and kinsmen of Ahmad were in turn executed (Hammer-Purgstall, *GdOD.* iii. p. 519).

[1] Ibrāhīm b. Muḥammad al-Ḥallabī, author of a hand-book on the *Furū'*, according to the Hanafī school of law, much used in Turkey. It is

was worn in Persia of seven *tarks*, called the *Saiyid-i-Jalāl*, after the eminent man of that name. This person was the founder of the Order of the Jalālīs,[1] who have no *takias* in Constantinople, though members of it often go there from Persia as travellers. There is still another cap sometimes worn by the Baqtāshīs, called *Shāhbāz-i-Qalandarī*, after the founder of the Qalandars, made of seven *tarks*, of white felt, said to have been assumed by a Shāh (king) of Balkh named Adham, and is called therefore the *Adhamī*. He is said to have abandoned his throne so as to become a Darvish. It is also said that to his time the Darvishes were all called after Junaidī, a holy man of that name resident in Baghdād, and there was then but one *tarīq*, or Order.

As a detailed description of the cap, I may add that the cap is called the *pīr* in honour of the founders of the various *tarīqs*, and that on it was originally written, " All things will perish, save His (the Omniscient's) face, and to Him will all return ", taken from the last lines of the 28th chapter of the *Qurān*.[2]

Around the top was written the *āyat-al-kursī*, from the 2nd chapter of the *Qurān*, and ending with the 256th verse.

Around its edges was written the 36th chapter of the *Qurān*, called the *Sūra-i-Yā-Sīn* [Y.S.].

Inside was written the 41st chapter of the *Qurān* ; near its

---

called the *Multaqā'l-Abḥur* and is mentioned on p. 79 *supra* (*E.I.* ii. p. 237). Ubicini translates the title of the work " the meeting of the two seas ", and this title doubtless expressed its attempt to reconcile all the decrees from the foundation of Islām concerning law and theology that had proceeded from the doctors of law before the time of Ḥalabī, who died in A.D. 1549 (*Letters on Turkey*, i. p. 139). But the connexion is by no means certain.

[1] The Indian order of the Jalālīs is ascribed to the saint Saiyid Jalāl-ud-Dīn, a disciple of Bahāwal Haqq, the Suhrawardi of Multan. Born at Bukhara in 595 H. (A.D. 1119), or in 1188, he is said to have lived till 1383, and is buried at Uch Sharīf. A prolific writer, he played a great part in the spread of Islam in the Punjab and Sind. His followers have many curious practices. At initiation they shave completely the head, face, and body, burn their clothes, and are branded on the right shoulder. They also wear glass bracelets like those worn by women. The order claims to be an offshoot of the Suhrawardi, and is regarded as one of the orthodox fraternities which conform to the shara'. In India, however, it does not appear to wear the cap with seven *tarks*. Nothing is recorded of the Isḥāq Jalālī mentioned on p. 142 *supra*.

[2] *Qurān*, ch. xxviii. v. 88 ends : " Everything shall perish except Himself : unto Him belongeth judgment, and before Him shall ye be assembled at the last day ". Cf. also ch. ii. v. 157.

edge the 53rd verse, " We will cause our miracles to shine over the different countries of the earth ".

On its front, the 109th [115th] verse of the 2nd chapter, " To God belongs the east and the west ; turn to whichever side you will, you will meet His countenance ; God is immense, and knows all things ".

On the other side was written the Mussulman Confession of Faith, " There is no God but Allāh, and Muhammad is the Prophet of Allāh ", and " 'Alī is the *walī*, or Friend of Allāh ".

Behind it was written the 29th verse of the 2nd chapter of the *Qurān* : " God taught to Adam the names of all beings, afterwards He brought them before the angels, and said to them, ' Name them to him if you are sincere ' ".

A stone which the Baqtāshes wear suspended on their necks is called the *taslīm-tāshī* or ' stone of submission '. One of the interpretations given regarding it is, that it is worn in remembrance of the bestowal of Fātima, the daughter of the Prophet, upon his nephew 'Alī. It is said that on this occasion her father took her hair in his hand, and giving it into that of 'Alī, delivered her up to him.

In their ears they wore another stone called the *mangosh-tāshī*, of this shape , or that of a *new moon*, in remembrance of the horseshoe [1] of 'Alī. Around their waists they wore belts called *qambarīa*, made of dark-coloured goats' wool or hair, with several knots, which, passing through a ring attached to one end of it, serve to fasten it. These knots are called as aforestated.

On their legs they wear leather gaiters, called *dolāq*,[2] from one of the principal disciples of Baqtāsh, named Bābā 'Umar (Dolāqī), who wore them.

Suspended from their belt is a small bag called *jilband*,[3] made after the following form , on which is embroidered the name of 'Alī, and serves to contain papers and books. It is said that the Prophet gave such a bag to his uncle Hamza,[4] in Makka.

[1] But, it is generally said, the Arabs did not shoe their horses, as owing to the hardness of the hoof they did not require to be shod.

[2] *Dolāq* (*dolak* in orig.) for *ṭolāq* (pron. *dolāq* in Turk.) " a long strip of cotton or woollen, etc., wound round the leg in lieu of a stocking or gaiter " (Redhouse, *Turk.-Eng. Lex.*, p. 1260).

[3] *Jilband* in Turk. = a portfolio.

[4] Hamza was son of 'Abd al-Muṭṭalib, uncle of the Prophet, and so his cousin. Tradition also makes him his foster-brother (*E.I.* ii. p. 254).

A Baqtāsh is not allowed to beg; and if he ever does, it is after fasting three days, and then only at seven doors. If these give him nothing he must cease. When begging, they are called Salmān, after Hazratī-Salmān-i-Fārsī, and must carry their *kashgol*, or beggar's cup, under their clothes.

An Oriental friend gives the following extract from a journal kept by him during an excursion in Asia Minor, referring to the founder of this Order.*

" Tūzkyöy, *i.e.* ' Salt Village ', situated in a volcanic part of the country, contains about one hundred houses, the inhabitants of which are all grazers, and possess many cattle, sheep, and Angora goats. The name originates from the salt-mines about a quarter of an hour distant, and which are still worked. According to tradition, they have been created by the famous Hājī Baqtāsh, the founder of the Order of that name, who on passing through this village was regaled with unsalted meat. When he asked the cause of the absence of savour to his meat, he was informed that the inhabitants had no salt, whereupon he struck upon the ground with his stick; and so produced, miraculously, a salt-mine. Up to the present time, annually about 1000 *batmāns* (17,000 lbs.) of salt are delivered to the *takia* opposite, on the river Kizil Irmak, near to the village of Hājī Baqtāsh, where also the shrine of this founder is to be seen. On the height which dominates the city there is a number of buildings, among which is a Mosque, and the tomb of Saiyidi Ghāzī Battāl,[1] a *madrasa*,

* Dr. Mordtmann.

[1] Sīdī Baṭṭāl Ghāzī, son of Ḥusain Ghāzī, possesses one of the most important Arab tombs in Asia Minor. It lies six hours south of Eskishahr, on the pilgrim's way from Constantinople to Makka. In the latter part of the sixteenth century ' Sīdī Baṭṭāl ' was the war-cry of the Turkish armies. As a historical personage 'Abdullāh Abū'l Ḥusain al-Antakī, al-Baṭṭāl, ' the valiant ', fell in battle at Afiūm Karā Hissār in A.D. 740, but a vast mass of legend has gathered round his name (Hasluck, *Annual*, B.S.A. xix. pp. 184, 186 f.). Later historians give his name differently (*E.I.* i. p. 680).

The ancient Nakoleia, known in Saljuqian times as Kala'-i-Masīhiya, ' the Christians' Castle ', Sayyid-i-Ghāzī, was named after Ja'far bin Ḥusain Sayyid-i-Ghāzī, though it is doubtful whether he fell there. His *mashhad*, however, appears to have been erected there in A.D. 1207 or 1208 by the mother of 'Alā-ud-Dīn Sulṭān of Qonia, but, if we are to credit the *Wilāyat-nāma* of Ḥājim Sulṭān, it had fallen into decay when Ḥājī Baqtāsh commissioned Ḥājim to found there a refectory for the poor, and Ḥājim declared his purpose of " bringing new life to Sayyid Ghāzī " (*Türk. Bib.* No. 17, pp. 30 and 80). But this design was opposed by its incumbent the Shaikh

and a *takia*, inhabited by some four or five Darvishes of the Baqtāsh Order. A verandah, built of marble, leads to the interior of this building, and the traveller is shown here two relics of Hājī Baqtāsh, viz. : in the well, the impression of his mouth and teeth, which, to judge from the size, must have been of the dimensions of those of a buffalo ; and in the entrance gate, an impression of his hand and finger."

The hall of a convent or *takia* of the Baqtāsh Order is always a square. In its centre is a stone with eight corners, called the *maidān-tāsh*,[1] in which, on occasions of ceremony, stands a lighted candle ; around this are twelve *pōsts* or *pōstakīs*,[2] seats consisting of white sheepskin. Whenever a *murīd* is to be initiated the candle is removed from the stone, and one is placed in front of each of the *pōsts*. Among the explanations given of this stone is the following : "The Prophet used to put a stone in his girdle to suppress, by its pressure, the cravings of hunger, and that this one, as well as that worn in the girdle of the fraternity of this Order, is in remembrance of his practice. It is said that

---

Qara Ibrāhīm, and Ḥājim had to slay him by lightning out of a clear sky. Nevertheless, he accepted his widow's gift of her son Ḥasan, apparently as his father's successor. Otherwise, the successor is not named. The marks of teeth on the sill of the well are here attributed to Ḥājim Sulṭān (*ib.*, p. 94). As a matter of history Sulṭān Orkhān seems to have restored the shrine and granted it to Ḥājī Baqtāsh. It was again restored by the Michal-oghlūs, a Christian family converted to Islam, in the fifteenth and sixteenth centuries. It has two daughter shrines, Shujā'-ud-Dīn, built in A.D. 1515, and Urian Bābā. At the former one Muruwwat Bābā lies buried. A fourth shrine in the same locality is that of Malak Ghāzī, an old Byzantine cloister converted in A.D. 1058, and situate on the Qirq-qiz Dāgh, 'hill of the forty virgins' (Bulzinger, *Drei Bektaschi-Kloster Phrygiens*, pp. 1-10 and 60 f.). It is noteworthy that in legend Sayyid Ghāzī's spirit greets Ḥājim Sulṭān in the form of a noble gazelle-like stag, reminding us of Geiklī Bābā (*Wilāyat-nāma*, p. 88).

[1] *Maidān*, lit. 'a plain' in Persian, in Turkey denotes an oratory or a room for common worship (Hasluck in *Annual*, B.S.A. xx. p. 95). For much lore on its significances see Thorning in *Türk. Bibliothek*, No. 16, p. 119 ff. He also renders it Kampfplatz, which would make it closely analogous to the Indian term *akhāra*, 'arena'. Tschudi points out that it also means the 'assembly' as well as the place in which it meets (*Türk. Bibliothek* No. 17, p. 32). Hence *maidān-tāsh* must mean the 'stone of the oratory or assembly', and it may typify 'Alī as the *maidān*. 'Alī is a very common feature in initiations.

[2] *Pōst* is a skin, tanned, and so a seat or throne ; *pōstakī*, Turk., a sheepskin (cf. p. 252 *infra*).

Ḥājī Baqtāsh called the candlestick which stands on this stone his eye, the candle his face, and the room his body."

In the *takia* is a stick, called the *challik*,[1] of this shape,  with which the members are punished in case of need. It is in remembrance of the stick with which 'Alī punished his groom *Kambarīa*,[2] and the latter ever afterwards carried it in his belt.

The twelve *pōsts* are in remembrance of the twelve Imāms, and are as follows : [3]

1. Is the seat of the Shaikh who personifies 'Alī.

[1] *Challik*, translated 'whip' on p. 197 *infra*. Redhouse, however, has only *chālīk*, "the child's game of tip-cat", "the stick called the cat", and *chelīk*, "a piece of wood or metal bevelled or tapering at one or both ends; especially a boy's tipcat" (*Turk.-Eng. Lex.*, pp. 709 and 729). Turk. *chal-mak*, however, = 'to strike'. Lane described the *firqilleh* as "a whip with a thick twist of cords" (*Modern Egyptians*, p. 249). The word may be connected with the name of the mystic Russian sect called the Chlysty, 'scourgers', who hold gatherings which are outwardly at least comparable to those of the dancing *darvishes*. The less reputable rites of the sect have, however, nothing in common with those of the Maulavīs (H. L. Strack, *The Jew and Human Sacrifice*, p. 39).

[2] *Qanbarīa*, explained as 'cord' on p. 178. 'Alī's groom was named Qanbar, as stated in the text below. Qanbar is probably the patron-saint of all grooms and those who have to do with horses, but Evliya informs us that the patron of the Arab grooms (*sa'īs*) is Kanbūr 'Alī, who is also patron of the *mekkārī* (*mukyārī*), otherwise called *kirājī*, 'horse-jobbers'; and he or his translator correctly translates *qanbūr* 'Alī as 'hunch-backed 'Alī'. The shrine of Qanbur Dada, near Hafsa, had become so popular as a place of pilgrimage that in 1667 the Sultan ordered its destruction at the instigation of the Khoja of Van (von Hammer, *GdOR.* iii. p. 593-4).

The origin of this name as applied to 'Alī does not appear, but one of the Rifā'ī *takias* at Constantinople is called 'Alī Kuzī *takia-si*, and *kūz* (Pers., in Turk. pronunciation *kyūz*) means 'a hump-back'.

[3] This passage is greatly illuminated from the late Mr. F. W. Hasluck's papers in the *Annual* of the British School at Athens, especially vol. xxi. p. 87, where he wrote: "Under the Dede [Akhi] Bābā and eight other Bābās, each having a separate 'residency' (*konak*), who preside over the various departments of work carried on in the tekke, directing the labours of the probationers under them. Their respective spheres are the buttery (Kilerdji Bābā), the bakery (Ekmekdji Bābā), the kitchen (Ashdji Bābā), the stables (Atadji Bābā), the guest-house (Mehmandār Bābā), the mausoleum of Balum Sultān (Balum Evi), and the vineyards (Dede Bāgh, Hanbāgh)." Hence in Brown's text Bahīm (Baheem) appears to be a misprint for Balum Sulṭān, a reforming saint who lived two generations after Hājī Baqtāsh and was buried at Pirevi (*ib.*, p. 88, n. 3). Balum is specially venerated by the Baqtāsh, and is the patron of the celibate branch.

2. Of the cook, called the *pōst* of Said 'Alī Balkhī, one of the Caliphs of the Order.

3. Of the breadmaker, called after Bahīm Sultān.

4. Of the *naqīb* (Deputy Shaikh), named after Gai Gusūs.[1]

5. Of the *maidān*.[2] It is occupied by the superintendent of the *takia*, who represents Sarī Ismāīl.

6. Of the steward of the *takia*, called after Kulī Achik Hājim Sultān.[3]

[1] The Gai Gusoos of the text is the Kaigousouz [Kīghūsūz] Sultān of Hasluck (*ib.*, p. 98). He was a pupil of Abdāl Mūsā and carried the Baqtāshī faith to Egypt. By repute of princely birth he bore in the world the title of 'Sulṭānzāda Ghaibī' or 'The Concealed Prince'. He is in charge, apparently, of some department of the kitchen, as he gives his name to the *pilāf* or dry stew among the Baqtāsh, and they call it 'Kaigousouz' (*ib.*, p. 98). E. G. Browne spells his name Qayghusuz (*J.R.A.S.*, 1907, p. 573).

In Turk. *qāygū* or *qāygī* = 'care' or 'anxiety', and *qāygū-suz* would apparently mean 'free from care'. *Kai* in Persian = 'king' or 'monarch', but *ghusuz* has no meaning, unless it is a corruption of *gyūzsuz*, 'sightless'. When sent to Egypt Kīghūsūz took the name of 'Abdullāh, and became known as the Shaikh 'Abdullāh al-Maghaurī, *i.e.* 'he of the grotto or cave', from Ar. *maghāra*, 'cave'.

In the passage quoted from Hasluck the term Kilerdji means 'holder of the larder', from Turk. *kilar* or *kilār*, 'store-cupboard'; Ekmekdji from Turk. *akmak* or *etmek*, 'bread'; Ashdji, from Turk. *āsh*, 'soup', 'a repast'; Atadji, from Turk. *āt*, 'horse'; and Mehmāndār, from the Persian, 'a receiver of a guest', *mihmān*. Hence these are not proper names like Balum.

[2] The *maidān* is the oratory; and Sarī Ismā'īl Ṣulṭān, one of the *khalīfas* of Ḥājī Baqtāsh, buried at Daouas in the Smyrna *wilāyat* (*ib.*, p. 92).

[3] Kolu (*sic*) Atchik Hādjim Ṣulṭān was a Khalīfa of the Baqtāsh and is buried at Rajab (Redjeb) in the Brusa *wilāyat* (*ib.*, p. 94).

Achiq, 'open', 'uncovered', 'free, saucy or impudent (in manner or conduct)': Redhouse, *Turk.-Eng. Lex.* p. 32. But this is not the explanation recorded in the *Wilāyat-nāma of Hājim Sulṭan*, so well translated by Rudolf Tschudi in No. 17 of the *Türkische Bibliothek*. That work, indeed, gives no rendering of the term, but Tschudi cites one from other sources. According to them Ḥājī Baqtāsh gave Sulṭān Ḥājim a wooden sabre wherewith the latter proceeded to cut the mule of a *dervish* in two. To punish him Hājī Baqtāsh made him *cholāq* or *qolāq*, 'one-armed' or 'paralysed in one arm'. But as he repented and his fellow-disciples interceded for him, the Ḥājī restored to him the use of his mutilated arm, and said that in future he should be known as 'Qolī achaq', or declared that "the arm of the Ḥājim should grow again"; so he was styled Qolū Achiq, "he with the arm which had grown again" (*op. cit.*, p. 33). Cholāq is the fore-name of a Khalwatī saint, Hasan (*v.* p. 463 *infra*).

Brown's information was that Ṣulṭān Ḥājim was steward of the *takia*, but his name means literally 'one who cups or scarifies'. And in the *Wilāyat-nāma* we find a curious rôle assigned to him. Usually it is the

7. Of the coffee-maker, called after Shāzilī Sultān.[1]

8. Of the bag-bearer, called after Kara Daulat Jān Bābā.[2]

9. Of the sacrificer, called after Ibrāhīm Khalīl-Ullāh, or the prophet Abraham of the Old Testament.

10. Of the ordinary attendant of the services, called after Abdāl Mūsā.[3]

---

superior who shaves the head of an inferior in the mystic ritual (*op. cit.*, p. 30). But Ṣulṭān Ḥājim is described as shaving the head of Ḥājī Baqtāsh, or, more precisely, as being about to shave it when his miraculous aid is invoked from a sinking ship (*ib.*, p. 31). Then follows the incident of the wooden sabre. We might understand that Ḥājī Baqtāsh bestowed on Ṣulṭān Ḥājim the mystic razor, and that the sabre was returned to the Ḥājī. But here again authorities differ, and the Ḥājī is said to have made Ṣulṭān Ḥājim the executioner (*jallād*) of the *maidān*, the 'assembly of the brethren' of the order, under restrictions (*ib.*, p. 32). Ḥājim was the third son of the Imām-zādā Ḥusain, son of the Imām 'Alī Naqī. His brothers were Sayyid Jihānī and Sayyid Sulṭānī, his own name being really Rajab Sultān (p. 5).

[1] The question whether coffee is a lawful beverage has been much debated by Moslem jurisprudents. Introduced from Persia (not Abyssinia as in *Oxford Dict.*, *s.v.*) into Aden by Muftī Jamāl-ud-Dīn (*ob.* 1470) and Muḥammad al-Hadrawī, it was subsequently brought into Egypt from Yaman by *darvishes.* It was used by them to prevent sleep during their vigils, but its use was often condemned by the religious authorities, as, for instance, at Mecca, and prohibited by the Sultāns Sulaimān II. and Murād III. Indulgence in it was sometimes punished with the bastinado. Ash-Shāzilī's views on this question do not appear to be on record, but the fact remains that he is the patron saint of the coffee-makers (*Le Voyage de l'Arabie Heureuse*, by Jean de la Roque, Amsterdam, 1716, p. 287 f.).

Evliya, however, while admitting that he does not know the name of the Shaikh of the coffee-merchants, "because coffee is a new invention", says "the drinking it comes from Sheikh Shādeli" (*Travels*, i. pt. ii. p. 214).

[2] This may be the Qara Bābā of the *Wilāyat-nāma of Ḥājim Ṣulṭān.* The legend about him is that he was a learned and excellent man, a Jalā-lī, 'a stalwart', of Khorāsān. Now that land was afflicted by famine after Ḥājī Baqtāsh and Ḥājim Ṣulṭān had taken away the wallet and other insignia. Qara Bābā volunteered to recover the wallet from Ḥājim Ṣulṭān, but the latter slew him with his own arrow and buried him somewhere in or near the Shaikhlū plain. But Qara Bābā's disciples entered the service of Ḥājim Ṣulṭān, and on a leafy tree just over his head Ḥājim hung the wallet, and for forty years it supplied food to those who put their faith in him (*Türk. Bib.* No. 17, p. 102 f.). This would explain his function as bag-bearer.

[3] 'Abdāl Mūsā was a very celebrated saint, a pupil of Yatagan Bābā, whose shrine is at Yatagan in the Smyrna *wilāyat.* Abdāl Mūsā is buried in the town or district of Elmali, the centre of the tract inhabited by the primitive Shī'a tribes known as the Takhtajī ('wood-cutters'). He was the teacher of Kaighousouz (*Annual*, B.S.A. xxi. pp. 91-3).

11. Of the groom, called after Qambar, the groom of the Caliph 'Alī.

12. Of the *mihmāndār*, or the officer charged with attending upon the guests of the *takia*, called after Khizr.[1]

The apartment of the Shaikh is called the *Shaikh hujrāsī*, or 'cell of the master'. He seldom resides in the *takia*, but occupies a separate house with his family. He, however, sometimes makes a vow of celibacy, called the *iqrār mujarrad*, in which case he resides in the convent. A Baqtāsh Darvish on making this vow is asked by the Shaikh whether, if he breaks it, he is willing to come under the sword of 'Alī (the *Zūlfikār*), and he answers in the affirmative, and adds that he may be cut asunder by the sword of our *Shāh-i-wilāyat*, or supreme 'spiritual chief', who is 'Alī. This is one of the secret vows of the Order. The number twelve is a mystical one for the Baqtāshes, for whenever any one makes a vow, called the *nazr*, he always incurs the penalty of twelve punishments should he fail to keep it; he swears by the twelve, pays money in twelves, and strikes twelve blows as a punishment. This, I am told, is done simply in imitation of the practice of the Founder. The *zikr ullāh*, or Prayers of the Brethren in the *takia*, are always silent, and have, it is said, the following origin:

It is related as coming from 'Alī—may God bless him with His Divine Satisfaction!—"I once asked of the Prophet, 'O Prophet of Allāh, instruct me in the shortest way to God, and facilitate me in the proper way to worship Him'. He replied, 'O 'Alī, the proper way is to mention, or call upon His Name'. I asked how I should mention Him, and he answered, 'Close your eyes and listen to me, repeating after me, *Lā illāha ill' Allāh* (there is no God but Allāh)'. These words the Prophet uttered three times with his eyes closed, speaking with a loud voice, and I imitated him".

It is said that once when the Prophet and 'Alī were alone

[1] Khizr would naturally be the guide of strangers. He must not be confused with Kilerdji Bābā, a disciple of Abdāl Mūsā and buried at Gilevgi in the *wilāyat* of Qonia (Hasluck in *Annual*, B.S.A. xxi. p. 92). These offices may be compared or contrasted with those of a Greek monastery such as that of Laura on Mt. Athos, as described by John Covel in 1677 (*ib.*, xvii. p. 109 f.). Covel alludes to a round stone or rose of stones in the Quire before the ὡραῖαι πύλαι ('fair gates'). This stone he calls σολέα (p. 111), but it rather denotes a flat or sunk arena. This may foreshadow the *maidān-tāsh*.

together, the former knelt, and 'Alī did the same before him, so that their knees met. The Prophet commenced reciting the preceding, three times; the first time with his face turned over his left shoulder, the second with his face over his breast, and the third with his face turned to his left shoulder; his eyes were closed, and his voice raised, confirming his *hadīs*, or saying, "The best of mentions or prayers is, 'There is no God but Allāh'".

This form of prayer is called the *jihrī*, or audible, and is common to many other Orders also. The silent one is called the *hiffī* [*khafī*],[1] and had its origin in the commands of the Prophet to Abū-Bakr when they were concealed together from their enemies in a cave. It may be added the 40th verse of the 9th chapter of the *Qurān* is the basis of the form of prayer of all the Darvishes, *i.e.* "They were both in a cave, and he (the Prophet) said to his companion, 'Be not grieved, for God is with us; He has caused his protection to descend from on high, and sustained him with invisible armies, and he overthrew the word of the infidels. The Word of God is much the highest,—He is powerful and wise'".

The members of a Baqtāsh *takia*, who offer the name of an individual to the Shaikh for acceptance, are called *rahpars*,[2] or 'guides'; those who accompany him in the *takia* during the initiation are called *tarjumāns*, or interpreters, and the latter are armed with a weapon called *tabar*, of this shape . The cord which is put round his neck when first entering the *takia* is called the *dehband*, or *taiband*. The horn which the Baqtāsh blow is called the *luffar*; it is also called after one of the titles of God, *Wadūd*, or the Loving.

One of the secret signs of the Order are in the two words *tabran* and *tūlan*,[3] 'near and far', signifying 'near in affection

[1] According to Petit (*Les Confréries Musulmanes*, Paris, 1902, p. 51) the *zikr-al-khafi* has been adopted by the Khāladiya, a Turkish branch of the Naqshbandīs.

[2] *Rahbār*, a guide. "Be a guide (*rahbār*), not a brigand (*rahbur*)", was a *mot* of Fātima, wife of the mystic Abū Ḥamid Aḥmad b. Khadruya al-Balkhī (*Kashf ul-Mahjūb*, p. 120).

[3] *Tūlan*, literally 'lengthwise'; *tabran*—is not easily explicable. It may be that there is some obscure allusion here to the theory of the tūl and 'arz, or *sayhūr* and *dayhur* of Ḥusain Manṣūr. Ṭūl = 'length', and 'arz = 'breath'. Ḥusain's work, the *Kitāb al-Ṣayhūr, fī naqẓ al-Dayhūr* means literally "The Book of the Cone of Shadow, wherein is eclipsed the Moon on the destruction of the Ages". (But *naqẓ* suggests 'deliverance' or 'salvation' as well as, or rather than, 'destruction'.) As Massignon points

and far in conceit'. The second *tie* called *bāgh*, or *band*, is in the words : " He was the sovereign of the *talqīn* (spiritual or mystical instructors of all the *pīrs*, or founders of Orders, and of their vows", and its execution is the *'ahd-i-wafā*[1] (performance of vow).

THE TWELVE IMĀMS OF THE BAQTĀSH

" It is related that the blessed Prophet told his confidential companions (the *aṣḥābs*) that he did not require of them either the performance of the *namāz* (prayers), the *saum* (fast), the *hājj* (pilgrimage to Makka), or the *zakāt* (bestowal of alms to the poor), but only that they should look after the members of his family".

The Prophet had but one daughter, Fātima, whom he married to his nephew 'Alī. The 'Alīide Darvishes, and especially the Baqtāsh, declare that the Prophet designed him to be his successor (*khalīfa*) or ' Caliph ', whilst the orthodox Mussulmans deny it. This daughter bore two sons, named Hasan and Husain, to whom the Prophet, who had no male children, was warmly attached. These are the first Imāms of Islamism, for although many deny their rights of succession, their direct descent from the Prophet surrounds them with a halo of veneration, respect, and affection. Hasan was poisoned,[2] and lies interred at Madīna, and Husain was killed by Yazīd bin-Muāwia, and is buried at Karbalā.[3]

---

out, Ḥusain had in view the Hellenistic doctrine of the eternity of the world ; and he was, moreover, affirming its duality—of spirit and matter. Hence he seems to have been insisting on the temporary or apparent occlusion of the ages and their essential indestructibility. The simile of the eclipse in the Cone of Shadow in his work only develops the line of thought expressed in his theory of the *lāhūt* and *nāsūt*, in the story of Adam's creation and in that of Iblīs's refusal to do him reverence, as the reflected image of his Creator. The crescent-shaped halberd of the Baqtāsh may thus symbolise man's nearness to God as the moon reflects the light of the sun. The Baqtāsh could not adopt the complete phrase *'arzan tūlan* without exposing themselves to the suspicion that they had fallen into heresy. Hence they seem to have coined a new word from their symbol, the *tabr*, to express unity with the divine by reflected light (*v.* Massignon, *Kitāb al-Ṭawāsīn*, pp. 141-5, and 138). But *v. n.* on p. 460 *infra*.

[1] *Wafā-i-'ahd.*

[2] Ḥasan died of consumption, though an attempt was made to throw the responsibility for his death on Mu'āwia (*E.I.* ii. p. 274).

[3] Ḥusain's death was deplored by Yazīd, and he treated the survivors of the massacre at Karbalā with honour (*ib.*, p. 339).

The fourth Imām was Zain-ul-'Abidīn,[1] and son of Husain; he was killed by Marwān,[2] the son of Yazīd, and is buried at Madīna.

The fifth, Muhammad Bāqir, was killed by Hishām, son of 'Abd-ul-Malik, and interred at Madīna.

The sixth, Ja'far-as-Sādiq, was killed by Mansūr-i-Kufr, and is buried at Madīna.

The seventh, Mūsā-al-Kāzim,[3] was killed by Harūn-ar-Rashīd, with poisoned grapes, and is buried at Baghdād. The spot is still called *al-Kāzimain*.[4]

The eighth was 'Alī ibn Mūsā-ur-Rizā; [5] he was killed by the

[1] Zain-ul-'Ābidīn, 'Ornament of the Faithful'.

[2] Marwān, the Ummayad Caliph, reigned from 683-85, and was succeeded by his son 'Abd-ul-Malik in 685 H.

[3] Called Mūsā al-Qazam incorrectly. Mūsā ibn Ja'far, see the list in *E.R.E.* 11, p. 455.

[4] For El Kiazzemain (the Turkish pronunciation) in original. Kāẓim, 'he who controls or suppresses (anger)', was a title of the seventh of the twelve Imāms of the Shī'as, and was also borne by his grandson. Both are buried at Kāzimain, which is sometimes described as a suburb of Baghdād, sometimes as a village near it (cf. Redhouse, *Turk.-Eng. Lex.* i. p. 1516). (The spelling Qādhimain sometimes adopted appears to be incorrect.)

The two martyrs, Mūsā al-Kāẓim and his infant grandson were not the only Alid martyrs, whose number is often given as fourteen. They are known as the Ma'sūm-i-Pāk, or 'Pure Innocents', *ma'ṣūm*, 'innocent', having also the meaning of 'an infant, a little child'. Hasluck records a curious transference of this cult at Siwās: "In the town is a recent *tekke*, called Maksoumler ('the infants'), or Maksoum Pāk (Pers. *pāk* = 'pure'), founded by a certain Halil Pasha, afterwards Governor of Beyrout. About fifty years ago a darvish is said to have discovered by revelation the graves of two infants (*maksoum*), who were identified with 'Ali Eftar, son of the fifth Imām (Mahommed Bakir), and Sali, son of the seventh (Mousa Kiazim); these infants are regarded as martyrs" (*Annual*, B.S.A. xxi. pp. 95-6). Here *maksūm* appears to be a popular corruption of *ma'ṣūm*, but it may be an error for *makẓūm*, 'sad', which is formed from the same root (*kaẓama*) as *kāẓim*.

The title Maisum borne by the rulers of Tabasaran, west of Darband, in the fifteenth century was explained as the Ar. *ma'ṣūm* (*E.I.* i. p. 889).

Hardly less seldom than the twelve Imāms are mentioned the fourteen *ma'ṣūm-i-pāk*, 'the pure innocent children'. They include Muḥammad Akbar, a son of 'Ali and Fātima; 'Abdullāh, a son of Ḥasan; both, like many Imāms, buried in the Baqī' al-Gharqad at Madīna; also 'Abdullah, a son of Ḥusain; and Khadīja and Fātima make up the total. But these two last may be Alid girls who died young, *e.g.* the Fāṭima buried at Qūm in 816 H. is called *al-ma'ṣūma*. She was a sister of the Imām 'Alī Rizā (Jacob, *Die Bektasch.* p. 41).

[5] 'Alī ibn Mūsā ar-Rizā was named his successor by the Caliph al-Mamūn, and married to his daughter, but he, too, was got rid of by poisoned grapes according to the Shī'as (*E.R.E.* 11, p. 454).

Caliph Mamūn, and is buried at [in] Khurāsān, now called Mashhad-i-a'lā.

The ninth, Muhammad Tāghī,[1] was killed by the Caliph Mastaqīm, and is buried at Sāmarrā, near Baghdād.

The tenth, 'Alī Nākhi',[2] was killed by the Caliph Mastaqīm, and is interred at the same place.

The eleventh, Hasan-al-'Askarī,[3] was killed by the Caliph Muta'ammid, and is buried at the same place.

The twelfth, Mahdī, who is said to have mysteriously disappeared the 15th day of Sha'bān, and the 266th year of the Hījrā [A.D. 878], at Sāmarrā,[4] and there is a cave at that place from which, it is supposed, he will reappear. All the Darvishes confidently expect this and so do most devout Mussulmans, and that he will reign as a temporal sovereign.

These were all sons [descendants] of the Imām Husain. Hasan also had children. The grandchildren of both escaped from these massacres, and from them descended the Saiyidāt, or the Saiyids (Cids), who wear green turbans as a family distinction, a colour which, it is said, Allah commanded the Prophet to use. There were two kinds of Saiyids (sometimes called also *amīrs*, commanders) ; they are *Saiyidāt 'Alīwīa*, or those born to 'Alī by another wife, and not by Fātima. They all have a jurisdiction, in many respects, separate from ordinary Mussulmans, under the

---

The eighth Imām, Rizā, a photograph of whose shrine at Mashhad may be seen in Major P. M. Sykes's *Ten Thousand Miles in Persia*, p. 24, had innumerable brothers, *e.g.* one Shāhzād Ḥusain, buried at Jupār near Rigabād in Karmān, another at Nagar, a third, 'Abd-ur-Rahmān, at Takia, and sisters, Fāṭima at Qum in Central Persia, and Bībī Hayāt between Kākh and Kirwān. A descendant, Kamāl-ud-Dīn, has a shrine at Saiyidābād near Sirjān, the ancient capital of Bardsīr. Sirjān is termed by Ṣūfīs the Lesser Syria from its many ancient graves (Major P. M. Sykes, *op. cit.* pp. 425, 427, 435, 444, 433 and 158).

[1] Tāghī, ' rebellious ', is, of course, impossible. Taqī, ' pious ', is meant. He appeared in a vision to Khwāja 'Alī the Ardabīlī (*v.* note on p. 85 *supra*).

[2] Nākhi', ' learned '. But his real title was an-Naqī, ' the pure ' or ' excellent '. He died in A.D. 868.

[3] Al-'Askarī was so named from his place of birth and death, the camp *'askar*, at Sāmarrā.

[4] Sāmarra, the scene of W. Beckford's *Vathek*. Supposed to have stood on the site of Nimrod's tower, it was refounded by the Caliph Mutasim when he found Baghdād untenable owing to disputes between its inhabitants and his Turkish slaves (Beckford's *Vathek*, p. 99).

direction of a functionary called the *naqīb-ul-ashraf*, who resides at Constantinople. Every Mussulman claiming to be a Saiyid is required to possess a document establishing his genealogy.

The following is a translation from a MS. of the Baqtāsh, and is an account of their various prayers at their *takia*:

1. The *takbīr* (*Allāhu akbar*), 'God or *Allāh* is the greatest of all Gods', on putting on the *tāj* or cap.
2. Similar.
3. Ditto.
4. When he visits the *takia* as a guest.
5. On arriving at the sill of the inner door.
6. On entering it.
7. On taking the first step inside it.
8. " second "
9. " third "
10. " fourth "
11. On approaching the *murshid* (Shaikh).
12. On offering him a present.
13. On standing before him, with the arms crossed on the breast, one hand over each shoulder, and the right toe over the left toe, called *Dār durmak*.[1]
14. Similar, called the *Dār-i-Mansūr*, after Mansūr, who was killed.
15. On the same occasion.
16. For sins.
17. "
18. Called the *gunāh-i-gulbank*,[2] or prayer for sins of omission, and to thank God for His bounties.
19. Called *takbīr-i-khirqa wa pōst*, or ['magnification'] for the mantle and seat.
20. Ditto, for the *khirqa* only.
21. " "

[1] *Dar durmak* in original. The word is not given by Redhouse, but cf. Persian *dardar kardan* or *dar-ā-dar kardan*, 'to remain firm, fixed (steadfast or immovable)': Johnson's *Dict.* p. 551. Cf. p. 252 *infra*, note on *būyūn kasmak*.

[2] For *gulbank-i-gunāh*, *gulbung* or *-bāng* is a loud shout or war-cry: or the noise of a drum (Johnson, p. 1044).

22. For the *fanāī*,[1] or cap.

23. For ditto.

24. A *tarjumān*, of the *taslīm-tāsh*.

25. Ditto.

26. „

27. A *takbīr*, on the *alif-lām-ad* the *tannūra*, [petticoat], the *palank*.

28. On the *palank*.

29. „ „

30. On the *alif-lām-ed*.[2]

31. „ *kambarīa*.

[1] *Fanāī, fenaee* in original: the word seems to be derived from *fanā*, 'annihilation', 'extinction', a suggestion borne out by the interpretation given on p. 199 *infra*. Thus the *fanāī* would signify 'self-extinction'. With this possible allusion may be compared that suggested for the *istiwā* on p. 244 *infra*.

[2] The usual conjunction is *lām-alif*, and these two letters are regarded as one or as two but united. The name of Allāh is composed of the five letters, *alif*, *lām* (*bis*), *alif* again and *he*. The *ed* in the text might be regarded as a mistake for *he*, but on p. 113 the *ed* is replaced by *end*, hence this suggestion is untenable. Moreover it fails to explain the conjunction *alif-lām*. The conjunction *alif-lām* might possibly be regarded as a picture of the two first fingers, and it is noteworthy that in early Christian art one of the three positions of the hand in Benediction was the first and second fingers elevated, the other two being the thunb and first finger or all four fingers raised (*E.R.E.* vi. p. 497). But in the *alif-lām* the two letters are disjoined, so that it is difficult to think that there is any suggestion of a gesture with the hand (cf. C. Huart, *Textes Houroufis*, p. 13). But for this difficulty it would be tempting to see in the *alif-lām* a revival of the 'symbolic hand' so fully described in Elworthy's *Horns of Honour*, pp. 194 ff., the *alif* representing the second finger, the down-stroke of the *lām* the first, and the up-stroke the thumb. In the Ḥurūfī system the Arabic alphabet with its twenty-eight letters was regarded as incomplete and only fulfilled by the addition of the four peculiar to the Persian, but the ligature *lām-alif* in some unexplained way anticipated those four letters (Jacob, *Die Bektaschijje*, p. 47). These four letters have twelve diacritical points and are symbols in the Baqtāsh doctrine of the twelve Imāms (*ib.* p. 40).

In the Ismailian catechism one of the questions was: Why does man's carriage, when he stands upright, represent an *alif*, and why, when he kneels, does he become like a *lām*, and when he prostrates himself like a *he*? In such wise that that forms a book which presents the name of God, *ilah* (ALH). Among the Mughairīs, a sect of the Mushabbihs, God was conceived of as a man of light, with a crown of light on His head, His members like the letters of the alphabet, and His feet like an *alif* (de Sacy, *Exposé de la Religion des Druzes*, i. pp. 86 and 47).

32. On the *kambarīa*.
33. „ *tannūra*.[1]
34. „ *mangosh*.
35. *Chirāgh*, or candle, after the *dalīl* ['proving'], or ceremony at the outer door.
36. Ditto.
37. „
38. „
39. On the *challik* or whip.
40. „ *kashgūl* [*kashkūl* [2]] beggar's cup.
41. „ *pōstakī* of the *nāib*.
42. „ „ of the cook.
43. „ *chahār yār*, or four direct Caliphs.
44. „ *qurbān*, or sacrifice.
45. On asking permission of the Shaikh to go to the table.
46. On spreading the table.
47. On the table.
48. On his seat at the table.
49. On the *maidānjī*, or sweeper of the hall of the *takia*.
50. *Tarjumān*, or [? of] the *ghusul*, or ablutions.
51. On the door.
52. „ *Dār-i-Mansūr*.
53. „ Drink-giver.
54. „ *salām* (salutation).
55. „ Attendants.
56. „ Flag and lamentations for the cruel fate of Hasan and Husain.
57. On the flag.
58. „ *chirāgh* [lamp] of the centre stone.
59. On emptying the *kashgūl* on the table.

[1] *Tannūra* is a dress, 'like a furnace, of leather worn by *dervishes* from their middle' (Johnson, *Pers.-Arab. Dict.* p. 387). *Tannūr* means an oven, but is also used for lantern; *e.g.* in the mosque at Jerusalem the Great Lantern (*Tannūr*) contained 500 lamps (G. Le Strange in *J.R.A.S.* xix. pt. ii. p. 41).

The *tannūr* (Osm. *tandūr*), in Pers. *kursī*, was a frame of wood made round a stove on which a rug or felt was thrown; it was used for warming the feet in seasons of intense cold (Cl. Huart, *Les Saints des Derviches tourneurs*, p. 198).

[2] Generally made in the form of a boat.

60. On the *tabar*,[1] the *fignī*,[2] and the *challik*, peculiar instruments used by the Baqtāsh when on a long journey.

61. When putting on the girdle.

62. On the *'ishq-i-mangosh*, or love for the horse-shoe of 'Alī, used as an ear-ring.

63. On the *jamjama*,[3] or skin thrown over the shoulders of the Baqtāsh when travelling.

64. On the *tarjumān-i-dolāq*, or leggings.

65. ,, *lawank*, or long shirt worn by them.

66. ,, *muliffa*,[4] a wide dress worn by them.

(These two latter refer to the garments worn by the Prophet when he declared : " 'Alī is my body, blood, soul, and flesh: my light and his light are one ".)

67. Of the *dahband*, or the rope which is put round the disciple's neck when first introduced into a *takia*.

68. On the *sharbat*, or drink.

69. Ear-rings.

70. ,, sacrifice.

71. On shaving.

72. On entering a *takia*

73. ,, the door.

74. ,, some steps.

75. On approaching the Shaikh.

The following are translations of a few of the preceding prayers. Some of them are ordinary Islām prayers, and many so closely

[1] *Tabr* or *ṭabr*, Pers., 'an axe or mattock', the halberd figured on p. 191 *supra*.

[2] *Fignī*, a word not traceable in the Lexicons, may be a corruption of or a mistake for the Ar. *fanīqa*, 'a large ḥair sack' (Redhouse, *Turk.-Eng. Lex.* p. 1398).

[3] *Jemjemeh* in original. Redhouse gives no such meaning as 'a skin thrown over the shoulders', but defines *jumjume* as 'a kind of shoe', Pers. *jumjum*, 'a sandal or foot covering of rope, old clouts, etc.'. But it is not impossible that Brown's translation is right, and that the word is of Indian origin, being a corruption of *chamrā*, 'skin'. Tschudi cites the *Köder* (? *yem*) as a part of the *dervish* equipment from Evliya, iii. p. 14, but that seemingly means 'heel-leather' (*Türk. Bibl.* No. 17, p. 8.)

'Shoes of cotton soled with linen-rags (*jumjum*)' were worn by Abū Sa'īd ibn Abī'l Khair, who was born in A.D. 967 (Nicholson, *Studies in Islamic Mysticism*, p. 45).

[4] *Muliffa*, Ar. *milaff*, 'anything in which people wrap themselves when going to sleep', 'a blanket' (Johnson, p. 1244). It may be that the form *muliffa* denotes 'shroud', but the Lexicons give no such form or meaning.

resemble each other as not to be of any particular interest as explicative of the Darvish Orders. The word *tarjumān*, or 'interpreter', has also the signification of a prayer, though only with relation to spiritualism.

1. *Tarjumān* of the door sill: "I have placed my head and soul (heart) on the sill of the door of repentance, so that my body may be pure as gold. My request is that you, O Shaikh, deign to turn your eyes for an instant on this *faqīr*."

2. *Tarjumān* on presenting an offering to the Shaikh: "The ant brought as an offering to Sulaimān (son of David), the thigh of a grasshopper; thou, O Shaikh, art Sulaimān, and I am thy ant; pray accept of my humble offering".

3. *Tarjumān* on saluting the Shaikh and Darvishes: "*Salām-alaik* (peace to thee), O ye followers of the true path; ye elders of the light of truth; ye disciples of true knowledge".

4. On asking forgiveness of a fault: "I have failed, O Shaikh,—pardon me for the sake of 'Alī-ul-Murtaza, with whom God was satisfied; for the sake of Hasan, the martyr of Karbalā. I have wronged myself, O Shaikh!"

5. On putting on the cap, called *fanāī*: "Sign of the glorious Uwais-ul-Karanī; of Qambar the groom of the sublime 'Alī,—of those who are dead, of the great family of the Imām Rizā—permit me to put on this cap; for I fully believe in its efficacy".

6. On putting on the eight-angular stone, called the *taslīm-tāsh*:[1] "O Allāh, the rites of the *Aranlar*[2] (disciples) have become my faith; no doubt now exists in my heart; on putting on the *taslīm* I have given myself up to Thee".

7. Ditto on the ear-ring: "End of all increase, ring of the neck of all prosperity, token of those who are in Paradise, gift of the martyr Shāh (Husain), curses upon Yazīd" (who killed him).

8. A *takbīr* of the *taslīm-tāsh*: "Allāh! Allāh! In the name of Allāh, the Merciful and the Clement! God commanded him (Moses) to strike the stone with thy staff, and twelve fountains were suddenly opened by the blow (*Qurān*, 2nd chapter, 57th verse). We sent a cloud over your heads,—we sent you manna and quails, saying, Eat of the delicious food which we have sent you; you have more wronged yourself than me."—*Qurān*, ii. 54.

[1] Cf. Palmer's *Quran S.B.E.* vi. pp. 7 and 8.

[2] *Erenler* in original: pl. of *aran*, 'one instructed in the truth'.

9. A *takbīr* of the *alif-lām-ad* and the *palank*: "God has been satisfied with the believers who have given thee their hand under the tree, as a sign of fidelity. He knew the thoughts of their hearts. He gave them tranquillity, and recompensed them with a speedy victory," and ending with the exclamations, "O Muhammad! O 'Alī".—*Qurān*, xlviii. 18.

10. Ditto of the *alif-lām-and*, on taking the vow of celibacy: "I abandon all matrimony, and obligate myself with this belt to do so". (He then recites chapter cxii. of the *Qurān*, and the Shaikh declares to the *murīd*, "God does not engender nor bring forth (and so may men tell of thee), and no one is equal to Him".)

11. A *tarjumān* of Kambar: "I am become a *kambarī* in the footsteps of thy steed. Under thy feet I have long suffered. 'I have become the leader of all prophets', says Muhammad. Thou (the Shaikh) seest all things; thou knowest all things; thou art all things to me."

12. A *tarjumān* of the *tannūra*: "O thou who art devoted to the Path, cling to thy *pīr*, and wander not about. From thy heart follow the noble Haidar ('Alī); attach the stone to thy ear; be a servant; come to the Shāh of the *arans*, and become the ostler of the ostler of 'Alī."

13. A *tarjumān* of the *chirāgh* (light). This is given after a lesson from the *pīr*, on the proper method of extinguishing it. "Allāh is my friend. Haqq! Hū! Arans! 'Āshiq! Faithful! Those who burn with Love! The Awake! The 'Ain-i-Jam'!" (This latter is the name of the place where they meet.) "The abiders in Love! Splendid Light! The Pride of all Darvishes!" (This is said to refer to the custom of 'Alī, who caused his friends to meet him, and lit a candle in their midst.) "Laws of all Mankind! Shāh of Khurāsān! By the beauty of Muhammad! The perfection of 'Alī! Hū! Dōst!"

14. On the same: "Allāh! Allāh! We have lit this light—the pride of all Darvishes, for the love of God,—the love of the Lord of both worlds,—the seal of all prophets,—the love of Him who gives water from the fountain of Kausar (in Paradise),—'Alī, the chosen of Khadīja, the best of women (the Prophet's first wife), of Fātima,—the twelve hearts of the *pīrs*,—the leaders of the Saints,—the sons of 'Alī, and the Imāms Hasan and Husain—for the fourteen pure victims, sons of the Imām Husain, and

the family of *al-'Abā*."[1] (This refers to the circumstance that the Prophet once collected under his *'abā* or cloak 'Alī, Hasan and Husain, and Fātima, himself being the fifth.) "For the love of the *Hazrat-i-khūnkiār*,[2] the *Qutb-i-Auliā*! May it burn and enlighten to the last of days the love of Hājī Baqtāsh Walī,—by the beauty of the Prophet and the perfection of 'Alī! Hū!"

15. Ditto: "Light of the saints! light of the heavens! May this spot be like the mountain of *Thūr*[3] (Sinai), where Moses saw the divine light, and worshipped it! Whenever thou art lit, may the lighter offer up a prayer for Muhammad and 'Alī!"

16. Ditto of the *challik* (stick): "Death to all those who believe in the Trinity! Say it does not open, except by 'Alī,—there is no sword but that of *Zūlfikār*." (This is from a verse of the *Qurān*.[4])

17. Ditto of the *kashgūl*; "Poor of the door of 'Alī; beggars of the *kashgūl* of the *darkiāh*[5] (*takia*); *sanad* (bond) of the lovers! In the name of 'Alī! Hū! Dōst! Ai Wallāh!"

18. Ditto of the *pōst*: "I look upon the face of a fair friend. O elevated man (the Shaikh), thou hast the two lines (the eye-

[1] 'Abā is explained to be a mantle worn by *darvesh*: *qabā*, 'a coat worn by ordinary people' (*Kashf*, p. 48).

[2] Hazrat-i-Khūnkiār, Jalāl-ud-Dīn Rūmī (also styled Mulla Khūnkār on p. 268 *infra*). Khūnkiār, literally 'a shedder of blood', means a king, as one having power of life and death. It is said to have been used as a title of the Grand Turk (Johnson, p. 545). According to Evliya the title of Khūnkiār was bestowed on Muḥammad II. in 857 H. (A.D. 1453) by Āq Shams-ud-Dīn, who also directed that he should be called Sulṭān instead of Beg, the title borne by the Osmānlī chiefs since the days of Osmān (*Travels*, i. pt. i. pp. 48, 47).

The title, like the name Jalāl-ud-Dīn, is hereditary in the head of the Maulavī order (Hasluck in *Annual*, B.S.A. xix. p. 215, citing Slade's *Travels in Turkey* (2), p. 376 f.; and Hasluck, *op. cit.* p. 209). For the ceremony of girding the Sultans of Turkey with the sword see App. to Chap. X.

The title of Khūnkār as borne by the Maulavīs recalls that of Tyrannos as borne by the god Mēn (Sabazios) whose cult was widespread in Asia Minor (P. Foucart, *Les Associations Religieuses chez les Grecs*, pp. 119 ff.). One hardly dares to suggest any connexion between Mēn and the brother of Hājī Baqtāsh who was called Mentish (*v.* p. 164 *supra*).

[3] The allusion is to Sura 3, *v.* 75 f., which refers to the legend borrowed from Talmudic sources that God assembled all past, present, and future prophets on Mt. Sinai and entered into a compact with them (Palmer's *Qurān S.B.E.* vi. p. 57 n.).

[4] The allusion apparently is to Sura 4, v. 169; 5, v. 78; or 4, v. 116.

[5] Darkīāh, the Turkish form of the Persian *dargāh*.

brows), thy seat is the seat of the *ellest.*"[1] (This refers to the 171st verse of the 3rd [7th] chapter of the *Qurān*. It is their belief that the light of the prophets descended from God upon the foreheads and between the eyes, and the pious Darvish, closing his eyes, becomes absorbed in thought, so as to produce, in imagination at least, on his own forehead, the form and figure of the *pīr* of his Order. This *āyat* or verse is considered as forming an *iqrār*,[2] or vow of faith. The *postakīs* of the four angels are the seats of God,—these are, 1st, *sharī'at*, 2nd, *tarīqat*, 3rd, *haqīqat*, and 4th, *ma'rifat*.) " By the present and the absent ; the *ain-i-jam'* ! Aranlar ! Hū ! "

19. Ditto of the *qurbān* : " By the sacrifice of Ismāīl (Ishmael), ordered by God through the angel Gabriel ! Hū ! Dōst ! Ai, Wallāh ! "

20. Ditto of the table. (This is entirely the 8th and 9th verses of the 77th chapter, and the 114th verse of the 5th chapter of the *Qurān*.)

21. Ditto, in entering the *takia* for the purpose of asking hospitality : " Allāh is our friend ! Joy to the dwellers in the *takia* ! Love to those who are joyful ! To all those *faqīrs* now present ! To the *pīrs* and the *ustāds* (masters). To the *nāibs* ! To the dwellers in this house of the Shāh ('Alī) ! "

22. The following is the *gulbank*, or grace before meals, of the Order : " O God ! O God ! by the horn of the archangel Isrāfīl ! —by the meaning of Qambar !—by the light of the *masjid* (Prophet), and the *mihrāb* and the *minbar* (altar and pulpit, the former pointing towards Makka),—by our Sovereign *pīr*, Hājī Baqtāsh Wali, Sarwar (General[3]),—by the Breath of the 3, the 5, the 7, and the 40 true Saints,—we thank Thee ! Hū ! "

These numbers refer to the *rijāl-i-ghaib* (or the unseen men), who every morning are supposed to attend at the Ka'āba (Caaba) of Makka, and who wander over the whole world, by Divine command, to superintend the affairs of mankind. Of the first

[1] For Alast—' Am I not ? (your Lord) ', *Qurān*, vii. v. 171. This verse is constantly alluded to in Persian mystical poetry as *roz-i-alast*, " the day of ' Am I not ? ' " (Palmer, *S.B.E.* vi. p. 87).

[2] Iqrār is usually ' confession ' (*v. E.I.* ii. p. 401, where the sense ' agreement ' is not noticed). At p. 208 *infra*, *iqrār-nāma* means ' deed of agreement '. Confession is known in Islām, and *hadia* is used for a death-bed confession.

[3] ? Generous.

three, one is called the *qutb*,[1] or centre,—the second and third the *umanā*, or the Faithful. One stands on the right and the other on the left of the *qutb*, and they all stand on the summit of the Ka'āba. They are also called the *ahl-i-tasarruf*[2] (Owners or Masters of Destiny), and they never leave Makka. There are also four others, called *autād*[3] (the Great or Eminent), who wander over the world. The seven are called the *akhiār*, or the 'Very good', who equally wander over the surface of the globe. The 40 are called the *shuhadā*,[4] or the victims, and their mission is equally the same. There are also 70 others, called the *budalā* (plural of *abdāl*), or the servants of Allāh; also eight, called the *nuqba*, or the deputies, and their duties are much like those of the others.

All of these go to Makka every morning, and report the result of their previous day's peregrinations to the *qutb* or centre, offer up prayers, and set out anew.

The horn of the Baqtāsh, called thc *luffar*, alluded to in the prayers, is the shape of a wild goat's horn. It is probably in remembrance of the horn of the angel Isrāfīl. By it the fraternity are called to refreshment, and warned of danger. It is, as aforementioned, also called *Yā Wadūd* (O Loving God)!

On the Asiatic side of the Bosphorus, inland from the town of Kadi Kūī (ancient Chalcedon), is a small village called Mardavan Kūī, much visited by pious, as well as simply superstitious, Mussul-

[1] This account does not agree with that of the Ṣūfī hierarchical order of saints given in *E.I.* i. p. 67. At its head is the Qutb, after him the two assistants (al-Imāmān); the five *autād* or *'umud*; the seven *afrād*, 'incomparable'; the *abdāl*; the seven *nujabā*, 'preferable'; the 300 *nuqabā*, 'chiefs'; the 500 *'aṣā'ib*, 'troops'; the *ḥukamā'*, 'wise', or *mufradūn*, 'lonely'; and the Rajabīyūn. The *abdāl* are also called al-Ruqabā, 'guardians', and dwell in Syria (*E.I.* i. p. 67). One or two of these terms were adopted for office-holders in guilds or orders. *E.g.* in the Egyptian orders the *naqībs*, who form the lowest rank of the organisation, are divided into three grades—the *naqīb al-ikhwān*, *naqīb* 'of the brethren', also called *naqīb al-qahwe*, 'of the coffee', and *naqīb al-mā*, 'of the water'; next are the *nuqaba az-zai*, *-ash-shama'*, 'of the lanterns', and highest of all are the *nuqaba al-majlis* or *-al-kabīr*, also styled *al-ustād*, 'the masters of the ceremonies'. (*V.* Kahle, in *Der Islam*, vi. pp. 163 ff.) But cf. Thorning in *Türk. Bibl.* No. 16, pp. 105 ff. and Index.

[2] Here we have *taṣarruf*, which might be rendered 'self-determination' or 'freewill'.

[3] Lit. 'pegs'.

[4] Pl. of *shahīd*.

mans, on account of a tomb which it contains. This tomb contains the dust of a Darvish of the Baqtāshī Order, named 'Azbī Chāūsh, once a public messenger of the Government in the time of the Shaikh-ul-Islām Vānnī, and the reign of Sultān Ahmad.

This *chāūsh*, or messenger, was ordered to carry into exile, to the town of Illimiya, an individual named Musrī Niāzi Effendi.[1] On their way the messenger perceived that, whenever his prisoner performed the *bismillāh* prayer, his fetters fell off his wrists, and, supposing he had a secret method of effecting this, doubled them. Notwithstanding this precaution, the same thing occurred. He therefore became aware that it was to be attributed entirely to his great sanctity, and his respect for him became in consequence very profound.

After reaching Illimīya, he resigned his office of *chāūsh*, and resided there with this pious man some fifteen years. At the expiration of this period, the exile told his companion that he was about to die. He presented him with his *taslīm-tāsh*, which he had always worn around his neck, and the *kamar*, or girdle,

[1] The Muhammad Niāzī Miṣrī of p. 271 *infra*. He is also known as Misrī Effendi, " a seventeenth century poet and heresiarch with a leaning towards Baqtāshī doctrines " (Hasluck, in *Annual*, B.S.A. xxi. p. 100, n. 1, citing Cantemir, *Hist. Ottomane*, tr. Joncquières, ii. 218, 228 ff. ; Hammer-Hellert, *Hist. Emp. Ott.* xi. 335 ; and Gibb, *Hist. of Ottoman Poetry*, iii. 312). To say, as one writer does, that he was a celebrated Khalwatī Shaikh of Brūsa who had leanings towards Christianity and was put to death with twenty-two of his followers in 1649, is incorrect. •The saint who was converted by an Arabic translation of the Gospel and was martyred with twenty-two followers in that year was an unnamed Shaikh of Āq-Ḥiṣṣār, whose order, as well as his designation, has not come down to us. Hammer-Purgstall gives a full account of his life and doctrines. Son of a Naqshbandī, he was born in a village near Malatia and studied in Diarbekr, at Cairo (under the head of the Qādirīs), and at Elmelī in Anatolia (under Umm Sinān, head of the Khalwatī order). By the latter he was deputed to represent that order at Ushshāqī near Smyrna, but his chief activities were displayed at Brūsa, Adrianople, and Constantinople, where his predilection for Kabbalistic prophecies led to his banishment to Rhodes. In all he was thrice banished and eventually died in exile in Lemnos in 1699. His attitude towards Christianity is obscure, but probably he only had a belief in the coming of Christ as the precursor of the Mahdī (*GdOD.* iii. pp. 587 ff.). In the text the town of Illimiyeh (as the original has it) is certainly Lemnos, Ilmelī in Turkish. The form Musrī in the text almost suggests that Muḥammad Niāzī was really styled Brūsī or Brūsawī, but he had some connexion with Egypt in his youth. The sect founded by him is called the Niāzīa-Masrīa according to Le Chatelier (*v.* note on p. 450 *infra*).

from his waist, and begged him to return to Stambūl, where his wife was about to marry another person, and to eat of her *zarda pilāf* (or wedding dish). He reached the capital just as the wedding was about to be consummated, and, having convinced his wife of his identity, was accepted as a husband in the place of the other person whom she had designed marrying. On his decease, 'Azbī Chāūsh was interred at the village of Mardavan Kūī, and, from having become an eminent Baqtāsh, his grave is much visited.

All the various *tarīqs* of the Darvishes profess to base their creeds on the *Qurān* and the *hadīsāt*, the latter being the sayings of the Prophet, collected after his decease from among the *aṣḥābs*, or intimate friends, who enjoyed familiar intercourse with him. Many of these were procured from second and third, or even many more persons, who having had them the one from the other, enabled the compilers to trace them back to their prophetical origin. They consist in a great measure of axioms, some proverbial, others moral or religious, and others relating only to what men supposed to be his own private wishes, not expressed in the *Qurān*, the contents of which were conveyed to the Prophet directly from God by the archangel Gabriel. Mystical as are many of the verses of the *Qurān*, several of these traditional sayings of the Prophet are much more so; and to those who desire to learn the condition of the mind of the Arabs during his time, they offer a wide field for gleanings. They also serve to show the character of Muhammad, and the weight of his mental abilities. The collection exists in Arabic, and, I do not doubt, also in Persian, with commentaries and translations in Turkish. Whatever may be the wanderings of the Darvish Orders from the teachings of the *Qurān*, they all profess to belong to one or the other of the four great commentators on that work. The peculiar devotion of the Baqtāshīs to the fourth direct caliph 'Alī is shown by the preceding account, as well as their strong attachment to the twelve Imāms, all descended from him. Among the 'Sayings of the Prophet', which they quote, are the following:

"I am the city of science (religious or spiritual), and 'Alī is its portal." "'Alī is the portal of a vast country; whoever enters therein is a true believer, and whoever departs from it is an infidel who disbelieves God."

This is said to be the spiritual signification of the 55th verse of the 2nd chapter of the *Qurān*. "Enter into this city, enjoy the wealth which is there to your entire satisfaction ; but on entering, prostrate yourselves and say, Pity us, O Lord ! and He will pardon your sins, for he has said, 'He will bestow our gifts upon the just'."

"'Alī, and those who follow him, will find salvation in the Day of Judgment."

The Initiation of a Baqtāshi

The *murīd* must be well recommended to the *murshid* (Shaikh) of the *takia* by two members of the fraternity, called the *rahpars* or guides, previously mentioned. On the night appointed for his reception, he takes with him a sheep for sacrifice, and a sum of money according to his means, as an offering to the Shaikh, which is subsequently divided among the functionaries of the *takia*, twelve in number. The sheep is sacrificed at the sill of the door, and a rope is made from its wool, and put round his neck. The remainder is preserved for the purpose of being made into a *taiband* for his subsequent use. The flesh is kept for the meal, of which all partake after the ceremony. As the meetings of the Order are all secret, care is taken that no listeners are concealed about the *takia*, and two of the fraternity keep guard outside the door. Three others are *en service*, inside the *takia*.

The *murīd* is deprived of nearly all his clothing, and care is taken that he has nothing on his person of a metallic or mineral character, showing that, on entering the Order, and offering himself to the *murshid*, he makes a voluntary sacrifice of the world and all its wealth, and other attractions. If he designs taking the *iqrār mujarrad*, or vow of celibacy, he is stripped entirely naked, whilst, in case he does not, his breast alone is bared. The rope is put around his neck, and he is led into the hall of the *takia* by two *tarjumāns*, or spiritual interpreters, *en service*, inside of it. He sees before him twelve persons, all seated, one of them is the *murshid* (Shaikh), and before each a lighted lamp or candle. He is led to a stone of twelve angles in the centre of the hall, called the *maidān-tāsh*, and directed to stand upon it, with his arms crossed on his breast, and his hands resting on his shoulders. This is called *boyun kasmak*, or 'bending the neck in humble respect and perfect submission'. His right great toe is pressed over the left great toe, and his head is inclined towards his right shoulder, his whole body leaning towards the Shaikh.

One of the *tarjumāns*, addressing the Shaikh, announces to him that he has brought him a *qūl*, or slave, and asks whether he will accept of him, to which the Shaikh acquiesces. Addressing the Shaikh, he repeats the following prayer after the guide :

" I have erred,—pardon my fault, O Shāh ! for the sake of the accepted one ('Alī), of the exalted place,—for the sake of Husain, the martyr of Karbalā. I have done wrong to myself, and to our lord, and I implore pardon of him."

His fault is in having deferred becoming a member of the Order. The Shaikh recites the prayers prescribed in the Litany aforementioned, and the disciple responds to them from the same, taught him previously by the two *rahpars* who recommended him to the Shaikh. At their conclusion, the two *tarjumāns* lead him off the stone, and holding him by the arms, conduct him to the Shaikh, before whom he bows low, and then prostrates himself. He then kneels before the Shaikh in a peculiar position, the former taking his hand into his own.

The *maidān-tāsh* represents the altar on which, in obedience to the Divine command, Ibrāhīm (Abraham) was about to offer up his son Ismā'īl (Isaac). The kneeling position of the *murīd* is that which, it is said, was taken by 'Alī before the Prophet, his knees touching those of the Shaikh ; each holds the other's right hand, the two thumbs raised up in the form of the letter *alif* (*a*), the first of the Oriental alphabet. He places his ear near to the Shaikh's mouth, and the latter recites to him the 10th verse of the 48th chapter of the *Qurān* : " Those who, on giving thee their hand, swear to thee an oath of fidelity,—swearing it to God ; the hand of God is placed on their hands. Whoever violates his oath, does so to his hurt, and he who remains faithful to it, will receive from God a magnificent recompense."

The two *rahpars* who conducted the *murīd* to the *takia*, remain outside of the door, armed with the weapon formerly described, called *tabar*.

Some say that, as the Baqtāshīs believe in a certain principle of a pantheistical character, the Shaikh whispers in the ear of the disciple a doctrine to which he must consent, under the penalty of death, and that he must admit that 'there is no God', meaning, however, that all living nature is God; but others deny it, and from a good Darvish source I have learned that it is not correct.

I have also been told that there are other secrets of the Order which are imparted by the Shaikh to the *murīd,* under a fearful penalty in case he imparts them; but as these are not printed, nor even written, they are known only to those of the Order. These form the *iqrārnāma,* or vows of the fraternity. The Baqtāshīs call the Shaikh ''Alī', and the *rahpar,* 'Muhammad', thus placing, in their spirito-mystical category, the Prophet lower than the Caliph. It is also said that the *murīd,* before his acceptance, is placed under surveillance for a full year, and has imparted to him certain false secrets, so as to test his powers of fidelity. He is, during this period, called a *mahakk,*[1] *i.e.* one who is being verified. In the meantime he frequents the *takia,* but learns none of the real mysteries of the Order. None are present at the initiation beyond the Shaikh, the representatives of the other eleven Imāms, and the *tarjumāns.* It is called the *iqrār*; and whenever a Darvish is asked to whom he made his *iqrār* (vow), he names the *pīr* or founder of the Order, and not the Shaikh. No other reply is ever expected, or given.

I am also informed that each Shaikh establishes a particular sign by which the members of his own *takia* may be recognised when knocking for admittance, and that it is responded to from within. This is not general, but is local and conventional.

Among the *iqrārs* which the Shaikh recites to the *murīd,* and which by him are repeated, is the following. It throws some light upon the ritual: "In the name of Allāh, the Merciful and the Clement, I beseech Allāh's forgiveness" (repeated three times). "I have come to implore pardon; I have come in search of the Truth; I ask it for the sake of God" (the word used is Haqq, the 'True' or 'Just'); "truth is the true path which leads to God,—the All True whom I know; what you call evil is the evil which I also know, and will avoid taking with my hand what belongs to another. I repeat (three times) 'Repent of your

[1] Muḥiqq is 'one who confirms or establishes', 'a speaker of the truth'. *Maḥakk* appears to mean 'one who is proved or tested'; *miḥakk* is a touchstone or a test. *Muḥaqqiq* is an adept—one proved (cf. *Kashf al-Maḥjūb,* p. 46). A *muḥaqqiq-i-asr* is 'a searcher of truth' (Nassau Lees, *Nafaḥāt-ul-Uns,* p. 3).

sins unto God,—a repentance without any return to sin.' " (From the *Qurān*).

The Shaikh adds, " Eat nothing wrong ; speak no falsehoods ; quarrel with no one ; be kind to those below you in life ; show respect to your superiors, and be good to those who visit you ; do not criticise the faults of others, if you see them conceal them ; if you cannot do this with your hand do so with your skirts, your tongue, and your heart. Be among the correct towards the twelve Orders of Darvishes ; we acknowledge each of the other eleven, for this is according to the precept of the *Qurān*, ' A day will come when nothing will benefit you—neither wealth, nor family,—nothing except submission to God with a pure heart.' "

The *murīd* replies by kissing the hand of the Shaikh, who continues : " If you now accept me as your father I accept you as my son ; hereafter the pledge of God (*'amānat-ullāh*) be breathed in your right ear ".

Among the *Qādirīs*, *Rifā'īs*, *Badāwīs*, *Maulavīs*, etc., all of the original twelve Orders, the *iqrār* is simply the *talqīn*, or the name Allāh.

The conclusion of the *iqrār* is the following : the *murshid* says to the *murīd*, who repeats it, " Muhammad is my *rahpar* (conductor)," " 'Alī is my *murshid* (spiritual guide) ".

The Shaikh then asks him : " Do you accept of me as your *murshid* ? " (in the place and as the representative of 'Alī).

The *murīd* replies : " I accept of thee as my *murshid*."

The Shaikh responds : " I then accept of thee as my son."

These words may seem to be of little import, yet they have to devout Mussulmans a signification of an impious and awful nature ; for they place the blessed Prophet and the *Qurān* inferior to 'Alī, and the Shaikh, as his representative, in the place of the Prophet.

After having been once admitted as a Darvish, the only salutation on entering the *takia* is to incline the head gently towards the Shaikh, and lay the right hand across the breast, near to the neck, in sign of perfect submission to him. When meeting in public, I am informed, and have verified it by observation, that Darvishes recognise each other by placing the right hand, as if unintentionally, on the chin. Some, and I believe it is a general rule, on entering a *takia*, or meeting a brother, place the right hand upon the heart, and with a gentle inclination of the body, exclaim, Yā Hū, aranlar! The reply is: *Ai Wallāh! Shāhim* (or) *Pīrim.*

The former [phrase] means, 'O! Him (God or Jehovah), arans' (noble fellows), and the latter, 'Good, by Allāh, my *Shāh*, or my *pīr*'.

On making an inquiry of the health, they say Kaiflar[1] Jumbushlarim! 'Health, my Joys', and the reply is, Ai Wallāh, aranlarim! 'Good, by Allāh, my arans'.

On meeting, they say, Hū Dōst, aranlar, 'Him, friend, arans', and the reply is, Ai Wallāh, aranlar. On departing, to take leave, they exclaim, Ai Wallāh! and the response is, Hū Dōst.

I may here add, that these salutations are common to other Orders than the Baqtāshīs, though generally, in private life, they all use the ordinary Islām one, of *Salām alaikum,* 'Peace be with you', and the reply is, *Alaikum-us-salām,* 'With you be peace'.

The following extract from the same MSS. is explicative of some of their forms. It is the address of the *murshid* to the neophyte:

"Come near and learn the manner in which we lead you in the True Path to Allāh. Those who come to the Avowal, are well understood by us; hearts respond to hearts; one person is needed who knows the way to be pursued,—one to initiate,—and one to act the part of a friend; those to be present will all be there (in the *takia*), and we then lead the *murīd* in the Path; one on his right and one on his left, who are called *rahpars,* and remain by your side; three persons act as servants, called *Parwānas,*[2] and so now we open the wonderful *takia* for labour.

[1] *Kaif*: in his *Dar-ul-Islam,* p. 175, Mark Sykes gives an amusing list of the meanings of this untranslatable word. It denotes all sorts of enjoyment from drunkenness to the delights of friendship, recreations like a short ride, a banquet, a happy meeting, home, a brown study (? ecstasy or contemplation), love in idleness, opium (and its effects), tobacco, and repose, *e.g.* after a Turkish bath. *Junbush,* vulg. T. for Pers. *junbish,* 'pleasurable excitement'.

[2] Parwāna, literally a 'moth': a 'messenger', 'supervisor or inspector'. The title of Parwāna was also applied to one Mu'īn-ud-Dīn, "governor (apparently) of Qonia . . . (moth or fly-wheel, viz. of the far-distant Mughal emperor, resident at the court of the king)" (according to Redhouse, *Mesnevi,* p. 37; but no authority is there cited). The Parwāna was not a mere envoy but a resident who exercised control over a tributary State. The term seems to occur first under 641 H., when the Mongols made Iconium pay tribute and accept a Parwāna (Ameer Ali, *A Short Hist. of the Saracens,* p. 387).

Twelve persons must be there, well knowing the four Columns of the Order ; give up all worldly knowledge, and confide your souls to us ; the *rahpars* conduct you to the *dār* (or the *maidān tāsh*), and there you make your vow. You then know what a *murshid* is, and we also know the same ; you enter by the four doors (the columns), and serve under them with warmth and fidelity ; be not a hypocrite, or we will know how to punish you ; the *murshid* will address you from the texts of the *'ahd* or 'covenant' (*Qurān*, vii. 171) ; receive his words with all your heart, or he will cut off your head. If those who know not God, or the *pīr*, learn from you your secrets, you will be led by them to the prison, and the asylum of the insane, or cause your death, and we will be with you in the hour of merited punishment. Be careful not to follow the dictates of your personal passions, and so wrong the four Columns of our Order ; your place will at first be that of the lowest degree, and if you are faithful, we will raise you to the Pleiades ; associate only with those who, like yourself, have learned the secrets and taken the vow of our Order ; others will divulge what you tell them, denounce you to the public, and cause us to degrade you for your weakness. Follow in the path, and keep the secrets of the arans, and so sustain the high standing of the Order ; whatever comes to your heart regarding the true path, keep it for communion with us ; to us you have made your vow, and from us learn the knowledge which you and we must possess.

"Whenever your true friends, the *rahpars* and the brethren present, are of one mind and heart, they become *ahl-i-bait*, or members of the family of the Prophet (a degree), such as those who were *ahl-i-'abā*, or those who were covered by him with his mantle (a degree),—or all of the 3, the 42, and the 73 in number (a degree). The *rahpars* must have a sword, the *zūlfikār* ; your offering to the *murshid* must be consistent with your means, and will form your *nazr* (votive offering) ; place this in the hand of the bearer of the *tabar*, it is to cleanse your heart, and fill it with purer thoughts ; one-half of it is for the *shāh* (Shaikh, who represents 'Alī), and the rest will be divided into four parts, of which the half is for the arans, and the other half for the expenses of the *takia*."

The night of meeting is called that of the *'ain-i-jam'* ; the five persons (the *rahpars* and the *parwānas* or *tarjumāns*) must all be of one soul, and of the degree of the *ahl-i-'abā*, for they are the lights of the congregation, and are called 'Alī, Zahrā,[1] Shepper[2] (or Hasan), Shāh Pīr (Husain), and the Hazrat-i-Kubrā (the Mahdī).

They say that there are four[3] distinct worlds,—the first, *'ālam-i-misāl*, or the world of dreams or assimulations; the second, the *'ālam-i-ajsām*, the present, or world of bodies; the third, the *'ālam-i-malkūt*, or world of angelic beings; and the fourth, the *'ālam-i-nāsūt*, or the world of mortals. Man's existence is divided into three parts,—wakeful existence, when all the mental faculties are vigorous; sleep, when the faculties of life are lulled or annihilated, but the spirit is wakeful; and death, when the body has entirely ceased to possess animation or existence, and the spirit is freed from its mortal ties. The *'ālam-i-misāl* is also a state of ecstaticism, when the spirit or soul has perceptions, though the body is not lulled by sleep, of spirituality or of the beautiful in thought. It then may have wakeful visions, of which it is incompetent in ordinary hours, and consequently approaches its Creator.

In the work aforementioned, called the *Rashahāt*,[4] the writer remarks that the *Sūfia* Shaikhs are those who, through the medium of a perfect conformance to the blessed Prophet, arrive at a degree of approximity to the Divinity, and after this desire to return and inspire others with the wish for the same *tarīq* or path which led themselves to Him. These perfectly pious or devout individuals become, by the grace and favour of God, submerged in the *'ain-i-jam'* of His unity, and wrecked in the

[1] Al-Zahrā, Fāṭima, *v.* p. 396 *infra.*

[2] Shappar, Pers. 'excellent'.

[3] This is a simplified version of the *'Awālim-i-khamsa* or 'five worlds' of the Ṣūfīs. In that system the third plane is the *'ālam-i-miṣāl* or 'world of similitudes', also called the *'ālam-i-malakūt* or 'world of angels'. *Malakūt* might also signify 'kingship', 'dominion', or 'possession'. *Mulkūt* would be 'the invisible world', 'Heaven'. The fourth plane is the *'ālam-i-shahādat* or 'visible world', often styled the *'ālam-i-mulk* or 'physical world'. This is the world in which we move, and it is the antithesis of the *ḥazrat-i-ghaib-i-mutlaq* or 'plane of the absolutely invisible'. The fifth is the *'ālam-i-insān* or 'world of man', in which the microcosm epitomises the whole universe. Hence the text rightly places 'the world of mortals' last. For a full account of the Ṣūfī system and its variants see Gibb, *Hist. of Ottoman Poetry*, i. pp. 54 ff.

[4] Nāshihāt in original.

depths of the sea of the indubitable truth of the One God only, and their mission is to lead others from the snares of corruption and uncertainty to the exalted shores of perpetual safety. There is, however, another sect, who, having reached the shores of perfection, are not required to retire and seek the salvation of others. They only continue engaged in devout piety, and spend their precious lives in perpetual praises and calling upon the holy name of the Eternal. The former are the *ahl-i-sulūk*, or advocates of the true path, and are divided into two classes, the *mutasūfia* and the *malāmīa*,—the one aspiring to *Jannat*, or the celestial Paradise of spiritual felicity, and the other to the *Ākhirat*, or that last period of spiritual existence which never ends. The former, through their incessant adoration and praise of the Omnipotent Allāh, become freed from some of the ordinary attributes of humanity, and gifted with some of the characteristics which belong only to spiritual beings, so that they naturally prefer to withdraw from the scenes of life, and spend their days in contemplating that Omnipresent Deity, who is hidden by the veil of mortality from ordinary sight, and to whom they have by this means approached. Though still hanging on the skirts of temporal existence, their souls become reunited, to a certain extent, with the all-pervading Spirit of the Creator.

The *Malāmīūns*, on the other hand, strive to lead lives of strict virtue and benevolence towards themselves and all mankind. The performance of the virtues of this life, as well as of acts of supererogatory excellence, are deemed by them essential to the path which they adopt, and in this they care but little for the commendation and admiration of the public, for all their acts are performed in reference only to the Divine satisfaction. With them, sincerity, free from all hypocrisy, is the essential object of their lives, and God only is the judge of their conduct. They abstain from all possible rebellion against His commands, the idea even of which is a sin; they are said to expose good and conceal evil, and among them are persons of great excellence of character, commendable for all the virtues and excellences of life; but yet the veil or curtain of mortality is not withdrawn from their eyes, and their vision is that which belongs only to temporal existence. They, therefore, do not possess the same distinct perception as the Sūfias of the Divine unity.

APPENDIX C TO CHAPTER VII

An Account of the Baqtāsh

Evliya says there is no doubt that Ḥājī Baqtāsh was descended in direct lineage from the Prophet, and he gives the following as his pedigree :

Imām Mūsā al-Kāẓim (who had 37 children).
|
Saiyid Ibrahīm al-Murtezā.
|
Saiyid Mūsā Ebi Sebha.
|
Saiyid Ibrāhīm Mokerrem al-'Askerī.
|
Saiyid Isḥāq as-Sākin.
|
Saiyid Mūsā Nishabūrī ×[1] Khatmeh, daughter of Shaikh Aḥmad.
|
Saiyid Muhammad Ḥājī Begtāsh.

He adds that Ḥājī Baqtāsh was entrusted as a boy to the care of Luqmān, a disciple of Aḥmad Yasawī, and that Luqmān had been invested with the religious habit of Imām Ja'far by Bāyazīd Bistāmī. Luqmān in turn invested Ḥājī Baqtāsh with it. Hence, he says, the Begtāsh wear the crown or turban with twelve folds in remembrance of the twelve Imāms, and the white *abba* with sleeves like a *jubbeh*.

Evliya also describes how from Mūsā al-Kāẓim the gift of direction to bliss (*irshād*) and the symbols of darvishship passed to Aḥmad Yasawī and from him to Ḥājī Begtāsh. What has become of these symbols does not appear, but Evliya hints that they are at Oṣmānjīk, also on the Kizil Irmāk, where Ṣulṭān Bāyazīd built a convent, etc., at the bidding of the true successor of Ḥājī Begtāsh, the great saint Qoyūn Bābā, who accompanied Ḥājī Begtāsh from Khurāsān and obtained his name because he bleated like a sheep once in twenty-four hours, which was the signal for prayer. At Oṣmānjīk pilgrims are given a *khirqa*, *sajjāda*, 'carpet', standard, drum, *pālahank*, 'halter', *assa*, 'stick', and *tāj*, as symbols of darvishship. Evliya speaks highly of this convent, though he says the Baqtāsh *darvishes* are generally in bad repute (*Travels*, ii. pp. 20 and 97).

The Baqtāshīs, as an order, owed all their importance to their asociation with the Janissaries. According to C. Huart, Orkhān betook himself to Ḥājī Baqtāsh at Amasia, after the foundation of that corps by his brother and chief minister, 'Alā-ud-Dīn. The *darvesh* placed the sleeve of his mantle on the head of one of the soldiers and conferred on the newly raised infantry the name of Yeni-cheri. Thenceforth the Janissaries wore a piece of stuff behind the white felt which served as their head-dress and ornamented it with a spoon of wood. But it has been shown that this tradition lacks historical support. Huart speaks of the ornament in the

[1] The sign × means married.

head-dress as a ‘ spoon ’, but Jacob says nothing of the kind : on p. x he speaks of a piece, doubtless of wood, one ell long and two fingers broad, which the Janissaries wore in their hat of white wool. (Huart, *Textes Ḥouroûfîs*, p. xii ; Jacob, *Die Bektaschijje.*)

On the death of Hājī Baqtāsh certain of his followers took counsel together. These were Kuyūn Bābā (‘ Father Sheep ’), who dwelt near ’Usmānjīk ; Abdāl Mūsā, near Elmalī ; Shujā’-ud-Dīn, near Eski-Shahr ; Kizil Delī, of Dimetoka ; and Sarsam ’Alī Bābā, at Kalkandelen ; and they agreed that the *kulas* to be worn in the convents should be two-, three-, and twelve-sided, according to the place. This, it will be seen, gives the shape of the Baqtāsh cap a merely local significance, independent of the sub-order (Jacob, *Beiträge*, pp. 85-6).

Rycaut tells a curious story of the origin of the custom of kissing the Sulṭān’s sleeve. Bektāsh was preacher to Murād (I., 1360–1389, must be meant), and warned that Sulṭān against trusting the Serbians, but the victorious sovereign allowed Vilvo (Milosh Kobilovitch) to approach and assassinate him. Bektāsh, knowing that the fulfilment of his prophecy and his proximity to the Sulṭān’s person would involve his own death, made no effort to avert his fate, but prepared himself for it. He provided himself with a robe of white with long sleeves, and this he proffered to all his proselytes to be kissed as a mark of obedience to him and to his institutions. Hence, somewhat inconsequently, arose the custom of kissing the Sulṭān’s sleeve (*Present State*, p. 148). Rycaut adds that the Bektāsh wear white caps of several pieces with turbans of wool, twisted in the fashion of a rope, and that they go clothed in white. The sect, he records, observed constantly the hours of prayer, which they perform in their own Assemblies, but, he then continues, their order is most abhorred by the Kadizadelis, because Bektāsh left it to the free will of his disciples to observe the constant hours of prayer or not, a licence naturally taken full advantage of by the Janissaries. The Kadizadeli (? Qāzī-zāda-lī) sect is described as having been founded by one Birgalī Effendi in the time of Sulṭān Murād, and as chiefly affected by renegade Russians and other Christians who retained some beliefs in Purgatory, and so invented many ceremonies in praying for the souls departed, at the burial of the dead (*ib.* p. 129). After describing the Potures, Rycaut says that a subtle point about the Divine Attributes begot a sect amongst the Janissaries, called the Bektāshī, who began, it is said, in the time of Sulaimān the Magnificent (1529–66). Some people called them Zeratī, *i.e.* those who have copulation with their own kindred, while the vulgar dubbed them *mumsconduren* or ‘ extinguishers of the candle ’. The sect observed the law of Muḥammad in divine worship with a strictness and superstition above any of the Precisians of that religion, but held it unlawful to adjoin any attributes to God, by saying that God is great, or God is merciful, because His nature cannot be apprehended. The practice of intercourse with their own children was defended on the principle that he who had planted the vine was entitled to taste of the fruit (*ib.* p. 131). This passage recalls the curious sect called Pertolī by Hammer-Purgstall. That body justified intercourse with a daughter on the precedent set by Lot (*GdOD.* ii. p. 422). Its name may really have been Pardalī, or ‘ concealed ’, but no explanation of it is given. It is said to have been a mystical sect of Sofia, whose leader or founder was one Sh. Isḥāq. Possibly the name is a corruption of Potur.

In view of the close connexion between the Baqtāshīs and the Janissaries, it is curious to find a Turkish writer taxing a Baqtāsh with a pacifist propaganda among the troops in 1690–91, contrasting the hardships they were enduring with the luxurious life which the Sulṭān was leading (Jacob, *op. cit.* p. 7, quoting from Es'ad Effendi's *Uss-i-Zaer*, p. 204).

Baqtāshism is said to teach that no life should be wantonly taken, and a really devout Baqtāshī of the old school wears bells on his shoes to warn the little creatures of the grass to avoid his footsteps (H. N. Brailsford, *Macedonia*, p. 245). The writer says the suggestion of Buddhist influence here is irresistible, but the idea is Jain rather than Buddhist. It must not, however, be forgotten that some Buddhistic ideas reached the Balkan Peninsula some time before the Moslem conquest (Gaster, *Roumanian Bird and Beast Stories*, pp. 23 ff.).

Tradition locates the burial-place of Ḥājī Baqtāsh at Ḥājī Bektāsh Takia, near Qirshahr. By the Christians who frequent his shrine he is here identified with S. Charalambos, who is powerful in respect of plague. But the Ḥājī is also equated to S. Eustathius, probably on account of some connexion with hunting (Hasluck in *Annual*, B.S.A. xx. p. 103). It is significant that the Baqtāsh at their *takia* at Istranijā in the hills N.E. of Constantinople were purveyors of game to the Sulṭāns (*ib.* xxi. p. 100, n. 9). The lack of historical evidence for Ḥājī Bektāsh's existence makes the origin of the above tradition of some interest. Evliya or his translator says that he was buried in Sulṭān Orkhān's presence in the capital of Crimea, where a Tatar princess raised the monument over his tomb (*Travels*, ii. p. 21). Here Crimea is almost certainly a mistake for Qaramania. Hasluck states simply that the 'capital of Crimea' is obviously a mistake for Qirshahr, and in all probability he is right. Mokissos, refounded by Justinian as Justinianopolis, became in the Byzantine period one of the chief cities of Cappadocia, and Qirshahr, a city in a fine situation, is the modern metropolis of the same division of Cappadocia (W. M. Ramsay, *The Hist. Geography of Asia Minor*, p. 300). It seems to have been the capital of Qaramania, though express authority for this cannot be cited, and though the Saljuqian capital was Qonia, while Qonia and Laranda (Qaramān) formed the principality of the Qaramānūghlī, or 'princes of Laranda and Qonia' (Ramsay, *op. cit.*, pp. 332 and 336; and Redhouse, *Eng.-Turk. Dict.* p. 1443). Qaramania was so imperfectly Turkicised that it gave its name to the Qaramānlījā script or Turkish written in Greek characters. Such a city would naturally be chosen for the shrine of a legendary saint, or it would be located in its environs, and, as a fact, the shrine is at the ancient Doara or Odogra, once the seat of a bishopric (Ramsay, *op. cit.*, pp. 268-9, 297).

At Ḥājī Bektāsh pilgrims make the passage of a natural rock tunnel with a view to proving their sincerity of purpose. The aperture is narrow, and it is customary for the pilgrim to remove his arms before making the attempt. An Albanian bey, who succeeded in passing through it armed, died early as a punishment for his presumption (from *Columns of Ordeal*, by the late F. W. Hasluck). A somewhat similar rite is observed by visitors to the shrine of Baba Farīd Shakar-ganj (*d.* 664 H., A.D. 1266), at Pakpattan, ‘ the holy ferry ’ in the Punjab. This saint was a Ṣufi of the Chishti sect. The pilgrim passes through ‘ the Gate of Paradise ’, the key of which is in charge of a Brahman. Lives used to be lost in the crush, though the ‘ gate ’ is not unduly narrow (*J. Punjab Historical Society*, i. p. 75). S. Pelagia, known to Moslems as Rabahat bint Hasan al-Basri, is buried in a crypt in the Church of the Ascension at Jerusalem. Her tomb is against the wall with a narrow passage between, and through this penitents squeeze, their ability to do so being a proof of grace. The tomb of Hasan Basri has a similar peculiarity, but it is not clear that a similar rite was performed there. The *qubba* originally built to him fell twice, and then he appeared and declared that he desired no qubba, but a tower, and that his tomb should be set against the wall to prevent circumambulation.

The meaning of the statement on p. 166 that Baqtāsh made over his powers to the Khātun (Lady) Anādur probably is that from her are descended the heads of the Baqtāsh order. The present Chalabī claims to be the actual descendant of Ḥājī Baqtāsh, and his office is hereditary in his family, following the usual Turkish rule whereby the senior surviving brother is preferred to the eldest son. But his claim is disputed by the party of the Dede Bābā, who hold that Ḥājī Baqtāsh left no physical off-spring, though they admit that a lady conceived by drinking the Ḥājī's blood. Her name, however, is given as Khātun Jikāna, the wife of a *khoja*. Ḥājī Baqtāsh himself is also said to have been of miraculous birth, being a *nafs-uglu* or ‘ son of the breath ’ (of God).

It may be that Chalabī is derived from Ar. *ṣalab* or *ṣulb*, ‘ loins ’, the term denoting his physical descent from Hājī Baqtāsh. In Persian *ṣulabīy* or *sulbīy* means ‘ own ’, ‘ real ’, as in *farzand-ī-ṣulbīyash*, ‘ his own son ’ (Richardson, *Pers. Ar.-Eng. Dict.* p. 790). The title goes back to the days of Tīmūr at least. It was borne by Sulaimān Chalabī, oldest son of Bāyazīd (1389–1403 : H. A. Gibbons, *The Foundation of the Ottoman Empire*, p. 195) ; while the ‘nickname’ of Kirī-chalabī (Girī-jilibī) was borne by Muhammad, the son whom Bāyazīd esteemed second only to Sulaimān, though it does not appear whether he was his second son by birth. Kirī-Chalabī seems to mean ‘ post ’—or ‘ after ’ Chalabī (from *kari*, Turk. ‘ after ’ or ‘ behind ’, but Gibbons styles it a nickname (*ib.* p. 252, n. 4). Girjilibī is Rabbi Joseph's form of the word (*Chronicles*, i. p. 257). It may be conjectured that Chalabī meant ‘ heir-apparent ’ or heir-designate, while Kirī-Chalabī meant the next heir after him : cf. the Sanskrit series of terms for heir-apparent, next heir (*dwistania*), and so on. In *E.I.* i. p. 832 the article on Chelebi does not allude to this ‘ nickname ’, but it discusses the history of the word at length.

In Turkish *chālāb* or *chalab* undoubtedly means ‘ God ’, and Redhouse defines *chelebī* as (originally, in Tartary) a religious man, a Christian man, a priest or monk, worshipper of the crucifix (*Turk.-Eng. Lex.* p. 728). But Evliya says that in Brūsa, being in Asia, the language is related to the Turkish, hence they say : ‘ *Chepū* instead of . . . *Chelebī* ’ (*Travels*, ii. p. 17). It is difficult to think that the word is derived from Ar. *ṣalb*, ‘ cruci-fixion ’, as the *ṣalb* by no means denoted a crucifix in the Christian sense (*v.* F. Babinger in *Der Islam*, xi. p. 74). The term Ṣalbī never seems to have been generally applied to Christians, though a little-known Bedouin tribe supposed to be descendants of Crusaders is called Solibah in the desert near Mosul (*Man*, 1921, p. 122). *Ṣalbī* (if such a word ever existed) would connote both the degradation of an out-caste Christian and the fate of a convicted criminal.

In Ar. *shalabī*=Turk. *chelebī* (*Der Islam*, ix. p. 72). But this is doubtless the Arabicised form of the Turkish term.

The above explanation is the late Mr. F. W. Hasluck's (*Annual*, B.S.A. xx. p. 103, n. 7, and xxi. pp. 87 and 88, n. 1). But it is not easily reconciled with that of Aḥmad Rif'at as given in Jacob's *Die Bektaschijje*, pp. 22 ff. According to that writer, who published his *Mirāt ul-Maqāṣid fi daf'il-Mafāsid* in 1876, Hājī Bektāsh was succeeded by the Shaikh Khizr Lāla Sulṭān, the youngest of the three sons of Idris Faqīh, and he in turn by his physical descendants until their line apparently died out. Then Bālim Sulṭān became head of the order. He, dying in A.D. 1516, was succeeded by 23 Shaikhs, of whom 17 appear to have been appointed and not to have attained the office by natural descent. Then in or about 1731 Shāh Quli Sulṭān became head of the order, and his descendants have succeeded him down to the present day. But besides the Chelebīs there were at the Mother-convent celibate Bābās (*mujarrad bābāsī*) beginning with Sarsam 'Alī, who assumed office in 958 H. (A.D. 1551), and their line, too, continued to the present day. Jacob regards the dynasty of Idrīs Faqīh as an invention of the eighteenth century, but it is based on the same authority as Aḥmad's other data. Whence that writer got them does not appear, though a vague reference is given to 'Bektāshī sources'. If, however, we take the lists as they stand they are not devoid of interest. That of the Chelebīs is patently one that indicates regular, uneventful succession until we get to Bālim Sulṭān.[1] His successor is given as the Shahīd Ganj Qalandar Effendi, and the term 'Shahīd' suggests that he was executed, and Jacob is probably right in identifying him with the Qalandar Chelebi who claimed to be a descendant of Ḥājī Bektāsh, and in 1526–27 led the fierce Qaramānian revolt against the rule of Sulaimān the Magnificent. With less certainty he is identifiable with the Qalandar Shāh whose *turbat* is in the Mother-convent. Quite possibly he was or claimed to be a descendant of Ḥabīb Effendi, the eldest brother of Khizr Lāla. This fact or claim gives a hint that Idrīs Faqīh was regarded as in some way a physical son of Hājī Bektāsh. After Qalandar, too, the order continued to have a stormy history, for in 1729–30 'Abd-ul-Qādir, and in 1824–25 Faiz-Illāh, Grand-Masters of the order, met with violent deaths, as they are also designated 'Shahīd'. The death of the last named clearly formed part of the steps taken to suppress the Janissaries. Turning to the list of the *mujarrad bābās*, it is noteworthy that it excludes all the prominent Baqtāsh saints who stand high in popular esteem, none of Hājī Bektāsh's four *khalīfas* being shown in it. Sarsam 'Alī is the sole exception.

According to the *Wilāyat-nāma* Ḥājī Baqtāsh had five *khalīfas*, but in the *Mīrāt ul-Maqāsid* the number is only four (Jacob, *Die Bektaschijje*, p. 42). It may well be that the original number was five, following the Buddhist

[1] There is, indeed, some reason for regarding Bālim Sulṭān as the real founder of the Baqtāsh order. He died in 922 H. (A.D. 1516).

precedent, and that it was subsequently reduced to four to conform to the Naqshbandī practice, wherein each of the great teachers of that sect had that number of *khalīfas*, a usage based again on the model of the first four Caliphs, the Chahār Yār (in Turk. *durt yār*) or 'Four Friends'.

According to Jacob the chief of the four *khalīfas* was Saiyid Jamāl Sulṭān, who is buried near Balukisir or Balikesri in Karasi. This *khalīfa* may be the 'Said 'Alī Balkhī' of the text.

The second was Kolu Achiq Hājim Sulṭān, whose real name was Rajab, and who is buried at Rajab, so called after him, not far from 'Ushshāq. His name seems to mean 'ashen-coloured', from *kyullu*, 'ashy', and *achiq*, 'light (in colour)'. He was a cousin of Baqtāsh.

The third *khalīfa* was Sarī Ismā'īl Sulṭān, whose tomb is at Davas, south of Denizli. One authority makes him the *ibrīqdār*, 'ewer-holder', of Ḥājī Bektāsh (*Türk. Bibl.* No. 17, p. 16).

The fourth Rasūl 'Alī Sulṭān or Rasūl Bābā is buried at Besh Karish, near Altyn Tāsh.

All these, it will be observed, bear the title of Sulṭān (*Bektaschijje*, p. 27; cf. also Hasluck in *Annual*, B.S.A. xxi. pp. 92, 94).

But the title of Sulṭān was subsequently given to a number of Baqtāshī saints. In addition to Bālim Sulṭān we have Patūk Sulṭān at Qīrshahr, Taslīm and Dede Sulṭāns at Denīzlī; 'Abdī Bey Sulṭān at Yatagan, Aqbiyik Sulṭān at Brūsa, Sidim Sulṭān (?), who seems to have given his name to a convent of bare-headed and bare-footed Baqtāsh near Tchorum, Imrān Yūnūz at Beybāzār (Yūnūz Imre, who is placed early in the fourteenth century), and the famous Qaighusuz Sulṭān of Cairo (Hasluck, *op. cit.*, pp. 91, 92, 93, 94, and 89-90).

But these 'Sulṭāns' were not always the most influential Baqtāshī saints. Soon after the death of Ḥājī Baqtāsh, if not immediately after it, five prominent Baqtāsh saints met to decide on the forms which the principal convents were to adopt for their distinctive head-dresses. These were Quyūn Bābā, Abdāl Mūsā, Shujā'-ud-Dīn of Eskishahr, Sersem 'Alī Bābā of Kalkandelen, and Kizil Deli of Dimetoka, of whom only the last named appears to have borne the title of Sulṭān (Jacob, *Beiträge*, pp. 85-86). All this suggests that the title was not used in the original organisation of the order. It was certainly not confined to the Baqtāshīs, but was affected by such saints as Karānjī Bābā Sulṭān, apparently a Hamzawī. Evliya also mentions Sīdī Bilāl (p. 38), Jujī and Qāzī Beg (*ib.*), Chekirka (p. 27), and a 'Bābā Sulṭān' (p. 29) in his *Travels* (ii.), but does not specify their orders. Then there is the saint Dūmlī (Bābā or) Sulṭān, at the source of the Euphrates, closely connected with an Umūdūm Sultan (*ib.* pp. 179 and 187). In the English translation Dūmlī appears as Rūmlī, but cf. *Der Islam*, ix. pp. 228-229. The names Dūmlī and Umūdūm are not explained. The latter may be connected with '*umud—vide* note on p. 203.

Shaikh Geiklī Bābā Sulṭān is expressly mentioned by Evliya as a *darvish* of the Baqtāshīs, a companion of Abdāl Mūsā and a disciple of Aḥmad Yasawī. He came from Azarbaijān, and was buried at Brūsa, in the great convent built by Orkhān (*Travels*, ii. pp. 21 and 24). His name Geiklī means 'deer', and when the poet Ghazālī, 'he of the gazelle', assumed that title he seems to have done so in imitation of Geiklī Bābā, for on his banishment, due to the Rabelaisian tendencies of his poems, he installed himself as Shaikh in the cell of that saint on the slopes of Mt. Olympos (Gibb, *Hist. of Ott. Poetry*, iii. p. 38). Nevertheless, the precise connexion between Ghazālī and the Baqtāsh is obscure, and it is, moreover, doubtful whether Geiklī Bābā was really an adherent of Ḥājī Baqtāsh. The Bābā "used to ride on wild roes in the woods, and load gazelles with his baggage after he had harnessed them", says Evliya. Geiklī Bābā was a Persian by birth, from Khoī, a disciple of the Sh. Iliās (von Hammer, *GdOR.* i. pp. 111-12).

'Usmān built cells for the *darvishes* Torud and Abdāl Kumral. His example was followed by Urkhān, who built a cell for Geiklī Bābā, east of Brūsa, on a spur of Mt. Olympos, and higher up the grave of Doghlī Bābā, the 'Buttermilk father'. On the western side of the town he also built the cloister of Abdāl Murād, by the Qaplīja, the 'covered-in hot springs', as well as that of Abdāl Mūsā, under the town walls.

This account of the saint certainly recalls the Chinese being Shou Hsing, 'the Star of Longevity', whose figurine, mounted on a stag, is common in China, and even sold in India. Major W. Perceval Yetts, to whom this information is due, doubts, however, if Shou Hsing is connected with Geiklī Bābā. In three examples known to me the stag is distinctly turning his head to speak, as it were, to Shou Hsing. Major Yetts suggests that the pictures of Tao Tzŭ, who rides an ox which did turn its head round and speak to him, may have influenced those of Shou Hsing. Curiously enough, his place in Karmān, where villagers offered Hājim Sulṭān animals, is called Geikli-lar jamā'atī, though deer could hardly have been included in the gifts. *Geiklī* thus seems to mean oxen or cattle as well as deer, and Geiklī Bābā may have affinities to both the Chinese beings (*Wilāyat-nāma*, p. 79).

Even this does not exhaust the list of Baqtāsh Sulṭāns. Evliya mentions Kari Aḥmad Sulṭān and (? or) Shaikh Kara Aḥmad Sulṭān, a Persian prince who was initiated by Hājī Baqtāsh, and is buried at Aq-Hissār; Sh. Geiklī Bābā Sulṭān, a follower of Aḥmad Yasawī and a great tamer of wild animals, who is buried at Brūsa; Sh. Sulṭān Ramazān Bābā, buried in a Baqtāsh convent at Brūsa; Abdāl Mūsā Sulṭān, another companion of Ḥājī Baqtāsh and a disciple of Aḥmad Yasawī, whose tomb is also at Brūsa; and Abdāl Murād Sulṭān, whose walk is situate in a valley high up on Mount Olympus, whence the finest view of Brūsa is obtained, and who must be a Baqtāshī (*Travels*, i. pt. 1, pp. 20-21, 24, 27; ii. 24, 14, and 8).

Olympos in Bithynia is the modern Keshish Dāgh, or "perhaps some point on the south-eastern skirts of Keshish Dāgh rather than the main summit" (W. M. Ramsay, *Hist. Geography of Asia Minor*, p. 187). *Primâ facie* this accords with the description given of the walk of Abdāl Murād Sulṭān. Keshish is the Ar. *qasīs*, "a Christian priest or monk" (F. Babinger in *Der Islam*, xi. p. 15). Evliya gives a picturesque description of it (*Travels*, ii. pp. 14 f.).

The history of the word Sulṭān may give a clue to its real significance. Meaning literally 'ruler', the title was first bestowed by Wāṣiq (Vathek) upon the commandant of his Turkish guards (Ameer Ali, *A Short Hist. of the Saracens*, p. 411). In Evliya's time it denoted a local ruler. He says explicitly that in Georgia Shabūrān was the seat of a Sulṭān, "which is the same as a *sanjāq* Beg in Turkey". Shamākhī again had 40 Sulṭāns and

40 judges attached to it. At Magū he found 2000 musketeers, commanded by a Sulṭān (Beg) subordinate to the Khān (Pāshā, governor) of Erivān (*Travels*, ii. pp. 165, 159, and 122). These uses of the title seem to have been confined to the northern parts of Asia Minor. Babinger suggests that the term had no secular or spiritual significance, but was merely used like a term of affection (*Kosenamen*); but among the Baqtāsh its prevalence may point to a division of the whole area of their activities into dioceses, quite a common phenomenon in Oriental sects, though such an act of ecclesiastical administration would not necessarily be openly avowed. Indeed, some orders in India are known to have mapped out the country into 'provinces', etc., but do not disclose their boundaries or more than they can help about their organisation. In any case the military rank of a Sulṭān was important, as Evliya speaks of his commanding at least 1000 men (*e.g.* p. 130).

The history of the term 'Sulṭān' prior to the Saljūqs is not yet clear. Before the ninth century the title is used to denote the holder of an office, *amīr* if the person is meant. The events of the eleventh century promoted the term 'Sulṭān'. No longer, as in the tenth century, was it applied to every petty ruler; only the head of an independent dynasty could so style himself. The Sulṭān became 'the shadow of God' on earth, while the Imām, deprived of secular power, was still 'the representative of God'. This theory was based on a *hadīs* of the Prophet. Early in the fourteenth century the concept that the Khalīfas should not intervene in the things of the transitory earthly government first appears. (Arnold, *The Caliphate*, App. D, and Index.)

From the *Wilāyat-nāma* of Ḥājim Ṣultān the following pedigree may be gleaned:

Sayyid Nūr-ud-Dīn of Sivri Hissār.

Bāyazīd Bisṭāmī.	Qaraja Aḥmad, the *giuzji*, 'patron-saint' of Rūm.	Bājī-Fāṭima.
‖	|	×[1]
A disciple. . . .	Ḥājī Togrul.	Khoja Idrīs.

What the precise relations of Qaraja Aḥmad with Hājī Bektāsh were is not clear. The Hājī gave to every *darvish* his lot (*naṣīb*), and that of Qaraja Aḥmad was the little demon. Reserving to himself the sound or healthy part of Rūm, to Aḥmad he consigned 'the part beset by a demon'. This seems to mean that, like Qara Bāba, Qaraja Aḥmad was taken over by the Bektāsh, just as his son also is said to have submitted to the Ḥājī (*Türk. Bibl.*, No. 17, pp. 20, 23, and 29). This tradition strongly supports Hasluck's view that the Khoja Aḥmad of the local legend preserved by Crowfoot in *Journal Anthropological Inst.*, 1900, p. 309, is really Qaraja Aḥmad, the Ḥaidar us-Sulṭān of the Qizzilbāsh, who gives his name to the Qizzilbāsh shrine and village of that name on the eastern bank of the Halys in the Angora province (*Annual*, B.S.A., xx. p. 121). Assuming this view to be correct, the Qizilbāsh must have been in existence before the advent of

[1] × = married.

Ḥājī Bektāsh to Cæsarea. Moreover, if the *Wilāyat-nāma* is to be trusted, Qaraja Aḥmad was the patron-saint of (all) Rūm and therefore an important personage. But he was never, surely, recognised as such by the Turks, or rather by the Osmānlīs. At Ḥaidar us-Sulṭān the Saljūqs are held in pious memory, and the Maulavīs and Bairāmīs claimed almost as kinsmen (Crowfoot, *op. cit.* p. 309). All this makes the legends told about Ḥaidar Sulṭān highly significant. Not only did he take a Christian wife, but his shrine stands on the site of an older Christian monastery (Crowfoot, *op. cit.* p. 306). Further, the well there impregnated with sulphur is used for divination by a Shaikhin, a prophetess who receives this gift but is not necessarily a member of the Shaikh's family. Whether Qaraja Aḥmad was a historical person it is impossible to say, but he certainly had several tombs (Hasluck, *op. cit.* p. 121). As a contemporary of Ḥājī Bektāsh, Qaraja Aḥmad can hardly have survived the middle of the fourteenth century, and he must not be confused with Shaikh Ḥaidar of Ardabīl, who was killed in 1488, though much of the latter's history may have been transferred to the former. *E.g.* both are said to have been Persian princes. Shaikh Ḥaidar is said to have married a lady of the Greek dynasty of Trebizond.

Aflākī mentions a Shaikh Isḥāq as an 'inspector' of Ḥājī Baqtāsh, who was sent by the Ḥājī to Jalāl-ud-Dīn Rūmī to protest against his teaching. Aflākī states that his informants told him that a certain group called the Ḥājī 'Bābā Rasūl-Ullāh', or 'the father sent by God', but that his tenets did not follow the law of the Prophet. The Ḥājī, however, was constrained to humble himself before the miraculous strength of Jalāl-ud-Dīn (Cl. Huart, *Les Saints des Derviches tourneurs*, i. p. 296). Who this Sh. Isḥāq was does not appear.

It is not certain that the Baqtāsh have degrees, but from a passage in the *Maqālāt* of Hājī Baqtāsh quoted by Vīrānī Bābā, men are divided into four grades, the *'ābid*, who revere God, the *zāhid*, who override legal observances, the *'ārif* or 'gnostics', and the *muḥibb* 'lovers', or Ṣūfīs (Jacob, *Die Bektaschijje*, in *Abhandl. der K. Bayer. Akademie der Wiss.*, 1909, p. 4). Hasluck, however, says that though the hereditary *shaikhs* of the Kizilbāsh *takias* of Asia Minor are consecrated by the Chelebi, they are regarded with some contempt by the other branch of the Baqtāsh, who call them Ṣūfī, and look upon their organisation as lax and their doctrines as superstitious (*Annual*, B.S.A. xxi. p. 88). Yet there can be no doubt that the *muḥibb* ranks highest in the esteem of the Baqtāsh, an instant of his *munājāt*, 'whispered prayer', being equal to seventy years of self-abnegation in the *'ārif*; as a moment's self-abnegation in the *'ārif* is equivalent to seventy years of *'ibādat* in the *zāhid*. But the real relations between the Kizilbāsh and the Baqtāsh are by no means clear.

Fāsil Izzat Bey, a Bektāshī, formed the acquaintance of Voltaire and other Encyclopædists. On his return to Constantinople he introduced into the Order, already a secret society, certain philosophical, or even free-thinking views, which had a prodigious influence on the entire body. The Bektāshīs issued many revolutionary pamphlets, and alarmed not only the *mullahs* but S. Murād (? Mahmūd I., 1730–54) himself.[1]

[1] Davey, *The Sultan and his Sujects*, p. 155.

After the suppression of their order by the Sulṭān Maḥmūd in 1824–25, he made over their property (at least in Constantinople) to the Naqshbandīs. During the next thirty or forty years the Baqtāshīs ostensibly mingled with the Sa'adīas, Rifā'īs, Qādirīs and Naqshbandīs. But by 1872 they resumed public profession of their doctrines and actually printed the *Jāwidān.*

The Baqtāshīs have four sub-orders, or branches, one of which was founded by Balum Sulṭān, according to Hasluck (*Annual,* B.S.A. xxi. p. 86). But it does not appear that the branches formed regular sub-orders; and their names cannot be traced. The Qarmatīs were far more ancient than the Baqtāsh. The Ḥurūfīs may be regarded as affiliated to the Baqtāsh, and the Nuqtīas were an offshoot from them:. they evolved a science of dots—*'ilm-i-nuqta*—judging even numbers to signify a thing permitted, and odd numbers something prohibited. Moreover, Fazl Hurūfī left nine *khalīfas,* one of whom, 'Alī al-'Alā, taught the doctrine of *nafs-i-ammāra*—'the ruling passion', corresponding to the Gr. ἐπιθυμία; and to this they gave the name of *sirr,* 'mystery' or 'secret'. 'Alī al-'Alā died in A.D. 1419. His followers seem to be the 'Alī-Allāhs of Jacob, or the 'Alī-ilāhīs of Persia, who hold men to be swayed by two forces, *'aql,* 'reason', and *nafs,* 'lust'. But they are divided into eight sects, not nine: these including the Khamūshīs and the Dā'ūdīs—the latter being found about Qazwīn and the villages towards Rasht. The 'Alī-Allāhs have a spiritual head at Kirmānshāh, in and around which town they make no secret of their doctrines (Jacob, *Beiträge,* pp. 46-8, 42-5; *E.I.* i. p. 292).

The modern Baqtāsh are for the most part Hurūfīs. Hājī Baqtāsh left no writings, but one of his disciples relates some anecdotes about him in the *Wilāyat-Nāma.* The Shi'as do not recognise the Hurūfīs as co-religionists, alleging that by 'Alī, whom they profess to recognise, they mean Fazl (*Textes Houroufis,* Gibb Memorial Series, ix., by C. Huart and Rizā Tevfīq, p. 270). Gul Bābā was a notable Hurūfī, who wrote *The Key of the Invisible* (cf. p. 94 *supra*). Another Baqtāshī-Hurūfī was Zarīfī Bābā (*ib.* p. 228). The Hurūfī literature is considerable, comprising the *Mahram-nāma-i-Saiyid Isḥāq,* or '*Book of Confidences of S. Isḥāq*', 1425; the *Nihāyat-Nāma,* or '*Book of Ends*'; ar-Rasāil, or short tracts; *Dar ta'rīf-i-Zarra,* or '*Definition of the Atom*'; and the *Iskandar-Nāma,* a poem on Alexander's search for the waters of youth, composed by Fazl himself. But Isḥāq gives a different list: the six *Jāwidān,* of which Fazl-Ullāh composed the first and his disciples the remaining five; one by Firishta-Ughlū being called the *'Ishq-nāma*; the *Haqīqat-nāma,* in Turkish, by Shaikh Safī; the *Māhshār-nāma* by Amīr 'Alī al-'Alā, who died in 822 H. (A.D. 1419). A Hurūfī of note, 'Abd-ul-Majīd ibn Firishta, got his training from Bāyazīd, he from Shams-ud-Dīn, and he from Fazl. He died in 874 H. (A.D. 1469). Their connexion with the Hurūfīs may explain why a claim for greater antiquity is made for the Baqtāsh. According to Isḥāq Effendi they are spiritual descendants of the Qarmatians. As already stated, Hājī Baqtāsh left no books, and in the fifteenth century Fazl-Ullāh Hurūfī of Astarābād, who was put to death by Mīrān Shāh, a son of Tīmūr, believed himself to be an incarnation of the Deity. All his theology was derived from the twenty-eight letters of the Arabic alphabet and the four added to it by the Persians. One of Fazl's disciples, 'Ali-al-'Alā, went to Asia Minor and instructed the Baqtāsh, presenting Fazl's ideas as those of the Hājī. Hence the Baqtāsh are called *ahl-i-fazl*, as opposed to the *ahl-i-haqq*. They have neither *ward* nor *zikr*. Fazl deciphered the Pentateuch, Psalms, Gospels, and *Qurān* according to Isḥāq's *Kāshif-ul-Asrār*.

The foregoing is Huart's account of the Hurūfī literature in his *Textes Houroufis*, but E. G. Browne's earlier paper in *J.R.A.S.*, 1907, pp. 533 f., should also be consulted, as it gives much additional information. According to Isḥāq Effendi the Hurūfī doctrines began to be promulgated in A.D. 1397–98, and Fazl's death is assigned to 1401–02. But Fazl may have been born as early as 1339–40, and have been martyred in 1394–95—which would make him almost a contemporary of Hājī Baqtāsh. If the tradition that he was executed by Mīrān Shah is true, he must have perished before the death of that prince in 1400–01.

It may be not without significance that the *Jāwīdān* was the name of an ancient book, attributed to Husheng, grandson of the founder of the oldest Persian monarchy. The name means 'eternal (wisdom)': Redhouse, *Turk. and Eng. Lex.*, pp. 639 and 640.

CHAPTER VIII

THE MALĀMIYŪN [1]—THE SECTARIAN RITES OF THE MUCH-LOVING TARĪQ OF THE MALĀMIYŪN—ON THEIR ASSEMBLIES—THANKS FOR FOOD—ACQUISITION OF THE MEANS OF EXISTENCE

THE original founder of this Order in Constantinople came from Brūsa. His name is Shaikh Hamza, and on that account they are sometimes called Hamzāwīs.[2] The author of the Order, *i.e.*

[1] The Malāmīa became known as the Ḥamzawīa after their reform by Shaikh Ḥamza, a *mullāh* of Brusa, in the sixteenth century. They remained, however, a secret Order, with an organisation strikingly like that of the Freemasons. Their tombs are often marked by triangles, curiously arranged (Petit, *Confrèries Musulmanes*, p. 18).

Goldziher's view is that the modern Malāmīs have no connexion with the Malāmīas of mediæval Islam. But though this is doubtless true of the extreme types of Malamatism, the claim of the latter-day Malāmīs that they teach nothing new and only revive ancient doctrine seems justified by one of their main tenets—that the followers of the Order should not be bound by ceremonies or hampered by forms—which was professed by their precursors. In his *Risālat al-Malāmatīya* As-Sulami begins by dividing the faithful, the *arbāb al-'ulūm wal-'aḥwāl*, into three classes: (1) the *'ulamā' ash-shar' wa a'imat ad-Dīn*, the learned in the law; (2) the *'ahl al-ma'rifa*, who are the elect; and (3) the Malāmatīya, who are at one with God (R. Hartmann, in *Der Islam*, viii. pp. 203 and 158).

The Malāmīa and other classes of holy men are subject to the *aqtab* and the saints of the next Order (? *abdāl*), according to the *Fasl-al-Khitāb* of Sulṭān ul-'Ārifīn Imām Muḥammad Parsā, who is followed by 'Alī, Muṣṭafā b. Aḥmad 'Alī (died 1008 H. = A.D. 1599) (*Cat. of Turkish MSS. in B.M.* p. 19, and *GdOD.* iii. p. 115). The former appears to be Khwāja (Abufer, according to Vambéry in *E.R.E.* 8, p. 887) Parsā, "a pupil of Bahā-ud-Dīn (d. 845 H.), whose grave at Balkh is a place of pilgrimage, particularly for Afghāns". Jāmī wrote a commentary on him (Browne, *Lit. Hist. of Persia*, iii. p. 515).

[2] The information available concerning the Ḥamzawīs is scanty, as usual in the case of a suppressed Order. The name Malāmīyūn seems to be unquestionably derived from *malāmat*, 'blame': indeed, Redhouse defines

the *pīr*, came from Persia, and his tomb is in the cemetery of Silivria Qapūsu, beyond the walls of the capital. They say that

---

the Melāmetiyye as "A sect of darvishes who court public reproach by neglect of the rites and duties of outward religion". The doctrine of blame appeared somewhat early in Ṣūfiism. It was spread abroad by the 'Shaikh of his age', Ḥamdūn Qaṣṣār, who said: "Blame is the abandonment of welfare", *al-malāmat tark al-salāmat*. Blame was of three kinds; it might result (1) from following the right way (*malāmat-i rāst raftan*), or (2) from an intentional act (*malāmat-i qasd kardan*), or (3) from abandonment of the law (*malāmat-i tark kardan*). The emphasis laid on the third of these definitions by the sect itself or by its opponents seems to have led to its persecution. The doctrine was apparently not confined to the Qaṣṣārīs, as Abū Ḥanīfa's renunciation of the office of Qāẓī is described as an act showing the soundness of blame, and others also "travelled on the road of blame" (Nicholson, *Kashf al-Maḥjūb*, pp. 62-9, 183-4, 94, 100).

But the same writer has also pointed out that the saint "who above all others gave to Ṣūfī doctrine its permanent shape" was a Malāmatī, *i.e.* he concealed his piety under a pretended contempt for the law. This saint was Zū'l-Nūn al-Miṣrī, who earned the title of 'he of the Fish' (*nūn*) by a miracle. His real name was Abū'l-Faiẓ Saubān b. Ibrāhīm or al-Faiẓ b. Ibrāhīm, and he was the son of a native of Nubia, or of Upper Egypt, who had been adopted by the Quraish tribe. He is said to have been a pupil of Mālik b. Anas, but his master in Ṣūfiism was either one Shuqrān al-'Ābid or a Maghribite named Isrāfīl. Though styled 'the Egyptian' (al-Miṣrī), he was regarded by the majority of the Egyptians as a *zindīq* or freethinker, but after his death in 245 H. (A.D. 860) he was canonised; and one of his followers, Ḥamdūn al-Qaṣṣār, founded the sect of the Malāmatīs or Qaṣṣārīs in Nīshāpūr before his death in 271 H. (A.D. 885). This sect proved its sincerity and devotion to God by cloaking it under an affected libertinism. Ẓū'l-Nūn was, however, a many-sided man, and his successors must have found in his teachings material for the doctrines of more than one sect or school of thought. He was an alchemist and magician. He claimed, moreover, to be able to decipher ancient Egyptian figures and inscriptions. He attached great importance to the doctrine of *gnōsis*. Prof. Nicholson's conclusion is that on its theosophical side Ṣūfiism is mainly a product of Greek speculation. It undoubtedly owed much to Neo-Platonism, but "Neo-Platonism itself had absorbed many foreign elements in the course of six centuries"; and Ẓū'l-Nūn may well have drawn, not only upon its teachings, but also directly upon so much of the old Egyptian learning as the Copts had been able to preserve. In any case, it is important to bear in mind the fact that the Copts were Christians. Prof. Nicholson points out that the correspondence between Neo-Platonism and Ṣūfiism is far more striking than that between Ṣūfiism and the Vedanta system, and that there is no historical evidence that Indian thought exercised any influence upon Islamic philosophy at the time when Ṣūfiism arose. Further, he calls attention to the fact that though Ma'rūf al-Karkhī came of Persian stock (he died in 200 H. or A.D. 816), the characteristic theosophical mysticism of the Ṣūfīs was first

the chief of all the Orders is Hasan Basrī of Basra, where he died, and that he received his spiritual powers directly from 'Alī.

The Malāmiūns had a *takia* in Scutari, in the Divijilers,[1] called

formulated by his successors, Abū Sulaimān al-Dārānī and Ẓū'l-Nūn, men who passed their lives in Syria and Egypt, and who had probably not a drop of Persian blood in their veins (*J.R.A.S.*, 1906, pp. 303 ff.). But whatever were the sources of the Malāmatī doctrines, they certainly essayed to reconcile the sects which from the beginning distracted Islam. Ḥamdūn, in expounding the doctrine of *malāma*, said that it was a compound of the Hope which characterised the Murjiyyas and the Fear which was incident to Qadarī tenets. His position was that unmixed fear induced despair, while unalloyed hope led to a lack of humility (H. F. Amedroz, "Notes on some Sufi Lives," in *J.R.A.S.*, 1912, p. 562). What part the Malāmatīs played in the disappearance of these earlier sects of Islam is as yet not fully known.

In Constantinople the Malāmīyūn hardly formed a regular Order. Evliya mentions "the Sulṭān of the contemplative saints (Molamyun) Kapānī Muḥammad Effendi, otherwise called Kīsūdār Muḥammad Effendi, because, though bare-footed and bare-headed, he used to wear his hair in thick bushes. Winter and summer he wore nothing but a white coarse cloth, and carried a hatchet in his hand. . . . He . . . spoke the purest Bosnian. At Qonia, he was one of the disciples of Erlī-zāda. . . ." Then he gives some account of "a famous saint, Shaikh Hadāyī Maḥmūd, Mahmūd Effendi, who was born at Sīvrī Hissār in Anatolia and got the name of Hadāyī 'through his spiritual teacher, the celebrated Kīsūdār'. After making 170 disciples and writing 100 volumes of spiritual songs (*ilāhī*) on *tasawwuf*, he died in 1038 H. = A.D. 1629" (*Travels*, i. part 2, pp. 24 and 83).

Kīsū-dār simply means 'long-haired', from Pers. *kīsū*, 'tress', and is equivalent to *ṣāchlī* in Turkish and to *gīsū-darāz*, a term applied to an Afghān saint. For two instances of its use in India, *v.* Crooke, *Islam in India*, pp. 141 and 210. The term seems to be connected with *kes-dhārī*, the Sikh title for those who strictly abstain from cutting the hair.

It will be observed that at least two of the quondam Malāmatī *takias* at Constantinople are held by the Bairāmīs, not one only as stated in the text. On p. 232 'Abd-ul-Bāqī is also said to have been originally a Bairāmī.

[1] Divijī-lar, apparently for *devejī-lar*, 'camel-sellers or owners', may be the Diyunjī-lī, at Scutari, where the Bairāmīs have a *takia* (*v.* p. 459 *infra*).

The Himmat-zāda *takia* appears in the list on p. 460. It must be ascribed to Himmat Effendi or to the saint, who was presumably his son (-zāda), Himmat-zāda.

Himmat, well rendered 'the spirit of enterprise', came in 1607 from Boli to Constantinople. At first a schoolmaster, he subsequently entered the Khalwatī order and was named by Shaikh al-Haj Ahmad at Boli as his successor. The *dafterdār* Ibrāhīm-pāsha built him a cloister near the new Garden Gate at Constantinople. After holding various positions as preacher he died in 1684 and was buried at Scutari. Al-Haj Ahmad was the Shaikh

that of Himmat Effendi ; another in Stambūl at Yanī Baghcha, near Naqqāsh Pasha. The latter is called Himmat-zāda Takia-sī, and is in appearance like any common dwelling. It bears at present the name of Bairāmia. Another at Qāsim Pasha, near Qūlāqsiz, is called 'Sāchlī Hāshim Effendi Takia-sī'. One of their great men is buried at the cemetery of Shahīdlar,[1] above the Castle of Europe, on the Bosphorus; he was named Ismā'īl Ma'shūkī. Another *takia* existed in Constantinople, at Āq-Sarai, called Ūghlānlar Shaikhī.[2] Its Shaikh was Ibrāhīm Effendi, and was immediately behind the *corps de garde* of that locality. He was put to death by order of Sultān Sulimān I. on account of his writings, which were considered anti-orthodox. It is said that he had forty *murīds*, all of whom, voluntarily, were decapitated at the same time that he was put to death. On the tombs of the Malamiūns are peculiar signs, the origin and signification of which I have not been able to learn. For instance, on that of al-Hājī 'Umr Āghā, deceased 1122 H. (A.D. 1710), and that of Abbaji al-Hājī 'Abdullāh Agha, deceased 1137 H. (A.D. 1725), which have been shown to me, there is a double triangle of this shape ⧖. Others have a single triangle, thus △, and some with the addition of one or more dots above and beneath the angles.[3] Many have also the *muhr-i-sulaimān*, or 'Sulimān's seal', thus, one triangle covering another, ✡, but without dots or

---

of the Karāmīs, followers apparently of one Ibn-ul-Kirām (Hammer-Purgstall, *GdOD.* iii. p. 533).

Le Chatelier's informant speaks of the 'Khalwatīa Bairāmīa Hinnatīa' (? for Himmatīa) and Khalwatīa Bairāmīa Ughlān-Shaikhia as two sub-Orders of the Khalwatī (*v.* note on p. 450 *infra*).

[1] Shahīd-lar, 'the martyrs': ? Shahīdlik, originally a Baqtāsh foundation (*Annual*, B.S.A. xxi. p. 100). Called simply Hāshmī on p. 460 *infra.*

[2] Ughlānlar Shaikhī—the Ughlān-Shaikhīa of the Khalwatīa-Bairāmīa group of Le Chatelier (*vide* p. 450 below). Ūghlān ('the young') Shaikh, or Ibrāhīm Effendi, was executed under a *fatwa* of Ibn Kamāl by order of Sulaimān the Magnificent (*Textes Houroufis*, p. 255). The son of a merchant of Egerdir, he affected the Shaikh of the Khalwatīs at the cloister at Egri Qapū, who nominated him to the cloister inside the walls near Āq-Sarāī. His charity to orphans and the poor earned him his title of Boys' Shaikh, and his death occurred in 1654 (Hammer-Purgstall, *GdOD.* iii. p. 406).

[3] In Moslem magic the triangle when inverted means the moon, but none of the figures given in the text appear to be strictly magical: *v.* the article on 'Magic' by E. Rahatsek in *J. Bombay Branch R. Asiatic Soc.* xiv. No. xxxvii. (1880) p. 215).

points. Some say that the original Order was the Khalwatīs, from whom descended the Bairāmīs, and from these the Hamzāwīs,[1] by which name the Malāmiūns are now known in Constantinople.

Like the Order of the Baqtāshīs, that of the Hamzāwīs is almost under prohibition at Constantinople, though from widely different causes. The latter, it is said, hold their meetings in secret, in houses in nowise resembling *takias*, and for this reason it is thought by some persons that they are Mussulman Freemasons. It has even been said that the Malāmiūns have several lodges in the Ottoman empire, under warrants from a Grand Lodge existing on the Lake of Tiberias, in Palestine, where it was taken after the destruction of Jerusalem.

The word *Malāmiūn* signifies 'the condemned', or 'the reproached',—a title assumed by this Order. Their litany shows them to be a very sincerely pious sect, conscientious in all their dealings, and living much for themselves and their doctrine,

[1] A sect of the Ḥamzevīs is mentioned by Evliya as if it were still existing in his day in the village of Shaikh Shāmī, 'whose name was Ḥamza'. His tomb, said by some to be the saint's own handiwork, was remarkable for its carvings of flowers and arabesques, and before it was a spring called the Spring of the Staff, because it had been produced by the saint's staff. Evliya states that this saint was a Bairāmī. He adds that his son Shaikh 'Abdullāh, who also seems to have been styled Karānjī Bāba Sulṭān, is buried at Kūrbāghli, a village in the same region in the territory of Kānghrī and the district of Kala'ajik'. The Shaikh's name, Shāmī or Shām, would suggest that he was a Syrian by origin, but in writing of Muḥammad Shām Ghāzān, Evliya says that Shām Ghāzān is a corruption of the Mughal language, in which that prince was called Shanb, whence Shām originated (*Travels*, ii. pp. 226-7 and 143).

Evliya also has a curious note on the Ettel tribe, who were settled near Mārdīn in 'the *sanjāq* of the mountains', and who pretended to be of Ḥamza's sect. Ettel, he says, means 'dog's tongue', and the tribe practised polyandry, not apparently of the type in which the husbands are all brothers. Paternity was assigned to the husband to whom the infant gave an apple. Then he goes on to say that the famous sect of the candle-extinguishers must be a branch of them, because he heard nothing of it elsewhere. This sect he calls Mom-sonduren (from *mūm*, 'wax', and *sundurmek*, 'to extinguish'), a term which recalls the fanciful derivation of Urmar, said to mean 'lamp' (*ur*) - 'extinguisher' (*mar*). The Urmar are a mysterious tribe or community found in Wazīrīstān, who speak a Ghalchah dialect distinct from Pashtū, but have a tradition that they came from Yaman (Rose, *Glossary of Punjab Tribes and Castes*, iii. p. 483). Evliya says the Ettels are very obedient to their Shāhs (by which he must mean priests), out of whose shoes they drink (*Travels*, ii. p. 157).

without any regard for the opinion of the world. They even disregard external appearances, so much so, that any poor and miserable object, as destitute of intellect as of the garments necessary to cover his person, is now called in Stambūl a *Malāmiūn*.

Shaikh Hamza [1] was put to death on a *fatwā*, or religious sentence of the Muftī Abū-Sāūd, 969 H. (A.D. 1553). His remains are buried near the Silivria Gate, in a spot known only to his brethren and particular friends. As his accusation was a strange one, and little understood by the public, he is generally considered either as a very revered martyr, or as an impious disbeliever in Islamism. His crime was that of neglecting to repeat in his prayers the full *ismā-i-Sharīf*, which are seven in number, he always omitting the three last. Various traditions are still prevalent in Constantinople about his piety and wonderful spiritual powers; and 'Abd-ul-Bākī, the author of the following *risāla*, or pamphlet, has also composed a work, the *Sarguzashta 'Abd-ul-Bākī*, giving an entire history of the Order.

He narrates that his grandfather, named Sārī 'Abdullāh Effendi,[2] and the writer of a celebrated commentary on the *Masnavī Sharīf*, told him that his father, Hājī Husain Āghā, once addressing him, said, " I am now an old man, and hope before leaving this world to make you acquainted with my friends of God ". I was then not yet arrived at the age of puberty. He told me, " When you go to see them with me, and are asked what you came for, say,

[1] Shaikh Ḥamza was executed soon after the accession of S. Murād (III.), apparently in 1575 (von Hammer, *GdOR*. ii. p. 594). The ground for his condemnation was said to be his excessive reverence for the Lord Jesus, and he was sentenced to be stoned at the Hippodrome, but, out of fear of a popular outbreak, as soon as he was brought out of his prison his throat was cut. One wonders if he was influenced by Qābiẓ, founder of the Khubmasīhiṣ, a sect which held Jesus to be morally superior to Muḥammad. He, too, had been executed with exemplary promptitude in 1527 (*E.I.* ii. p. 592).

Abū Sa'ūd also gave the *fatwa* under which some executions of Janissaries took place. At any rate he ruled that he who held that a Janissary was a true believer was an infidel, and that it was no offence to call one a pagan (Rycaut, *Present State*, p. 149).

[2] Sārī 'Abdullah, whose poetic title was 'Abdī (VI.), was also styled Shāriḥ-al-Mesnevi, or ' Commentator of the Mesnevi '. He also wrote two ethical and three mystical works. He died in A.D. 1669, and was buried outside the Top Qapū in the cemetery of Mal-Tepe, adds Gibb, *Hist. of Ott. Poetry*, iv. p. 79 (Hammer-Purgstall, *GdOD*. iii. p. 482). His father, Sa'īd Muḥammad Effendi, the learned Ra'īs Effendi, came from Mauritania.

'My desire is God'". So we both performed the *ābdast*, or Islamic ablution before prayers, and accompanied him. We were perfectly alone, and without any servant to attend upon us; we went to a place called Kirk Chashma [1] in Constantinople, to the *khān* called the Pashtimāl 'Odalārī, and there entered a chamber in which was an aged man engaged in weaving. My father saluted him, and kissed his hand; I did the same; my father told him that I was his son, and that he had brought me in so that he might 'look into my heart'. The old man asked my father whether he had the permission of the Shaikh to bring me, and he replied that he had not, but could bring me without it. On hearing this, the old man struck the wall with his hand, and all the *ustāds*, or labourers in the *khān*, entered the room where we were, to the number of twelve, forming a circle, in the midst of which they placed me, and asked me why I had come there. I replied as previously directed by my father, 'My desire is God.' The old man then addressing me, said, "If you have come for that purpose, drive away all else from your heart, and turn your thoughts entirely to Him, and we will see what our Lord the *pīr* will do in your behalf.' All of those present thereon commenced the *murāqaba* and the *mutawajjiīn*,[2] 'contemplation' and 'supplication', and the old man bade me do the same, which I did, thinking only of Allah. After some time I opened my eyes, and saw a light turning round the circle, and I cried out 'Allāh!': at the same instant the feeling that my heart was filled with the love of God became so impressed upon me that I swooned away, and was quite senseless for an hour. At the end of this time I revived, and looking round me found that all those who had been with me had disappeared, except the old man, who, as previously, was engaged at his work, and my father who sat near me. My father, so soon as I could rise, bade me go with him. My heart was still filled with *light*; I kissed the hand of the old man, and so as to conceal myself I wrapped my cloak over my breast, at seeing which the old man told me no one could see it, and that I must strive always to keep it there.

"On our way, I tried to think who our Shaikh was, and, though I had never seen him, wondered whether I should ever

[1] Kirk Chashma, Forty Fountains or Fountain of the Forty 'Saints' (cf. Hasluck, in *Annual*, B.S.A. xix. pp. 221 ff.).

[2] *Mutavejieen* in original.

behold his face, at the same time feeling a warm affection for him. I was ashamed to ask my father who he was, but my affection for him increasing, I was, one Friday, requested to accompany my father to the mosque of Ayā Sofiāh, and there perform our prayers. After these were terminated, we left the mosque; my father covered himself, and looked behind him with much respect on account of some person then present. Just then, I perceived an aged man come out of the mosque, who, in passing, saluted us, and inquired of my father who I was, and whether I was not his son. He looked fixedly at me, and immediately I felt like a *jazbah*, or crazed person; the people in the way collected round us, and my father told them that I was suffering under a complaint which at times thus affected me. I had to be conveyed home, where I remained in a state of insensibility. After my recovery, I asked my father who the individual was whose regard had so strangely impressed me, and he told me that he was our Lord and Chief, Idrīsī 'Alī Effendi, the *Qutb-i-Zamān*,[1] and the bestower of the *jazbah-i-Rahmān*,[2] and that the brethren whom we had seen at the Kark Chashma were his disciples."

A Translation of the Risāla (*pamphlet or tract*) *of the Hamzāwīs, otherwise known as the Malāmiūn, written by La'lī Effendi-zāda 'Abd-ul-Bākī,*[3] *who is buried at the mosque of Aiyūb al-Ansārī,—on whom be the Divine satisfaction. He entered the Qalandar-khāna in the vicinity of the said mosque, near the* takia *of the Bhoharalīs.*[4] *His tomb is near to its doorway. He*

[1] 'The Pole of the Age.'

[2] 'The ecstasy of the Merciful.' Majẓūb, 'one whose thoughts are attracted to God, so as to be careless of earthly things; hence (vulgar) crazy' (Redhouse, *Turk.-Eng. Lex.* p. 1748).

[3] La'lī Effendi-zāda 'Abd-ul-Bāqī, most probably the poet 'Ārif (VI.) 'Abd-ul-Bāqī, who died in A.D. 1713, and is buried at Aiyūb. He wrote several metaphysical works (Hammer-Purgstall, *GdOD.* iv. p. 72). But 'Ārif does not seem to have been styled La'li or to have had any special connexion with the Bairāmīs. Moreover, the date of his death is rather too late.

[4] Bhoharalīs should probably read 'the *takia* at Baharia Keui', near the cemetery to the north of Aiyūb.

was originally of the Bairāmīa Order, and subsequently joined that of the Malāmīas. This Risāla *contains, in detail, the rites of the latter Order, their intercourse, and great love for God.*

Chapter I

THE SECTARIAN RITES OF THE MUCH-LOVING *TARĪQ* OF THE MALĀMIŪN

The following is the advice which the *faqīr*, or elder member of the *tarīq*, gives to the disciple :

" If, after having performed the *ahkām-i-sharī'at*, or religious ordinances, the *lawāzim-i-tarīqat*, or exigencies of the Order, any one commits an act growing out of the feebleness of the human passions, and contrary to the *sharī'at* and the Order, and permits himself to use improper language, or commits a sinful act, he will be expelled from the Order ; he will not be permitted to re-enter it ; but if, after this, he acknowledges his fault, and promises not to commit the same again, and begs to be restored to his place, the way to arrive at it will be pointed out to him, and he will renew his *bai'at*, or confirmation. He must conform strictly to the commands given him,—to the law of God,—the *aqwāl*, or directions of the inspired Prophet, and the *tarīqat* of the saints ; he will undergo the disciplinary punishment of the Order, to be re-accepted as before in all love. If, on the contrary, he refuses to do this, he must remain for ever rejected.

" God forbid such an occurrence ! Should any one who believes in the *ahl-i-tauhīd*,[1] or unity of the Divinity, so far err as to admit the erroneous doctrine of the *Wahdat-ul-Wujūd*,* or the

[1] *Ahl-i-tauḥīd* means 'people of unification', *i.e.* those who believe in the unity of God.

* Pantheism. [Waḥdat-ul-wujūd, literally 'solitude of being'.]

It is curious that Brown should translate the term by 'pantheism', as it means 'unity of being'. An important school of Ṣūfīs, whose watchword is *waḥdat-ul-wujūd* or *ittiḥād,* hold that reality is one, and that the phenomenal is the outward manifestation of the real. The views of this school were expounded in the fifteenth century by 'Abd-ul-Karīm al-Jīlī, who taught that man was the microcosm in which all the attributes of reality are united, and in man alone does the Absolute become conscious of itself in all its diverse aspects (*E.R.E.*, art. on Ṣūfīs by R. A. Nicholson). In a sense, then, *waḥdat-ul-wujūd* implies pantheism, or rather that man partakes

existence of the Divine Creator in all things of His creation, and thus fall from the true path into impiety, persisting, at the same time, in the correctness of his course, adding that *al bait bait Ullāh* and *al zait zait Ullāh*, it is the duty of every correct person to strive, by gentle means, to withdraw him from such an error, by showing him his fault and the dangers which he incurs, and telling him clearly that, so long as he continues in such a sin, he cannot be of us. He must also be cut off from all intercourse with his former friends and associates, so that no one will commune with him. They must even avoid his presence. Should the Almighty, in His bountiful mercy, again draw him into the true path, and he repent of his sin, the whole false doctrine of his heart will disappear, and he again become a bright light. He will come to his Shaikh, and admit his sins, and return to the discipline of the Order. The *siāsāt-i-Sūfīa*, or punishments of the Sūfīs, are numerous, and are all well known to the Shaikh, so that he can prescribe them according to the fault which the erring one may have committed. After this, he is re-admitted, and the past is forgotten.

"Alas! that whilst at one time it was so necessary to be secret in the matters of our Order, everything has become public. Up to the time of the venerable Muhammad Hāshim, one of the Shaikhs of our Order, there was no need for secrecy: the *ādāb-i-tarīqat*, or moral rules of the Order, and the *ahkām-i-sharī'at*, or holy commands of the law, were brilliantly executed by the *faqīrs*, and no reference was ever made to the judges and governors of the sovereign; everything was done by the command of the Shaikhs of our Order; the faulty admitted their errors and sins, repented of them, and suffered their expiation in this world so as not to do so in the other; their repentance was accepted of God,—their hearts were filled with the light of love, and, as before, they performed the *zikr-i-khafī*, or silent call upon God's name, whilst alone, and the audible call, or *zikr-i-jihrī*, when in the midst of the congregation.

"By command of the Most High, after the occurrence of the

---

of the divine. But L. Massignon renders the word by 'monisme' (*Kitāb al-Ṭawāsīn*, p. xxiv). That it underwent a change of meaning and fell into some disrepute is clear from the fact that *fanā fī waḥdat al-Wujūd* was condemned as one of the two impious modalities of annihilation (*ib.* p. 162). For the microcosm, *v.* p. 140.

saintly martyr Bashir Agha, who is interred in Scutari,—may his secret be blessed !—the hearts of the brethren became troubled and sorrowful ; they diminished in number ; few sought for the path of love ; sloth overcame others ; the 'Self-Reproaching' and the 'Living Ones' (titles of the Order) fell into faulty habits, —daily they became degraded, and it was absolutely requisite to form systems of secrecy for the benefit of the Order. This necessity was declared by Bashir Agha[1] as growing out of the *asrār-i-qazā*, or secret Providences, and yet it was hoped that a time would again arrive when the secret (*bātin*) would be known (*zuhūr*), through the brethren who labour for that purpose."

The *Rūh-i-'Ālam* and the *Khalīfa* of the blessed Prophet, who is the *Sāhib-i-Zamān*, receives his bounties and grace by the will of God. This person is called the *Qutb* (Centre), and is a spiritual being placed by Allāh over the spiritual world. He sees every place, and knows all things by Divine permission. Of this there is no doubt ; whatever be the will of God, he makes apparent, and the faithful must inevitably submit to that will.

The Shaikh must restore the feeble sinner to his original position ; he must know the mental condition of each disciple, and this he is able to see through the light of the *wilāyat* (spiritual power of the *pīr*), and he must see and know all things through the light of the truth (*haqq*). The light given by the blessed Prophet is peculiar to the Perfect ; the holy body and precious heart of the latter become the mirror of God. All the sayings of the Prophet (*hadīsāt*) and his degrees (*maqāmāt*) are revealed to the truly devout. These degrees are explained to me as being seven in number, of which there are also seven branches ; in all fourteen. To each of them is prescribed one *asmā*, name or title of God, and they are also called the *atwār-i-sabi'ah*. "O God, all favour is from Thee, so is the true path of love and sanctity ; show then this true path to those who seek after the All-Just, to those lovers of the All-Beautiful, and lead them to the object of their desires ; preserve them from shame and indifference ; intoxicate them with the wine of reunion to Thee and love ; open to their sight a glimpse of Thy perfect beauty, O thou Living One, Thou Aider, through thy Friend (the Prophet), and the Seal of the universe, on whom be prayers and salvation, and on his family and all his friends. Amen."

[1] Bashīr Āghā, who has a *takia* named after him at Stambūl.

ON THEIR ASSEMBLIES

Whenever those who follow in this path, and who love the unique God, to the number of two or three, or more, meet together and join in the *tauhīd* and the *zikr*, and their hearts are occupied with their worldly affairs, they should, on their way to the place of meeting, employ their minds with thoughts of God, in all sincerity and purity, and also beg their *pīr* to lend them his spiritual aid, so that when they reach the meeting they may all, small and great, with humility and contrition, embrace the hand of each other, and devoutly join in the contemplation of the Deity, and turn their faces towards the Grace of the All-Just (*Haqq*), the ever-rising love of Allāh, without harbouring in the tongue, in the mind, or otherwise, any thoughts respecting worldly concerns, but, with perfect hearts and active spirits, take part in these pious ceremonies.

They must next offer up those prayers which are conformable with the rules of the Order, seat themselves, and, if there be among them any one possessing a pleasant voice, let him peruse ten verses of the great *Qurān*, and interest the company with some account of the prophets and saints, or even of the Deity. No one must feel concern about his worldly affairs ; all their remarks must be relative to the love of God, of pious fervour (here the name used is *jazbah*, which signifies craziness, or that condition in which the mind and intellect is taken away from the body by Divine favour, as in idiots) ; no one not of the Order must be admitted, and should any such be present, the peculiar gift of God (*faiz-Ullāh*) will not rest there. After this the assembly must disperse, and each return to his proper worldly occupation. Every one must, even when thus employed, preserve in his heart the love for God. Should other thoughts than these enter his mind, he must forsake his occupation and seek converse with the *ahl-i-fanā* [1] (those who have abandoned the world) and the *fuqrā* (Darvishes), and they must not be satisfied with themselves until they have in this manner freed their hearts. When they casually

[1] Fanā, ' annihilation '. The doctrine of *fanā* and *baqā*, ' subsistence ', was developed by Abū Sa'īd Kharrāz, who gave his name to the Kharrāzī sect. In mysticism *fanā* means the annihilation of one attribute through the subsistence of another attribute, as annihilation of substance, *fanā-i-'ain*, is impossible (*Kashf al-Maḥjūb*, pp. 244-5).

meet each other, let their conversation be always about God, and never consider themselves as being superior to any one else ; but, on the contrary, regard themselves as poorer, lower, and more humble than all others—as insignificant, even, as an ant. Following this course, they must, as much as possible, withdraw from all intercourse with the world, seek to gain their living honestly, always endeavouring to lead spiritual lives. They must not divulge the secrets to their families (wives and children), nor to any one who is not a seeker of the truth (*tālib sādiq*),[1] and ask for assistance in attaining to the path of God (*Haqq*). In that case violence must not be used towards him who does divulge them to another in the view of engaging him to join the Order and finds that he refuses ; but such cases are rare.

THANKS FOR FOOD

It is one of the rules (*arkān*) of the Order, obligatory on all its members, whenever he is at meals with a brother, or even alone, to retain in his heart the remembrance of God, and, after the conclusion of his meal, to offer thanks to God in a devout prayer. For this purpose he must sincerely turn his thoughts to Him, and pronounce the *zikr-Ullāh* (*Qurān*, xxiv. 37, 38 : " Men celebrate His praises, whose traffic does not divert their minds from remembrance of Him,—from the observance of prayer, and from the giving of alms, who fear the day wherein man's heart and eyes shall be troubled, so that God may recompense them according to the utmost merit of what they shall have wrought, and add unto them of His abundance a more excellent reward ; for God bestoweth on whom He pleaseth without measure "), so that the food of which he has partaken may strengthen him with the love of God. Thus, each mouthful speaks with the tongue, and says, " O God, give us the favour of an humble and faithful believer ". In case you do not do this, you will have done violence to the truth ; the food will prove ungrateful to you, and seem to say, " This violent person has abandoned Him ", and it will complain against you to the Giver of all bounties. Should the food be vegetables or meats, and you seem to ask whether they can speak, learn from the verse (*Qurān*, xvii. 46), " The seven heavens, and

[1] Literally ' seeker of the truthful or sincere ' one : ' seeker of the truth ' would be *ṭālib-uṣ-ṣidq*.

all that they contain, as well as the earth, celebrate His praises. There is nothing which does not praise Him ; but you do not comprehend their songs of praise. God is humane and indulgent." Those who do understand their praises are the spiritual, the devoutly loving, and the perfect—through the attributes of the prophets and the saints. In case of need, they cause even those who do not believe to hear His praises. When this occurs, and comes from the blessed Prophet, it is called a miracle ; and if from the saints, a favourable demonstration. When the prophets call infidels to the true faith, they are ordered to perform miracles, as an evidence of their conversion. It is not proper to aspire to the performance of miracles, or favourable demonstrations (*karāma*), except when directly ordered by God, and He will decide as to the necessity. The saints are few in number ; they are empowered to make animals, vegetable and even inanimate things, speak ; and such are found in the history of their lives.

ACQUISITION OF THE MEANS OF EXISTENCE

The faithful, who devoutly seek for the path of God and the love of Him, will find, regarding the acquisition of the means of existence, in the *hadīs*, the saying of the Prophet, " The seeker of gain is the friend of God ". Those who are busily engaged in the daily acquisition of their own existence in this world, must, in the event of their acquiring much wealth, return to their homes, reject from their minds the idea of the value of gold, and turn their thoughts, with deep piety and with a pure heart, towards God,—giving themselves up entirely for the time to feelings of devotion.

There is a difference in the sentiment of pious ecstasy. Ecstatic feeling is derived from a deep contemplation of the heart of God, and of the *murshid.* A sense of sincere satisfaction is the result, and the person feels a conviction of personal helplessness, which he will enjoy immensely. This kind of feeling is most acceptable to God. Ecstasy is also that state of the heart which arises from a fervent desire to drive away from it all anxiety about worldly store. It comes from a profound contemplation and reflection of the Deity, and an absorption in sincere prayer to Him : from tears and a sight of repentance ; from the performance of the *zikr* ; from a convulsive movement of the body ;

from a frequent repetition of the word *hū* ; from a seeking devoutly after the same state (*wajd*) ; and when in this search, from the opening of a door to the seeker, through which he receives what is called the *jazba-i-rahmān*, or the merciful attraction of God, and is filled with intense joy and delight. The termination of this ecstatic state is called *wajd*, the close of this is called the *wajdain* (two *wajds*), meaning worldly and eternal ecstasies, which leads to the *wujūd*, or undying state of existence, in which there is no death. Regarding this subject, I have been given two *hadīses* of the Prophet. *Jazbat*, or attraction, comes from the attraction of the All-Merciful, and the recipients of this grace abandon all care or thought of this world and their future existence.

It is related that the Caliph 'Alī, when absorbed in this state, was told that he had lost his senses. He immediately fell down in prayers of thankfulness to God, declaring that he had at last reached the condition mentioned in the Prophet's *hadīs* above stated.

The second *hadīs* says : " The faithful do not die ; perhaps they become translated from this perishable world to the world of eternal existence ".

It is said that on this account Darvishes implore the help of the *auliā*, or saints. This state, however, must not be shown to strangers or the public ; it is proper to be enjoyed in private, amongst the lovers of the same.

When engaged in conversation about the *tauhīd* (unity of God) with the brethren, and the heart is in its appropriate state, there is no impropriety in exciting the occurrences of this ecstasy ; but, among the brethren to excite it, in the view of having it spoken of to their praise, and that they are *ahl-i-'ishq* (lovers of God), is hypocrisy equal to that of *shirkat* (saying that God has an associate), for it will have had its source entirely in the *personal* ambition of the individual, and not in the *spiritual*. It gives rise to all kinds of spiritual disease ; and when your sins are taken into account at the Day of Judgment, the tricks of your body will, by the excellence of God, be made apparent, and seem like dark spots on the surface of pure milk. However, it may be added, that those who do fall into such errors are not fully perfected in the brotherhood. Besides these, the saints are the *ahl-i-fanā*, who have given up all care for this world ; and the *mukhlisīn*, or the freed from worldly anxieties, are pure and faithful, and not liable to this sin. They may even use those members of the body which provide for its wants; but their hearts must, nevertheless, be always occupied with God. They arrive at nothing through the medium of mental superiority (science or knowledge); no one can comprehend their real state through the ordinary sources of calculating intelligence, as they are only commissioned to be seekers of piety through the deepest sincerity of the heart, and through the spiritual guidance of the Shaikh, who, in consequence, keeps them always in his pious remembrance (his prayers).

"O God! facilitate us through the favour of the *ahl-i-fanā* and the *baqā*."

This *baqā* (a condition in which there is no death) is the source out of which the *fanā* originates. The *wujūd* is also that which is referred to in the verse of the *Qurān* where God says:

"Be it known that those who search for the pathway of God, find it through the *tawakkul*, or confidence in His mercy, and in the *kasb*, or acquisition of the means of existence"; but the former is only proper to the *ahl-i-fanā*. The *ahl-i-tawakkul* is that person who, on his admission to the Order, considers himself as dead, and regards all his worldly interests as wholly given up and perished, and abandons himself, spiritually and temporally, to the guidance of his Shaikh. He must not give any thought to himself; he must consider his wife and children, his servants and dependants, as lost to him, or as if they never existed. He must abandon all his sources of gain, and place his entire dependence and confidence in the Bestower of all gifts; he will then be shorn of all worldly connexions, so that he will be registered, by God's command, on his *pīr*; he will be in a state of annihilation; but this is a very difficult rule of conduct to pursue. Now, according to the *hadīs, al-kāsib habīb-Ullāh,* or 'the gainer is the friend of God', this condition is better than the former, and it is better to gain an honest livelihood by proper means, depending always upon Him for success in your endeavours. The 'Lover' and 'Faithful', in thus using the means necessary for gaining an existence, do this, not simply with the idea of depending wholly upon God, but rather in obedience to the commands of the 'First Cause of all causes'. The servants of God in all things acknowledge their own poverty in the sight of God. Those who become faithful followers of the Prophet—on whom be the Divine satisfaction—were all, individually, occupied in the acquisition of an existence, and it is necessary that each person, in honour of God, should be thus engaged ; yet there are some idle persons who employ their time in no useful occupation,—abandon even the name of Darvish, and call themselves *zuhd*, or ascetics.[1] These give themselves up to idleness and inactivity. God has covered His saints with a veil—such as are worldly employments—which conceals their real character from public gaze, so that those whose spiritualism has not been touched with *kuhl* (collyrium) of the

MAULAVĪ DARVISH OF DAMASCUS CROSSING HIS ARMS BEFORE BEGINNING TO DANCE

light of Muhammadanism, are unable to distinguish them, and to recognise in them the true saints of God. Thus it is only through the light of Muhammadanism that the saints recognise each other; none other can distinguish them ; and for this reason the lovers of God (*'ushshāq-Ullāh*) have abandoned all causes of hypocrisy.

[1] *Zuhd*, 'asceticism'; *zuhhād*, 'ascetics'. Perhaps a better rendering is 'renunciation'; *zuhd* was the 'station' of Noah (Nicholson, *Kashf al-Maḥjūb*, p. 371).

CHAPTER IX

REAL AND FALSE DARVISHES—THE KHIRQA, OR MANTLE—THE PALANK, OR STONE WORN IN THE GIRDLE—THE POST, OR SEAT

(TRANSLATED FROM A MS.)

THERE is as much difference between the real and false Darvish as between heaven and earth. The right-minded man can recognise them, and draw the distinction.

To the question, "What is true repentance shown by ?" the reply is, "Goodness of heart"; and this is qualified by "the abandonment of all pride and pretension, and by following a line of straightforwardness in the Path of the Most High". The number of the columns of the Path are six—viz. 1. Repentance, 2. Resignation, 3. Fidelity to the Order, 4. Increase of internal devotion, 5. Contentment with your lot, and 6. Devout retirement from the world. The Precepts of the Order are also six in number, viz. 1. Knowledge, 2. Generosity, 3. Nearness to God, 4. Fidelity, 5. Meditation, and 6. Trust in God. The Rules of the Order are equally six: 1. Knowledge, 2. Meekness, 3. Patience, 4. Submission to superiors, 5. Good breeding, and 6. Purity of heart.

The Rules of the *tarīqat* are six, viz. 1. Benevolence, 2. Calling upon God (the *zikr*), 3. Abandoning evil (the *tark*), 4. The abandoning of all worldly enjoyments, 5. Fear of God, and 6. Love of God.

The ablution of the *tarīqat* is a total abnegation of all worldly goods, and contentment with the will of the Shaikh. The truthful ablution is 'to increase in love for God'.

A question was once put to the Imām Ja'far as to the peculiar characteristics of a *faqīr* (Darvish), and he replied: "It is the characteristic of the Prophet, and of love; for he has said in a *hadīs*, 'Bear the characteristics of God', the tree of which is straightforwardness, and its fruit is to know one's self. Its jewel is utter poverty, or a total disregard of self. Now one who possesses these certainly knows himself, and can do anything he pleases, but abandons all for devotional retirement. The Caliph 'Alī has said, 'Whoever knows himself, knows his God'."

The *tark* or abandoment required by the *tarīqat* is thus explained: To abandon the world, its comforts and dress,—all things now and to come,—conformably with the *hadīs* of the Prophet, *i.e.* "The world is forbidden to those of the life to come; the life to come is forbidden to those of this world; and both are forbidden to the true servants of God", which is thus explained: The true Darvish in heart not only willingly abandons all the joys and pleasures of the world, but he is willing also to give up all hope of the pleasures of Paradise, and to be satisfied with the enjoyment derived from a submissive and devout contemplation of the beauty of God, and the hope of attaining to that private Paradise, occupied only by the pious, the holy, and the prophets.

Abandonment of the world is also to neglect to comb the hair, to regulate the eyebrows, to cleanse the beard and moustaches; and whoever pays attention to these personal comforts has already determined to return to the world and given up the hope of seeing God hereafter. Not to shave the head in the presence of the *murshid*, shows that the *murīd* knows himself. To suspend a *charkhā*,[1] or circle, to the neck, means, "I have resigned myself entirely to the will of God, for blessing or for punishment"; to suspend the *mangosh*, or ear-rings, to the ears, signifies, "I believe the language of the saints is that of the Most High, and that their words are my laws, or my *mangosh*, and is ever hung over my heart". If ever any one is asked whose son and Darvish he is, he must reply, "I am the son of Muhammad 'Alī", the proof of which is in the *hadīs*, "I am of that people to which I belong".

The *arkān*, or columns of the Order, are based upon the following: When it is asked what Darvish means, the reply is, "One who asks nothing of any creature, and to be as submissive as the earth which is trodden upon by the feet, to serve others before yourself, to be contented with little, to do neither good nor evil, to abandon all desires, to divorce even his wife, to submit hourly

[1] Charkhā, for *charkh*, a wheel, a collar, or anything round, *e.g.* the circular dance of the Muhammadan *darvishes* (Johnson, p. 451). In Turkish, *charkhah* means a skirmish or whirlwind.

to all occurrences of misfortune and accident, not to drink wine nor to lie, not to commit fornication, not to touch what does not belong to you, to know the true and the false, and to restrain the tongue and speak little ".

The rules of the *tarīq* are thus explained: 1. To change the thing desired to whatever is wished for miraculously; 2. to divorce his wife and live secluded, because to become a true *murshid* this must be done so as to enable the aspirant to that position to devote himself wholly to the love of Allāh; the disciple, though married, must become a benedict if he hopes to be a good *murshid*. (This is not now followed, for Shaikhs are favoured with visions, in which they receive permission to keep their wives, or to take one if they have none.) This is founded upon the principle contained in *Qurān*, xxvi. 87, 88: " Do not dishonour me in that day when all mankind will be resuscitated; that day when all riches and offspring will be of no value; it is only for him who comes to God with an upright heart that Paradise will be opened and approached by pious men ".

In reply to the question as to what is a *tāj* (crown or cap) it should be said, " Honour and respect "; to that as to their number, say, " There are two, the *tāj-i-jāhil* and the *tāj-i-kāmil* ", viz. the 'Crown of the Ignorant' and the 'Crown of the Perfect' in spiritual knowledge. The principle of *khalwat* and *'azlat*[1] signifies retirement from the eyes of the world, and cessation from seeking the honour and respect of any one. The 'Crown of the Ignorant' means to frequent the public streets and bazaars, and to possess the esteem and honour of every one, whilst that of the Perfect signifies to have the esteem of no one.

The form (turban) which is wrapped round a crown is called *istiwā*.[2] Its centre, or *qubba*; its border; its diameter; the letters which form its name, *t*, *ā*, *j*; its upper surface,

[1] From same root as Mu'tāzilī, 'seceder'. It connotes an abrupt breaking away.

[2] *Istiwā*, lit. 'equality', 'a plane surface', apparently from the same root as *āyat*, the literal meaning of which is 'sign' or 'token'. But there is probably a play on the word *istawā*, which means 'He stood straight or erect', or 'He set himself upon (the throne)' (see Palmer's *Qurān S.B.E.* vi. p. lxxix). On p. 245 *infra*, *istiva* (as Brown transliterates it) is rendered 'parable'; but Redhouse does not give this meaning or that of 'turban'. His definitions include 'a being or becoming upright, steadfast, firm', 'a becoming perpendicular' (*Turk.-Eng. Lex.* p. 105).

qibla;[1] its ablutions, its key, its religious duties, commanded by God; its services, directed by the Prophet; its soul, its interior,—all have their respective significations.

1. The *istiwā*, ' parable ', means to change evil deeds and actions to those of an exalted and pious nature.

2. The *qibla*, ' The position facing you at prayer directing to Makka ', is the *pīr*, or founder of the Order.

3. The *kanār*, or ' border ', is the faculty of spiritual command in both worlds, viz. to pray with a devout heart to God for the release of any one in danger, for God accepts an intercession for the latter, and it relieves him from the danger.

4. The *langar*,[2] or ' capacity ', means to point out (by the Shaikh) the true path to his disciples.

5. The *kalima*, or ' letters of the word *tāj* ' (*t*, *ā*, *j*), means to implore pardon from God according to the *āyat*, or verse of the *Qurān*, " God is the rich, but we are the poor ".

6. The *qubba*, or ' summit of the cap ', means the point of truth, which signifies that the owner knows all things; the ' Summit of the Sphere of the Universe ' (God) allowing the observer to see and know all things.

7. The *ghusl*, ' ablution ', means not to mingle with the public, and so remain pure.

8. The *qilīd*,[3] or ' key ', means to open the secret and difficult. The Shaikh interprets and explains by it all dreams and visions of his disciples.

9. The *farz*, or ' obligation ', means the conversation and communication with the *pīrs* and the brethren (*arans*).

10. The *sunnat*, ' order of the Prophet ', means honour and respect.

11. The *jān*,[4] or ' soul ', means to keep the commandments of the *pīr* or Shaikh, and to abstain from hurting the feelings of any one, and to withdraw from the world.

12. The *muwāt*, or 'dying', means to touch the living creature's hands, as on the initiation of a *murīd*.

13. The *far'*, ' branch or decoration ', is to refrain from all females.

[1] *Qibla*, ' direction to which one turns (in prayer) '.

[2] *Langar*, an anchor, a house or monastery of the Qalandars or Muhammadan monks. It has come to mean ' refectory ' further East.

[3] *Qilīd* for *miqlad* or *iqlīd*.

[4] *Yān* in original.

On the *tāj* is written, " There is no God but Him, the Living and the Eternal ". In the front is written, " All things perish except the face of God ". In the middle, " I swear by the learned book (*Qurān*) ".

There is another question as to the number of the *tājs*. These, as aforestated, are two, viz. that of the learned and that of the ignorant. The former means to strive to reach the secrets of Muhammad and 'Alī, for the blessed Prophet has said, " I and 'Alī are made of the same light ", and to *see* that they are made of one light, and the All-Just at the same time. Do not, therefore, understand like those who wear the crown of the ignorant. And yet God knows all with goodness.

THE KHIRQA, OR MANTLE

It is related that the Imām Ja'far[1] having been interrogated on this point of spirituality, and what is the true faith of this garment—its *qibla* and *ghusl*, its ' existence ', ' prayers ', and ' divine obligation ', its ' duty ', as prescribed by the Prophet (*sunnat*) ; its ' soul ', as well as the proper method of putting it on the body, its collar, and interior and exterior, he replied as follows :

" Its point of faith is to regard it as a covering for the faults and weaknesses of others ;

" Its *qibla* is the *pīr* ;

" Its *ghusl* the ablution from sins ;

" Its prayers are manhood (among the Darvishes, I am informed, there are male and female characteristics, from which a man is called ' manly ', and also ' feminine ') ;

" Its ' obligations ' are the forsaking of the sin of cupidity ;

" Its ' duty ', to be easily contented and satisfied with one's lot in life ;

[1] The influence of the Imām Ja'far in Central Asia is still very great, especially in Khotan, and Sir M. A. Stein has described his curious desert shrine at the end of the Niya River in his *Ruins of Desert Cathay*, i. pp. 266 ff. and in *Ancient Khotan*, i. p. 312.

In Khotan is a shrine of Imām Musa Kasim, situate at Kosa, where it probably occupies the site of the Virochana-Sangharama, once famous as one of the earliest sanctuaries of Buddhism in Khotan (Stein, *Sand-buried Ruins of Khotan*, p. 267). Near Somiya also is a shrine of Bowa-Kambar, the groom of 'Alī (*ibid.*, p. 267). This, too, probably lies on the site of an old Buddhist shrine.

"Its 'soul', to give one's word, and keep it sacredly;
"Its 'key', the *takbīr*;
"Its 'putting on, or tying', an inducement to serve others;
"Its 'perfection', uprightness and correctness of conduct;
"Its 'border' is the condition of a Darvish;
"The 'edges of its sleeves', the *tarīqat*, or Order;
"Its 'collar', submission to God's will;
"Its 'exterior', light; and
"Its 'interior', secrecy."

On the collar is written *Yā! 'Azīz, Yā! Latīf, Yā! Hakīm.* On its border, *Yā! Wahīd,*[1] *Yā! Fard, Yā! Samad.* On the edges of its sleeves, *Yā! Qabūl, Yā! Shukur,*[2] *Yā! Karīm, Yā! Murshid.* Also the 'visible' and the 'invisible'. The former alludes to those who are visibly submerged in the goodness and mercy of God, and the latter seclusion.

A real Darvish is he who desires for himself nothing, has no egotism, and is meek and lowly, and willing to accept all things as coming from God. The gains of a Darvish are seclusion and retirement, refraining from the utterance of all profane language, reflection, contentment, patience, silence, and resignation, and to watch and obey the will of Allāh; to keep the commands of the *murshid*; to war with his own wild passions; to change his evil feelings for those which are good, and to be faithful to his Order, according to *Qurān*, xxix. 69: "We lead in our paths all those who are zealous in propagating our faith, and God is with those who do good. We make the lesser war (of this world), and also the greater (upon our own wild passions), and this is true the word of God."

The better conduct is that of the pious, and the worse that of the impious. The Man is he who serves (girds up his loins). To serve the *pīr*, for the science of the Lord, is half of the path of a Darvish, according to the axiom, "The service of kings is one-half of the path". "To gird up the loins" is to serve the *pīr* in such a manner as never to neglect his orders so long as he lives, so that both in this world and in the other he may protect and guard him.

[1] See pp. 130-4, Nos. 9, 31, 47, 68, 36, 43: names of God. *Wahid*= *Wāhid* (67); *Fard*='One'; *Qabūl* would be 'He who accepts'.

[2] *Sic* in original. *Shakr*, 'gratitude', can hardly be meant. *Shakūr*, 'generous': 'He who requites'.

THE PALANK, OR STONE WORN IN THE GIRDLE

This stone signifies contentment and resignation to hunger. A *khirqa* cut short means to have given up the world. To wear the *tannūr*, or the full and wide skirts of the Maulavīs, means to have drawn his head out of the oven of misfortune. (The word *tannūr* means an oven.) [1]

The numerical value of the eternal path (*tarīq abadī*) is ten.

1. To grow old in the science of the *pīr*.

2. To sow seeds of knowledge.

3. To tell the joys of the Darvish heart, of the pleasures of the path which has been pointed out to him.

4. To reap in the field of abstinence.

5. To be well bred, and to follow this rule in a meek and lowly manner.

6. To pronounce the *kalima tauhīd* to the *murīd* until he becomes satiated.

7. To reap with the sickle of humility.

8. To beat out the grain in the barn of Divine acquiescence.

9. To blow away the tares with the mind of alacrity.

10. To measure with the bushel of love.

11. To grind in the mill of godly fear.

12. To knead with the water of reply (this refers to the replies made by the *pīr* to the dreams of his disciples).

13. To bake in the oven of Patience.

14. To burn therein all evil feelings, and come out purified by the fire.

THE PŌST, OR SEAT

The *pōst* (or skin seat of the *pīr*), with its head, feet, right and left side, has its condition, middle, soul, law, truth, etc.

The head signifies submissiveness.

The feet service.

The right—the right hand of fellowship, at initiations.

The left, honour.

The east, secrecy.

The west, religion.

[1] But *tannūra*=petticoat (see p. 197). There is a play on the words *tannūra* and *tannūr* or *tandūr*, 'an oven'.

The condition (obligatory) to bow the head before the *arans*.

The middle is love.

The *mihrāb*[1] is to see the beauty of God.

The soul is the *takbīr*.

The law is to be absorbed in Divine Love and adoration, so that the soul leaves the heart (body), and wanders away among the other spirits with whom it sympathises.

The *tarīqat* is to enter into that which has been established.

The *ma'rifat* is the fear of the *pīr*.

The *haqīqat* is whatever the *pīr* orders to be done, and is the indubitable duty of his disciples.

[1] Miḥrāb, from *ḥarb*, 'war'. The niche indicating the direction of the Qibla is the instrument of war. *Jāwidān*, cited in *Textes Ḥouroūfīs*, Gibb Mem. S., ix. 63.

CHAPTER X

THE ORDER OF THE MAULAVĪS

THE founder of this eminent order of Darvishes is Maulānā Jalāl-ud-Dīn Muhammad al-Balkhī ar-Rūmī.[1] It is commonly called by foreigners, 'The Dancing or Whirling Darvishes', from the peculiar nature of the devotions.

He was, as his name designates, a native of the city of Balkh, and was born in the 6th day of the month of Rabī'-ul-awal, 604 H. In the work aforequoted, called the *Nafahāt-ul-Uns*, by Maulā Jāmī, it is stated that the spiritual powers of this celebrated *Pīr* were developed at the early age of six years, and that those spiritual forms and hidden figures, viz. those angelic beings who inscribe the acts of mankind, and the pious *jinns* and illustrious men who are concealed beneath the domes of honour, became visible to his sight, and drew allegories before his eyes. Maulānā Bahā-ud-Dīn Walad writes, as an example of the circumstance, that once on a Friday, Jalāl-ud-Dīn was at Balkh, on the roof of a house, in company with some other youngsters of his own age, when one of them asked him whether it would not be possible to jump from the place on which they stood to another house-top. Jalāl-ud-Dīn replied that such a movement would be more suitable to dogs and cats, and other similar animals, but woe to the human being who should attempt to assimilate himself to them. "If you feel yourselves competent to do it, let us jump upwards towards heaven!" and then, setting the example, he sprang upwards, and was immediately lost from their sight. The youths all cried out as he disappeared, but in a moment more he returned, greatly altered in complexion and changed in figure and he informed them that whilst he was yet talking with them

[1] See Appendix D at end of this Chapter.

a legion of beings clothed in green mantles seized him from amongst them, and carried him in a circle upwards towards the skies; "they showed me strange things of a celestial character, and on your cries reaching us they lowered me down again to the earth".

It is also narrated that during this year he only partook of food once in three or four days. When he went to Makka he communed with the Shaikh Farīd-ud-Dīn 'Attār, then at Nishabur. This Shaikh gave him an *Asrār-nāma*, or 'Secret Epistle', in the form of a book, which he always carried upon his person.

The *Hazrat-i-Maulavī*, viz. Jalāl-ud-Dīn, stated that he was not of the body which the *'āshiqs* or devout 'lovers' of God beheld; "Perhaps I am that Joy and Delight which the *murīds* experience when they cry out, 'Allāh! Allāh!' therefore seek that delight and taste of that joy; hold to it as to riches, and be thankful that it is me". He once is said to have remarked that a bird which flies upward does not reach the skies, yet it rises far above the roof of the house, and so escapes. So it is with one who becomes a Darvish, and though he does not become a perfect Darvish, still he becomes far superior to common men, and far exalted above ordinary beings. He likewise becomes freed from worldly cares and anxieties, and is exhilarated above all ordinary human sensations.

Each *takia* of every Order of Darvishes has a particular day or days in the week for the performance of the religious exercises of the brethren. As there are several *takias* of the same Order in Constantinople, the brethren of one are thus enabled to visit and take part in the ceremonies of the others. The brethren of other Orders frequently join in the services of the *takias* not their own, nothing forbidding it, except, as with the Maulavīs, the want of practice and skill.

A Qādirī who can perform the services of a Maulavī, on entering a *takia* of the latter, goes to the *hujra*, or cell, of one of the brethren, and receives a cap called a *sikka*, or cap made in a 'mould', from which it takes this name. It is made of camel's hair, or otherwise wool; he also receives a *tannūra*, which is a long skirt like that of a lady's dress, without arms, and a *dasta gul* (literally a bouquet of roses), or a jacket with sleeves made of cloth or other material; around his waist is fastened the *alif-lām-and*, or girdle of cloth some four fingers in width, one and a half *archins* [1] in length, edged with a thread (*chārit* [2]), and a piece of the same at its ends serves to tie it round the body ; over the shoulders is thrown a *khirqa* or cloak (mantle), with long and large sleeves, and thus equipped he enters into the hall of the *takia*, called *samā'-khāna*.

With regard to their services, it may be said—1. that they all perform the usual *Islām namāz* ; 2. that they offer up certain prayers, of the same character ; 3. the Shaikh proceeds to his seat, his book lying in the direction of the *qibla* (that of Makka) ; then standing upright, he raises his hands, and offers a prayer for the *pīr*, asking his intercession with God and the Prophet in behalf of the Order.

4. The Shaikh then leaves his *pōstakī*, or sheepskin seat, and bends his head in humility to the *pīr* (the *Boyun Kasmak* [3] alluded to in the chapter on the Baqtāshīs), towards the side of the *pōstakī*, and then makes one step forward, and turning again towards the same seat on his right foot, bows to the same, as that of the *pīr*, were he in existence. After this he continues round the hall, and the brethren, in turn, do the same, all going round three times. This ceremony is called the *Sultān Walad Daurī*, after the son of *Hazrat-i-Maulānā*, their founder or *pīr*.

5. The Shaikh next takes his position, standing in the *pōstakī*, his hands crossed before him, and one of the brethren in the *mutrib* [4] (upstairs) commences to chant a *na't-i-sharīf*,[5] or holy hymn, in praise of the Prophet. At its termination the little orchestra in the gallery commences performing on the flutes (called *nāis*), the *kamāns* [6] and *qudūrs* [7] (the latter small drums).

[1] Archin, for Turk. *arshūn* or *arshīn*, an ell, about 28 or 29 inches in length.

[2] Chārit, doubtless Turk. sharīṭ, 'a ribbon or strip'. In Arabic *sharīt* means a rope made of palm bark fibre.

[3] Boyun kas-mak, from Turk. *būyūn*, 'neck', and *kas-mak*, 'to lower, abase'. This rite must be the analogue of the Baqtāsh *dar durmak* of p. 195 *supra*.

[4] Muṭrib = 'minstrel' or 'singer', or who or what causes to 'dance and skip'. On p. 257 *infra mutrīb* is translated 'place of excitement', but the dictionaries give no noun of place from *ṭariba*, 'was excited' (cf. Johnson, p. 1202). The word should apparently be *muṭrib-khāna*, 'musicians' room' (Evliya, i. p. 181).

[5] Na't, lit. 'laud' : *na't* = 'encomium'.

[6] Kamān, in Turk. 'a violin'.

[7] Qudūr, pl. of *qidr*, lit. 'a pot or kettle'.

6. One of the brethren, called the *samā'-zan*, goes to the Shaikh, who has proceeded to the edge of his seat, and bows to him, his right foot passing over the other—kisses the hand of the Shaikh, recedes backwards from him, and standing in the middle of the hall, acts as a director of the ceremonies about to commence.

7. The other Darvishes now take off their *khirqas*,—let fall their *tannūrīs*,—go in single file to the Shaikh, kiss his hand, make an obeisance to the *pōstakī*, and commence turning round on the left foot, pushing themselves round with the right. If they happen to approach too near each other, the *samā'-zan* stamps his foot on the floor as a signal. Gradually the arms of the performers are raised upward, and then extended outward, the left hand turned to the floor, and the right open, upward to heaven ; the head inclined over the right shoulder, and the eyes apparently closed. The Shaikh, in the meantime, stands still on his *pōstakī*. The brethren, whilst turning round, continually mutter the inaudible *zikr*, saying *Allāh! Allāh!* and the musicians play for some twenty minutes or half an hour, chanting a hymn called the *'ain-i-sharīf*. Often they perform only some ten minutes, when having reached a certain part of the chant, in which are the words *Hai Yār!* (O Friend !), they cry it out loudly, and suddenly cease. The Darvishes below at the same time stop in their course, so that the *tannūra* wraps around their legs, so as to quite conceal their feet, and all inclining lowly, perform obeisance again to the Shaikh. The *samā'-zan* taking the lead, they all march slowly round the hall, bowing low to the Shaikh, turning completely round as they pass him. If any fall, overcome by the performance, this repose affords them an opportunity to withdraw, which some few do ; soon after this the music recommences, and the same performance is renewed until arrested as before. This is done three times, after which they all sit down, and the *samā'-zan* covers them with their mantles.

8. Whilst thus seated, one of the brethren in the gallery reads or recites a part of the *Qurān* ; the *samā'-zan* rises, and going into the middle of the circle, offers up a prayer for the Sultān, with a long series of titles, mentioning also a good number of his ancestors. At its conclusion the Shaikh rises from the *pōstakī*, and after all have saluted him, retires from the *takia*.

It may be added that the Qādirīs and Khalwatīs have the

same form of worship, without music; that is to say, they all take each other's hands, or put their arms over each other's shoulders, and turn round their hall, performing the audible *zikr*.

Foreigners who are not Mussulmans are admitted into many of the *takias* as spectators, either in a particular part of the gallery, or in a small apartment on a level with the hall. In the latter they are expected to stand upright during the performance, and to leave their overshoes or shoes outside the door in charge of a man stationed there for that purpose, and to whom a trifle is handed on departing. They, however, are admitted only after the conclusion of the *Islām namāz*.

The apartment of the Shaikh is called the *Shaikh hujra*, and the large hall the *samā'-khāna*, or the hall or house where brethren hear celestial sounds, and enter into a state of ecstatic devotion.

The Maulavīs have also another apartment, called the *ism-i-jalīl hujra*, where they perform their ordinary morning and evening *namāz*, or prayers; also the *ism-i-jalīl* (the beautiful name of Allāh), or the *zikr*; and this is not to be found in any other *takia*. The performance before described is always the third daily prayer, called in Turkish the *īkindī*,[1] and commences about ten [? two] o'clock p.m.

A properly constructed Maulavī *takia* should have eighteen chambers, and the vows are also always eighteen. Each occupant of a chamber receives eighteen piastres *per diem*. The *murīd* must serve in the kitchens of the convent 1001 days, and his room is then called the *chillā*[2] *hujrasī*, or 'cell of retirement', wherein the neophyte is supposed to be under probation, and much occupied in prayer and fasting. They have no other officer than the Shaikh, and perhaps his *nāib khalīfa*, or deputy, and one who superintends the expenses of the convent, called the *khazīnahdār*. The office of Shaikh is hereditary, but in Turkey, as with all the other orders, it requires the confirmation of the Shaikh-ul-Islām,[3] or Supreme Head of the Islam religion.

[1] Īkindī, Turk. 'middle of the afternoon'. See too Redhouse, *s.v.*

[2] *Chilla* (or–*ā*) means a fast of 'forty days' duration' (*Kashf*, pp. 51, 324). In Persian *chihil*=40, and in Arabic *jill* is said to have the same meaning, though the usual word is *arbi'ūn*.

[3] The office of Shaikh-ul-Islām was first constituted at Constantinople by Muhammad I., the Conqueror, who bestowed the title on the *muftī* of that city, according to *E.R.E.* 8, p. 906. But Macdonald states that the

I have been unable to learn any creditable reason for their peculiar form of worship. The short biographical sketch of the founder, Maulā Jalāl-ud-Dīn, shows the facility with which, through his extraordinary spiritual powers, he could become invisible to ordinary sight, and his proneness to rise upward. It is a tradition of the Order that, whenever he became greatly absorbed in pious and fervid love for Allāh, he would rise from his seat and turn round, much as is the usage of his followers ; and that on more than one occasion he began to recede upward from the material world, and that it was only by the means of music that he could be prevented from entirely disappearing from amongst his devoted companions. His celebrated poem, called *Masnavī Sharīf*, is that kind of poetry which is composed of distichs corresponding in measure, each consisting of a pair of rhymes, and each distich having distinct poetical terminations. It is written in the Persian language, and though it has been commented upon, it is too mystical to permit of a close translation. It is, in fact, filled with the most mystical reflections—mostly on the subject of Divine love, and breathes in every line the most ecstatic rapture. These raptures are supposed to be holy inspirations, which carry the creature aloft to the Creator, with whom he holds spiritual communion. The soft and gentle music of the *nāi*, or mystical flute of the Maulavīs, is made from a cane or reed, this being the music of nature, and is used also for the purpose of exciting the senses.

Sir William Jones gives the following translation of a few lines of the *Mathnavī Sharīf* of this Order :

> "Hail, Heavenly Love ! true source of endless gains !
> Thy balm restores me, and thy skill sustains.
> O ! more than Galen learned, than Plato wise !
> My guide, my law, my joy supreme, arise !
> Love warms this frigid clay with mystic fire,
> And dancing mountains leap with young desire.

---

dignity was first created by Muhammad II. in A.D. 1453 (*Muslim Theology*, p. 113). On the other hand it seems to have been already known in India in the thirteenth century (Raverty, *Tabaqāt-i-Nāsirī*, Trans., ii. pp. 713, 622, 707), though chronological difficulties arise regarding its devolution. It was also bestowed in India, but not officially, on the Suharwardī saint Bahā-ud-Dīn Zakarīa of Multān on account of his miraculous powers.

Blest is the soul that swims in seas of love,
And longs for life sustained by food above.
With forms imperfect can perfection dwell?
Here pause, my song, and thou, vain world, farewell."

Regarding the tall felt *kula* or cap of the Maulavīs, it is stated that before the world was created as an abode for man, another one existed, known as the *'ālam-i-arwāh*, or spirit-world. A soul is supposed to be a *nūr*, or light, without bodily substance, and consequently invisible to the mirror-like eyes of humanity. During the previous state, the soul of Muhammad is said to have existed, and that the Creator placed it in a vase also of light, of the form of the present cap of the Maulavīs.

The author of the work called the *Shaqqāiq Nu'mānia*, already alluded to, says, in regard to this Order: "The Maulavīs are those who join together as brethren, and by the love of Allāh, worshipping Him in a house of love, to the melodious sound of the flute, which expresses the harmony of His creation, and revolve round like His empyreum, dancing for joy, and uttering the soft sound of affectionate sighs and lamentations, the result of their ardent desire to be united to Him. Revolving round and round the *samā'-khāna* of sinful abandonment and spiritual isolation, they free themselves from all unworthy passions, and are detached from all the subtile minutiæ and associations of religion."

The usual services of the Maulavīs are as follows:

1. The usual *namāz*. Before commencing it they make what is called the *niyat*, or vow, to go through the appropriate prayers.

2. The *Allāhu-akbar*, the *subhān-naka*, the *auzū billāhī*, one *bismillāh*, one *fātiha*, the *zumr-sura*[1] or any other *sura* (verse of the *Qurān*), which may be selected.

The *Allāhu-akbar* is made standing upright at first, and at the close is repeated kneeling, saying three times, *subhān Rabī-ul'*-

[1] Zamee in orig. The 39th chapter of the *Qurān* is called *zumar*, or 'the troops'. But the root *zamara* means 'he played the flute', and it is not unlikely that there is really an allusion to that meaning. In v. 24 the words rendered 'by iteration' may be translatable as 'by rhyming couplets' (Rodwell's *Koran*, p. 257, n. 1, and p. 116, n. 2).

In 'or any other *sura* which may be selected' one suspects an allusion to Sura 73, *muzammil*, 'the enfolded', which begins: "O Thou enfolded in thy mantle" (*ibid.* p. 24).

azīm, etc., "Blessed be Thou, O great Lord God", and adds, *sami'a Allāhu*, etc., "Hear us, O Lord God, whilst we offer up to Thee our praises, for Thou art the greatest of all gods!" and then prostrates himself upon the floor.

After this performance, which composes the *namāz*, they recite the *aurād*. In the morning, before the sun has risen, they perform the *sabāh* [' dawn '] *namāzī*, and as it rises above the horizon, some ten minutes or so after it is up, perform two *rak'ats* (prostrations), called the *ishrāqīa*, or the sun-rising,—another called the *wird ishrāq*. At noon they perform the usual *namāz* of all Mussulmans, generally of ten *rak'āts*, four of which are *sunna*, four *farz*, and two also *sunna* (the former ordered by the Prophet, the second a Divine ordinance, and the third also by the Prophet, with peculiar injunctions). At the *īkindī*, or third prayer of the day, they perform eight *rak'āts*, four of which are *sunna*, those said to have been performed by the Prophet himself, four more *farz*. The evening service is composed of five *rak'ats*, three being *farz* and two *sunna*. After this latter prayer they perform another called the *ism-i-jalīl*, which consists of three *tauhīds*, and as many *ism-i-jalīls* as they who are present please to recite.

Previous to the commencement of their sectarian devotions, the *murīds* are all seated, piously engaged in meditating on their *pir*, which occupation is called the *murāqaba* and the *tawajjuh*, whilst those in the gallery, named the *nāizan* (musicians), chant a holy hymn. This gallery is called the *mutrīb* (place of excitement), and those stationed there are attentive to the directions made by their Shaikh with his hands.

As the whole principle of the Order is the *'ishq Ullāh*, or Love for God, their usual compliment is, for instance after drinking, *'ishq olsūn* (may it be love). None are allowed to beg, but many are seen in the streets bestowing water on the thirsty, *fī sabīl* and *li 'ishq Ullāh* (' in the path ' of God, and ' for the love of God ').

In a small treatise by a learned Shaikh of the Maulavī Order, lately deceased, there is a clear and distinct explanation of the ' spiritual existence ' as believed by them. He explains and draws his proofs from the *Qurān*, that all mankind were created in heaven, or in one of its celestial spheres, long before God created the present one, and perhaps any of the planets; that in this world they continue to exist in varied conditions before assuming that of humanity; and that moreover they will continue hereafter to exist in other forms before they finally return to their original ones in the sphere of blessedness, near to the Creator from whom they emanated. He shows from a verse of the *Qurān*, wherein God says in reference to the Prophet, " Had it not been for you I would not have created the world ", that he pre-existed, and only became human in this world. Adam, he says, was created from

A MAULAVĪ ORCHESTRA

earth—a mineral, and corporeally returned to it, though his spirit proceeded on its course of existence elsewhere. He, as well as all Mussulmans, maintain that Jesus Christ was of a Divine origin, that is to say, that He was the *Rūh Allāh*, or the Spirit of God, though not God in any manner, as this would necessarily imply a plurality of Gods, which Muhammad constantly denied. He declares that the spirit of man has no knowledge in this life of its condition or existence in any previous one, nor can it foresee its future career, though it may often have vague impressions of past occurrences which it cannot define strongly resembling those happening around it.

APPENDIX D

JALĀL-UD-DĪN'S DESCENT AND TEACHING

The spiritual pedigree[1] of Jalāl-ud-Dīn is thus given by el-Eflaki in his *Acts of the Adepts*, pp. 135, 133:

'Alī

||

Imām Ḥasan of Baṣra (*ob.* A.D. 728).

||

Habīb the Persian (*ob.* A.D. 724).

||

Dā'ūd at-Tā'ī (*ob.* A.D. 781).

||

Ma'rūf Karkhi (*ob.* A.D. 815).

||

Sarī Saqatī (*ob.* A.D. 867).

||

Junaid (*ob.* *c.* A.D. 909).

||

Ash-Shiblī (*ob.* A.D. 945).

||

—thus far following the usual sequence of Ṣūfī descent. Then begins a divergence—

Abū-'Amr Muḥammad, son of Ibrāhīm Zajjāj, 'the Glazier', of Nīshāpūr (*ob.* 348 H. = A.D. 959).

||

Abū Bakr, son of 'Abdullāh of Tūs, the Weaver

||

Abū Aḥmad (Muḥammad), son of Muḥammad al-Ghazzālī (*ob.* 504 H. = A.D. 1110).

||

Aḥmad al-Khatībī, great-grandfather of Jalāl-ud-Dīn.

|

Ḥuṣaīn Jalāl-ud-Dīn. — Imām as-Sarakhsī (*ob.* 571 H. = A.D. 1175).

| ||

Muḥammad, Bahā-ud-Dīn, the 'Sultān-ul-'ulmā', known as Bahā-ud-Dīn Walad or Bahā Walad (*ob.* A.D. 1231).

|

MAULĀNĀ JALĀL-UD-DĪN RŪMĪ, surnamed KHUDĀVANDGĀR (b. A.D. 1208, *ob.* 1273–74).

|

'Alā-ud-Dīn. — Bahā-ud-Dīn Sultān Walad. — ḤASAN HUSĀM UL-HAQQĪ WA'D-DIN (b. A.D. 1225, *ob.* 1284).

||

Sultān Walad (b. A.D. 1226, *ob.* 1312)

|

Chelebi Amīr 'Ārif. — Jalāl-ud-Dīn (*ob.* A.D. 1320).

The last named was succeeded by 'Ābid and another, his half-brothers, following the usual Turkish custom of succession, and then it reverted to Amīr 'Ālim 'Shāhzāda', the eldest son of Amīr 'Ārif.

[1] The single rules (|) denotes natural, the double ones (||) spiritual, descent.

It will be observed that the rule of natural descent eventually prevails, after a struggle, over the usage of purely spiritual adoption. Jalāl-ud-Dīn's spiritual teacher was the Shaikh Saiyid Burhān-ud-Dīn, 'the Proof of the Faith', surnamed Sirr-dān al-Muhaqqiq al-Ḥusainī, 'the Knower of secrets, the Prober of truth, of the branch of Ḥusain', son of 'Alī. Burhān-ud-Dīn is said to have been himself a pupil of Bahā Walad, but according to other authorities this Bahā-ud-Dīn was named Muḥammad ibn Ḥusain al-Khatībī al-Bakrī and was a courtier, not a professed saint (*E.R.E.* 7, p. 474). Redhouse, however, points out that the title of al-Khatībī, borne by Aḥmad (as well as by Bahā Walad) implies that its holder was a son, or descendant, or a client, of a public preacher, *khatīb*. Again, Jalāl-ud-Dīn was succeeded by one of his disciples, and it was only on the death of Husām-ud-Dīn that his son,[1] Ṣultān Walad, inherited the headship of the Order. Ṣultān Walad was the author of a mystical poem, the *Rabābnāma* or 'Book of the Rebeck', and the procession or dance described on p. 252 *supra* is doubtless called after him.

Bahā-ud-Dīn also appears to have been eminent. Sultān Alā-ud-Dīn Saljūq invited him to settle at Qonia, and he obtained the title of Sultān ul-'ulmā or 'sovereign of the learned', a title also borne by Jalāl-ud-Dīn (Garnett, *Mysticism and Magic in Turkey*, pp. 154-6, citing Eflāki in Redhouse's translation, p. 10).

Regarding some of the titles mentioned, Maulāna, 'our lord', is that usually given to Jalāl-ud-Dīn, and Hazrat-i-Maulāna may be translated 'His Highness our Lord'. That his son should be styled 'Walad' or 'Son' is natural enough, but it is not easy to see how this title came to be applied to his father. Possibly in his case the correct title is Wālid, 'father', just as Jalāl-ud-Dīn's mother was styled Wālida Ṣultān (*v.* p. 284 *infra*). After his death Bahā Walad received the title of Maulāna Buzurg, 'the greater or elder master' (Redhouse, *op. cit.*, p. 7), but *buzurg* would more literally denote 'ancestor'. Lastly, it may be noted that Husām-ud-Dīn also bore the title of Chelebi.

Eflaki gives several indications that Jalāl-ud-Dīn came under Indian influences. In memory of his murdered friend, Shams-ud-Dīn of Tabrīz, he instituted his peculiar order of *darvishes*, with their special dress, the Indian garb of mourning (Redhouse, p. xii). Jalāl-ud-Dīn was a contemporary of the Slave dynasty of Delhi (1206–90). It was the century of the great Mughal invasions, though the Mughals did not establish their power in India until much later. The poet Sanā'ī, of Ghazni in Afghānistān, was regarded by some as a non-Muslim, but Jalāl-ud-Dīn and his followers revered him, and an oath on his *Ilāhī-nāma* was esteemed more binding than one on the *Qurān* (*ib.* pp. 64-5). But the moving spirit of the new Order seems to have been Shams-ud-Dīn, a native of Tabrīz, the Ṣultān of Mendicants, the Mystery of God on earth, the Perfect in word and deed, the Parinda, or 'winged', because he had wandered in many lands seeking

[1] And *not* by his elder son, 'Alā-ud-Dīn, who had been slain in the riot at Quonia which resulted in Shams-ud-Dīn's arrest and disappearance, during his father's lifetime (Redhouse, *Mesnewi*, p. x). Indeed one suspects from Eflaki's story that 'Alā-ud-Dīn attorned to Shams-ud-Dīn, who was opposed to Bahā Walad. Yet on p. 284 *infra*, 'Alā-ud-Dīn is said to be prayed for by the Maulavīs as his father's vicar (*i.q.* successor or *khalifa* ?} So tradition seems to contradict Eflaki. But Jalāl-ud-Dīn's real relations with Shams-ud-Dīn are obscure.

spiritual teachers (*ib.* pp. 99 and 24). Shams-ud-Dīn forbade Jalāl-ud-Dīn to study the writings of his father, Bahā Walad (*ib.* p. 102). Eflaki's account says that Jalāl never again used his father's writings during the lifetime of Shams-ud-Dīn, but the Indian tradition is that the latter recovered the books, which had belonged to Bahā Walad, from the tank into which he had flung them (Rose, *Glossary of Punjab Tribes and Castes*, i. p. 545). Much uncertainty prevails regarding Shams-ud-Dīn's origin, but he is said to have been put to death in A.D. 1247, a date which accords with Eflaki's relation. On p. 94 *supra* Brown styles him Qalandarī, but he is not claimed as its founder by that 'order' (*v.* p. 299 *infra*). His namesake, a great saint of Multān in the Punjab, is said to be really Shams-ud-Dīn *tap-rez*, the 'heat-pouring', because he brought the sun nearer to that spot than to any other on earth. Jalāl's friend was very possibly an Indian. In any case the story of the nosegay of flowers from Ceylon points to Jalāl's having come into contact with Indian, and probably Buddhist, ideas (Redhouse, *op. cit.* p. 27).

Jalāl-ud-Dīn appears to have regarded himself as especially destined to be a missionary to the Greeks, and to have cited a prayer of Abū Bakr, the first Caliph, in answer to which God made them a chief receptacle of his mercy. The Maulavī dances are also said to be devised to attract their mercurial temperament (Redhouse, *Mesnewi*, 27, § 13).

Eflaki does not describe very clearly the dress adopted by the Maulavīs. He says Shams-ud-Dīn wore black felt and a peculiar cap (*ib.* p. 23), and that Jalāl adopted, as a sign of mourning for his loss, the drab hat and wide cloak since worn by the order (p. 25), but as noted above it wore the Indian garb of mourning. But he also describes its adoption of the turban called the *shakar-āwēz*. In the time of Ṣultān Walad the son of the guardian of the Prophet's tomb, himself a descendant of the Prophet, visited Qonia. He wore a singular head-dress, one end of his turban hanging down in front to below his navel, while the other end was formed into the *shakar-āwēz* of the Maulavī *darvishes*. This fashion they had already adopted in imitation of Jalāl. The term means lit. 'sugar-hanging' (*ib.* pp. 79-80). The one end of the turban seems to be worn as a veil, while the other is folded to represent a mass of liquid sugar, as it would appear when falling from the sugar-mill. The term *Aba-posh*, or 'felt-clad', does not seem to be commonly applied to the Maulavīs, but it was assumed by Bali, of the house of Germian (Gibb, *Hist. of Ott. Poetry*, i. p. 423 and p. 181 *supra*).

M. Hartmann gives the following succession from Sultān Wald. It differs from the above version in calling his son Jalāl-ud-Dīn Ulu. Set forth in tabular form it proceeds thus :

(3) Sultān Wald.

(4) Ulu 'Ārif (b. 660, d. 719 H.). (5) Amīr Shams-ud-Dīn 'Ābid (682–739). (6) Ḥusām-ud-Dīn Amīr Wājid (689–742).

(7) Amīr 'Ālimi Kabīr (692–751). (8) Amīr 'Ādili Kabīr (695–770).

(9) Amīr 'Ālimi Ṣānī ('2nd'), son of (5) (715–798).

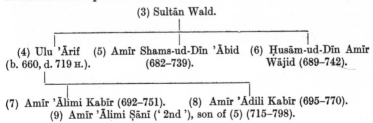

(10) Amīr 'Ārifi Ṣānī (II), son of (8) (745-824).
(11) Amīr 'Ādili Rābī' (*sic*, lit. '4th'), son of (9) (781-865).
*(12) Jamāl-ud-Dīn Ṣānī (II), son of 'Ādili Khāmis (841-915).
(13) Khusrau ibn Qāzī Muḥammad Pasha (886-969).
|
(14) Faraḥ Muḥammad (923-1010).
|
(15) Bōstānī Awwal Muṣṭafā (961-1040).
*(16) Abū Bakri Awwal, son of (14) (965-1053).
(17) Muḥammad 'Ārifi III. (Ṣāliṣ), son of the Wald Chelebī'i II. (Sānī) (1006-1050).
(18) Pir Ḥusain, grandson of (14) (988–1074).
(19) 'Abd-ul-Ḥalīm, grandson of (16) (1035–1090).
(20) Ḥājjī Bōstānī Sānī (11) (1055–1117).
|
(21) Muḥammad Ṣadr-ud-Dīn (1080–1124).
(22) Muḥammad 'Ārifi Rābi' (IV.) ibn 'Abd-ur-Raḥmāni Ṣānī (II) (1090–1159).
|
(23) Ḥājjī Abū Bakr Ṣānī (1133–1199).
(24) Ḥājjī Muḥammad, great-grandson of (18) (1156–1230).
|
(25) Muḥammad Sa'īd Hamdam (1222–1275, having succeeded at the age of 8).
(26) Maḥmūd Ṣadr-ud-Dīn.

The accession of the two marked * is not certain. As Hartmann says, the tendency to form a dynasty is unmistakable. But there is pretty strong internal evidence in the above dynastic list itself that the whole history of the headship has not come down to us. An 'Adil III. has been struck off the roll, for some reason not recorded. With (13) a new element seems to come in. With (17) the old line appears to regain its spiritual throne. But the four *interreges* did not reign undisturbed, for we are told that Farrūkh Chelebi, doubtless the Faraḥ Muḥammad (14) above, was deprived of the mystical throne at Qonia by an usurper (Hammer-Purgstall, *GdOD.* iii. p. 126). We may conjecture that this usurper was the Wald Chelebī'i II., or his father, *v.* (17) above. The title Chelebī'i seems to imply that he was the Wald by physical descent, though he was never actually installed or recognised.

The fact that Abū Bakr I. (16) only held office for ten years and was the only *pōstnishīn* of all the Pīr-i-Sajjādas who was not buried at Qonia indicates that he was deposed or ousted from the possession of the *asitāna*. He lies in the Maulavī-khāna of the New Top Qapūsi, Stambūl, (Hartmann, *op. cit.* iii. p. 193).

APPENDIX E

Girding the Sultan

The origin of the ceremony of girding the Sultān of Turkey at the particularly sacred mosque of Abū 'Aiyūb Ansārī in Constantinople is discussed by Hasluck in *Annual*, B.S.A. xix. pp. 208–12 (cf. *E.I.* i. p. 871). The traditions are not easy to reconcile with the historical facts, but the clue to the puzzle they present may lie in the weakness of the title of the Ottomān Sultāns to the Caliphate. Bāyazīd I. was only recognised by the Caliph Mutawakkil as Sultān of Rūm, just as in 1219 Alā-ud-Dīn I. had been recognised as the Caliph's representative in Rūm. The Sultāns of Turkey never acquired a clear title to the Caliphate, as they were not Arabs of the tribe of the Quraish, though the Abbassid Caliph surrendered the sacred relics of the Prophet to the Sultān. But the head of the Maulavī order appears to have had a claim to the powers of the Caliphate, and this may explain why it is said that if he actually entered Constantinople he would *ipso facto* become Sultān and Caliph. He has accordingly, from time to time, invested the *de facto* Sultān with the temporal power symbolised by the sword. When, however, the Sultān has leaned to the policy of emphasising his claim to the Caliphate he has naturally dispensed with the Maulavī's investiture. It may be doubted whether the Maulavī can be regarded rightly as the nearest approach to a Sunnī Pope next to the Khalif (H. C. Lukach, *City of Dancing Dervishes*, p. 22). The Sunnī Caliph could not tolerate any rival in the religious headship of Islām. The Maulavī Chalabi appears to claim the supreme religious headship, without the title of Khalīfa, since he has not entered Constantinople; and he has never assumed the title of Caliph but only that of Amīr Sultān, just as he assumed that of Khūnkār (Hasluck, *op. cit.* p. 210).

It must, however, be suggested that, like many Oriental rites, the ceremony is commemorative rather than symbolical. Early in the eighteenth century the Mughal emperor Bahādur Shāh " created a new dignity, the ' Juliana ', or the dignity of crowning the Emperor, a privilege which became hereditary in her family " (the family of the lady Juliana Dias da Costa) (the Rev. H. Hosten in *Jour. Punjab Hist. Soc.*, vii. p. 39). This ' dignity ' was instituted to commemorate that lady's services. The ceremony could have had no analogy to the non-Moslem rites of consecrating a king (*v.* " Über die Königsweihe, den Rajasūya ", by A. Weber, in *Abh. der K. Akademie der Wissenschaften*, 1893, pp. 701 ff.). Pirzāda Muhammad Husain states that a crown in the technical sense of the word was never worn by any Muhammadan sovereign, and that " Amīr Tīmūr was the first Mughal king to get himself seated on the throne by the Muhammadan clergy instead of by his near relations, but his descendants did not think the employment of the clergy necessary at all ", so they only attached importance to the reading of the *khutba* (*J.R.H.S.* i. pp. 141 and 148). It is at best doubtful whether the girding of the Sulṭān of Turkey with the sword was designed to transfer to him any spiritual authority, and Hasluck's note on the mystical importance attaching to the girdle in Bektāshī doctrine overlooks the fact that the Sulṭān was not invested with a girdle but with the sword [1] of 'Oṣmān (*Annual*, B.S.A. xix. p. 213). The basic idea was possibly that the girding ratified the Sulṭān's claim to the Caliphate, or rather to its temporal powers, while it may well have originated in a ceremony commemorative of the aid rendered to the House of 'Oṣmān by the militant *darvish.* The whole question of the origin and descent of the title of Khalīfa has now been exhaustively discussed in Sir Thomas Arnold's work, *The Caliphate* (Clarendon Press, 1924).

[1] Writing of the tombs of Aiyūb, Evliya says: "Sh. Jalīl 'Alī b. Khizr, celebrated by the name of Fāzil 'Alī Beg; he was of the family of Edebalī, the famous Shaikh of Sulṭān 'Usman's time; he girded S. Ahmad I. [1603–15] with the sword in the mosque of Sultān Aiyūb, where he lies buried" (*Travels*, i. pt. 2, p. 36). Hasluck seems to have overlooked this reference.

CHAPTER XI

D'OHSSON ON THE RISE AND SPREAD OF DARVISH ORDERS

MR. D'OHSSON, in his celebrated work on the Ottoman Empire, gives the following account of the rise and spread of the Darvish Orders :

" The enthusiasm with which Muhammad was able to inspire his disciples, exalting their imagination by the picture of the voluptuous enjoyments which he promised them in the other world, and by the victories with which he sustained in this his pretended mission, gave rise among all the believers in the *Qurān* to a host of cœnobites whose austerity of life seemed to render them, in the eyes of a credulous people, entire strangers to the earth.

" In the first year of the Hijra forty-five citizens of Makka joined themselves to as many others of Madīna. They took an oath of fidelity to the doctrines of their Prophet, and formed a sect or fraternity, the object of which was to establish among themselves a community of property, and to perform every day certain religious practices, in a spirit of penitence and mortification. To distinguish themselves from other Muhammadans, they took the name of Sūfīs. This name, which later was attributed to the most zealous partizans of Islamism; is the same still in use to indicate any Mussulman who retires from the world to study, to lead a life of pious contemplation, and to follow the most painful exercises of an exaggerated devotion. The national writers do not agree as to the etymology. Whilst some derive it from the Greek word *sophos* (sage), others say it is from the Arabic word *sūf* (coarse camel's wool or hair cloth), or stuff used for clothing by the humble penitents of the earlier days of Mussulmanism ; others from the Arabic word Safā, the name of one of the stations around the Ka'ba of Makka, where many of the neophytes passed whole days and nights in fasting, and prayer, and macerations. To the name of *Sūfī* they added also that of *faqīr* (poor), because their maxim was to renounce the goods of the earth, and to live in an entire abnegation of all worldly enjoyments, following thereby the words of the Prophet, *al-faqr fakhrī*, or ' Poverty is my pride '.

" Following their example, Abū-Bakr and 'Alī established, even during the lifetime of the Prophet, and under his own eyes, congregations over which each presided, with peculiar exercises established by them separately, and a vow taken by each of the voluntary disciples forming them. On his decease, Abū-Bakr made over his office of president to one Salmān Fārsī, and 'Alī to Hasan Basrī, and each of these charges were consecrated under the title *khalīfa*, or successor. The two first successors followed the example of the caliphs, and transmitted it to their successors, and these in turn to others, the most aged and venerable of their fraternity. Some among them, led by the delirium of the imagination, wandered away from the primitive rules of their society, and converted, from time to time, these fraternities into a multitude of monastic orders.

" They were doubtlessly emboldened in this enterprise by that of a recluse who, in the thirty-seventh year of the Hijra (A.D. 657), formed the first order of anchorites of the greatest austerity, named Uwais Karanī, a native of Karn, in Yaman, who one day announced that the archangel Gabriel had appeared to him in a dream, and in the name of the Eternal commanded him to withdraw from the world, and to give himself up to a life of contemplation and penitence. This visionary pretended also to have received from that heavenly visitor the plan of his future conduct, and the rules of his institution. These consisted in a continual abstinence, in retirement from society, in an abandonment of the pleasures of innocent nature, and in the recital of an infinity of prayers day and night. Uwais even added to these practices. He went so far as to draw out his teeth, in honour, it is said, of the Prophet, who had lost two of his own in the celebrated battle of Uhud. He required his disciples to make the same sacrifice. He pretended that all those who would be especially favoured by heaven, and really called to the exercises of his Order, should lose their teeth in a supernatural manner ; that an angel should draw out their teeth whilst in the midst of a deep sleep ; and that on awakening they should find them by their bedside. The experiences of such a vocation was doubtless too severe to attract many proselytes to the Order; it only enjoyed a certain degree of attraction for the eyes of fanatic and credulously ignorant people during the first days of Islamism. Since then it has remained in Yaman, where it originated, and where its partisans were always but few in number."

Notwithstanding its discredit, this singular association contributed greatly to the institution of other Monastic Orders, all of which originated in the two great congregations of Abū-Bakr and 'Alī,—the founders of which were the most ardent and ambitious of their successors. Each gave his name to the Order which he thus instituted,—taking the title of *pīr*, synonymous to that of Shaikh, both words meaning 'Deacon' or 'Elder'. Their disciples bore the name of darvish, a Persian word, the etymology of which signifies the 'sill of the door', and metaphysically indicates the spirit of humility, of retirement, and perseverance, which should form the principal characteristic of these anchorites. Each century gave birth, in all Mussulman states, to some of these societies, nearly the whole of which still exist in the Ottoman empire,—the most distinguished of which are some thirty-two in number. The following is the chronology, with the names of their founders, and the year of their decease:

Shaikh 'Ilwān died at Jedda in 149 H. (A.D. 766); founded the 'Ilwānīs.

Ibrāhīm [b.] Adham died at Damascus in 161 H. (A.D. 777); founded the Adhamīs.

Bāyazīd Bustāmī died at Jabal Bustām, in Syria, in 261 H. (A.D. 874); founded the Bustāmīs.

Sarī Saqatī died at Baghdād in 295 H. (A.D. 907); founded the Saqatīs.

'Abd-ul-Qādīr Gīlānī died at Baghdād in 561 H. (A.D. 1165); founded the Qādirīs. He was the *zāwiadār* or guardian of the tomb of the Imām A'zam Abū-Hanīfa, the Islām jurisconsult, in Baghdād.

Sa'īd Ahmad Rifā'ī died in the woods between Baghdād and Basra in 578 H. (A.D. 1182); founded the Rifā'īs (called by the public the 'Howling Darvishes').

Shahāb-ud-Dīn Suharwardī died at Baghdād in 602 H. (A.D. 1205); he founded the Order of the Suharwardīs.

Najim-ud-Dīn Qubrā died at [in] Khwarazm in 617 H. (A.D. 1220); founded the Qubrāwīs.

'Abd-ul-Husain [Hasan b. 'Abd-ul-Jabbār] Shāzilī died at Makka in 656 H. (A.D. 1258); founded the Shāzilīs.

Jalāl-ud-Dīn ar-Rūmī Maulāna, called the Mullā Khūnkār, died at Qonia in 672 H. (A.D. 1273); founded the Maulavīs, generally called the 'Turning' or 'Dancing Darvishes'.

'Abd-ul-Fatān[1] Ahmad Badawī died at Tanta, in Egypt, in 675 H. (A.D. 1276); founded the Badāwīs.

Pīr Muhammad Naqshbandī died at Qasr-i-'Ārifān, in Persia, in 719 H. (A.D. 1319); founded the Naqshbandīs.[1] He was a contemporary of 'Usmān I., founder of the Ottoman empire. [The correct date of his death is 791 H. (A.D. 1388), but the order may be older.[2]]

Sa'd-ud-Dīn Jabrāwī [Jabanī] died at Jaba, near Damascus, in 736 H. (A.D. 1335); founded the Sa'dīs.

Hājī Baqtāsh Khurāsānī, called the *walī* or 'saint', died at Kir-shahr, in Asia Minor, in 759 H. (A.D. 1357); founded the Baqtāshīs. He lived several years at the court of Orkhān I., and it was he who blessed the Janissaries on the day of their creation.

'Umar Khalwatī died at Qaisarīa in 800 H. (A.D. 1397); founded the Khalwatīs.

Zain-ud-Dīn Abū-Bakr Khāfī died at Kūfa in 838 H. (A.D. 1438); founded the Zainīs.[3]

'Abd-ul-Ghanī Pīr Bābāī died at Adrianople in 870 H. (A.D. 1465); founded the Bābāīs.

[1] Simply Ahmad al-Badāwī in *E.R.E.* 10, p. 724.

Aḥmad al-Badawī (not-āwī) Sīdī was so called because he wore the face-veil like the African Bedouins. In Mecca he was called al-'Aṭṭāh', 'the intrepid horseman', and the same meaning may underlie his title of Abū'l-Fityān (not Abd-ul-Fatān): for those and other titles *v. E.I.* i. p. 192. His followers are called Ahmadīa, but there are at least four branches or sub-orders (*ib.* p. 194). His disciples were called *aṣḥab-ul-saṭḥ* or *suṭūḥīya* from their habit of living on the roof. The term Badāwī (? for Badawī) in Brown's text appears to be still used in combination with Aḥmadīa (*E.R.E.* 10, p. 724). Ahmad's teaching was in many respects remarkable. It inculcated compassion and the requital of good for evil. He wore a mantle (*bisht*) of red wool; and a turban (*imāma*) which was handed on to his *khalīfa* or 'successor' as the insignia of his succession (for its significance *v.* p. 59 *supra*).

[2] Jacob, *Beiträge*, p. 80.

[3] The Zainīs became famous by their twelve saints, called '*ibad*, 'servants.'

Hājī Bairām Anqirawī died at Angora [1] in 876 H. (A.D. 1471); founded the Bairāmīs.

Sa'īd 'Abdullāh Ashraf Rūmī died at Chīn Iznīk in 899 H. (A.D. 1493); founded the Ashrafīs.

Pīr Abū-Bakr Wafāī [2] died at Aleppo in 902 H. (A.D. 1496); founded the Bakrīs.

Sunbul Yūsuf Bolawī died at Constantinople in 936 H. (A.D. 1529); founded the Sunbulīs.[3]

Ibrāhīm Gulshanī died at Cairo in 940 H. (A.D. 1533); founded the Gulshanīs.[4] This order is called the Roshanī, from the name of Dada 'Umr Roshanī, preceptor and consecrator of Ibrahīm Gulshanī.[5]

[1] Angora, called Angira by the Arabs and Enguriya by the Turks. Its most notable building is the mosque of Hājī Bairām, dating from the time of Sultān Sulaimān (probably Sulaimān I., the Magnificent, 1520 to 1566) (*E.I.* i. p. 354). Bairām, according to other authorities, died in 833 H. = A.D. 1429–30 (*ib.* p. 595).

[2] D'Ohsson gives also a later date for the death of Pīr Abū Bakr Wafā'ī, viz. 909 H. = A.D. 1503–4 (*E.I.* i. p. 608). The Bakrīs are apt to be confused with the Baqrīa, the Khalwatī sub-order, founded by Mustafā al-Baqrī, a Syrian Khalwatī who died in A.D. 1709. He was a professor in the Azhar University at Cairo. He, too, is apt to be confused with another Khalwatī named al-Bakrī. Mustafā b. Kamāl-ud-Dīn b. 'Alī ul-Ṣiddīqi ul-Ḥanafī ul-Khalwatī Muḥyī-ud-Dīn who, born in 1688 at Damascus, lived till 1749 A.D. (*E.I.* i. p. 608).

[3] A popular saint, Simbillī (from *zanbil*, a 'basket'), Alī Effendi died about the same time as Sumbul Yūsuf, in the year 932 H. His shrine is at Stambūl near the Zairak Jāmī', and it is visited by the fever-stricken. He was so named because he carried his library on his back in a basket when he went as Qāzī to Baghdād (Schrader, *Konstantinopel*, p. 96).

[4] Evliya observes that there are many thousand ways and religious orders, and that after the Khalwatīs and Naqshbandīs rank the Bairāmī, Wāhidī, Zainī, Maulavī, Roshanī, Gulshanī, Baqtāshī, Ni'amatullāhī, Nūrbakhshī, and 140 other orders of *darvish*. He derives all these from the Naqshbandis, except apparently the Khalwatīs. Then he goes on to say the most famous orders are the Gulshanī, Maulavī, Khalwatī, Jilwatī, Sinānī, and Baqtāshī. According to Evliya the Khalwatīs trace their origin to 'Alī, as the Wāhidī trace theirs to 'Umr, and the Zainī to 'Uthmān (*Travels*, ii. p. 29). For the Wāhidī, see p. 57 *supra*.

[5] Shaikh Ibrahīm Gulshanī, a native of Azarbaijan, was a celebrated mystic of the Khalwatī order. He left Tabrīz for Cairo when Shāh Ismā'īl proclaimed the Shī'a creed the state religion of Persia, and was subsequently invited to Constantinople by Sultān Salīm I. in 1528–29, dying there five years later. He wrote his great mystic poem, the *Ma'anawī*, in answer to the *Masnawī* of Jalāl-ud-Dīn Rūmī (*E.I.* ii. p. 183). The word *gulshanī*

Shams-ud-Dīn Ighith-bāshī[1] died at Magnesia, in Asia Minor, in 951 H. (A.D. 1544); founded the Igith-bāshīs.

---

means 'rose-garden', Roshani 'Illuminated'. The Roshani Umr Dede must have died about 1500, so that he lived till within twenty-five years of the birth of the Afghān Bāyazīd Anṣārī, the Pīr Roshan who thought that *pirs* are supreme manifestations of God (*ib.* i. p. 686).

A sect of this name had some vogue in North-Western India at or about the same period. Of its origin little is known. At Jālandhar in the Panjab an ancient Islamic college is mentioned as existing in the twelfth century, and that town was also a famous school of saints, dating from the end of the thirteenth century. These were of Afghān or kindred stock, and from one of them was descended an Ansārī Shaikh named Bāyazīd, but better known as the Pīr-i-Roshan, or 'the Saint of Light'. Born in 1526, about a year before Bābur overthrew the Afghān dynasty of Dehli, Bāyazīd's parents were forced by the rise of the Mughal power to seek a refuge in Wazīristān. This story suggests that the family was, to some extent, associated with the Afghān supremacy in India, and that Bābur compelled it to flee to the Afghān hills, where, it may be surmised, it would find hereditary adherents. But Bāyazīd, destined to become the leader of a considerable revolt against the Mughal power, was himself a dissenter from his ancestral sect. His father had been a follower, it would seem, of Shaikh Bahā-ud-Dīn Zakarīa, himself a disciple of Shaik Shihāb-ud-Dīn Suhrawardī, but Bāyazīd became an Ismailian of pronounced ultra-Shī'a tendencies. According to Amīr Alī these Roshanīas were the exact counterpart of the Illuminati of Christendom, and Bāyazīd himself had acquired a taint of Manichæism from the Ismailians who were then still to be found in the hills of Khurāsān, but later on his teaching was that all existing objects are but forms of the Deity, that the *pīr* represented Him, and that the ordinances of the law had a mystic meaning. He also taught that perfection being once attained through the *pīr's* instructions and religious exercises, the exterior ordinances of the law cease to be binding (*The Spirit of Islam*, pp. 314-5). Politically Bāyazīd preached communism of all property, including, of course (according to his enemies) that in women, with some form of the metempsychosis. Whatever his real teaching was, he and two generations of his descendants headed a formidable resistance to the Mughal power, inflicting at least one grave defeat upon it, and probably succeeding in preventing the complete subjection of the Afghān hills by the Mughals, a historic fact of cardinal importance, as it was the failure of the Mughal dynasty to hold Afghānistān which contributed largely to its ultimate downfall (*v.* Rose, *Glossary of Punjab Tribes and Castes*, i. pp. 496 and 516, and iii. pp. 335-8).

The Gulshani tenets which had been regarded as errors were brought from Egypt by the poet styled Usuli, who died in A.D. 1538. He also composed poems in the spirit of Nasimi and of the Jawidnama of Fazl-ullah the Persian poet, whereby he was also called the Second Nasimi and Fazl-ullah (Hammer-Purgstall, *GdOD.* ii. p. 221).

[1] Yagit-bāshī, Yakit (pron. *yiyit*)-bāshī = 'chief of the young men', and so a foreman (Redhouse, *Turk.-Eng. Lex.* p. 2206). In the guild organisa-

Shaikh Umm-Sinān[1] died at Constantinople in 959 H. (A.D. 1552); founded the Ummī-Sināns [-Sinānīs].

Pīr Uftāda[2] Muhammad Jalwatī died at Brūsa in 988 H. (A.D. 1580); founded the Jalwatīs.

Husain-ud-Dīn 'Ushhāqī died at Constantinople in 1001 H. (A.D. 1592); founded the 'Ushhāqīs.

Shams-ud-Dīn Siwāsī died in the environs of Madīna in 1010 H. (A.D. 1601); founded the Shamsīs.

'Alim Sinān Ummī died at Elmaly in 1079 H. (A.D. 1668); founded the Sinān-Ummīs.[3]

Muhammad Niāzī Misri died at Lemnos in 1106 H. (A.D. 1694); founded the Niāzīs.

Murād Shāmī died at Constantinople in 1132 H. (A.D. 1719); founded the Murādias.

Nūr-ud-Dīn Jarrāḥī died at Constantinople in 1146 H. (A.D. 1733); founded the Nūr-ud-Dīnīs.

Muhammad Jamāl-ud-Dīn Adirnawī died at Constantinople in 1164 H. (A.D. 1750); founded the Jamālīs.

Three of the Orders—the Bustāmīs, the Naqshbandīs, and the Bektāshīs—descend from the congregation of Abū-Bakr (the first Caliph). The fourth Caliph, 'Alī, gave birth to all the others.

---

tion the order of precedence was: Shaikh, *naqīb, pīr, agha, kiāya, yigitbāshī* and *chāūsh*; or Shaikh, *naqīb, chāūsh,* and *yigitbāshī* (*Evliya*, i. pt. 2, pp. 102 and 128).

The title is reminiscent of the *ephebarch,* which occurs in the list of honours borne by a citizen of Colossai in the course of his career. It was merely a title, not an office, like *princeps juventutis* (W. M. Ramsay, *Cities and Bishoprics of Phrygia,* p. 212, n. 2, citing Th. Reinach, *Rev. Ét. Gr.*, 1893, p. 162).

[1] Sinān, lit. 'a steel spear-head' in Ar. Used in Persian to translate the Egyptian name Joseph, the name is frequently bestowed on a Christian convert who was originally called Joseph, its full form being Sinān-ud-Dīn Yūsuf, though the reason for this association is not clear (*v.* Babinger's note in *Der Islam*, xi. p. 20; and cf. Hammer-Purgstall, *GdOD.* ii. p. 329). Redhouse also gives *sinān* the meaning of 'a whetstone' (*Turk.-Eng. Lex.* p. 1080), and Evliya says *sinān-khāna* (?) = 'a room for religious exercises', among the Maulavīs (*Travels*, i. pt. ii. p. 30).

[2] Uftāda, Pers. lit. 'fallen', may mean 'loving', in which sense it is used in Turkish. It might also mean 'humble', as in Pers. *uftādagī* means 'humility'.

[3] The Sinan Ummis were founded the year after the shrine of Qanbur Dada at Hafsa was destroyed, so it must be supposed that they were at least tolerated by the Khoja of Van (von Hammer, *GdOR.* iii. p. 594).

Their affiliation is seen in the tables drawn up by different Shaikhs. They are called the *silsila-ul-Auliā-Ullāh*, or the 'genealogy of the saints of God'. The most recent and highest esteemed is that of 'Abdī Effendi, the Shaikh of the Jamālīs, who died at Constantinople in A.D. 1783. We have drawn it up in a more methodical order, and present it to our readers as an object of curiosity. Some of the Shaikhs are omitted, who were not founders of Orders, because writers who have noticed their genealogies do not agree as to their real names. This, however, does not change at all the exactitude which reigns in the original, or the series and general organisation found in the list.

In this multitude of Monastic Orders, the Naqshbandīs must be distinguished. The successful establishment of the first of these Orders caused the insensible extinction of the two fraternities out of which they originated. But in the commencement of the eighth century of the Hijra, Pīr Muhammad Naqshbandī made a merit of restoring it. With this view he instituted the Order which bears his name, and which is only a religious association. It is based upon the principles of the two ancient ones, and particularly upon that of the Caliph Abū-Bakr. Like them, this new congregation was composed only of men of the world. Devotion engaged citizens of all the Orders and men of the highest rank then, as it does even now, in all parts of the empire. The first duty of the members of this Order is to recite, daily, particular prayers,[1] called the *khatam Khojagiān*; once, at least, the *istaghfār*; seven times the *salāmat*; seven times the *fātiha* (1st chapter of the *Qurān*); and nine times the [3rd] chapter (of the *Qurān*) called the *alam* [A.L.M.] *nashr'alaika* ['He has sent down to thee'], and the *Ikhlās-i-sharīf* [112th]. To these are added certain practices wholly voluntary, consisting of the recital of the common prayers, or rather, in the meeting together of a certain number of the brethren, once a week. Ordinarily, this is on Thursday, and after the fifth *namāz* of the day, so that it occurs after nightfall. In each city, each suburb, each quarter, the members of this new association, divided into different bodies, assemble at the house of their respective deacon or Shaikh, where, seated on the sofa, they perform this pious exercise with the most perfect gravity. The Shaikh, or any other brother in his stead, chants the prayers which constitute the association, and the assembly

[1] ? Salawāt, pl. of *salāt*, 'prayer'; or *salāt-i-salām*.

respond in chorus 'Hū!' or 'Allāh!' In some cities the Naqshbandīs have especial halls, consecrated wholly to this purpose, and then the Shaikh only is distinguished from the other brethren by a turban, in form like that of the Shaikhs of the mosques.

Each of the other Orders is established on different principles. Each founder gave to his Order a distinctive character, with rules, statutes, and peculiar practices. These characteristics extend even to the garments worn by their followers. Each Order has, in fact, a particular dress, and amongst the greater

A BUSTĀMĪ SHAIKH.

part of them this is chosen so as to mark a difference in that of the Shaikh from that of the ordinary Darvishes. It is perceived principally in the turbans, the shape of the coat, the colours, and the nature of the stuff of which the dresses are made. The Shaikhs wear robes of green or white cloth; and any of those who in winter line them with fur use that kind called *petit gris*, and zibaline [isabelline, 'greyish yellow'] martin. Few Darvishes use cloth for their dress. Black or white felt, called *'abā*, such as is made in some of the cities of Anatolia, are the most usual. Those who wear black felt are the Jalwatīs and the Qādirīs. The latter have adopted it for their boots and the muslin of their turbans. Some, such as the Maulavīs and the Bakirīs, wear tall caps called *kulas*, made also of felt; and others, such as the Rifā'īs, use short caps called *tākkia*,[1] to which is added a coarse cloth. The head-dress of almost all the other Darvishes is called *tāj*, which signifies a crown. There are turbans of different forms, either from the manner in which the muslin is folded, or by the cut of the cloth which covers the top of the head, and is in several gores. Some are of four, as the Adhamīs; some of six, as the Qādirīs and the Sa'dīs; the Gulshanīs have eight; the Bektāshīs twelve; and others even eighteen, such as the Jalwatīs.

Generally, all the Darvishes allow their beards and mustachios to grow. Some of the Orders — the Qādirīs, Rifā'īs, Sa'dīs, Khalwatīs, Gulshanīs, Jalwatīs, and the Nūr-ud-Dīnīas—still wear long hair, in memory of the usage of the Prophet and several of his disciples. Some allow their hair to fall over their shoulders; others tie it up in the form of a Hū, and put it up behind their turban. These cœnobites are distinguished under the name of *sāchlīs*,[2] or the 'long-haired', and they live separate, even in their convents. If private Mussulmans are in the habit of holding rosaries of beads as a pastime, the Darvishes do the same, only in a spirit of religion and piety. These must have thirty-three, sixty-six, or ninety-nine beads, which is the number of the attributes of the Divinity. Some have them always in their hands, others in their girdles; and all are required to recite, several times during the day, the particular prayers of their Order.

Whilst attending upon the fastidious details respecting the particular spirit of each one of these Orders, we will limit ourselves to an exposition of the principal rules and practices on which they are based. The statutes of nearly all require the Darvish to repeat often, during the daytime, the seven first attributes of the Divinity, called by them the *asāmī*[3] [names] *Ilāhī*, consisting of the following words:

1. *Lā ilāha ill' Allāh*! (There is no God but Allah), a confession of His unity.

[1] Tāqī, Pers. 'a high-crowned cap or mitre'; but its derivation from *tāq*, 'arch', would suggest that Brown is right and that this cap is low and arched rather than high. In Turkish *tāqia* means simply a cap or skull-cap of cloth.

[2] Sāchlū; cf. p. 227.

[3] Pl. of *ism*, 'name'.

2. Yā Allāh ! (O God), an exclamation referring to Him, the Almighty.

3. Yā Hū ! (O Him), He who is. An authentic acknowledgment of His eternal existence ; the Jehovah of the Hebrews.

4. Yā Haqq ! (O just God).

5. Yā Hai ! (O living God).

6. Yā Qayyūm ! (O existing God).

7. Yā Qahhār ! (O revenging God).

These words allude to the seven heavens, called the *sab'a-samā*,[1] and the seven Divine lights, called the *anwār Ilāhī*, from which, they say, emanate the seven principal colours, viz. white, black, red, yellow, blue, deep green, and light green.

It is by means of these mysteries that they proceed to the initiation of the Darvishes in the greater Orders. The individual who desires to enter an Order is received in an assembly of the fraternity presided over by the Shaikh, who touches his hand and breathes in his ear three times the words, *Lā ilāha ill' Allāh* (' there is no God but Allāh '), commanding him to repeat them 101, 151, or 301 times each day. This ceremony is called the *talqīn*. The recipient, faithful to the orders of his chief, obligates himself to spend his time in perfect retirement, and to report to the Shaikh the visions or dreams which he may have during the course of his novitiate. These dreams, besides characterising the sanctity of his vocation and his spiritual advancement in the Order, serve likewise as so many supernatural means to direct the Shaikh regarding the periods when he may again breathe in the ear of the neophyte the second words of the initiation, *Yā Allāh !* (O God), and successively all the others to the last, *Yā Qahhār !* (O avengeful God). The full complement of this exercise, which they call *chilla*, requires six, eight, or ten months, sometimes even longer, according to the dispositions, more or less favourable, of the candidate. Arrived at the last grade of his novitiate, he is then supposed to have fully ended his career, called *takmīl sulūk*,[2] and acquired the degree of perfection for his solemn admission into the corps to which he has devoted himself. During all his novitiate the recipient bears the name of *kūchak*, and the Shaikh who directs him in this pretended

[1] Samā, pl. *asmiyat*, 'sky.' The word is not to be confused with 'samā', 'audition.'

[2] Lit. ' completion of the path '

celestial career takes the title of *murshid*, which is equal to 'spiritual guide'.

The founder of the 'Ilwānīs laid out the first rules of this novitiate; they were subsequently perfected by the institution of the Qādirīs, and more so by the Khalwatīs. The Darvishes of these two last societies are distinguished from all others by the decoration of their turban, on the top of which are embroidered the words *Lā ilāha ill' Allāh*.

The tests of the novice among the Maulavīs seem to be still more severe, and the reception of these Darvishes is attended with ceremonies peculiar to their Order. The aspirant is required to labour in the convent or *takia* for 1001 successive days in the lowest grade of the kitchen, on which account he is called the *karra kolak*[1] ('jackal'). If he fails in this service only one day or is absent one night, he is obliged to recommence his novitiate. The chief of the kitchen, or *ashjibāshī*,[2] one of the most notable of the Darvishes, presents him to the Shaikh, who, seated in an angle of the sofa, receives him amid a general assembly of all the Darvishes of the convent. The candidate kisses the hand of the Shaikh, and takes a seat before him on a mat which covers the floor of the hall. The chief of the kitchen places his right hand on the neck and his left on the forehead of the novice, whilst the Shaikh takes off his cap and holds it over his head, reciting the Persian distich, the composition of the founder of the Order:

"It is true greatness and felicity to close the heart to all human passions; the abandonment of the vanities of this world is the happy effect of the victorious strength given by the grace of our holy Prophet."

These verses are followed by the exordium of the *takbīr*, after which the Shaikh covers the head of the new Darvish, who now rises and places himself with the *ashjibāshī* in the middle of the hall, where they assume the most humble posture, their hands crossed upon the breast, the left foot over the right foot, and

[1] Karra Kolak must represent the Turkish words *qarah qulāq*, 'black ear', and so mean jackal. In Persian, however, the *siāh-gosh*, 'black ear', is the lynx or panther.

[2] Ashji-bāshī, the Baqtāsh also have an 'Ashdji' Bābā or abbot in charge of the kitchen (Hasluck in *Annual*, B.S.A., xxi. p. 87; cf. p. 188, n. *supra*).

the head inclined towards the left shoulder. Then the Shaikh addresses these words to the head of the kitchen :

" May the services of the Darvish, thy brother, be agreeable to the throne of the Eternal, and in the eyes of our *pīr* (the founder of the Order) ; may his satisfaction, his felicity, and his glory grow in this nest of the humble, in the cell of the poor ; let us exclaim ' Hū ! ' in honour of our Maulānā."

They answer ' Hū ! ' and the accepted novice, arising from his place, kisses the hand of the Shaikh, who at this moment addresses to him some paternal exhortations on the subject of the duties of his new condition, and closes by ordering all of the Darvishes of the meeting to recognise and embrace their new brother.

Among the Baqtāshīs the novitiate is also required to be 1001 days ; but the practices observed in the reception of the candidates are different.

Each institution imposes on its Darvishes the obligation to recite certain passages at different times of the day in private, as well as in common with others. Several have also practices which are peculiar to themselves, and which consist in dances, or rather religious circular movements. In each convent there is a hall, all of wood, consecrated to these exercises. Nothing is simpler than its construction ; it contains no ornaments of any nature ; the middle of the hall, turned towards Makka, contains a niche which serves as an altar ; in front of it is a small carpet, mostly made of the skin of a sheep, on which the Shaikh of the community reclines ; over the niche the name of the founder of the Order is written. In some halls this inscription is surmounted by two others—one containing the confession of faith, and the other the words ' Bismillāh ', etc. (In the name of God, the Most Clement and Merciful). In others are seen on the wall to the right and the left of the niche tablets on which are written in large letters the name of God (Allāh), that of Muhammad, and those of the four first caliphs. At others are seen the names of Hasan and Husain, grandsons of the Prophet, and some verses of the *Qurān*, or others of a moral character.

The exercises which are followed in these halls are of various kinds, according to the rules of each institution ; but in nearly all they commence by the recital by the Shaikh of the seven mysterious words of which we have spoken. He next chants various passages of the *Qurān*, and at each pause, the Darvishes, placed in a circle round the hall, respond in chorus by the word 'Allāh!' or 'Hū!' In some of the societies they sit on their heels, the elbows close to those of each other, and all making simultaneously light movements of the head and the body. In others the movement consists in balancing themselves slowly, from the right to the left, and from the left to the right, or inclining the body methodically forward and aft. There are other societies in which these motions commence seated, in measured cadences, with a staid countenance, the eyes closed or fixed upon the ground, and are continued on foot. These singular exercises are consecrated under the name of *murāqabah* (exaltation[1] of the Divine glory), and also under that of the *tauhīd* (celebration of the Divine unity), from which comes the name *tauhīd-khānah*, given to the whole of the halls devoted to these religious exercises.

In some of these institutions—such as the Qādirīs, the Rifā'īs, the Khalwatīs, the Bairāmīs, the Gulshanīs, and the 'Ushāqīs—the exercises are made each holding the other by the hand, putting forward always the right foot, and increasing at every step the strength of the movement of the body. This is called the *daur*, which may be translated the 'dance' or 'rotation'. The duration of these dances is arbitrary—each one is free to leave when he pleases. Every one, however, makes it a point to remain as long as possible. The strongest and most robust of the number, and the most enthusiastic, strive to persevere longer than the others; they uncover their heads, take off their turbans, form a second circle within the other, entwine their arms within those of their brethren, lean their shoulders against each other, gradually raise the voice, and without ceasing repeat '*Yā Allāh!*' or '*Yā Hū!*', increasing each time the movement of the body, and not stopping until their entire strength is exhausted.

Those of the Order of the Rifā'īs excel in these exercises. They are, moreover, the only ones who use fire in their devotions. Their practices embrace nearly all those of the other Orders; they are ordinarily divided into five different scenes, which last more than three hours, and which are preceded, accompanied, and followed by certain ceremonies peculiar to this Order. The first commences with praises which all the Darvishes offer to their Shaikhs, seated before the altar. Four of the more ancient come

[1] 'Vigilance'; cf. p. 144, n. 2.

forward the first, and approach their superior, embrace each other as if to give the kiss of peace, and next place themselves two to his right, and two to his left. The remainder of the Darvishes, in a body, press forward in a procession, all having their arms crossed, and their heads inclined. Each one, at first, salutes by a profound bow the tablet on which the name of his founder is inscribed. Afterwards, putting his two hands over his face and his beard, he kneels before the Shaikh, kisses his hand respectfully, and then they all go on with a grave step to take their places on the sheep-skins, which are spread in a half-circle around the

RIFĀ'Ī DARVISHES RECITING THE AURĀD OR PRAYERS TO THE PROPHET

interior of the hall. So soon as a circle is formed, the Darvishes together chant the *takbīr* and the *fātiha*. Immediately afterwards the Shaikh pronounces the words *Lā ilāha ill' Allāh*, and repeats them incessantly; to which the Darvishes repeat 'Allāh!', balancing themselves from side to side, and putting their hands over their faces, on their breasts and their abdomen, and on their knees.

The second scene is opened by the Hamdī[1] Muhammadī, a hymn in honour of the Prophet, chanted by one of the elders placed on the right of the Shaikh. During this chant the Darvishes continue to repeat the word 'Allāh!' moving, however, their bodies forward and aft. A quarter of an hour later they all rise up, approach each other, and press their elbows against each other, balancing from right to left, and afterwards

[1] Ḥamdī, from *ḥamd*, 'praise'.

in a reverse motion—the right foot always firm, and the left in a periodical movement, the reverse of that of the body, all observing great precision of measure and cadence. In the midst of this exercise, they cry out the words '*Yā Allāh !*' followed by that of '*Yā Hū !*' Some of the performers sigh, others sob, some shed tears, others perspire great drops, and all have their eyes closed, their faces pale, and the eyes languishing.

A pause of some minutes is followed by a third scene. It is performed in the middle of an *ilāhī*, chanted by the two elders on the right of the Shaikh. The *ilāhīs*, as has already been said, are spiritual *cantiques*, composed almost exclusively in Persian by Shaikhs deceased in the odour of sancity. The Darvishes then hasten their movements, and, to prevent any relaxation, one of the first among them puts himself in their centre, and excites them by his example. If in the assembly there be any strange Darvishes, which often happens, they give them, through politeness, this place of honour ; and all fill it successively, the one after the other, shaking themselves as aforesaid. The only exception made is in favour of the Maulavīs ; these never perform any other dance than that peculiar to their own Order, which consists in turning round on each heel in succession.

After a new pause commences the fourth scene. Now all the Darvishes take off their turbans, form a circle, bear their arms and shoulders against each other, and thus make the circuit of the hall at a measured pace, striking their feet at intervals against the floor, and all springing up at once. This dance continues during the *ilāhīs* chanted alternately by the two elders to the left of the Shaikh. In the midst of this chant the cries of '*Yā Allāh !*' are increased doubly, as also those of '*Yā Hū !*' with frightful howlings, shrieked by the Darvishes together in the dance. At the moment that they would seem to stop from sheer exhaustion, the Shaikh makes a point of exerting them to new efforts by walking through their midst, making also himself most violent movements. He is next replaced by the two elders, who double the quickness of the step and the agitation of the body ; they even straighten themselves up from time to time, and excite the envy or emulation of the others in their astonishing efforts to continue the dance until their strength is entirely exhausted.

The fourth scene leads to the last, which is the most frightful of all, the wholly prostrated condition of the actors becoming converted into a species of ecstasy which they call *hālat*. It is in the midst of this abandonment of self, or rather of religious delirium, that they make use of red-hot irons. Several cutlasses and other instruments of sharp-pointed iron are suspended in the niches of the hall, and upon a part of the wall to the right of the Shaikh. Near the close of the fourth scene, two Darvishes take down eight or nine of these instruments, heat them red-hot, and present them to the Shaikh. He, after reciting some prayers over them, and invoking the founder of the Order, Ahmad-ur-Rifā'ī, breathes over them, and raising them slightly to the mouth, gives them to the Darvishes, who ask for them with the greatest eagerness. Then it is that these fanatics, transported by frenzy, seize upon these irons, gloat upon them tenderly, lick them, bite them, hold them between their teeth, and end by cooling them in their mouths! Those who are unable to procure any seize upon the cutlasses hanging on the wall with fury, and stick them into their sides, arms, and legs.

Thanks to the fury of their frenzy, and to the amazing boldness which they deem a merit in the eyes of the Divinity, all stoically bear up against the pain which they experience with apparent gaiety. If, however, some of them fall under their sufferings, they throw themselves into the arms of their *confrères*, but without a complaint or the least sign of pain. Some minutes after this the Shaikh walks round the hall, visits each one of the performers in turn, breathes upon their wounds, rubs them with saliva, recites prayers over them, and promises them speedy cures. It is said that twenty-four hours afterwards nothing is to be seen of their wounds.

It is the common opinion among the Rifā'īs that the origin of these bloody practices can be traced back to the founder of the Order. They pretend that one day, during the transport of his frenzy, Ahmad Rifā'ī put his legs in a burning basin of coals, and was immediately cured by the breath and saliva and the prayers of 'Abd-ul-Qādir Gilānī; they believe that their founder received this same prerogative from heaven, and that at his death he transmitted it to all the Shaikhs his successors. It is for this reason that they give to these sharp instruments, and to these red-hot irons, and other objects employed by them in their mysterious frenzy, the name of *gul*, which signifies 'rose', wishing to indicate thereby that the use made of them is as agreeable to the soul of the elect Darvishes as the odour of this flower may be to the voluptuary.

These extraordinary exercises seem to have something prodigious in them, which imposes on common people, but they have not the same effect on the minds of men of good sense and reason. The latter believe less in the sanctity of these pretended thaumaturges than in the virtue of certain secrets which they adroitly use to keep up the illusion and the credulity of the spectators, even among the Darvishes themselves. It is thus, perhaps, that some assemblies of these fanatics have given, in this age of light, and in the heart of the most enlightened nation, the ridiculous spectacle of those pious and barbarous buffooneries known by the name of convulsions. At all times, and amongst every people of the earth, weakness and credulity, enthusiasm and charlatanry, have but too frequently profaned the most holy faith, and objects the most worthy of our veneration.

After the Rifā'īs, the Sa'dīs have also the reputation of performing miracles, pretty much of the same sort as the preceding. One reads in the institutes of this Order, that Sa'd-ud-Dīn Jabāwī, its founder, when cutting wood in the vicinity of Damascus, found three snakes of an enormous length, and that, after having recited some prayers and blown upon them, he caught them alive, and used them as a rope with which to bind his fagot. To this occurrence they ascribe the pretended virtue of the Shaikhs and the Darvishes of this society, to find out snakes, to handle them, to bite them, and even to eat them without any harm to themselves. Their exercises consist, like those of the Rifā'īs and other Orders, at first in seating themselves, and afterwards in rising upright; but in often changing the attitude, and in redoubling their agitation even until they become overcome with fatigue, when they fall upon the floor motionless and without knowledge. Then the Shaikh, aided by his vicars, employs no other means to draw them out of this state of unconsciousness than to rub their arms and legs, and to breathe into their ears the words, *Lā ilāha ill' Allāh.*

The Maulavīs are distinguished by the singularity of their dance, which has nothing in common with that of the other societies. They call it *samā'* in place of *daur*, and the halls consecrated to it are called *samā'-khānas*. Their construction is also different. The apartment represents a kind of pavilion, sufficiently light, and sustained by eight columns of wood. These Darvishes have also prayers and practices peculiar to themselves. Among them the public exercises are not ordinarily made by more than nine, eleven, or thirteen individuals. They commence by forming a circle, seated on sheep-skins spread upon the floor at equal distances from each other ; they remain nearly a half-hour in this position, the arms folded, the eyes closed, the head inclined, and absorbed in profound meditation.

The Shaikh, placed on the edge of his seat on a small carpet, breaks silence by a hymn in honour of the Divinity ; afterwards he invites the assembly to chant with him the first chapter of the *Qurān*. "Let us chant the *fātiha*", he says, "in glorifying the holy name of God, in honour of the blessed religion of the prophets ; but above all, of Muhammad Mustafā, the greatest, the most august, the most magnificent of all the celestial envoys, and in memory of the first four caliphs, of the sainted Fātima, of the chaste Khadīja, of the Imāms Hasan and Husain, of all the martyrs of the memorable day, of the ten evangelical disciples, the virtuous sponsors of our sainted Prophet, of all his zealous and faithful disciples, of all the Imāms, *mujtahids* [1] (sacred interpreters), of all the doctors, of all the holy men and women of Mussulmanism. Let us chant also in honour of [the] 'Hazrat-i-Maulānā', the founder of our Order, of [the] 'Hazrat-i-Sultān-ul-'Ulamā' (his father), of Saiyid Burhān-ud-Dīn [2] (his teacher), of Shaikh Shams-ud-Dīn (his consecrator), of [the] Wālida Sultān

[1] *Mujtahid*, lit. 'strenuous', 'diligent', from the same root as *jihād*, 'holy war'. The most ancient *mujtahid* was the renowned Shī'a lawyer Abū 'Abdullah Muḥammad b. Muḥammad al-Nu'mānī, the Shaikh Mufīd or Ibn Mu'allim, who wrote the *Irshād* and many other legal works. His death in 413 or 416 H. (A.D. 1022 or 1025) was the occasion of rejoicing to the Sunnī jurisprudents (Beale, *Or. Biogr. Dict.*, p. 16). Another leading *mujtahid* of the Imāmīa or Shī'a sect was Abu Ja'fer Muḥammad b. Hasan al-Tūsī, Shaikh, author of the *Kutab Arbā'* or 'Four Books' on the Shī'a traditions. He also wrote a commentary on the *Qurān* in 20 volumes, and other works (but of these two, the *Mabsut* and *al-Muhit*, are also assigned to Abū Bakr Muḥammad al-Sarakhsī). The greater part of his works were publicly burnt in 1056, and he died in A.D. 1067 = 460 H. (*ib.* pp. 21 and 19). For the position of the *mujtahids* in Persia see *E.R.E.* 11, p. 457.

[2] Saiyid Burhān-ud-Dīn had been a pupil of Bahā-ud-Dīn during his residence at Balkh. Thence he went to Tirmīz, and eventually to Qonia. He was styled Sirrdān, or 'knower of secrets' (Garnett, *op. cit.* p. 158, citing Eflaki, in Redhouse, pp. 14-15).

(his mother), of Muhammad 'Alai-ud-Dīn Effendi (his son and vicar),[1] of all the Chalabīs (his successors), of all the Shaikhs, of all the Darvishes, and all the protectors of our Order, to whom the Supreme Being deigns to give peace and mercy. Let us pray for the constant prosperity of our holy society, for the preservation of the very learned and venerable Chalabī Effendi (the general of the Order), our master and lord, for the preservation of the reigning Sultān, the very majestic and clement emperor of the Mussulmān faith, for the prosperity of the Grand Wazīr, and of the Shaikh-ud-Islām, and that of all the Muhammadan militia, of all

A MAULAVĪ DARVISH OF DAMASCUS.

the pilgrims of the holy city of Makka. Let us pray for the repose of the soul of all the institutors, of all the Shaikhs, and of all the Darvishes of all other Orders; for all good people, for all those who have been distinguished by their good works, their foundations, and their acts of beneficence. Let us pray also for all the Mussulmans of one and the other sex of the east and the west, for the maintenance of all prosperity, for preventing all adversity, for the accomplishment of all salutary vows, and for the success of all praiseworthy enterprises; finally, let us ask God to deign to preserve in us the gift of His grace, and the fire of holy love."

After the *fātiha,* which the assembly chant in a body, the Shaikh recites the *fātiha* and the *salawāt,*[2] to which the dance of the Darvishes succeeds. Leaving their places all at once, they

[1] *V.* note on p. 260.

[2] Pl. of *salāt.*

stand in a file to the left of the superior, and, approaching near him with slow steps, the arms folded, and the head bent to the floor, the first of the Darvishes, arrived nearly opposite the Shaikh, salutes, with a profound inclination, the tablet which is on his seat, on which is the name of Hazrat-i-Maulānā, the founder of the Order. Advancing next by two springs forward, to the right side of the superior, he turns toward him, salutes him with reverence, and commences the dance, which consists in turning on the left heel, in advancing slowly, and almost insensibly making the turn of the hall, the eyes closed, and the arms open. He is followed by the second Darvish, he by the third, and so on with all the others, who end by filling up the whole of the hall, each repeating the same exercises separately, and all at a certain distance from each other.

This dance lasts sometimes for a couple of hours; it is only interrupted by two short pauses, during which the Shaikh recites different prayers. Towards the close of the exercises he takes a part in them himself by placing himself in the midst of the Darvishes; then, returning to his seat, he recites some Persian verses expressive of good wishes for the prosperity of the religion, and the state. The general of the Order is again named, also the reigning Sultān, in the following terms:

"The emperor of the Mussulmans, and the most august of monarchs of the house of 'Othman, Sultān, son of a sultān, grandson of a sultān, Sultān . . . . . , son of Sultān . . . . . , Khān", etc.

Here the poem mentions all the princes of blood, the Grand Wazīr, the Muftī, all the Pāshas of the empire, the '*ulamās*, all the Shaikhs, benefactors of the Order, and of all the Mussulman *pīrs*, invoking the benediction of heaven on the success of their arms against the enemies of the empire.

"Finally, let us pray for all the Darvishes present and absent, for all the friends of our holy society, and generally for all the faithful, dead and living, in the east, and in the west."

The ceremony terminates by chanting the *fātiha*, or first chapter of the *Qurān*.

All these different exercises, in each institution, ordinarily take place one or twice in a week. Among the Rifā'īs it is on Thursday, the Maulavīs Tuesday and Friday, others on Monday, etc. All meet at the same hour, viz. immediately after the second *namāz*, or noonday prayer. It is only the Naqshbandīs who meet at night, at the close of the fifth (evening) *namāz* ; and the Bektāshīs, who only perform during the night. These Bektāshīs follow the usage of celebrating their ceremonies, like the Persians, on the anniversary of Karbalā, the 10th of Muharram, a day consecrated among them under the title of *yaum-i-ashūrā* ('tenth day'). At the close of a solemn prayer all the Darvishes of the Order anathematise the race of the Mu'āwiya as having been the implacable enemy of that of 'Alī, the fourth caliph, and the nephew and son-in-law of the Prophet.

It must not, however, be imagined that these dances are everywhere exercised in silence. In some of the Orders they are performed to the sound of soft music. Sa'd Shams-ud-Dīn,[1] the immediate successor of 'Abd-ul-Qādīr Gilānī, founder of the Order of the Qādirī, was the first to give an example of this kind. In 1170 he allowed his Darvishes to use tambourines, only, however, to mark the measure of their steps, and to sustain the vivacity of their movements. This practice, though repressed by Islamism, was, nevertheless, at length adopted by the Rifā'īs, the Maulavīs, the Badāwīs, the Sa'dīs, and the Ashrafīs. The Maulavīs have added the flute, which is open at either end, called by them the *nāi* ; the greater number of the Darvishes of this Order play on it exquisitely ; they are the only ones whose exercises are accompanied by various airs, all of a soft, tender, and pathetic expression. The convent of the general of this Order is distinguished from all others by a band of music composed of six different instruments. Besides the *nāi* and the tambourines, the Darvishes of the house (convent) established at Qonia play on the psalterim, the sister of the bass-viol, and the drum of the Basque.

As in each institution these public exercises are performed at different days, several Darvishes have the habit of visiting and assisting each other reciprocally in their religious dances. They, moreover, hold it as a duty to take part in them, so as to participate, as much as possible, in the merit of the good deed. The Darvishes who are the musicians are almost always attentive to join their *confrères* with their instruments ; and those even which are the most scrupulous about the use of music are good enough to allow them to play during their services. This compliance is

[1] Sa'd, possibly Saiyid, Shams-ud-Dīn, was 4th in descent, not 1st: *v.* p. 102, n. 2.

the more remarkable with reference to the Maulavīs, who never visit any other Order without taking their flutes with them. They are, however, very strict in not allowing the brethren of any other Order to join in their dances ; and the Baqtāshīs are the only ones who hold their services with closed doors, whilst they, on the other hand, are free to assist in those of all the other Orders.

Such is the spirit or general system of these different congregations. If the prayers which are there recited are analogous to the principles of Islamism, and the high idea which the sectarians of the *Qurān* possess of the Supreme Being, the practices which accompany them lead them, nevertheless, away from the maxims of their Prophet, and prove how much the human mind is susceptible of being misled when it gives itself up, without rule and measure, to the illusions of an enthusiastic zeal and the promptings of an exalted imagination. It is probable that these innovations had their origin, among Mussulmans, in the sacred dances of the Egyptians, the Greeks, and the Romans of the lower empire.

But these practices, common to and obligatory on the Darvishes of all the Orders, are not the only ones which their devotion exercises. The more zealous amongst them devote themselves voluntarily to the most austere acts ; some shut themselves up in their cells, so as to give themselves up, for whole hours, to prayer and meditation ; the others pass, very often, a whole night in pronouncing the words Hū and Allāh, or rather the phrase, *Lā ilāha ill' Allāh.* The seven nights reputed as holy, as also those of Thursday and Friday, and of Sunday and Monday, sanctified among them by the conception and the nativity of the Prophet, are especially consecrated to these acts of penitence. So as to drive away sleep from their eyes, some of them stand for whole nights in very uncomfortable positions. They sit with their feet on the ground, the two hands resting upon their knees ; they fasten themselves in this attitude by a band of leather passed over their neck and legs. Others tie their hair with a cord to the ceiling, and call this usage *chilla.*

There are some, also, who devote themselves to an absolute retirement from the world, and to the most rigid abstinence, living only on bread and water for twelve days successively, in honour of the twelve Imāms of the race of 'Alī. This peculiar exercise is called *khalwat.* They pretend that the Shaikh 'Umar

Khalwatī was the first to follow it, and that he often practised it. They add that one day, having left his retirement, he heard a celestial voice saying, " O 'Umar Khalwatī, why dost thou abandon us ? " and that, faithful to this oracle, he felt himself obliged to consecrate the rest of his days to works of penitence, and even to institute an Order under the name of Khalwatīs, a name signifying ' retirement '. For this reason, Darvishes of this Order consider it their duty, more than any others, to live in solitude and abstinence. The more devoted among them observe sometimes a painful fast of forty days consecutively, called by them the *arba'īn* (forty). Amongst them all their object is the expiation of their sins, the sanctification of their lives, and the glorification of Islamism ; the prosperity of the state, and the general salvation of the Muhammadan people. At each occasion they pray Heaven to preserve the nation from all public calamities, such as war, famine, pests, sins, earthquakes, etc. Some of them, especially the Maulavīs, have it also as a maxim to distribute water to the poor, and for this reason are called *saqqās*.[1] With a vessel of water on their backs, they walk about the streets crying out, *fī sabīl-illāh*,[2] which means, " In the path of God ", or rather in the view of pleasing God, and give water to all those who wish it, without asking for any payment. If they, however, receive anything, it is only for the poor, or, at least, to be partaken of with them.

The most ancient and the greatest of the Orders, such as the 'Ilwānīs, the Adhamīs, the Qādirīs, the Rifā'īs, the Naqshbandīs, the Khalwatīs, etc., are considered as the cardinals ; for which reason they call themselves the *usūls*, or ' originals '. They give to the others the names of the *furū'*, or ' branches ', signifying thereby secondary ones, to designate their filiation or emanation from the first. The Order of the Naqshbandīs and Khalwatīs hold, however, the first rank in the temporal line ; the one on account of the conformity of its statutes to the principles of the

[1] The Saqqā in general bears a semi-sacred character, and in Egypt his place is largely taken by the *ḥamālī* or carrier, who is a Rifā'ī or Baiyūmī *darvesh*. The *ḥamālīs* there outnumber the *saqqās* (Lane, *Modern Egyptians*, p. 329).

[2] Fī sabīl Allāh, 'for the love of God, for sacred uses' (Johnson, *Pers.-Arab. Dict.*, p. 681). *Sabīl* has also come to mean colloquially a public drinking-fountain, and in India the place for ablutions in a mosque.

ten first confraternities, and to the lustre which causes the grandees and principal citizens of the empire to incorporate themselves in it ; and the other, because of its being the source of the mother society which gave birth to many others. In the spiritual line, the Order of the Qādirīs, Maulavīs, Baqtāshīs, Rifā'īs, and the Sa'dīs, are the most distinguished, especially the three first, on account of the eminent sanctity of their founders, of the multitude of the miracles attributed to them, and of the superabundance of the merit which is deemed especially attached to them.

Generally, all these societies of anchorites are to be found spread over the different portions of the empire. They have, moreover, everywhere convents called *takias*, *khānaqās*, and

GHĀZĪ HASAN BĀBĀ, AN ABDĀL OR SANTON OF TRIPOLI, BARBARY

zāwias ; they are occupied each by twenty, thirty, or forty Darvishes, subordinate to a Shaikh, and nearly all are endowed by benefactions, and continual legacies left them by charitable persons. Each community only gives, however, to its Darvishes food and lodging. The former consists only of two dishes, rarely ever three. Each one takes his meal in his own cell, though they are nevertheless allowed to unite and dine together. Those who are married have permission to have a private dwelling ; but they are obliged to sleep in the convent once or twice a week, particularly the night preceding their dances or religious exercises. The monastery of the general of the Maulavīs is the only one which allows any deviation from this universal usage. It is not even allowed to the married Darvishes to pass the night there. As to the dress and other necessaries of life, they must provide them for themselves ; and it is for this reason that many among them follow a trade or profession. Those who have a fair handwriting copy books, or the more *recherché* works. If any one among them has no resource whatever, he is sure to find aid from his relations, the generosity of the great, or in the liberality of his Shaikh.

Although all of them are considered as mendicant Orders, no Darvish is allowed to beg, especially in public. The only exception is among the Baqtāshīs, who deem it meritorious to live by alms; and many of these visit not only private houses, but even the streets, public squares, bureaux, and public-houses, for the purpose of recommending themselves to the charity of their brethren. They only express their requests by the words *shayid Ullāh*, a corruption from *shaiyun-l'Illāh*, which means 'Something for the love of God'. Many of these make it a rule to live only by the labour of their hands, in imitation of Hājī Bektāsh their founder; and, like him, they make spoons, ladles, graters, and other utensils of wood or marble. It is these also who fashion the pieces of marble, white or veined, which are used as collars or buckles for the belts of all the Darvishes of their Order, and the *kashgūls*, or shell cups in which they are obliged to ask alms.

The wealthier convents are held to aid the poorer of the same Order. The Maulavīs are the best endowed of all. The monastery of the general possesses considerable lands, given him as *waqfs*, or pious legacies, by the ancient Seljukide Sultāns, and confirmed by the house of 'Usman, or the Ottoman princes when they conquered Karamania.[1] Murād IV. added more liberalities to those of his ancestors. In 1044 H. (A.D. 1634), when marching against Persia, and passing through Qonia,[2] in Asia Minor, he

[1] From Qaramān, once the capital of a Turkish dynasty. Until after A.D. 1386 Karamania was a far more important amirate in Asia Minor than that of the Osmānlīs. The Qaramānlīs were the actual successors of the Saljūqs, and maintained themselves in Qonia. Karamania long maintained power and refused to do homage to the Ottoman sovereigns during the first half of the fifteenth century (H. A. Gibbons, *The Foundation of the Ottoman Empire*, pp. 289-90).

[2] Although Moslem tradition places Plato's tomb at Qonia and associates his name with a river in its neighbourhood, the folk-lore of the Qonia plain preserves little of his philosophy. It has rather converted him into a magician of the type of Michael Scott or an engineer who caused the sea to leave the plain of Qonia and formed the lake of Egerdir (see F. W. Hasluck, "Plato in the Folk-Lore of the Konia Plain," *Journal* of the British School at Athens, xviii. pp. 265 f.). With considerable probability Hasluck traces the Moslem veneration for Plato at Qonia to Maulavī influence (*ib.* xix. p. 192).

bestowed many favours and distinctions upon the general of this Order, and gave to his community, as a perpetual *waqf*, the full amount of the poll-tax of the tributary subjects established in that city. Considerable as the resources of a convent may be, its superiors never allow for themselves any luxury or ostentation. The surplus of the revenues is distributed among the poor, or is employed in the establishment of private and charitable buildings. The Shaikhs and Darvishes are scrupulously attached to this inviolable principle of their Order. Habituated from their youth to all sorts of privations, they are all the more faithful in the observance of its statutes.

Although in no wise bound by any oaths, all being free to change their community, and even to return to the world, and there to adopt any occupation which may please their fancy, it is rarely that any one makes use of this liberty. Each one regards it as a sacred duty to end his days in the dress of his Order. To this spirit of poverty and perseverance, in which they are so exemplary, must be added that of perfect submission to their superior. This latter is elevated by the deep humility which accompanies all their conduct, not only in the interior of the cloisters, but even in private life. One never meets them anywhere but with the head bent and the most respectful countenance. They never salute any one, particularly the Maulavīs and the Baqtāshīs, except by the names '*Yā Hū !*' The words *aib'Allāh* (thanks to God) frequently are used in their conversation ; and the more devout or enthusiastic speak only of dreams, visions, celestial spirits, supernatural objects, etc.

They are seldom exposed to the trouble and vexations of ambition, because the most ancient Darvishes are those who may aspire to the grade of Shaikh, or superior of the convent. The Shaikhs are named by their respective generals, called the *raīs-ul-mashā'ikh* (chief of shaikhs). Those of the Maulavīs have the distinctive title of 'Chalabī Effendi'. All reside in the same cities which contain the ashes of the founders of their Orders, called by the name of *asitānia*, signifying 'the court'. They are subordinate to the Muftī of the capital, who exercises absolute jurisdiction over them. The superior head of the Mussulman religion, called the Shaikh-ul-Islām, has the right of investing all the generals of the various Orders, even those of the Qādirīs, the Maulavīs, and of the Baqtāshīs, although the dignity be hereditary in their family, on account of their all three being sprung from the blood of the same founders of their Orders. The Muftī has likewise the right to confirm the Shaikhs who may be nominated by any of the generals of the Orders.

To arrive at the grade of Shaikh, the rights of seniority must also be sustained by talents, virtues, and an exemplary life. The person must even be reputed as holy, and especially favoured by heaven. In nearly all the Orders the generals never name any one to the office of Shaikh except after having prayed, fasted, and asked light of the Most High. They then consider the choice made as being the effect of a supernatural inspiration, which they owe to the powerful intercession of the Prophet, as the founder of the Order, sometimes even of the venerable Shaikh 'Abd-ul-Qādir Gilānī. These considerations, strengthened by prejudices, are the motives which decide the Muftī (Shaikh-ul-Islām) to respect the choice made by the generals, and never to refuse to invest the persons proposed to him by them.

On these grounds also the generals are at liberty to name Shaikhs without monasteries and functions. These titular officers, who may be called *in partibus*,* go to the city, or the suburb, which, according to the visions of the general, are considered as predestined to possess a convent of such and such an Order, and there wait the period of its being established. Their hopes are never deceived ; a noble emulation leads its more wealthy and pious citizens to join in so meritorious a work. Some erect the building at their own expense ; others provide for its support by the donation of perpetual *waqfs* ; others, uniting their zeal to that of the Shaikh (*in partibus*), do all they can to strengthen the new institution. It is in this manner that formerly the greater part of these institutions were got up, and such even now is the case in various parts of the empire.

In former times the preference was given to those of the Orders which sanctioned neither dances nor music. The others, far from being famed by such acts of benevolence, experienced, on the contrary, much ill-will from many of the citizens. They were even the objects of malice, and were openly accused of following practices forbidden by religion and law ; their exercises were regarded as profane acts, and their halls as so many temples

* Not necessarily *in partibus infidelium*. It would be more correct to say ' called unbeneficed '.

devoted to the maledictions of heaven ; all were scrupulous about entering them ; such was even the effervescence of the public mind that under several reigns, particularly that of Muhammad IV., rigid Mussulmans proposed the abolition of all of these Orders, and the entire destruction of all of their convents and dancing halls. But those who were armed with the principles of religion so as to combat against these institutions, were, in turn, combated with other principles, drawn from the same source. The majority of the nation has always regarded these Shaikhs, the Darvishes, and, above all, their founders, as so many beloved sons of heaven, and in intimate relations with the spiritual powers, these opinions having for basis the belief (still in vogue at the present time) that the different Orders originated in the two congregations of Abū-Bakr and 'Alī (the second and fourth Caliphs) ; the grace which these had received from the Prophet, both as his relatives and vicars, was transmitted, miraculously, down to the series of Shaikhs who from age to age have governed the monastic societies. It is also generally believed that the legion of 356 saints who, according to the Mussulmans, perpetually exist among mankind, and who form, in an invisible manner, that spiritual and celestial Order, sacred in the nation under the august name of the *Ghaus-i-'ālam*, is principally composed of the members of these different fraternities, and so to abandon, condemn, and destroy them, as was the unanimous voice at the period of the crisis alluded to, would be but to call upon them and the whole empire the anathemas of all the holy saints who have lived, and still live, in pious retirement. The less enthusiastic, or the less favourable to the cause of the Darvishes, did not dare to declare themselves against them ; they held this mixture of religious practices and profane exercises to be a mystery which all Mussulmans should adore in silence. The superstitious ideas which the Darvishes themselves have the talent to perpetuate in their nation have always served as their shield ; they have maintained their institutions by drawing upon them the veneration and the generosity of credulous souls.

It is for this reason, according to these opinions, that a host of citizens hasten to join the different Orders. If, in the beginning, they preferred those which have no dancing nor music, for some time past they have incorporated themselves indistinctively with all of them. There are some who, not content with the advantages of belonging to one of them, cause themselves to be admitted into several. Some believe that they can add to the merit of their initiation by joining in the dances of the Darvishes; others go so far as to mix up with them, and take part in their exercises. Those whose zeal is restrained by their occupations, and the regard due to their position in life, are satisfied with the recital, in their own houses, of a portion of the prayers used in the society to which they belong; and so as to purchase, in some manner, this involuntary absence from the convent, they wear two or three times a week, if only for a few minutes at a time, the cap of the order.

The grandees seem to have a preference for the Maulavīs, and those who are of that Order never fail to leave off their turban when alone, and to wear the great *kula* of these Darvishes. This practice goes back as far as the time of Sulaimān Pāsha, son of Usmān I. It has already been seen that this prince addressed himself to the general of the Maulavīs, at Qonia, to ask the blessings of heaven in favour of the expedition which he was about to make against the Greeks of the lower empire; that this prelate covered the head of the prince with one of his caps, reciting prayers, and assuring him that victory would accompany his steps; that Sulaimān Pāsha had this cap covered with embroidery of silver, and ordered turbans of nearly the same form for himself and all the officers of his army; and finally, that this cap, which became the ceremonial turban of all of the grandees of the court, and also of the sultans, who wore theirs embroidered in gold, was abandoned by Muhammad, and given up to the officers of the staff of the Janissaries. The opinion which was entertained of the happy influences of this head-dress is still retained by all the grandees who protect the Maulavīs. They consider it as a duty to associate with them, and to wear now and then this cap, in all its primitive simplicity.

The militia, especially the Janissaries, have a particular devotion for the Order of the Baqtāshīs, on account of the circumstance that, on the day of their creation, under Orkhān I., Hājī Bektāsh, the founder of the Order, spread the border of his cloak over their heads, and showered his blessings on them. This is the cause of the veneration which the Janissaries have for that institution. On this account they are also called Bektāshīs, and the title of the colonel of the 95th *oda*, or 'chamber' of that force, called *jamā'at*,[1] is borne by all of the generals of this order. From this also arose the custom of those troops of lodging and boarding eight Bektāshī Darvishes in the barracks of Constantinople. These have no other duty than to pray, morning and evening, for the prosperity of the empire and the success of its arms. In all the ceremonies of the Janissaries, and above all, during the days of the Dīwān of the Seraglio, they marched on foot before the horse of the Aghā of the corps, all dressed in green cloth, their hands closely crossed over their stomachs. The elder of them cried out incessantly with a loud voice the words, 'Karīm Allāh!' 'God is merciful!' to which the others responded, *Hū!* and this gave rise to the distinctive name of *Hū-kashāns*, or 'Him scatterers', borne by the Janissaries.

As to the rest of the citizens, though their feelings are pretty much the same with regard to all of the Orders, many, nevertheless, appear to make a distinction in favour of the Khalwatīs, the Qādirīs, Rifā'īs, and the Sa'dīs. The greater portion of those who do not care to incorporate themselves in these Orders are still attentive to assist occasionally at their dances. One sees among these simple spectators people of every condition of life, of both sexes. The custom is to take places in the corners of the halls, or in separate tribunes; those to the right are for the men, and those to the left for the women. The first are exposed, whilst the latter are covered with blinds. Christians, who in other respects are not allowed to enter the mosques during the holy service, are admitted, without any difficulty, among these Darvishes,—particularly strangers and people of distinction. One of the elders receives and shows them into the tribunes. As I have frequently assisted at these exercises in several convents of Constantinople, I can vouch for their urbanity.

After these very general opinions as to the sanctity of these religious Orders, one must not be astonished if the greater portion of the people have so much veneration for the Shaikhs of the Darvishes. Whenever they appear they receive the most distinguished tokens of welcome, and though, from principle, they never ask for anything, they nevertheless never scruple to accept the liberal donations of charitable individuals. There are some who reserve their alms for these pious recluses. Others, who hold it as a duty to seek for such as are the most recommendable in the

[1] Jamā'at, *v.* n. on p. 9 *supra*.

Orders, form acquaintances with them, see them often, and supply their wants. Many even lodge and board some in their own houses, in the hope of drawing upon themselves, their families, and fortunes, the blessings of heaven. In time of war this devotion becomes more general and more fervent. One sees Pāshas, Beys, and officers, as well as high functionaries of the Court, engage one or more of these cœnobites to follow them during the campaign. They pass whole days and nights in their tents, wholly occupied in offering up vows for the success of the Mussulman arms.

Moreover, whenever a warlike expedition is to be got up, a host of Shaikhs and Darvishes of nearly all the Orders hasten to follow the army as volunteers. The Government encourages them, as by their presence, their example, and the mortifications to which they subject themselves, they animate the courage of the troops, and maintain a religious enthusiasm among them on the eve of an action : they spend the night in prayers and tears, go among the ranks, exhort the officers and soldiers to perform well their duty, or in calling to their minds the ineffable benefits promised by the Prophet to all Mussulmans who fight for the defence of the faith, or who die in arms. Some cry out, "Yā Ghāzī!—Yā Shāhid!" ("O ye victorious!—ye martyrs!") Others repeat the words, "Yā Allāh!" or 'Yā Hū!" More than once, when they thought the *sanjāq* * *sharīf*, or 'holy standard' (made out of the garments of the Prophet), was in danger, they have been seen to press around this holy object, strengthen the lines of the Emirs and officers stationed as its guard, sustain their efforts, and even themselves perform prodigies of valour.

Independent of these general considerations, which render the whole corps of the Orders so commendable to the nation, the miraculous virtues attributed to the greater part of their Shaikhs inspire especial devotion to them. They claim the power of interpreting dreams, and of healing, by means of spiritual remedies, both mental and bodily diseases. These remedies consist in exorcisings and prayers. Ordinarily, they put their hand on the head of the invalid, make mysterious breathings on his person, touch the suffering parts, and give the individual small rolls of paper, on which hymns have been written of their own composition, or passages taken from the *Qurān*—generally from the

* *Sanjāq*, or *sanjūq*, 'flag'.

two chapters which refer to the work of malevolence, enchantments, witchcraft, etc. They order some to throw them into a cup of water, and to drink the liquid some minutes afterwards ; to others they recommend that they should carry them on their persons, in their pockets, or to hang them around their necks for fifteen, thirty, or sixty days, reciting, now and then, certain prayers.

They believe that these exorcisms may be traced back to the time of the Prophet. Indeed, the historian Ahmad Effendi relates that, in the 10th year of the Hijra, 'Alī, the fourth Caliph, having to march against the province of Yaman, the army of which was superior to his own, expressed some anxiety as to the success of his expedition ; that Muhammad, to reanimate the courage of his son-in-law ('Alī), covered his head with one of his own turbans, and then pressed his hands on his breast, adding these words : "O my God ! purify his tongue, strengthen his heart, and direct his mind". Since then religious traditions have sanctified these words as a fruitful source from which all the exorcising Shaikhs draw the virtue and efficacy of their remedies. It is not only to the sick that they give these cabalistic writings ; they distribute them to persons in good health, as so many preservatives against physical evils and moral afflictions. Those who have recourse to these talismans flatter themselves that they have the virtue of curing the plague (smallpox), and generally all kinds of evils, even the wounds of an enemy. Some retain them on their person all their lives in small trinkets of gold and silver ; others festoon them on their arms, place them on the upper part of their caps, or on their turbans ; others again suspend them around their necks with a cord of gold or silk, and between the shirt and the vest.*

All these rolls are called *yāftas*,[1] *nuskhas*, or *hamā'ils*,[2] and possess virtue, so say the Shaikhs, only when given by their own hands. The superstitious of all classes, men and women, zealously call upon them, and they never fail to bestow upon the former (the Shaikhs) marks of their generosity in the shape of silver,

* Kara Mustafā, whose head is in the Museum of Armour at Vienna, wore a shirt covered with cabalistic Darvish writings, as a preservative.

[1] Yāfta, an illuminated text: the word is Persian, and also means a diploma or privilege of immunity from taxes.

[2] Ḥamā'il, a talisman, and in Turkey the same as the *yāfta* or *nuskha*, according to the *E.I.* ii. p. 243, where a full account of them is given. They often contain magic squares, *wifq*, or figures. *V.* n. on p. 311 *infra.*

stuffs, or provisions of all kinds. Whatever may be the success of these remedies, nothing changes the faith of the meek-minded, because those who administer them require as the chief condition the strongest faith on the part of those who ask for them ; so that, by accusing them of failing in this point, they are always able to screen themselves from the reproaches which the recipients might feel disposed sometimes to utter against their efficacy.

The public attribute to some of the Shaikhs the secret faculty of charming snakes, of discovering their nests in houses, of indicating thieves and pickpockets, of destroying the magical tie (*bāg*) which, it is believed, prevents newly married husbands from consummating their marriage ; finally, of preventing the unhappy effects of every sort of malevolence by drawing with collyrium the letter *alif* (*a*) on the foreheads of women, and especially of children.

If, on the one hand, these reveries, which are prescribed by Islamism, attract at the same time the devotion and money of the superstitious, on the other they only serve to discredit them in the minds of people of reason and good sense. What adds still more to this personal disfavour is the immorality of many of these same Shaikhs and Darvishes. It is observed that they unite together debauchery and the most severe acts of austerity, giving to the public the scandalous example of intemperance, dissoluteness, and the most shameful excesses. The least reserved of all are those travelling Darvishes, called *saiyāhs*, or travellers, about whom something remains to be said.

These recluses adopt the system of wandering over all Mussulman countries in the three portions of the globe, and are divided into three classes. One, principally Baqtāshīs and Rifā'īs, travel for the purpose of making collections, and of recommending their Orders to the liberality of the pious and charitable. The others are individuals expelled from their Order for misconduct, and who, retaining the garb of a Darvish, beg a subsistence from town to town. The third are foreign Darvishes, such as the 'Abdālīs,[1] the 'Ushshāqīs, the Hindīs, etc., for whom the Ottomans entertain but little devotion, on account of their not descending, like the others, from the original congregations during the lifetime of the Prophet.

[1] By Abdālī may be meant Afghan, as the Abdālī or Durrānī tribe claim descent from Khwāja Abū Ahmad, an *abdāl* or saint of the Chishtī order (*E.I.* i. p. 67).

To this latter class belong also the Uwaisīs, the most ancient of all, and the Qalandarīs, whose founder was Qalandar Yūsuf Andalūsī, a native of Andalusia, in Spain. He was for a long time a disciple of Hājī Baqtāsh, but, having been dismissed from his Order on account of his haughty and arrogant character, he made vain efforts to be admitted into the Maulavīs, and ended by establishing on his own authority an Order of Darvishes, with the obligation of perpetually travelling about, and of entertaining an eternal hatred against the Baqtāshīs and the Maulavīs.

The title of Qalandar, which he himself assumed, and after-

A WANDERING DARVISH OF THE QALANDARĪ ORDER

wards gave to his disciples, signifies pure gold, in allusion to the purity of the heart, to the spirituality of the soul, and to the exemption from all worldly contamination which he required of his proselytes. The rules of his Order compelled them to live wholly upon alms, to travel about mostly without shoes, and to practise the severest acts of austerity, so as to merit the favour of Heaven, especially in a state of ecstasy, of light, of perfect sanctity, which makes, he declared, the portion of every cœnobite, renders him truly worthy of his vocation, of the name of a Qalandarī, or that of a Maulavī. It is, therefore, given to all the Darvishes of the other Orders who are distinguished by their brethren for acts of supererogation, for revelations, and for supernatural grace. It is this class of enlightened beings of the various Orders which has produced so many fanatics in every age of Muhammadanism. From it came the assassin of Sultān Bayazīd II., and of many ministers and grandees of the empire. Out of it came, under various reigns, so many false *mahdīs*, who, under this name, have got up the most audacious enterprises, and desolated entire countries by misleading the minds of the public through their impositions, their revelations, and pretended prophecies.

To secure the State and public from similar calamities, the light of the age in which we live should penetrate into this nation where vulgar prejudices have prevailed, as yet, even over the laws, and at the same time triumphed over all the projected reforms made from time to time by wise, enlightened men, though, it must be added, with feeble and tremulous hands. But if fanaticism has its schools, irreligion has also its precipices. If, then, it is in the destiny of the Ottomans to return at some future day to a better order of things, we entertain the hope (and it is only humanity which inspires us) that he who shall undertake this salutary reform will avoid, with prudence, extremes equally disastrous, by combining with his plan the principle of wise moderation. This is the only means whereby, in point of policy, abuses of religion and vices of government among any people may be corrected, and effect a concurrence of legal authority and doctrinal tenets, in favour of the prosperity of the State, the glory of its chiefs, and the happiness of all individuals.

CHAPTER XII. being merely a selection of extracts from E. W. Lane's The Manners and Customs of the Modern Egyptians, *a work first published in* 1836 *and frequently reprinted, is not reproduced here. Notes on the Orders dealt with by Lane and also connected with the present work will be found in their place. A handy edition of* Modern Egyptians *is that in the Everyman's Library to which the references have been made.*

CHAPTER XIII

MUSSULMAN SAINTS

I AM somewhat deviating from the object of the present work, by devoting a chapter, however small, to the subject of Mussulman Saints. These, nevertheless, are so intimately connected with the spiritualism of the Darvishes, that I do not see how it can be properly avoided. The subject has already been alluded to in Chapter III., and I avail myself of the information given in Mr. Lane's *Modern Egyptians* for details which confirm what I there stated.

"The Muslims of Egypt, in common with those of other countries, entertain very curious superstitions respecting the persons whom they call *walīs*. I have often endeavoured to obtain information on the most mysterious of these superstitions, and have generally been answered, 'You are meddling with the matters of the tarīka' (*tarīqat*), or the religious course of the Darwishes; but I have been freely acquainted with general opinions on these subjects, and such are perhaps all that may be required to be stated in a work like the present; I shall, however, also relate what I have been told by learned persons, and by Darwishes, in elucidation of the popular belief (Ch. x. p. 235).

"The Egyptians pay a superstitious reverence not to imaginary beings alone; they extend it to certain individuals of their species, and often to those who are justly the least entitled to such respect. An idiot or a fool is vulgarly regarded by them as a being whose mind is in heaven, while his grosser part mingles among ordinary mortals; consequently he is considered an especial favourite of Heaven. Whatever enormities a reputed saint may commit (and there are many who are constantly infringing precepts of their religion), such acts do not affect his fame for sanctity; for they are considered as the results of the abstraction of his mind from worldly things, his soul, or reasoning faculties, being wholly absorbed in devotion ; so that his passions are left without control. Lunatics who are dangerous to society are kept in confinement ; but those who are harmless are generally regarded saints. Most of the reputed saints of Egypt are either lunatics, or idiots, or impostors. Some of them go about perfectly naked, and are so highly venerated that the women, instead of avoiding them, sometimes suffer these wretches to take any liberty with them in a public street ; and, by the lower orders, are not considered as disgraced by such actions, which, however, are of very rare occurrence. Others are seen clad in a cloak or long coat composed of patches of various coloured cloths, which is called a *dalq*, adorned with numerous strings of beads, wearing a ragged turban, and bearing a staff with shreds of cloth of various colours attached to the top. Some of them eat straw, or a mixture of chopped straw and broken grass, and attract observation by a variety of absurd actions. During my first visit to this country, I often met in the streets of Cairo a deformed man, almost naked, with long matted hair, and riding upon an ass led by another man. On these occasions he always stopped his beast directly before me, so as to intercept my way, reciting the *fātiha* (or opening chapter of the *Qurān*), and then held out his hand for alms. The first time that he thus crossed me, I endeavoured to avoid him ; but a person passing by remonstrated with me, observing that the man before me was a saint, and that I ought to respect him and comply with his demand, lest some mischief should befall me. Men of this class are supported by alms, which they often receive without asking for them. A reputed saint is commonly called *shaikh*, *murābit*, or *walī*. If affected with lunacy or idiotcy, or of weak intellect, he is also, and more properly, termed *majzūb*, or *maslūb*. *Walī* is an appellation correctly given to an eminent and very devout saint, and signifies a favourite of heaven ; but it is so commonly applied to real or pretended idiots, that some wit has given it a new interpretation, as equivalent to *balīd*, which means a ' fool ', or ' simpleton ', remarking that these two terms are equivalent both in sense and in the numerical value of the letters composing them ; for *walī* is written with the letters *wáw*, *lám*, and *ye*, of which the numerical letters are 6, 30, and 10, or together, 46 ; and *balīd* is written with *be*, *lám*, *ye*, and *dál*, which are 2, 30, 10, and 4, or, added together, 46. A simpleton is often called a *walī* (pp. 234-5).

" In the first place, if a person were to express a doubt as to the existence of true *walīs*, he would be branded with infidelity; and the following passage of the *Qurān* would be adduced to condemn him : ' Verily, on the favourites of the God no fear shall come, nor shall they grieve '. This is considered as sufficient to prove that there is a class of persons distinguished above ordinary human beings. The question then suggests itself, ' Who, or of what description, are these persons ? ' and we are answered, ' They are persons wholly devoted to God, and possessed of extraordinary faith ; and according to their degree of faith, endowed with the power of performing miracles ' (p. 235).

" The most holy of the *walīs* is termed the *Qutb* ; or, according to some persons, there are ten who have this title ; and again, according to others, four. The term *qutb* signifies an axis ; and hence is applied to a *walī* who rules over others ; they depending upon him, and being subservient to him. For the same reason it is applied to temporal rulers, or any person of high authority. The opinion that there are four Qutbs, I am told, is a vulgar error, originating from the frequent mention of 'the four Qutbs', by which expression are meant the founders of the four most celebrated Orders of Darwishes (the Rifá'īa, Qádirīa, Ahmadīa, and Baráhima), each of whom is believed to have been the Qutb of his time. I have also generally been told that the opinion of there being two Qutbs is a vulgar error, founded upon two names, ' Qutb al-Haqīqa ' (or the Qutb of truth), and ' Qutb al-Ghaus ' (or the Qutb of invocation for help), which properly belong to but one person. The term ' al-Qutb al-Mutawallī ' is applied, by those who believe in but one Qutb, to the one ruling at the present time ; and by those who believe in two, to the acting Qutb. The Qutb who exercises a superintendence over all other *walīs* (whether or not there be another Qutb—for if there be, he is inferior to the former) has under his authority *walīs* of different ranks, to perform different offices,—*naqībs*, *badīls*, etc., who are known only to each other, and perhaps to the rest of the *walīs*, as holding such offices (p. 236).

" The Qutb, it is said, is often seen, but not known as such ; and the same is said of all who hold authority under him. He always has a humble demeanour and mean dress ; and mildly reproves those whom he finds acting impiously, particularly those who have a false reputation for sanctity. Though he is unknown to the world, his favourite stations are well known ; yet at these places he is seldom visible. It is asserted that he is almost constantly seated at Makka, on the roof of the Kaaba ; and, though never seen there, is always heard at midnight to call twice, 'O thou most merciful of those who show mercy ! ' which cry is then repeated from the mád'nehs of the temple by the *muaddins* : but a respectable pilgrim, whom I have just questioned upon this matter, has confessed to me that he himself has witnessed that this cry is made by a regular minister of the mosque, yet that few pilgrims know this : he believes, however, that the roof of the Kaaba is the chief *markaz* (or station) of the Qutb. Another favourite station of this revered and unknown person is the Gate of Cairo, called Báb Zuwaila, also called Báb Mutawallī. Though he has a number of favourite stations, he does not abide solely at these ; but wanders through the world, among persons of every religion, whose appearance, dress, and language he assumes ; and distributes to mankind, chiefly through the agency of the subordinate Walīs, evils and blessings, the awards of destiny. When a Qutb dies, he is immediately succeeded in his office by another (pp. 236-8).

" Many of the Muslims say that Elijah, or Elias, whom the vulgar confound with al-Khidr, was the Qutb of his time, and that he invests the successive Qutbs ; for they acknowledge that he has never died, asserting him to have drank of the fountain of life. This particular in their superstitious notion respecting the Qutbs, combined with some others which I have before mentioned, is very curious when compared with what we are told in the Bible of Elijah, of his being transported from place to place by the Spirit of God ; of his investing Elisha with his miraculous powers and his offices, and of the subjection of other prophets to him and to his immediate successor."[1] Al-Khidr, according to the more approved opinion of the learned, was not a prophet, but a just man, or saint, the *wazīr* and counsellor of the first Zū'l Qarnain, who was a universal conqueror, but an equally doubtful personage, contemporary with the patriarch Ibrāhīm, or Abraham. Al-Khidr is said to have drunk of the fountain of life, in consequence of which he lives till the day of judgment, and to appear frequently

[1] Pp. 237-8.

to Muslims in perplexity. He is generally clad in green garments, whence, according to some, his name of Khidr.

I may here add that in a work which I possess in MS., entitled *Hadīqat al-Jawāmi'*, or ' An account of the mosques, *takias*, etc., of Constantinople ', it is stated in the description which it gives of the mosque of St. Sophia, that " in the centre of the holy mosque, under the Tōp Qandīl, and between the Muslā gate and the Minber, there is a picture of a door in the wall, marking the Maqām, or ' place ' of Khidr ; and that by the command of Hazrat-i-Khidr, the grandson of the celebrated pious Mussulman Divine Aq Shams-ud-Dīn, named Hamdī Effendī, translated the tale of Yūssuf and Zulaikhā of Mullā Jāmī, in the centre of the mosque." (See 1 Kings xviii. 12, and 2 Kings ii. 9-16.)

Much veneration is shown in the East for the tombs of *walīs*, Shaikhs, and other deceased pious persons. Throughout Constantinople one frequently meets with similar tombs, on which a lamp is kept suspended and lit at nightfall. Others are within *turbas*, or mausoleums, more or less splendid, covered with costly shawls or embroidered silks, and, either on the tombstone or on a framed inscription, the names and titles of the deceased are narrated at length. On the windows are seen pieces of rags, tied there by those who believe they may profit by the spiritual powers and holiness of the deceased. These petty native offerings are called *nazr*, or vows. On this subject Mr. Lane says (pp. 242-7) :

" Over the graves of most of the more celebrated saints are erected large and handsome mosques ; over that of a saint of less note (one who by a life of sanctity or hypocrisy has acquired the reputation of being a *walī* or devout Shaikh) is constructed a small, square, whitewashed building, crowned with a cupola. There is generally directly over the vault in which the corpse is deposited an oblong monument of stone or brick (called *tarkība*), or wood (in which case it is called *tábūt*), and this is usually covered with silk or linen, with some words from the *Qurān* marked upon it, and surrounded by a railing or screen of wood or bronze, called ' maqsūra '.[1] Most of the sanctuaries of saints in Egypt are tombs ; but there are several which only contain some inconsiderable relic of the person to whom they are dedicated, and there are few which are mere cenotaphs. The Egyptians occasionally visit these and other sanctuaries of their saints, either

[1] Lit. ' an enclosed dwelling '.

merely with the view of paying honour to the deceased, and performing meritorious acts for the sake of these venerated persons, which they believe will call down a blessing on themselves, or for the purpose of urging some special petition, such as for the restoration of health, or for the gift of offspring, etc., in the persuasion that the merits of the deceased will insure a favourable reception of the prayers which they offer up in such consecrated places. The generality of the Muslims regard the deceased saints as intercessors with the Deity, and make votive offerings to them. The visitor, on arriving at the tomb, should greet the deceased with the salutation of peace, and should utter the same salutation on entering the burial ground. In the former case the visitor should front the face of the dead, and consequently turn his back to the Kibla. He walks round the *maksūra*, or the monument, from left to right, and recites the *fātiha* inaudibly, or in a very low voice, before its door, or before each of its four sides. Sometimes a longer chapter of the *Qurān* than the first (*fātiha*) is recited afterwards ; and sometimes a *khatma* (or recitation of the whole of the *Qurān*) is performed on such an occasion. These acts of devotion are generally performed for the sake of the saint, though merit is likewise believed to reflect upon the visitor who makes such a recitation. He usually says at the close of this, 'Extol the perfection of thy Lord, the Lord of Might, exempting Him from that which they (the unbelievers) ascribe to Him' (namely, the having a son or a partaker of his Godhead) ; and adds, 'And peace be on the Apostles, and praise be to God, the Lord of all creatures. O God ! I have transferred the merit of what I have recited from the excellent *Qurān* to the person to whom this place is dedicated,' or 'to the soul of this *walī*'. Without such a declaration, or an intention to the same effect, the merit of the recital belongs solely to the person who performs it. After this recital the visitor, if it be his desire, offers up any prayer for temporal or spiritual blessings, generally using some such form as this—'O God ! I conjure Thee by the Prophet, and by him to whom this place is dedicated, to grant me such and such blessings' ; or, 'My burdens be on God and on thee, O thou to whom this place is dedicated'. In doing this, some persons face any side of the *maqsūra* and the Kibla ; but I believe that the same rule should be observed in this case as in the salutation. During the prayer the hands are held (raised upwards and open) as in the private supplications after the ordinary prayers of every day, and afterwards they are drawn down the face. Many of the visitors kiss the threshold of the building, and the walls, windows, *maqsūra*, etc. This, however, they disapprove, asserting it to be an imitation of a custom of the Christians. The rich, and persons of easy circumstances, when they visit the tomb of a saint, distribute money or bread to the poor, and often give money to one or more water-carriers to distribute water to the poor and thirsty for the sake of the saint. On these occasions it is a common custom for the male visitors to take with them sprigs of myrtle : they place some of these on the monument, or on the floor within the *maqsūra*, and take the remainder, which they distribute to their friends. At almost every village in Egypt is the tomb of some favourite or patron saint, which is generally visited on a particular day of the week by many of the inhabitants, chiefly women, some of whom bring thither bread, which they leave there for poor travellers, or any other persons. Some also place small pieces of money on these tombs. These gifts are offerings to the Shaikh, or given for his sake. Another custom common among the peasants is to make votive sacrifices at the tombs of their Shaikhs. For instance, a man makes a vow (*nazr*) that, if he recover from a sickness, or obtain a son, or any other specific object of desire, he will give to a certain Shaikh (deceased) a goat, or a lamb, or a sheep, etc. : if he obtain the object, he sacrifices the animal which he has vowed at the tomb of the Shaikh, and makes a feast with its meat for any persons who may happen to attend. Having given the animal to the saint, he thus gives to the latter the merit of feeding the poor. It is a custom among the Muslims, as it was among the Jews, to rebuild, whitewash, and decorate the tombs of their saints, and occasionally to put a new covering over the *tarkība* or *tábūt* ; and many of them do this from the pharisaic motives which actuated the Jews."

Besides the care taken to keep up, and in good order, the tombs of deceased holy Shaikhs, Darvishes, etc., in the East, these are frequently watched over by a pious-living brother Darvish, who abandons the world and its attractions for this purpose. Himself of undoubted purity of conduct and character, his prayers are solicited by those in need of religious and spiritual consolation and aid—often of a purely worldly nature—such as the procuring of office, the favour of the Sultan, or other person high in office. These guardians of holy tombs may themselves be Shaikhs, and have with them one or more *murīds*, to whom they give 'spiritual' instruction. They are of various *tarīqs* or 'paths', Naqshbandī, Badāwī, Khalwatī, or Qādirī, etc.; and considerable rivalry exists among them, which degenerates into calumny and ridicule.

A humorous story has been told me regarding a Shaikh near one of the larger cities of Asia Minor, who for many years had watched over the tomb of a deceased Darvish saint, attended by a youth, or *murīd*, to whom he was supposed to impart his spiritual knowledge. The Shaikh possessed an extensive reputation for piety, and even spiritual power and influence, and was consequently much frequented by the peasantry, and even the neighbouring gentry—especially the female part of the community. The *turba* over the grave was a conspicuous object, and contained two or three small rooms, in which lodged the Shaikh and his disciple, and served as a dormitory for any wandering Darvish who, on his way to and from places of pilgrimage in various parts of Asia Minor, might claim his hospitality. A lamp hung suspended at the head of the grave, and this was always kept burning at night, and even on certain days—such as, for instance, that of the birth of the deceased—and on Fridays, when visitors were most apt to frequent the Shaikh for the purpose of presenting various gifts, of imploring his prayers and blessings, and of offering prayers over the sainted remains. The windows of the little mausoleum were literally covered with bits of rags tied there by the many persons who made vows or *nazrs* to the saint; and the reverence shown for both the living and the dead saint, brought quite a revenue to the former and his humble *murīd* or disciple. The Shaikh for many years had possessed a comely ass, on which he was wont to make visits to his friends in the vicinity, and a small amount of the veneration bestowed on its master was even vouchsafed to his humble animal. As to the *murīd*, he became well versed in the routine of the affairs of the *turba*, and was supposed to exercise considerable influence with his principal. He wore the cap of the *tarīq*, or Order of the Shaikh, though the rest of his costume was rather the worse for long years of wear; but this by no means affected his reputation—indeed, on the contrary, poverty is so well known an attribute of the 'poor Darvish', and gives so much interest to his career, that it forms the chief capital of the fraternity, and enables them to wander over the world free from all fear of robbery, or of a want of daily subsistence. It formed the ' pride ' of the blessed Prophet, and therefore might readily do as much for a humble Darvish, who, though generally sadly deficient in cash, never had occasion to complain of the want of food, as this flowed into the *turba* in abundance, especially on Fridays, through the benevolence and piety of the visitors. As to the Shaikh himself, he wore the full costume of his Order, and even added the green turban which designates descent from the family of the Prophet, through his only child and daughter Fātima, the wife of 'Alī, the nephew as well as son-in-law of the Prophet, and who finally succeeded him as the fourth of the direct Caliphs of Islamism. This turban constituted him a Saiyid—*amīr* or a *sharīf*—of the family of Muhammad, and tended to add greatly to his claims to popular veneration. Whether he possessed the necessary *sanad*, or *silsila-nāma* (genealogical register), to support his assumed descent from so honoured a source might have been questioned ; but no one cared or perhaps dared to entertain, much less put in doubt, such a matter with regard to the honoured Shaikh who passed his days, and even much of his nights, in prayers over the sainted tomb of the Darvish, whose name and good character were fully described in the epitaph at its head.

The disciple, whose name was 'Alī, had never been much remarked for any superior intelligence : but for piety, and acquaintance with the duties of his position, no fault could possibly be found with him. He had gradually assumed the sedate and calm exterior of a pious Darvish, and always possessed a dignity of demeanour which was quite impressive on the minds of the visitors of the *turba*. It was predicted that some day he would be sure to figure as an eminent Shaikh, and destiny seemed to press him strongly in that direction already. Quite as little was known of his origin and parentage as of those of the Shaikh, his superior ; but these are of little use to a Darvish, who, it is well understood, has no claims to celebrity other than those acquired by his own spiritual powers and personal reputation. The Shaikh was his immediate spiritual director, or *murshid*, and all the knowledge which he possessed was due to the oral instruction received from him. From him he had taken the *bai'at*, or initiation ; he had spent long nights in prayer and meditation, and the visions of the latter had been duly reported to and interpreted by him, much to his own satisfaction and encouragement. The time had therefore fully arrived when, according to the rules of the Order, he must set out on his travels, for the purpose of performing pilgrimages to various holy tombs situated throughout Islam lands, or to extend his wanderings as far even as that of the blessed Prophet and the Ka'ba, or the shrines at Karbalā, where are interred the remains of the grandsons of the Prophet, Hasan and Husain, and others of the victims of the cruel usurpers of the Caliphate, after the death of the fourth Caliph, 'Alī.

One Friday evening, after the visitors had all departed, and the Shaikh and his pupil remained quite alone in the *turba*, the former renewed a topic which had already been slightly touched upon on some previous occasions, viz. of the necessity which existed for the latter setting out upon his travels. This time a decision was come to, and it was mutually agreed upon that on the following Sunday the young neophyte should take his departure. " I have instructed you with much care, my son," said the Shaikh, " and taught you all that it is necessary for you to know, and your further continuance here is not only of no use to you, but even detrimental to your career. As you well know, I possess but little of the world's goods, but of what I have you shall receive a bountiful share. You have now grown up to manhood, and will be able to make your way in the world, and by your pious appeals to the benevolent and the wealthy, not fail to receive all the assistance of which you may stand in need. On the morning aforenamed I will be prepared to equip you for your long and tedious journey, and to bestow upon you my blessing." So much goodness deeply impressed the heart and mind of young 'Alī, and so overcame him, that, in place of any answer, he devoutly pressed his Shaikh's hand to his lips, and retired to meditate upon his future prospects, and cultivate whatever spiritual visions might be sent him by the *pīr* of the Order, or even by the blessed Prophet himself.

Early on Sunday morning 'Alī arose, and awaited the conclusion of the Shaikh's slumbers. The latter was not long behind him, and after the usual salutations and morning prayers, he gave his pupil some excellent advice, and then quite overcame him by the declaration that he had decided to offer him an evidence of the great friendship which he had always entertained for him, by the gift of his own long-treasured companion the ass, on which he had rode for so many years, with its pack-saddle, one of his own *khirqas*, or mantles, and a wallet of provisions sufficient for some days' use. Besides these, he presented him with a *keshgūl*, or alms-cup, a *mu'īn*,[1] or arm-rest, made of iron, in which was concealed a goodly dagger with which to defend himself against wild animals or in any other danger—for it was not to be supposed that it could possibly ever be used as a means of offence in the hands of a pious Darvish like himself, travelling over the world only for the most peaceful and honest motives—and a tiger's skin to throw over his shoulders, as some protection against the heat of the sun and the colds of winter. But the most precious of all his gifts was a *nuskha* or *hamā'il* [2] (amulet), which the Shaikh had long worn suspended to his own neck in a small metal cylinder, which seemed to be of some precious metal, much resembling silver, greatly admired and revered by the visitors of the *turba*, in which so many of his days had been spent. As to the ass, it had peculiar claims to his consideration on account of its age and truly venerable appearance. They had long served together, and often suffered, especially during the winter season, from the same cause, viz. a want of food ; and even now its lean condition seemed to indicate that pasture was scarce, and a more nourishing diet decidedly on the decline. Whether this was the case, or rather that its teeth were imperfect, cannot be now stated with any degree of accuracy ; but there was one thing quite apparent to 'Alī, and which he now remembered with reflections to which the coming future gave rise, that he and the ass were nearly about the same age, and therefore could readily sympathise with each other in whatever lot their lives might hereafter be cast during their united pilgrimage.

The ass was soon got ready for the journey, and its load now consisted only of the wallet, the *keshgūl*, and the mantle, for 'Alī decided to start on his wanderings on foot, like any ordinary Darvish, and so not accustom himself, at the outset, to the luxury

[1] Mu'īn, a helper, especially God. This may be compared to the Indian arm-rest, which takes two forms, the crutch or *bairāgan* and the T-shaped rest.

[2] *Hamīla* (*hamileh* in orig.) and *ḥamāla* both have the plural *hamā'il*, which is used as a singular. Both denote a baldrick, a sword-knot, and the root simply means a carrier, anything to hold something to be carried, *e.g.* a *Qurān*. *Pace* the *Oxford Dict.*, p. 295, it is tempting to see in the word the origin of our ' amulet '.

of a conveyance. The Shaikh took a deep interest in all his preparations, and when these had been got ready for the departure, he accompanied his pupil some half a mile or so from the *turba*, and then, coming to a standstill, took his hand in his own and devoutly blessed him, reciting the *fātiha*, or first chapter of the *Qurān*, with a tone of peculiar benevolence. Then, bidding him farewell, he slowly returned to the *turba*, and 'Alī bent his way, not to the town, but across the neighbouring valley, and towards the distant mountain range which bordered the horizon.

For some days 'Alī journeyed onwards over the public route, without much regard to its possible termination, and with a very vague idea of the direction which he was taking. His provisions were becoming low, and his companion's strength was failing from the want of a better nourishment than that offered by the way-side. His nights had been spent in true Darvish style, under the cover of a hospitable tree, or beside a bountiful spring of water, and few had been the alms which he, thus far, had received from passers-by. Hunger, however, had not as yet rendered it necessary for him to appeal to the benevolent for assistance ; and as he was naturally of a timid disposition, he rather had avoided than sought companionship on his way. Indeed, it is so usual to meet with wandering Darvishes in the great routes of Asia Minor, that his appearance attracted no particular notice. But one day, towards nightfall, 'Alī was much fatigued by the exertions which he had been compelled to make to induce his companion to proceed : and, indeed, the ass had several times actually lain down by the way-side from sheer exhaustion. The day had been extremely warm, and little shelter or pasture had been found for their relief. Finally, age and its infirmities overcame the animal, and falling down, it seemed to fail rapidly. A few minutes of heavy breathing, then a quivering of all its limbs, a gurgling in its throat, and a reversion of its eyeballs, and all was over. 'Alī was left alone in the world by the side of a dead ass, with no one to sympathise with him in his loss, or from whom to seek consolation in his grief. Overcome by his feelings, he folded his arms across his breast, and gave vent to his sorrow in a copious flood of tears. The vast plain in the midst of which he stood now appeared to him peculiarly desolate, and his thoughts reverted to the distant *turba* in which so many years of his life had glided away, free from care or anxiety. To this he could, however, no more return, and the dead ass served as the last link which connected him with his deserted home and venerated instructor, its pious Shaikh. It might be said that this was the first time he had ever experienced real grief, and his lonely condition added to its poignancy.

Whilst the young Darvish was thus situated, he beheld on the distant horizon a small cloud of dust rise, which indicated the approach of visitors, and gave to him the reflection that, lest he should be held responsible for the decease of his late companion, he would do well to drag him away from the public road ; and, as well as he was able, under the circumstances, to conceal his remains beneath its sandy soil. It did not take him long to put this plan into effect, and so, in a short space of time, he had succeeded in digging a hole sufficiently deep to contain the thin body of the deceased animal. When this was done he sat down by the side of the newly made grave, and indulged in a fresh flow of tears.

In the meantime, the small cloud of dust which 'Alī had seen in the distance, and which had excited his apprehensions, gradually increased, and speedily approached him. Seated by the grave of his late companion, the ass, his mind became filled with reflections of a desolate and alarming nature ; friendless and alone in the wide and desert world that surrounded him, he watched the arrival of the coming interruption to his grief with no ordinary interest. Although not very near to the road, he was not so distant as to be able to hope to escape the notice of those who were approaching, and a vague feeling of danger greatly agitated him. He began to regret that he had buried the ass from view, and half determined to disinter it, so that there could be no misapprehension as to the truth that the deceased was only an ass, dead from sheer age and exhaustion, and not a human being, whose death might be attributed to violence. In case of suspicion, thought he, they can readily remove the thin cover of earth which conceals its remains, and so verify the fact of my assertion of innocence. With this reflection he had almost recovered his composure, and modified somewhat his grief, when, the dust rising higher and higher in the air, he could distinctly perceive emerge from it quite a numerous cavalcade of Mussulman travellers, none of whom, as yet, seemed conscious of his existence. In advance of the group was one who seemed to be the most prominent of the company ; either from the unpleasantness of the heat and atmosphere, or from fatigue, the party hastily rode on in silence, and he hoped that it would pass him by unnoticed. From, however, an intuitive impulsion of respect, common to all the people of the East in the presence of even possible superiors, as it neared him he rose to his feet, and so, perhaps, attracted the attention of the whole company. Surprised by so sudden an apparition, their faces were all immediately directed towards 'Alī, some nods were exchanged amongst them, and the leader of the group, having suddenly come to a halt, he turned to one of his attendants and directed him to ride up and see who the lonely individual was.

Now the party in question was that of a wealthy Bey of the neighbourhood, returning from a distant visit to the governor of the province, attended by a numerous retinue of his own servants, and by several of the principal inhabitants of the little town in which he resided, not many miles off, among the hills, which, in a clearer atmosphere, were visible from the spot on which 'Alī stood. Though somewhat fatigued by the ride over the dusty plain, and overcome by the heat of the day, now almost spent, the Bey was not insensible to the wants of others, and thought that the individual in question might be some wayfaring traveller in need of assistance. Mussulman hospitality and generosity is never more prominent than on those occasions when it is asked for by silent respect ; and to have passed 'Alī by unnoticed would have been a strange deviation from this noble characteristic of the Eastern gentleman. The attendant had only to approach 'Alī to discover, from his Darvish cap, his tiger skin, and the *kashgūl* suspended at his side, that he belonged to one of the fraternities of the Islam Orders. So, turning back to the Bey, he informed him that the stranger was a poor Darvish. On hearing this, the whole company followed its leader to the spot where 'Alī stood, trembling with apprehension, and his countenance still showing the grief which he had so recently felt for the loss he had sustained.

After the exchange of the usual Mussulman salutation, the Bey was struck by the circumstance that the poor fellow was standing beside a newly made grave, undoubtedly that of a recently deceased brother Darvish ; and he was struck with the strange fate or providence that had led them to so desolate a spot, the one to die there, and the other to inter his remains, where neither water could be procured for the requisite ablutions of the dead prescribed by Islam holy law, nor an Imām to assist at so touching a ceremony. He made inquiry of 'Alī as to the time of the decease, and learned that it had even occurred during the present day; and to the question as to how long they had been companions, 'Alī, with much emotion, added that, from his earliest youth, they had almost been inseparable. Deeply touched by so tender an attachment and devotedness between two brothers, the Bey deemed it unnecessary to make any more inquiry as to the history of the deceased. After a few words exchanged between him and one or two of the better-dressed companions of his journey, turning towards 'Alī, he stated to him that he regarded the whole circumstance as one of a particularly providential character, intended as a blessing to the whole neighbouring country, which had never possessed, he added, any of the advantages always derived from the protection and spiritual influence of the grave of a holy man; and that one such was greatly needed by the community. We beg you, therefore, he continued, to consent to remain amongst us; and if you do so, we will, without any loss of time, have a goodly *turba* constructed over the sainted remains of your deceased brother, which shall remain under your own especial care. Too much affected by the recent occurrence of the day to enter into any explanations of the real facts of the case, or perhaps fearful that an exposition of the truth might be so mortifying to the Bey as to result in an immediate and severe exhibition of arbitrary power upon his own person, for having conferred the honours of burial upon an ass, which are only due to a human being, 'Alī was unable to utter a word of remark. Perhaps, also, he was not dissatisfied with the favourable turn which had thus, unexpectedly, occurred to his fortunes, and found that silence neither committed him to a falsehood, nor betrayed imprudent truth. He, therefore, said nothing, and only by his countenance and a low salutation, consented to sacrifice any private desire he might entertain for the prolongation of his travels, and pilgrimages to holy tombs, for the spiritual benefit to the pious Mussulmans of the surrounding country. "Remain here, and watch over the remains of your deceased brother," said the Bey, "and we will have the *turba* commenced without delay. I will even, to-night, have some provisions and drink sent you from my own family, and you shall, henceforth, be in want of nothing necessary for your comfort."

With these parting words, the Bey turned his horse again towards his route, followed by all of his company, and gradually receded from sight. In the course of an hour or two he reached his home, and the news of the decease of a pious Darvish on the plain, and of the intention of the Bey to erect a *turba* over his hallowed remains, soon became known over the little town or village in which he and his companions resided.

As to 'Alī, he made a frugal meal from the now almost empty wallet bestowed upon him by his venerated Shaikh ; and as the sun was descending behind the hills of the distant horizon, devoutly spread his tiger skin (the hair of which, from long use, was quite worn off) upon the earth, beside the grave of his lamented companion, and performed the *namāz* appropriate to the fourth period of the day prescribed by the Islam Prophet. Having no water with which to perform the requisite *ghūsl*, or ablutions, he, according to usage, made use of sand for that purpose, and so acquitted himself of his religious duties. These he had been instructed never to omit, and to perform them as strictly in a crowd as in a desert place—in the *turba*, or by the way-side—and thus leave no room to doubt his piety and strict observance of all the injunctions of the 'Path', or Order to which he belonged, and to religion in general. Then placing his *kashgūl* under his head, and his *mu'īn* by his side, as a means of defence in case he should be attacked by any wild animal during the night, his skin serving him for a bed, and his mantle for a cover, he sought relief and calmness in sleep from the sorrows and anxieties of the past day. Some time before midnight he was roused by the sound of a human voice and the noise of an animal's feet, and, jumping up, he was addressed by a Mussulman peasant, sent by the Bey, with an abundant supply of food and water for his use. The bearer stayed but a short time, and on delivering the provisions, told 'Alī that he had also been directed to repeat to him the desire of the Bey, that he should continue to watch by the remains of his deceased brother, over which a *turba* was to be commenced as soon as possible. Then devoutly kissing 'Alī's hand, and pressing it to his forehead, in token of deep respect, he begged his blessing and prayers, and set off for the place from which he came.

On the following day 'Alī had occasion to review the labours of the previous one, and to place the remains of his late companion considerably deeper in the ground than he had primitively done, and also to raise the earth above them in such a manner as to give to the spot more the appearance of a properly constructed grave. He also threw some water over the fresh earth, either as an oblation or to harden the surface. Whilst thus engaged, he was not surprised to perceive in the distance the approach of visitors, perhaps of travellers, perhaps of workmen, sent for the construction of the *turba*. With more calmness and composure than on the previous occasion, he quietly watched their approach, which was but slow; and perceiving that the company was formed of waggons heavily laden, drawn by oxen and buffaloes, and the drivers pointing to himself, he became convinced that he was the object of their visit. Lest he should not have time to perform them, after their arrival, he now spread his skin beside the grave of his lost friend, and was busily engaged in the performance of his *namāz* when the waggons drew near, and out of respect for his evident piety, the drivers stood at some little distance from him, until their completion. It was readily seen how forcible was the impression which this simple act of piety made upon them, for, after saluting 'Alī, they each came forward and kissed his hand. A little group was soon formed around the newly made grave, and two pieces of plank were at once erected at its head and foot by one of the workmen. The loads were next discharged, the circumference of the building was laid out, and the construction of the *turba* at once commenced.

We must now pass over a period of several years. The *turba*, or mausoleum, had long since been constructed, and 'Alī been constituted the *turbadār*, or keeper of the holy tomb of the deceased, whose venerated remains rested peacefully beneath its little dome. The structure seemed to be formed much after the model of the other one, in which he had spent so many days of comfort with his Shaikh; and if he had really any part in shaping it, there is no doubt but that the resemblance was intentional. In place of two pieces of wood, an equal number made of marble now marked the grave of the deceased. On the one at its head was inscribed an epitaph, commencing as usual with "Him, the Creator and the Eternal", and adding, "This is the tomb of the celebrated *qutb*, or axis, of eminent piety, the renowned Shaikh

'Abd-ul-Qādir, of the *tarīq*, or Order, of the Qādirīs. Say a *fātiha* (the opening chapter of the *Qurān*) for his soul." As if so eminent a Santon could not possibly be equalled in stature by ordinary humanity, the length of the grave was considerably extended, and full ten feet of space showed the size of the great man whose bones were considered so great a blessing to the locality in which they reposed.[1] The tomb was surrounded by a wire network, to keep it from the pollution of impure hands; and not unfrequently a costly shawl or a rich silk article of apparel was

[1] This recalls the *naugazas* or '9-yard' long shrines found in India. There these tombs actually vary in length from 10 to upwards of 50 ft., and they appear to 'grow', perhaps because they are lengthened by the devout, like cairns. Sir Alexander Cunningham opined that every such tomb was described as that of a Ghāzī and Shahīd, 'Champion and Martyr', but he also records that two graves at Ajudhia are ascribed to the prophets Sīs and Aiyūb (Seth and Job), and one at Lamghān, in Afghānistān, to Lamech, so they are clearly ascribed to ancient prophets as well as to more modern martyrs. He also says those two places are the extreme limit of their occurrence, but Doutté depicts and describes the tomb of a giant prophet in Morocco (*En Tribu*, p. 379). He also refers to his *Merrākech*, i. p. 293, and to Pettazoni, *Religione primitiva in Sardegna*, pp. 4 f., in support of the statement that Moslem ruins are often assigned to the idolaters of the times of ignorance, regarded as a race of giants (*ib.* p. 381). So to in India Cunningham suggested a Buddhist origin for such shrines (*Archaeological Survey Rep.*, V. pp. 130-1, 106).

In Moslem belief a dead person when put in his grave will be asked and if he replies that he bore witness that Muhammad was the servant of God and His Prophet, his tomb will be expanded 7000 yards in length and as many in breadth, and a light will be placed in it. Then he will be told to sleep. Hence it seems hardly necessary to postulate a Buddhist origin for such tombs.

In the early years of the present century Chevalier describes a *takia* at the town of the Dardanelles as containing a *cerceuil* 40 feet in length and ascribed to a giant whose remains form the relics for which it appears to be revered (*Voyage de la Propontide*, p. 14, quoted by Hasluck in *Annual*, B.S.A. xxi. p. 95). Hasluck considered this tomb to be possibly identical with a ruined and deserted *takia* outside the village of Seraidjik, in the valley of the Rhodius, which was probably a Baqtāshī centre before 1826. It bears the name of the saint interred in it, Indje or Indjir Baba. This name is not explained, but *injīr*='fig'. *Inje* would, however, mean 'slender', but possibly the saint's correct name is Īnjī or Īnjū, 'pearl', or 'the lily of the valley'.

N. of Hayil . . . upon a height . . . is the Kabr es-Sany, 'the smith's grave', laid out to a length of three fathoms. "Of such stature was the man; he lived in the time of the Beny Helal; pursued by the enemies' horsemen, he ran before them with his little son upon his shoulder, and fell there" (Doughty, *Wanderings in Arabia*, i. p. 265. Abridgement, 1908).

spread over this, to remain there, however, only for some days, and receive for its future wearer the benefit of the spiritual powers of the revered and holy deceased. A lamp hung suspended within the enclosure, which at nightfall was carefully lighted, and a pious lady of the neighbouring town had, just before her decease, appropriated a sum of money as a *wakf*, or votive offering, from which to support the expense of keeping up this lamp. Other *wakfs* had also been left for the support of the *turba* generally, and to ensure the comfort of the pious individual who watched over the tomb. In the windows of the *turba* could be seen innumerable pieces of cloth and cotton fabrics tied there in evidence of the *nazrs*, or vows of the visitors who had come to ask spiritual aid from the deceased ; many of them from young Mussulman maidens, who, not being able orally to make known their affection for the objects of their preferences, sought, through the spiritual powers of their renowned Shaikh, to reach their hearts in an indirect manner—an usage unknown to or unpractised by the now Islam world ; or from married ladies, to secure the wavering affections of their husbands—or acquire the cares of maternity—through his intercession. Few persons ever passed by the *turba* without stopping to offer a prayer at its tomb, and such visits were a source of no little emolument to 'Alī, who now bore the full title of ' 'Alī the Shaikh ' It was not uncommon for persons highly placed in official as well as social position throughout the neighbouring country, to send him a present, and ask his interprocession with the deceased saint in their behalf, and for the promotion of their worldly interests. The Shaikh 'Alī, much to the dissatisfaction and mortification of sundry maidens and wealthy widows of the neighbourhood, had refused to join his lot in life with theirs, and change his solitary position for one more in harmony with their own desires and regard for his welfare. Following the example of the Shaikh by whom he had been educated, he preferred passing his life in a state of celibacy, his only companion being a comely youth, then of some twelve or fourteen years of age, whom he had found destitute and an orphan, in one of the villages of the vicinity.

Shaikh 'Alī's renown had spread far and wide over the surrounding country. His eminent piety, and the innumerable miraculous occurrences at the *turba*, all attributed to his prayers and the spiritual powers of the holy Santon over whose tomb he presided, tended greatly to acquire for him and it an enviable celebrity. News of it had reached even as far as the *turba* in which he had been educated, and created no little surprise in the mind of its Shaikh. He had never heard of the presence nor of the decease of any eminent member of his own fraternity, much less of the existence of so pious a Shaikh as the one must be who presided at his tomb. Curiosity, as well perhaps as jealousy, deeply penetrated his heart, and finally decided him to make a pilgrimage in person to a tomb so renowned for its sanctity. One fine autumn day the now venerable old Shaikh closed his *turba* and set out on a journey which, at his time of life, was not free from much inconvenience and fatigue. The object in view, however, was so important to his own interests, both temporal and spiritual, that he considered it quite providential, and worthy of his declining days. At least, so he gave out to the usual visitors at his own shrine; and the painful effort which it required greatly enhanced his own already high reputation. He therefore set out, with the prayers and blessings of all his friends and admirers. Travelling by easy stages, the aged Shaikh finally reached the object of his little pilgrimage, and on Friday noon arrived at the *turba* by the way-side.

There were many visitors present on the occasion in question. Ladies had come there in such wheeled conveyances as the country furnished; others rode there on horseback, quite in the same fashion as the men; not a few bestrode gentle donkeys, especially the more aged and infirm; and men came, some on horseback, and some even on foot. A few trees, which had grown up under the care of Shaikh 'Alī and the protection of the holy tomb, afforded these visitors some shade during the heat of the day, and copious draughts were imbibed from a well which had been sunk in close proximity to the tomb, the waters of which had become widely celebrated for their healing qualities. Mingling among the crowd, the old man attracted but little attention, and after the performance of the usual prayers at the holy tomb, he sat down in quiet beside it, his mind filled with pious meditations on the Prophet, the *pīr* of his Order, and the holy deceased in general. As Shaikh 'Alī passed frequently by him, he had abundant opportunity of seeing his features, now considerably changed by time, and a goodly beard which ornamented his features, and greatly added to the venerableness of his appearance.

Although his head was covered by a green turban of considerable dimensions, showing his direct descent from the blessed Prophet, more than once it flashed across the mind and memory of the old man that he had seen him under other circumstances and in some other part of the world. Indeed, he at one moment almost thought that he had some resemblance to his former pupil, but as he had never heard from, or of him, since his departure, he concluded that it was only accidental, and that 'Alī must have long since joined the list of the deceased. Gradually the visitors departed, and towards nightfall the two eminent Shaikhs remained alone at the *turba*, attended only by the comely youth afore alluded to. It was only then that any communication took place between them, and very soon the old man became fully convinced that the younger Shaikh was none other than his former pupil. The former made no difficulty in admitting the fact, and an intimacy soon was renewed between them. The flourishing condition of his late *élève* was a source of much satisfaction to the old man, and dispelled any feelings of envy which he might have previously entertained. Shaikh 'Alī, on his part, seemed to be extremely happy on receiving the visit of his former master, and treated him with much respect and consideration. They freely talked over the interests of their particular *turbas*, and the old man admitted that the growing celebrity of the newer one had considerably affected that of the old. The old man, being now no longer able to restrain his curiosity, begged Shaikh 'Alī to be so good as to inform him who was the revered member of their Order whose remains were interred in the *turba*. But on this point his former pupil made some objection to enlighten him. Pressed, however, to inform him of what so deeply interested the character and welfare of their common Order, 'Alī, after exacting a most formal promise of secrecy, narrated to his late master the entire history of his journey thus far, on the pilgrimage on which he had originally set out, its sudden termination, with the untimely death of the aged ass which he had so generously bestowed upon him, and the manner in which its remains had been canonised by popular favour, he having only to offer no opposition to what he verily believed was brought about by a direct intervention of Providence for some wise purpose, the ass having perhaps been the receptacle of the soul of some re-embodied saint. To this frank avowal the old man did not make even a show of surprise, and received the information with his usual calm and dignified demeanour. At this 'Alī was somewhat astonished and alarmed, lest it might prove ominous to the continuance of his heretofore most peaceful and prosperous career as a Shaikh. With this reflection he thought he would venture to inquire, for the first time in his life, what holy man was interred at the *turba* of the old Shaikh, his former master, but found him equally uncommunicative on such a subject. As a matter of reciprocity and mutual confidence, he pressed him for information on so deeply interesting a subject; and it was only after having given him a most solemn pledge of secrecy that he learned, with no little surprise, that the remains of the deceased saint over which the venerable Shaikh had presided for so many years, and to which so many of his own earlier prayers and supplications had been offered, were those of none other than the father of his own once so lamented companion, and now so highly venerated saint, the ass, which had been bestowed upon him by his master, with his blessing.

CHAPTER XIV

PERSIAN DARVISHES — SPIRITUAL EXERCISES — HASHĪSH — THE OCCULT SCIENCES — A LIST OF DARVISH CONVENTS AT CONSTANTINOPLE

It has been heretofore shown that the principles entertained by the more modern *tarīqs,* or Orders of the Darvishes, first became prominent in Persia and Bukhāra, though it is scarcely to be doubted that they originated in Arabia. From thence they travelled into Turkey, Syria, and Egypt, and even along the shores of the Mediterranean, as far as Morocco.

In Malcolm's *History of Persia* are found some interesting details of the original Orders of the Sūfīs, taken from Persian manuscripts, which may be fully depended upon for their accuracy. It is therein stated that the original sects were two in number, viz. the Hulūlī, or the ' Inspired ', and the Ittihādī, or the ' Unionists ', out of which grew five branches. Of these, the first is the Wusūlīa, or the ' United ' ; the second, the 'Ashiqīa, or the ' Loving ' ; the third, the Talqīnīa, or the ' Learned ' ; the fourth, the Zurīqīa, or the ' Penetrating ' ; and the fifth, the Wahdatīa, [Wāhidīa], much resembling the Ittihādīa, the chief principle being the great primitive dogma of mankind, the Unity of the Deity.[1]

The first branch maintains that God has entered or descended into man, and that the Divine Spirit enters into all those who are of a devout and intelligent mind.

The second believes that God is one with every enlightened mind, and that the immortal part forms its union with God, and becomes God. They say that the divine nature of Christ, who is called by all Mussulmans the *Rūh Allāh,* or ' Spirit of God ', was derived from the Spirit of the Deity having entered the womb of the Virgin Mary. The third and fourth have no very distinct dogma.

[1] Cf. p. 54 ff.

The fifth maintains that God is in everything, and that everything is in God. They admit that their principles are the same as those of the ancient Greek philosophers of Hellas, especially of Plato, who, they assert, maintains that God created all things with His own breath, and that everything is thus both the Creator and the created. This principle, in many of the modern writings of the Darvishes, is called the *nafs*, or ' breath of God ', and, as applied to man, is deemed to be the human part of animated nature, and distinct from the *rūh*, or ' soul ', the immortal part.

There are many Darvish Orders in Bukhāra, nearly all of the Sunnī, or orthodox kind, more closely attached to the dogmas of the *Qurān* and its Prophet than those of Persia, which are almost all Shī'a, and advocates of the Caliph 'Alī. The people of these two countries are much divided by their religious sentiments, though with 'Othman those of Bukhāra have a strong sympathy. I regret to be unable to give any account of the Darvish Orders of the latter country, and believe that they are particularly fanatic and hostile to all non-Mussulmans.

M. le Cte. A. de Gobineau, formerly secretary of the French Embassy in Persia, in 1859 published a small work called *Three Years in Asia*, and on the subject of the religion of the people of Persia, gives some interesting accounts, from which I borrow the following summary:

" The first sovereign of the dynasty of the Safāwīs, who mounted the throne in the sixteenth century, was not a Mussulman. He was a Sūfī. The partiality of the Persians for 'Alī had already given birth to several sects, which extended as far even as Syria, the greater part of which were Shiites. The *mullāhs* of Persia had always a tendency in that direction. The new dynasty, in accordance with them, made it the religion of the State, modified considerably the oral doctrine (of the *hadīs*, or traditions), and broke off from the rest of Islamism. From this moment the interpretation given by the Persians to the law of Muḥammad received a consecration. They became legitimists. The existence of an ecclesiastical body, the exaggerated cult of the Imāms—a theology as refined and exuberant in developments as the *Qurān* is simple—and the veneration of saints, out of whom they made demi-gods, was all formed into a doctrine, now not only tolerated and favoured, but even commanded. The *mullāhs*, in fact, became the absolute masters of the empire. These, however, having assumed a despotic sway over the people, they became the object of satire and invectives, out of which grew a struggle; and the sovereign having taken the part of the latter, these prevailed, and increased the civil power at the expense of the religious."

The Eastern idea that the spirit or soul returns to this world and lives again in a new body, long after the decease and decay of its primitive corporeal form, is held as true by many of the modern Shaikhs of Persia. With them the belief in the re-existence of the Imām Mahdī is stronger than among any other Muḥammadans. They are, as aforementioned, with few exceptions, 'Alīides, and attach the greatest importance to all of the members of his family—the twelve Imāms. The transmigration of the soul from one body to another is fully developed in their estimation of the Mahdī. It is, perhaps, borrowed from a parallel in Christianity, or may even be traced to the Old Testament.* The Mahdī, according to them, still lives, and will again reappear in a new body. It forms the chief principle of the religion of the Druzes, who hold that the great apostle of their faith, Hākim bi Amr Allāh,[1] possessed the soul of the 12th Imām. The Persians place but small faith in some of the dogmas of the *Qurān*, and having superseded its founder by the person of 'Alī, are disposed even to doubt the authenticity of certain portions of it, or at least to interpret it after the manner of the Sunnīs. The Darvish orders of Persia are less good Mussulmans than the people at large, and carry the principle that the " spiritual part of man emanated from God, and will return to Him ", and will as that man, through a state of extreme piety and religious fervour, becomes re-united, or near to God, to an extreme degree. This same approach to the Divinity is supposed by them to give to the pious Darvishes great ' spiritual power ', so as to enable them to overcome the ordinary laws of nature, and therefore to perform superhuman, or otherwise ' miraculous ' acts. The most remarkable of these Darvishes, however, are not actually Persians, but come from India. M. de Gobineau describes one of these, who visited Teheran, from Kashmīr, as " dressed in a cotton robe, much torn, his long and thin arms penetrating two sleeves, which scarcely held to the body ; he was barefooted ; his head covered

* Elias.

[1] See p. 121.

with a mass of black shaggy hair; his eyes of a surprising brilliancy, and teeth of the greatest whiteness, offering a striking contrast to his dark Eastern complexion." He had travelled all over India, Turkistān, and the whole Eastern world; and public report declared that he was possessed of the most extraordinary secrets.

The Nusairīs of Persia seem, from M. de Gobineau's account of them, to be those who entertain the most extreme principles of the 'Alīide Darvishes. They call their religion that of the *ahl-i-haqq*, or the 'people of truth'. The Arabs and Turks call them Nusairīs,[1] the Persians 'Alī-Illāhīs. The former assimilate

[1] For a full account of the Nuṣairī see *Histoire et religion des Noṣairis*, by René Dussaud, Paris, 1900. Their origin is obscure. Dussaud rejects the derivation of the name from *naṣrānī*, Christian, which would make it a diminutive, = 'little Christian'. He accepts the derivation from Muḥammad ibn Nuṣair, a disciple of the 11th Imām, Ḥasan-ul-'Askarī (p. 9).

The Nuṣairī are found mainly in the mountainous country bounded on the E. and N. by the Orontes, and on the W. by the sea in Northern Syria. The Maronites and Greek Syrians tend to push them to the North. Often called Anṣārīs, but quite incorrectly, they are not descended from the Ismailians, though in the very centre of the Jabal-an-Nuṣairia the remnants of that sect are to be found about Qudmus and Māṣiyād. Dussaud has shown that de Gobineau's view that two-fifths of the population of Persia are Nuṣairī was incorrect (pp. 1-5).

The Nuṣairīs make 'Alī God, Muḥammad his creation—and with Salmān al-Fārsī the three form a trinity, which one of their sects, the Shamālī, equates to the heaven, sun, and moon. The good Nuṣairī go to the stars, the bad suffer a long series of transmigrations, but even the good have to be transformed seven times before they can reach heaven. Like the Ismā'īlī in general they divide the world-history into seven ages, in each appearing an embodiment of deity. The Ismā'īlīs further taught that in each of these periods there appeared a prophet or *nātiq* ('utterer'), who was followed by an inferior (*asās*) who affirmed his law. But the Nuṣairīs have postponed the *nātiqs* to their chiefs, so that their bases are Abel, Seth, Joseph, Joshua, Asaph, Peter (?), and 'Ali, and the *nātiqs*, Adam, Noah, Jacob, Moses, Solomon, Christ, and Muḥammad. The Nuṣairī sects are at least four in number. The first, the Shamālī, are also called Shamsī—from the sun-god. Another sect is the Ghaibī, for the present is the time of God's 'absence', and the Absent is the true God, equated with the air or sky. A third sect, the Kalāzī, holds that 'Alī dwells in the moon—whence it is also called Qamarī, from *qamr*, 'moon'. It denies that 'Alī resides in the sun. One of its tenets is that by drinking wine one reaches a closer relation with the moon—a possible parallel to the identification of the moon with the Vedic *soma*. The fourth and most advanced sect is the Haidarī, which has accepted extraneous beliefs freely, however little it may preserve their ancient rites, while it admits that Muḥammad is the sun and Salmān the moon (p. 77).

them to the Christians of the East, whilst the latter suppose that they consider 'Alī as God, and so adore him. There are numbers of this sect in Constantinople, mostly from Persia, and the same exist in various parts of Asia Minor. He states that the 'Alī-Illāhīs (believers in the divinity of 'Alī) are different from the *ahl-i-haqq*, inasmuch as the former distinctly declare that the son-in-law of the Prophet was an incarnation of the Deity, and it is for this reason that they are considered by the more rigid Mussulmans as assimilated to the Christians, who attribute the same divine character to Jesus Christ, whilst the *ahl-i-haqq* consider that every one may, by superior piety and love of God, become joined to Him, or even become God.

I make special mention of these two sects of Persia, whence came almost all of the Darvish orders now in the Ottoman empire —and refer particularly to the principles entertained by the Baqtāshīs before described. They have but little respect for Islamism, though they hold themselves to be Muḥammadans. The *ahl-i-haqq* carry the dogmas of the Baqtāshīs to an extreme degree; they consider the Quraishite Prophet (Muḥammad) as an impostor, and do not either frequent the mosques nor perform the prayers, except when it is absolutely necessary. They pretend to a purely spiritual religion, and are very tolerant to other religions. They differ from ordinary Mussulmans by not believing in any legal impurity, and so have no need of the ablutions prescribed by the former. They divide themselves into the *ahl-i-sharī'at*, or those of 'religious legal law'; the *ahl-i-ma'rifat*, or those of 'religious knowledge or wisdom'; the *ahl-i-tarīqāt*,[1] or those of the 'destructive orders'; and the *ahl-i-haqīqāt*, or *ahl-i-haqq*, or those of the 'true faith', or 'truth'. By their theory, the first are those who follow the ordinances of the religious law, and among them are considered the Jews and Christians; the second are those who still seek for higher and more extensive knowledge, among whom are the Sūfīs, whose beliefs are quite pantheistic; and by considering each human soul as a Divine

[1] *Tārikāt* in original. It is difficult to get the meaning 'destructive orders' out of this form. Probably it is merely an error for the usual *ahl-i-ṭarīqat*, 'people of the path'. But the possibility that the text is correct must not be overlooked. There may be an allusion to the 86th chapter of the *Qurān*, the Ṭāriq, or 'Night-comer'. But the whole passage is full of typographical mistakes, *me'ārifet*, *hakeekāt*, repeated. Just below the original has shee'at for *sharī'at*.

emanation, expose themselves to much persecution by an assumption which would, *in extensis*, place them superior to ordinary humanity. As this incarnation of man originates in India, this doctrine may be considered semi-Hindu—semi-Ghabr. The second (*ahl-i-ma'rifat*) are those who seek for divine knowledge and, having obtained it, are superior to the ignorant; whilst the third (*ahl-i-tāriqāt*) are those who have found and entered upon the true path, which leads to divine inspiration.

Malcolm, in his *History of Persia*, on the subject of the Darvish principles (Sūfīism) also says: "So as to secure fidelity and secrecy, the *murīd* or novice is required to place himself under the guidance of a Shaikh or Master of the Order, who is regarded as possessing a peculiarly holy character, and to place implicit confidence in his tuition, as well as to submit to his will, quite—to use the Darvish expression—'like a dead body in the hands of an Imām'".

Darvishes represent themselves as entirely devoted to *Haqq*, or 'the Truth', and as being incessantly occupied in the adoration of Allāh—a union with whom they desire with all the ardour of a Divine love. The Creator is, according to their belief, diffused over all His creatures. He exists everywhere and in everything. They compare the emanations of His Divine Essence and Spirit to the rays of the sun, which they conceive to be continually darted forth and reabsorbed. It is for this reabsorption into the Divine Essence—to which their immortal parts belong—that they continually aspire. This return to the Deity is fully carried out in a verse [151] of the *Qurān* (2nd chap.), which says: "All mankind are *of*, and will return *to*, Him". This verse is the basis of much of what is peculiar to the Darvish doctrine. They believe that the soul of man, and the principle of life, which exists throughout all nature, is not *from* God, but *of* God. In their sophistry they use the term *'Ālam-i-khiāl* ('delusive world') to signify that we are continuously in a state of delusion with regard to the *māda*, or 'matter', of which the universe is formed; that the 'Light of God' is the animating principle which enables us to see the latter—viz. the 'matter'—just as would be the case did not light shine upon all objects, and so render them visible to the eyes; and that God having poured His Spirit over the universe, its light became diffused everywhere, and intelligence beamed upon the mind of man. This is also called the *Wahdat-ul-Wujūd*, or 'unity of being'—the One God being everywhere and in all things.

Their doctrine teaches that there are four stages or degrees, called the four columns of the Order, through which living man must pass before he can attain to the highest grade—that of 'Divine Beatitude'—when his corporeal veil will be removed and his emancipated soul will rejoin the glorious Essence from which it had been *separated*, but not *divided*. The first of these stages is that of humanity, called the Sharī'at, or that of 'holy law', which supposes the *murīd* or disciple to live in obedience to the written law, and to be an observer of all the established rites, customs, and precepts of the (Islām) religion, which are admitted to be useful in regulating the lives and restraining the vulgar mass within the proper bounds—as souls cannot reach the heights of Divine contemplation, and might be corrupted and misled by that very liberty of faith which tends to enlighten and delight those of superior intellect and more fervent devotion.

The second stage is called the *tāriqāt*, or 'paths', which may be called that of the 'mystical rites', in which the *murīd* or disciple attains power or strength. He who arrives at this leaves that condition, in which he is only admitted to admire and follow a *murshid*, or 'spiritual teacher', and enters the pale of the mystical Sūfiism before-mentioned. He may now abandon all observance of strictly religious form and ceremonies, because he exchanges *practical* for *spiritual* worship. But this cannot be attained without great piety, virtue, and fortitude, as the mind cannot be trusted in the neglect of religious or legal usages and rites necessary to restrain it, whilst yet weak, until it has acquired strength from habits of mental devotion, grounded on a perfect knowledge of its own dignity, and of the divine nature of the Almighty.

The third stage is that of the *ma'rifat*, or 'Knowledge', and the disciple who arrives at, or is deemed to have attained to, supernatural knowledge—or, in other words, to have become as one inspired—is supposed when he reaches it to be on an equality with the angels in point of knowledge.

The fourth and last stage or degree is called the *haqīqat*, or that of the 'Truth', at which the disciple is supposed to have arrived when he has become completely united to the Deity.

In these four degrees the disciple must be under the guidance of a *murshid,* who on his part must be of great piety and virtue, and himself reached them, through the spiritual teachings of another. For this purpose he attaches himself to a learned Shaikh and seeks instructions from his wisdom, just as, in the times of the Greek philosophers, young men, anxious to learn the principles of a particular master, attached themselves to him and sought knowledge from his mouth—or like St. Paul at the feet of the learned Jewish teacher Gamaliel.

The *murīd* must, mystically, always bear his *murshid* in mind, and become mentally absorbed in him, through a constant meditation and contemplation of him. The teacher must be his shield against all evil thoughts. The spirit of the teacher follows him in all his efforts, and accompanies him wherever he may be, quite as a guardian spirit. To such a degree is this carried that he sees the master in all men and in all things, just as a willing subject is under the influence of the magnetiser. This condition is called 'self-annihilation' into the *murshid* or Shaikh. The latter finds, in his own visionary dreams, the degree at which the *murīd* has reached, and whether or not his soul or spirit has become bound to his own.

At this state of the disciple, the Shaikh passes him over to the spiritual influence of the *pīr*, or original founder of the particular *tarīq* or 'path' to which they belong, long since deceased, and he sees the latter only by the spiritual aid of the former. This is called 'self-annihilation' into the *pīr*. He now becomes so much a part of the *pīr* as to possess all of his spiritual powers, and may perform even all of his supernatural acts.

The third grade also leads him, through the spiritual aid of the Shaikh, up to the Prophet himself, whom he now sees in all things. This state is called, like the preceding, 'self-annihilation' into the Prophet.

The fourth degree leads him even to God. He becomes a part of the Divinity, and sees Him in all things. Some, in this state of ecstacism, have gone so far, in Persia, as to declare themselves to be the Deity, and for this have forfeited their lives,—such as Mansūr [1] and Nasīm,[2] both celebrated mystical Darvishes. It is related that Junaidī of Baghdād, the *pīr* of all the modern 'Alīide

[1] Manṣūr al-Hallāj is doubtless meant: see note on p. 84 *supra*.

[2] Nusīmī, a Turkish Ṣūfī poet, a fervent admirer of Hallāj, and a member of the Ḥurūfī sect (*E.R.E.*, art. Ṣūfīs).

Orders, believed himself to be in this state, and allowed his disciples to cut at him with a sword. It is said that they could not hurt him, but made, nevertheless, so many wounds on their own persons.

The Shaikh, after this remarkable proof of spiritual teaching, next brings the *murīd* back to his original state, like the physician who, after reducing the patient, by natural remedies restores him to health, and puts upon him the *tāj*, or cap of his Order, or confers upon him the grade of *khalīfa,* which, in his case, is an honorary degree. He now again performs all of the rites of ordinary Islamism. Few ever reach the fourth degree, though many do the second. Although in all the various Orders there are differences of usages and forms of worship, still, in the chief principles they agree with each other,—particularly in those which inculcate the necessity of an absolute obedience to inspired teachers, and the possibility, through fervent piety and enthusiastic devotion, of attaining (for the soul, even when the body inhabits this world) to a state of celestial beatitude. Among the first acts required of the *murīd*, or disciple, is that of spending much of his time—with some forty days and nights—in retirement and prayer, invoking the name of Allāh, after which he will see visions, the spiritual interpretation of which he receives from the Shaikh of his *takia.* Among their points of belief are the following. Some maintain that God has entered or descended into the Devout, and that the Divine Spirit enters into all those who are of a truly pious and intelligent mind.

Some believe that God is as one with every enlightened mind, and that the immortal part forms its union with God, and becomes God. They say, as before stated, that the Divine nature of Christ, who is called by all Mussulmans the *Rūh Allāh,* or ‘ Spirit of God ’, was derived from the Spirit of the Deity entering the womb of the Virgin Mary. Others, as before stated, hold that God is in all things, and that everything is God. They say that the Prophet was a Sūfī, or believer in mystical religion, of a high order, and quote many of his *hadīsāt*, or ‘ traditional sayings ’, to sustain the same. They declare that the Caliph ’Alī was thoroughly acquainted with their doctrines, and deputed two of his sons, Hasan and Husain, and two other holy men of his time, named Kumāil ibn-Zaid[1] and Hasan al-Basrī, to teach and

[1] Kumail ibn Zaid, ? ’Abdullah al-Kāmil (*J.R.A.S.*, 1903, p. 158. But see p. 156).

perpetuate them. From these, they maintain, many of the principal founders of *tarīqs* or paths received their intuition, and their *khirqas*, or mantles, as symbols of their spiritual orders. This symbol reminds us of the mantle of Elijah which descended upon Elisha, and the cloak or garment of Christ.

I may also add a fact of some significancy. As among the more recent Orders of Darvishes, the head of the *takia* is called the Shaikh, or *murshid*, and his successor the *khalīfa*, or caliph, so is it with regard to the political head of the State who has received the mantle of the Prophet, and becomes his caliph, or 'successor'. Sultān Salīm I. received the *khirqa sharīf*, or holy mantle, from Muḥammad, the last of the Abbassides, of the Prophet's lineage, when he conquered Egypt; and this revered relic is carefully preserved in the old seraglio at the present time, under the charge, I am assured, of a descendant of the *asḥāb*,[1] or friendly companions of the Prophet, named *rais*, on whom he bestowed it.

To arrive at the second grade or degree of office in a *takia*, that of *khalīfa*, it is, as before stated, necessary to spend much time in fasting and prayer, and in complete abstraction from all worldly pursuits. The man must die, so to say, before the saint can be born. To this degree of spiritual perfection, as well as to his supposed familiarity with all the mystical dogmas and tenets of the Order, he must possess the respect, reverence, and entire submission of all of the *murīds*. By constant prayer, his breath, even his touch, must possess a sanctifying influence, and be believed to have the superhuman power of performing miracles. This is peculiarly the case with the Rifā'ī, or 'Howling Darvishes'. If, in the course of his devotional probation, the *murīd* who seeks advancement succeeds in seeing a vision, the *pīr* of his Order, by whom its import is interpreted, may terminate his seclusion; and though much reduced in bodily strength (but strengthened spiritually), his trial has not ended. He must wander from place to place; visit holy tombs, at which to seek further inspiration, perform the pilgrimage to Makka and Madina, and even proceed to the revered tombs of Karbalā, near to Baghdād.

Among some of the Orders, the Shaikh is free to leave his mantle of succession, at his death, to whomever of his *murīds* he deems most worthy of it. But in the Ottoman empire, the office

[1] This seems to be a mistake for *aṣḥāb-ul-ra'ī* (*J.R.A.S.*, 1906, p. 325).

of Shaikh has generally become hereditary in the family of the *murshid*, though in default of a son and heir the members may elect a successor from among themselves; or all the Shaikhs of the same Order meet and select one, subject, however, to confirmation by the Shaikh-ul-Islām, or head of the Islam Faith, who resides at Constantinople, and is appointed by the Sultan.

The *zikr*, or repetition of God's Name by the Darvishes and Moslems generally, which has been explained elsewhere, may be traced to the habit of the Prophet himself, who frequently recited various portions of the *Qurān*, with an audible voice, both in moments of prayer and in those of danger, to his followers. To the efficacy of this recitation he evidently attached great importance, and believed in their merit with the Creator. During several of his battles he observed this custom, either designing thereby to encourage his forces, or to obtain a Divine manifestation through the pious act. As he, doubtlessly, fully believed in his own inspiration, and that the verses which he recited had come to him from the Creator, through the medium of a celestial messenger, whom he called the Angel Gabriel during his periods of pious fervour and ecstasy, he also believed in their value near Him from whom they emanated. It is not, therefore, surprising that his followers should still entertain the same conviction. Such a belief finds some confirmation in the practice of pious Christians, when they call upon God and Christ in the language of the Old and New Testaments. In his last illness the Prophet often recited various *sūrahs*, or chapters, some of the longest of the *Qurān*, especially in the quiet of the night, in praise of the Lord. It is related that he suffered greatly during his periods of mental excitement and agitation attending the reception of the revelations conveyed to him by the Angel,—such as the chapters called the 'Hūd' [xi], the 'Inevitable' [lvi], and the 'Striking' [ci], designated as the 'terrific' *sūrahs*; and he is said to have attributed his grey hairs to them. It is difficult to suppose that he composed these long chapters and committed them at the same time to memory, and yet such must have been the case. He pretended to no superhuman powers at such seasons, nor did he ever recite them in the view of imposing on his friends, disciples, or any others, differing widely from the Darvishes.

I would refer the curious reader to the *Life of Mahomet*, by William Muir, Esq., of the Bengal Civil Service, for the most interesting and truthful biography ever written of this wonderful man. I regret not to have found in it any allusion to the origin of the *tarīqs*, or 'paths' of the Darvishes.

Whenever the origin of these *tarīqs* cannot be found in the practices of the Prophet, or in the interpretation of the verses of the *Qurān* by their *pīrs* or founders, it may be taken for granted that it is contained in the *hadīs*, or traditions, collected in the first and second centuries of the Hijra. So far as I know, no collection of these has been translated into Turkish or any European language. They would, doubtlessly, well repay the labour of translation, especially could they be arranged chronologically, and with reference to the historical events which gave rise to them.

SPIRITUAL EXERCISES

The ordinary state or condition of pious contemplation and prayerfulness is called *murāqaba*. This is possessed in wakeful moments, when the soul and body are united, and the senses of the latter are enfeebled by superior powers of the soul. There is, however, another condition, called *insilā*, when, it is held, the soul of man leaves the body, and wanders about without regard to time or space. It was in this latter that the Prophet is supposed to have ascended in the spirit to heaven, borne there on an imaginary celestial animal, called the Barāq.[1]

The celebrated Shaikh, Muhyī-ud-Dīn al-'Arabī, relates regarding the *insilā*: "Once when I was in the vicinity of the holy and reverend Ka'ba (Caaba), it happened that, absorbed in mental reflections on the four great jurisconsults of Islamism, I beheld a person who continuously made the *tawāf* or circuit of that holy building. His height was quite as elevated as the Ka'ba itself. Two other individuals were engaged in the same occupation, and whenever these were near to each other, the power would pass between them, without, however, separating them. From this I concluded that the individual must belong to spiritual bodies only. As he continued his circuits, he recited the following: 'Truly, we have been, for many long years, engaged in walking round this holy house, but you only are doing it now' (*Qurān*, cxxiii).

[1] See note at p. 28.

"On hearing these words, I formed a desire to know who he was, and to what tribe he belonged. So I fixed him with my eyes, after the manner called *habs-i-nazr*,[1] and when he had ended his circuit, and desired to depart, he was unable to do so. Finally, he came to my side, and feeling that I was the cause of his detention, begged me to allow him to depart. I answered him with the words, *Bismillāh ur-Rahmān ur-Rahīm*, 'In the name of God, the merciful and the clement', and added, 'I will allow you to go only after you have let me know what kind of a being you are, and to what tribe or people you belong'. He replied, 'I am of mankind'. I next asked him how long it was since he left this world. He replied, 'It is now more than forty thousand years'. Surprised, I added, 'You say it is so long, whilst it is only six thousand years since Adam's time, and yet you state that you are of mankind'. He answered, 'The Adam you speak of was the father of the human race, and though since his time only six thousand years have elapsed, thirty other worlds preceded him. In the Traditions of the Pride of all Beings (the Prophet), and the Sovereign ('Alī), it is said, 'Certainly God created the Adam (Man) you know of, after the creation of an hundred thousand others, and I am one of these'."

The principles of this writer are peculiarly spiritual. He believes that the world was inhabited by many other species of human beings previous to the creation of Adam and Eve, all differing from each other, and some of them also of various degrees of stature and spiritual faculties. The spirits of mankind, separted by death from the body, continue to people the vast space which surrounds the world on which we dwell, but are wholly invisible to the ordinary organs of vision; that some persons of a high spiritual power are, however, able to behold them, and that a superior spiritual faculty possesses an influence and power over an inferior one; and that visions are not connected with the ordinary senses of the body, but are wholly spiritual, so that oftentimes during our corporeal slumbers, when the senses are lulled into repose, the soul leaves the body and wanders over the world, with a velocity which knows neither time nor space, and can see objects extremely distant; whilst ordinary dreams are but an effect of the senses—such, for instance, as memory—when in a state of half repose, and are common to all

[1] Habs-i-nazar, lit. 'holding of the sight'.

animated nature, in which expression are understood those animals which do not possess immortal souls or spirits.

In connexion with the preceding account of the principles of Muhyī-ud-Dīn, of arresting any one by a 'spell', it may not be out of the way to add the following summary of a little work by Ibn-'Īsāī, as an explanation of what has only been given as a theory.

Ibn-'Īsāī was born, so says the MS., at Ak-Sīai, in Asia Minor, and emigrated thence to Tripoli of Barbary, where he founded the Order of the 'Isāwīs.[1] He was originally of the Order of the Bairāmīs. [Aq-Sarāī must be meant.]

An abridged account of his theory:—

Tālib[2] signifies the Darvish.

Matlūb[3] is the person whom you wish to appear before you.

Mulāhaza is the action of thinking of the latter in such a manner as to make him appear.

Tawajjuh is the producing of the person in question.

Ahl-i-hāl, those who have the power of making others appear.

Ahl-i-tasarruf are the holy people who possess that power.

Murāqaba is much the same as the *tawajjuh*.

Hāl is the state of ecstasy into which the person goes who makes the absent appear to him.

[1] The Īsāwīa of Lane (*Modern Egyptians*, p. 466 f.). Founded by Sīdī Muḥammad ibn-'Isā, the Īsāwīa eat glass as well as fire.

For their curious rites, reminiscent of those practised in India by the Aghorīs and others, see *E.R.E.*, 10, p. 721. This account differs seriously from the one given by E. Montet, who says that Muḥammad b. 'Īsā was born of a Sharifian family in Mekinez (Morocco), where he also died in 1523-24, and became a member of the Shāzilī-Jazūlīa order. (Al-Jazūlī, who died in *c.* 1465, was a native of Sus, the author of a famous work called the *Dalā'il al-Khairāt*, but his sub-order has almost ceased to exist as an organised community in Morocco.) The 'Īsāwīa, on the other hand, became one of the most important in Africa. Mystical in doctrine, it has some remarkable ritual practices, which include the seated dance resulting in ecstasy so acute that the spirit of the founder of the Order is believed to have gained control over a disciple prostrated by it. In this state the ecstatic is proof against the effects of broken glass, cactus leaves, etc., which they devour, and even against poison. The Bukharā (pl. of Bukhārī), descendants of the famous Black Guard, instituted by the Sulṭāns of Morocco, belong to this Order, now, at least, a negro aristocracy. The Order thus recalls the Baqtāsh relations with the Janissaries (*v. E.R.E.*, 10, pp. 719, and 8, p. 882). See also *E.I.* ii. p. 527.

[2] Lit. 'seeker'.

[3] Lit. the 'sought'.

Kāl [1] is the condition of perfect submission of the person thus appearing to the power of the *hāl*.

Shughl [2] is the performance of this act of power.

Wifq [3] is the science of mystical numbers.

Istidrāj [4] is the acquisition of certain illegal and diabolical powers, by the abandonment of the purifications and prayers required by religion.

In the fourteenth chapter of his work he explains the spiritual powers of 'fascination', viz. the producing of an effect upon an absent individual for a good or an evil purpose. He calls it that faculty of the soul of the *tālib*, or active agent, which by the power of the will, or profound contemplation (*mulāhaza*), can produce the *matlūb*, or passive object, before him. The method of exercising this peculiar power, he says, can best be taught practically by a Mushaikh (Shaikh). One of the rules, however, is for the *tālib* to place himself in operation (*shughl*); the name of the *tālib* and the *matlūb* must be drawn up according to the science of the *wifq* (or the mystical numerical value of the letters of their respective names) calculated and placed upon the left knee; he must gaze upon them with deep fixedness, and think constantly on the figure and form of the *matlūb*; he must blow, as it were, at the mouth of the *matlūb* and recite his incantation, and so continue to bring the figure nearer and nearer to his vision. After this he must look at the *wifq* and recite the *wird* (an Islam prayer); now and then close his eyes, and blow at the mouth of the *matlūb*; then recite the *fātiha* (2nd [5] chapter of the *Qurān*), without, however, for a moment allowing the figure to escape from his sight. To thus gaze upon the *wifq* is the same as to gaze upon the *matlūb*; to gaze upon the figure is an evidence of the *hāl*, and to neglect to follow this rule is a proof that the *tālib* is in a

[1] Kāl, apparently *qāl* for *iqālat*, 'annulment', or 'self-abandonment'.

[2] Shughl, fr. *shaghala*, 'was busied in', 'engrossed in'.

[3] Wifq, apparently = harmony (cf. Salmoné, *Arab. Dict.*, p. 1222, where this form is not given). The form *wafq* means more especially 'a magic square', but (if it is intended) it is very rightly given a much wider meaning in the text (*v.* W. Ahrens, "Studien über die magischen Quadrate der Araber", in *Der Islam*, vii. p. 215).

[4] Istidrāj, x. of *daraja*: lit. 'was beguiled'. The term may well be translated 'misdirection'. It is found in As-Sulamī's "Risālat al-Malamatia" (*v. Der Islam*, vii. p. 173).

[5] The 1st chapter.

state of *istidrāj*. When the figure is by this means brought near to the *tālib*, he can describe it to any persons who may be present.

It is related that Nimrūd, who, Orientals say, was a great apostate, was once desirous of effecting an evil upon a king, and for this purpose had his portrait made and placed before him. By continuously gazing upon this figure, and by the exercise of his 'power of the will', he so seriously affected the health of the king that he would certainly have died, had he not sent and begged him to cease, offering to submit entirely to his will.

The *tawajjuh* is produced by the *ahl-i-sulūk* [1] (the Darvish) fixing his gaze upon the heart of the *matlūb*. If he looks upon the left breast, he will perceive the figure appear from out of the heart; then the act of the *tālib* is completed. He must then look upon the left breast whilst in a dark and quiet apartment; many erroneous thoughts will arise in his own mind, and after they have vanished, a *raf'at*, or true state,[2] will come upon him; the figure of the *matlūb* will rise before him, and as it will be perfectly submissive to his will, he can readily effect whatever purpose he may have in view.

Another mode of the *tawajjuh* is the following: This is not by looking at the heart, but by turning the thoughts to the Almighty. You must pray to Him, and give yourself up entirely to Him. Whether the figure of the *matlūb* appear or not, the *tālib* must persist in his act of the *shughl*, and pray and weep with much warmth, until it does finally appear. The moment it begins to show itself, he must blow, as it were, in its mouth, recite the invocation, lament and beg, and excite his own feelings excessively. The *tālib*, nevertheless, must be calm in mind, and not suffer his fervour to overcome him. Besides this, he must never have any doubt of the efficacy of his effort, but place entire faith in its certainty.

Every *dāïra*, or 'mystic circle', has its *tawajjuh*; that of the *tālib*, who seeks the right path, is called 'of the heart'. When once attained, its possessor can perform spells over the feebler wills of others, especially of females. When he reaches the *dāïra* of the spirit, he can bewitch men and lovers; on reaching that of the 'mind', he can bewitch aged persons, the *'ulamā* (doctors of law), the *fuzlā* (pious), the *zāhid* (the devout). By the

[1] Lit. 'people of the way'.
[2] Apparently *rufa't*, 'elevation', or *raf'āt*, 'high pitch'.

secret circle he can enchant the learned, poets, and those who spend their lives in the pleasures of love. By it, also, he can ensorcillate Shaikhs, people in a state of ecstatic fervour, the *tasawwuf*, and even the *ahl-i-sulūk* (Darvishes). In the circle of the Jalāl (name of the Deity), these powers are used for purposes of revenge ; in that of the *jamāl* (beauty), for purposes of kindness ; and all of these are known to the *ahl-i-hāl*. As it sometimes happens that through the power of the *tālib* the figure of the third person is produced, this one is apt to suffer from it, and may even die ; it is, therefore, necessary that the operator be made thoroughly acquainted with the process, lest danger be incurred. Should the *tālib* produce the figure of a fiend, or of his beloved, he must cease and recite the *ikhlās* (a Moslem prayer), and so preserve him or her from any injury. At other times the *tālib* effects the *tawajjuh* and the *tasawwur* (imagining), and when the figure of the *matlūb* appears, he can arrest it by a spell, by simply crying out its name, blowing in its mouth, and, looking fixedly at its heart, reciting a prayer.

The powers of the Shaikh ibn-'Isā were certainly thus most extraordinary, for after reciting the *wird*, he would gaze fixedly upon the *wifq*, so as to produce, before his own vision, the figure of the person desired. He could so affect any person present, as to perfectly subdue him or her to his will, and then take any revenge on him or her that he pleased. No one could withstand the ardour of his gaze, and he could impress any one so as to hold him completely under his control.

Another *tawajjuh* is when the *tālib* is desirous of bestowing something upon a *matlūb*, and he can then so influence the latter by his powers as to impress him beneficially. This is generally done to the *sāliks*, or neophytes under his instruction. The Shaikh ibn-'Īsā, during the course of his instructions, would bestow the benefit of the prayers of his circle upon his pupils, and so enable them to produce the same results on others. This he could do from a distance as well as near, and he could so influence them, that they assumed whatever condition he pleased, of joy or grief.

The preceding is quite sufficient to show the nature of the 'spiritual powers' of this Shaikh, who is quite renowned in Tunis and Tripoli, where there are many adherents of his Order. They seem to be of a magnetic character, and resemble those of

Muhyī-ud-Dīn al-'Arabī, mentioned in a preceding part of this chapter.

HASHĪSH

Heretofore I have endeavoured to explain how, among the Darvishes, the mental excitement and enthusiastic germ is ascribed by them entirely to divine inspiration, growing out of the *zikr*, or invocation of the Deity. Among some of them, however, material means are also resorted to for the purpose of exciting, if not the mental faculties, at least the brain, so as to produce visionary glimpses of what is considered by them at least a foretaste of future happiness and enjoyment, in that existence which the more sensible hold to be entirely of a 'spiritual' character. On this subject a writer in the *Levant Herald*, of Constantinople, makes the following observations:—

"The peculiar pleasures affecting especially the nerves, and produced by narcotics, tobacco, and opium, belong apparently to modern times—that is to say, that it is only in modern times that we find them in general use. Amongst the ancients there is very little doubt of their existence, but they were the secrets of the priests, or of the initiated. We read, for instance, of certain temples in Cyprus or in Syria, to which the votaries thronged from all parts of the world, in expectation of having their wishes gratified. Those wishes generally were in such cases interviews with some beloved object, or visions of future happiness. The votary was bathed, dressed in splendid robes, given some peculiar food, after which he inhaled a delicious odour, and was then laid on a couch strewn with flowers. Upon this he probably went to sleep; but in all events such an intoxication of the mind was produced that the next morning he rose satisfied that in the night all his desires had been realised. The worship of the Paphian Venus, of the 'Syrian goddess', be she Astarte, or known by whatever other name, and of other mystical divinities, was full of these rites, in which the effects on the mind could only have been produced by narcotic stimulants."

The first intention of *hashīsh* was evidently not as a stimulant. It was intended as a 'spiritual' soporific producing that quiescence of soul so dear to Orientals, and known throughout all the regions under Arabian influence by the name of *kaif*.[1] But

[1] 'Intoxication', 'carouse': see note on p. 210 *supra*.

this stolid annihilation of ideas was not sufficient for the more exalted natures ; these found a higher power in the drug—that of raising the imagination until it attained to a beatified realisation of the joys of a future world. This last effect could only be produced by mixing other noxious ingredients with *hashīsh*, already sufficiently noxious of itself, and the effect of the delirium was mentally worse than that of opium itself. The mind (brain), utterly prostrate after the effect had ceased, required still more imperatively than in the case of the opium-eater a fresh supply to the diseased imagination ; the dose was heightened as the craving for beatitude became stronger, and half-a-year's indulgence ended in a madness of the most moody and miserable kind—all the more miserable that, unlike the opium-eater, the inhaler of hashīsh in this form preserves his corporeal strength and activity. The lovers of this vice present few of the hideous forms of humanity exhibited by a Chinese opium-house ; but, on the other hand, the mental effect is wilder, more terrible, and yet more difficult of cure.

The use of *hashīsh* prevails in the Levant to an extent very little suspected by the common observer, so carefully is it concealed, or veiled under the pretence of ordinary smoking. The word *hashīsh* is of Egyptian or Syrian origin (*khashkhāsh* in the Arabic language signifies simply the poppy). At Constantinople it is known by the name of *asrār*,[1] which word means a secret product or preparation ; the name of *hashīsh* in European Turkey being confined to the poppy from which the product is obtained. The cultivation of this plant is carried on with much activity in many parts of the Ottoman dominions ; it thrives best and in most abundance in the provinces of Asia Minor, and especially Nicomedia, Brussa, and in Mesopotamia, near Mosul. The dealers in *asrār* repair to these countries towards the end of May, in the first place, to examine the state of the vegetation and to suggest improvements in its cultivation ; and in the second, to overlook the harvest, and themselves to collect the dust which forms the staple of this commodity. The merchant, as soon as he arrives at the spot, sends the company he brings with him into the fields to cut off the heads of the plants, in order that the leaves which contain the precious material may have more force. Fifteen days

[1] Especially a preparation of Indian hemp (Redhouse, *T.-E. Lex.*, p. 109). But it is also used of opium (Massignon, *Lexique technique*, p. 86).

after this operation the plants are gathered in, after care has been taken to ascertain that the leaves are large, and feel viscous to the touch. The plants are cut down, not rooted up, for fear of damaging the leaves ; they are then taken into a shed, where the leaves are carefully picked off, and spread out to dry upon a long coarse carpet, made of wool, and called *kilīm*.[1] When the leaves are sufficiently dry, they are collected together upon one-half of the carpet, the other half being left free for the purpose of beating the leaves till they are reduced to dust. The first product is immediately collected, forming the choicer portion of the *asrār*, and is called *sighirmā*. The fibres of the leaves are then, by means of a second and third pounding, reduced to dust. This dust,

A BAQTĀSH DARVISH INHALING *HASHĪSH*.

called *honarda*, is in less esteem ; so much so that, while the first dust sells at forty francs the kilogramme, the second is not worth more than ten, it being not only as the refuse, but lying under the suspicion of adulteration. It is sent to Constantinople in double sacks—the outside one of hair, the inner one of skin ; the entire quantity is not there consumed, much of it being sent to Egypt and Syria. Before being brought into the market, the *asrār* is differently prepared, according to the tastes of the different countries. In Egypt and Syria the extract is preferred in a fatty form, prepared with butter. At Constantinople the rancid and viscous flavour produced by this process is greatly disliked, and the *asrār* is sold in the form of syrup, or in pastiles to be smoked with *tombeki*[2] (in the *nārghīli* or water-pipe). The simple syrup still retains something of the fatty and viscous flavour, and for

[1] Kilīm, *gilīm*, 'a woollen frock', *Kashf-ul-Maḥjūb*, p. 45.
[2] Vulg. for *tanbākū*, 'tobacco of Shirāz' (Redhouse, p. 597).

that purpose some aromatic productions, as *bahārāb*, are introduced into the preparation. This last addition is of great importance, as by the nature of its excitement it impresses the mind of the imbiber, in addition to the ecstatic delirium of the pure *hashīsh*, with a series of visions of the joys of paradise and other scenes of future life, much prized on this account by the true believer. This last preparation is extremely expensive, and is therefore only in the reach of the rich ; it is chiefly used by the grandees of Asia Minor, who, being more devout than those of Europe, carefully abstain from fermented liquors, but consider *hashīsh*, which produces the same effects in a very aggravated form, to be in perfect accordance with the law of the Prophet.

The inhabitants of the capital (Constantinople) are less impulsive, and for the purpose of producing that state of mind so desirable, and known in the East by the name of *kaif*, they add the effects of *rāqi* and other fermented liquors. The pastiles for smoking are thus prepared. A certain quantity of *asrār* is put into an iron pot, and warmed slowly over a brazier. A peculiar acrid odour is then given forth, upon which the operator puts his hand, enclosing a portion of the dust, into a vase full of a strong infusion of coffee, with which he carefully moistens and kneads the dust. After having been thus mixed, the dust becomes a paste, having the smell and colour of coffee ; it is then taken from the fire and put upon a marble table, where it undergoes a long process of manipulation until it is made thoroughly homogeneous ; it is then cut in pieces, and moulded into the form of small cylinders or rolls. Pastile cylinders, weighing four grammes, are sold for a piastre (or four cents), and one is more than enough to throw any person not habituated to the practice into the most complete delirium. This last form of *hashīsh* is the most common and the best appreciated in the country. The reason of the preference is partly the cheapness and partly its colour and form, which allow it to be carried about and used without discovery. The pastiles are commonly soaked for use in the *nārghīli* with the *tombeki*, or Persian tobacco, but those who require a more decided action prefer the mixture with common tobacco, for which reason the dealers in *asrār* sell cigars impregnated with this substance to those who are not used to it. According to precise returns, the quantity of *asrār* dust collected in the aforenamed localities commonly exceeds 25,000 kilogrammes.

THE OCCULT SCIENCES

Education in the East is removing from the minds of Moslems many of the superstitious ideas which they attached to what may be called the 'hidden arts', and to the value of amulets, talismans, charms, etc. I have found, however, that these are still cherished by most of the lower classes, and especially among the Darvishes. Mr. Lane, in his excellent work afore-quoted called the *Modern Egyptians*, gives a minute account of these, and I would recommend the curious and patient reader to refer to it for what I spare him in the present humbler book.

So much sanctity is attached by Moslems generally, and especially by Darvishes, to particular verses of the *Qurān* as to lead them to believe in certain 'spiritual powers' possessed by each one of these, differing according to their application. On many of the more magnificent palaces and *qunāqs*, or the dwelling-houses of the wealthy, it is usual to suspend a writing for the protection of the same. Sometimes a few words are written on an angle of the building, and in these cases the words are generally some of the names of the Deity, or a pious invocation, such as *Yā! Hāfiz!* 'Oh! protector!'; at others the writing is composed of several words, or even of a full verse of the *Qurān*. In addition to these it is not at all uncommon to see suspended from an angle of the same edifice—even a royal one—an old shoe or a bunch of garlic, the latter sometimes painted blue. Even an old horseshoe is supposed to possess certain vague powers of protection against fire and ill-luck; and as it cannot be supposed that the intelligent owner of the *qunāq* really believes in its efficacy, it must be attributed to a 'popular superstition', against which he does not care to offend. The 'pious invocation' arises from a higher motive, inasmuch as it is a part of that strong principle of Islamism which teaches its disciples a perfect submission to the will and providence of God, and to look to Him only for protection and preservation under all the circumstances of life. The religious amulets or *tilasms* generally known as 'talismans' are stones of various kinds, such as agates and cornelians, or even those of a more precious character. On these are engraved various verses of the *Qurān*, or even some of its shorter chapters, and vary according to the peculiar belief of the engraver or the wearer. These are suspended to the neck, attached to the arm, or worn as a ring. Sometimes they are also an invocation of the Caliph 'Alī, or of all of the four direct caliphs —of even the Prophet; and when the former are sectarian, they generally are of a Persian or Darvish character. Verses of the *Qurān* are also written on parchment or paper, and are worn in the same manner and for the same purpose. These are called *nuskhas*, or amulets, and are worn by an immense number of Mussulmans of every position in life.

There is, however, another class of talismans, which are entirely of a mystical or cabalistic character, drawn up according to what is called the *'Ilm Wifd*,[1] or 'Science of Calculation'. To these the public, and especially the Darvishes, still attach extraordinary powers.

This is the science of drawing up figures in a mystical manner. All the letters of the Arabic alphabet have a numerical value, like in our own; V is 5, X is 10, etc., and it is therefore easy to draw up an invocation or a prayer in figures; chronograms are written in a similar manner, and in most public inscriptions the last line, though written and possessing a signification of a special character, if calculated, also gives the date of the writing. In this manner, if I am not mistaken, the inscription on the marble slab sent by the late Sultān 'Abd-ul-Majīd to the Washington Monument explains the period of the contribution in the last line. It is only necessary to ascertain the numerical value of each letter, and these when added together form the date. The letters 'Baktāsh' make the date of his Order 738 H.

It is also believed that each letter of the alphabet has a servant appointed by Allāh to attend upon it. These, it is supposed, may be invoked in case of need. Particular writings are equally attended by mysterious beings, who, though they may not actually appear when invoked, are nevertheless present, and are supposed to obey implicitly the commands of the invoker. Some of these writings in numerals are for evil as well as for good purposes. They must be drawn up on certain days and hours, at certain periods of the moon, or on certain positions of the stars, without which their powers are lost. They are also engraved upon stones taken from certain localities, such as in the vicinity of the holy cities of Makka and Madīna, in Arabia, or near the

[1] ? *wifq*.

tombs of celebrated saints or founders of the Darvish Orders. Those from the neighbourhood of the grave of Hājī Bektāsh are highly esteemed. Besides verses from the *Qurān*, are often seen invocations to 'Alī or the other caliphs, and to the Prophet ; and mystical numerical calculations inscribed in and on drinking-cups, so that they may arrest the eye of the drinker. In case a charm is drawn up for the purpose of inspiring some one with the divine passion (love), the servants, or, as they are called, the *jinns*, attendant upon the letters which compose it meet together and devise a series of influences which, though invisible, are believed to have the power of compelling the devoted person to obey them. The only means of protection to be used in such cases is to draw up a counter charm, the *jinns* attendant upon which either overcome the others or come to a compromise, and so relieve the afflicted object.

Various calculations are made of an abstruse nature, involving a series of cubes and squares, subtractions and divisions, multiplications and additions, of a conventional character, to learn a result, either odd or even. If odd, the result is considered unfortunate ; whilst if even, it is fortunate.

The *tasbīh*, a Mussulman rosary, composed of ninety-nine beads (some of those of the Darvishes are much greater), represent so many names of the Deity, which are invoked by the devout. Its use is taken from the 41st verse of the 33d chapter of the *Qurān*, viz. : "O, believers [in the unity of Allāh, and the mission of His Prophet], repeat the name of Allāh, and count His names, night and morning".

Another peculiar belief has been thus explained to me by a Darvish friend, in connexion with the mystical character of Letters, based upon the principle that the faculties of reason and speech being peculiarly Divine gifts bestowed upon man, letters also were given to him as a means of expressing himself, and of perpetuating knowledge, and were practically used by God himself, in His communications to some of the prophets, as in the writing of the Ten Commandments.

The four elements, viz. water (*āb*), earth (*turāb*), fire (*nār*), and air (*hawā*), possess twenty-eight letters, as follows :—

A, 1 ; *b*, 2 ; *j*, 3 ; *d*, 4 ; *h*, 5 ; *v*, 6 ; *z*, 7 ; *h*, 8 ; *t*, 9 ; *y*, 10 ; *k*, 20 ; *l*, 70 ; *m*, 40 ; *n*, 50 ; *s*, 60 ; *'a*, or *'ain*, 70 ; *f*, 80 ; *z*, or *zād*, 90 ; *k*, 100 ; *r*, 200 ; *sh*, or *shīn*, 700 ; *t*, 400 ; *th*, or *thay*,

500 ; *h*, or *heh*, 600 ; *z*, or *zeh*, 700 ; *dz*, 800 ; *zh*, 900 ; and *gh*, or *ghain*, 1000.

These are divided into four classes, each of a different temperament. Fire has seven letters, *i.e.* *a*, *h*, *t*, *m*, *f*, *sh*, and *dz*, all supposed to be of a hot temperament. Earth has seven letters, *i.e.* *d*, *h*, *l*, *'ain*, *r*, *khah* or *k*,[1] and *gh* or *ghain*, which are of a dry temperament. Air has seven letters, *i.e.* *b*, *v*, *y*, *t*, *s*, *n*, and *dz*, all of a cold temperament. Water also has seven letters, *i.e.* *j*, *z*, *s*, *k*, *kāf*, *t*, and *th*, all of moist temperaments. The letters of the element water are considered as being the principal ones, and all the others as their branches; for God says, in the *Qurān*, "All things have been made by us from water".

These are called the *'Anāsir-i-arb'ā*, or the four elements of Nature, and are much considered in many of the modern sciences, such even as medicine and chemistry, among not only the Darvish Orders, but even among the more educated classes of Mussulmans generally.

[1] Or *kh*?

CHAPTER XV

UBICINI'S "LETTERS ON TURKEY"[1]—THE HINDI, OR THE WANDERING DARVISHES OF INDIA

ONE of the most interesting and correct writers on the East, Mr. M. A. Ubicini, devotes a chapter in his book entitled *Letters on Turkey*, to the subject of the Darvishes. I should commit an act of injustice did I not mention the valuable statements it contains. This author says :—

" If the *'Ulmā* [of Turkey] in its actual condition represent on the one side the secular clergy, the Orders of the Darvishes may also be assimilated, on the other, to the regular clergy of our own ecclesiastical society. Spread, from the Atlantic to the Ganges, over a vast space, under the name of Darvishes, Santons, Sūfīs, and *faqīrs*, they are the religious members of Islamism, in the same manner as the *'ulmā* are its theologians, and form, with these latter—although they be irreconcilable enemies to each other—the opposing force in Turkey.

" It is necessary, however, not to carry this assimilation too far. The Darvishes are individuals who voluntarily deprive themselves of their worldly goods for the purpose of devoting them to the benefit of the poor. The word *Darvīsh*, according to the Persian etymology, signifies a beggar (*dar* signifies door, and *vīsh* spread, or extended, meaning, in fact, the poor, who, having no asylum, stretch themselves at night upon the sills of doors to sleep), thus denoting the poverty of the profession, and also one who reduces himself to mendicity for the purpose of aiding others.

" The Khalīfa Alī was the first among Mussulmans who gave the example of this voluntary renunciation of worldly store, not,

[1] Translated from the French by Lady Easthope. London : Murray, 1856.

as might be supposed, as an act of penitence, but to accomplish literally the maxim of the *Qurān*, which says, 'The best of men is he who is useful to mankind'. His example led a large number of Mussulmans in the same path, who formed an association, of which he became the chief. These were called the *Safā-sāhibī*, from the Arabic adjective *safī*, 'pure', to express the poverty of their lives and conformity to the moral law of the *Qurān*. Little by little, however, the Darvishes departed from their original design; attracted by the charms of contemplative life and the example of the solitary individuals of India and Greece to the practice of acts of benevolence, they substituted the ravings of ecstasism, and began to withdraw from the rest of society. Soon afterwards they formed communities, which adopted practices, some of an austere, and some of a fantastical character; and it was then that, under the double influence of rules and mysticism, there was developed amongst the Darvishes the character which assimilates them to our religious Orders.

"Two things must be distinguished among the Darvishes—doctrine and institution. The first is nothing else than the Sūfīism which existed in the East long previous to the coming of Muhammad. Perhaps, if we wish to trace it to its origin, we must go back even to the most remote theocracies of Egypt and India, through the secret schools of the Pythagoreans, and the Neo-Platonism of Alexandria. It is easy to convince oneself, if attention be paid, that under the confusion of fantastical names, times, and often of doctrines, the Greek trace does not cease to be visible in the Arabian philosophy alongside of an Indian impression. It is thus that we see, more than a century before Muhammad, the two great sects which divide it: the *meschaïouns*[1]

[1] Meschaïouns, *mushayī*, 'one who follows and overtakes', 'who conforms to, or agrees with', 'an adherent', from the same root as Shī'a. The resemblance to the Peripatetics is not very obvious. Some points of contact may, however, be traced.

As stated on the next page, the *mushayī* continued in the *mutakallim*, a term which may be partially translated 'disputants' (Macdonald, *Muslim Theology*, p. 147). But the doctrine of Ḥusain Manṣūr was a *mazhab kalamī*; he was regarded as one of the Mutakallimun, and a good account of his teaching will be found in L. Massignon's *Kitāb al-Ṭawāsīn* and in his *La Passion d' al-Hosayn-ibn-Mansour al-Hallaj*.

The mutakallimūn cannot, however, be regarded as distinct from the Ṣūfīs, or as a school which taught any one definite doctrine (*Der Islam*, vi. p. 37 ff.).

(the walkers), and the *ischrachaïouns*[1] (contemplatives), reminding us, by the similarity of the names, of a certain point, and by the conformity of doctrines of the two great philosophical schools of Greece, represented by their illustrious chiefs (*muallim awwal*),[2] of the grand master Aristotle, and Aflatūn īlāhī (' the divine Plato ') ; nor is it less true, notwithstanding this title of Divine, which has been religiously preserved in the ὁ θεῖος Πλάτων of the Greeks, that Plato, seated amidst his disciples, and rising to the highest practical truths of morality and religion, was but a Plato doubled up by Diogenes, bent up in a tub, and causing virtue to consist in absolute inaction and the annihilation of all the faculties. The almost simultaneous apparition of the *Qurān*, and the writings of the ancient philosophers, which as yet were only known through tradition, marks a new era in the history of Arabian philosophy. The religious element joined the rational element which had, until then, reigned without partition ; and, under the combined influence of these causes, the two primitive sects, becoming each transformed in the sense of its doctrine—the *meschaïouns* continued in the *mutakallim*, or metaphysicians, and the *ischrachaïouns* in the Sūfīs. What is the correct origin of the name of Sūfīs, on which so many dissertations have been written? Does it come, as well as the word given to the association of which Alī declared himself to be the head, from the Arabic adjective *safī*, or from *sāfā*, one of the stations around the Kaaba, or from *sūf* (wool, or that which is made from wool), in allusion to the woollen garment adopted by this new sect, either through humility, or so as to distinguish it from the other rival sects? Or rather must it be attributed, more naturally, to a corruption of the Greek word σοφοί? This question of etymology merits less our attention than the examination of Sūfīism itself."

The beginning of Sūfīism is nothing else than pantheism, as shown in the exclamation of Maulānā Jalāl-ud-dīn, addressed to his spiritual master, " O my master, you have completed my doctrine by teaching me that you are God, and that all things are

[1] Ischrachaïouns ; under this formidable term is concealed a simple enough word, meaning in effect *illuminati*, from the *ḥikmat-ul-ishrāq*, a kind of neo-Platonic mysticism. *Mushriqīa* is the philosophy of illumination on which Avicennes wrote his *al-Ḥikma al-Mushriqīa*. It is noteworthy that the alchemists also called their science *ḥikma* (*E.I.* ii. p. 305).

[2] *Muallim eyel* in original.

God". Whilst the philosophers of India and Greece limited themselves to teaching, under a diversity of myths and systems, the immortality of the soul, the emancipation of Divine intelligence, its fall, its terrestrial condition, and reunion to its source, the Sūfīs had reached only to the sight, in material forms, of the emanations of the Divine essence, resembling, they say, the rays of the sun, which are continuously darted forth and re-absorbed; applying thus to the entire creation that which Seneca had said in magnificent terms regarding the soul, in which a particle of the Divinity,—"*Quemadmodum radii solis contingunt quidem terram, sed ibi sunt unde mittuntur: sic animus magnus et sacer . . . conversatur quidem nobiscum, sed haeret origini suae*".—Sen. *Epist.* xl. Comparisons of this nature abound in the books of the 'Spirituality of the Sūfīs'. I will cite a few of those which are the most familiar.

"You say 'the sea and waves', but in that remark you do not believe that you signify distinct objects, for the sea when it heaves produces waves, and the waves when they settle down again become sea; in the same manner men are the waves of God, and after death return to His bosom. Or, you trace with ink upon paper the letters of the alphabet, *a*, *b*, *c*; but these letters are not distinct from the ink which enabled you to write them: in the same manner the creation is the alphabet of God, and is lost in Him."

The Shaikh Shublī, contemporaneous with Murād II., whose disciple Ahmad-ud-dīn was condemned by a sentence of the *ulmā* to be skinned alive, publicly taught that the human soul absorbed in God, mixed with Him, just as rain does with the water of the sea.

Spinoza undertook at a later period to show in proper terms the identity of God with matter. From that comes the necessity of a perpetual adoration of the Creator in His works. The Sūfīs inculcate the doctrine, 'Adore God in His creatures'. It is said in a verse of the *Qurān* which I have already cited: "It is not given to man that God should speak to him; if He does so it is by inspiration, or through a veil". Thus all the efforts of man should tend to raise up the veil by the force of divine love and the annihilation of the individuality which separates him from the Divine essence; and this expression, 'raise up the veil', has remained in the language of the East as expressive of the greatest intimacy. Must one say, however, that the *Sūfīs*, by leaning upon the passage of the *Qurān*, and upon another where it is said that " God made the creation as an emanation, and will afterwards cause it to re-enter Himself " (*Qurān*, v. 4), pretend to the consecration of this dogma ? On the contrary, the dogma had perished in their hands. They did not deny the divine mission of the Prophet, but they reduced his precepts to an allegorical sense, the key of which alone could give the interpretation. In our times even the Wahhābites, whom Sultān Mahmūd could not wholly destroy, and who are still spread over the Persian Gulf, admit no other authority than that of the *Qurān* as interpreted by human individual reason, and without any submission to the prophets or the Imāms.

Moreover, the Sūfīs regained in the beginning all that such a doctrine could possess of the dangerous by teaching the strictest morality. They incessantly preached union, sobriety, universal benevolence, and offered in themselves an example. They said that evil only came into the world through ignorance, and is the cause of error and disunion among men. Some of them cited on this subject the following tale: " Four travellers—a Turk, an Arab, a Persian, and a Greek—having met together, decided to take their meal in common, and as each one had but ten *pāras*, they consulted together as to what should be purchased with the money. The first said *uzum*, the second *ineb*, the third decided in favour of *inghur*, and the fourth insisted upon *stafilion*.[1] On this a dispute arose between them, and they were about to come to blows, when a peasant passing by happened to know all four of their tongues, and brought them a basket of grapes. They now found out, greatly to their astonishment, that each one had what he desired."

" I do not know," adds M. Ubicini, " for my part any more abominable doctrine than this deceptive idealism which tends to substitute the creation for the Creator, and arrives by an irresistible slope at the destruction of all faith and all morality ; all the more dangerous as it veils its corruption under the most

[1] A. *'uzum*, lit. ' husks of grapes '. A. *'inab*, a grape. P. *angūr*, grape. Gr. *σταφύλι*, grape.

There may be a subtle hit at the Turk in the reply attributed to him. The word *'uzum* is pure Arabic, not Turki, and does *not* mean grape (see Salmoné, *Arab. Dict.*, p. 560).

amiable exterior, and so it misleads, unknown to themselves, the best minds: '*eo perniciosior, quod abundans dulcibus vitiis*', as Quintilian said of the diction of Seneca. The materialism in which it finally terminates, with the unheard-of niceties of sensuality, is a hundred times less to be feared, because it at once revolts the secret instincts of the human conscience, whilst mystical reveries so full of seductions are a snare laid for the inclinations of the most unsuspecting and the most noble of our nature. It is this point which gives so much authority to the words of Bossuet, combating, in the name of the immutability of dogma and the integrity of morality, the quietism of Fénelon. These fermentations of dissolution, which Sūfīism had thrown into the bosom of Mussulman society, did not at once manifest themselves, tempered, moreover, as I have just said, by the ardent, though sincere, enthusiasm, and the austerity of morals of its first adepts. But they gradually gained ground, and little by little entered the veins of the social body. In fact this spirit of holy abstraction upon which Sūfīism is based; this ardent mysticism so marvellously adapted to the imaginations, at the same time wildly unsteady and sensual, of Orientals, and of which the Bible offers more than one trace, could not fail to gain for him many proselytes. Egypt, once the cradle of monastic life, after the folly of the desert had succeeded, among the first Christians, to the folly of the cross, was again filled with Thebaides. With the only substitution of the name of Allāh for that of Jesus, it was the same life, or rather the same absence of life, '*Vitae mori ac vivere morti*'—the same austerities, the same exaggerations. Mount Olympus, on the Asiatic coast, nearly opposite Mount Athos, where there were erected innumerable Greek monasteries, held thousands of these solitarians, lost in the contemplation of themselves and of nature, and whose memory is still venerated as that of holy persons. From thence they passed over into Arabia, to Persia, as far as the extremity of India, wherever there was Muhammadan power. Always this enthusiasm, like that of the earlier times of Christianity, spread towards the desert, fleeing from the world in contempt of temporal things; it neither strove to reverse authority nor to invade established powers. Sūfīism did not take this character until when, from being a doctrine, it became an institution."

It was in the second century of the Hijra, near 129, that a

Sūfī reputed for his virtue and knowledge, Shaikh 'Ilwān, founded the first religious Order, to which he gave his name. This innovation met with great opposition on the part of the legislators and the truly orthodox of Islāmism, who recalled the formal declaration of Muhammad, 'No monkery in Islām'. Though this sentence, because in some sort proverbial, was received at the same time as an article of faith by all Mussulmans, the inclination of the Arabs for a solitary and contemplative life carried it against orthodoxy. Other Orders were soon founded in imitation of the first. The number grew rapidly from the second to the seventh century, and also in subsequent epochs. Hammer counts up thirty-six, which he enumerates according to D'Ohsson. Of this number twelve are subsequent to the Ottoman monarchy, the eighteen others arose from the commencement of the 14th to the middle of the 18th century.

Sūfīism modifies itself, like all systems, by passing from theory to action. There were, as has been always practised in the divers schools of Theosophists and Thaumaturgists, two doctrines—the one public, which precedes the initiation; and the other secret, for the adepts only. A strict observance of religion and of all the social virtues was required of the candidate for his initiation. Later, when by a long suite of proofs and mortifications, above all by the absolute annihilation of his individuality, he was supposed to have arrived at the desired degree in which to contemplate the truth face to face, and the veil, until then spread over his vision, suddenly fell, they taught him that the Prophet in his book had only presented, under the veil of allegory, maxims and political precepts; that the *Qurān* without the interpretation was only an assembly of words void of sense; that once the habit of mental devotion contracted, he could reduce his worship to a purely spiritual one, and abandon all forms and external ceremonies.

"When one is out of the Ka'ba (the Ka'ba in the allegorical language of the Darvishes is 'Divine Love'), it is good to direct our regards towards it; but for him who is in the Ka'ba, it imports little to what direction he turns." This is the language of Jalāl-ud-Dīn in his *Masnavī Sharīf*. The whole passage is too remarkable not to be cited here entire.

"Moses once met with a shepherd, who, in the fervour of his soul, addressing God, exclaimed, 'O my Master! my Lord! where art Thou, that I may become Thy servant,—that I sew

Thy shoes,—that I comb Thy hair,—that I wash Thy robes,—that I serve up to Thee the milk of my goats,—to Thee whom I revere? Where art Thou, that I may kiss Thy beautiful hand,—that I rub Thy beautiful feet,—that I sweep out Thy chamber before Thou retirest to rest?' Thus spoke the simple shepherd. Moses, warmed by zeal for the religion which he had been sent to proclaim, reproached this man for blasphemy, telling him that God has no body, that He has no need of clothing, of nourishment, or of a chamber, and ended by declaring that he was an infidel. The shepherd, whose intelligence could not rise to the comprehension of a Being who had not, like himself, a body subject to all the same wants, was stunned by the reproaches of the envoy of God, gave himself up to despair, and renounced all adoration. God addressed Moses, and said, 'Thou hast driven My servant away from Me; I had sent thee to draw others near to Me, and not to divide them. Each being has received a mode of existence, and a different means of expressing himself. What thou findest blameable, is praiseworthy in another. What thou callest poison, is honey in his sight. Purity, impurity, slowness, precipitation,—all these distinctions are beneath Me. The Indian language alone is good for the Indian, the Zend for the Zend. Their expressions cannot stain Me; they, on the contrary, are purified by the sincerity of the homage which they offer to Me. Words are nothing to Me; I regard the heart, and if it is humble, what do I care if the tongue tells the contrary? The heart is the substance of love—words are only accidents. My servant embraces the heart of My love, and cares nothing for thought, nor for expressions. The compass only serves to direct the prayers of those who are outside of the Ka'ba, whilst within it no one knows the use of it.'"

M. Ubicini, in giving this beautiful extract of the *Masnavī Sharīf* of the founder of the Maulavī Order of Darvishes, which shows in a very clear manner the purity of its Spiritualism, adds the following note: "Saint Theresa, in her ecstatic rapture, cries out in the same manner: 'O my Friend! my Lord! my well-beloved! O life of my life!' When she beholds Jesus Christ during her devotional exercises, that which strikes her above all others is the incomparable beauty of His hand, the whiteness of His feet, the penetrating softness of His voice, of His look, etc. The language of the mystical of all religions is the same."

I may here add another somewhat similar quotation from the writings of Jalāl-ud-Dīn ur-Rūmī.

"During the reign of an Eastern sovereign, he remarked that the learned and pious men of his times differed widely in their estimate and comprehension of the Deity, each ascribing to Him characteristics differing the one from the other. So that this prince had an elephant brought in secret to his capital, and encircled in a dark chamber; then, inviting these learned men, he told them that he was in possession of an animal which none of them had ever seen. Descending with them to the dark abode of the elephant, he requested them to accompany him. On entering it, he said the animal was before them, and asked them if they could see it. Being answered in the negative, he begged them to approach and feel it, which they did, each touching it in a different part. After returning to the light, he asked them if they believed the animal really existed, and what it was like. One declared it was a huge column; another, that it was a rough hide; a third, that it was of ivory; a fourth, that it was huge flaps of some coarse substance, etc.; but not one could correctly state what the animal was. Now, returning to the same chamber, to which the light of heaven fully penetrated, these learned men beheld, for the first time, the object of their curiosity, and learned that, whilst each one was correct in what he had said, all differed widely from the truth.

"Such, now, said the prince, is God; men judge of Him according to their sensual capacities, differing from each other, but all equally true, when they feel and search for the truth, without doubting of His existence."

Similar doctrines came to light in the fourteenth century, in Christendom, among the Béguins, condemned by the Council of Vienne, in Dauphiné, and which taught, among other anti-social principles, that the practice and the observance of the law is only for the imperfect, and that the perfect are exempt from it. Like these latter, the Darvishes tend to the overthrow of all authority, political or religious. "Men who conduct themselves according to the laws of society form one class,—those who consume the love of God form another. The lovers of God are the people of no other than God."

"The last fragment of the dogma had thus departed, at the same time that the foundation of all morality was destroyed. One only principle remained, and marked the ruin of religious enthusiasm and sacerdotal imposture. This was submission to their inspired institutor (the *pīr*), which took the place amongst the Darvishes of the individual interpretation, which is the basis of Sūfīism. I have already cited the narration of the Founder of the Maulavīs, regarded by all the Darvishes, indistinctively, as one of the greatest masters of the spiritual life. 'O my master, you have completed my doctrine by teaching me that you are God, and that all is God.' Already nearly four centuries previous, Bāyazīd of Busṭām, the founder of the Bustāmīs, had identified himself with the Divinity, when he cried out, in the presence of his disciples, alluding to his own person, 'Glory to me! I am above all things!'—a formula which, in the language of Orientals, is applied exclusively to God. The adoration of the Master replaces also for the Darvishes the worship of the Divinity; the end of the being no longer dwelt in the intimate union of the soul with the Creator, but in an absolute conformity to the thoughts of the Shaikh. 'Whatever you may do, whatever you may think, have always your Shaikh present in your mind.' Such is the first obligation, the only one, so to speak, imposed on the Darvish, and expressed by this species of mental prayer, called *rabūta*,[1] to which he is not less exact in the performance than the ordinary Mussulman is to his *namāz*."

"The consequences of such a doctrine did not fail to be soon felt, and produced these sectarians, half religious, half political, who call themselves, according to the places, the *reds*, the *whites*, the *masked* (*burqā'ī*[2]), the *intimates* (*bātinī*), the *allegorists*, or *interpreters* (*muta-awwil*), *Karmathites*, *Ismailites*, etc., and of which traces in history, from the second to the seventh century of the Hijra, are marked with blood and ruins. The orthodox designate them by the generic name of Mulhād[3] (rascals), or of

[1] Rabūṭa, cf. Marabout: like it the word appears to be post-classical, but *rabīṭ*, 'monk', and *ribāṭ*, 'hospice', are recognised Arabic words.

[2] Burqā'ī, 'veiled', a term borne by a sect in Transoxiana where the Veiled Prophet of Khurāsān first spread his doctrines. That prophet was called al-Burqā'ī (or al-Muqanna' because he wore a golden mask: von Hammer, *Hist. of the Assassins*, Eng. trans., London 1835, p. 26). For a sect called the Burqa-pōsh, see Rose, *Glossary of Punjab Tribes and Castes*, i. pp. 583-84.

[3] Mulhād, from s. *mulḥid*, 'heretic': *mulāḥidah* is the most usual plural form. *Mutāawwil*, cf. *tāwīl*, 'interpretation'.

Sindīq [1] (strong minds). The most celebrated were the Ismailites, or assassins (derived from Hashāshīn, eaters of the *hashīsh*), who originated, as is well known, in Persia ; the remains of whom are still to be seen in the mountains above Tripoli (of Syria) and of Tortosia. In fact, Persia was the classic land of Darvishism, both from the decided inclination to mysticism, which always distinguished its inhabitants, and from the effect of the Shī'ite dogma, where the belief in the hidden Imām (the Mahdī), and who is still expected, like the Messiah among the Jews, favours the ambition of the impostures of the sectarians. Add to this the *éclat* of the names of Sa'di and Hāfiz, and the great number of the celebrated poets of Persia, who were all either Darvishes or affiliated to their Orders, and whose works are placed in the highest rank of the books on Spirituality. They represented, moreover, in their writings, rather the philosophical than the political side of the doctrine. These are dreamers, inspired songsters, moralists sometimes of a singular character ; they are neither ambitious sectarians nor repining hypocrites. But one must read their *ghazls* (odes), each line of which is filled with ecstatic ravings, to comprehend how far mysticism may be carried in poetry, to surpass by the sensuality of expression and the crudity of images the material paintings of a most voluptuous nature. Nothing of this kind, not even the invocation to Venus by Lucretius, equals the passage of the *Masnavī*, where the poet shows us, in the soft Persian idiom, all Nature filled with that Divine love by which the humble plant even is excited to seek after the sublime object of its desires. The adoration of the creature, under that of God ; the terrestrial love taught as the bridge over which all must pass who seek for the beatitude of divine love ; the apotheosis of matter under the glorification of the mind : such are the familiar reveries of the Persian poets. These are Sūfīs rather than Darvishes. At the same time, they show themselves careful, for the most part, to preserve the purity and sincerity of the doctrine. The eighth chapter of the *Gulistān* of Sa'di is full of instruction for Darvishes, and of reprimands

[1] Zandīq, in original Sindeeq, 'free-thinker': *zaddīq* is an Aramaic word meaning 'righteous', and equivalent to the Ar. *ṣiddīq*, which, however, means 'veracious'. In Persian *zaddīq* took the form *zandīq*. Originally applied to the Manichaeans, who had an elect class called *zaddīq*, it is used occasionally of the Buddhists (Nicholson, *A Literary Hist. of the Arabs*, p. 375).

for those who make of spiritual life an act of hypocrisy. These austerities and mortifications—this dirty and neglected exterior—this affected contempt of all ordinary decency, does not inspire him with any confidence. 'Have', he says, 'the virtues of a true Darvish, and afterwards, in place of a cap of wool, take, if you choose, the felt of a Tartar,' for the Turks have a proverb which says, *Darvishlik khirqā dan billi dagil dir*, *i.e.* 'The Darvish is not known by the mantle which he wears' ".[1]

He next seeks to describe and define the ecstasy which he regards, in the same manner as all of the Sūfīs, as the end of the being, and the last effort of our nature. " But how render, with the language of man, that which is beyond human powers? The words which we use cannot express other than what is common to our material and gross ideas. He who enjoys ecstasy and returns again to his ordinary state, does not retain any idea of it, because he has again become man, whilst previously Divine love had consumed in him all that belonged to human nature. The poet comments thus upon his idea with the aid of an allegory. 'A Darvish, interrogated with derision by one of his brethren, as to what marvellous gift he brought back with him from the garden of delights out of which he had come, replied : " I intended, on arriving at this rose-bush (the sight of God), to fill the skirt of my robe with roses, so as to offer them as a present to my brethren ; but when I was there, the odour of the rose-bush so intoxicated my senses that the border of my robe escaped from my hands." The tongue of that man is dulled who has known God.'

" Such was the favour which the Darvishes enjoyed in Persia, that one of them, Shāh Ismā'īl Safawī, who pretended to be descended from Mūsā, the seventh revealed Imām, reached the throne in the 10th century of the Hijra (A.D. 1501), and founded the dynasty of princes, known in Europe under the name of the Sophees. The Ottoman Sultāns, and the Khalīfs their predecessors, had only waited until then to act against the Darvish system ; and, justly alarmed at its progress, took it upon themselves to do all in their power to suppress it. The *'ulmās*, in turn, also excited, under the plea of defending Mussulman orthodoxy, but in reality to maintain its spiritual supremacy, became their

[1] Cf. the saying of Jalāl-ud-Dīn Rūmī quoted by Nicholson, *A Literary Hist. of the Arabs*, p. 298. *Mard-i-Khudā shāh buvad zer-i-dalq*, " a man of God is a King 'neath darvish cloak ".

auxiliaries in a struggle wherein the altar and the throne, the power of the sovereign and that of the mosque, were equally in danger. It even happened that the people, at certain moments, adopted the same, as the result of the deep antipathy which the Sunnīs entertained against the Shī'as. This triple intervention of political power, of the 'Ulmās, and of popular instinct, presents the matter under three different aspects.

" Political power acted directly, by brute force,—as, for example, on the occasion of the attempt made, in 1656, under the Grand Vazirat of Muhammad Kuprulī, to destroy entirely the Maulavī Darvishes, the Khalwatīs, Jalwatīs, and the Shamsīs.[1] But in general these attempts proved unsuccessful, and only served to show more and more the impotency of the Government and the growing credit of the religious Orders. One remarks that the first is afraid ; its acts of violence, even, accuse its pusillanimity, or at least embarrass its situation ; it fears revolts, defections ; it fears, above all, the Janissaries, who were united by a kind of fraternity, to the Darvishes,—especially to the Bektāshīs. This fraternity dated back even to the origin of this militia. When the second Sultān of the Ottomans, Orkhān, created, in 1328, the Yenicharīs (new troops)—the name which Europeans have changed into ' Janissaries '—he wished, conformably with the same political principles which led the Khalīfs to have their ordinances sanctioned by the *fatwā* of the *muftī*, to impress a religious seal upon this military institution. Hājī Bektāsh, a venerable Shaikh, and founder of the Bektāsh Darvishes, blessed the troops by putting on the heads of the principal officers the sleeve of his robe, which has since then figured in the head-dress of the Janissaries, as a piece of felt which hung down behind their cap; and since then, also, an indestructible solid feeling was established between the Darvishes and the Janissaries, who considered themselves as possessing a common origin ; and that, as a double expression of the same idea, they were, at the same time, both a religious and a military body.

" The intervention of the *'ulmās* was more pacific in its form, yet more hostile, more constant, and more systematic. There existed, in point of fact, not only a rivalry of interests, but also one of doctrines. Ambition, pride, fanaticism, *amour propre*,—

[1] The Shamsī or Shamālī are a sub-sect of the Nusairī, but the followers of Shams-ud-Dīn Siwāsī must be meant.

all the human passions were brought into play. It was both a battle and a dispute. The *'ulmās* being unable to attack the basis of the Darvishes, so long as it continued to remain secret, fought, in the name of the *Qurān* and the *sunna*, the principles which served as a basis to the Institution,—such as abstinence, vows, music and dances used in the *takias*, the gift of miracles and communication directly with God, claimed by the Shaikhs, as contrary to the letter and spirit of Islamism. They recalled the example of the first disciples of the Prophet, of Othmān, 'Alī, and 'Abd-ur-Rahmān,[1] who was the first to vow not to approach his wife Asmah, from one sunrise to another; the second, not to sleep until morning; the third, not to take any food for twenty-four hours; and the Prophet reprimanded them for it with a *hadīs*, since become celebrated. Soon after this, as it happens, the Darvishes abating in the prudence and severity which form a rule of their Orders, as their influence increased, let out the last word of their doctrine. This last word, the dominant idea of the Institution, was nothing less, one may say, than an attempt at a Christian priesthood and a divine church, clearly designated by the Living God, who figures among the seven attributes of the Darvish symbol, viz.

1. There is no God, except God.
2. The Omnipotent God.
3. The Eternal God.
4. The Judging God.
5. The Living God (upon Earth).
6. The Existing God (in Heaven).
7. The All Omnipotent God;—

attributes figured in the seven firmaments, and the seven principal colours, *i.e.* white, black, red, yellow, blue, deep green, and light green. At the same time, it became known that it terminated with certain prayers anathematising the Ummayad Khalīfs, and glorifying 'Alī. Then their adversaries could knowingly accuse them, not only of wishing to introduce a new dogma, but also of mixing up impious dogmas and abominable practices; to give themselves up to orgies of every kind, in the *takias*; to blaspheme the *Qurān*; to deny even the existence of God; to preach disobedience to all established temporal powers, and to trample upon

[1] 'Abd-ur-Rahmān bin 'Auf, one of the Hawārī or apostles (*E.I.* ii. p. 293). He was one of the six chief companions (Sale's *Al Koran*, i. p. 59).

all divine and human laws. The Middle Age has put upon record similar accusations, which public opinion proclaimed against the Templars before their condemnation.

" Popular opposition held, as I have said, to the puritanism of Sunnite orthodoxy, and to the horror which zealous Mussulmans have professed at all times against the Shī'ites, whose doctrines they willingly confounded with those of the Darvishes ; but this was neither general nor regular ; its habitual mode of expressing it was by mockery. Turkish literature is full of tales and satires upon the Darvishes, in which they are little better treated than our monks were in the fables of the tenth and eleventh centuries. These consist in jocosity and drolleries, so to speak, in entire freedom of thought and language. One author says, in allusion to the Darvishes, 'An ill-dressed body, hands without a farthing, and an empty stomach, are the characteristics of those whom God honours with His intimate friendship'.—'If you wish to know', says another, 'some of the qualities of a good Darvish, they are the following : he must have ten of those which are peculiar to the dog, viz. always hungry, homeless, sleepless at night, no heirs after death, to bark at passers-by,' etc. Moreover, by a contrast which confirms the reconcilement which I have just pointed out, one does not see that these constant jokes at the expense of the Darvishes affect in any manner their credit with the people, and matters go on exactly in Turkey as they did in France and Italy during the Middle Ages, where the monks were never more powerful than when they were the object of public raillery.

" It is thus that the Darvishes continued to exist, notwithstanding the odium and ridicule with which it was attempted to cover them, having, at the same time, the *firmāns* of the Sultān, the *fatwās* of the *muftīs*, the jeers and curses of the public, whilst daily they beheld their authority increase, in the face even of all the vain efforts of their enemies to destroy them. Sultān Mahmūd was the first to strike them a severe blow, by the abolition of the Janissaries ; but this was only a prelude to a more precise and personal attack. Twenty-six days after, the 10th of July 1826, he took advantage of a revolt which occurred in consequence of the suppression of the Janissaries, and in which the Bektāshīs were accused of being mixed up, to finish with these fanatics. After having consulted with the *muftī* and the principal *'ulmār* the three chiefs of the congregation were publicly executed, the Order was abolished, the *takias* were reduced to ruins, the greater part of the Darvishes exiled, and those who were allowed to remain in Constantinople were made to leave off their distinctive costume. This bold step spread terror among the Darvishes. At one moment they thought that all of their Orders would be immediately dispersed, and they remained noiseless, waiting the advent of their last day, 'devoured with anguish, and their backs leaning against the wall of stupefication'.

"Unfortunately Sultān Mahmūd hesitated. 'He who had not feared', so says the historian of the massacre of the Janissaries, 'to open with the sword a road to public happiness, cutting away the thorny bushes which obstructed his way and tore his Imperial mantle,' stopped before the sole measure which could ensure success to the completion of his work. The opportunity once passed, could not be regained. The Darvishes renewed their audacity with their hopes, and silently recommenced to agitate the public. Even the Sultān came near falling a victim of the fanatic zeal of one of them. One day, in 1837, whilst he was crossing, surrounded by his guards, the bridge of Galata, a Darvish, known by the name of Shaikh Sāchlū (the Hairy Shaikh), and whom the people venerated as a saint, sprang forward in front of his horse, and cried out in a fury, 'Ghiour Pādishāh' (infidel sovereign), 'art thou not yet satisfied with abominations? Thou wilt answer to Allāh for all thy impieties; thou destroyest the institutions of thy brethren; thou revilest Islamism, and drawest the vengeance of the Prophet upon thyself, and upon us.' The Sultān, who feared the effect of such a scene upon the public, commanded one of his officers to rid the way of such a man, whom he declared was a fool. 'Fool!' screamed out the Darvish with indignation; 'me a fool? It is yourself and your unworthy councillors who have lost your senses. To the rescue, Mussulmans! The spirit of God which anoints me, and which I obey, compels me to declare the truth, and promises me a recompense given to the saints.' He was arrested and put to death, and the next day news spread over the whole city that a brilliant light had been visible during the whole night, over the tomb of the martyr.*

* It is, however, well known that Sultān Mahmūd was an affiliated member of the Maulavī Takia of Pera, and frequently visited it. He also

"It is by the pretended miracles which are daily renewed under the eyes of the authority that the Darvishes keep alive in the public mind their ancient superstitions and the idea of their supernatural powers. An Ottoman filling an eminent position in the State once remarked to me, 'Our ministers labour in vain for that civilisation which will never enter Turkey so long as the turbehs (holy tombs) are in existence'. We were at the time at Skutari, where we had assisted at a representation of the 'Howling Darvishes'. We had observed various individuals brought into the *takia* from without, sick and infirm, women, aged persons, and even children as young as two or three days, who were laid on their backs before the Shaikh for him to cure them, not by the imposition of his hands, but of his feet. When he had finished and left the inside of the *takia*, not only did the crowd prostrate themselves before him and kiss his robes, as they would have done to a saint, but the guards actually presented arms and beat their drums in honour of him. 'See,' said my companion, 'the government which hates the Darvishes, and only desires to get rid of them, not only tolerates them and keeps well with them, but even aids them to be powerful by causing military honours to be shown them. You can scarcely imagine, after what you have seen, the impudence of these rascals. Lately, a Darvish of Bukhāra (you must know that these surpass all others in fanaticism) presented himself before Rashīd Pāsha, and there publicly, in the path itself, heaped upon him abuse and threats, calling him a dog, an infidel and disbeliever, and invoking upon his head the lightning of heaven and the dagger of every true Mussulman. The *wazīr*, so as to remove all pretext for a commotion, which began to show itself, had to content himself with putting him out of his room by a *khwās*; and that, too, politely, as he would have done to any poor fellow who had lost his senses. You are astonished? There is scarcely a month or a week that some of the ministers have to submit to the remonstrances of any Darvish who is pleased to push himself forward at his audiences for the purpose of abusing and threatening him. It is the effect of this fanaticism, nourished by the Darvishes, and this freedom

---

frequently visited a Naqshbandī *takia* at Fondukli, where he witnessed the ecstatic swoon of the Shaikh. The latter on one occasion revived, much to his amusement, on learning that the Sultān was about to leave, so as to secure a royal present.

of language, which the people use in the presence of public authority, that creates the explosions during the month of Rāmazān. Here this is nothing, where the Government has its eyes upon them ; but in certain provinces, at Baghdād, in Arabia, in Egypt, their daring and cynicism is carried beyond all limits. Will you believe that I saw at Cairo, in full daylight, one of these miserable creatures who run about the streets half-naked, stop a woman in the street and glut his brutality upon her, in the presence even of passers-by, who turned their faces away, some out of respect, others from disgust, without one calling upon the aid of the police. I do not know which carries the palm among these bandits, hypocrisy or fanaticism, two things which seem, however, to exclude each other. May God preserve you from ever meeting one of them in the public road, for these vagabond Darvishes who, under the name of *sayyāhs* (travellers) infest most of the routes, where they live by begging and robbery. Many of the most dangerous of them are strangers ; they travel by the order of their superiors to collect money, or have been dismissed from their convents for grave causes : these are Qalandars whose statutes do not allow them to have any fixed abodes—in fact, they are no better than unknown individuals or criminals, who, under the cover of a Darvish cloak, escape punishments richly merited by their actions.'

" My interlocutor added many things on the difficulties of the position of the case in general. I was struck with the consideration which he finally expressed : ' What we lose is the want of faith in our work ; some are discouraged into inertia, others hasten to arrive at a goal which has no stability. You say that God is patient because He is eternal ; but we are impatient because we fear that we have but a few hours to live, and we feel the future fly away from us.'

" But let us return to the subject of the Darvishes by attempting to resume the idea of this latter and the preceding one. The two bodies of which religious society in Turkey is composed—the *'ulamā* and the Darvishes—are the enemies of all reform. The danger, however, is not equal on both sides, neither for the government nor for society. The *'ulamā* speak in the name of the law, of which they pretend to be guardian and the depository; they say, ' Touch nothing which has been established, borrow nothing from the infidels, because the law forbids it '. The Shaikh says, 'There is no law', or rather, 'The law is I; all is good that I commend, all is evil that I forbid. You must kill your mother, your sovereign, if I bid it, for my sentence is the sentence of God.' One thus sees the difference between the two doctrines. On the one hand, the Government may hope to have the *'ulamā* on its side; many of them are not wanting either in acquired information or in natural light. The example of the Shaikh-ul-Islām and the principal chiefs of the magistracy in Turkey, who form a part of the Government, may do much with them. Old prejudices commence to lose ground, especially among the *'ulamās* of Constantinople in contact with Europeans. One of them—a most wonderful thing—has actually allowed himself to be sent to Paris by the Dīwān, which desired to show him that civilisation which he and his brethren reject without possessing any knowledge of it. This new attempt on the part of Rashīd Pasha will do more, if it succeeds, for the emancipation of Turkey than has been as yet done by the mission to Paris and London of many young Turks to study there; and who, having left there without any direction or fixed rule of action, have badly answered in general to the hopes placed upon them. The *'ulamās* may be thus brought to comprehend that, even by sacrificing their privileges, there still remains to them a fair place in the State, and that their interests are actually the same as its own. But this cannot be said of the Darvishes; between them and it there is a mortal conflict."

As it has been my object throughout the present little work to enable the curious and patient reader to judge of the Darvishes both by what they say of themselves and by what others say regarding them, I would not terminate my extracts without placing before their eyes the words of that eminent Orientalist, Sir William Jones—than whom, perhaps, no greater has ever lived—on the subject of the leading principles of the Darvishes, *alias* Sūfīism. In his lecture "On the Philosophy of the Asiaticks" this wonderful Eastern linguist says:

"From all the properties of man and of nature, from all the various branches of science, from all the deductions of human reason, the general corollary admitted by Hindus, Arabs, and Tartars, by Persians, and by Chinese, is the supremacy of an all-creating and all-preserving Spirit, infinitely wise, good, and powerful, but infinitely removed from the comprehension of his most exalted creatures ; nor are there in any language (the ancient Hebrew always excepted) more pious and sublime addresses to the Being of beings, more splendid enumerations of His attributes, or more beautiful descriptions of His visible works than in Arabic, Persian, and Sanscrit, especially in the *Qurān*, the introductions to the poems of Sa'di, Nizāmi, and Firdausi ; the four *Vedas*, and many parts of the numerous *Purānas* ; but supplication and praise would not satisfy the boundless imagination of the Vedānta and Sūfī theologists, who, blending uncertain metaphysics with undoubted principles of religion, have presumed to reason confidently on the very nature and essence of the Divine Spirit, and asserted in a very remote age—what multitudes of Hindus and Mussulmans assert at this hour—that all spirit is homogeneous, that the Spirit of God is in *kind* the same with that of man, though differing from it infinitely in *degree*, and that as material substance is mere illusion, there exists in this universe only one generic spiritual substance the sole primary cause, efficient, substantial, and formal of all secondary causes and of all appearances whatever, but endowed in its highest degree with a sublime providential wisdom, and proceeding by ways incomprehensible to the spirits which emanate from it ; an opinion which Gautama never taught, and which we have no authority to believe ; but which, as it is grounded on the doctrine of an immaterial Creator supremely wise, and a constant Preserver supremely benevolent, differs as widely from the pantheism of Spinoza and Toland as the affirmation of a proposition differs from the negative of it; though the last-named professor of that insane philosophy had the baseness to conceal his meaning under the very words of St. Paul, which are cited for a purpose totally different by Newton, and has even used a phrase which occurs, indeed, in the *Veda*, but in a sense diametrically opposite to that which he would have given it. The passage to which I allude is in a speech of Varuna to his son, where he says, ' That Spirit from which these created beings proceed, through which having proceeded from it they live ; towards which they tend and in which they are ultimately absorbed ; *that* Spirit study to know ; *that* Spirit is the Great One '."

In the " Sixth Discourse on the Persians " he says :

" I will only detain you with a few remarks on that metaphysical theology which has been professed immemorially by a numerous sect of Persians and Hindus, was carried in part into Greece, and prevails even now among the learned Mussulmans, who sometimes avow it without reserve. The modern philosophers of this persuasion are called *Sūfīs,* either from the Greek word for a *sage,* or from the *woollen* mantle which they used to wear in some provinces of Persia ; their fundamental tenets are, that nothing exists absolutely but God ; that the human soul is an emanation from His essence, and though divided for a time from its heavenly source, will be finally reunited with it ; that the highest possible happiness will arise from its reunion, and that the chief good of mankind in this transitory world consists in as perfect an *union* with the Eternal Spirit as the incumbrances of a mortal frame will allow ; that, for this purpose, they should break all connexion (or *taālluk,*[1] as they call it) with extrinsick objects, and pass through life without attachments, as a swimmer in the ocean strikes freely without the impediment of clothes ; that they should be straight and free as the cypress, whose fruit is hardly perceptible, and not sink under a load like fruit-trees attached to a trellis ; that, if mere earthly charms have power to influence the soul, the *idea* of celestial beauty must overwhelm it in ecstatick delight ; that, for want of apt words to express the divine perfections and the ardour of devotion, we must borrow such expressions as approach the nearest to our ideas, and speak of *beauty* and *love* in a transcendant and mystical sense ; that, like a *reed* torn from its native brook, like *wax* separated from its delicious honey, the soul of man bewails its disunion with melancholy *musick,* and sheds burning tears like the lighted taper, waiting passionately for the moment of its extinction, as a disengagement from earthly trammels, and the means of returning to its only beloved. Such in part (for I omit the minuter and more subtil metaphysicks of the Sūfīs which are mentioned in the *Dabīstān*) is the wild and enthusiastick religion of the modern Persian poets, especially of the sweet Hāfiz and the great Maulavi (Mevlevee); such is the system of the Vedānta philosophers and best lyrick poets of India ; and, as it was a system of the highest antiquity of both nations, it may be added to the many other proofs of an immemorial affinity between them."

" On the Philosophy of the Asiaticks," he says :—

" I have already had occasion to touch on the Indian meta-

[1] *Ta'alluq.*

physicks of natural bodies according to the most celebrated of the Asiatic schools, from which the Pythagoreans are supposed to have borrowed many of their opinions ; and as we learn from Cicero that the old sages of Europe had an idea of centripetal force and a principle of universal gravitation (which they never indeed attempted to demonstrate), so I can venture to affirm, without meaning to pluck a leaf from the never-fading laurels of our immortal Newton, that the whole of his theology and part of his philosophy may be found in the *Vedas*, and even in the works of the Sūfīs ; that *most subtil spirit* which he suspected to pervade natural bodies and lying concealed in them, to cause attraction and repulsion, the emission, reflection, and refraction of light, electricity, calefaction, sensation, and muscular motion, is described by the Hindus as a *fifth element* endowed with those very powers ; and the *Vedas* abound with allusions to a force universally attractive, which they chiefly ascribe to the sun, thence called Aditya, or the attractor, a name designed by the mythologists to mean the child of the goddess Aditi ; but the most wonderful passage in the theory of attraction occurs in the charming allegorical poem of *Shīrīn and Farhād, or the Divine Spirit and a Human Soul disinterestedly pious*, a work which from the first verse to the last is a blaze of religious and poetical fire. The whole passage appears to me so curious that I make no apology for giving you a faithful translation of it :—

" ' There is a strong propensity which dances through every atom, and attracts the minutest particle to some peculiar object ; search this universe from its base to its summit, from fire to air, from water to earth, from all below the moon to all above the celestial spheres, and thou wilt not find a corpuscle destitute of that natural attractibility ; the very point of the first thread in this apparently tangled skein is no other than such a principle of attraction, and all principles beside are void of a real basis ; from such a propensity arises every motion perceived in heavenly or in terrestrial bodies ; it is a disposition to be attracted which taught hard steel to rush from its place and rivet itself on the magnet ; it is the same disposition which impels the light straw to attach itself firmly to amber ; it is this quality which gives every substance in nature a tendency toward another, and an inclination forcibly directed to a determinate point.' "

From the preceding extracts of this learned scholar, and those of the first chapter of the present work, the intelligent reader will readily perceive the strong affinity which exists between the principles of the *Vedas* of India and the metaphysical and philosophical writings of the Sūfīs. The religion of Brahma has been carried into Persia and even Arabia, and been engrafted upon that of Islāmism by the Darvishes. It would be interesting to trace the connexion which existed between the ideas of the sages of Greece and those of India. Whilst with these the original oneness of the Deity became extended into an infinity of secondary gods, Islāmism has retained the purity of the Mosaic principle of a One Supreme, Omniscient, and Omnipotent Creator, possessing a great number of *attributes*, which are not personified as with the Hindus and the Greeks. In the religion of the former it is impossible not to perceive traces of the creation, of the history of man as revealed to Adam, handed down to his posterity, and chronicled by the earliest historian of the human race—Moses.

In support of this assertion I would add the following extract from Sir William Jones's lecture "On the Gods of Greece, Italy, and India":—

"That water was the primitive element and first work of the creative power is the uniform opinion of the Indian philosophers; but as they give so particular an account of the general deluge and of the creation, it can never be admitted that their whole system arose from traditions concerning the flood only, and must appear indubitable that this doctrine is in part borrowed from the opening of *Birasit*,[1] or Genesis, than which a sublimer passage from the first word to the last never flowed, or will flow, from any human pen.

"'In the beginning God created the heavens and the earth. And the earth was void and waste, and darkness was upon the face of the deep, and the Spirit of God moved upon the face of the waters. And God said, Let light be, and light was.'

"The sublimity of this passage is considerably diminished by the Indian paraphrase of it, with which Manu, the son of Brahmā, begins his address to the Sages, who consulted him on the formation of the universe.

"'This world,' says he, 'was all darkness, undiscernible,

[1] Hebrew *Bareṣit*, 'in the beginning', the first word of Genesis, i. 1. The Book of Genesis is called *Sifr-ut-takwīn*.

undistinguishable, altogether as in a profound sleep, till the self-existent, invisible God, making it manifest with five elements, and other glorious forms, perfectly dispelled the gloom. He, desiring to raise up various creations by an emanation from His own glory, first created the waters, and impressed them with a power of motion.'

"To this curious description, with which the *Mānava Śàstra* begins, I cannot refrain from subjoining the four verses which are the text of the *Bhāgavat*, and are believed to have been pronounced by the Supreme Being to Brahmā.

"'Even I was, even at first, not any other thing (existed), that which exists unperceived, supreme; afterwards, I am that which is; and He, who must remain, am I.

"'Except the first cause, whatever may appear, and may not appear in the mind, know that to be the mind's *māyā* (or delusion) as light and darkness.

"'As the first elements are in various beings, entering, yet not entering (that is, pervading, not destroying), thus am I in them, yet not in them.

"'Even thus far may inquiry be made by him who seeks to know the principle of mind, in union and separation, which must be everywhere always.'

"The Hindus believe that when a soul leaves its body, it immediately repairs to Yāmapur, or the city of Yāma, when it receives a just sentence from him, and either ascends to Swarga, or the first heaven, or is driven down to Nārak, the region of serpents, or assumes on earth the form of some animal, unless its offences had been such that it ought to be condemned to a vegetable, or even to a mineral poison."

THE HINDĪ, OR THE WANDERING DARVISHES OF INDIA

In the list of the various *takias* of Constantinople given previously, mention is made of that called the Hindīlar Takiasī. This is also a *masjid*, or chapel, situated near the Mosque of Murād Pāsha Jāmi'sī. It is the refuge of all those wandering Darvishes who, from the distant clime of Hindustan, visit Stambūl.

A Darvish friend informs me that the greater part of these belong to the Order of the Naqshbandīs, Qādirīs, Chishtīs Kubrāwīs, Ni'āmatullāhīs, and Qalandarīs.

These natives of India, after performing the *bai'at*, or initiation required by the Order of their profession, and receiving the blessing of its Shaikh, set out on their travels, depending upon the alms and charities of the public for a subsistence. But few make the journey by land, and mostly take passage from Bombay to Jidda, in the Red Sea, on their way to the holy cities of the Hijāz. They there perform the usual *hājj*, or pilgrimage of all Mussulmans, and next proceed across the country by land to Baghdād. Some re-embark at Jidda for Basra, in the Persian Gulf. The object of this journey is to visit the holy graves of Hazrat-i-'Alī, Hazrat-i-Husain, Imām 'Abbās, and the other sons of the fourth Caliph 'Alī. At Baghdād they remain at the Takia and *jāmī* of Hazrat Shaikh 'Abd-ul-Qādir Gilānī, the founder of the Qādirīs. Some of them sit as night-watchers (*bakjīs*[1]) in the bazaars of Baghdād, and do not beg. At other times their home is the great establishment of the Qādirīs aforementioned. At the entrance to this is the grave of Hazrat-i-'Abd-ul-Jabbār, son of the founder, before which the newly-arrived Hindī spends three days, as a trial of his faith, and if he prove to be a *majūsī*,[2] or 'idolater' in disguise, it is said that he cannot possibly support the ordeal of prayer and fasting. A superior spiritual influence is supposed to be exercised against him, and before the termination of that period, he is self-condemned, and flies from exposure and ill-treatment.

It is only after he has visited the other sacred tombs, and performed all the devotionary exercises required, that he really begins his career of mendicity. By some he is called a *faqīr* (poor man), and it may be added that the greater number are not affiliated in any particular Order or *tarīq*, but simply indigent Mussulmans, who have vowed to make a visit (*ziyārat*) to certain holy tombs in the distance, and difficulties in which he finds religious merit. To do this, these *faqīrs* abandon father, mother, wife, children, and friends, and all they may possess. This abnegation of all the pleasures and comforts of life places them above the ordinary *convenances* of society, and they affect to respect no one, whatever may be his official position; and their poverty and miserable appearance preserves them from punishment when their remarks are insolent.

[1] Bakjī, T., 'sentinel', 'guardian'. 'Abd-al-Jabbār, youngest son of 'Abd-ul-Qādir Jīlānī, died in 575 H. (1179–80 A.D.): *E.I.* i. p. 42.

[2] Magian, fire-worshipper.

Among the anecdotes relating to Darvishes of this category, I add the following:—

"Once, when a king was passing near a Darvish, the latter, who was seated on the ground, neither arose to his feet nor otherwise offered any tokens of respect; so that the king, being of an irascible temper, was offended by his want of regard, and exclaimed, 'These ragged individuals are no better in manners than so many wild beasts.' The *wazīr*, or minister of the king, cried out to the Darvish, and asked him why he thus failed in respect to the king? 'Tell your master,' replied the Darvish, 'to look for respect from those who need his bounties, and that, as sovereigns are for the protection of the people, the latter are under no obligation to court their duties by external marks of respect.' On this reply, the king directed the *wazīr* to ask the Darvish what he could do for him, and, in reply, the latter said that all he wished was to be let alone."

"A Darvish, speaking to a king who entertained but little respect for persons of his condition, said: 'We have neither the strength, nor the power, which you possess in this world; but I am sure we are all the happier for it. After death, we are all equals; and after the day of judgment, we are your superiors.'"

"A thief once asked a *faqīr*, if he was not ashamed to stretch out his hand and beg alms of passers-by? The latter replied, that it was better to do that, than have his hand cut off for thieving."

"A king had vowed that, if he should succeed in an affair which he was about to undertake, he would distribute a handsome sum of money among the poorer Darvishes of his capital. Having met with the desired success, he confided the distribution of the money to one of his officers. The latter, not being favourably impressed with the character of the Darvishes, kept the money until nightfall, and then returned it to the king, remarking that he had not been able to find any such in his capital. The king was much surprised, and said that there must be several hundreds; but the officer replied, 'Darvishes do not accept money, and those who do are not Darvishes'."

A Darvish, as above said, should possess ten of the characteristics of a dog, viz.: he should be always hungry; he should have no home; he should not sleep even at night; he should leave no inheritance at his death; he should never forsake his master, even if the latter ill-treat him; he should be satisfied with the lowest and most humble place; he should give up his place to whoever wishes it, and take another; return to whoever beats him, when he offers him a piece of bread; he should remain at a distance when food is served up; and he should never think of returning to the place he has left, when he is following his master.

Conformably with the preceding, a Darvish, after having been frequently invited to a great man's house, was often driven away by his servants; and when the master, to whom the fact became known, apologised for such ill-treatment, and expressed his admiration for the humility and patience which he had shown, the Darvish remarked that it was not a merit, but only one of the characteristics of a dog, which always returns, when driven away.

CHAPTER XVI [1]

ON THE TASAWWUF, OR SPIRITUAL LIFE OF THE SUFĪS

TRANSLATED FROM THE TURKISH OF MUHAMMAD MISRĪ

THE word *sūf* signifies in Arabic 'wool', and Mr. Lane, in his 102nd note on the 10th chapter of *The Arabian Nights*, says that the so-called Sūfīs derive their title either from their wearing woollen garments, or from the Greek word σοφός, because of their philosophical tenets. He adds, that "there is an Order of Muslim Darweshes called Sūfīs, 'who make profession of a more regular and more contemplative life than Darweshes in general; and many of this class have written books of spirituality, of devotion, and of contemplation, which mostly bear the title of *tasawwuf*, that is, of spiritual life.' . . . The Sunnī Sūfīs are in a great degree mystical and latitudinarian; but not so much so as the Sūfīs of the Persian sect."

In all the *takias*, or convents, of the various sects which I have visited the members sit on sheep-skins, called *postakīs*. Many also wear white felt caps made of wool, and even their cloaks are of an uncoloured stuff of the same material.

The Order of the Baqtāshīs, which was intimately connected with the Yanicharīs, wear white felt caps, and believe in the *tanāsukh*, a system of metempsychosis.

TRANSLATION

" A few remarks on the subject of the *tasawwuf* (lit., profession of Sūfīism, or spiritual life), by the learned and pious Muhammad Misrī—may his precious grave be blessed!

" In the name of the Clement and Merciful God.

[1] This chapter originally appeared in the *Journal of the American Oriental Society*.

"Praise be to the Lord of the Universe (lit., the present and future world). Prayers and Peace [from his people] be upon our Saiyid (Lord) Muhammad [the Prophet], and 'Alī [his cousin and son-in-law], and all other prophets, and the family and *aṣḥābs* (companions) of Muhammad.

"[*Question.*]—Should any person ask what is the beginning of the *tasawwuf*, the answer is :

"[*Answer.*]—Faith, which has six columns, to wit : 'The existence of God', 'His Unity', 'the Angels', 'the Prophets', 'the Day of Resurrection', and 'Good and Evil through His Predestination'—all of which are to be spoken with the tongue, and acknowledged with the heart.

"[*Q.*]—What is the conclusion and end of the *tasawwuf* ?

"[*A.*]—It is the pronouncing with the tongue of faith the six preceding columns, and the confirming of them with the heart, as was said by Junaidī, in answer to an interrogation on the subject of the end of the *tasawwuf*.

"[*Q.*]—What is the distinction between the *suffā* (lit., the clarified) and common people ?

"[*A.*]—The knowledge [which is the foundation] of the faith of the latter is only an imitation of these six columns, whilst the faith of the *suffā* [1] is the true, as is shown by the evidences of the *'ulmā-i-uzamā* [2] (doctors of the sects).

"[*Q.*]—In what does this imitation consist ?

"[*A.*]—This imitation is what has been learned from their fathers, the *imāms* (preachers) of the quarters in which they live, or from one of the *'ulmā*, and so believed ; but they do not know why it has become a fundamental rule to believe in these columns

[1] Salmoné, *Arab. Dict.*, p. 452, gives no such form as *ṣuffā*. *Ṣafī*, pl. *aṣfīā*=pure, chosen, elect, from *ṣafā*, 'was pure'. There is a play on the roots *ṣafā* and *ṣūf*, from the latter of which is derived *ṣūf*, 'wool'.

Nicholson translates *ahl-i-ṣuffā* by 'people of the verandah', and explains the term *ṣuffā* to mean 'bench'—*ahl-i-suffā* being the title given to poor Muslims who used to take shelter in the covered bench outside the mosque built by the Prophet at Medina. It seems to be equivalent to *aṣḥāb-i-ṣuffā* (*Kashf-ul-Maḥjūb*, pp. 81 and 30, and *E.R.E.*, art. *Sūfīs*).

[2] Uẓama, not apparently pl. of ẓimma but of *ẓimām*. Zimām=bridle or reins. Hence=control or check. *Ẓimām* (zāl)=protection. In Spain the Kātib uẓ-ẓimām was entrusted with the protection of the ahl-uz-ẓimma or ẓimmis. In 192 H. Mahdi established the diwān azzimah (ḍ or z ?) or (?) azzimmah (Ameer Ali, *A Short Hist. of the Saracens*, p. 619).

of faith, nor how salvation is obtained thereby. It is not known that, whilst walking in the public streets, one has found a jewel which many sovereigns sought after unsuccessfully—conquering the world from one end to the other, and finding everything else but it. He who has found it, has found a light brighter than the sun, when it obscures the lesser lustre of the moon, and found an alchemy which converts copper of a thousand years old into pure gold. The finder, however, knows not its real value, and considers it only as a false jewel, which its possessor, if thirsty, might give away for a drink of water.

"[*Q.*]—What is the proof of faith?

"[*A.*]—The proof consists in a search made for the origin of each of the six columns above named, and one's arrival at the truth (*haqīqat*). The *'ilm-i-tarīqat* (science of the sects) is the distinctive path existing between a *taqlīd* village and a *taqlīd*[1] city [*i.e.* only leads from one authority to another]. Many persons follow on that path for ten, others for twenty, others thirty, others forty years, wandering away from the truth, and entering each upon a different road of error. Some become *ahl-i-jabrī*[2] (persons who believe that God compels each action of man, and leaves no room for free will); some become *ahl-i-qadrī* (persons who hold that man has power to do good and evil); others are *ahl-i-mu'tāzalī*; some again become *mujassamīs* (anthropomorphists); and others, *mushabbahīs*[3] (those who define the appearance of

[1] Taqlīd, 'imitation', 'mimicry', 'authority'. The term means mechanical repetition of prayers or doctrine. For the Mu'tazilites see Macdonald, *Muslim Theology*, pp. 135 f. They denied that God pre-destined the actions of men.

[2] The more usual form is Jabariūn or -īa, who were extreme fatalists. Their strongest defender was Jahm b. Safwān Abū Muḥriz al-Tirmizī (or al-Samarqandī), put to death in 128 H. (A.D. 745-46). As a theologian he occupied an independent position, as he accepted the Murjite teaching that belief is an affair of the heart, and the Mu'tazilite denial of all anthropomorphic attributes to God. His followers, the Jahmīa, eventually became Ash'arites (*E.I.* i. pp. 1001 and 985). The Ash'arites were moderate fatalists. The Qadarīas (*ahl-i-qadr*) adopted a doctrine of free-will (Zwemer, p. 105, and Shedd, p. 77).

[3] Mushabbiḥa, from *shabah*, 'form' or 'shape'. *Mushabbiḥ* = 'comparer', *mujassim* = 'corporealizer' (Macdonald, *Muslim Theology*, p. 191; cf. also Sale's *Koran* (Wherry's recension), i. pp. 257-58). About the Mushabbiḥa Shahrastānī has much to say. From the first intervention of the devil arose the doctrines of the Hulūlīas, Tanāsukhīas, or believers in transmigration, Mushabbiḥa, and the Ghulāt, or extremists, among the Shī'as, because

God by portraits or otherwise). There are, in all, seventy-three ways or sects; each one following one of these wanders off, without ever arriving at the city of the true faith; only one of these seventy-three parties is in the right, called the *firqā-i-najīa* [1] (party of salvation), and it is those alone who follow this way that reach the proper goal. Through their perfect subjection to the directions of the blessed Prophet, these know the real value of the jewel found by them. Their faith is manifest; and whilst proceeding, as it were, with a lamp, they have reached the sun. Though at first only imitators, they have finally found the truth. After finding the true faith, they turn their attention to the imitation (or semblance), and familiarise themselves with its interior. They find that the *tarīqat* (paths of the Darvishes) and the *sharī'at* (laws of Islām) are coincident. They have as yet only received sufficient inspiration from God to enable them to see the truth, which is hidden from those who still wander in the path of imitation. Comparing the two with each other, they consider them as being like the soul and the body, according to the words of the blessed Prophet: 'Whoever is deficient in one of his

---

they ascribed divine attributes to the Imām. From Satan's second interference came the tenets of the Qadarīas, Jabarīas and Mujassima, who attributed human qualities to God. Then he goes on to point out that these groups overlap, in that the Mu'tazilites are Mushabbiḥa in respect of God's dealings, while the Mushabbiḥa are Ḥulūlīs in regard to His attributes (Haarbrucker, *Religionspartheien*, i. p. 12). He also classes them in some degree with the Shī'as (*ib.* p. 216). But Tāhir-al-Isfarāini gives even more details. According to him the Mushabbiḥa were divided into two groups, one comparing God's Being with other beings, the second likening His Being to the attributes of other beings. The first extreme Mushabbiḥa were the Sabā'īya (the name seems incorrectly written as Sabābīa) who revered 'Alī as God, and of whom a number were burnt by him. (In their defence they cited a text of the *Qurān* applying the epithet 'Alī to Allāh; they held 'Alī to be an incarnation of the divine, and believed that Muḥammad would reappear (Margoliouth, *Early Development of Islam*, p. 209 and Index). Among other groups of the Mushabbiḥa was that of the Muqanna'īa, "the Mushabbiḥa of Māwarānnahr (Trans-Oxiana)", who looked upon the Veiled Prophet as God, while another group, a sect included in the once generic term of Ḥulūlīa, worshipped every fair form, holding that God was manifest in it (*ib.*, p. 403).

[1] Najīa = *najāt*, 'deliverance'; from the same root as *najwī*, p. 424. It is often said that Islām has 72 sects, and each sect asserts that all of them have gone astray and that the only true Order is the 73rd, itself, the *firqa-i-najāt*—according to Muhammad's prophecy.

faculties, is deficient in one of his parts,' from which it is clear that whoever is deficient in the *sharī'at*, cannot be perfect in the *haqīqat*.

" [*Q*.]—In matters of faith and forms of worship, to what sect are the *suffā* attached?

" [*A*.]—Most of them are of the Muslim faith, and of the sect of the *ahl-i-sunnat* (those who observe the traditionary precepts of the blessed Prophet), and accept the *jamā'at* (prescribed forms of public prayer), according to the *mazhab* (creed) of the celebrated Shaikh Abū Mansūr Mātarīdī.[1] Most of the Arabs are of the creed of the Shaikh Abūl-Hasan, al-Ash'arī,[2] and are *ahl-i-sunnat*, and accept the *jamā'at*, as understood and practised in conformity with one or other of the four rites, adopted in the country to which they belong (*i.e.* either the Hanafī, Hanbalī, Shāfi'ī, or Mālikī).[3] For instance, those of the country of Rūm are Hanafīs, so called from Abū-Hanīfa, who derived his articles of faith from the *Qurān* and the *hadīsat* (traditional sayings) of the blessed Prophet; those in Arabia, Egypt and Aleppo, as well as in the two holy cities, are Shāfi'īs; all the people of Tunis and Morocco, and as far as Andalusia, as well as some in Arabia, are Mālikīs; most of the people of Baghdād, Irāq, and a part of Arabia, with some of the inhabitants of the holy cities, follow the Hanbalī Imām. There are some differences between these, but only such as refer to forms of worship; as regards dogmas, they all agree. The blessed Prophet designated those who observe the *sunnat*

[1] Abū Manṣūr Muḥammad b. Maḥmūd al-Ḥanafī, entitled Imām al-Hudā, 'the director', was born in the Mātrīd quarter of Samarqand, in which city he died in 333 H. (A.D. 945). For a brief account of his doctrine see Macdonald, *op. cit.* p. 193.

[2] The teacher before whom the Mu'tazilite system went down (Macdonald, *Muslim Theology*, p. 187). Abū'l Ḥasan 'Alī, born at Basra in 260 H. (A.D. 873-74), was a Mu'tazilite till his fortieth year, but thenceforth championed the orthodox view against that sect. Yet "for the rest", it is said, "he belonged to the *maẓhab* of the Shāfi'ites", meaning apparently that "his method found acceptance with that sect especially". Rightly described as the founder of orthodox scholasticism (*kalām*), it would seem that in his legal principles he was a Shāfi'ī and in other respects a Ḥanafī, since his contemporary al-Maturīdī, who was preferred by the Hanafites, only differed from him on minor points. Among his followers were al-Qushairī, al-Juwainī (the Imām al-Ḥaramain), and the famous al-Ghazālī (*E.I.* i. p. 480). He died at Baghdād in 935.

[3] The geographical distribution of these schools of law is not quite as definite as the text suggests (*v.* note on p. 79 *supra*).

and *jamā'at* by the title of *ahl-i-najāt* [1] (the saved), and these four are all of this kind. All the *suffā* belong to the *ahl-i-najāt*. It is a point of belief among the *suffā* that it is not for every one who is of the *ahl-i-Allāh*, or a *karāmāt sāhibī* (*i.e.* either a believer in the Divinity, or particularly gifted by the Divinity), to attain to the character of sanctity belonging to the four great doctors of the holy law, much less to that of one of the *ahl-i-Kuzīn* (the Twelve Imāms). The only means of arriving at their degrees of perfection would be to follow their creed until one surpassed it, and then to establish, by God's sanction, a new one superior to theirs—which, as yet, no one has ever been able to do.

" [*Q*.]—When Bāyazīd al-Bustāmī was asked of what sect he was, he replied : ' I am of the sect of Allāh.' What did he mean by this answer ?

" [*A*.]—All of the sects of Allāh are those just mentioned. They are called (for example) the sects of [Abū Hanīfa] the Greater Imām (Nūmān ibn Sābit al-Kūfī) and of the Shāfi'ī Imām, but are in reality sects of Allāh ; and so Bāyazīd spoke truly when he said he was of His sect.

" [*Q*.]—Most of the Sūfīs, in their *qasīdas*, use certain words which we hear and understand as showing that they were of the *ahl-i-tanāsukh* (Metempsychosians). They say : ' I am sometimes Lot,[2] sometimes Rayu, sometimes a vegetable, sometimes an animal, at other times a man.' What does this mean ?

" [*A*.]—Brother ! the blessed Prophet has said : ' My people, in the eternal life, will rise up in companies '—that is, some as monkeys, others as hogs, or in other forms—as is written in a verse of the *Qurān* (chap. lxxviii. v. 18) which has been commented on by Qāzī Baizāwī [3] (this commentator cites a tradition to the effect that at the resurrection men will rise up in the form of those animals whose chief characteristics resemble their own ruling passions of life : the greedy, avaricious man, as a hog ; the angry, passionate man, as a camel ; the tale-bearer, or mischief-maker, as a monkey) ; because, though these men, while in this life, bore the human form externally, they were, internally,

[1] Ahl-i-Najāt, for ahl-ee Vejah in original. See note on page 378.

[2] Lot, apparently for *laut*, Ar., ' concealment '. *Rayu* possibly for *rūyā*, ' revelation ', or *rūya*, ' vision '. The *rūya* is alluded to by Macdonald, *Muslim Theology*, pp. 310 and 314 (citing *Qurān* vii. 139).

[3] Al-Baidhāwī.

nothing different from the animals whose characters are in common with their own. The resemblance is not manifest during one's life, but becomes so in the other existence, after the resurrection. Let us avoid such traits; repentance before death will free any one from these evils. The blessed Prophet said with regard to this: 'Sleep is the brother of Death'. The dying man sees himself in his true character, and so knows whether or not he is, by repentance, freed from his ruling passion of life. In like manner, he will see himself during his slumbers still following in the path of his passion. For instance, the money-calculator, in sleep, sees himself engaged in his all-absorbing occupation; and this fact is a warning from God, not to allow himself to be absorbed in any animal passion or degrading occupation. It is only by prayerful repentance that any one can hope to see himself, in his sleep, delivered from his ruling carnal passion, and restored to his proper human, intellectual form. If in your slumbers you see a monkey, consider it as a warning to abandon or abstain from the passion of mischief; if a hog, cease to seize upon the goods of others; and so on. Go and give yourself up to an upright *murshid* (spiritual guide), who will, through his prayers, show you in your slumbers the evil parts of your character, until one by one they have passed away, and have been replaced by good ones—all through the power of the name of God, whom he will instruct you to invoke: at length you will only see in your slumbers the forms of holy and pious men, in testimony of that degree of piety to which you will have attained.

"This is what is meant by that expression of certain poets, referring to one's condition previous to the act of repentance, when the writer says: 'I am sometimes an animal, sometimes a vegetable, sometimes a man'; and the same may be said by the Soffees, in application to themselves, of any other part of creation, for man is called the *ākhir-i-maujūdāt* (the climax of beings): in him are comprised all the characteristics of creation. Many mystical books have been written on this subject, all showing that man is the *nuhā-i-kubrā* (the larger part), and the world, the *nuhā-i-sughrā* (the smaller part), of God's creation. The human frame is said to comprise all the other parts of creation; and the heart * of man is supposed to be even more comprehensive than

* Orientals consider the heart as the seat of mental capacity; and the liver, of the affections.

the rainbow, because, when the eyes are closed, the mental capacity can take in the whole of a vast city : though not seen by the eyes, it is seen by the capacious nature of the heart. Among such books is the *Hauz-ul-Hayāt* (Well of Life), which says that, if a man closes his eyes, ears, and nostrils, he cannot take cold ; that the right nostril is called the sun, and the left the moon ; that from the former he breathes heat, and from the latter cold air. There is also a treatise entitled *Nuskha-i-kubrā,* wholly on the subject of the superiority of man, which is one of the favourite works of the Sūfīs.

"[*Q.*]—Explain the distinctive opinions (*mazhabs*) of believers in the *tanāsukh,* and of the Sūfīs.

"[*A.*]—We say that this system of metempsychosis has nothing to do with the *barzakh* [1] (a name given to the intermediate period between death and the resurrection, mentioned in the 23rd chapter of the *Qurān,* 102nd verse, in which departed souls receive neither rewards nor punishments : here, however, it means only a state of total indifference to all future life, into which some men fall in consequence of the vicious nature of their lives, or their spiritual demoralisation). It is believed to be operative in eternity, or in the future state ; it is declared that it does not exist in the present life. For example, it is said that some men take the character of certain animals, not their forms, and that, when they die, their souls enter the bodies of such animals as they already resembled in character, and so, by natural propagation, they become the animals themselves, visible to the eye, and never again really die, or cease to exist in this world. In this manner, mankind leave the human form, and become, in turn, various animals, either through natural propagation, or by one animal devouring another, perpetually. Such is the belief of the Metempsychosians, and it is wholly inconsistent with the true faith. On this point 'Umar ibn-ul-Farīd has said : 'He who believes in transformation and transmigration stands in need of God's healing—keep thyself far removed from his belief ! '

"O brother, keep far from such a belief, and have no connexion with it. Of the seventy-two erring sects, before alluded to, this is the worst. God preserve us, in this life and the one to come, from participating with, or even beholding, such sectaries !

"[*Q.*]—These persons regard certain things as legally proper,

[1] Lit. 'isthmus'.

which are forbidden. For instance, they command the use of wine, wine-shops, the wine-cup, sweethearts; they speak of the curls of their mistresses, the moles on their faces, cheeks, etc.; and compare the furrows on their brows to verses of the *Qurān*. What does this mean?

"[*A.*]—Just as these Sūfīs leave the true faith for its semblance, so they also exchange the external features of all things for the internal (the corporeal for the spiritual), and give an imaginary signification to outward forms. They behold objects of a precious nature in their natural character, and for this reason the greater part of their words have a spiritual and visionary meaning. For instance, when, like Hāfiz, they mention wine, they mean a knowledge of God, which, extensively considered, is the love of God. Wine, viewed extensively, is also love: love and affection are here the same thing. The wine-shop, with them, means the *murshid-i-kāmil*[1] (spiritual director), for his heart is said to be the depository of the love of God; the wine-cup is the *talqīn* (the pronunciation of the name of God, in a declaration of faith, as: There is no God but Allāh), or it signifies the words which flow from the *murshid's* mouth respecting divine knowledge, and which, heard by the *sālik* (the Darvish, or one who pursues the true path) intoxicates his soul, and divests his mind (of passions), giving him pure spiritual delight. The sweetheart means the excellent preceptor, because, when any one sees his beloved, he admires her perfect proportions, with a heart full of love: the Darvish beholds the secret knowledge of God which fills the heart of his spiritual preceptor (*murshid*), and through it receives a similar inspiration, and acquires a full perception of all that he possesses, just as the pupil learns from his master. As the lover delights in the presence of his sweetheart, so the Darvish rejoices in the company of his beloved preceptor. The sweetheart is the object of a worldly affection; but the preceptor, of a spiritual attachment. The curls, or ringlets, of the beloved are the grateful praises of the preceptor, tending to bind the affections of the Darvish-pupil; the moles on her face signify that when the pupil, at times, beholds the total absence of all worldly wants on the part of the preceptor, he also abandons all the desires of both worlds—he perhaps even goes so far as to desire nothing else in life than his preceptor; the furrows on the brow of the beloved

[1] 'The perfect *murshid*'.

one, which they compare to [verses of] the *Qurān*, mean the light of the heart of the *murshid*: they are compared to verses of the *Qurān*, because the attributes of God, in accordance with the injunction of the Prophet: 'Be ye endued with divine qualities', are possessed by the Shaikh (or *murshid*).*

"[*Q*.]—The *murshid* and other Darvishes say: 'We see God'. Is it possible for any other than the Prophet to see God?

"[*A*.]—It is not possible. What they mean by this assertion is that they know God, that they see His power; for it is forbidden to mortal eyes to behold Him, as is declared in the *Qurān* (ch. vi. v. 103): 'No sight reaches Him: He reaches the sight [but he perceives men's sights [1]]—the Subtle, the Knowing'. The blessed Prophet commanded: 'Adore God, as thou wouldst didst thou see Him; for, if thou dost not see Him, He sees thee'. This permission to adore Him is a divine favour, and they say that they are God's servants by divine favour. The blessed 'Alī said: 'Should the veil fall from my eyes, how would God visit me in truth'! This saying confirms that no one really sees God, that even the sainted 'Alī never saw Him.

"[*Q*.]—Can it possibly be erroneous to say that, by seeing the traces of any one, he may be beheld?

"[*A*.]—One may certainly be thus seen. When any person sees the brightness of the sun, he may safely say that he has seen the sun, though indeed he has not really seen it. There is another example, namely: should you hold a mirror in your hand, you see a figure in it, and you may therefore say that you see your own face, which is really an impossibility, for no one has ever seen his own face, and you have asserted what is not strictly correct.

"[*Q*.]—Since every one sees the traces of God, as every one is able to do, how is it that the Darvishes declare that they only see Him?

"[*A*.]—Those who make this statement do not know what they see, and have never really seen Him. A person who has

* During the wars between Alī and Muāwia, the latter, on being once beaten, elevated the *Qurān* on a lance, and begged for mercy. On this being reported to Alī, he declared that he himself was the living and the speaking *Qurān*, whilst the one raised upon the lance of his enemy was only a painted, or imitated one.

[1] Palmer's *Qurān* S.B.E. vi. p. 128.

eaten of a sweet and savoury dish, given to him, but of which he knows not the name, seeks for it again with a longing desire after it, and thus wanders about in search of what has given him so much delight, ignorant of what it is. So are those who seek after God, without knowing Him, or what He is.

"[*Q.*]—Some Darvishes declare: 'We are neither afraid of Hell, nor do we desire Heaven,—a saying which must be blasphemous. How is this?

"[*A.*]—They do not really mean that they do not fear Hell, and that they do not wish for Heaven. If they really meant this, it would be blasphemous. Their meaning is not as they express themselves; probably they wish to say: O Lord, Thou who createdst us, and madest us what we are, Thou hast not made us because we help Thy working: we are therefore in duty bound to serve Thee all the more devotedly, wholly in obedience to Thy holy will; we have no bargaining with Thee, and we do not adore Thee with the view of gaining thereby either Heaven or Hell. 'God has bought the goods and persons of the Faithful, and given them Paradise in return' (ch. ix. v. 112, of the *Qurān*), which signifies that His bounty has no bounds, His mercy no end; and thus it is that He benefits His faithful servants. They would say: Thou hast no bargaining with any one; our devotion is from the purity of our hearts, and is for love of Thee only. Were there no Heaven, nor any Hell, it would still be our duty to adore Thee. To Thee belongs the perfect right to put us either in Heaven or in Hell, and may Thy commands be executed agreeably to Thy blessed will! If Thou puttest us in Heaven, it is through Thine excellence, not on account of our devotion; if Thou puttest us in Hell, it is from out of Thy great justice, and not from any arbitrary decision on Thy part; so be it for ever and for ever! This is the true meaning of the Sūfīs, when they say as before stated.

"[*Q.*]—Thou saidst that there is no conflict between the *sharī'at* and the *haqīqat*, and nothing in the latter inconsistent with the former; and yet these two are distinguished from one another by a something which the *ahl-i-haqīqat* (believers in the truth) conceal. Were there nothing conflicting, why should it be thus hidden?

"[*A.*]—If it be concealed, it is not because there is a contrariety to the *sharī'at*, but only because the thing is contrary to the human mind : its definition is subtle, and not understood by every one, for which reason the blessed Prophet said : ‘ Speak to men according to their mental capacities ’, for, if you speak all things to all men, some cannot understand you, and so fall into error. The Sūfīs therefore hide some things conformably with this precept.

“ [*Q.*]—Should any one not know the science which is known to the Sūfīs, and still do what the *sharī'at* plainly command, and be satisfied therewith, would his faith (*imān*) and *islām* be less than that of the Sūfīs ?

“ [*A.*]—No. He would not be inferior to the Sūfīs ; his faith and *islām* would be equal even to that of the prophets, because

DARVISHES OF THE MAULAVĪ ORDER

faith and *islām* are a jewel which admits of no division or separation into parts, and can neither be increased nor diminished, just as the portion of the sun enjoyed by a sovereign and by a *faqīr* is the same, or as the limbs of the poor and the rich are equal in number : just as the members of the body of the sovereign and the subject are precisely alike, so is the faith of the *ahl-i-Islām* the same in all and common to all, neither greater nor less in any case.

“ [*Q.*]—Some men are prophets, saints, pure ones, and others *fāsiqs* (who know God, but perform none of His commands) ; what difference is there among them ?

“ [*A.*]—The difference lies in their *ma'rifat* (knowledge of spiritual things), but in the matter of faith they are all equal : just as, in the case of the sovereign and the subject, their limbs are all equal, while they differ in their dress, power, and office. As to the humanity of men, that depends upon their dress of knowledge, and their spiritual power ; in these only are they men, and not simply animals. The character of the sovereign does not depend upon his humanity, which is the same as that of all other men, but upon his office and rank."

CHAPTER XVII

A BIOGRAPHY OF THE FOURTH CALIPH 'ALĪ

THE reader will have perceived the intimate connexion existing between the Darvish Orders and the Fourth (Direct) Caliph 'Alī. Indeed, nearly all of these are 'Alīides, as if he had been the great originator of them, and the advocate and patron of their peculiar principles. Whether this was the case or not, much that is of a 'spiritual' character is attributed to him, and even in those Orders that are *sunnī*, or orthodox, 'Alī is held in high respect. I have therefore thought it necessary to devote a chapter especially to him, and for this purpose have translated a short biographical sketch of him from the work in the Turkish language, entitled The *Chahār Yār*, or the "Four Friends", by Shams-ud-Dīn Sīwāsī[1] (of Sīwās, in Asia Minor). From this sketch the reader will readily imagine why such honour is paid by a large portion of the Islam world, and by the Darvish Orders in particular,—so much so as to give him the sublime title of 'Alī al-Ilāhī, or "'Alī the Divine".

"'Alī bin-Abū-Tālib ibn-'Abd-al-Muttalib was of the same lineage as the Blessed Prophet,[2] being the son of the uncle of the latter, and therefore his cousin.

"He was born in the revered city of Makka, in the thirtieth year of the era of the Arabs, known as the 'Year of the Elephant', and the 910th of the Alexandrian era. Perwas[3] (the Sassanian king of Persia) had ceased to reign eight years.

"His mother, Fātima binti-Asad bin-Hāshim (so it is related), one night saw in a dream that her chamber was filled with light,

[1] Shams-ud-Din Sīwāsi's work is available in a lithographed abridgement: 1312 H.

[2] Muhammad himself was born in the 'Year of the Elephant', as to which see Palmer's *Qurān* S.B.E. vi. p. xviii.

[3] Khusru Parviz.

and that the mountains which surrounded the holy Ka'ba (Caaba) were worshipping it ; that she had held in her hands four swords, all of which having fallen out of them, lay scattered before her. One of these swords fell into water ; a second flew up into the air, and disappeared from her sight as it rose upwards towards heaven ; and a third, as it fell, attempted to do the same, but suddenly became converted into a lion, which fled away towards the mountains, alarming every one by its ferocity, so much so that no one ventured to approach it, except the Prophet of God,—on whom be the Divine satisfaction!—who, going up to it, seized upon, and so subdued it, that it followed after him, licked his blessed face and feet, and voluntarily served his wishes.

" Four months after this dream, the Prophet of God visited Fātima, and looking her in the face, exclaimed, ' O mother ! what ails thee, for I see a change in thy countenance ? ' She replied, ' My son, I am pregnant ; aid me to have a male child '. The Prophet replied, ' O mother ! if you have a son, give him to me, and I will pray for you '. On hearing these words, Fātima vowed to Allāh, that in case her child was a son, she would give him to the Prophet. Abū-Tālib (her husband) confirmed the vow, by making one similar to it.

" The Prophet therefore blessed her, and the fruit of her conception was 'Alī al-Murtazā, or ' 'Alī the Agreeable '.

" On the occasion of 'Alī's birth, a light was distinctly visible, resembling a bright column, extending from the earth to the firmament.

" Upon receiving news of his nativity, the Prophet immediately visited the dwelling of his parents. On seeing, for the first time, the little infant, he took some spittle from his own lips and rubbed it upon those of the child, and it immediately swallowed it. It is believed that from this 'Alī derived all of his great knowledge and power, as well as miraculous capabilities. By it, he became victorious in all his battles, and a perfect sovereign for conquest and heroic deeds. He also was thus gifted with all of the most eminent qualities of manhood ; and the most noble and loveable traits of character were certainly united in him.

" The Prophet also recited in his ears the *takbīr* and the *tahlīl* [' glorification '], at the same time giving him the name of 'Alī (the sublime or exalted). His mother, in remembrance of her dream, also called him Haidar (lion), and the Prophet declared that he would become the 'Lion of God'. Taking off his own turban, he wrapped one end of it around the child, and rolled the other about his own head, so that it became a crown of glory to him. None of the Faithful have ever had so great a distinction bestowed upon them as this.

"By some it has been related that when the mother of 'Alī was about to be confined, she went into the 'Bait-i-sharīf', or the holy temple of Makka, for the purpose of there being delivered; and that it being impossible to remove her, the child was actually born within its sainted precincts; but for this, we have only their report.

"Ayesha (the third wife of the Prophet, and daughter of Abū-Bakr, the first direct Caliph)—on whom be the Divine satisfaction! —relates that one day when the 'Pride and Glory of the World' (the Prophet) was seated, 'Alī happened to pass by him. 'Calling my attention to him, he declared to me, that 'Alī was the Saiyid (Cid) of the Arabs. But, I asked, are you not their Saiyid? He answered, "I am the Saiyid of all, that is, of the Turks, the Tartars, the Hindis,[1] the Arabs, and the 'Ajamīs;[2] but 'Alī is especially the Saiyid of the Arabs"'. This favoured lady also adds that the Prophet was fond of rocking the cradle of 'Alī, and would often lift him out of it, and carry him about in his arms; so that even when asleep, on hearing the approaching footsteps of the Prophet of God, he would awake, press his little arms out of their ties, and raise them up towards him. On such occasions the Prophet would hasten towards the child, take it from its cradle, and press it, with great tenderness and affection, to his breast. Its mother more than once chided him for it, and begged him to allow her to nurse and look after the child, as became her duty; but the Prophet would as often remind her that even before its birth she had given it to him, and that, consequently, he must, for the present and the future, consider him as his own. It is related that one day the 'Joy of the World' (the Prophet) —on whom be the blessings and salutations of the Most High!— was seated in the Holy Temple, holding the child 'Alī on his knees. Many of the most valiant men of the day were assembled there, boasting of their deeds. Pointing to the child, he told them that it would become the most heroic man of his time, and

[1] Hinds in original. For Hindi or Hindu = Indian.
[2] 'Ajems in original. For 'Ajamī, people of 'Ajam, Persia.

that no one would be his equal on the face of the globe. Surprised and irritated by these words, they expostulated with the Prophet; 'O Muhammad al-Amīn! we always thought you were a wise and truthful man; pray how can you speak thus of a little child, about whose future career in life you can foresee nothing?' In reply, the Prophet only bade them remember his words, and that in a few years they would see them verified.

"It is related that, at the age of three years, 'Alī would perform the *namāz* (prayers) with the Prophet. On seeing this, Abū-Tālib made no remark regarding the precocity of his child, but the mother was much pleased, and exclaimed, 'See! our child worships the Ka'ba with Muhammad, and does not adore our idols'. Abū-Tālib replied, 'O Fātima! we have given him up to Muhammad,—whatever he does will be right in the sight of the All-Just; he is still a child, and will be of whatever religion Muhammad is; let them be brothers, and inseparable'. One day, also, when the revered Prophet and 'Alī were performing their prayers together, Abū-Tālib approached them on horseback, and remarked that 'Alī was on his right side. Now Ja'far Taiyār [1]—on whom be the Divine satisfaction!—was close behind his horse, and Abū-Tālib, addressing him, bade him go and place himself to the left of the Prophet, and pray with them, 'for in this manner you will become an eminent person'. Ja'far immediately left Abū-Tālib and proceeded to the left side of the Prophet, and stood there, on seeing which the latter was much rejoiced, and after prayers, addressing Ja'far, said, 'Rejoice, O Ja'far, that the Most High has given you two wings, with which you may fly away to Paradise, and be the companion of the *hūr-i-ayīns* (houries), and be near to the Lord of the Universe'.

"According to some narratives of holy note, it is stated that

[1] Ja'far Ṭaiyār, fi'l-Jannat, 'the rapid flier, who flies into Paradise', fell at the battle of Mu'ta. In spite of the loss of both his hands he held the standard until he was slain, pierced with fifty wounds. The Prophet said 'he has two wings in Paradise'—whence his designation. He is also called Zū'l-Janāḥain, or 'he with two wings', and in India has become a *jinn* who offered his assistance to Ḥusain before he was killed and is invoked in magic. The book *Al-Jafr* is attributed to him (Mathews, *Mishcat ul-Masabih*, ii. p. 781; D. B. Macdonald in *J.R.A.S.*, 1901, p. 203). The followers of his son 'Abdullāh formed the sect of the Janāḥīa, which believed in the doctrines of incarnation, metempsychosis, and allegorical exposition of the *Qurān* (*E.I.* i. p. 1013).

'Alī was born thirty years after the era of the Elephant, on the 13th day of the Moon of Rajab, which fell on Friday, and that it occurred within the holy Ka'ba; that there was in Yaman a very aged and pious person, named Mīram, whose heart was free from all worldly desires, and who spent the great life of 190 years in adoration and prayer. He cared nothing for worldly wealth, and his only pleasure consisted in pious occupations; he never turned his eyes in any other direction than that of the *minbar* (the point of Makka). One day this person prayed to God that He would bless his country with some one from among the residents of the Holy Temple, and those who were eminent among the chiefs of the Ka'ba. His prayer was accepted, and by Divine direction, Abū-Tālib, then one of the most prominent individuals of Makka, was led to travel, and visit his country. After learning who his visitor was, he thanked God for having accepted his prayer and sent him so distinguished an individual as Abū-Tālib, son of 'Abd-ul-Muttalab, of the tribe of the Banī Hāshim, and a native of the city of Makka. He then told him that from ancient times there was a tradition to the effect that 'Abd-ul-Muttalab would have two grandsons, one from the loins of 'Abdullāh, and that he should be a prophet, and the other from those of Abū-Tālib, who would render easy the enigmas of the *walāyat* (spiritual holiness); and that when the Prophet would have reached his thirtieth year, the *wālī* would come into the world,—and that a prophet like whom none other had ever yet appeared. To this Abū-Tālib replied, 'Oh! Shaikh, that Prophet has been born, and is now in his twenty-ninth year'. Mīram responded, 'Oh! Abū-Tālib, when you return to Makka, and approach the place of prayer, take with you my salutations, and say that Mīram has always borne testimony to the unity of the one universal Creator, who is without any equal, and that he is His prophet. Take also my salutations to the one who is born to you.'

"Abū-Tālib, seeing opposite him a dry pomegranate tree, as a temptation to the Shaikh, requested him to cause it to put forth leaves and fruit, as a proof of the truthfulness of his words. The Shaikh turned his face upwards in supplication to God, and prayed, that for the sake of the *nabī* (Prophet) and the *wālī* ('Alī), about whom he had just declared words of sincerity, there might be a demonstration of Divine power over Nature. In a minute the tree became covered with leaves and fruit, from which he presented his visitor with the fresh pomegranates. Of these the Shaikh gave one to Abū-Tālib, which he broke open and ate two grains. It is related that the juice of these two grains became the source from which sprang the bodily existence of 'Alī al-Murtazā.

"Abū-Tālib, much rejoiced with what he had heard from the Shaikh, returned to Makka; and his wife, Fātima binti-Asad, soon proved to be pregnant. During her pregnancy (as she stated) 'I was one day engaged in making the turn (called the *tawāf*) around the holy house, and had an attack of the spleen. The blessed Prophet saw and understood what ailed me, and addressing me, asked whether I had terminated my circuit (the *tawāf*). I replied that I had not. He then added, "Continue, and if you feel fatigued, enter into the Ka'ba"'. It is also narrated in the book entitled *Siyar-al-Mustafā*, that whilst Fātima binti-Asad was thus engaged in making the *tawāf* of the Harām-i-Ka'ba, Abbās ibn-al-Muttalab and all the Banī Hāshim, following behind her, did the same; she suddenly had an attack of the spleen, and, being unable to go out, prayed, 'Oh, Lord, give an easy confinement'. Suddenly the wall opened, and Fātima became lost from sight. In the view of learning something about her, I entered the Ka'ba, but was still unable to do so, because for three days she could not be found; on the fourth day she came out, bearing in her arms 'Alī bin-Abū-Tālib,—on whom be the Divine satisfaction!

"The Imām-ul-Haramain ('Imām of the two holy places'[1]) states that before this case, never was any one blessed with such a favour; for it has never been heard that any other one was born in the Harām. Fātima conveyed 'Alī to her dwelling, and bound him in a cradle. Abū-Tālib was present, and, desiring to

[1] 'Imām of the ten holy places' in the original. Abu'l Ma'āli 'Abd-ul-Malik al-Juwaini, who bore the title of Imām al-Ḥaramain, 'Imām of the holy places of Makka and Madina', was born in 419 H. (A.D. 1029) near Nīsābūr. He adopted the teaching of al-Ash'ari, and during the persecution to which the Rāfiẓi were subjected in the Saljuq empire he left his native town and went to Baghdad, Mecca, and Madina, but eventually returned to Nisabur, where the Nizāmīa College was founded for him. He died in 478 H., A.D. 1085 (*E.I.* i. p. 1067). He was also a jurist, and wrote a work on the differences between the Hanafite and Shāfi'ite schools, called the Viae (al-Asâlib), and left other books on law unfinished (Wüstenfeld, *Der Imam el-Schafi'i*, p. 21).

see the child's face, attempted to raise up the veil which covered it, but 'Alī, with his own hand, prevented him, and even scratched his face. His mother, on observing this, approached, and endeavoured to compel the child to submit, but it still refused, and even wounded her in the face also. Abū-Tālib was much surprised at such conduct, and, asking Fātima what name they should give to their child, she replied, 'Oh, Abū-Tālib, it has the strength of a lion's claws, and if we call it a lion, it will be very proper'. Abū-Tālib answered, 'I wish to name it Zaid'. So soon, however, as the 'Pride of the Universe' heard of the birth of the child he hurried to the house, and having inquired what name had been decided upon for it, and heard all that was said on the subject, remarked that it was his desire that he should be an honour to the 'elevated people' ('Alī signifies elevated). Fātima, on hearing this, exclaimed, 'I also heard a voice (*hātif*[1] is the unknown and mystical voice) saying the same name'.

"Another report is that a dispute occurred between the parents regarding the name to be given to this child; and in the view of asking Divine counsel on the subject, they both went to the Ka'ba, where Fātima prayed: 'O Lord! for the child whom Thou givest me in the Harām-i-sharīf, or Holy House, let me beg of Thee a name'. Just then a voice was heard as from the roof of the Ka'ba directing her to call it 'Alī, which they did.

"The blessed Prophet having desired to approach the cradle of the child, Fātima begged him not to do so, for it had all the ferocity of a lion, and might act uncivilly towards him; but to this the blessed Prophet replied, 'O Fātima! this child respects in me the regard due to the True Path'. 'Alī al-Murtazā having in the meantime fallen asleep, the Prophet gazed attentively at its face, on which was already impressed the light of Divine Truth. Afterwards he raised it up out of the cradle, and with his own hands washed it, thus performing the religious ablution called the *ghusl*; and when Fātima, with surprise, inquired the cause, the Prophet replied, 'I have now performed this for 'Alī at his birth, and he will do the same for me at the end of my life'. It was thus that he acted towards the child, taking the deepest interest of an uncle in its future welfare.

"When 'Alī was five years old, a great drought occurred in

[1] From *hatafa*, 'cooed': for a full account of the term *hātif* see *E.I.* i. p. 287.

the Hijāz, from which the inhabitants suffered severely. Abū-Tālib had many persons in his family. The Prophet one day remarked to 'Abbās, 'O! uncle, you are a man of wealth, whilst Abū-Tālib is poor and has a large family; during the present distress we should each take charge of one of his sons and aid him with provisions'. Just then they fell in with Abū-Tālib, and told him what they had designed doing. 'Leave 'Uqail[1] with me, and you may do with the rest of my sons as you please', was his reply; so 'Abbās took Ja'far Taiyār, and the Prophet took 'Alī al-Murtazā, and he remained with him until the angel Gabriel (Jibrāīl) gave him permission (to leave this world). He became an acceptant of the *imān* (true faith) after Abū-Bakr. May God have mercy upon them both, and upon all of the Aṣḥābs (friends) of the blessed Prophet!"

"The Prophetship was given to the Glory of the World (Muhammad) on the second day of the week (Monday), and on Tuesday the *imān* (true faith) was accepted of the Imām 'Alī. Abū Bakr thus preceded him, and before him no one had accepted it. 'Alī was, as just said, the second, and he was then ten years of age, though some pretend that he was only seven years old. At no time did he ever worship idols, and from this great sin the Almighty preserved him.

"It is related that he once said: 'When I was still in my mother's womb, she went to a church (*kanīsa*) for the purpose of worshipping an idol; but, by special divine power, a pain suddenly came upon her, and she was compelled by it to forget her design, and seek relief from her suffering.' The Imām 'Alī was brought up by the Prophet, and 'Abbās relates that no less than 300 *āyats* (verses of the *Qurān*) descended from heaven in honour of him."

"The Imām 'Alī has several names. One of these is Abū'l-Hasan,[2] one Abū'l-Husain, one Haidar, one Karrār, one Amīr-al-

[1] 'Uqīl was 'Alī's brother and father of Abū Muslim (*v.* note on p. 90 *supra*). Abū-Tālib surrendered 'Alī to be adopted by the Prophet, contenting himself with 'Uqīl. This is the arrangement hinted at, though adoption is not recognised by strict Muhammadan law.

[2] Abū'l-Ḥasan means 'Father of Ḥasan', and Abū'l-Ḥusain, 'Father of Ḥusain' (*v. E.I.* i. p. 73, *s.v.* Abū). Ḥaidar and Karrār should be one title, Ḥaidar-i-Kerrār, 'the impetuous lion' (*ib.* p. 284).

Nuhl,[1] one Abū'l-Rahānain,[2] one Asad-Ullāh,[3] and one Abū'l-Turāb ;[4] but he always said that he liked none so well as the last (which signifies 'the Father of Dust'), because it was given him by the 'Glory of the World' himself. The occasion on which he gave it was the following. It happened that one day Fātima al-Zahrā[5] and the Imām 'Alī had an altercation, and on account of it the latter went to the *masjid* (chapel) and lay down on the dry earth. Much grieved with this, she forthwith went in search of the Prophet, and related to him what had happened, adding that the fault was her own. The Prophet immediately walked around the *masjid*, and observing 'Alī reposing on the ground, addressing him, exclaimed, 'Arise, 'Alī, arise!' 'Alī, on hearing the voice of the blessed Prophet, at once got up, and the latter seeing some earth on his face, with his own blessed hands wiped it off, and said, 'Abū-Turāb (father of earth), arise!' But, in the *Shawāhid-al-Nabūwa*[6] it is stated that one day the blessed Prophet went to the house of Fātima—on whom be Divine satisfaction!—and, not finding 'Alī there, inquired where he was; Fātima replied that, having been troubled, he had gone out, perhaps to the *masjid*. On hearing which the Prophet forthwith went there, and seeing 'Alī lying on the bare ground, his mantle fallen off, and his body covered with dust, he bade him arise, calling him for that purpose Abū-Turāb, and with his own hands wiped the dust off him."

[1] Amīr al-Nuhl, 'Lord of the gift.' But in the Nusairī catechism Amīr an-Nahl is rendered 'Prince of Bees', and explained to mean that "the true believers are like bees, which seek the best flowers. Therefore is he so called" (Rev. S. Lyde, *The Asian Mystery*, p. 275).

[2] Abu'l Rahānain would mean 'father of pledges', from *rahān* or *rihān*, but rūḥānain, 'blessed spirits' is probably meant, the dual alluding to Ḥasan and Ḥusain.

[3] Asad-Ullāh al-Ghālib means 'the lion of God, the Victorious' (*E.I.* i. p. 284).

[4] The title Abū Turāb, 'father of dust', said to have been bestowed on 'Alī by Muḥammad, is regarded by the Shī'as as an honorific surname (*E.I.* i. p. 111). *Turāb*, 'earth', is one of the four elements (*v.* note on p. 475 *infra*).

[5] Fātima al-Zuhrā, 'the beauteous', to distinguish her from Fāṭima the mother of 'Alī. Burton, however, gives a different explanation of the title, which he equates to al-Batul, 'the Virgin' (*Pilgrimage*, ii. pp. 90-91). The account in the text is not noticed in the interesting art. in *E.I.* ii. pp. 85-88.

[6] 'Evidences of Prophecy'.

"The marriage of 'Alī with Fātima-al-Zahrā (the fair), daughter of the Prophet, occurred as follows:

"The blessed Prophet had six children born to him by Khadīja al-Kubrā (the great), two of which were boys and four were daughters; and it was after the birth of Fātima that she left this perishable world for that of eternity. The blessed Prophet nursed this last child until she reached the age of puberty, and himself educated her (morally). One day, whilst she was engaged in serving her father, he remarked that she had reached an age when it was necessary to marry her, and he felt sad to think that he had not the mother, whom she greatly resembled, to attend to the matter for her. It may be added that Fātima had always been a pious and serious-minded girl, and was in consequence much beloved by her parent. Whilst this thought was still in his mind, the messenger of the Most High (the angel Gabriel) appeared before him, and saluting him on the part of the Almighty, said, 'Be not troubled, O Muhammad! I will prepare a dowry for Fātima out of the treasures of Paradise, and bestow her upon one who is a good and faithful servant to Me'. These words greatly affected the blessed Prophet, and so soon as he had offered up thanks and adoration to God for his great mercies, the angel disappeared from sight but for a moment, for he soon returned, bearing in his hand a golden vessel, covered over with a golden cloth. Behind him followed 1000 angelic cherubim (*karūbīyūn*), with the angel Mīkhāīl (Michael) in their rear, also bearing a similar vessel, covered over like the first; after them came the same number of cherubim, followed by the angel 'Izrā'īl, similarly laden, and each laid their burthens as an offering before him.

"On beholding this apparition the Prophet, addressing Gabrāīl, said, 'Oh! Brother, tell me what are the commands of the Most High, and what I am to do with these vessels!' The angel replied, "O! Prophet of God, He salutes thee, and commands that 'thy daughter of Paradise, Fātima al-Zahrā, be given to 'Alī; for from the great arch of the heavens I have married them together'. He has likewise commanded that you betroth her in the presence of the *asḥābs*; let her be dressed in the garments contained in one of the vessels; and make a feast for the guests (*asḥābs*) from the food contained in the others."

"The blessed Prophet, on hearing these divine commands, addressing the angel, exclaimed, 'O! Brother Gabrāīl, pray inform me distinctly as to what I must do regarding the wedding'. The angelic messenger replied, 'He has commanded that the gates of Paradise be thrown open; that Paradise be splendidly ornamented; that the doors of the criminals be closed; that all of the angels, *muqarribīn*,[1] *karūbīyīn*,[2] and *rūhānīn*[3] (those nearest to God, the cherubim, and the blessed spirits), in the seven spheres of heaven and earth, assemble together in the shade of the great arch, under the Tūbā trees. He has also commanded that an odoriferous breeze shall blow over the angels, the sweetness of which is indescribable, and that when it blows it put in motion the leaves of the same trees, in such a manner as to create the most pleasant harmony, intoxicating the senses of those who hear

[1] *Makribeen* in original: for *muqarrabūn*, 'those who are allowed to approach, especially to the divine presence of God, the Cherubim, the archangels, etc.' The *-īn* is the oblique form used in Turkish as a nominative.

The saints, *muqarrabūn*, who have not to be judged, being justified in advance, are assessors to the Judge. They are enthroned with the *salām* or *qaul*, 'salutation', as special symbols (Massignon, *Lexique technique*, p. 88).

According to Ḥasan Baṣri and others they are the mysterious *ahl al-a'rāf* of the *Qurān* (vii. 44-6). Ḥasan himself declared them to be the martyrs and ascetics: Tustarī, more precise, specifies them as the mystic saints, the *ahl-i-ma'rifat*. The Sunni view is that they are the prophets and the *khalīfas*: while the Imamites make them the prophets and the twelve *imāms* (Massignon, *Al-Hallaj*, ii. p. 688).

Ṣūfīs often use the term *muqarrab*, lit. 'one who is brought near (to God)' to describe the highest class of saints. The *muqarrab* prefers union to separation, whereas in perfect union there are no contraries. The term is borrowed from the *Qurān* (Nicholson, *Studies in Islamic Mysticism*, p. 230).

In the Nusairi system this earthly world contains seven degrees of believers:—

The *muqarrabīn*, 'near ones', numbering seventeen thousand.
,, cherubims.
,, *ruhiyīn*, 'spiritual'.
,, *muqaddasīn*, 'sanctified'.
,, *saiyīn*, 'ascetics'.
,, *mustama'īn*, 'listeners'.
,, *lahihīn* (? *lāhiqīn*), 'followers', each degree being one thousand more numerous than the one above it, so that the grand total amounts to 119,000. This hierarchy is, of course, below the luminous, spiritual hierarchy of the Abwāb, etc. (Lyde, *The Asian Mystery*, pp. 111-12).

[2] 'Cherubs'. But the only cherubim known to orthodox Islam are the four, Gabriel, Michael, Rafael (Isrāfīl), and Azrael as Christian guardians of the points of the compass (Evliya, i. Pt. 2, p. 18).

[3] For *Rūḥānīūn*, pl. of *rūḥānī*, 'spiritual'. The name was bestowed on the first Sunnī mystics (Massignon, *Al-Hallaj*, ii. p. 662).

them ; and He also has commanded the birds of the gardens of Paradise to sing sweetly.' All of which was done accordingly.

" The angel also said to the Prophet : ' O ! Friend of God, the Most High has likewise commanded me as follows : " O ! Gabrāīl, be thou the *wakīl* (representative at the marriage ceremony) of My lion 'Alī, and I will be the *wakīl* of My servant Fātima ; and these, My angels, be witnesses that I have freely bestowed My servant Fātima in marriage upon My lion 'Alī. Thou, Gabrāīl, as his *wakīl*, accept of the betrothal ". In this manner, these two are to be married from heaven ; and He (God) has commanded that you assemble here all of the *asḥābs*—on whom be the Divine satisfaction !—and proceed to the performance of the nuptial ceremony.' The blessed Prophet again offered up adoration and thanks, and called together all of the *asḥābs*, and then addressing the angel, said, ' O ! Brother Gabrāīl, my thoughts are much occupied with my daughter Fātima ; it is not proper that she should wear in this world the clothes of Paradise ; take them, therefore, back there '.

" When the *asḥābs* came together, they inquired who would be the *wakīls* of the Prophet and 'Alī. Just then the Angel Gabriel descended, and addressing the Prophet of God, said, ' O Prophet of God ! He salutes thee, and commands that 'Alī performs the *khutba*' (the solemn prayer of noon, on Friday, and in Bairām).[1] 'Alī thereupon recited this prayer, after which he was married to Fātima, for the dowry of four hundred *āqchas* [2] (silver pieces). When Fātima received information of her marriage she was dissatisfied; and the angelic messenger descending again, said, ' O Prophet of God ! He commands that in case my servant Fātima be not satisfied with the amount of four hundred *āqchas*, let it be four thousand '. This change being communicated to Fātima, she still expressed discontent ; and Gabriel, again returning, directed that the portion be made four thousand *āltūns* [3] (gold pieces). As she was still dissatisfied,

[1] Bairām is an Osmānli-Turkish word which denotes the two great Musulman festivals, that on the breaking of the fast (*'īd ul-fitr*) of the lesser 'Īd, and the *qurbān bairām* or ' feast of the sacrifice ' (*E.I.* i. p. 594).

[2] Āqcha, Turk. ' silver ' (cf. *āq*, ' white '). It is now used to denote a rouble, at least in W. Turkistān. But it is also used of copper coin (*E.I.* i. p. 229).

[3] Āltūn, Turk. ' gold ' ; also used of gold coins (*E.I.* i. p. 322, *s.v. altin* or *altun*).

Gabriel returned, and directed the Prophet to go in person to his daughter and ask her what she desired. On hearing this, the Prophet arose, and having gone to her, his daughter, asked her what she wished done on the occasion of her marriage; she replied, 'O Friend of God! I wish that in the same manner that you are the intercessor for rebellious men, at the Day of Judgment, to render them faithful, so may I intercede for women, and place them in Paradise' (*jannat*). On this the Prophet withdrew, and made known to Gabriel what his daughter desired. The Angel departed, and conveyed to the presence of the All-Glorious her reply: he soon returned, and reported to the Prophet that her wishes had been acceptable to God; and He had commanded that, at the Day of Judgment, she might intercede for women. He added that there was a verse in the ancient books, and in the Great *Qurān*, to that effect, serving as a *hujjat* or title in her behalf. The Prophet having inquired where the title was to which he alluded, the Angel begged leave to convey his question to the Most High, and receive His commands,—which he did, and immediately returned, bearing in his hand a roll of white silk, which he handed to the Prophet. The latter, on opening the roll, perceived in it a document, in which was written, 'By this Title, I appoint my servant Fātima to be the intercessor, in the Day of Judgment, in favour of the *mūmina* (faithful females)'. The Prophet of God now took this roll and conveyed it to Fātima; she accepted it, and declared that she was now satisfied with her marriage. It is, however, related that the Imām 'Alī did not put any faith in this title. At the Last Day, he may therefore be asked what became of it. It is also related that when the Prophet married Fātima to 'Alī, he presented to her eighteen *āqchas*, together with a spotted robe, and that as he wept, she put it on, and inquired the cause of his tears, and he replied by asking her what account she would be able to give of her nuptial presents when she came to appear before the Almighty? He likewise added that if the thoughts of such small presents gave him so much pain, what must be the reflections of those parents who expend hundreds,—perhaps even thousands,—upon the bridal suits of their daughters."

"The Imām 'Alī was somewhat smaller than the middle size, with broad shoulders and light-coloured eyes; his blessed beard was of a sandy colour, and plentiful in quantity, and his breast was rather large. Whenever infidels beheld his countenance, their hearts failed them and caused them to tremble like autumn leaves. He not unfrequently remained without food from three to four, five, and even seven and eight days, and so remarkable was this peculiarity, that the blessed Prophet was once questioned as to the cause. He answered that 'Alī possessed a holy strength, which preserved him from the cravings of hunger, so that during the Holy Wars, in which he took an active part, he seldom partook of any food, and occupied himself entirely with the promotion of the war,—the subject of food never for a moment troubling his mind. No such war occurred without his taking part in it; and whenever a fortification held out, or the enemies proved to be strong, the Prophet would give him his own flag, and telling him that he had commended him to the Most High, bade him take the former and conquer it, which he never failed to accomplish."

"There was a very numerous Christian tribe called the Banī Buhrān,[1] which, notwithstanding the repeated advice of the blessed Prophet, continued dissatisfied and held out against him. Their pertinacity and rebellious conduct increasing, it was impossible to strive against them. Finally, the illustrious *āyat* (verse) of the *ibtihāl* (obedience) descended from heaven, and they were thus divinely commanded to submit.[2] It is stated in the *sura* (chap. iii. of the *Qurān*, 54th verse) called the *al-'Imrān*: 'To those who shall dispute with thee on this subject, since thou hast received perfect knowledge, reply: "Come, let us call our children and yours, our wives and yours, come, we and you, and

[1] Muir describes the Beni-Bahra as 'a Christian or semi-Christian tribe near Tadmor' (*Annals of the Early Caliphate*, p. 103; cf. *The Life of Mahomet*, p. 381). The lithograph reads 'Najrān'.

There may have been a Christian tribe so named, but the Banu Burhān or Barhān, as it is spelt on page 403, appear to be the Ethiopians. Abraha, the viceroy or ruler of Yaman, is the subject of chap. cv. of the *Qurān*. Kings Abrahā and Aṣbaḥā are still saints in the Ethiopic Calendar (Adrian Fortescue, *The Lesser Eastern Churches*, p. 295).

The fortress of Bakhrā', Baḥrā', or Baḥr, on the frontier of Palmyra, may, however, be alluded to (cf. *E.I.* i. p. 600).

[2] *Bahala*, 'he left free, at large'. *Bahalat* is a curse or imprecation. *Ibtihāl*, 'the humbling one's self in prayer'.

let us pray to the Lord, each one apart [then we will imprecate], and call down curses upon the liars" '.[1]

"This signifies that whosoever disputes with thee on the subject of Jesus,—on whom be peace!—after the knowledge which has come to thee respecting Jesus, who is the servant and apostle of the Most High, know that the expression *abnāanā*, of this *āyat*, means Fātima, and *anfusanā* means the blessed Prophet's pure breath, which is none other than 'Alī himself; because among the Arabs it is customary to call the son of an uncle *nafsī* (breath or person). God has said, *Wa lā talmaizu anfusakum*, meaning, 'And do not defame your uncles' sons', 'your brothers', in which is understood all those who are of the true religion; and ibn-'Abbās,—on whom be Divine satisfaction!—declares that *summa nabtahil* signifies, 'Let us pray and implore'. Gulebee[2] (an author) says this means 'to pray and war excessively,' whilst Kasāī[3] and Abū 'Ubaida[4] say it means, 'Let it curse them together', for *ibtihāl* signifies 'the curse', and *Fa-naj'āl la'nat Allāhi 'alāi'l-kāzibīna* means, 'Let us, we and you, all of us, call down God's curses upon the liars'.

[1] Palmer's *Qurān* S.B.E. vi. p. 54. The *sura* is called the chapter of 'Imrān's family.

The full verse is: "*Faman ḥājjaka fīhi min ba'di mā jāaka min al'ilmi faqul ta'āl-wā nadu' abnāanā wa abnāakum, wa nisāanā wa nisāakum, wa anfusanā wa anfusakum, ṣumma nabtahil fanaj'al lla'nata Allāhi 'ala-i al-kāzibīna*" (*The Qoran with the Commentary of al-Zamakhshari*, by Nassau Lees, i. pp. 207-8).

[2] Gulebi, Muḥammad b. Sa'ib al-Kalbī, the traditionist who transmitted traditions derived from Ibn 'Abbās and which were recorded by Ishāq b. Ibrāhīm b. Manṣūr b. Khalaf un-Nīsābūrī, author of the *Qiṣaṣ al-Anbia'*. He died in 146 H.=A.D. 764 (*Cat. of Turkish MSS. in B.M.*, p. 143). But Abū Thaur, Ibrāhīm b. Khālid b. Abū'l Yaman al-Kalbī, mainly a follower of Shāfi'ī, who died in 240 H., may be meant (Wüstenfeld, pp. 53-55).

According to the author of the *Mawahib al-Ludunia* Kalbī's traditions have been rejected as his veracity was suspect (Syed Ahmed Khan, *Essays on the Life of Mohammed*, Ess. on M. Traditions, p. 41). He does not seem to have derived all his lore direct from Ibn 'Abbās, but through intermediaries such as Abū Sālih.

[3] 'Ali b. Hamza Al-Kisā'i died in 189 H. (A.D. 805). He was an authority on the correct reading of the *Qurān* and taught at Kūfa (Wüstenfeld, *Der Imam el-Schafi'i*, p. 49).

[4] Abū 'Ubaida, a celebrated companion and one of the ten Asharah, who died in 639 H. Matthews gives his name as Āmir b. 'Abdullah b. ul-Jarrāh al-Kahadi-al-Qūrashī (*Mishcat*, ii. p. 310; cf. *E.I.* ii. p. 293), where he is called Abū 'Ubaida bin al-Jarrāh, one of the Ḥawārī or apostles.

"The Prophet of God read this verse on the people of Bahrān, and invited them not to curse his faith; whilst on their part they replied, 'Let us return to our people, and take counsel together regarding our affairs, and to-morrow we will come'. So they assembled together, and finally the more sensible amongst them said, 'Do you not believe in the words of the Messiah?' To which the Prophet replied, 'Oh! Nazarenes, you confirm the congregation (of the Messiah), and that Muḥammad is the Prophet sent by the Most High, and yet call upon yourselves His curses. If you thus continue, you will all meet death; so return to your Master, and remain in the belief of His words.'

"On the following day they came with 'Alī before the blessed Prophet, whom they found holding Husain in his arms, and Hasan by his hand, whilst Fātima followed him. He bade these to exclaim, 'Amen!' whenever he prayed. Now when the Nazarene chiefs approached him, he, addressing them, said, 'Oh! congregation of Nazarenes, I of a truth thus view the case: if you ask of God to remove a mountain, He will do so, in honour of Himself; guard against maledictions, or you will meet destruction, and not a Nazarene will remain on the earth's surface from this to the end of time'. On hearing this, the chiefs begged Abū'l Qāsim to advise them what to do, and added that they had decided not to curse Muhammad. 'We will leave you in your religion, and continue firm in our own.'

"The Prophet of God commanded, 'Since you have decided to refrain from curses, become Mussulmans. You are in need of that which they possess, and you will then participate in the same.' This they refusing to do, he added, 'Prepare then to die, for we will certainly put you to death'. They now declared that they were unable to war with the Arabs, and preferred to make peace with them, and have their lives spared. 'Do not', they said, 'frighten us, nor seek to cause us to abandon our religion, and we will yearly pay you 2000 suits, 1000 in the month of Safar, and 1000 in that of Rajab.' So the blessed Prophet consented to their proposal and made peace with them, and declared, 'My person is in His hands. Punishment has been turned away from the people of Bahrān. Had they cursed, they would have been turned into monkeys and pigs, and been consumed with flashes of fire; in fact, God would have destroyed both Bahrān and its inhabitants; and even the birds on the trees would not have survived one year.'"

"Mīr Husain Wā'iz [1]—on whom be Divine mercy!—in his work in the Persian tongue, a commentary called *Kasf*, when commenting on the *sura* 'Baqr' (of the *Qurān*, chap. ii. v. 275), 'Those who give alms day and night, in secret and in public, will receive their reward from God; [2] fear will not descend upon them, nor will they be afflicted,' says, in regard to the 'causes of descent', that 'Alī al-Murtazā once had four *dirhams*; one of these he publicly gave away in alms; one he gave away secretly, one he bestowed during the darkness of night, and one he bestowed during the light of day. The Most High thereon caused that *āyat* to descend, and the blessed Prophet inquired of 'Alī what kind of alms he had been giving. He replied, 'I have not gone beyond these four paths in their bestowal; I took them all upon myself, so that at least one of them may meet with acceptance'."

"In the *sura* ''Alam Sijda' [3] ('Adoration'), on the subject of the "Signs of descent" (ch. xxxii. v. 18), 'He who has believed, will he be like him who has given himself up to sin? Will they both be equal?' The commentator, Muhyī al-Sunna [4]—on whom be mercy!—says, 'This verse descended in favour of 'Alī

[1] Mīr Ḥusain Wa'iẓ Kāshifī, also author of the more famous *Anwār-i-Suhailī*, or 'Lights of Canopus'. Like Mir Khwānd, he was one of the brilliant group of writers and painters at the court of the great king of Khurāsān, Ḥusain Mīrza—1469–1506 A.D.—(*E.I.* ii. p. 343).

[2] "Those who expend their wealth by night and day, secretly and openly, they shall have their hire with their Lord" (Palmer's *Qurān* S.B.E., vi. p. 44).

[3] Ch. xxxii. is the *surat us-sijda*, and it is prefixed by the latters A.L.M. which could not possibly be read *'alam*, 'sign'.

Sijda lit. = 'prostration', and from the same root come *masjid*, 'mosque', and *sajāda*, 'prayer-carpet'.

[4] Muhee el Seneh in original. Muḥyī 'l Sunna, or 'the restorer of orthodoxy', was a title of al-Baghawī (Abū Muḥammad al-Ḥusain b. Ma'sud b. Muḥammad al-Farrā'), an Arab *faqīh* (jurist) of the Shāfi'ite school, who, in addition to the *Muṣābiḥ ul-Sunna*, wrote a commentary on the *Qurān* called the *Ma'ālim ul-Tanzīl*. He was born in Khurāsān and died in A.D. 1117 or 1122, when upwards of eighty years of age (*E.I.* i. p. 562; *v.* note on p. 409 and *infra*). Al-Baghawī also wrote the *Sharḥ-us-Sunnat* and *Jāmi' bain-ul-Saḥīḥain*. He was styled al-Farrā because he was a vendor of furs (Beale, *Or. Biogr. Dy.*, p. 28).

bin-Abū-Tālib, and Walīd bin Abū Ma'īt,[1] who, on his mother's side, was related to 'Othman (the third direct Caliph). A quarrel occurred between 'Alī and Walīd, on which occasion the latter made a remark to 'Alī, and directed the latter to be silent, saying, 'You are but a youth; I for the want of a tongue am silent, and in point of years am your senior; my heart is more courageous than yours, and in war I am braver'. To this 'Alī replied, 'Be you silent, for you are certainly a wicked man. The Most High has sent down this verse, but said *they* in the *plural*, and not *they* in the *dual*, for He did speak of one faithful and one evil-minded, but alluded to *all* the faithful and to *all* the wicked.'"

"On the same subject (the *ma'lam tanzīl*),[2] or the 'signs of the descent', the Imām Baghāvī, regarding the ch. lxxvi. v. 1, 'Has much time passed over man without his being thought of?' and the eighth verse of the same chapter, 'Who, though themselves sighing after the meal, give food to the poor, the orphan, and the captive', says there has been much disputation regarding these verses, and the cause of their descent. Majāhid [3] and 'Atā ibn-'Abbās [4] relate that they came down for 'Alī, and in a succinct

[1] Walīd bin Ukba, one of the companions and, according to Matthews (*Mishcat ul-Masabih*, ii. p. 366), a brother of the Caliph 'Othmān, who made him governor of Kūfa.

[2] *Me'lem* in original; *ma'lam*, for *ma'ālim*, pl. of *'alam*, 'sign'. *Tanzīl* lit. means 'descent', but its meaning here is 'revelation' or 'inspiration', alluding to the Prophet's claim that his teaching was inspired. For this Imām Baghawī see note on p. 404 *supra*. An Imām Bāghawī has a tomb at Qonia with which certain stones are associated. These are two drums of an angle-pillar from a classical colonnade. The pillar . . . had its two antæ worked as half-columns, so that the section of each drum is heart-shaped. With the angle uppermost the two present some resemblance to a saddle, from which circumstance they are supposed to represent the horses of the Imām turned to stone, and cures are wrought by contact with them in the posture thus suggested (Hasluck in *Annual*, B.S.A., xxi. p. 73). Who this Imām may be does not appear. In Turk. *bāghū* = 'a spell'. The title Baghawī was also borne by Abū Ja'far Aḥmad b. Mani' b. 'Abd-ar-Raḥmān al-Baghawī, the deaf, and by his cousin Isḥāq b. Ibrāhīm b. 'Abd-ar-Raḥmān al-Baghawī; the former settled at Baghdād and passed on traditions from al-Bukhārī: *d.* 256 H. (*J.R.A.S.*, 1901, p. 205).

[3] *Majāhid*, *v.* note on p. 33.

[4] 'Atā ibn-'Abbās, apparently an error for 'Aṭā b. Abī Rabāḥ Aslam al-Makkī al-Qurashī, who was celebrated for his learning and virtue as one of the *tābi'ūn*, in spite of his physical deficiencies (Matthews, *Mishcat*, i.

manner state the fact ; whilst in other commentaries it is narrated in detail. Hasan and Husain (sons of 'Alī) having fallen ill, the holy and revered Prophet and all of the *aṣḥābs* went to see them, and 'Alī and Fātima were addressed by the Prophet, and requested to make a vow in favour of their beloved children ; this was also done by the maiden slaves of the parents, named Surūr and Fazah, and they all together vowed that if God would restore them to health, they should fast for three days. After they had recovered they had nothing to eat, and 'Alī went to a Jew and purchased on credit three bushels of barley, which, in performance of the vow, he devoted to their fast. One of the three measures Fātima ground, so as to make five cakes. When their term of fasting had ended she gave one to 'Alī, one to Hasan, one to Husain, and another to the maid Fazah, whilst she kept one for herself. Just then a miserable beggar appeared, and exclaimed, 'Oh ! family of the Prophet of God, I am a most miserable Mussulman ; give me of your food, and God will recompense you by bestowing on you the choicest meats of Paradise'. On hearing these words, they gave him the cake that was in their hands and contented themselves with a cup of water, and fasted till the day following. Fātima again ground another measure and made five more cakes. When they were about to partake of these, an orphan came along and asked for food, so they gave them to it, rejoicing its heart by the gift, and again contented themselves with a drink of water, and went to sleep. On the day following, she ground the third measure of barley and made five cakes, and just as they were about to eat them, a captive made his appearance and asked for food, saying, 'It is three days that I am without food, and have been kept tied without anything to eat ; pray, for God's sake, have pity on me'. So they all gave the starving man their cakes, and contented themselves with water. Some say that this captive was a believer in the Trinity, and the narrative goes to prove that to feed a suffering captive, even if he be a Trinitarian, is a good action, and must be so regarded. It is said that on the morning of the fourth day, 'Alī

---

p. 350). According to the *Mishcat* he handed down a tradition connected with Ibn 'Abbās. He died in 114 H. (A.D. 732) (*J.R.A.S.*, 1901, p. 203, n. 2). But according to Margoliouth, who ascribes to him the introduction of music into devotion, his death occurred in 710 A.D. (*Early Development of Islam*, p. 178).

took his two [1] sons in his hands, and went to the blessed Prophet, who remarked that hunger had reduced them so much that they trembled like young birds ; and he said to 'Alī, ' Oh, 'Alī, how deeply you have afflicted me ! ' Then, taking them with him, he went to Fātima, whom he saw in the *mihrāb* (pulpit),[2] her stomach stuck to her back, and her eyes were sunken. His grief was thereby greatly increased. Just then the Angel Gabriel, descending, addressed the blessed Prophet, and said, ' Take this from the All-Just ', handing him the chapter [lxxvi] entitled *Insān*, or ' man '.

" It is related that when the Prophet once visited Fātima, he said to her, ' My daughter, it is now four days since your father has partaken of any food '. He had, in fact, left Madìna, and met with an Arab engaged in drawing water from a well ; and, addressing him, asked whether he would employ him to draw up water for him, and, having consented, an agreement was made by which he was to receive two dates for each bucket of water, so that the most blessed Prophet of the Most High Almighty was actually employed, for a given stipend, to draw water from the well. After drawing as much water as was needed, by Divine providence the cord broke, and the bucket fell into the well : on seeing which the Arab struck his blessed face a blow, and paid him all of the dates which he had earned. The Prophet now reached his hand down into the well and pulled out the bucket, and, after handing it to the Arab, departed to visit Fātima, to whom he now presented the dates. Whilst eating them, she remarked traces of the blow upon her father's face, and asked the cause of it. The Prophet replied that it was nothing, and sought to conceal the fact from her knowledge. Now it happened that when the Arab struck the blessed Prophet, and saw him draw up the bucket from the well, he was greatly surprised, and reflected that if the individual was not God's Prophet he could certainly not have done this. ' The hand which has done such a dishonour to a Prophet must not be mine ' ; so he at once cut it off, and set out in search of the Prophet whom he had wronged. Knocking at the door, 'Alī was surprised to see before him a man with one hand held in the other, and blood flowing from the arm from which it had been amputated. Having informed the Prophet of the circumstance, he smiled, and said that this was the Arab

[1] Ten in original. [2] Translated ' altar ' on p. 202, *q.v.*

who had struck him so severely as to leave traces of the blow on his face. He also bade 'Alī permit the man to come in; and on his entrance he was much pained by the sight, and asked the Arab why he had committed such an act? The Arab wept, and implored forgiveness of his fault, and the blessed Prophet, putting the two ends of the arm and hand together, prayed over them, and so they became reunited. By God's providence, thus the Arab recovered the full use of his arm."

"Fātima relates that once the blessed Prophet asked 'Alī whether he loved God. 'Alī replied that he did. The Prophet next asked him whether he loved him, and 'Alī made the same answer. He next asked him whether he loved Fātima, and he replied again in the affirmative. He then inquired whether he loved Hasan and Husain, and he answered as before.

"The Prophet now asked him how his heart could contain so much love, and he was unable to reply. Troubled by his want of ability, 'Alī went to Fātima and explained the same to her. She remarked that he did not need to be troubled, for love for God came from the mind; that for the Prophet from faith; love for her came from human passion, and that for their sons from nature.

"'Alī now returned forthwith to the Prophet, and having given him this answer, the latter exclaimed, 'This is not the fruit of faith, but of the prophetship', thereby meaning that the answer did not proceed from himself, but from Fātima. In fact, her explanations were full of wisdom, merit, and deep reflection."

"Fātima also relates that when 'Alī al-Murtazā had captured the fortress of Khaibar, and with his *Zūl-fiqār* (a sword presented to him by the Prophet) had cut off the heads of the infidels, and returned sound, and with much booty, he told Fātima to remark that he owed the capture to that sword. She answered, 'Oh, 'Alī, I know the *Zūl-fiqār* far better than him'. 'Alī went to the Prophet and repeated to him what had occurred and the words of Fātima; and he arose, and going to see her, asked how it was she knew better the *Zūl-fiqār* than 'Alī. Fātima replied, 'Oh, most excellent and respected parent, the night in which you went up to heaven and saw your Lord, you reposed under a tree of Paradise, from which you gathered two apples, one of which you gave to my mother, and the other you ate. I am the fruit of those two apples. At the time the sword of *Zul-fiqār* hung upon the tree.'

"The Prophet was much gratified by her answer, and on leaving her, exclaimed that it was a blessing for any person to have such a daughter."

"In the work entitled the *Masābīh Sharīf*[1] it is related as an anecdote, coming from Sa'd ibn-Abī Waqqās,[2] that the blessed Prophet once remarked to 'Alī, 'Thou art to me what Aaron was to Moses, and of a truth after me there is no prophet'. Thur Pishtī[3] states that on the occasion of the war of Tabūq,[4] the Prophet appointed 'Alī as his *khalīfa* (lieutenant) over the people, and directed that he should preside over their affairs. The hypocrites having learned this, declared that he had not appointed 'Alī as *khalīfa*, and it was only to rid himself of worry that he so named him. When 'Alī heard of this he put on his sword and went directly to the Prophet, then at a place called Jarf, and asked him whether what the hypocrites had said regarding his appointment, viz. that it was only to free himself from worry, was true? The Prophet declared that they were all liars, and that he had named his *khalīfa* in consequence of his intended absence from Madīna; that he should return, and act as such for him, even if his own wife (Khadīja) and that of 'Alī should refuse to accept of him. 'For you are to me what Aaron was to

[1] Doubtless the *Maṣābīḥ-us-Sunna* or 'Lamps of the Sunna', a celebrated collection of traditions of al-Baghawī (Huart, *Textes Houroufis*, p. 56). Baghawī's work has had the unusual honour of being translated into English in its recension by Walī-ud-Dīn al-Tibrīzī called the *Mishkāt al-Maṣābīḥ*, 'The Niche of the Lamps' (*v.* A. N. Matthews' *Mishcat al-masābīh, or a Collection of the most authentic Traditions regarding the Actions and Sayings of Muhammad*, Calcutta, 1807–10).

[2] His name was Mālik b. Wahīb az-Zaharī al-Karashī, and he was the seventh person to embrace Islam (Matthews, *Mishcat*, i. p. 144). Sale calls him one of the six principal *aṣḥab*, 'companions', of the Prophet (*Koran*, i. p. 200).

[3] Thur Pishtī, possibly Sufyān ath-Thawrī, one of the *tābi'īn*, son of Sa'īd, an inhabitant of Kūfa. Born in 99 H. he became of high authority in tradition and died in 161 H. = A.D. 778 (Matthews, *Mishcat*, i. p. 452).

[4] Tabūq, a town half-way between Madīna and Damascus. The expedition took place in the 9th year of the Hijra under very unfavourable conditions (Sale's *Koran* in Wherry's recension, ii. pp. 374, 291 ff.). It ended in the submission of the Christian prince, John of Aylah.

Moses, just as it is said in the holy *āyat*, " And Moses said to his brother, be my *khalīfa* among the people ".' All commentators and confirmers of this *āyat* held this to be a legal deed in favour of 'Alī. Even the Rāfizīs [1] and the Shī'as hold to this, to show that the Caliphate belonged to 'Alī, and that he thus accepted it. At a later period, disagreements arose between them, and the Rāfizīs declared that the *aṣḥābs* were guilty of blasphemy, and others again accused 'Alī of the same crime. According to their statement, 'Alī had a full right to the Caliphate ; and, if so, why did he not arise and demand it? All of this (says the author) I must most surely condemn as entirely erroneous.

" Qāzī [2] states that ' there is no room to doubt of the blasphemy of those who make such a declaration ; for any one who would thus injure his whole people, and debase the highest authorities, denies the holy law itself, and destroys Islāmism '. The fact is that the *āyat* (before quoted) in no manner served as a deed to their declaration in favour of 'Alī ; it can only serve, at best, as a proof of his excellent character, but cannot be quoted to show that he was *the* best, or even equal to the other successors of the blessed Prophet. On the occasion of the war of Tabūq he was named *khalīfa* only for the reasons assigned, just as Aaron acted for Moses for a particular period. It is well known that Aaron did not become *khalīfa* after Moses, and there is good reason to believe that he died full forty years previous to Moses, and only was appointed to lead the prayers when the latter went to be with the Lord."

" It is also related, as an anecdote in the *Masābīh*, that 'Alī stated : ' Glory be to that Most High God, who causeth the grain to grow, and who created man, on account of the words which the blessed Prophet used in my behalf, " because he loved only the

[1] The term Rāfiẓī came to be applied to all schismatics who spoke against any of the companions of the Prophet, but historically it has a narrower application. The Rāfiẓīs were a sect of the Shī'as of Kūfa who abandoned Zaid b. 'Alī, a descendant of 'Alī the 4th caliph, because he forbade them to speak against the first two caliphs (D. B. Macdonald in *J.R.A.S.*, 1901, p. 237 n.). Shī'as : for Shey'ee (Shi'ī) in original, but they may not be meant. Their collocation with the Rāfiẓī, ' an extreme Khārijite sect ', and usually regarded as heretics, suggests that the Asha'rites or followers of al-Ash'arī are meant. Both sects were joined in the same anathema *c.* 450 H. (Macdonald, *Muslim Theology*, p. 212).

[2] Kāzī, probably al-Kisā'ī ; *v.* p. 402.

faithful, and despised the hypocritical" '; the correct signification of which *hadīs* is that the person who only regards 'Alī on account of his connexion with the Prophet, and for the love which the latter bore for him, and from the influence which the acts of 'Alī had upon the conquests of Islāmism, and loves him because of them, has in these so many evidences of the healthy faith of the believer. He who is happy on account of the coming of Islāmism, and renders obedience to the things which the blessed God and His Prophet have exhibited, but who opposes 'Alī on account of the same, entertains a feeling which is the reverse of what it should be, and is a gross hypocrite; his mystical faith will be evil in the extreme,—from all of which may God preserve us!"

"Tahil bin Sa'd [1] relates that on the occasion of the battle of Khaibar, the blessed Prophet said he would provide a standard for the day following, which, in the hands of one who, under God's blessing, would carry it to a victory,—a man who is beloved of God and His Prophet, and who also loves them.

"Now the morning of that day came, and the people ran in haste to the Prophet to ask and implore him for the promised flag. The Prophet asked for 'Alī; and being informed that his eyes pained him, he bade them call him. On his arrival, the blessed Prophet of God rubbed his eyes with his own fingers, and the pain at once left them, so that they suddenly became perfectly cured. He then handed him the flag. 'Alī asked him whether he should destroy the infidels, after the usual mode of warfare: and the Prophet directed him to approach their country quietly and gently, and then to invite them to accept of Islāmism, or prepare to meet the young lion who advances against them on the part of the Most High God; for it is a good deed, he added, to be the medium of directing even one man in the true faith."

"On the same subject of the qualities of 'Alī, it is related in the *Masābīh*, as coming from 'Amrān bin Husain,[2] that the

[1] Tahil bin Sa'd, Sihl b. Sa'd, when almost the sole surviving companion of the Prophet, imbued Mālik ibn Ānas with his extreme veneration for the traditions. But how far he is to be regarded as responsible for the collection of traditions called the *Muwatta* does not appear (Beale, *Oriental Biographical Dy.*, p. 238).

[2] 'Imrān bin Ḥusain, Abū Nujaid, who embraced Islam in the year of the war of Khaibar (7 H.). He lived at Baṣra, and died in 52 H. at that place (Matthews, *Mishcat*, i. p. 116).

blessed Prophet once declared, 'Of a certainty 'Alī is from me, and I am from 'Alī, and he is the *walī* of all the Faithful'. In the excellent commentators of these words, it is found stated by Qāzī, 'The Shī'a people declare that 'Alī is the *walī* (possessor), and that the meaning of this *hadīs* is that 'Alī was worthy of possessing all the things that the Prophet possessed. The affairs of the Faithful appertained to these, and 'Alī was therefore their Imām.' To this we reply that he could not correctly bear the *imāmat* over their concerns during the life of the Prophet, because he was the Imām, and, consequently, his *walāyat* was only one of love and affection.

"The same work states, as coming from ibn-'Umr,[1] that the blessed Prophet declared the *aṣḥābs* should all be as brethren to each other. 'Alī on learning this, wept, and asked of the Prophet, why, as he had made them to be brethren, he had made him brother to no one? To this the Prophet replied, 'You are my brother, both in this life and in the life to come'. The Imām Tirmīzī[2] relates the same as a 'remarkable' *hadīs* (*hadīs gharīb*), or one not fully confirmed.

"On the subject of this same *hadīs*, Inis[3] relates that once the blessed Prophet had a roasted bird before him, of which he was about to partake, and exclaimed, 'O God! send to me him

[1] Ibn 'Umr, 'Abdullāh, son of 'Umr ibn al-Khattāb (Matthews, *Mishcat*, i. p. 3).

[2] Abū 'Abdullāh Muḥammad b. 'Alī al-Tirmīzī, also called Muḥammad Ḥakīm, founder of the Ḥakīmī, a Ṣūfī sect, died in 285 H. (A.D. 898). It is said that the apostle Khizr used to visit him every Sunday. He studied jurisprudence with a friend of Abū Ḥanīfa, and was the author of several works on Sufiism. His principal tenet was that a knowledge of servantship, *'ubūdīyat*, is essential to a knowledge of the nature of lordship, *rubūbīyat*, explained to mean that self-knowledge must precede knowledge of God, and a recognition of the contamination of human qualities a recognition of the purity of divine attributes (Nicholson, *Kashf al-Maḥjūb*, p. 141). He also maintained the superiority of Jesus, as Khātim al-wilāyah, over Muḥammad as Khātim al-nubūwah, a doctrine in which he was followed by Manṣūr al-Ḥallāj, a text of whom represents the second coming of Jesus, charged to establish the supreme prayer, etc. The Ṣūfīs awaited the second advent as the triumph of the real Islām (L. Massignon, *Kitāb al-Ṭawāsīn*, p. 161). But Abū 'Īsa Muḥammad b. 'Īsa al-Tirmizī, the compiler of a great collection of traditions, may be meant. He died six years earlier, in 279 H. (Wüstenfeld, *Der Imam el-Schafi'i*, p. 85).

[3] Inis, called apparently Enis on p. 431 *infra*, is probably Ānas bin Mālik (*v.* note on p. 428 *infra*). But the name Ānas is sometimes confused

whom Thou lovest most among Thy creatures, so that he may eat of this bird with me.' At that moment 'Alī came to the Prophet, and they ate the bird together. Tirmīzī states that this is a remarkable and beautiful *hadīs* ; and Thur Pishtī,[1] on commenting on it after alluding to it with much eloquence and excellence, says, 'Innovators have wasted much breath on this *hadīs*, and have blown the feathers quite off the wings of the bird, making a great deal of very little. Without wishing to cast any blame on the Caliphate of Abū Bakr, this *hadīs* should, on the decease of the Prophet, have been the first principle on which to unite the Mussulman people together, for it would have consolidated them, and sustained them.'

"To this we reply that the *hadīs* in question does not at all strengthen those which are of an obligatory character. As to the precedents, as well as all the good things that arose in the Caliphate of Abū Bakr, they condemn these holy *hadīses*, notwithstanding the most exact information which we possess from the whole of the *aṣḥābs* whose remarks on them still exist. It is, however, not proper to deny the *hadīs* in question, and one of these persons, Inis, quotes the fact that it was actually uttered, and no one disputes it. The real sense and signification of it is, therefore, that God should send him one of His most beloved, for his personal excellence and superior intelligence. There is nothing in the holy law showing that 'Alī was the most beloved of all of God's creatures, for among these was the blessed Prophet himself. We must then only accept what is comformable to the holy oracles of the *Qurān*, and known to the community of the people, then with the Prophet. It must, therefore, be read as we have stated above, or as it was understood by the children of the Prophet's uncle (Abū Bakr), whom he loved very much; because he often spoke freely, but always attentively, and never with negligence. In the *Masābīh* it is related in connexion with this

---

with Unais, as in the case of 'Ānas b. Abū Marthad Ghanawī', one of the *sahabah* who was present at the conquest of Makka and the battle of Hunain (*d.* 20 H.) (Matthews, *Mishcat*, ii. p. 721). Another Ānas, bin Nudr, uncle of Ānas b. Mālik and brother of Rabii, slain at Uhud, was one of the most illustrious of the *sahabah* (*ib.* p. 161). But neither of these appear to have left any traditions on record.

[1] Thur Pishtī, *v.* note on p. 409 *supra.*

hadīs, that 'Alī himself stated: 'Whenever I asked anything of the blessed Prophet, he would answer me; and if I remained silent, he would commence a conversation explaining his meaning'.

"It is also related in the *Masābīh*, as subsequent to the preceding *hadīs*, that the blessed Prophet once said with regard to Alī, 'I am the house of Wisdom, and 'Alī is the door'. Tirmīzī states that this also is a *hadīs gharīb*;[1] and Muhyī-'l-Sunna, who is the author of this book, declares that it was not known to any one of the companions of the Prophet. The Shī'as say that it was the intention of the Prophet that instruction in metaphysics (*hikmat*) should be peculiar to 'Alī; that no one else had this faculty, and that it could only be acquired by his medium. God, in His own firm words, has said, 'Piety does not consist in your entering your house through a door in its rear; but, in the fear of God, enter therefore by its proper portals' (chap. ii. v. 185). There is, in fact, no need of this at all, for Paradise is widely open to those acquainted with spiritual wisdom (*hikmat*), and it has eight portals for their admission. In the *Masābīh* it is related as coming from Jābir,[2] that the blessed Prophet called 'Alī, the day that he sent him to Tā'if,[3] and spake with him secretly. Though this conversation was a lengthy one, he said to his uncle's sons, 'I did not conclude with him, but God did'. Now the expression 'to conclude' signifies to 'converse secretly'. The commentator, Tāyibī,[4] says that these words mean that 'God commanded the Prophet to converse secretly with 'Alī'; and I

[1] For *garbee* in original. But this is not a recognised term in the science of the traditionists. *Gharīb*, 'strange, rare, foreign', on the other hand, is regularly used of such traditions as are 'isolated, do not date from one of the companions of the Prophet, but only from a later generation' (*E.I.* ii. p. 141, and cf. p. 192 *ib.*). Matthews defines it as resting on the testimony of a single narrator (*Mishcat ul-Masabih*, i. p. ii), and that is generally its meaning. See also note on p. 78 *supra.*

It is difficult to think that it ever meant traditions 'whose narrators have related but very few hadeeses', which is Syed Ahmed Khan's definition (*Essays on the Life of Muḥammad*, Essays on Traditions, p. 10).

[2] Jābir, Abū 'Abdullāh Jābir b. 'Abdullāh al-Anṣārī died in 74 H. = A.D. 693–94 (Matthews, *Mishcat*, i. p. 13).

[3] Ta'if, 60 miles east of Makka, was Muḥammad's place of refuge in the 11th year of his mission.

[4] Tāyibī, the Qāzī Abū-'ṭ-Ṭayyib aṭ-Ṭabarī, died in 450 H. = 1058 A.D. (? A.D. 834–923) (*J.R.A.S.*, 1901, p. 200, n. 1).

truly believe that it was by Divine command that he spoke with him of secret things. The same work relates, on the part of Umm Atīa,[1]—on whom be the Divine satisfaction!—that the Prophet of God sent troops in a holy warfare, and that 'Alī was among them. On that occasion the blessed Prophet elevated his hand, and prayed, 'O God, do not kill 'Alī, but send him back to me'.

"On one occasion the *aṣḥābs* inquired of the blessed Prophet the cause and reason of his great love for 'Alī, so that, in conformance with it, they might also increase their affection for him. In reply, he bade them go and call 'Alī to him, and learn the cause from himself. One of them went and called him; and whilst he was gone, the Prophet said, 'O my companions! should any one do good to you, what would you do in return to him?' They replied that they would do good to him. He then asked them what they would do if any one did harm to them; and they answered that they would still do him good. The Prophet repeated the latter question, and they bent down their heads, and made no reply. Just then 'Alī appeared, and the blessed Prophet asked him what he would do if any person should do him evil in return for his own goodness. 'Alī replied, 'O Prophet of God, I would do him good.' 'Should he again do you evil, what would you do?' added the Prophet; and 'Alī replied as before. This question was put for the seventh time by the most excellent of prophets, and 'Alī always replied the same, and finally added, 'O Prophet of God, I swear by that Almighty One, and there is none other, that should such a person harm me, a thousand years, in return for my own kindness, I would always continue to do him good'. On hearing these words, the *aṣḥābs* all agreed that the love of the Prophet was well founded, and they offered up a prayer for the object of his affection.

"Beware from supposing that the question of the *aṣḥābs* was caused by any feeling of jealousy, for it was only so as to know the cause of the particular affections the blessed Prophet bore for 'Alī.

"Once, three persons visited the Prophet of God, one of the people of Ibrāhīm, one of Moses, and one of Jesus. The first

[1] Ami Atieh in original: was the lady who took charge of the sick and wounded during the Prophet's wars (Matthews, *Mishcat*, i. p. 314).

asked the Prophet, 'How shall we know that you are indeed what you declare yourself, *i.e.* the greatest and most excellent of prophets, and the most acceptable of God,—for God said to Ibrāhīm (Abraham), Thou art my friend (*khalīl*)?' To this one the Prophet replied by saying, 'The Most High has said to me, Thou art my beloved friend (*habīb*),[1] which therefore is the nearest to any one; His friend (companion or associate), or His beloved?' The individual was amazed and unable to make any reply. Then looking upon the blessed face of the Prophet, he, from the bottom of his heart, pronounced the confession, 'I bear testimony that there is no God but Allāh. He is unique, and without any associate, and that Muḥammad is His servant and apostle.'

"Next came the individual of the people of Moses, and asked, 'Oh, Prophet of God, when you say that your place is the most exalted of all the prophets, and that you are their joy and sovereign, how shall it be known that this is really so? I have heard that the All-Just said to Moses, You are my *kalīm*[2] (interlocutor, or one who speaks with me), and that whenever He was up in Mount Sinai, he spoke with God.' To this the blessed Prophet replied, 'When God called Moses his *kalīm*, He called me His *habīb*, and though he went up on Mount Sinai, He sent me the angel Jabrāīl (Gabriel) with Barāq, ornamented with caparisons of Paradise, and, seated on him, in a short space of time I visited the world, the heavens, the celestial vault, the throne, Paradise, and Hell, as well as the whole Universe and all Creation, from the *Kāb Kausar* (cup of a stream of Paradise called *Kausar*) to the smallest object. The Most High spoke with me, and showed me the greatest kindness, so much so that there is no cause for modesty with Him on my part. Blessed be God for His great mercy in having chosen this humble and insignificant servant from among His people! God also promised me that whoever should pray every day one hundred times to my pure spirit, and he should never abandon or neglect this habit, He will pardon and have mercy on him one thousand times, and give him an exalted place in Paradise. His sins will a thousand thousand times be more pardoned than if he had given as many alms to the poor.'

[1] Habīb, 'beloved'.

[2] 'One who speaks', 'a familiar': hence Moses' name of Kalīm-ullāh, 'one who speaks to God'.

"Abū Huraira[1] relates, on the part of [Ānas] ibn Mālik, that on hearing the preceding, the individual was quite overcome; that he fell at the feet of the blessed Prophet, and then raising up his hands, recited with great joy the Confession of Faith.

"Next came the individual who was of the people of Jesus, and asked, 'When you say, I am near God, and am beloved of Him, and am the Lord of the beginning and of the ending; and that Jesus was the Spirit of God (*Rūh Allāh*), and that he resuscitated the dead in God's name, how are we to know the truth of this?' To this the blessed Prophet and the Apostle of the oppressed answered, 'Go and call 'Alī.' On hearing this command, one of the *aṣḥābs* went and bade 'Alī come to the Prophet; and on his arrival the latter directed the individual to point out to 'Alī one of the very oldest cemeteries. This person replied that in such a place there was a grave one thousand years old. 'Go,' said the blessed Prophet to 'Alī; 'go to that grave, and cry out three times, and wait patiently until you see what God will do.' 'Alī proceeded to the spot, and cried out once, 'O Jacob!' The grave immediately opened; he cried out the same once more, and the grave became completely open; on calling the same once more, lo! an aged man, with a bright countenance, came out of the grave, with hair so long that it reached from his head to his feet; and standing upright, he cried out with a loud voice the Confession of Faith. He next accompanied 'Alī to the presence of the Prophet of God, where, at the sight of so extraordinary a miracle, a large number of infidels accepted the true faith. As to the individual of the people of Jesus, he joined the people of the Prophet and became a Mussulman.

"Regarding these traits or sketches of 'Alī's character, it will suffice to add that when the blessed Prophet was commanded by the Most High to emigrate (the Hijra) from Makka to Madīna, He directed 'Alī to occupy his bed, and that he should be his lieutenant in the holy Ka'ba; to watch over his family, to

[1] Abū Huraira, one of the companions (*aṣḥāb*) of Muḥammad: so called from a favourite kitten which he had. His name was 'Abd-ur-Raḥmān b. Ṣakhr: he died in A.D. 678 at the age of seventy-eight, and according to Evliya was buried at Jiza in Egypt (*Travels*, i. Pt. 2, p. 111). However this may be, he became the patron of the deliverers of tradition. No less than 3500 are attributed to him, and though the greater part of these may have foisted on him he transmitted a greater number of *hadīs* than any other companion (*E.I.* i. p. 93).

distribute among their owners all the objects deposited in the keeping of the Prophet, and to take care of such *aṣḥābs* as should remain in the Ka'ba. That same night the miserable infidels attacked the dwelling of the blessed Prophet; but God, in His infinite mercy, sent a sleep upon them. The Devil (Shaitān)—on whom be maledictions—was with them, and he also fell asleep. 'Alī, together with Abū Bakr, went out of the house, and walked about. The Most High commanded the angels Mīkhāīl (Michael) and Isrāfīl (on whom be the Divine salutation of peace) to hasten to His lion, 'Alī, because the infidels wished to commit a crime. In the wink of the eye these two exalted angels appeared—Michael stood by 'Alī's head and Isrāfīl at his feet, where they prayed. Soon afterwards the devil awoke, and cried out aloud, 'Muhammad has escaped'. To the infidels this accursed one having appeared in a human form, they, addressing him, asked, 'How should we know it?' and he replied, 'It is now so many thousand years since I have had any rest that I slept to-night, and it is possible that Muhammad has bewitched me, and put me to sleep'. After this, all of the infidels having fled away, the people entered the house of the Prophet of God; and 'Alī arose from his bed, and standing up they beheld that the Prophet of God was really gone, and that in his place was 'Alī, who came suddenly out. On the following day he proceeded to the Ka'ba and took up the place in which the blessed Prophet was used to stand, and from thence cried out that whoever had any objects deposited with the Prophet of God they should come forward and receive them, which, on producing the tokens received for them they did, and took them away, so that not one remained. All of the *aṣḥābs* in the holy Ka'ba sought protection of 'Alī, and not one had reason to complain of any wrong. As the Prophet's dwelling was inside the Ka'ba, 'Alī made it his abode. Some time after this the Prophet commanded that 'Alī should take his family and proceed to Madīna, which he did; and going to the congregation of the infidels of the Quraish, he told them of his intention to set out on the day following, and that if any one had anything to say let him speak. All lowered their heads, and not one had a word to answer.

"After the departure of 'Alī, Abū Jahal [1] (on whom be curses)

[1] Abū Jahal, the enemy of the Prophet who attempted his life (Margoliouth, *The Early Development of Islam*, p. 252). He was, however, it is

asked them, 'O, ye great men of the Quraish! why did you not speak out whilst the family of Muhammad was still here, for it can do us no harm?' They then assembled around Abū Jahal and discussed the matter, and finally proceeded to 'Abbās, and begged him to advise his brother's son ('Alī) not to remove the family of Muhammad, lest trouble should arise in consequence of its departure. 'Abbās found the *Shāh-i-mardān* [1] (the king of men, 'Alī), and spoke with him on the subject; but the latter answered that, 'Inshallāh! on the morrow he would remove the family of the Prophet'. This he did, and was followed by four or five of the Quraish mounted on horses. Previous to 'Alī's departure, however, he declared that he would fight whoever attempted to prevent him carrying into effect the orders of the Prophet. On hearing this from 'Abbās the infidels were greatly troubled, and formed a compact among themselves not to permit 'Alī to leave the city. So that when they met 'Alī and ordered him to return, he refused, and having mounted his charger commenced fighting them, and through Divine assistance was enabled to beat them all. He now continued on his way, and next met with Miqdād bin-Aswad,[2] who also commenced fighting him. But the Imām 'Alī, in the most fearless manner, withstood the attack, and soon dismounted him. Placing his foot upon this man's breast, he invited him to accept of the true faith, which he at once most cheerfully did, and became a Mussulman. This person's son became a martyr in the defence of the Imām Husain ('Alī's son) at Karbalā; and beside being a most heroic man, subsequently became one of the most excellent of the *aṣḥābs*. If any one wishes to know more about this story they will please refer to the work entitled the *Siyar-un-Nabī* [3] (a biography of the Prophet), where it is given in a detailed manner.

---

said, prevented from doing him bodily harm by miraculous visions, and was eventually killed at Badr by Muāz b. Amr b. al-Jamūh (*E.I.* i. p. 83).

[1] Shāh-i-mardān, 'king of heroes' (Pers. *mard*, pl. *mardān*). Johnson has 'King of valour, 'Alī', incorrectly (*Dict.*, p. 734).

[2] Miqdād b. al-Aswad, one of the ahl-i-suffā (Nicholson, *Kashf al-Maḥjūb*, p. 81).

[3] *Siyar un-Nabī*, 'The Virtues of the Prophet', by Sa'īd Shaikh Kazrūnī. *Tārīkh-i-Rashīdī*, p. 145.

This may be the work referred to, rather than the *Siyar un-Nabī* of the Turkish poet Zātī (Bakhshī or 'Iwaz, *d.* 1546). This title Gibb translates

" The Imām 'Alī, in consequence of having heard the ' Friend of God', in the Prophet, declared in a *hadīs*, that ' Poverty was his pride', became extremely poor. From that moment he took no interest in worldly concerns, so much so, that if he became possessed of 1000 pieces of gold, he would, by the morrow, not have one of them, for all would be given away to the poor. The blessed Prophet therefore used to say of 'Alī, that he was the ' Sultān of the Liberal'. 'Alī once said to the pure Fātima, ' O best of women, and the daughter of the Prophet of God, have you nothing to give your husband to eat, for I am extremely hungry ?' Fātima replied, ' O father of Hasan, I declare to you by that Allāh, beside whom there is none other, I have absolutely nothing ; but in the corner of that tomb you will find six *āqchas* (pieces of silver): take them, go to the bazaar, and buy something for yourself to eat, and also some fruits for our sons Hasan and Husain'. 'Alī departed, and on his way met with two Mussulmans, the one holding the other by the collar of his robe, rudely pulling him, and claiming the payment of a debt, and declaring that he could wait no longer, and must have his money. Approaching them, 'Alī asked how much was the debt, and on hearing that it was just six *āqchas*, he thought to himself that he would free this Mussulman from his affliction, and yet was embarrassed as to what he would say to Fātima, who expected him to return with food. Nevertheless he paid over the sum, and so relieved the Mussulman. He reflected for a moment on the answer which he should give to Fātima, and was much troubled by his painful position. With the idea in his mind that she was the best of women, and the Prophet's daughter, he returned empty-handed, and had scarcely reached the door, when he saw their sons, Hasan and Husain, running towards him, in the full expectation that their father had brought them some fruit for food, and, on seeing that he had none, they both wept. He now explained to their

---

'Acts of the Prophet' (*Hist. of Ottoman Poetry*, iii. p. 50; cf. Hammer-Purgstall, *GdOD*. ii. p. 240). Or again the reference may be to the *Durrat-ut-Tāj fi Siratī-Sāḥib-il-Mi'rāj*, 'the Pearl of the Crown concerning the Life of the Lord of the Ascension', of the Turkish poet Uvais (Veysi), who died in 1627–28. This work, generally known as the *Siyar-i-Veysi*, is still popular, although it has been condemned by the Modern School in Turkey (Gibb, *op. cit.* iii. p. 208).

mother what use he had made of the money which she had given him, and how he had freed a Mussulman from a most painful predicament. 'You have done well,' she exclaimed, 'and I am delighted that you have done so good an action,' though, at the same time, she was pained at heart; and in place of adding, 'How great are our necessities! and how strangely you have acted!' she only said, 'The Most High and Noble Allāh will provide for us'.

"As to 'Alī, remarking that his wife was much afflicted, and that his two sons wept from pure hunger, his heart became troubled, and he left the house, in the design of proceeding to the blessed Prophet of God, to see what would follow; for it was well known that, should any one be oppressed with ten thousand sorrows, the sight of the countenance of the blessed Prophet at once removed them all, and in their stead he became filled with innumerable joys. On his way he met with an Arab leading a fatted camel, who asked him whether he would not purchase it, and 'Alī replied that he did not possess any ready money with which to pay for it. To this the Arab replied that he would credit him for the amount; and as 'Alī requested to learn the price, he added that it was 100 *āqchas*. 'Alī accepted the offer, and the Arab delivered him the animal. Taking its bridle in his hand, he proceeded on his way, and soon met with another Arab, who, addressing him by name, inquired whether he would not sell it. 'Alī replied that he would, and the Arab asked him whether he would accept of 300 *āqchas* for it. Having consented, he handed over the camel to the purchaser, who forthwith counted him out the sum thus agreed upon.

"'Alī, much delighted, proceeded at once to the bazaar, where he purchased an abundance of food and fruit, and thence returned to his house. Opening the door, his children clung to him, delighted with the prospect of partaking of a bountiful meal. Their mother inquired of him how he became possessed of so much money, and 'Alī related to her the preceding occurrence. After satisfying their hunger, they all returned thanks to that Sublime and Blessed Allāh who thus provided for their pressing wants. 'Alī then arose, and after telling his wife of his intention, proceeded to the residence of the Pride of the Universe, the most blessed Prophet of Allāh. The latter having, however, just left his house, 'Alī met him on the way to his own premises, where, he told the *aṣḥābs* near him, he desired visiting his daughter and son-in-law. So soon as the Prophet beheld 'Alī, he smiled, and exclaimed, 'O 'Alī, from whom did you buy the camel, and to whom did you sell it ?' and 'Alī replied, 'God and His Prophet know'. The Prophet now informed him that the seller was the angel Gabrāīl, and the purchaser the angel 'Isrāfīl, and that it was one of the camels of *jannat* (Paradise); that the all-just Allāh had bestowed upon him fifty favours for the one he had granted to that afflicted Mussulman; and that those which were in store for him, in eternity, were only known to God.

"During the *Mi'rāj-i-sharīf* (or the Ascension) of the blessed Prophet, he beheld a lion in the seventh heaven, of so terrible an appearance, that it was perfectly indescribable. He inquired of the angel Gabrāīl what lion it was, and was informed that it was not a wild animal, but was the 'spirituality' of the Imām 'Alī; adding, 'O friend of Allāh, remove your ring from off your finger, and cast it in its mouth', which he having done, the lion, with great humility and many caresses, took and held the ring in its mouth. On the day following the Ascension, the Prophet gave an account of the same to the *aṣḥābs*; and whilst relating the frightful appearance of the lion, and the matter of the ring, 'Alī, who was also present, withdrew the latter from his own mouth and handed it to him, greatly to the surprise of all the spectators. From this remarkable occurrence they were enabled to understand the sublimity of his character, and their love and affection for him became greatly increased.

"Of the *āyats* (verses of the *Qurān*) sent in honour of 'Alī, one refers to the following occurrence. Some of the learned '*ulmā* state that the *Amīr al-Mūminīn*, or 'Commander of the Faithful' ('Alī), was once engaged praying in the *masjid*, or chapel, when a beggar approached him, and asked for something. 'Alī, turning aside his face, withdrew a ring from off his finger and handed it to the man. This act of generosity having been agreeable to the Most High, the following *āyat* descended from heaven, chap. v. v. 60: 'Your protectors are God and His Prophet, and those who believe, who perform the prayers exactly [who are steadfast in prayer],[1] who give alms, and who incline themselves before God'.

[1] Palmer's *Qurān* S.B.E., vi. p. 105.

"Another *āyat* was the subject of a dispute between 'Abbās and Talha.[1] The former said, 'I am of those excellent persons who supply the pilgrims with water'; and the latter declared, 'I am of those excellent ones who have charge of the key of the holy house (Ka'ba), and, if I choose, I can spend the night therein'. To this 'Alī remarked, 'What do you say? It is now more than ten months since I have turned my face towards this *qibla* (the Ka'ba), and you were not here even then'. It was on this occasion that the following *āyat* descended from heaven, chap. ix. vv. 19-20: 'Will you place those who bear water to the pilgrims and visit the holy oratory on the same footing with those who believe in God and in the Last Day, and fight [are strenuous in] in the path of God? Now, they will not be equal before God; God does not direct the wicked. Those who have left their own country, who fight in the path of God with their property and their persons, will fill a more elevated place before God; they will be the happy.'[2]

"There is another *āyat*, commanded by God, relative to 'Alī bin-Abū Tālib, Fātima, and Hasan and Husain, chap. xlii. v. 22: 'This is what God promises to His servants who believe and do good. Tell them, All that I ask of you in return for my ministrations is some[3] for my relations. Whoever shall have performed a good deed, we will raise in value; God is indulgent and thankful.' Qatāda[4]—on whom be the Divine satisfaction—states that the *mushriks*, at a meeting, declared, 'Let us see whether Muhammad wishes for a recompense?' On these words, that *āyat* descended, as is stated by Sa'īd ibn-Jabīl.[5] Ibn-'Abbās[6] remarks that, in the expression 'relations' are comprised 'Alī, Fātima, and Hasan and Husain; and no one must ever feel an ill-will for them.

"Another *āyat* is that in which the Most High shows the purity of the religious sentiments of 'Alī, chap. xv. v. 47: 'We will remove all falsehood from out of their hearts; living together as brothers, they will repose upon beds, viewing each other face

[1] Ṭalḥa b. Ubaid-ullāh, one of the Ḥawārī or apostles (*E.I.* ii. p. 293).

[2] Palmer, *op. cit.*, p. 175. The word translated 'fight' means 'to be strenuous', and does not inculcate the *jihād* or holy war.

[3] The word 'love' should be supplied. Cf. Rodwell's *Koran*, p. 272.

[4] Abū Qatāda, 60–117 H. (A.D. 680–737).

[5] Sa'eed ibn Jebeel in original.

[6] Ibn 'Abbās, *v.* note on p. 426 *infra*.

to face'. Some of the learned have said that this *āyat* referred to 'Alī, Mu'āwīa,[1] Talhā,[2] Zubīr,[3] and the faithful 'Ayesha.

"Another *āyat* of the Most High is chap. lviii. v. 13: 'O ye who believe: when you go in private to consult the Prophet, prior to your visit bestow an alms, for this will be better for you, and more suitable; but, if you have not wherewith to do it, know that God is indulgent and merciful'. The champions of Islāmism state that no one acted upon this *āyat* except 'Alī, who, whenever he desired to consult the Prophet, conformably with this verse, always bestowed something previously in alms.

"Ibn-'Umr[4] relates that 'Alī possessed three things, of which, said he, 'had I only one, it would have made me much beloved'. One of these was the daughter (Fātima al-Zahra) of the Prophet, given to him in marriage; the second, the gift which the Prophet made to him of the standard of victory, at the battle of Khaiber; and the third, that he put in performance the holy *āyat*, called the *najwī*.[5] It is said of 'Alī, that he would take a *dinār*, divide it into ten *dirhams*, and so bestow it in alms on ten poor persons; that he also once asked of the Prophet ten questions, confidentially, one of which was, 'How shall I pray?' and the Prophet replied,

[1] Mu'āwia b. Abī Sufyān, the Ommayad.

[2] Talhā, *v.* note on p. 423.

[3] Possibly Zubair ibn al-Awwām, cousin-german of the Prophet and one of the ten Ashara Mubashshara to whom he gave certain assurance of Paradise; but his conduct is a difficulty, for having started the revolt against 'Alī he was persuaded by him to take a solemn oath that he would not war against the Caliph. His son, however, induced him to free a slave by way of atonement and then break his pact (Matthews, *Mishcat*, i. p. 428, and Margoliouth, *Early Development of Islam*, p. 60). The *āyat* quoted hardly seems applicable to him.

Another Zubair, ibn-Ārabī, was one of the *tābi'ūn* (Matthews, *op. cit.*, p. 618).

[4] Ibn 'Umr, *v.* note on p. 412.

[5] *Najwī*, 'secret', from the same root as *najīa* on p. 378, and *najāt*, 'salvation'. *Najwā* is 'secret conversation' or 'the concealment of imperfections from the knowledge of other (than God)' (Nicholson, *Kashf al-Maḥjūb*, pp. 352 and 385. But the term *najwī* (pron. *najwā*) was also applied to the voluntary contributions, peculiar to the Bātinīs or Isma'īlīs, and abolished by Ḥākim bi-amr-Allah (de Sacy, *Exposé de la religion des Druzes*, i. p. cccxliii, where his *Chrestomathie arabe*, p. 132, vol. i., is referred to). The context indicates that the verse alluded to is v. 211 of *sura* ii. (Rodwell, p. 361), read especially with v. 13 of *sura* lviii., which Rodwell renders: "O ye who believe! when ye go to confer in private with the Apostle, give alms before such conference. . . ." (p. 452).

'With fidelity and purity'; the next, 'What shall I ask of God?' and the reply, 'Health in this world and in the other'; the next, 'What do I need most?' and the answer was, 'To keep God's laws, and the commands of His Prophet'; 'What, O Prophet of God, must I do to secure my own salvation?' and the former replied, 'Do no wrong to others, and speak the truth'. He next inquired, 'What is truth?' and the blessed Prophet answered, 'Islām, the *Qurān,* and to act correctly up to the close of your life'. He then asked him, 'What is joy?' and he replied, 'Paradise'; 'What is comfort?' he added, and heard that it was 'To behold God'. 'What is rebellion?' he next asked, and the blessed Prophet told him, 'To be a *kāfir*' (or otherwise to be unfaithful to the Most High God); and he added the question, 'What is fidelity?' to which he received the reply, 'To bear testimony that there is no God but Allāh, and that Muhammad is the Prophet of Allāh'; for He is that God who honours and degrades men; and where His Prophet so admonished the people of Makka, they would turn their faces away, and declare otherwise; for it is said in the Great Book (*Qurān*), chap. xli. v. 25: 'The infidels say, Do not listen to the *Qurān,* and speak loudly so as to drown the voice of those who read it'. In the end, God so elevated him, that He commanded, 'He is most dear to me, and you must hear and obey everything that he directs'. On this head the *āyat* says: 'When you visit the Prophet, before entering near him, bestow an alms, for your own welfare' (chap. lviii. v. 13). 'Do not address him a word until he comes out of his room.' The *āyat* says also (chap. xlix. v. 4): 'Those who call thee with a loud voice, whilst thou art still within thy apartments, are, mostly, people of no sense.' Also (chap. xlix. v. 4): 'Do not raise your voice above that of the Prophet'. Also (chap. xxxiii. v. 9): 'He was at the distance of ten arcs, or nearer'. God placed him in so elevated a position, that the angel Gabrāīl and all the other angels, though they went round it, were unable to reach it. Those who falsely swear, who shout within the limits of the *Harām-i-sharīf,* at Makka and Madīna, or are deficient in their prayers and fasts, must bestow alms upon the poor, and thus acquire the satisfaction of the Most High. The holy verse says (chap. xlv. v. 20): 'Those who do evil, think that we will treat them equally with those who believe,—who do good; and that for either, life and death is the same: they judge badly'.

"An *āyat* descended for 'Alī, whose faith was correct, and all his acts were good and praisable, without hypocrisy, and unheard-of for perfection. The Christians (*mushriklar*)[1] said to him: 'If what you declare (about God and His Prophet) be true, you will be greater than we in this world, and in the other' (chap. xxxiii. v. 33). 'Remain quiet in your houses; adopt not the luxuries of the times of Ignorance; observe the hours of prayer; give alms; obey God and His Prophet. God only wishes to free you from abominations, and give you perfect purity.'

"Sa'īd bin-Jabīr[2] relates, on the part of 'Abdullāh bin-'Abbās,[3] as coming from Ibn-'Abbās,[4] that when the holy verse descended, 'Thou givest fear, and to each people there is a director in the true path', the blessed Prophet stated, 'I am the one who gives the fear, and 'Alī is he who directs in the true path. O 'Alī, those who are directed will be directed by thee.'

"Rabīyat bin-Najd relates that 'Alī once stated: 'The blessed Prophet read over me and said, You resemble Jesus, the Son of Mary, inasmuch as the Jews hated him, and calumniated his mother. The Nazarenes loved him so greatly as to declare that he had no post or grade among the prophets, but was really God.' To this 'Alī responded: 'Many persons destroy their souls for love of me; some love me very much, and are inimical to the other *aṣḥābs*; I do not love these, and some who love the other *aṣḥābs* hate me; both of which are of the people of hell. I am not a prophet; on me no inspiration descends, and yet, with all the strength given to me, I conform to God's book.'

[1] Turk. plur. of *mushrik*, 'polytheist', or 'syntheist, one who attributes a partner or partners to God' (Redhouse, *Turk.-Eng. Lex.*, p. 1867).

[2] Sa'īd bin Jabīr, mentioned on p. 32 *supra*.

[3] 'Abdullāh b. 'Abbās, one of the most learned of the Companions, was entitled Tarjumān ul-Qurān or 'Interpreter of the *Qurān*', and Sulṭān ul-Mufassirīn or 'Prince of Commentators'. He became governor of Baṣra, and was the ancestor of the Abbasside sovereigns. He is also celebrated as the Doctor (Rabbi) of the Community (Ḥibr al-Umma), and is called the 'sea'. He died in 68–79 H. (A.D. 687–90). Estimates of his trustworthiness as a traditionalist vary, but he became the patron of the *mufassirīn* or commentators on the *Qurān* in the Turkish guild-system (Evliya, i. pt. 2, p. 111). For his life and titles *v. E.I.* i. p. 19, and Margoliouth, *Early Development of Mohammedanism*, p. 138.

[4] Ibn 'Abbās should, no doubt, be al-'Abbās b. 'Abd al-Muṭṭalib, surnamed Abū'l Fazl, uncle of the Prophet and father of 'Abdullāh b. al-'Abbās, surnamed Abū'l 'Abbās.

The blessed Prophet now added : 'All that I order you to do is to conform to the will of the Most High, either through your own free will, or from misery and compulsion. If I should ever order you to do what is contrary to this, do not obey it ; for who obeys me, obeys Him.'

"Another narrative is that of Qais bin-Hārith.[1] An individual asked a question of Mu'āwīa bin-Sūfyān, and for reply was directed to make the same interrogation of 'Alī ; 'for he knows better than myself'. The individual, nevertheless, persisted in receiving an answer from him, 'for I shall love it more,' he added, 'than any that 'Alī can give me'. The [Caliph] Mu'āwia, however, declined, and said to the individual, 'You speak falsely, and are a wicked man ; for you show an aversion for him who enjoys, to an eminent degree, the respect and regard of the Prophet of God, on account of his great knowledge of Him, respecting whom the Prophet has declared : "O 'Alī, after me, you occupy the place of Aaron after Moses ; with the difference that, after me, there will be no other prophet"'. I have also observed that 'Umr often took counsel with him ; and whenever any doubts arose, he would say, ''Alī is present ; let us ask him'. So Mu'āwia—on whom be the Divine satisfaction—said to the individual, 'Depart, and may the blessed Allāh not give any strength to your steps' ; and so he departed.

"Another narrative is by Sa'd bin-Abī Waqqās. 'Once, Mu'āwia came to me, on account of some personal need. He mentioned 'Alī, and I told him that 'Alī had three peculiar characteristics, of which, had I but one, I would be greatly beloved. These I heard stated by the blessed Prophet himself. 1. "'Alī is the *walī* (friend) of whomsoever I am the *walī*." 2. The Prophet declared, the day of the battle of Khaibar, "To-morrow I will give the standard to one who is beloved of God and His Prophet", and gave it to 'Alī. 3. "You are to me what Aaron was to Moses."'

"Jābir bin-'Abdullāh relates that the Prophet once stated : 'The night during which I went up to heaven (*al-mi'rāj*), I passed by the porters, and heard a voice behind them say, "O Muhammad, goodly is your father Ibrāhīm, and how goodly is your brother 'Alī bin-Abū-Tālib ; leave him a testimony from you that he had done good"'.

[1] Kais b. Hārith in original.

" Hasan Bahrī relates that Uns bin-Mālik [1] heard it from the Prophet: 'There are three persons whom Paradise desires ardently to receive, viz. 'Alī bin-Abū-Tālib, 'Ammār bin-Yāsir,[2] and Salmān Fārsī'.

" Sa'd bin-Abī Waqqās once said: 'Mu'āwia [3] asked me, "Do you love 'Alī?" and I replied, "Why should I not love him? Have I not heard the Prophet say to him, 'O 'Alī, after me, you are what Aaron was to Moses'". At the battle of Badr he came out of the fight, and a voice came forth from his belly, declaring that God would ever be with him; and he never ceased fighting, until he had coloured his sword with the blood of the infidels.'

" 'Amir bin-Sherbīl al-Sha'bī [4] states: 'Alī once remarked, Zaid ibn-Serha,[5] at the battle of Jamal,[6] was in the following condition. He had fallen down in his blood; 'Alī stood over his head, and exclaimed to him, 'O Zaid, may the Most High have mercy upon you; I did not know you, except as one recommended to me; I now know you for your good deeds, and as one to whom the Prophet has given the good news (of faith) and Paradise'. Zaid was still covered with blood, and raising up his hands, he exclaimed, 'O Amīr of the Faithful, may thine also be good news; for to thee has the Prophet of God given the same assurances. I swear by the truth of God, I have never had an occasion to fight with you in any battle, where I could destroy

[1] Abū Ḥamza bin Naṣr al-Anṣārī, surnamed Ānas bin Mālik, 'the last of the Companions': (Matthews, *Mishcat,* i. p. 4). His death is variously ascribed to 91–3 H. (A.D. 709–11), but it is fairly certain that he died at Basra, at the age of 97 or even 107. He was one of the most prolific of the traditionists but not one of the most trustworthy, and Abū Ḥanīfa is said to have denied his authority (*E.I.* i. p. 345). On the other hand, Beale says he was one of the six most approved for Muhammadan traditions, and that he died at the age of 103, in 91 H. (A.D. 710), leaving 100 children (*Oriental Biographical Dy.*, p. 19, where his name is printed Aus).

[2] 'Ammār bin-Yāsir, one of the Companions; for some details of his life see Matthews, *Mishcat,* i. p. 105. He was saved from torture by fire by the Prophet and slain under 'Alī at Ṣaffīn in A.D. 657. Muḥammad had prophesied that he would be killed by usurpers (Margoliouth, *Early Development,* p. 240).

[3] Mu'āwīa b. Abī Sufyān al-Umawī, the Ommayad.

[4] 'Āmir b. Sharāhīl ash-Sha'bi, *v.* note on p. 33.

[5] Zaid ibn-Serha, as in original.

[6] Lahi al-Jamal was a village between Makka and Madīna (Matthews, *Mishcat,* i. p. 648), but the place where 'Alī encountered Ayisha is doubtless alluded to.

the ranks of the enemy, on account of the hypocrisy and falsehoods of the public against you ; and yet I have heard it as said by the Prophet, 'Alī is a *pathway* ; he is the destroyer of wickedness and has conquered the person who has conquered him, and put to flight him who would not aid him. I am happy at last to have found myself in battle with you, and to fight with you as a friend.' As he terminated these words, his soul left his body.

" 'Amrū bin-al-Jamūh [1] states : 'I was once in the presence of the Prophet of God, when he exclaimed, " O 'Amru " ; and I answered, " What are thy commands, O Prophet of God ? " He answered, " Do you wish me to show you the columns of Paradise ? " I replied that I did. Just then 'Alī passed by, and he, pointing to him, said, " The members of this person's family are the columns of Paradise ". It is also reported by 'Abdullāh ibn-'Abbās,[2] that the Prophet declared, " the chief of places was in his own body " '.

" 'Alī himself relates that the blessed Prophet declared : ' The night of the *mi'rāj*, the angel Gabrāīl held my hand, and led me to a splendidly ornamented position in Paradise, where he placed a quince before me. I took it up and smelt it, and whilst turning it round in my hand, it separated into two pieces, and from out of it came a *hūrī*. Never in my life had I seen so beautiful a being as this. So addressing me, she said, " Peace be to thee, O Muhammad ". In reply I asked her who she was, and she replied, " My name is Rāzia and Murzia [3] (consenting and consented, or satisfying), and the Most Glorious has created me out of three things : the upper part of me is made of ambergris, the middle camphor, and the lower musk ; I was joined together with the water of life, and thus was I created by the Sovereign Lord of the universe for your brother 'Alī bin-Abū-Tālib " '.

" Abū Zerr Ghifārī [4] also relates, as coming from the Prophet

[1] 'Amrū b. al-Jamūh, Mū'az bin-Āmar bin-Jamūh, one of the Anṣārs, who shared in the killing of Abū Jahal (*E.I.* i. p. 83). He died in the reign of 'Othmān (Matthews, *Mishcat*, ii. p. 810).

[2] *V.* p. 426.

[3] Rāzī, ' content ' or ' pleasing ' ; *murzi*, ' pleasant '.

[4] Abū Zar Ghaffārī (Zarr al-Ghifārī), one of the most esteemed of the Companions for his piety and veracity (Matthews, *Mishcat*, i. p. 12). His real name was Jundub b. Junāda al-Rabaẓī, but there are different versions of this and of his descent. He died at al-Rabaẓa near Madīna in 32 or 33 H. (A.D. 653) (*E.I.* p 82). After his death Abū Zurr's reputation increased

of God : ' Whoever is separated from me is separated from God, and whoever, O 'Alī, is separated from you is also separated from me'. Uns bin Malik states that 'The glory of all beings (the Prophet) mentioned 'Alī bin-Abū-Tālib adoringly'. Jābir bin-'Abdullāh mentions from the same source : ' It is written over the door of Paradise, "There is no God but Allāh ; Muhammad is His Prophet, and 'Alī is the aider of His Prophet" ; and that this was so written 2000 years before the erection of the heavens and the earth.'

" 'Abdullāh bin-Mas'ūd [1] relates : ' I was once in the company of the blessed Prophet, when he said of 'Alī, " Wisdom is divided into ten parts, nine of which are given to 'Alī, and one to mankind" '. 'Abdullāh bin-'Abbās relates that the Prophet one day came out of his house, holding the hand of 'Alī in his own blessed hand, and exclaimed, ' Beware that no one bear any hostile feelings for 'Alī, for such an one is an enemy of God and His Prophet ; whoever loves 'Alī, loves also God and His Prophet'. The same person relates that the Prophet once remarked : ' Whoever wishes to see the meekness of Abraham, the wisdom of Noah, the patience of Joseph, let him look upon 'Alī bin-Abū-Tālib'. Ānas bin-Mālik says : ' I was once seated in company with the Prophet, when suddenly 'Alī appeared and seated himself behind him. The Prophet called to him to sit before him, and addressing him, said, " O 'Alī, God has honoured and distinguished you with

---

and, like Miqdād al-Aswad and Salmān, he was honoured by all the secret sects, especially by the Nusairīs, who make him the 'left' of prayer as Miqdād is the right. The Ḥābiṭis, a professing sect of the Mata'zilīs, declared that Abū Zurr had been more continent and pious than the Prophet himself. This sect had on the one hand Christian leanings, regarding Jesus as the created God, while on the other it held that animals and even insects had their prophets, a tenet clearly connected with their belief in transmigration of souls (S. de Sacy, *Exposé de la religion des Druzes*, i. p. xlii. ff. and Lyde, *The Asian Mystery*, pp. 152–3).

Mu'āwia regarded Abū Zarr as all but a communist, and he certainly protested against the luxury which the newly gotten wealth of the Arabs induced. His own habits were ascetic (Muir, *The Life of Mahomet*, pp. 309, 310–11.

[1] 'Abdullāh bin Mas'ūd, one of those to whom Muḥammad gave assurance of Paradise (Matthews, *Mishcat*, i. p. 18). He is said to be the authority for 848 traditions, including one relied upon for a mild interpretation of the interdiction of wine. His death at Madīna or Kūfa is assigned to 32–3 H.

the gift of four qualities above my own". 'Alī rose to his feet and exclaimed, "May my father and mother be devoted to you; how can a servant be honoured above his Lord?" The Prophet replied, "O 'Alī, when the Most High and Blessed God desires to honour one of His servants, He bestows upon him those things which eye has not seen, ear has not heard, nor which have ever come into the mind of man". Ānas[1] says that he observed, on hearing this, "O Prophet of Allāh, explain this to us, so that we may understand it"; and he continued, "God has given him such a wife as Fātima, and not to me; He has given him two such sons as Hasan and Husain, and none to me; and He has given to him such a father-in-law (the Prophet himself) as He has not given to me"'.

"Sa'īd bin-Jabīr relates that once the Prophet took the hand of 'Abdullāh bin-'Abbās, and they together walked to the well of Zamzam, where a number of people were seated, indulging in improper remarks about 'Alī. He sent away ibn-'Abbās, and approaching them, stood still, and exclaimed, 'Who is it that dares to speak ill of God and the Prophet of God?' They replied, 'None of us have spoken ill of God, nor of His Prophet'. 'Who,' then added he, 'speaks ill of 'Alī bin-Abū-Tālib?' and some one answered, 'Yes, such has been spoken'. 'I know it,' he added, 'for I bear testimony that I heard it with my own ears, and whoever speaks ill of him speaks ill of me, and whoever speaks ill of me has spoken ill of the Most High, and He will cast him headlong into hell.'

"Atiet al Avkī[2] relates: 'I once went to see Jābir bin-'Abdullāh and found him much advanced in years, his eyebrows covering his eyes. I asked him a question about 'Alī, and on hearing his name, he raised up his head and smiled for joy and love of him, and exclaimed, "In the time of the blessed Prophet the only hypocrites we knew were those who were unfriendly to 'Alī, and we therefore considered them all as enemies"'.

"Sha'bī says: 'Once Abū Bakr al-Siddīq, on seeing 'Alī, remarked that "Whoever was well thought of by him ('Alī) and met with his favour, would be held in high consideration by the

[1] Enis in original.

[2] Atiet el Avkee in original. ? 'Ātika, aunt of 'Abdulla bin al-'Abbās (*E.I.* i. p. 20).

blessed Prophet; and whosoever 'Alī deemed truly spiritual, would be regarded by the Prophet as being near to God (in a spiritual sense)"'.

"'Ayesha relates that she once asked the blessed Prophet, 'Who, after him, was the best amongst the people, and he answered, Abū Bakr al-Siddīq; after him, I inquired, and he added, 'Umr; and next, I asked, and he said, 'Othmān. Fātima, on hearing this, exclaimed, "O Prophet of God, have you nothing to say for 'Alī?" and he replied, "I am 'Alī, and 'Alī is myself; have you ever heard any one commend his own self?"'

"Zaid-al-'Abidīn bin-'Alī Husain relates that he once heard 'Alī bin-Abū-Tālib declare, 'The Prophet of God has taught me a thousand doors of knowledge, each one of which has opened to me a thousand others'.

"'Abdullāh al-Kandī[1] relates, that Mu'āwia bin-Abū Sūfyān made the pilgrimage after the death of 'Alī, and coming among the congregation there, seated himself in the presence of 'Abdullāh bin-'Abbās and 'Abdullāh bin-'Umr. Mu'āwia placed his hand upon the knee of 'Abdullāh bin-'Abbās, and said, 'My affair is better than that of your uncle's son'. 'Abdullāh bin-'Abbās replied, 'Why did he say that about him who stated, "I am the nephew of the Prophet whom they unjustly put to death?" that is to say, 'Othmān bin-'Affān, on whom be the Divine satisfaction'. 'Abdullāh said, 'His presence is better than you for the Caliphate, for 'Alī's relationship is nearer than that of your nephew'. Mu'āwia, on hearing this, became silent; then turning toward Sa'd bin-Abi-Waqqās, he said, 'O Sa'd! do not separate the truth from the obsolete; will you be with or against us?' To this Sa'd replied, 'When I witnessed the darkness of violence committed, I said to myself, I will be patient until the daylight again appears, and then I will depart from here'. Mu'āwia on this, exclaimed, 'I swear by Allāh that I have read the most glorious *Qurān*, and found nothing of this in it'; and Sa'd added, 'Do you not accept the words which I myself heard from the mouth of the blessed Prophet on the subject of 'Alī bin-Abū-Tālib? "Thou art with the truth, and the truth is with me"'. Mu'āwia now bade him produce some person who had also heard these from the Prophet, or, added he, 'You will see what I shall

[1] Ya'qūb b. Iṣḥāq al-Kindī, styled 'the Philosopher of the Arabs' (*Failasūf-ul-'Arab*), flourished in the first half of the ninth century A.D.

do to you.' Sa'd said that Ami Salma[1] had likewise heard them, and so, going to him, Mu'āwia asked, 'O Father of believers! the public say many things which never were spoken by the blessed Prophet, one of which is a *hadīs* brought forward by Sa'd'. 'What is it?' inquired Ami Salma. 'What does he quote?' 'He states,' replied Mu'āwia, 'that the blessed Prophet was heard to say to 'Alī, "Thou art with the truth, and the truth is with me"'. Ami Salma at once exclaimed, 'He quotes correctly, for I heard him use these same words myself in my own house'. On hearing this, Mu'āwia turned away his face, asked pardon of Sa'd and others of the *aṣḥābs* of the blessed Prophet there present, and exclaimed, 'I swear by the Most High God, that had I known this I would have been the servant of 'Alī to the day of my death'.

"Another statement is from the mouth of the blessed Prophet, given by 'Abdullāh bin-'Abbās. He says that the former also declared, 'I am the scales of knowledge; 'Alī is its weights, Hasan and Husain are its cords, Fātima is its suspension; after me the Imāms (Hasan and Husain) are the columns which sustain it, and by these scales do we weigh the deeds of our friends'. Uns bin-Mālik states that the Prophet also declared, 'I am the city of knowledge; 'Alī is its gate, and Mu'āwia is its ring or circle'.

"Ma'az bin-Jabal[2] states that the Prophet likewise declared, 'The Most High has made a people pure from sins, as the head of a bald man is neat, and 'Alī is the first of that people'. Salmān Fārsī (an eminent founder of a Darvish *tarīq*) stated, ''Alī is the possessor of my secret'.

"'Alī relates that the Prophet of God once directed him, in case his head ever ached, to put his hands on his temples, and recite the *āyat*,—'We have caused this book (*Qurān*) to descend from heaven', from one end to the other, and the pain will cease. One day, when walking in the environs of Makka, the Prophet holding 'Alī by the hand, they met with several fine gardens. 'Alī relates that, having expressed his admiration of them, the Prophet assured him that a finer one awaited him in Paradise. Soon after, the Prophet, looking him steadfastly in the face, burst

[1] Ummī Salmā, a slave of Safīa bint 'Abd-ul-Mutallab, the Prophet's aunt and nurse to Fātima's children (Matthews, *Mishcat*, ii. p. 376).

[2] Mū'aẓ bin-Jabal, Mū'adh ibn Jabal, a famous Companion, appointed judge of Yaman by Muhammad, and employed in Syria by 'Umr (Matthews, *Mishcat*, i. p. 10).

into tears, on seeing which 'Alī was much affected, and also wept; and on inquiring the cause, the Prophet told him that he had a presentiment of his death, through the enmity of a certain tribe. 'I asked him,' adds 'Alī, 'whether the faith which I possessed would not secure me salvation in the life to come, and being assured that it would, I declared that I would then die contented'.

"When the blessed Prophet captured Makka, there were 1140 idols in it, which he designed to destroy; 360 of these surrounded the *Bait-i-sharīf*, and one large one was inside of it. It was made of stone, and was fastened to the wall with strong spikes and chains of iron. When the Prophet entered the Ka'ba, he recited a prayer, and commanded 'Alī to mount on his shoulders and pull out the spikes and chains, and so free that idol from its fastenings; but he declined to profane the person of the Prophet of God by such an act, and it was only on the repeated remonstrances of the latter that he finally consented, and in this manner the great idol of the infidels was destroyed.

"One day the blessed Prophet, calling to 'Alī, exclaimed, 'Good news to thee, O 'Alī! for God has commanded that at the Judgment Day the keeper of the treasure of Paradise shall give a deed (*tamassuk*) of entrance there only to such persons as have met with your approval, and shall refuse admission to all others'. On account of this remark, it once happened that Abū Bakr as-Siddīq (the first Caliph) falling in with 'Alī, observed that he had learned the preceding, and asked him whether he would not favour him with a document by which he could enter Paradise. 'Alī answered, 'Of a truth the blessed Prophet did make such a statement, but he even also said that I should not give any such deeds of admission without previous consultation with Abū Bakr. This, therefore, gives you a supervision over me in the matter, and you thus do not need to ask me for any permission.' These remarks were made in a kind and jocose manner, and they proceeded on their way together, pleased with the arrangement entered into."

APPENDIX I

SOME PROBLEMS IN NAQSHBANDĪ HISTORY[1]

THE history of the Naqshbandī Order would be of some interest if it could be recovered, not merely because it has played an important part in Muslim thought, but also because it has had no little influence on the political vicissitudes of India, Mesopotamia, and, to a less extent, Turkey. In order to unravel some pieces of the tangled skein it is essential to set forth the spiritual pedigree of the Order.

1. As usual in such pedigrees its line is linked up with that of the great Muhammadan mystics, ending in this case with Abū'l Qāsim Gūrgānī (quite incorrectly Karkiānī). Thence the line continues to—

2. Abū 'Alī al-Faẓl b. Muḥammad al-Fārmadhī: as to whom see Nicholson's *Kashf-al-Maḥjūb*, p. 169. He died in 470 H. (A.D. 1078), and he must not be confused with another Fārmadī who died in 537 H. (M. Hartmann, *Der islamische Orient*, vi.-x. p. 308).

3. His *khalīfa* (successor) Khwāja (or Shaikh Abū) Yūsuf Hamadānī (A.D. 1048–1140). In the *Rashaḥāt* Yūsuf Hamadānī is assigned three *khalīfas*: (1) Khwāja 'Abdulla Barqī, (2) Ḥasan Andāqī, and (3) Aḥmad Yasawi, who died in A.D. 1166–67 or perhaps in 562 H. (A.D. 1169). Aḥmad Yasawī was a saint of great importance. His disciple Luqmān al-Khurāsānī taught Muḥammad 'Aṭā bin Ibrahīm, called Hājī Bektāsh, subsequently the patron saint of the Janissaries. The date of his death is uncertain, but it occurred in the fourteenth century A.D. (M. Hartmann, *Der islamische Orient*, vi.-x. p. 309).

4. Khwāja 'Abd-ul-Khāliq Ghujduwānī (son of Imām 'Abd-ul-Jamīl and one of the best-known Naqshbandīs), born at Ghujduwān, six *farsakhs* from Bukhāra, in the twelfth century A.D. He died in 575 H. (A.D. 1179–80). Except that he studied under Shaikh Abū Yūsuf little is, however, really known of him, though

[1] Reprinted, with some additions, from *The Indian Antiquary*, vol. lii., 1923, pp. 204-211. For the precursors of the Naqshbandi mystics see the first Appendix to Chap. VI. (p. 156 *supra*).

MSS. of his works exist (*E.I.* i. p. 165). He laid down eight rules, which constitute the *tarīqa* of the Khwājas, but three more were afterwards introduced. They include *khilwat dar ānjuman*, *safr dar waṭn*, etc., which are explained in a mystic sense (*J.R.A.S.*, 1916, pp. 64-5). According to Hartmann, it was to 'Abd-ul-Khāliq that Khizr taught also the *ḥabs an-nafas* or 'restraining of the breath' exercises of the Naqshbandīs (*Der Islam*, vi. p. 67). This practice is naturally attributed to one of the forms of the Indian *yoga*, but it is not quite impossible that its origin is far older, both the Yogīs and the Naqshbandīs having revived a practice current among some forgotten sects of Central Asia. That Indian ideas did, however, influence the earliest Ṣūfīs seems to be unquestionable (*ib.* p. 51).

5. 'Ārif Rewgari, who took his title from Rewgar, a place six *farsakhs* from Bukhāra. His death is assigned to 715 H., but, as Hartmann points out, this cannot be correct, as his *pīr* died in 575 H., and assuming that he received the gift of 'light' from him at the early age of ten, he must have been 150 years old when he died ! (Hartmann, *op. cit.* vi.-x. p. 309).

6. Muḥammad Faghnawī, who appears in the *Tārīkh-i-Rashīdī* as Khwāja Maḥmūd 'Anjīr Faghrawī. His correct name seems to have been (Khoja) Maḥmūd Anjīr(ī) Faghnawī, from his birthplace, Faghn, three *farsakhs* from Bukhāra. But he lived in Wabkan, where his grave also is. There is much uncertainty as to the meaning of 'Anjīr, and also about the date of the saint's death, which is assigned to 670 H. or to 715 H. (A.D. 1272 or 1316) (Hartmann, *op. cit.* vi.-x. p. 309).

7. The Khoja Azīzān Shaikh 'Alī Ramitanī, who died in 705 or 721 H. (A.D. 1306 or 1321), and took his title from Ramitan (the name is variously spelt), near Bukhāra (Hartmann, *op. cit.* p. 310). He was also styled Pīrī Nassāj.

8. Khwāja Muḥammad Bābā-i-Samāsī, of the *Tārīkh-i-Rashīdī*, p. 401. The Khoja Muḥammad Bābājī Samāsī was born in Samāsī, a dependency of Ramitān lying three *farsakhs* from Bukhāra, and died in 740 or 755 H. (A.D. 1340 or 1354) (Hartmann, *op. cit.* p. 310).

9. Amīr Saiyid Kalāl (in the *Rashaḥāt* (*J.R.A.S.*, 1916, p. 62. Mīr Kalāl in the *Tārīkh-i-Rashīdī*, p. 401). His true name was probably Saiyid Amīr Kulāl Sokharī, from Sokhar, two *farsakhs* from Bukhāra, where he was born and buried. He worked as a potter (*kulāl*), and is said to have been also styled Ibn Saiyid Hamza. He died in 772 H. (A.D. 1371) (*op. cit.* p. 310).

10. The Khoja Bahā-ud-Dīn Naqshband was born in 718 H. (A.D. 1318) and died in 791 H. (A.D. 1389–90) at the age of 73 (*op. cit.* p. 311).

The Nūrbakhshīs

From the Naqshbandīs at a very early stage branched off another Order, that of the Nūrbakshīs. So far as I have been able to trace, this Order is not now known outside Kashmīr and the Hazāra District of the Punjab. Unfortunately its history is very obscure. The *Tārīkh-i-Rashīdī*[1] throws some light upon it. According to that work Saiyid 'Alī Hamadānī,[2] also called Amīr Kabīr 'Alī the Second, a refugee from Hamadān, appeared in Kashmīr about A.D. 1380. He and his Order are said to have been expelled from Persia by Tīmūr, and to him is attributed the conversion of Kashmīr (although it had been at least begun by Sulṭān Shams-ud-Dīn, who came there disguised as a Qalandar, about forty years earlier). However this may be, Saiyid 'Alī is stated to have died at Pakhlī,[3] the seat of a half-legendary Arab kingdom, about A.D. 1386. He became " a sort of patron saint of the Muhammadan section of the population ", but the people were all Hanifī, we are told, until about A.D. 1550, one Shams, who came from Talish (? Gīlān) in Irāq, introduced a new form of religion, giving it the name of Nūrbakhshī. Shams wrote a work called the *Fikḥ-i-Ahwat*, which does not conform to the teachings of any sect, Sunni or Shi'a, and his sectaries regarded him as the promised Mahdī. That Saiyid 'Alī Hamadānī was a historical personage is confirmed by the Turkish authorities, but I have failed to connect him with Sh. Abū Yūsuf Hamadānī. His full name was Amir Saiyid 'Alī b. ush-Shihāb (Shihāb-ud-Dīn) b. Mīr Saiyid Muḥammad al-Ḥusainī of Hamadān, " founder of an order of Ṣūfīs, especially known as the apostle of Kashmīr " ; and he entered Kashmīr in 781 H. (A.D. 1380) with 700 disciples, acquiring great influence over Sulṭān Qutb-ud-Dīn. Dying in 786 H. (A.D. 1385) at the age of 73, he was buried at Khuttilān (*not* at Pakhlī). He was the author of the *Zakhīrat-ul-Mulūk*, a treatise on political ethics (*Cat. of Persian MSS. in the British Museum*, ii. p. 147). These fragments of history perhaps justify a conjecture that S. 'Alī Hamadānī played an important part in the resistance to Tīmūr and his descendants. In the Punjab Shāh Rukh, for instance, never seems to have been able to extend his sway much beyond the Salt Range, and his failure to penetrate Kashmīr may have been largely due to the Naqshbandī opposition or resentment.

Who ' Shams ' was it is not easy to say. But in all prob-

[1] Pp. 432-7 of Denison Ross's Trans.

[2] Cf. p. *supra* 124, where he appears as ' Sa'eed 'Alee Hemdanee '.

[3] Wherever Saiyid 'Alī may actually have been interred, he certainly has still a shrine (*ziārat*) at Nankoṭ in the Pakhlī plain of Hazāra, and to it women bring children suffering from *parchhāwān* to be passed under an olive-tree. The saint also has some resting-places (*nishast-gāhs*) in Kashmīr (Rose, *Glossary of Punjab Tribes and Castes*, i. p. 594). The tradition that the saint was buried at Khuttilān may be explained ; Khutlān, as it is also spelt, was the seat of Khwāja Iṣhāq (see page 438). Unfortunately the *Mirāt at Muqāṣid*, though mentioning the Nūrbakhshīs on p. 3, gives no account of them that I can trace.

ability he is to be identified with Saiyid Muḥammad, son of Saiyid Muḥammad of Qātif, a descendant, of course, of the Imām Mūsā Kāẓim. Born at Qa'in 795 H. (A.D. 1393) he was initiated by the Khwāja Isḥāq Khutlānī, who was a disciple of Saiyid 'Alī Hamadānī, and from him received the title of Nūrbakhsh. In 826 H. (A.D. 1423) he proclaimed himself Khalīf in Khutlān and was imprisoned by Shāh Rukh at Herāt in that year. He died at Rai in 869 H. (A.D. 1465). So far all is plain sailing, but when we come to his successors the facts are obscure. Saiyid Muḥammad is said to have been followed as head of the Order by his son, Shāh Qāsim. Well treated by Shāh Isma'īl Safawī, he died in 927 H. (A.D. 1521). But it is also said that S. Muḥammad's principal *khalīfa* was Asiri (Shaikh Shams-ud-Dīn) Muḥammad b. Yaḥyā of Lahījān in Gīlān, and that he settled in Shirāz, where he built the Khānqāh Nūria. A friend of Dawani, Shāh Isma'īl visited him, too, in 910 H. (A.D. 1505). Besides a *Dīwān* Asiri left a commentary on the *Gulshan-i-Rāz*. His son Fidā'i died in 927 H. (A.D. 1531) (*Cat. of Turkish MSS. in the British Museum*, p. 650). It is fairly obvious that the Nūrbakshīs continued to exercise some influence in Persia under the Safawīs, but that fact would not endear them to the Turkish authorities and amply explains why there is no allusion to Shāh Qāsim or Asiri and their protectors in such a work as Brown's *Darvishes*. Nevertheless, another disciple of S. Muḥammad, one Shaikh Khalīl-ullāh Baqlānī, is mentioned in the spiritual pedigree given in the *Sabḥat ul-Akhbar*, a work which was actually translated from the Persian into Turkish in 952 H. (A.D. 1545) (*ib.* p. 323).

The Disruption of the Naqshbandīs

We now come to a crisis in the history of the Naqshbandī Order, which so far has not been explained. According to the *Rashaḥāt* its real founder was the saint Khwāja 'Ubaidullāh, by name Nāṣir-ud-Dīn, but commonly known as the Khwāja Aḥrār or Ḥaẓrat Īshān. This work makes Bahā-ud-Dīn Naqshband merely a learned expositor of the principles of the Order. Yet it ascribes Khwāja Aḥrār's investiture to Ya'qūb Charkhī, himself a disciple of Bahā-ud-Dīn. Other authorities, however, ignore Ya'qūb Charkhī [1] and make Khwāja Aḥrār 5th, not 3rd in spiritual descent from Bahā-ud-Dīn, thus :

[1] A minor problem concerning Ya'qūb Charkhī is the place of his burial. From 'information received' I stated in *A Glossary of Punjab Tribes and Castes*, iii. p. 548, that he was one of the four important disciples of Bahā-ud-Dīn Naqshband and was interred at Malafko in the Hiṣṣār Dist. of that province. But according to the *Rashaḥāt* he lies buried at Hamalghatū (or -nū) in Hiṣṣār-Shādmān, Transoxiana, and east-south-east of Samarqand, though he was born in the Ghazni district of Afghānistān (*J.R.A.S.*, 1916, p. 61). This suggests that a Ya'qūb (but not Charkhi) was buried at

Bahā-ud-Dīn Naqshband.

|

Alai-ud-Dīn al-Attār.

|

Niẓām-ud-Dīn Khāmūsh. The *Tārīkh-i-Rashīdī* speaks of a Maulāna Niẓām-ud-Dīn Khāmūsh or -ī (*op. cit.* p. 194). I have failed to trace any other details of his personality, but the 'Alī-ilāhīs still have eight sects, one of which is styled Khamūshī (*E.I.* i. p. 293).

|

Sulṭān-ud-Dīn al-Kāshgharī[1] (but his real name was almost certainly Sa'īd-ud-Dīn, and the *Tārīkh-i-Rashīdī* calls him Sa'd-ud-Dīn[2]). He is, however, sometimes described not as a disciple of Niẓām-ud-Dīn Khāmūsh, but of Saiyid Sharīf 'Alī b. Muḥammad al-Jurjānī, who died in 816 H. (A.D. 1414), and was the author of the *Sharh Muwāqif* (Nassau Lees, *Nafahāt al-Uns*, pp. 6, 2-3).

|

'Ubaid-ullāh Samarqandī (Khwāja Aḥrār).

Malafko. The doubtful passage in Bābur's *Memoirs* makes mention of a Ya'qūb as a son of Kh. Yaḥyā. Whether he was Yaḥyā's third son or not, this Ya'qūb may be the saint of Malafko.

[1] Here Le Chatelier, who actually cites the *Rashaḥāt* as his authority, has fallen into a twofold error. On p. 150 of his *Confréries musulmanes du Hedjaz*, he gives an account of "Sulṭān-ud-Dīn al-Kāshgharī and his resistance to Baber". But the future conqueror of India was not opposed by the Naqshbandī Shaikh. The prince in question was Mīrza Bābur, and the Shaikh who opposed him was not Sultān-ud-Dīn al-Kāshgharī but Khwāja Aḥrār. So far from being hostile to the branch to which the great Bābur belonged, the Khwāja Aḥrār fended off Mīrza Bābur's attack in the interests of Abū Sa'īd Mīrza, grandfather of the future emperor (H. Beveridge in *J.R.A.S.*, 1916, p. 69). And so far from being opposed to the great Bābur at Samarqand, the latter asserts that Khwāja Aḥrār appeared to him in a dream and foretold his second capture of the city (*Memoirs*, i. p. 139). Strangely enough, Brown (*The Dervishes*, p. 136) makes "our Lord Maulāna Sa'īd-ud-Dīn Kāshgharī" the opponent of Mīrza Bābur, and this, too, on the authority of the *Rashaḥāt*, thus endorsing one of Le Chatelier's errors. It seems then possible that more than one recension of that work exists, but even if that be so, a consideration of the dates involved proves that it was Mīrza Bābur, and not the conqueror of India, who was thwarted at Samarqand by a Naqshbandī Shaikh. The great Bābur made his first attempt on the city in A.D. 1498, and could not possibly have been opposed by the precursor of Khwāja Aḥrār, who had died in A.D. 1490, at least eight years earlier.

[2] The *Tārīkh-i-Rashīdī* adds that Sa'd-ud-Dīn had a disciple in the 'Shaikh al-Islām', Maulāna 'Abd-ur-Raḥmān Jāmī (p. 194). This was, of course, the famous Persian poet Jāmī' (A.D. 1414–92) (*E.I.* 7, I, p. 1011). To the poet he is credited with having appeared in a vision.

Le Chatelier again assigns not only Alai-ud-Dīn and Ya'qūb Jarhi (Charkhī obviously) as disciples or rather successors to Bahā-ud-Dīn, but also gives him a third successor in Nasr-ud-Dīn of Tāshkand. Thus it seems clear that the Order began to show symptoms of disruption on the death of Bahā-ud-Dīn. Le Chatelier, however, says that it was under the pontificate of Nasr-ud-Dīn Tāshkandī (who is not at all generally recognised as a *khalīfa* of Bahā-ud-Dīn) that the Order split up into two branches, that of the West under him as Grand Master, and the other of the East under another *khalīfa*, Sulṭān-ud-Dīn al-Kāshgharī. But the Turkish versions of the pedigree seem to acknowledge only the last named.

The Western Naqshbandīs

Of the fate of the Western Naqshbandīs little seems to be recorded in Turkish literature. From 'Ubaid-ullāh al-Samarqandī the 'descent' passes to Sh. 'Abdullah Alahī (as he was known in poetry), Ārif billah 'Abdullah, "the God-knowing servant of God", of Simaw. He followed the jurisprudent 'Alī of Tūs to Persia, quitting Constantinople; and devoted himself to the secular sciences until he was impelled to destroy all his books. His teacher, however, induced him to see them all with the exception of one containing the dealings of the Saints, and give the proceeds in alms. From Kermān he went to Samarqand, where he attached himself to the great Shaikh Ārif billah 'Ubaid-ullah (the 'little servant of God'), and at his behest he accepted the teaching of the Naqshbandīs from their Shaikh Bahā-ud-Dīn. Later he went to Herāt, and thence returned to Constantinople, but its disturbed condition on the death of Muḥammad II drove him to Yenija Wardar, where he died in A.D. 1490. He left at least two works, the *Najāt al-Arwāḥ min Rasan il-Ashbāh*, 'The Salvation of the Soul from the Snares of Doubt', and the *Zād al-Mushtāqīn*, 'The Victuals of the Zealous', sometimes described as the *Zād al-Ṭālibīn* or the *Maslik aṭ-Ṭālibīn* ('The Victuals of the Seekers', or Regulations for them) (Hammer-Purgstall, *Geschichte der osmanischen Dichtkunst*, i. p. 207). This sketch does not hint that Alahī was *head* of the Western Naqshbandīs.[1] But it suggests that the Order was not popular with the imperial

[1] Rycaut has a good account of an order which he styles the Ebrbuharee. Its founder, Emir Ebrbuhar, was a disciple of Naqshband, and taking with him 'Abdullah, Ilạhi and Wafa, preachers and heads of other convents, he came out of Asia to propagate their doctrine in Europe. Here Ilahi may be the poet Alahi, but if so Rycaut reversed his relation to Amir Bukhari, for he brought that Shaikh to Constantinople. To him Sulṭān Bāyazīd (II. 1481–1512, must be meant) in 911 H. built a mosque and convent at that city. Rycaut lays stress on the saint's abstinence and the morals of his sect, whose members fasted for the most part on Mondays and Thursdays (*Present State*, p. 141).

authorities at Constantinople in his day, and that people who wrote about its history were obliged to omit facts of cardinal importance in it.

From Alahī we are taken to Sh. Sa'īd Aḥmad al-Bukhārī, as to whom I fail to find any record. Thence we come to Sh. Muḥammad Chalabī (the Turkish cognomen is noteworthy), "nephew of Azīz", and so to Sh. 'Abd-ul-Latīf,[1] nephew of Muḥammad Chalabī. Here it is patent that the pedigree is quite fragmentary.

These data and omissions suggest that by Evlia's time the Naqshbandīs had fallen under the disfavour of the imperial government, that the heads of the Western Naqshbandīs were only recognised by it when they were harmless, and that, while that Government did not venture to abolish the convents of the Order in the capital or elsewhere, it suppressed any leading institution which was likely to recall memories of the great names in the Order or increase the influence of its independent heads for the time being.

The connection with the Eastern Naqshbandīs was similarly discouraged, if not entirely broken off. None of the great Naqshbandīs of India are commemorated by foundations at Constantinople. There is, indeed, one Hindīlar [2] ('Indians') *takia* at Khorkhor near Āq Sarāī in Stambūl, just as there is an Usbeklar *takia* there too. But most of the Naqshbandī convents bear names that are merely picturesque,[3] or only commemorate latter-day saints of the Order who were, frankly, nonentities. And so, when the author of the Turkish *Mirāt al-Muqāsid* gives a list of the Naqshbandī saints of modern times, he has to omit all allusion to their chequered history in the West and fall back on the Indian *silsila*, which never had any real jurisdiction in Turkey and was certainly not recognised there by the imperial authorities.

The Eastern Naqshbandīs

To turn now to the Eastern Naqshbandīs, we have first to deal with the Khwāja Aḥrār. In his youth this saint had a vision of

[1] Was this the 'Aḥd-ul-Latīf Naqshbandī who died in 971 H. (A.D. 1564), according to the *Mirāt al-Kā'ināt* of Nishānjī-zāda Muḥammad b. Aḥmad b. Muḥammad b. Ramaẓān, a Qāzī of Adrianople who died in 1031 H.? (*vide Cat. of Turkish MSS. in the British Museum*, p. 30). If so, we have again the curious fact that his headship of the Order is suppressed.

[2] Evliya mentions two Indian convents, one of the Hindus, 'worshippers of fire', where bodies could be burnt, and the other, the convent of the Indian Qalandars, at the head of the bridge of Kāghidkhāna (*Travels*, i. pt. 2 p. 87).

[3] *E.g.* the Agvān-lar Takia-sī, near the Chīnīlī Mosque at Scutari, seems to be so named from the Pers. *akawān*, 'flower of the *arghawān* (red) Judas-tree' (Johnson, *Pers.-Ar.-Eng. Dict.* p. 144, and Redhouse, *Turk.-Eng.-Lex.* p. 69). Evliya's translator calls it the Syringa.

Christ, which was interpreted to mean that he would become a physician, but he himself declared that it foretold that he would have a living heart. Later on he obtained great influence over Sulṭān Abū Sa'īd Mīrza, a great-grandson of Tīmūr and ruler of Māwara-un-Nahr from A.D. 1451–68. This sovereign was then the most powerful of the Tīmūrids in Central Asia: and Herāt his capital was famous for its institutions and its learning. The Khwāja acted as envoy to the rivals of this ruler who were also descendants of Tīmūr. For the nonce he succeeded in making peace between them, but it was not permanent. The Khwāja died in A.D. 1490 or perhaps a year later.[1]

His descendants were:

(Khwāja Aḥrār, 'Ubaid-ullah.)

- Khwājakā Khwâja.
- Khwāja Yaḥyā, whom Babur styles Kh. Kālān: his father's successor.
  - Zakarīa.
  - 'Abd-ul-Bāqī.
  - Muḥammad Āmīn.
  - ? Ya'qūb.

(Zakarīa and 'Abd-ul-Bāqī:) both, with Kh. Yaḥyā, murdered by Uzbegs in A.D. 1500.

Regarding the sons of Kh. Ahrār, Bābur makes a significant statement. Between them enmity arose, and then the elder became the spiritual guide of the elder prince (Baisanqar Mīrza) and the younger the guide of the younger (Sulṭān 'Alī Mīrza). Khwājahkā Khwāja had stoutly refused to surrender Baisanqar when that prince had sought sanctuary in his house. Kh. Yaḥyā, on the other hand, gave shelter to Sulṭān 'Alī Mīrza, his rival. It is further stated by Bābur that *his* "teacher and spiritual guide" was a disciple of Kh. Aḥrār, by name 'Abdullah, but better known as Khwāja Maulāna Qāzī. Now this adviser was murdered by Bābur's enemies in 903 H. (A.D. 1498). Thus we see that there was a tendency for the sons and disciples of the religious chief each to attach himself to a member of the ruling house descended from Tīmūr. Khwāja Maulāna Qāzī was apparently hanged for no better reason than that he had been active in defence of Bābur, a fate from which his religious character did not save him. But the tendency mentioned was not the universal rule, for we read of yet another disciple of Kh. Aḥrār, Ḥaẓrat Maulāna Muḥammad Qāzī, author of the *Silsilat al-Ārifīn*, who was honoured by the "Hazrat Īshān" with the title of Īshān (though he does not appear to have been recognised as his spiritual successor) and died in A.D. 1516 without having attached himself to any prince. On the other hand Kh. Aḥrār, it is said, also left a grandson, "Khwāja Nūra" or Hazrat Makhdūmī Nūra, who was named Maḥmūd from his father and Shahāb-ud-Dīn from his grandfather (*sic*), but received the title of Khwāja Khawand Maḥmūd. This saint followed Humāyūn to India, but found

[1] *J.R.A.S.*, 1916, p. 66.

that he had been supplanted in favour by the sorcerer-saint Shaikh Bahlol.[1] To this refusal on Humāyūn's part to recognise Khwāja Nūra's claims to his hereditary veneration, the author of the *Tārīkh-i-Rashīdī* hints that all that emperor's misfortunes were due (*J.R.A.S.*, 1916, pp. 59 ff. and *Tārīkh-i-Rashīdī*, pp. 212 and 398-9).

After the murder of Khwāja Maulāna Qāzi, Bābur seems to have had no spiritual guide for a time. He declares that in 905 H. he was negotiating with Khwāja Yaḥyā, but he admits that the Khwāja did not send him any message, though several times persons were sent to confer with him, *i.e.* in plain English, to attempt to seduce him from his allegiance to Sultān 'Alī Mīrza. Whether the Khwāja was inclined to listen to such overtures must remain uncertain. At the worst, all that can be reasonably regarded as proved against him is that when Sultān 'Alī Mīrza was betrayed by his mother and it became clear that Samarqand must fall either to Bābur or to Shaibānī Khān, the Khwāja deserted Sultān 'Alī and ostensibly went over to Shaibānī. But his tardy submission did not save him from the suspicion (possibly well-founded) that he was really favouring Bābur's claims, which were far stronger than Shaibānī's, to the possession of Samarqand. In so doing he would in fact have only been renewing an hereditary tie, for, Bābur informs us, his father had appointed Khwājahkā Khwāja keeper of his seal.[2]

The slaughter of Khwāja Yaḥyā with his two sons in A.D. 1500 did not, of course, bring the *silsila* or chain of spiritual descent of the western Naqshbandīs to an end, but how it continued is a mystery. The *Rashahāt* states that Yaḥyā had a third son, Muḥammad Āmīn, who escaped death. On the other hand a tradition was current that Yaḥyā had a third (or fourth) son, named Khwāja Ya'qub. This last is mentioned in Bābur's *Memoirs* as once appearing to him in a dream, but Beveridge holds that the passage is spurious (*J.R.A.S.*, 1916, p. 73). It is, however, possible that it is genuine, but that it was suppressed in the Persian translations in order to make it appear that Bābur was not under the spiritual protection of the Naqshbandī Shaikhs. But this suggestion finds no confirmation, it must be admitted, in the authorities known to me. These are two, the Panjāb traditions, and the Turkish work, the *Mirāt al-Muqāṣid*. Below, the spiritual pedigrees so preserved are set out in parallel columns :

[1] This saint, a brother of the better-known saint Muḥammad Ghaus of Gwalior, was, it is interesting to note, put to death by Mīrza Hindāl, brother of Humāyūn, in 945 H. (A.D. 1538) (Beale, *Or. Biog. Dy.* p. 370. On p. 265 Bahlol appears as Phul !).

[2] Bābur describes him as a man of learning, a great linguist and excelling in falconry. He was also acquainted with magic, *yadahgirī*, *i.e.* the power of causing rain and snow by magic (*Memoirs*, i. p. 68).

Mirāt al-Muqāṣid	The Panjāb Tradition
1. Maulāna Ya'qūb Charḥī Ḥissārī.	Ya'qub Charkhī.
2. Khwāja (a gap) Nāsir-ud-Dīn 'Ubaidullah Tāshkandī Samarqandī.	Nāsir - ud - Dīn 'Ubaid - ullah Aḥrār.
3. Muḥammad Ẓāhid.	Muḥammad Ẓāhid.
4. Maulāna Darvīsh.	Maulāna Darvīsh Muḥammad.
5. Maulāna Khwājagī Samarqandi.	Maulāna Khwājgī Amkinki (*sic*).
6. Maulāna Shaikh Muḥammad Samāqī.	Khwāja Muḥammad Bāqī-billah Berang.
7. Imām Rabbānī Mujaddid Alif - ṣānī Sh. Aḥmad Fārūqī b. 'Abd-ul-Wāḥid Fārūqī Sirhindī, *d.* 1074 H. (A.D. 1664).	Imām Rabbānī Mujaddid Alif-ṣānī Sh. Aḥmad Fāruqī Sirhindī.
8. Sh. Muḥammad Ma'sūm 'Urwah' - Waṣqā, Sāhib Maktūbāt: *d.* 1097 H. (A.D. 1688).	Kh. Muḥammad Ma'ṣūm.
9. Sh. Saif-ud-Dīn 'Ārif.	Sh. Saif-ud-Dīn.
10. Sh. Saiyid Muḥammad Nūrī Budaunī.	M. Hāfiz Muḥammad Muhsin Dihlawī.
	Saiyid Nūr Muḥammad Budaunī.
11. Sh. Shams-ud-Dīn Khān Jānān Mazhar.	Shams - ud - Dīn Habīb - ullah Mazhar Shahid.
	Mirza Janjanan.
12. Sh. 'Abdullah Dihlawī.	Mujaddid Miatusāliswal (?) Ashar Sayid.
	'Abdullah (Shāh Ghulām 'Alī Aḥmadī).
13. Ḥazrat Ẓiā-ud-Dīn Ẓū-'l-Jannāḥīn Maulāna Khālid, *d.* 1242 H. at the age of 50 (A.D. 1827). (Hence the Order is called Khālidīa.)	Shāh Abū Sa'id Aḥmadī.
	Shāh Aḥmad Sa'd Aḥmadī.
	Hājī Dost Muḥammad Qandhārī.
	Hājī Muḥammad 'Uṣmān—whose shrine is at Kulāchī in the Dera 'Ismā'īl Khān Dist., Panjāb.

The *Mirāt al-Muqāṣid*, it will be observed, omits all mention of the *silsila* of the Western Naqshbandīs, Alahi and his successors. Now the Naqshbandīs have always been numerous and important in Turkey. They have, or had when Brown wrote, 52 *takias* in Constantinople alone. In other Turkish towns also they had many foundations, *e.g.* three at Brusa (Evliya, ii. p. 8).

The *takias* at Constantinople include one named " Aḥmad

al-Bukhārī Takiasī", which must commemorate Sh. Sa'īd 'Aḥmad al-Bukhārī, Alahī's successor. It is in the Kabān Daqīq (Flour Weigh-House) at Stambūl.

They also include four called Amīr Bukhāra Takiasī. Who the 'Amīr Bukhāra' was, it is hard to say with any certainty. A Shams-ud-Dīn Bukhārī (not to be confused with Shams-ud-Dīn Muḥammad Bukhārī, the 'Amīr Sulṭān' of Bāyazīd I.'s reign) was a Persian who came to Constantinople in the time of Muḥammad II., and there rose to eminence as the Shaikh of the reign of Bāyazīd II. He lived as a Naqshbandī, and his cloister is one of the principal Naqshbandī foundations in the Turkish capital (Hammer-Purgstall, *GdOD*, i. p. 212). This must be the convent 'just outside the Adrianople Gate,' in which lies Shaikh Aḥmad 'Bukhāra' (? al-Bukhārī) in the mausoleum built for him by Murād III., near the Flower-Hall (Evliya, i. pt. 2 p. 21). If this Sh. Aḥmad was the head of the Order, it is clear that it was favoured by Murad III., though Evliya, who is very chary of details where the Naqshbandīs are concerned, does not say that Sh. Aḥmad Bukhāra belonged to that Order. But he adds: "Sh. Aḥmad Sādiq, from Tāshkendi in Bokhāra, who made the journey on foot three times from Balkh to Constantinople (and back again) is buried at the convent of Amīr Bokhara". And further: "Sh. Khāk Dada, the chief fountain of contemplation, born at Pergamus, was most famous by the name of Na'lbenji (the farrier)"; and at Rumelī Hissār is the *takia* of a farrier-saint, Na'lbar Maḥmad Effendi, a Naqshbandī.

In the religious teaching of the Naqshbandīs there was not much that would explain all this. They taught that a life could be purchased by the sacrifice of another life; and twice Khwāja Aḥrār was saved from death by men devoting themselves (becoming *fedā*) in order to restore him to health (*J.R.A.S.*, 1916, p. 75).[1] This example was clearly followed by Bābur, when he resolved to offer up his own life to save that of Humāyūn (*Memoirs*, ii. p. 442).

According to al-Nābulusī the Naqshbandīs at the present day practice telepathy. "Whilst engaged in silent meditation they converse spiritually and understand each other though no word is uttered" (see Nicholson, *Studies in Islamic Mysticism*, p. 201).

Bābur, like his descendant Aurangzeb, was buried in a tomb open to the sky. Whether Jahāngīr's tomb at Lahore was also hypæthral is still a moot question (*Journal of the Punjab Historical Society*, iii. p. 144). But it is noteworthy that Jahāngīr rebuilt Bābur's tomb in A.D. 1607–8 (*Memoirs*, ii. p. 426). This usage was certainly not confined to the Naqshbandīs, though Khwāja Bāqī-billah has no building over his grave at Delhi (Rose, *Gloss. Punjab T. and C.* iii. p. 550). It appears rather to have become

[1] For a much earlier instance of the practice *vide* R. Hartmann, *al-Qushairī's Darstellung des Ṣūfītums, Türk. Bibl.* xviii. p. 46.

a Chishti practice (*ib.* p. 530). (Qutb Shāh forbade a building to be erected over his tomb at Mihraulī near Dehli.)

But the political predilections of the Naqshbandīs may well have led to their persecution at the hands of the Sultans of Turkey. As we have seen, a Nūrbakhshī wrote a treatise on political ethics. Khwāja Aḥrār's dependents by their influence protected many poor defenceless persons from oppression in Samarqand, says Bābur (*Memoirs*, i. p. 40). In truth the Naqshbandī Khwājas seem to have sought to give new life to the old idea, that beside the secular King should stand a divinely-guided adviser, the keeper of his seal and his conscience, and the interpreter of the spirit, not merely of the latter, of the formal laws.

Early in the nineteenth century members of the Naqshbandī order penetrated into Daghestan and spread their doctrines there with great success ; about 1830 the leaders of the order started in the land of the Avars a movement which was directed against the ruling dynasty as well as against the rule of the Russians. The first leader of the rebels, Ghāzī Muḥammad, his successors Ḥamza Beg and the famous Shāmil Effendi (Schamyl), all apparently belonged to the order and ruled the part of Daghestan held by them as Shaikhs, endeavouring to govern by the strict *sharī'at* law and abrogating the customary law (*E.I.* i. p. 891).

The saint most reverenced by the Kurds, Sh. Khalid of Sulaimania, was a Naqshbandī. His sayings are styled *hadīs* (Garnett and Stuart-Glennie, *Women of Turkey*, ii. p. 141).

The Naqshbandīs were never a militant order, but, like the Zainīs and Baqtāsh, either had a militant section or tended on occasion to become militant. Thus at the final siege of Constantinople Ayā Dada was posted with 300 Naqshbandī *faqīrs* before the gate of Ayā, where he fell a martyr, and was buried at " our old court of justice the *takia* of Sirkehjī " (Evliya, *Travels*, i. p. 34). And the story of the order closes on this same note.

It remains to record that a Naqshbandī, Muhammad Māmūn ibn 'Abdul-Wahhāb al-Madanī, was endeavouring in 1924 to found at Pera a seminary for the '*moralisation*' of the Turkish *takias*, but his activities were cut short when the present Turkish government decreed the suppression of all the Orders in Turkey.

APPENDIX II

NOTES ON SOME OF THE ISLAMIC ORDERS LISTED IN CHAP. II., P. 51; IN CHAP. III., PP. 81-2; AND IN CHAP. XI., PP. 267-71. THE NOS. PREFIXED REFER TO THE LIST IN CHAP. III.

1. Uwais in original. The place assigned to the Uwaisī or to Uwais is highly significant. The Uwaisī can hardly be regarded as a religious order or sect at all, though Uwais (Awīs) bin 'Umar, al-Karanī, adopted the contemplative life at the bidding of Gabriel as early as 37 H. He had all his teeth extracted in memory of the Prophet, who had lost two of his at the battle of Uhud, and the same sacrifice is imposed on his followers. They observe night-long vigils: Petit, *Confréries musulmanes*, p. 6. (A slightly different version of this sacrifice is given on p. 98 *supra*.) Al-Hujwīrī makes no mention of it, but says Uwais was a solitary who never saw the Prophet. But 'Umar and 'Alī sought him out after Muḥammad's death in accordance with the Prophet's behest. They found him at prayer, and waiting until it was finished were shown the white marks, as large as a *dirham*, on his left side and the palm of his hand (Nicholson, *Kashf al-Maḥjūb*, p. 83). No other instance of such *stigmata* appears to be on record in Islam.

Uwais was pre-eminently the traditional patron of many of the patron-saints of the trade-guilds of Turkey. Indeed, Evliya states that he "tied on the girdle of no less than seventy individuals, who shall all be mentioned in their places", a promise unfortunately not fulfilled by any means completely (Evliya, i. pt. 2 p. 140).

It is, however, possible to detail some of the guilds which are under the patronage of Uwais. He is naturally patron of the barber tooth-drawers, as noted by Miss L. M. J. Garnett in her account of the *eṣnāf* or trade-guilds (*Mysticism and Magic in Turkey*, pp. 42-43). He is also patron of the bowmen and of the camel-drivers (Evliya, i. pt. 2 pp. 93 and 126). In India he re-appears as Omes Karīm (probably an error for Ovais Karanī), and is there said to be patron of the comb-makers.

2. "The legend of Shaikh 'Ilwān, who is said to have founded the first order in 49 H. (A.D. 670), may be safely rejected" (Macdonald, *Muslim Theology*, p. 268). But the Aulād 'Ilwān,

'sons of 'Ilwān or 'Ilwānīa', form a sect of the Rifā'ī, and Lane describes their practices. They thrust iron spikes into their eyes and bodies, break stones on their chests, and eat live coals, glass, etc. They also used to carry a log of palm wood filled with lighted rags soaked in oil and tar in processions, the flames curling over their heads and bodies without causing any injury. They also passed needles through their cheeks (*Modern Egyptians*, p. 248). But see also No. 14 below.

10. The Shādhilīyyah is an African order, or rather theological school, founded by Abū'l Ḥasan b. 'Abd al-Jabbār al-Shādhilī, born in Morocco or Tunis in 1197-98. He was a pupil of 'Abd al-Salām b. Mashīsh, a renowned Moroccan disciple of Shu'aib Abū Madian al-Andalūsī of Seville. The school is also represented in the Hedjaz, Syria and Turkey. The university of al-Azhar drew its inspiration exclusively from his teaching (*E.R.E.*, 10, p. 724). Another account is that Abū Ḥasan Alī ash-Shāẓilī, founder of this order, derived his title from Shāẓil (Shādal), a town near Tunis, where he went. His master was 'Abd-us-Salām, a disciple of Abū-Madian, a disciple of 'Abd-ul-Qādir Gīlānī. He died in 656 H. (A.D. 1258) (Petit, *Confréries musulmanes*, p. 12). For one of its thirteen sub-orders, the Isāwī, see p. 336 *supra*.

12. The Badawī are the Aḥmadīa of Lane. Also called the Badawiyyah-Aḥmadiyyah, this order is allied both to the Rifā'ī and Qādirī. It was founded by Aḥmad al-Badawī, who died in Egypt in A.D. 1276. Legend assigned to him power to cure barrenness in women (*E.R.E.* 10, p. 724). Lane describes the order as numerous and respected. It affects red turbans and banners. It has three main offshoots—the Bayūmīa, founded by Saiyid 'Alī al-Bayūmī, the Sha'rāwīa, founded by Shaikh ash-Sha'rāwī, and the Shinnāwīa, founded by Saiyid 'Alī ash-Shinnāwī; but it has many other sub-orders. The last-named train an ass to perform a strange part on the last day of the *mūlid* or birth-place celebrations, observed thrice a year, of al-Badawī at Ṭanṭā. The animal is taught to enter the mosque and advance to the saint's tomb, where it stands while its hair is plucked off as charms by the congregation. A militant—apparently—section of the Aḥmadīas are the Aulād Nūḥ or 'sons of Noah'. All young men, they wear *tartūrs* or high caps, with a variegated tuft on top, and numerous strings of beads, and carry wooden swords and a thick twist of cords called *firqilla*, 'a whip' (*Modern Egyptians*, pp. 129 and 246).

14. The Sa'dīs are clearly the same as the Sa'adīya, an Asiatic order founded in the thirteenth or fourteenth century by Sa'ad al-Dīn al-Jabanī of Damascus, and now found in Asia and Africa. Its Egyptian branch has adherents in the Sūdān. Another section, in Syria, seems less important, but its members are also found in the Hedjaz. It is an ecstatic order, allied to the Rifā'ī (*E.R.E.* 10, p. 724). Lane describes the Sa'adīya, founded by

Sa'd-ud Dīn al-Jibāwī, as a sect of the Rifā'īs, more celebrated than the 'Ilwānīya. They have green banners and turbans, or affect the sober colours of the Rifā'ī. They handle venomous snakes and scorpions, and even partly devour them. Many Rifā'ī and Sadī *darvesh* earn a livelihood by charming snakes away from houses. At the *dosa* ceremony the Sa'dīa *shaikh* rides on horseback over the prostrate bodies of his *darvesh* and others who throw themselves on the ground for the purpose (*Modern Egyptians*, pp. 248-49). The founder of the Sa'dī order died at Jabā near Damascus in 736 H. (A.D. 1335). He is said to have used snakes as cords to tie up his faggots (Jacob, *Beiträge zur Kenntniss des Derwisch-Ordens der Bektaschis*, p. 47). Paul Kahle, however, states that the Rifā'īs have no *furrū'* or sub-orders, each with a Shaikh at its head, but only three *buyut* or ' corporations ' (from *bait*, sing.), and he does not mention the Aulād 'Ilwān. Like the Aulād Nūh of the Ahmadīa, the Aulād 'Ilwān seem to be an association within the order, who take their name from the more or less legendary Shaikh 'Ilwān. Their designation can hardly be referred to the Sh. 'Ilwān of Shīrāz, a follower or, as some say, merely a friend of Hājī Bairām, who translated the *Gulshan-i-rāz* of Sh. Maḥmūd Tabrīzī Shabistarī, since Brown's list places the 'Ilwānīs immediately after the Uwaisīs and before the Adhamīs, making them much older than the Bairāmīs (*vide* Hammer-Purgstall, *GdOD.* i p. 64, and *Der Islam*, vi. p. 154).

16. The Khalwātiya owes its name, at least, to 'Umar al-Khalwātī, a Persian of the fourteenth century, but its doctrine goes back to al-Junaidī. Though an Asiatic order—or rather school—it soon took root in Egypt, where it threw out several sub-orders. It is one of the few Muhammadan orders which admit women (*E.R.E.* 10, p. 725). According to Petit, the founder, 'Umar-al-Khalwatī, who died at Caesarea in Syria in 800 H. (A.D. 1397), left the order without any hierarchic organisation, and it is said to have split up, in Turkey and the neighbouring countries, into as many as fifteen groups. These include the Bakrīa, founded in 909 H. (A.D. 1503); the Khafnawīa, founded in 1163 H. (A.D. 1749); the Rahmānīa, 1208 H. (A.D. 1793); and the Dardirīa, 1292 H. (A.D. 1875) (*Confréries musulmanes*, p. 19). Of these the Bakrīa are clearly the followers of Pīr Abū Bakr Wafāī, and are apparently still to be found. Rinn is probably wrong in regarding the Bakrīa as a Shāzalī sub-order (*Marabouts et Khouans*, p. 271). The much later sub-order called the Baqrīa (founded *ca.* 1700) is doubtless extinct, but it lived long enough to split up into three fresh groups, the Khafnawīa (above mentioned), the Sharqawīa, and the Sammanīa (according to Montet in *E.R.E.* 10, p. 725).

This account does not, however, agree with that of Paul Kahle, who makes the Sammānia a Shāzilī sub-order, omits the Sharqawīa, and gives the Khafnīa, Saba'īa, Ṣawīa and Ḍaifīa as the four daughter-orders of the Khalwatīs (*Der Islam*, vi. p. 155).

In Turkey the process of disruption was still more marked, for a spiritual pedigree compiled by Shaikh Muḥammad Salīm Naqshbandī, of Constantinople, gives the following affiliation of the fifteen Khalwatīa sub-orders for that empire and the neighbouring lands:

No. in text, p. 82 above	Name.
	Habīb Faramania ' Chougaia ' (Shūgāiā).
(23)	Gulshanīa ' Cizaia ' (Sizaia).
(28)	Shamsīa ' Souasiya Rouchdiya ' (Siwāsīa Rushdīa).
(28)	,, ,, ,, Siwās.
	,, ,, ,, Latifīya al-Bostān.
	,, ,, 'Abd-ul-Majadīa Nūria Sūsīa, Istambūl.
(? 34)	Shabānīa Naswīa Sharkāsīa Kash-Ataliwīa.
	,, ,, ,, Karawīa.
	,, ,, Badāia.
	,, ,, Rashidīa.
(22)	Sunbūlīa Markāsīa (Markazīa).
(30)	Niāzīa Masrīa.
(32)	Nūr-ud-Dīn Jarrāhīa.
(19)	Bairāmīa Khoja Hinnatīa (Himmatīa).
	,, Ughlān Shaikhīa.

(A. Le Chatelier, *Confréries musulmanes du Hedjaz*, p. 50.) In the above list there are several obvious misprints, and for ' Faramania ' Qaramānīa should also probably be read. Habīb Qaramānī was the first Shaikh at Constantinople and was " buried at the convent of Ja'ferābād at Sūlijeh, opposite Eyyūb ". He had 70,000 disciples (Evliya, i. pt. 2 p. 29). Another (?) Habīb Qaramānī was born at Ortakoī near Nikde and was buried at Karajelar near Erzerum. " He died a Shaikh of the Bairāmī in the reign of Muḥammad II." One of his disciples was Hamza Effendi, whose birthplace, Hāj Hamza, amongst the mountains on the banks of the Kizil Irmāk, was in ruins even in Evliya's time. At Karajalar he found the tomb of ' Sheat ' Bābā Sulṭān, in a meadow outside the town, to which pilgrimages are made (*ib.* ii. p. 95).

Down to Sh. Chelebi Khalīfa Jamāl-ud-Dīn the *Mirāt ul-Muqaṣid* gives the same descent for the Sha'bānīas as it does for the Sunbulīs. Then it adds the name of Sh. Khair-ud-Dīn Toqādī, and gives the founder's name as Sha'bān Walī (of) Qasṭamūnī, as usual. It omits the dates of his death, etc.

For the ' Chabaniya ' of Le Chatelier should no doubt be read ' Sha'bānīa ' (*v.* note on p. 51 *supra*). His ' Nassouiya ' (Naswīa) may refer to Shaikh Nusuhī Effendi, whose *takia* is at Scutari. His ' Cherkasiya ' (Sharkāsīa) may be identical with Brown's ' Eshrakī ', and if so that order is one of the Khalwatī sub-orders. His ' Kach-Ataliouiya ' suggests a connection with Adalia (Ar. Anṭālia, the ancient Attaleia), but on p. 466 *infra* we read of the

Khalwatī *takia* of Kush ' Adālī Ibrāhīm Effendi ', and though the identity of the two names is evident, the spelling ' 'Adālī ' is against any derivation from Adalia. ' Karaouiya ' (Karawīa) may be an error for ' Qaramānīa,' as the Khalwatīs have an ' Isḥāq Qaramānī *takia-si* ' at Sudlija (p. 467 *infra*).

For the Sunbulī saint Markaz *v.* p. 481 *infra*. Niāzī ' Misrī ' is discussed on p. 204 *supra*, where the Nūr-ud-Dīnīs are also mentioned.

Le Chatelier gives a very full account of the Khalwatī order, but it may have yet other sub-orders. *E.g.*, it has one called Hayātī, whose patron is Ḥasan of Baṣra, possibly identical with the Hayetti of Rycaut's *Hist. of the Present State of the Ottoman Empire*, p. 67. A heretical sect with Christian leanings, though the Khalwatī are orthodox, they penetrated into Southern Albania later than the Baqtāsh but certainly before the end of the eighteenth century (Hasluck in *Annual*, B.S.A. xxi. p. 116).

Finally, Jacob suggests that the Khalwatī may be a good deal older than 'Umr's time. Ibn Batūta describes the *zāwiyas* of the Akhīs or ' convents of the Brethren ' wherein he lodged, and the Shaikh Akhī Mīrim Khalwatī, who died at Kir-Shahr in 812 H. (A.D. 1409–10) is a possible link between them and the Khalwatī order. On the other hand, it may owe its foundation as a regular order to Yaḥyā-i-Shirwānī, who is styled " *pīr* of the Khalwatīs ", and who died at Baku in 869 H. (A.D. 1464–65) (*Beiträge zur Kenntniss der Bektaschis*, p. 80). Yaḥyā-i-Shirwānī was in a sense founder of the Gulshanī or Roshanī order also (*v.* note on p. 455 *infra*).

That the Khalwatī are of some antiquity is also apparent from their connection with a Pīr Iliās, a Shaikh buried at Amasia on an elevation called Sevadie near the town. One of the saints of Bāyazīd I., he went with Tīmūr to Shirwān. His mausoleum was erected by Bāyazīd II. Pīr Iliās had a son-in-law, Shaikh 'Abd-ur-Raḥmān b. Ḥusām-ud-Dīn, commonly called Gūmishlī-zāda, who foretold to Muḥammad II. his conquest of Constantinople. But his disciple was Zakarīa Khalwatī, who is buried near him. Evliya says he was his first disciple, and is buried near the saddlers' shops at Amasia. The son-in-law was also a Khalwatī, and Evliya styles him the Sulṭān of the faith, the Sīmurgh of truth ; he, too, tells how the saint signified his prevision that Muḥammad would ascend the throne, and adds that he left many poems on divine love. His poetical name was Hossāmī, a name adopted by other later poets ; and the poetess Mihrmāh Khātun was also descended from this family (*Travels*, ii. pp. 101-2 and 123). The last-named is the Ottoman Sappho, whose poetical title was Mihri (II.) (Hammer-Purgstall, *GdOD*. i. p. 306).

Brusa was a great Khalwatī centre, containing seventeen Khalwatī convents, including that of Uftādī Effendī, in the inner castle, wherein was the chief of the small mosques (*Evliya*, ii. p. 8).

The Khalwatī cloister of Yuwashja Muḥammad-Pāsha near

Shahr Amīnī seems to have disappeared. It was held by Sh. Nazim Effendi in the reign of Mustafa II., and then by Sh. 'Abd-ur-Raḥmān, the poet Rafia, murdered in 1720 (*GdOD.* iv. p. 135)

The Khalwatīs were irreverently styled *takhta-depen-ler*, or 'floor-kickers', by their detractors (Babinger in *Der Islam*, xi. p. 71).

The Khalwatī are described by Lane as in opposition to the Shāzilī, each community having its own Shaikh. The former derive their name from *khalwat*, 'retreat', which they practise. In retreat they pray before daybreak the *wird as-saḥr*, whereas the Shāzilī do so *ḥasb ash-Shāzilī*, "according to the Shāzilī (rite)", after it. The Khalwatī retreat may last forty days, spent fasting except at night in a solitary cell; though if it is spent in a cell at the sepulchral mosque of Shaikh al-Damirdāshī north of Cairo, three days appear to suffice, but only a little rice may be eaten. Certain secret prayers are in use, and the only reply vouchsafed to any one who speaks to them during the retreat is the *kalima*: "There is no god save God" (*Modern Egyptians*, p. 251). The Khalwatīs in Egypt have no *'alam*, 'standard', and the *zai* which is their distinguishing mark is the *qa'uq*, or head-dress, their only uniform (*Der Islam*, vi. p. 169).

In the life of the Turkish court the proclamation of a *khalwat* required all males to withdraw from the streets under pain of death, so that the ladies of the harem could pass through them unseen. Hence the term denotes a peculiarly sacred seclusion, just as *halwā* connotes the privilege of entertaining the Sulṭān (cf. von Hammer, *GdOR.* iv. p. 200).

17. The *Mirāt ul-Muqāṣid* gives the following as the line of Zainī descent:

Junaid.
,,
Shaikh Mimshād Dīnwarī.
,, Muḥammad Dīnwarī.
,, Muḥammad Bākrī.
,, Waṣīyy-ud-Dīn al-Qāzī.
,, 'Umr Bākrī.
,, Abū'l Najīb 'Abd-ul-Qāhir Ziā-ud-Dīn Muḥammad al-SUHARWARDI.
,, -ush-Shuyūkh Shihāb-ud-Dīn 'Umr b. Muḥammad Bakrī al-Suharwardī.
,, Najīb-ud-Dīn 'Alī b. Yazghīsh Shīrānī.
,, Nūr-ud-Dīn 'Abd-ul-Ṣamad b. 'Alī.
,, Najm-ud-Dīn Muḥammad Isfahānī.
,, Ḥusain Ḥisām-ud-Dīn.
,, Jamāl-ud-Dīn Yūsuf.
,, Nūr-ud-Dīn 'Abd-ur-Raḥmān.
,, ZAIN-UD-DIN Abū Bakr Khwāfī (Ḥwāfī in the lithograph).
,, 'Abd-ul-Latīf Qudusī Rūmī.

Shaikh Wafā Muṣtafā b. Aḥmad Wafā.
,, 'Alī Dada Wafāī.
,, Dāūd Wafāī Rūmī.
,, 'Abd-ul-Latīf Wafāī Rūmī.

The Zainīs were once an important Order. Evliya mentions as a divine of the time of Sulṭān Muḥammad I. (1413–21) the Shaikh 'Abd-ul-Latīf Mokadessi (Muqaddasī would mean 'of Jerusalem,' but Qudusī must be meant) bin 'Abd-ur-Raḥmān b. 'Alī b. Ghānim (*Travels*, ii. p. 22). But five pages farther on he mentions a Sh. 'Abd-ul-Latīf Mokadessi as the Imām of Ilderīm Khān. Then adding the title al-Anṣārī to the divine's names he describes how he built the Zainī-lar convent at Brūsa after he had visited the tomb of Ṣadr-ud-Dīn at Qonia, where the dead saint stretched out his hand from his grave and bade the Shaikh read the *sura* Yā-sīn. Under Muḥammad II. (1451–81) the Zainīs formed, like the Naqshbandis, a militant Order, and led by Jubbah 'Alī, the spiritual guide of the Sulṭān of Egypt, three hundred of them, unfurling the standard of Zain-ud-Dīn Ḥāfī, embarked on skins which floated on the sea, and attacked the enemy (*ib.* i. pt. i. p. 34).

That the Order took its name from Zain-ud-Dīn is certain, but its founder's title is variously given as Khāfī (cf. p. 268 *infra*) and Ḥāfī, which latter term means 'barefoot' (Beale, *Or. Biog Dict.*, p. 147). Born in Khurāsān in 757 H. (A.D. 1356) Zain-ud-Dīn taught at Aleppo, one of his would-be pupils being Āq Shams-ud-Dīn, who was, however, led by a vision to follow Hājī Bairām. Zain-ud-Dīn died in 838 H. (A.D. 1435) (Gibb, *Hist. of Ottoman Poetry*, ii. p. 139). His biography is in the *Shaqā'iq*. The Zain-ud-Dīn al-Khwāfī, 'the Secret', who wrote a Persian tract on Ṣūfī ethics called the *Ādāb-us-Ṣūfīyyat* and a work entitled the *Mirāt-u-Ṭālibīn*, mentioned by Prof. E. G. Browne in his article on "The Literature of the Hurufis" in *J.R.A.S.*, 1907, pp. 553 and 576, would seem to be our Zain-ud-Dīn. Zain-ud-Dīn Ḥāfī had a college at Brūsa named after him, and that city was a great Zainī centre.

The Zainis, however, claim to be much older than Zain-ud-Dīn. Evliya, indeed, describes them as "of the sect of Na'amān Ben Thābet", though elsewhere he says they trace their origin to Oṣmān, and became famous by their twelve Shaikhs called 'Ibād (*op. cit.*, i. pt. 2 p. 29, and ii. p. 8). His account of their 'sect' gives point to his remark that the famous jurist Mulla Khusrau ibn Khizr, author of the *Ghurar al-Ahkām* and the commentary on it, the *Durar al-Hukkām*, wrote his 'famous book' at the Masjid Zaini-lar in Brūsa, and he doubtless meant that the Order was attached to the legal doctrines of Abū Hanīfa (*ib.* pp. 27 and 28). Who the twelve '*ibād* or 'servants'[1] were does not appear, but

[1] This may indicate some affinity with the 'Ibādiyah, who were an offshoot from the original seceders of the early days of Islam, and who held

at Constantinople the Wafā Jāmī' mosque on the Golden Horn was built for the Zainīa Shaikh Muṣṭafā Wafā by Bāyazīd II. in 881 H. (1476–77), according to the *E.I.* i. p. 870, though as that Sulṭān's reign did not commence till 1481 there must be here an error in the date. Still, the erection of this mosque shows that the Zainīs were an Order of some importance down to the end of the fifteenth century.

19. Down to Sh. Abū'l Najīb Suharwardī the Bairāmī descent is the same as that of the Zainīs. Then come :

Shaikh Qūtb-ud-Dīn [Abū Zashd (*sic*) on p. 35] Abharī.
,, Rukn-ud-Dīn Muḥammad al-Bukhārī [Naḥāsī on p. 35].
,, Shihāb-ud-Dīn Muḥammad Tabrīzī.
,, Jamāl-ud-Dīn Tabrīzī.
,, Ibrāhīm Zāhid Gīlānī.
,, Ṣafī-ud-Dīn Abū Isḥāq Ardibīlī.
,, Sadr-ud-Dīn Mūsā Ardibīlī.
,, Khwāja 'Alī Ardibīlī.
,, Ibrāhīm Ardibīlī.
,, Ḥāmid Walī Aqsarāī Shams-ud-Dīn Mūsā.
,, Hājī Bairām, d. in 833 H.

A disciple of Hājī Bairām, Muḥammad, son of Sālih, wrote the *Mughārib uz-Zamān fi gharāib il ashia fil 'ain wal aian*, " Rareties of the Age and Rare Things for Eye and Mind ". This his brother Yāzījī-oghlī translated into Turkish under the title *Anwār ul-'Ashiqīn*, or " The Lights of the Loving ". The translator, who was known as Bījān, 'the lifeless,' also wrote the *Durrī maqnūn*, ' Hidden Pearls ' ; and Muḥammad the *Muhammadiat*, ' Muhammadanism '. Both contain much of dogmatic and mystic interest, and Hammer-Purgstall compares the latter to the *Divina Commedia* for the richness of its religious content (*GdOD*. i. pp. 127-28). These works were written before 853 H. (A.D. 1449), but Yāzījī-oghlī does not seem to have completed his Anwār till 855 H. (*Cat. of Turkish MSS. in the B.M.*, p. 18).

Muḥammad b. Muḥammad Āltī-Parmaq, ' the six-fingered ', author of a translation of the ' Stufen des Prophetenthums ' of the historical picture-gallery, was a Bairāmī. He died in Cairo in 1033 H. (A.D. 1623) (*Cat. Turk. MSS. in B.M.*, p. 26, and *GdOR*. ii. p. 842).

21. The Wafāīya were founded early in the eighth century (H.) or fourteenth century A.D. as an independent Shāẓilī order by Muḥammad Wafā, head of a Sharīf family in Egypt. Their principal form of worship is psalmody in unison (Petit, *Confréries*

---

that the watchword of the Islamic government should be ' efficiency ', and not descent from any particular tribe. They are recognised as a ' fifth rite ', alongside the four better-known schools, and are also called Yūsufīyah, at least in Morocco (T. H. Weir, *The Shaikhs of Morocco*, pp. xlii. and 124).

musulmanes, p. 13). Montet describes the Wafaiyyah (Ufaiyyah) as still under the control of its founder's family (*E.R.E.* 10, p. 724). (Muḥammad Wafā appears to be entirely distinct from Pīr Abū Bakr Wafā'ī, founder of the Bakrīa.) The order may, however, be referred to the Shaikh Wafā' or Wafā'zāda, the 'son of fidelity', Sh. Muṣliḥ-ud-Dīn Mustafā of Qonia, who died in 1493. At first a disciple of the famous saint of the tanners (apparently Husām-ud-Dīn Dabbāgh mentioned by Cl. Huart, *Les Saints des Derviches tourneurs*, pp. 334-35), which would connect him with the Maulavīs, he became an adherent of the Shaikh 'Abd-ul-Laṭīf al-Qudsī. His grave became a place of pilgrimage, and Bāyazīd I. built there the mosque still known by his name (*GdOD.* i. p. 316). Whether he founded any regular order or not is by no means clear, but occasionally a darvish is described as having joined it, *e.g.* Shammii the poet, who died in 1529 (*GdOD.* ii. p. 15).

22. Down to Sh. Pīr Muḥammad Arzinjānī the *Mirāt ul-Muqāṣid* gives the Sunbulī descent as virtually identical with that of the Niāzīs. Then it adds the name of Sh. Chelebī Muḥammad Jamāl-ud-Dīn as his successor, and gives that of the founder of the order as Sunbul Sinān Yūsuf al-Marzīfūnī, not Bolawī as on p. 269 *supra*. Sunbul Yūsuf died in 1529. The Sunbulīs may be the Ardabalīs of p. 85, since they hold the *takia* of Sinān Ardabalī in Scutari—see p. 480. *Sunbul* in Turkish 'hyacinth', and in Arabic 'spikenard'; al-Sunbula is also a sign of the zodiac (*E.I.* i. p. 135). The Sunbulīs also have a *takia* "at the Agha Chair near the Selivria Gate" (p. 481 *infra*), which may be the one alluded to in the text, and several others at Constantinople. They still hold one at Khoja Muṣṭafā Pāsha, in Stambūl, but none apparently at Psamatia.

Sunbuli (?) Muhammad Shaikh, son of the famous Shaikh of Balat of the reign of Sulaiman II., known in poetry as Wahyi (V). In 1688 he succeeded to the cloister inside the Balat Gate on his father's death, himself dying in 1717 (*GdOD.* iv. p. 100).

23. Also called Roshanī (see p. 269 *supra* and note).

Down to Ibrāhīm Zāhid Gīlānī the *Mirāt ul-Muqāṣid* gives the same descent for the Gulshanīs as for the Bairāmīs. Then come:

Shaikh Akhī Muḥammad b. Nūr Khalwatī.
,, Pīr 'Umr Khalwatī.
,, Fānī Akhī Khurram Khalwatī.
,, Fānī Akhī Miram Khalwatī.
,, Ḥājī 'Izz-d-Dīn Khaiāwī.
,, Ṣadr-ud-Dīn Khaiāwī.
,, Sayyid Yaḥyā Shirwānī.
,, Dada 'Umr Roshanī Tabrīzī.

The title Gulshanī, "the one of the rose-field", as Hammer-Purgstall translates it, was adopted by a Turkish poet before the time of Ibrāhīm Gulshanī (*GdOD.* i. p. 286). In mysticism there may be an allusion to the poetic simile "As wounds are poetically compared to flowers, he whose breast is torn through the anguish of love has but to look thereon so to find a garden" (Gibb, *Hist. of Ottoman Poetry*, iii. p. 10).

The poet Rindī (IV.), Shumlalī-zāda Aḥmad Effendi, the Shaikh of the Gulshanīs, took the vows of the order at Cairo, and on his master's death settled at Brūsa as Imām of the cloister of 'Alī Mast. He died in 1678 (*ib.* iii. p. 516).

The poet Ibrāhīm Gulshanī (III.), son of Samisjī-Dada of Magnesia, who was an adviser of the Sulṭān Muḥammad III., succeeded his father as Shaikh of the cloister at Adrianople, and at Ispahān enjoyed the society of Shaikh Bahā-ud-Dīn. He died in 1717 (*ib.* iv. p. 92).

The poet Safa'ī (IV.) whose name was Hasan, of Morea, devoted himself at Adrianople as disciple of the Shaikh La'alī Muḥammad Effendi of the Gulshanī order, and then became Shaikh of the cloister of Jabī Dada at Constantinople (*ib.* iv. p. 257). A chronogram composed by him fixes the date of the death of Sh. 'Ushshāqī Ṣādiq Effendi in 1682, so he must have lived on after that year.

The poet Kiāmī (VII.) was son of the Shaikh of Shaikhs Gulshanī Ibrāhīm Effendi, and by name Muḥammad Effendi, of Adrianople. Before his death in 1722 he wrote many works, including some on law. He does not appear to have joined the Gulshanī order, and he certainly held no Shaikhship in it (*ib.* iv. p. 114).

26. According to the *Mirāt ul-Muqāṣid* the Jalwatī descent was:

Shaikh Ismā'īl Ḥaqqī of Brūsa.
„ Sayyid 'Uṣmān Fazl-illāhī Āt-Bāzārī.
„ Ẕākir-zāda 'Abdullah Effendi.
„ Dizdār-zāda Aḥmad Effendi.
„ Ḥazrat Maḥmūd al-Hudāī.
„ Ḥazrat Muḥammad Uftāda.
„ Khiẓr Dada al-Muq'ad.

Ismā'īl Ḥaqqi, a prolific Jalwatī poet, born in 1652, son of Muṣṭafā and disciple of Sh. Fazlī-Ilāhī 'Uṣmān of Aidos, died in 1724 (*GdOD.* iv. p. 135).

30. The *Mirāt ul-Muqāṣid* also traces the descent of the Niāzīs (Miṣrīas) to Sayyid Yāḥyā Shirwānī; after whom come:

Shaikh Pīr Muḥammad Arzinjānī.
„ Tāj-ud-Dīn Ibrāhīm Qaisarī.
„ Qabāqlī Salāh-ud-Dīn 'Ushshāqī.
„ Yigīt-bāshī Shams-ud-Dīn Aḥmad.
„ Ṭālib Ummī.
„ 'Abd-ul-Wahhāb Almālī.
„ Aḥmad.
„ Sāzāī Almālī.

31. The Murādīs seem to be divided into three branches and to be themselves an offshoot of the Naqshbandīs (Le Chatelier, *Confréries musulmanes du Hedjaz*, pp. 50 and 155). On p. 271

supra their foundation is ascribed to Murād 'the Syrian', who died in A.D. 1719. They may, however, be an offshoot of the Baqtāsh founded by Abdāl Murād, a saint of the sixteenth century, described as a companion of Hāji Baqtāsh. Sulṭān Orkhān is said to have founded the *takia* of Abdāl Murād at Brūsa, but Hasluck regards his connection with the Baqtāsh as probably apocryphal (*Annual*, B.S.A. xxi. p. 93). The poet Murādī, of Bustām, 'a darvish', a descendant of Sh. Bāyazīd Bustāmī, died in 968 H. (A.D. 1560) (*GdOD*. ii. p. 285).

32. Down to Yigīt-bāshī Shams-ud-Dīn Aḥmad the *Mirāt ul-Muqāṣid* gives the Nūr-ud-Dīnīs the same descent as the Niāzīs. After him come :

Shaikh al-Hāj Qaramānī 'Alī 'Imād-ud-Dīn.
,, Qāsim Effendi.
,, Yāḥyā Qara-Hiṣṣārī.
,, Ramẓān Effendi.
,, Mastjī 'Alī Rūmī.
,, Mastji-zāda Ibrāhīm.
,, Dabbāgh Rūmī.
,, Fāzil 'Alī Rūmī Lūfajawī.
,, 'Alī Kūstandīlī.

33. Jamālī. This order was founded by Jamāl-ud-Dīn, who is styled Muḥammad Jamāl-ud-Dīn Adirnawī (' of Adrianople ') (see p. 271 *supra*). As he died in 1750 he cannot be the Jamāl-ud-Dīn mentioned on p. 90 above. One of the principal saints of the Jamālī order, 'Abdī Effendi, died in 1783 at Constantinople (see p. 272 above). An 'Abdī Bey Sultān, a Baqtāsh saint, is buried at Yatagan in the Smyrna *wilāyat*, but the date of his death is not recorded (Hasluck in *Annual*, B.S.A. xxi. p. 93).

34. Ashrākī (Eshrakee in original) would mean ' polytheist ', from *ashrāk*, ' an asserting that the Deity subsists in more than one person ' (Redhouse, *Turk. Eng. Lex.*, p. 121) ; *ishrāq* = ' a being illuminated ' (*ib.* p. 121).

In his account of the new and modern sects among the Turks Rycaut describes the Ishrāqī (Eschrakian) or ' illuminated ' as a purely Platonical sect, contemplative of the Divine Idea, and the number in God. They held the Unity, but did not deny the Trinity, a conception which they illustrated by three folds in a handkerchief. Some parts of the *Qurān* they styled ' abrogated ' (in Turkish ' *mensuca* '). They also contemned all fancies and gross conceptions of Heaven. Yet of this were all the Shaikhs or able preachers that belonged to the royal mosques. Constant in their devotions, abstemious, yet cheerful and of taking behaviour, great lovers of music and of an indifferent strain in poetry, they procured their disciples as much as possible to be men of comely and pleasing countenances and majestic presence, educating them in all their rules of abstinence, gravity and other virtues of the sect. Rycaut contrasts them with the Haireti or ' amazed ', a sect of doubters who condemned the Ishrāqī as dogmatical and obstinate, but were themselves so devoid of principle that when entrusted with the office of *mufti* they gave *fatwas* even on affairs of State so incautiously that they met with banishment or death a good deal oftener than their opponents (*Present State*, p. 135). Observe that he calls neither an Order.

35. Shāh Ni'āmat-Ullāh [Walī] is the title by which Saiyid [Shāh (Saiyid was his poetical title)] Nūr-ud-Dīn Yazdī is best known. A descendant of the Imām Bāqir, he was born at Aleppo in 730 H. (A.D. 1330) and travelled widely, spending eighty days in meditation on the summits of Dawāwand in winter and an equal period on Mt. Alwand, the Orontes of the Greeks. At Karbalā he lived on dust for forty days (the dust of Karbalā is sacred). Thence he visited Najaf and stayed seven years at Makka. Joining Shaikh 'Abdullāh Ja'far he travelled with him, possibly visiting India (or more probably Afghānistān). Tīmūr sent him into an honourable interment at Māhun, in Karmān, where his shrine is still a great place of pilgrimage. His death is assigned to A.D. 1430. One of his prophecies contributed largely to the Indian Mutiny (Major P. M. Sykes, *Ten Thousand Miles in Persia*, pp. 148-49). (Yazdī, 'of Yazd', has no connection with Yazīdī.)

His followers are described on p. 371 *infra* as of importance in India.

Beale describes him as a descendant of Imām Mūṣā Kāzim and a disciple of Sh. 'Abdullah [b. 'Abd-ul-] Yāfa'ī, but a follower of the tenets of the Imām Shāfi'ī. He also assigns his death to 827 H. (A.D. 1424) or to 1431, saying that he was only seventy-five at his demise. The date of his birth must have been later than 1330. The Imām Yāfa'ī, 'Abdullah b. As'd, styled the Quṭb of Makka and Yāfa'i Nazal al-Ḥaramain, born at Yāfa' in Syria, died in 767 H. (A.D. 1366) or possibly earlier, in 1354. The title of one of his works, the *Khulāsat al-Mufākhir fi Munāqib ash-Shaikh 'Abd-ul-Qādir*, indicates that he was a follower of 'Abd-ul-Qādir Gīlānī, but he wrote much else (*Or. Biogr. Dy.*, pp. 291 and 418).

Mir Khalil-ullah Hirwi was one of his descendants (*ib.* p. 212).

36. Haidarīa, founded by Qutb-ud-Dīn Haidar, of Zaūsh near Nisabūr in Khurāsān, early in the thirteenth century. They are closely akin to the Rifā'ī, and dance on fires. They also wear iron rings on the hands, neck, ears ; and even elsewhere—in token of their vow of chastity (Petit, *Confréries musulmanes*, p. 15).

APPENDIX III

A LIST [REARRANGED BY ORDERS] OF ALL THE DARVISH CONVENTS OR *takias* AT CONSTANTINOPLE, AND THE DAYS ON WHICH THEY PERFORM THEIR EXERCISES FOR THE GUIDANCE OF CURIOUS VISITORS.

THE BADAWĪS

'Hasīb Effendi Takia-sī', near Top Tāshī, Scutari. *Mondays.*
'Shaikh Mustafā[1] Effendi Takia-sī', near Tatavala in Ūzūn Yol. *Tuesdays.*

THE BAIRĀMĪS

'Abdī Bābā[2] Takia-sī', near Aiyūb. *Fridays.*
'Mehmed Āghā Takia-sī', in the mosque aforenamed (?). *Saturdays.*
'Yanez[3] Takia-sī', at Salajik, Scutari. *Sundays.*
''Abd-ul-Samad Effendi Takia-sī', at Khāgid-khāna [the Paper Factory]. *Mondays.*
'Bezjī-zāda[4] Muḥyī Effendi Takia-sī', at Diyunjīlī,[5] Scutari. *Tuesdays.*
'Tāvīl[6] Mehmed Effendi Takia-sī', near the Alti Mermer.

[1] Mustafā Effendi, ? Fasihi, *d.* 1694 (*GdOD.* iv. pp. 3-4).

[2] 'Abdī Bābā, apparently the La'lī Effendi-zāda 'Abd-ul-Bāqī of p. 232 *supra.* He was originally a Bairāmī. The poet 'Abdī, 'Abdullah, son of the great Shaikh Himmatzāda, may, however, be intended. Claimed both by the Khalwatīs and the Bairāmīs, he succeeded his father as Shaikh of the cloister in the New Garden in 1683, and died in 1708 (*GdOD.* iii. 570). An 'Abdī Bairām Effendi, *d.* 1709, lies buried at the Mosque of the Sultan Walida (*ib.* iv. p. 38).

[3] Yanez, *yañīz,* vulg. for *yāghīz,* 'brown' or 'dark'.

[4] Bazjī, 'linen-draper'.

[5] Diyunjīlī = *divijīlar, v.* p. 227 *supra.*

[6] Taveel in original, a term difficult to explain. *Tāwīl* means 'an explaining a word or expression by some slight but real analogy, so as to reconcile it with received doctrine' (Redhouse, *Turk.-Eng. Lex.* p. 482). The Metawalees also followed the *tāwīl* or 'allegorical interpretation of the *Qurān*'. Supposed by v. Hammer to be a sect of the Isma'ilia they are now found principally in and about Tyre and near the source of the Orontes. (Lyde, *The Asian Mystery,* p. 99). But it may be for *tawallī,* or more commonly *tawalla,* whereby the Baqtāshīs understand the devoted love of

'Jasīm[1] Laṭīf Takia-sī', at Āq-Sarāī. *Wednesdays.*
'Himmat-zāda Takia-sī', near Naqqāsh Pāsha. *Thursdays.*
'Hāshmī 'Uṣmān Effendi Takia-sī', at Qulaqsiz, in Qāsim Pāsha.

The Gulshanīs

'Tātār Effendi Takia-sī', at Top Khāna. *Mondays.*
'Kiorjī[2] Shaikh 'Alī Effendi Takia-sī', near Mulla 'Ashkī.[3] *Tuesdays.*
'Halwī[4] Effendi Takia-sī', at Shahr Amīnī.
'Saīd Effendi Takia-sī', in the Yāshjī[5] Mosque at Khassakī. *Wednesdays.*

The Jalwatis

Convent of Azīz Maḥmūd Effendi,[6] in Scutari. *Fridays.*

God, opposed to the *tabarra* (*-u*), the avoidance of evil (Jacob, *Die Bektaschijje*, p. 41). The conjunction of these two terms may explain the puzzle on p. 191 (*n.* 3) *supra*, where *tabran* and *tūlan* may be mistakes for *tabarra* and *tawalla*. Tawallī, 'the possessor of authority', was a *darvish* poet who wrote some antique *ilāhiāt* or hymns entitled 'the jewels of knowledge'. Nothing is known of his life (Hammer-Purgstall, *GdOD.* ii. p. 391). It can hardly be for *aṭāvil*, 'eminent'?

[1] Jasīm, apparently Ar. *jasīm*, 'bulky', 'immense', or 'important'.

[2] Kiorjī, apparently for Gyūrjū, 'Georgian'. Evliya says Kūrūjī = 'forest guard' (*Travels*, ii. p. 144). T. *qūṛjū* would = a man in armour, a cuirassier of the guard of the Shah of Persia. But cf. Babinger in *Der Islam*, xi. p. 86, n. 1, where Qurchi is rendered Kurd and *qūrjī* 'guardsman'.

[3] 'Ashkī, probably for 'Āshiq; but *'ashq*, usually pron. *'ishq* in Turk., means a wandering monk or *dervish* (Babinger in *Der Islam*, xi. p. 69).

[4] Ḥulvī (-wī), 'sweet': *ḥallī or ḥallū*, 'ecstatic'. Halwī was the poetic title of the son of a confectioner, born in 1574, who after his father's death became Shaikh of the Gulshanī convent at Old Mustafā-Pāsha. In Egypt he visited the Shaikh of the Gulshanīs, Najib-ud-Dīn Sa'īd Ḥasan; and on a second visit he received the rules of the order from the Gulshanī Shaikh, Ibrāhīm Effendi. A frequent preacher in the mosques of Constantinople, he also wrote a *Lama'āt*, 'Effulgences', a chronicle of the Gulshanī Shaikhs, He is buried in his father's house, which he turned into a convent, at Constantinople, dying there in 1653 (Hammer-Purgstall, *GdOD.* iii. p. 410).

[5] Yāshjī, *yāsh* = juice: but Evliya does not seem to mention any guild of *yāsh*-vendors, though he describes the *ighdajīs* or syrup-makers (*Travels*, i. pt. 2 p. 155).

[6] Aḥmad Effendi, son of the Shaikh of the Jalwatīs, Ismā'īl Effendi, was Shaikh of the Jalwati cloister at Little Aya Sofia. Known in poetry as Umidī, he wrote the *Majlis al-Aulia* and spiritual poems, dying in 1694 (*GdOD.* iii. p. 569). This convent seems to have disappeared.

A Shaikh Ibrāhīm Effendi followed the great Shaikh Maḥmūd into the cloister and so may have been a Jalwatī, but eventually he became a Naqshbandī: he lived from 1591 to 1666 (*GdOD.* iii. p. 465). His name in poetry was Sidqī.

Convent of Āq Shams-ud-Dīn, at Zairak.[1]
Convent of Ummī Sinān, at Shahr Amīnī.
Convent called ' *takia* ' at Topī Qapū.
Convent called ' Bandarwālī-zāda ', at the place called Inadia in Scutari.
' Dīwānī Muṣṭafā Effendi [2] Takia-sī ', in the Shaikh Jāmī ' (cathedral mosque), Scutari.
' Salāmī 'Alī Effendi Takia-sī ', at Ajī Badām,[3] in Scutari. *Saturdays.*
' Salāmī 'Alī Effendi Takia-sī ', Beshik Tāsh.[4] *Mondays.*
' Sir Tārik-zāda [5] Takia-sī ', at Kamerillī, in the vicinity of the Mosque of Muḥammad II. *Tuesdays.*
' Badjī-lar [6] Takia-sī ', near 'Azīz Maḥmūd Effendi, Scutari.
' Ibrāhīm Effendi Takia-sī ', in the Qizil [' Red '] Mosque, Bulghārlī.[7] *Wednesdays.*

1 Āq Shams-ud-Dīn, whose true name was Muḥammad, son of Ḥamza, was born at Damascus : of the family of Abū Bakr, Hammer-Purgstall says his father traced his descent from the famous Shaikh Suharwardī, executed at Aleppo (*GdOD.* i. p. 151), he " conversed with the most renowned Shaikhs, Suhrwardī and Hājī Bairām the saint, and foretold the day of the conquest of Constantinople " (Evliya, i. pt. 2 p. 2). How or why his convent came to be appropriated by the Jalwatīs does not appear. He left seven sons, who nearly all attained distinction : Sh. Sa'd-ullāh as a physician ; Sh. Fazl-ullāh, who plunged deep into mystic science (*d.* 1500) ; Amr-ullāh, who wrote many tracts, though he did not follow his father's sect ; Sh. Muḥammad Nūr-ul-Hada, the greatest saint among his brethren ; and Sh. Muḥammad Ḥamd-ud-Dīn, famed as the poet Hamdī (I.). The son of the last named, Sh. Muḥammad Zain-ud-Dīn, was also a great divine and a caligraphist. Evliya says that Aq Shams-ud-Dīn's successors were his eldest son and Sh. 'Abd-ur-Rahīm, author of a *Wahdat-nāma* or book on God's Unity ; also : " 'Abd-ur-Rahīm the Egyptian, and Mosslah-ud-Dīn Attār, who is buried in the town of Isklib, lived in retirement like Sh. Hamza, who obtained from their master, Aq Shams-ud-Dīn, permission to become his spiritual successor(s) ". Further, Sh. Ibrāhīm Tenūrī, the son of Sarrāf Husain, was also one of those who trod in Āq Shams-ud-Dīn's footsteps. But none of these had any recorded connection with the Jalwatīs. On the Golden Horn, the Zairak Jāmī' is named after Zairak Mulla Muḥammad, whose cell (*zāwiya*) was near by.

2 Dīwānī Muṣṭafā : a Shaikh, Mustafā Jalwatī, was father of the poet Suburī, ' the patient ', Muḥammad, born in 1638 at Philippopolis. In 1667 he became Shaikh of the cloister of The Three Fountains (Uch Bunār) at Bulghurlu, but Qadri Effendi built him a cloister of his own with a mosque inside the Adrianople Gate, and after holding various other offices he was inducted to the convent of Maḥmūd Effendi in 1711. He died in 1717 (*GdOD.* iv. p. 96).

3 Ajī Badam, ' bitter almond '.

4 Beshik Ṭāsh, a village on the Bosphorus.

5 ? Sirr-ṭārik, ' diviner of secrets ', ' magician ' : hardly ' distraught '.

6 Bājī-lar, ' the sisters or nuns ', ' the nunnery '.

7 Bulghārlī, or Bulghurlu.

'Salāmī 'Alī Effendi Takia-sī', at Chāmlījā.[1]
'Jalwatī Takia-sī', at Top Khāna, near Akarja.
'Fanā'ī Takia-sī', at Alājā Mināra,[2] in Scutari.

The Khalwatīs

'Kallanjī[3] Shaikh Amīn Effendi Takia-sī', at the Otakfilar,[4] in the Chayir-bāshī meadow. *Fridays.*
'Shaikh Nusuhī Effendi[5] Takia-sī', at the Toganjīlar,[6] Scutari.
'Aidīn-ūghlū[7] Takia-sī', near the Sublime Porte, Stambūl.
Called the 'Khalwatīa Takia-sī', inside the mosque of Kuchūk Aya Sofia (the lesser St. Sophia mosque), Stambūl.
'Faizī Effendi[8] Takia-sī', near Agach Kakan.[9]
'Sāchlī Ḥusain Effendi Takis-sī', near the Aḥmadīa meadow.

[1] Chāmlījā, from *chāmlī*, 'fir': Chāmlījā is a hill behind Scutari on the Asiatic side of the Bosphorus, celebrated for its view.

[2] Ālāja, 'variegated'.

[3] Kallanji, ? from *kalān*, 'chief'. Or possibly a mistake for *qalāījī*, 'an artizan who tins copper vessels'. Evliya has '*Hallanjīān penbe*', 'cotton-beaters', a guild with curious rites (i. pt. 2 p. 201).

[4] Otakfilar, in original, is clearly an error for Otāqjīlar, 'the tent-makers, or the quarter where they work' (Redhouse, *Turk.-Eng. Dict.*, p. 235. Cf. p. 479 *infra*).

[5] Muḥammad Effendi, the poet styled Nasūhī (III.), was one of the followers of Qarābāsh Walī and a Sha'bānīa, until he founded a sub-order of his own, the Nasūhīa, according to the *O.M.*, p. 176. Other authorities say that he served the Shaikh of the Khalwatīs, Qarābāsh 'Alī Effendi, as disciple, and became Shaikh in the convent built for him by Ḥasanpāsha at Scutari. In 1705 he was preacher at the mosque of Aiyūb, but in 1714 he was banished to Qastamūnī. Permitted to return two years later he died in 1717 and was buried in his cell (*GdOD.* iv. p. 99).

[6] For Ṭoghānjīlar, 'place of the falconers', where his convent was built.

[7] Aidīn-ūghlū, may be the poet Roshanī, 'the light or bright', a title which refers to his birthplace, Aidīn, 'the land of light'. At the behest of Khizr he went to Persia and thence to Bakū. In Shirwān he became a disciple of the Shaikh Yāḥyā (*GdOD.* i. p. 235).

[8] Faiẓī, 'the wielder of influence', was a title borne by some twenty Turkish poets. One of the best known of them was Faiẓi Ḥasn Effendi Sīmger-zāda (silversmith's son), who does not seem to have really belonged to any definite order. Undoubtedly a follower of 'Abd-ul-Āḥad Nūrī, he devoted himself to the spiritual life under Khalwatī, Naqshbandī, and Maulavī guidance, finally, according to some writers, joining the first-named order. But others say that he affected Sh. Bashīr and the Bairāmīa-Malāmīa tenets. He was, however, Shaikh of the Amīr Bukhāra *takia* in 1674, and there, not 'near Agāch Kākān', he lies buried. He died in 1102 H. (A.D. 1690) (*GdOD.* iii. p. 555 and *O.M.* p. 139).

[9] Agach Kakan, perhaps for Aghāj-qāqān, the 'green woodpecker'.

'Ujīlar [1] Takia-sī', at the Silivria Gate, Stambūl.
'Cholaq [2] Ḥasan Effendi Takia-sī', at the Idrīs Kiosk (Kuski).
'Chellak [3] Ṫakia-sī', in the Menkeuch [4] meadow.
'Sa'īd Wilāyat Ḥazraterī Takia-sī', near the plain or meadow, called 'Āshiq Pāsha Arzā-sī. *Saturdays.*
'Urdū Shaikhī Hāfiz Effendi [5] Takia-sī', near Hammām Chelebi Mehmed Āghā.
'Sa'dullah Chāūsh Takia-sī', at Ainalī Baqqāl, near the Silivria Gate [Silivrī Qapū-sī].
'Bulbuljī-zāda Effendi [6] Takia-sī', in the [New] Mosque of Nishānjī Pāsha Jadīd. *Sundays and Wednesdays.*
'Shaikh Faizullah Effendi Takia-sī', at Aḥmadīa, Scutari.
'Amīr-lar Takia-sī', near the Khassakī Mosque, Stambūl.
'Jamālī-zāda Takia-sī', outside the Egrī Qapū [the 'Crooked' Gate] near the Adrianople Gate.
'Yildiz [7] Takia-sī', near the Bāghcha Qapū-sī, Stambūl.
'Shaikh Sulaimān Effendi Takia-sī', near the Ṣūfī-lar.[8] *Sundays.*
'Ummī Sinān Takia-sī', near the Kurkjī [9] Mosque, at Top Qapū.

[1] Ūjī, 'a hunter' or 'light infantryman': pron. *avjī.*

[2] Cholāq, 'maimed or paralysed in one hand or arm'.

[3] Chellak, Pers. *chalāk,* 'quick, clever'.

[4] Doubtless *manqūsh,* 'ornamented with figures or designs'.

[5] Ordū, 'camp'. Shaikhī, a title borne by at least sixteen Turkish poets, of whom several were famous. It denotes eminence as well as devotion to the spiritual life. Of those who adopted it Shaikhī (V.) Siwāsī was an acknowledged Khalwatī. Born in 1563 near Siwās, he was named Majīd-ud-Dīn after the Shaikh who died about that time, and succeeded his uncle Sh. Shamsī as head of the Khalwatīs at Siwās. Summoned to the capital by Muḥammad III., he became a great preacher, and was made principal of the convent of Sh. Yausī, near the mosque of Selim I. Dying in 1639, he was buried at the Nishānjī Mosque near Eyūb. The title was, however, also adopted by Auḥad Shaikhī (*v.* p. 481 *infra*), and by other Shaikhs of convents not of the Khalwatī order (*GdOD.* iii. p. 286; cf. iv. pp. 132 and 264).

[6] Bulbuljī-zāda, 'son of the nightingale-seller'. The poet Fatḥī, 'the holder of victory', Shaikh Bulbuljī-zāda 'Abd-ul-Karīm, was a disciple of Shaikh 'Abd-ul-Aḥad Nūrī. A son of al-Ḥajj 'Abd-ul-Laṭīf of Qaramān, he was preacher at the New Mosque of Nishānjīpāsha among other places, and died in 1106 H. (1694). He composed hymns and spiritual songs (*GdOD.* iii. p. 570). The *O.M.* describes him as a disciple of 'Abd-ul-Laṭif (p. 140).

[7] Yildiz, 'star'.

[8] Ṣūfī-lar, apparently the Qūla Ṣūfīlarī: the Ṣūfī-lar were formerly a special class of servants in the Sulṭān's palace.

[9] Kurkjī, apparently *kiūrkjī,* 'fur-merchant' (*v.* note on p. 475). But at Stenia, Sosthenion, Schrader notes a Kurekjī-bāshi, or 'boatswain's' mosque, as well as one of the Dervish Ra'īs or 'Captain' (*Konstantinopel,* p. 219).

'Ḥājī Kadin [1] Takia-sī', at Psamathia.[2]
'Khamza-zāda [3] Takia-sī', near the [New] Mosque of Nishānjī Pāsha Jadīd.
'Hāfiz Effendi [4] Takia-sī', Beicos.
'Shaikh Hāfiz Effendi Takia-sī', near Qaraja Aḥmad,[5] Scutari.
'Khalwatī Takia-sī', at Qāsim Pāsha, in the lot called Bāb-i-Sail.
'Oksizja Bābā [6] Takia-sī', near the lot called Akarjā.
'Sir Tārik-zāda [7] Takia-sī', at Aiyūb, near the Nishānjī-lar.[8]
'Kausara [9] Mustafā Bābā Takia-sī', at the Chāūsh Dere ['valley'], Scutari.
'Matehka Takia-sī', at Beshik Tāsh. *Mondays.*
'Nūr-ud-Dīn Jarrāḥī [10] Takia-sī', near the Qara Gūmrūk ['Customs-house'], Stambūl.

[1] Ḥājī Qādim would mean the 'returning pilgrim'. Qādīn = 'lady'.

[2] Psamatia, Gr. *psamatha*, from the sand thrown up on the beach.

[3] Khamza, a word not traceable in the dictionaries. Possibly for Ḥamza, less probably for Ar. *khamaṣān* or *khumṣān*, 'gaunt' or 'slender'.

[4] Hāfiz Effendi, possibly the poet Hāfiz (V.), Sutjī-zāda (the milkman's son) 'Abd-ul-Laṭīf, who devoted himself to the Shaikh of the Khalwatīs, Ummī Sinān-zāda, and on his master's death made the pilgrimage to Makka, where he died in 1688 A.D. (*GdOD.* iii. p. 543).

[5] Qaraja, 'dark', 'swarthy'. "It is Qaraja Aḥmad, not Khoja Aḥmad, who generally figures as the pupil of Ḥājī Baqtāsh in Baqtāshī legend". Tradition makes him a saintly prince of Persia, and besides his reputed tomb in the great burial-ground at Scutari he has three more in the district of Ushā, and one in Rumelī near Uskub at Tekke Keūī. Evliya styles him Qara Aḥmad Sulṭān (*Travels*, i. pt. 2 p. 81), or Qaraja (p. 83). His shrine at or near Liyen in the Ushāk district is a famous place of healing. He has from an early period been confused with Khoja Aḥmad of Yasī. See Hasluck in *Annual*, B.S.A. xx. pp. 120 f. and 83, where numerous references are given. Evliya does not appear to mention his tomb at Scutari, but only his convent 'in the burial-ground'.

[6] Öksizja, *ūksizje*, 'orphan-like'. Redhouse (*T.-E. Lex.* p. 262) defines this adj. as a dim. of *ūksuz*, 'orphan'. If this rendering is correct it recalls the *aitām* (pl. of *yatīm*) or 'orphans' of the Nusairī. *Yatīm* meant a disciple who had lost his master, but it also denoted a rare or choice spirit, and was the title of the second grade of the celestial hierarchy (Lyde, *The Asian Mystery*, p. 133).

[7] Sir-tarik, see note on p. 461 *supra*.

[8] Nishānjī-lar, officers who affixed the Sulṭān's cypher to letters-patent.

[9] Kauṣarah, clearly from Kausar, 'abundance', or the River of Paradise. Qauṣara appears as an affix to the name of a *qāzī*, Najm-ud-Dīn, in the earlier history of the Maulavīs (Huart, *Les Saints des Dervishes tourneurs*, ii. p. 281).

[10] Nūr-ud-Dīn Muḥammad Jarrāḥī was a Ramaẓānīa Khalwatī before he founded a sub-order of his own. He owed his title to his birth in the Maḥalla Jarrāh Pāshā at Constantinople. The date of his death is given as 1133 H., not 1146 as on p. 271 *supra*. His devotion to the principle of *tauḥīd* earned him the title of Qutb al-Wāṣilain (*O.M.* p. 178).

Thursdays.

'Īplikji[1] Mehmed Effendi Takia-sī', near Otlāgjī[2] Yokushī.
'Suklī[3] Mehmed Pāsha Takia-sī', at the At Maidān, in Stambūl.
'Telloni[4] Takia-sī', near Inadia, Scutari.
'Haqīqī 'Usmān Effendi Takia-sī', near Egri Qapū.
'Khalwatī Takia-sī', near Arpa[5] Chashma-sī, Aiyūb.
'Chāmlījālī Mehmed[6] Effendi Takia-sī', near Chāūsh Dere, Scutari.
'Rūfi' Effendi[7] Takia-sī', at Toghānjī-lar, Scutari.
'Safwatī[8] Effendi Takia-sī', at Toghānjī-lar, Scutari.
'Qara-bāsh 'Alī Effendi[9] Takia-sī', in Eskī Jāmī' Wālida, at Scutari.

[1] Īplikjī, 'yarn-merchant' (Evliya, i. pt. 2 p. 203).

[2] Otlāq, 'pasture': hence Otlāqjī Yoqūsh must be 'Shepherds' Lane'.

[3] Suklī, probably Sokolli Muḥammad, the greatest of the Grand Wazīrs, assassinated in 1578. But he is not described as a Khalwatī, though he erected many pious foundations, including a mosque, etc., at Burgas. He is buried at Aiyub (Von Hammer, *GdOR.* ii. p. 470).

[4] Telloni, ? from Ar. *talawwun*, 'a changing hue or appearance': *talwīn* in the parlance of the mystics denotes a devotee's being filled with ecstasy by a glimpse of the divine favour (Redhouse, *Turk.-Eng. Dict.* p. 590). Villoison records Teloni (τελώνιον) as the name at Mykone of a water-sprite (Miss L. M. J. Garnett, *The Women of the Turkey and their Folk-Lore*, "Christian Women", p. 128). But this spirit is only one of the numerous ἀερικά, 'ἐναέρια τελώνια or aerial customs-officers', to appease whom τελωνιακά or 'dues paid at the customs' are distributed to the poor at a death (J. C. Lawson, *Modern Greek Folklore and Ancient Greek Religion*, pp. 283 f.).

[5] Arpa, 'barley'.

[6] Chāmlījālī, 'of the pine-wood'. Maḥmūd Effendi's convent was the largest at Scutari, and there 300 Khalwatīs night and day praised the Lord with cries, says Evliya (*Travels*, i. pt. 2 p. 80). He writes as if it no longer existed.

[7] Rufi, Rūfī Sayyid Aḥmad of Scutari, was a Shaikh of the Ramazānīa branch of the Khalwatīs. A disciple of Kostandīlī 'Alī Effendi, he died in 1171 H. (A.D. 1758) and was buried near the Toghānjīlar in the precincts of the mosque of Sinān Pāsha. He wrote hymns (*O.M.* p. 76). He must not be confused with 'Abd-ul-Ra'ūf al-Munāwī, who died in 1031 H. (A.D. 1622). He wrote a biographical work on Sufiism called *Al-kawākib al-durriyya fī tarājim al-sādat al-Ṣūfiyya.*

[8] Ṣafwatī, from *ṣafwat*, 'peace of mind'. In Turk. *ṣafvet*, 'purity': *Ṣafwat-ullāh* is a title of Muḥammad. This title was borne by the poet Mulla 'Ārif Muḥammad, son of 'Ārif Muḥammad, son of Asaad, (grand ?) son of the great Seaad-ud-Dīn, and he was buried at the tomb of the last-named near the mosque of Aiyūb, on his death in 1664. A Ṣafwatī Effendi also gives his name to the Khalwatī convent at the Toghānjīlar in Scutari (*v.* Hammer-Purgstall, *GdOD.* iii. p. 455).

[9] Qarah-bāsh, 'the French lavender', was a title borne by several *darvish*, *e.g.* by Qarabāsh Bābā, who has a *turbah* and mosque named after

'Sarmashik [1] Takia-sī', near the Adrianople Gate, Stambūl.
'Kush 'Adālī Ībrāhīm Effendi [2] Takia-sī', at the Sengli Baqqāl.[3]
'Shaikh Sulaimān Effendi [4] Takia-sī', at Beicos.
'Siwāsī [5] Takia-sī', near Sultān Salīm's Mosque, in Stambūl.
'Qara-Bāsh Takia-sī', in the Rūmēlī Hissār.
'Qara-Bāsh Takia-sī', at Top-khāna.

---

him in the Qara Gūmrūk quarter at the Adrianople Gate, and concerning whom F. Schrader records a folk-tale (*Konstantinopel*, pp. 95-96 and 225). Qarabāsh, too = 'a Christian bishop' (from his black head-dress) (Redhouse, *Turk.-Eng. Lex.* p. 1155). Qarabāsh 'Alī Effendi was Shaikh of the Khalwatī. The poet Nasūhī (III.), who died in 1717, was his disciple, but in 1705 Ḥasan-pāsha built him a new cloister at the Place of the Falconers (*GdOD.* iv. p. 99).

[1] Ṣārmāshiq, 'any thickly twining plant, especially ivy' (Redhouse, *Turk.-Eng. Lex.* p. 1155).

[2] Kūsh 'Adali, Qosh Āta-lī, is described in the *O.M.* (p. 151) as one of the Shaikhs of the Sha'bānīa Khalwatīs. He took his name from Qosh Āta, 'Bird Island'. The 'Kach-Ataliouiya' of Le Chatelier's informant are clearly his followers (*v.* note on p. 450 *supra*). Brown's spelling (Kush 'Adālee) almost suggests that folk-etymology has connected his title with Ar. '*idāl*, a balancing, vacillation'; originally, perhaps, the 'poising' of a hawk (*qūsh*). From the same root comes '*adl*, 'justice', etc.

[3] Senglī Baqqāl: *baqqāl*, formerly 'a greengrocer', now 'a grocer'.

[4] Saiyid (Sa'īd) Sulaimān of Alaiya was a Khalwatī who entered the order at Brūsa, and after being Shaikh of its cloister at Qāsimpāsha returned to Brūsa as successor to Shaikh 'Alī and was buried in his cloister on his death in 1654 (*GdOD.* iii. p. 411). But a Sh. Sulaimān Effendi from Diārbakr, who was immersed in the ocean of contemplation and dogmatic contest, seems to have been a Khalwatī, and his tomb is at Constantinople (Evliya, i. pt. 2 p. 20).

[5] Siwāsī may be the poet Shaikhī (V.). His name was 'Abd-ul-Majīd and he was born near Siwās in 1563. He was named 'Abd-ul-Majīd after the saint of that name recently deceased. He succeeded his uncle Sh. Shamsī as chief of the Khalwatī at Siwās, but was invited to Constantinople by the Sulṭān Muḥammad III., and after holding several important incumbencies died in 1639, being buried in a special cupola at the Nishānjī Mosque. He left many writings in prose and verse (*GdOD.* iii. p. 287). But the cloister probably takes its name from 'Shamsi', Shaikh Shams-ud-Dīn Siwāsī (Aḥmad b. Muḥammad), author of the *Gulshanābād* (in 996 H.) and of the *Manāzal ul-'Arifīn.* The former work was in praise of Abū Ḥanīfa. Dying soon after 1005 H. Shamsī was succeeded by 'Abd-ul-Majīd, who was called to the capital by the Muftī San'ullah (*Cat. of Turkish MSS. in the B.M.* pp. 181-89). But he was not a professed Khalwatī it would seem.

Nuri (V.) Sh. 'Abd-ul-Aḥmad, son of Ṣafa'ī Mustafā, grandson (Enkel) of Ismā'īl, the *muftī* of Siwās, the commentator on the *Multika,* and nephew of the Sh. Siwāsī Eff., was born in 1594. In 1622 he became Shaikh of the cloister of Muḥammad pāsha at Constantinople, and dying in 1650 was buried near his uncle, the Sh. Siwāsī. He composed a number of poems under the name of Nuri, which were mystical effusions (*GdOD.* iii. p. 400).

'Altūnjī-zāda [1] Takia-sī', at Ekshī Kara Tūt.[2] *Mondays.*
''Alā-ud-Dīn Takia-sī', near the Hammām Sūfī-lar.[3]
'Buzurgiān [4] Takia-sī', at Khoja Mustafā Pāsha.
'Hasan Effendi [5] Takia-sī', in the Mosque of Jahāngīr.[6]
'Isḥāq Qaramānī Takia-sī', at Sudlija.
'Fazl-ullāhī Āt-bāzārī 'Usmān Effendi [7] Takia-sī', at the Āt-bāzār ['Horse-market'], Stambūl.
'Fanā'ī [8] Takia-sī', at Mūlla Kiovānī.[9]

1 Altūnjī, ? 'dealer in gold' (not in Redhouse).

2 *Akshī*, 'sour', *qara*, 'black', *tūt*, 'mulberry' : ? blackberry.

3 In the convent of the Bath of the Sufis is buried Sh. Kamāl-ud-Dīn Effendi, the disciple of Sulaiman Effendi, Khalwatī (Evliya, i. pt. 2 p. 20).

4 Buzurgiān, 'holy ones'.

5 Hasan (IV.) Effendi, celebrated under the name of 'Ummi Sinānzāda, was taught by 'Abd-ul-Ahad Effendi and principal of the cloister at Shahr Amīni. He composed the *Majalis-ali-Sinani* or 'Collections of Sinani', and died in 1677 (*GdOD*. iii. p. 509). This cloister was clearly a Khalwatī foundation, as Wahdatī, the Khalwatī poet and astronomer, retired to it (*ib*. ii. p. 556).

6 Mosque of Jahāngīr, probably the Shāhzāda mosque built by Sulaimān I., 1520-66, in memory of his son Muḥammad. His son Jahāngīr was also buried there (Evliya, i. pt. 2 p. 9).

7 Fazlillahee in original, the Shaikh of the Horse-Mart, known in poetry as Fazlī (VI.) 'Uṣmān Effendi, was born at Shumna and died in 1687. Though he held high posts as a preacher he taught the poor at the Kuljāmī' mosque in the Horse-Mart, and was twice banished for his outspokenness, dying in Cyprus on his second banishment and being buried at Famagusta. Besides commentaries on several juridical works, he left spiritual *ilāhīs* (*GdOD*. iii. p. 541). In spite of a slight discrepancy in the date of his death this 'Uṣmān Effendi seems to be the person mentioned below.

'Usman Effendi Shaikh died in 1684 and was buried beside 'Umr Effendi in the cloister of the Dolmaja Junis, the court-dolmaja of Sulaimān the Law-giver. At first a disciple of Sh. Abd-ul-Ahad an-Nuni, he became *mulāzim* of Bostānzāda Yahya Effendi at (?) Scutari (*GdOD*. iii. p. 532). The cloister of Yunis, the court interpreter (*dulmàch*) of Sulaimān the Great, was at one time certainly a Khalwatī institution. Held once by 'Usmān Effendi Shaikh, who in 1634 attached himself to the Shaikh 'Abd-ul-Aḥad an-Nūnī and died in 1684, it was in 1683 under the Shaikhship of the poet Mahwī (IV.), Shaikh Īsā Effendi, who died in 1715 (*GdOD*. iii. p. 532, and iv. p. 82). This cloister seems to have disappeared, unless it be that in Tunus (*sic*) Bāgh, at Scūtari, held by the Qādirīs.

8 Fanā'ī, 'the possessor of self-annihilation', was a title borne by four Turkish poets. Of these Sh. Muḥammad Jannat Effendi, son of Isḥāq Effendi, whose elder brother was in the service of the great Sh. Maḥmūd Hudāyī, and who himself affected that saint, is clearly here in question. He held the Shaikhship of a convent at Scutari and died there in 1665 (*GdOD*. iii. p. 466). But possibly it is for *fināyī*, from *finā*, 'court-yard'.

9 Kiovānī, ? for Korānī.

'Mu'bir Hasan Effendi Takia-sī', near Eskī ['Old'] 'Alī Pāsha.
'Toghrāmaji [1] Takia-sī', behind the Zindān ['Prison'] of the Arsenal.
'Ismā'īl Effendi Takia-sī', at Yenī Kiūī. *Tuesdays.*
'Shavkī Mustafā Effendi [2] Takia-sī', near Mimar.
'Mimar Sinān [3] Takia-sī', at 'Āshiq Pāsha.
'Khoja-zāda al-Hājī Ahmad Effendi Takia-sī', at Zairak. *Wednesdays.*
'Ummī Sinān Takia-sī', at Aiyūb in the Dokmajī-lar.[4]
'Aq Bayik [5] Takia-sī', at Akhor Qapū-sī.
'Kashfī [6] Takia-sī', near Shāhzāda Bāshī.
'Turmish Dede [7] Takia-sī', at Rūmelī Hissār.
'Iskandar Bābā Takia-sī', near Āghā Hammām, in Scutari.
'Ummī Ahmad Effendi Takia-sī', near the Chinilī ['Faience'] Mosque, Scutari.
'Idrīs Effendi [8] Takia-sī', in Chāūsh Dere.

[1] Toghrāmajī, 'joiner'.

[2] Shavkī, from *shauq*, 'yearning', 'ardently yearning' (for God). Four Turkish poets were so entitled, but none of them was called Mustafa.

[3] Mi'mār Sinān, 'the architect Sinān', the famous Turkish architect who flourished in the sixteenth century.

[4] Dokmajī-lar 'brass-founders.' But J. von Hammer has Knopfmacher, 'button-makers'.

[5] Aq Bayik, Āq Biyiq Sulṭān, 'of the white moustache'. The convent at Brusa of this saint is assigned by Evliya to the Baqtāsh, and then again to the Bairāmīs. It will be noticed that at Constantinople the suffix 'Sulṭān' is dropped (*v.* Evliya, ii. pp. 8 and 26).

[6] Kashfī, from *kashf*, 'revelation'. The poet Kashfī, who was a Khalwatī, wrote a *Maulūd* or 'Birth Song'. He is alluded to by Gibb, *Hist. of Ott. Poetry*, ii. p. 375, and appears to be the Kashfī II. of Hammer-Purgstall, who died in 1538. Several other poets bore this title, *e.g.* Kashfi I. the censer-bearer who dispensed spiritual incense as well as material at the time when the mosque of Bayazid II. was built (*GdOD.* i. p. 284, and ii. p. 222). He was perhaps a Naqshbandī.

[7] Turmish, clearly Durmish, a sailors' saint who died in the reign of Aḥmad I. and was buried on the point of Rūmelī Hissār. His *takia* was originally held by the Baqtāsh (Hasluck in *Annual*, B.S.A. xxi. p. 100). Dūrmīsh was born at Akkermān, but carried off to Constantinople in his youth. He used to foretell the fortunes of those who went to sea (Evliya, i. pt. 2 p. 70). Dūrmīsh, as Tūr-mish is pronounced, may mean 'he who has ceased from motion': cf. ṭūr-maq, 'to remain quiet, at rest'; pron. *dūrmaq* (Redhouse, *T.-E. Lex.* p. 1254). The Durmish-lar are identified with the Ṭorlāq-lar (*v.* note on p. 158 *supra*). It was a name in use in Khwārizm in the fourteenth century, for we read of 'Turmish, brother of Turkan' (*Tārīkh-i-Rashīdī*, p. 44).

[8] Idrīs, Shaikh Pīr 'Alī, called Idrīs as being the son of a poor tailor (Idrīs being patron-saint of tailors), was a Bairāmī, a follower of Hussām-ud-Dīn of Angora, and was strangled and buried at an elevated spot in Qāsim Pāsha behind the Arsenal. Worker of many miracles, he founded

'Yahyā Kethoda[1] Takia-sī', at Qāsim Pāsha, near the Juma' Bāzār.
''Alī Effendi Takia-sī', at Ājī Chashma [' Bitter Fountain'], near the Adrianople Gate.
'Sa'īd Khalīfa Takia-sī', at Fanā'ī.

THE MAULAVIS[2]

or 'Turning Darvishes', in Pera.[3]	*Fridays.*
'Maulavī-khāna Takia-sī'.	*Saturdays.*
'Qāsim Pāsha Maulavī-khāna-sī'.[4]	*Sundays.*
'Yanī Qapū Maulavī-khāna-sī'.[5]	*Mondays.*
'Beshik-tāsh Maulavī-khāna-sī'.	*Wednesdays.*
'Yanī Qapū Maulavī-khāna-sī'.	*Thursdays.*

---

a number of pious institutions, including the Idrīs Kiosk on the north side of Aiyūb, but the building was levelled at Sultān Murād's death, leaving only the basin, fountain, and place of prayer (Evliya, i. pt. 1, p. 48).

[1] Kethoda, doubtless for *ket-khudā*, 'steward', the 'warden of a guild'. The poet Yahya III., son of the Shaikh of the Khalwatī, born in 1644, was himself Shaikh at the convent of Saad-Dīn at Aiyb. He died in 1699 (*GdOD.* iii. p. 580).

[2] The fact that there are only four Maulavī cloisters at Constantinople gives an inadequate idea of the importance of the order in the Turkish empire. It has or had fifty *khānqās* or *zāwiyas*, including the *āsitānia* or 'court' at Qonia (M. Hartmann, *Der islamische Orient*, iii. p. 194). The Galata Maulavī-khāna-sī, originally built in A.D. 1491-92, and finally rebuilt by Salīm III. in 1795-96, is the oldest settlement of this order in Constantinople. It contains the tomb of Ismā'īl Anqarawī (*E.I.* i. p. 875). Sh. Ismā'īl Dede (Rusūkh-ud-Dīn Ismā'īl b. Aḥmad) al-Maulavī al-Anqirawī was the author of the *Minhāj us-Sālikīn*, and also of the *Fātiḥ-ul-Abyāt*, a commentary on the *Mesnewi* of Jalāl-ud-Dīn. Shaikh of the Maulawī-khāna at Galata, he died in 1041 H. (A.D. 1632) (*Cat. of Turkish MSS. in the B.M.* p. 235, and *Cat. of Persian MSS.* ii. p. 790).

[3] A cloister called the Bāb-i-Qula was erected in Galata (which included Pera), was built in 926 H. = A.D. 1520 (M. Hartmann, *Der islamische Orient*, iii. p. 194).

[4] Evliya states that in the infidel time Qāsim Pasha was a monastery called Ayā Longa, but Muḥammad II. converted it into a burial-ground. Koja Piāla Pāsha, however, recolonised it. The Maulavi-khāna town was built by 'Abdī Dede, who himself worked at its building, *temp.* Murād IV. —1023-40—(*Travels*, i. pt. 2 pp. 45-46).

[5] Built in 1597-98 (*E.I.* i. p. 872). It was built for Kamāl Aḥmad-Dada, who died in 1601. Born at Āqshahar, a son of the Maulavī Khasii-ud-Dīn-dada, he served the Shaikhs Khusrau and Farrūkh-Chelebi as disciple until the last-named was deprived of the mystical throne at Qonia by an usurper, and then betook himself to Constantinople (*GdOD.* iii. pp. 12–16; *v.* p. 262).

The Naqshbandīs

'Amīr Bukhāra '[1] Convent, near the Mosque of Sulṭān Muḥammad, the conqueror of Constantinople. *Fridays.*
Convent of Kioshgiāri 'Abdullāh Effendi,[2] at Idris Kiosk.
A Qalandar-khāna, at Aiyūb.
Convent of the Shaikh-ul-Islām, at Aiyūb.
Convent called the 'Usmān Effendi', in Scutari.
Convent called 'Hindīlar[3] Takia-sī', at Khorkhor, near Āq-Sarai, Stambūl.
'Bashīr Āghā[4] Takia-sī', near the Sublime Porte, in Stambūl.
'Usbak Takia-sī',[5] near Bulbul Dara-sī, Scutari.
'Usbaklar Takia-sī', at the ascent of the Muḥammad Pāsha Yokushī, Stambūl.
'Izzat Mehmed Pāsha Takia-sī', Aiyūb.
'Amīr Bukhāra[6] Takia-sī', just outside the Adrianople Gate, Stambūl.

[1] *Vide* n. 6 *infra*.

[2] Kioshgiari, clearly for Kāshgharī, 'of Kāshghar'.

[3] Evliya mentions two Indian convents, one of "the Hindoos, worshippers of fire", where bodies could be burnt, and the other, the convent of the Indian Qalandars, at the head of the bridge of Kāghid-Khāna (*Travels*, i. pt. 2 p. 87).

[4] Beshīr, 'prophet', 'a bringer of good tidings', or 'pleasing in countenance'. Bashīr Agha is mentioned on p. 235 *supra*.

[5] The Usbeg must be the Naqshbandī Shaikh, the poet Haidar III., who settled in Scutari at the Nightingales' Hill and sang like one in Persian and Turkish. He died in 1700 (*GdOD*. iii. p. 596).

M. Hartmann mentions this cloister, which also appears to be called the Bukhāra cloister, as in the Ḥajja Ḥasna Khātun quarter in Scutari. In the beginning of the present century it was still visited by *darvishes* from Transoxiana. Its head was styled *Uskudarda Ka'īn Osbekler dergāhī pōst-nishīnī*, suggesting that only the Shaikh sat upon a *pōst* (*Der islamische Orient*, i. pp. 125 and 127). Another cloister at the Nightingale Valley was built by Diwijī-zāda Shaikh Muḥammad Effendi, a disciple of the great Sh. Maḥmūd of Scutari, for his son. The founder, whose poetic name was Thalib (V.), died in 1679 (*GdOD*. iii. p. 553).

[6] It will be noticed that four cloisters of the Naqshbandīs bear this name, but it should apparently be Shaikh Bukhāra or Sh. Bukhārī. Shams-ud-Dīn Bukhārī, who must not be confused with Shams-ud-Dīn Muḥammad Bukhārī, the Amīr Sulṭān of Bāyazīd I.'s reign, was a Persian who came to Constantinople in the time of Muḥammad II. under Sh. Alawī, and there rose to eminence as the Shaikh of the reign of Bāyazīd II. He lived as a Naqshbandī, a contemporary of the Shaikh Bābā Ni'āmatullah, the commentator of the *Gulshan-i-rāz* of Shabistarī, and of Sh. Dāūd of Modreni. His cloister is one of the principal Naqshbandī foundations in Constantinople (*GdOD*. i. p. 212).

The cloister 'outside the Adrianople Gate' was under the poets Faizī

'Shaikh Murād Takia-sī', near the Ortakjī-lar.[1] *Sundays.*
'Murād Mulla Takia-sī', in the Chahārshamba [Thursday] Market.
'Amīr Bukhāra Takia-sī', near the Egrī Qapū.
'Salāmī Effendi Takia-sī', in the place called Bābā Haidar, near Aiyūb.
'Mustafā Pāsha Takia-sī', outside the Adrianople Gate, Stambūl.
'Salim Bābā [2] Takia-sī', near Chinār [' the Plane '].
'Nūrī Effendi [3] Takia-sī', near the Top Qapū.
'Vānī Ahmad Effendi [4] Takia-sī', at Lālazār.[5]
'Raqm Effendi [6] Takia-sī', at Zinjīrlī Kiūī,[7] in Stambūl.
'Ardak [8] Takia-sī', near Dāūd Pāsha [Qapū-sī ?, formerly the Gate of S. Aemilianus].
'Mybekler [9] Takia-sī', at Salāmīa, in Scutari.
'Shaikh Sa'īd Effendi Takia-sī', at Qandīlī [on the Asiatic shore of the Bosphorus] in the valley.

---

and Shaikhī, father and son, in the seventeenth century. Faizī was the Shaikh Sinesh Hasan Effendi, a disciple of the great Shaikh 'Abd-ul-Aḥad Nūrī, and in turn a Khalwatī, a Naqshbandī, and a Maulavī, who finally joined the first named of those orders. Dying in 1690, he was buried at the cloister of Amīr Bukhāra, of which he was Shaikh (*GdOD.* iii. p. 555). His son Muḥammad 'Shaikhī', born in 1666, succeeded him. Faizī wrote the 'Lives of the Jurisprudents', a work continued by his son and grandson (*ib.* iv. p. 264). Whether this cloister was originally a Khalwatī foundationers or not does not appear, nor is it clear that Sinash Ḥasan Effendi is also still regarded as a Khalwatī.

1 So spelt by von Moltke on his map; but ? Otāqjī-lar, 'tent-makers'; Ortāq (not ortāqjī) would = 'partner'.

2 ? Salīm Dada, 'Alī, known as the Qurghu *darvish*, the 'fantasy' darvish, or as Qirq Darvish, 'the forty *darvish*', who died in 1688 (*GdOD.* iii. p. 544).

3 Nūrī Effendi, probably the Shaikh as-Said Ḥasan Effendi, born in 1619, who was placed at the head of the convent of Farrukh Kiaya at Constantinople in 1663, and died in 1688. He wrote spiritual and mystical poems (*GdOD.* iii. p. 550).

4 Vānī Ahmad, Khoja Ahmad of Vān, appears to be the poet Durri (VI.). Associated in some way with the cloister, etc., built by 'Alī Pāsha at Brūsa, and the cloister erected by Eidam 'Alī Pāsha at Constantinople in 1714, on which he composed chronograms; he also wrote a poem in defence of his orthodoxy which had been impugned (*GdOD.* iv. pp. 111-12).

5 Lāla-zār, 'abounding in tulips'.

6 Rakam in original: *raqm* may allude to the *raqm awwal* or 'the halo of divine glory whence proceeded the spirit of Muḥammad' (Redhouse, *Turk.-Eng. Lex.* p. 983). *Rāqim* would = 'writer'.

7 Zinjīrlī Kiūī, the prisoners' village.

8 Erdek in original.

9 Maibaklar, Mybekler in original, apparently for *māh-paikar*, 'beautiful as the moon'. But much more probably the convent of the *maqbar-bakjī-lar*, or 'watchers of the shrine' (*maqbar*) is intended (*v. Der Islam*, xi. p. 71, citing Zenker, ii. p. 870a, *s.v.* Maqbar). But the convent so named is at Stambūl.

'Jān-Fidā [1] Takia-sī', at Qubba Tosh.
'Dulger-zāda [2] Takia-sī, at Beshik Tāsh. *Mondays.*
'Naqshbandī Takia-sī', in the mosque of Kurshundi Mahsen,[3] Galata.
'Naqshbandī Karilar [4] Takia-sī', at Idrīs Kuskī.
Tuesdays.
'Kashfī Effendi [5] Takia-sī', in the Kéffélle Mosque,[6] at Deragma.
'Salih Effendi [7] Takia-sī', near Deragman.
'Chākir Dede Takia-sī', at Shāhzādabāshī. *Wednesdays.*
Thursdays.
'Yahyā Effendi Hazraterī Takia-sī', outside the Maulavī-khāna.
'Ahmad al-Bukhārī [8] Takia-sī', at the Kabān Dakīk,[9] Stambūl.

[1] Jān-Fidā, 'soul-redeeming' or 'life-ransoming'. Jān Fidā (Seelenopfer) was the Kiāya Haram or chief Lady of the Bedchamber of Murād III. She was styled Jān-fidā Kadun. In 1595 her brother Ibrāhīm was executed, and she herself shared the fate of the rest of Murād's harem (*GdOR.* ii. 443, 506, and 599).

[2] Dūlgar-zāda, 'house-carpenter and builder': apparently styled Dūlgar-ūghlū below. The Dūlgerzāda family possessed large estates near Uskub. To it belonged the poet Sidi or Sidi Chelebi (*d.* 1521), but he is not recorded as a Naqshbandī (*GdOD.* i. p. 187). A Dūlgarzāda, Sh. Dūlgarzāda Muḥammad Sidiq Effendi, initiated the poet Mekki into the Naqshbandī order, just as Mulla-ud-Dīn introduced him into that of the Ashrafīas (*ib.* iv. p. 196). This appears to be the cloister called Sinsan's at Beshik Ṭāsh whereof Mustafā, the mystic poet Rizā (II.), was Shaikh. His *Dīwān* enjoys a great, though perhaps undeserved, reputation, but it is clearly notable as an exposition of the Naqshbandī tenets (*ib.* p. 157 ff.).

[3] For Qūrshūnlū Makhzan, the old Customs House at Galata. This mosque is also called Yer Alti Jāmi' or 'the Underground Mosque', and it was discovered by a Naqshbandī Shaikh to whom its existence was revealed in a dream. But, as F. W. Hasluck showed, it was probably known before 1640, a century earlier than the alleged revelation. Its claim to be a pre-Turkish mosque containing the tomb of 'Abū Sūfiān', an Arab warrior who took part in the first Arab siege of Constantinople, rests on imaginary grounds (*Annual,* B.S.A. xxii. pp. 164-65).

[4] Doubtless Qārī-lar, 'professional readers of the *Qurān*'.

[5] Kashfī Eff., *v.* n. on Kashfī Khalwati.

[6] Sinope had a Kefeli mosque (Evliya, ii. p. 38). Kéffélee, apparently for *kaff 'Alī,* 'the hand of 'Alī'. Kaffah-lu (Kefeli) would be 'of the town of Kaffa'.

[7] Sālih Effendi may be the 'great Shaikh and poet Sālih (Shāhīn-dada)', author of the *Gulshan-i-asrār.* His grandfather Sālih had by a Christian wife a son, Khudāī-dada, who died in 1480. This Sālih devoted himself to the service of Sh. Saiyid Kamāl, sister's son of the great Sh. Amīr Sulṭān. But no further details about the younger Sālih are given (*GdOD.* i. p. 140).

[8] A Shaikh Aḥmad Bukhārī is associated in Turkish folk-lore with a Nālīn Bābā, but both are assigned to the Rifā'ī order. The latter performed a miracle and then disappeared. Sulṭān Maḥmūd I. (1730–54) set out to

'Beshikjī-zāda [1] Takia-sī', near the Mosque of Bikir Pāsha.
'Samani-zāda [2] Takia-sī', at Otlāqji Yokushī.
'Uluklu Bayir [3] Takia-sī', at Aiyūb.
'Amīr Bukhāra Takia-sī', at the Otāg[q]jī-lar.
'Salīmīa Takia-sī', at Scutari.
'Sadiq Effendi Takia-sī', at the Ālāja Mi'mārī, in Scutari.
'Mudanīali-zāda [4] Takia-sī', near the Bāb-i-humāyūn, in Stambūl.
'Tāhir Āghā Takia-sī', near Kas āb Bāshī Chashma-sī.
'Aghā Shaikh Takia-sī', near the Jebbeh Khāna.
'Sa'īd Bābā Takia-sī', near Khassakī.
'Derūnī [5] Takia-sī', near Bozdaghān Kemerī.
'Na'lbar [6] Mehmed Effendi Takia-sī', at Rūmelī Hissār.
'Bābā Haidar Takia-sī', near Aiyūb.[7]
'Alta Effendi Takia-sī', in Anadolī Bāzār.
'Mehmed Alta Allāh Effendi Takia-sī', at Kanlijik.[8]
'Sa'īdī Bey Takia-sī', near Yuksek Qaldirim.
'Ya'qūb-zāda Takia-sī', near Baila.
'Salīm Bābā Takia-sī', at Sultān Tepe-sī, Scutari.
'Dulger-ūghlū Takia-sī', near the Khaffāf-khāna.
'Agvan-lar [9] Takia-sī', near the Chinili Mosque, at Scutari.

---

look for him, and riding through all Stambūl reached the neighbourhood of Āyā Qapū where his horse jibbed and refused to go any farther. The Sulṭān had excavations made on the spot, and the body of Sh. Aḥmad was found there with that of Nālīn Bābā ten fathoms below the surface. Sh. Aḥmad's death is placed in 994 H. (A.D. 1586) (H. Schrader, *Konstantinopel*, pp. 83-84).

9 Qabān Daqīq, the Flour Weigh-House.

---

1 Beshikjī, 'a maker or seller of cradles'.

2 Samani, possibly for *ṣamānjī*, 'a dealer in straw', or for *semmān*, 'a maker or seller of clarified butter'.

3 Ūlūqlū Bāyir, 'channeled waste'?

4 Mudaniali, 'of Modania', the port of Brūsa (Evliya, ii. p. 2).

5 Derūnī, 'internal'. With the meaning 'esoteric' the title was borne by three of the earlier poets (16th century); none of whom, however, are said to have been Naqshbandīs (*GdOD.* ii. pp. 235, 282, and 417).

6 Na'lbar, 'a maker of horseshoes'.

7 A Naqshbandī cloister at Aiyub was built by the poet Bahir (II.), Mustafapasha, who was thrice Grand Wazir in the eighteenth century, but was eventually beheaded, his head being buried in his convent (*GdOD.* iii. p. 215).

8 Kanlijik, Qānlijiq?

9 Agvan, possibly for *akawān*, Pers., 'flower of the *arghawān* (red) 'Judas-tree' (Johnson, *Pers.-Ar.-Eng. Dict.* p. 144, and Redhouse, *T.-E. Lex.* p. 69). Evliya's translator calls it the syringa. It is abundant about Brūsa, and the annual assembly of Amīr Sulṭān is held when it is in perfection (*Travels*, ii. p. 5).

The Qādirīs

Fridays.

Yahyā Effendi [1] Convent, at Beshik Tāsh.
Convent called the 'Hakīm-ūghlū 'Alī Pāsha',[2] Stambūl.
Convent called 'Fauri',[3] at Bulbul Dara-sī, near Aiyūb.
Convent called 'Piali Pāsha [4] Takia-sī', near the Oq Maidān (archery ground),[5] behind the Navy Yard.
'Rasmī [6] Takia-sī', near the Adrianople Gate, Stambūl.
''Alī Bābā Takia-sī', near Piāli Kosha.

[1] Yāḥyā Effendi, apparently also affected by the Rifā'īs, was by origin of Trebizond and a foster-brother of Sulaimān, the Sulṭān, who had his son Muṣṭafā put to death, an act which Yāḥyā Effendi sturdily condemned. Known in poetry as Mudarris, 'the professor', he died in A.D., 1571 after he had beautified the walk above Beshikṭāsh (Hammer-Purgstall, *GdOD.* ii. p. 343). Evliya records, in his description of Trebizond, that "Sulaimān (the Great) . . . was the apprentice of a Greek called Constantine, who was the foster-brother of Yāḥyā Effendi, who is buried at Beshik-tāsh" (*Travels*, ii. p. 48). Like Selīm I., Sulaimān the Magnificent learned the art of a goldsmith from the famous workers in that art at Trebizond.

[2] Hakīm-ūghlī, 'the doctor's son', was a poet (Hammer-Purgstall, *GdOD.* ii. p. 409).

[3] The poet Faurī, 'the flowing', was originally a Christian slave, who became a Moslem with the name of Aḥmad b. 'Abdullah, and devoted himself to the spiritual life at the behest of Muḥyī-ud-Dīn al-Arabī, who appeared to him in a dream. He died in 1570 at Damascus (*GdOD.* ii. 499).

[4] Evliya informs us that this convent lay in a valley. It was surrounded by walls, and held, in its two storeys, 200 men. Handicraftsmen were there lavishly feasted (*Travels*, i. pt. 2 p. 46). This foundation would assign the great Koja Piāla Pāsha, the High Admiral who possessed 12,000 slave-prisoners, to the Qādirīs. However this may be, he continued Qāsim Pāsha's work and made his new suburb a Turkish Greenwich.

[5] At Oq Maidān Muḥammad II. built the old convent for the guild of the bowmen; it was renewed by Bāyazīd II. and by Mustafā Pasha under Murād IV. In a spacious valley the bowmen, disciples of Sa'd Wakkāss, their saint, assembled for archery. This convent must be the half-ruined Kamānkash Dargāhi mentioned by Schrader (*Konstantinopel*, p. 30). In 1818 its Shaikh was the Binyūsjī Hāfiz Effendi, so entitled from his prowess.

[6] Rasmī, apparently distinct from the Shaikh Rasmī of the Qādirīs (*v.* p. 476 *infra*). This title was borne by at least four Turkish poets, of whom Rasmī (IV.) Sa'd Muḥammad, son of Akhī Maḥmūd, the Āchiq-bāsh, or 'bare-headed', was a Naqshbandī, and Rasmī (IV.) a Khalwatī *darvish* (*GdOD.* iii. pp. 464 and 578). The former died in 1666, the latter in 1697. A Kirīdī Rasmī or 'Rasmī of Crete' wrote a Turkish *Ḥurūfī* treatise called the '*Uyūn al-Hidāyat*, but he seems to have been a Baqtāsh (*J.R.A.S.*, 1907, p. 563). Jacob suggests that his title was taken from Retyno, or Rasmo, on the north coast of Crete (*Abhandl. der K. Bayer. Akademie der Wiss.*, 1909, p. 9).

'Terābī Takia-sī',[1] near the Navy Yard.
'Kiurukjī[2] Takia-sī', at the Asmali Zokāk, in the Lālazār meadow. *Saturday.*
'Pashmakjī[3] Takia-sī', at Kūchūk Piāli Pāsha [in Qāsim Pāsha]. *Sundays and Wednesdays.*
'Yarmajī Bābā[4] Takia-sī', at Limān Pāsha, Scutari.
'Shaikh Meḥmed Khifāf[5] Takia-sī', at Baljī[6] Yokushi, in Kūchūk Ḥammām.
'Ghausī Effendi[7] Takia-sī', near the convent called Mimār Arzasī.

[1] Qalandar Turābī of Qastamūnī, teacher of the unfortunate prince Jam, who died in 1495, seems to be meant (Babinger, in *Der Islam,* xi. p. 16, citing Evliya, i. p. 385). Prince Jam was the brother of Bāyazīd II., and they were the sons of Muḥammad II. by a French princess according to many (? Christian) monks and patriarchs whom Evliya met on his journey to Vienna in 1663. The tale may have originated in the prince's captivity in France (Evliya, i. pt. 1 p. 40, and pt. 2 p. 23).

Turābī the poet wrote his verses on the walls of convents and taverns, slept in graves and wandered in the wastes (Hammer-Purgstall, *GdOD.* i. p. 214). Evliya merely says he was famous for his religious hymns (*Travels,* i. pt. 2 p. 1). Hasluck describes him as a fifteenth-century *darvesh* noted for his liberal views to religions outside Islām. Near Larnaca is a small mosque called the Arab Mosque by the Moslems and by the Greeks Saint Arab. The saint is now worshipped by Muḥammadans as Turābī and by Christians as S. Therapion (*Annual,* B.S.A. xxii. p. 170). This saint's real name has not come down to us. *Turāb* denotes 'dry earth', and Evliya's translator states that *turba,* 'a mound of earth', is derived from it. But the precise significance of Turābī as a title is obscure. The people of Morocco trace the four temperaments of men to the elements, and thus a *turābī* is a "*stiller, kalter Mensch*" (M. Quedenfeldt, *Verhandlungen der Berliner Gesellschaft für Anthropologie,* 1886, p. 671). The term is derived from *turāb,* 'earth'. For Abū Turāb as one of the names of 'Alī *v.* note on p. 396. *Turāb-i-layyin* = 'moist earth', *i.e.* the existence of God, '*wujūd*' (Wilberforce Clarke, *Ḥāfiz,* i. p. 11).

[2] Kiūrūkjī would mean a maker or seller of bellows, but Redhouse has no such word. It is probably a mistake for *kiūrekjī,* 'a maker or seller of oars or shovels', 'an oarsman or rower' (*Turk.-Eng. Lex.* p. 1587). Or it might be for kūrkjī, 'fur-merchant' (cf. Evliya, i. pt. 2 p. 204). The fur-merchants formed an important guild, and its members were dressed like *perīs* and *dīvs,* or represented captive animals in the annual procession of the guilds.

[3] Peshmāqjī, Evliya translates 'makers of women's shoes': *bashmāq* or *-aq* is a 'shoe'.

[4] Yarmajī, ? *yārimjī,* 'métayer' tenant.

[5] Khifāf for *khaffāf,* 'shoe-merchants' (Evliya, i. pt. ii. p. 210).

[6] Bāljī, 'a dealer in honey'.

[7] Ghausī, apparently Ghausī Aḥmad-dada, who entered on a spiritual life at Brūsa and became Shaikh of the convent at Galata in 1668. He died in 1697 (*GdOD.* iii. p. 579).

'Hamdī Effendi [1] Takia-sī', at Sinān Pāsha's.
'Haidar Dada Takia-sī', near the Serach-(Sarāj-) khāna (saddlery mart).
'Hilim [2] Gulem Takia-sī', Zinjirlī Kiūī, at Scutari.
'Jadīd Hājī Dada Takia-sī', in Tūnus Bāgh, at Scutari.
''Abd-ul-Salām Takia-sī', in Khwās Kiūi.
'Tāshjī [3] Takia-sī', in Qāsim Pāsha, in the lot called Bāb-i-Sail.
'Shaikh Khalīl Effendi Takia-sī', near the Altī Mermer ('Six Marble Columns').
'Nizāmī-zāda Takia-sī', near the Shahr Amīnī. *Mondays.*
'Paik Dede [4] Takia-sī', at the Silivria Gate.
'Chekeh-zāda Takia-sī', near Eskī 'Alī Pāsha.
'Shaikh 'Umr Effendi Takia-sī', at Hājī Ilyās, near the Egrī Qapū-sū, Stambūl.
'Tāshjī Takia-sī', near Dāūd Pāsha Eskele-sī.
'Qādirī Takia-sī', near Chagala-zāda Sarai.

Tuesday.

'Ismā'īl Rūmī Hazrateri [5] Takia-sī', Top Khāna, called also Bakadir Khāna.
'Kartal Ahmad Effendi [6] Takia-sī', at Bāzārbāshī, Scutari.
'Mahmūd Effendi Takia-sī', at Aiyūb, near the Dabag Khāna.[7]

Wednesdays.

'Shaikh Rasmī Takia-sī', at the Qara Gumruk, in Stambūl; also called Qubba Kollak.
'Ramlī [8] Takia-sī', near Shahr Amīnī.
'Yannik [9] Takia-sī', at Ferhad Āghā in Qāsim Pāsha.
'Qādirīa Takia-sī', at Top Khāna.

[1] Ḥamdī, 'the praised', a title borne by some ten Turkish poets. Of these, only one, Muḥammad Effendi, judge of Rumīlī, bore the latter title. He died in 1694, but appears to have had no bent towards mysticism. Ḥamdī I., a son of Āq Shams-ud-Dīn, can hardly have been styled Effendi. Ḥamdī II., a descendant of Shaikh Sa'dī, was precentor in the Mosque of Āyā Sofia. Ḥamdī VIII. had but a brief connexion with Sinān-Pāsha's college at Beshik Ṭāsh (*GdOD.* iv. p. 42).

[2] ? Halīm, 'gentle'.

[3] Tāshjī, 'stone-worker'.

[4] Paik, 'a messenger', 'a member of the Sulṭān's body-guard'.

[5] Hazrateri, apparently for Ḥaẓratlari, 'His Highness'.

[6] Qartāl, 'the vulture's feather used to feather an arrow'. Qartāl-dada was a dervish of Laranda, the son of a dervish and brought up as one, who took the poetic name of Deli-dada (the insane or ecstatic). His poetry is much esteemed by the Maulavis (Hammer-Purgstall, *GdOD.* iii. p. 125).

[7] Dabāg, dabbāgh, 'tanner': -khāna, 'tanyard'.

[8] Ramlī, possibly the *takia* of the Soothsayers, 'rammāli', Their patron is Imām 'Alī, whose divination is famous by the name of *raml 'Alī* (Evliya, i. pt. 2 p. 114).

[9] Yāniq, 'burnt'

'Nabati [1] Takia-sī', at Top Khāna.
'Mu'bir [2] Hasan Takia-sī', at Qāsim Pāsha.
'Dibilī [3] Kala Ahmad Effendi Takia-sī', near the new Maulavī-khāna.
'Shaikh Tai Effendi Takia-sī', near Khassakī. *Thursdays.*
'Hājī Iliās Takia-sī', near the Egrī Qapū, at Batgan.

The Rifā'īs

Fridays.

Convent called Qubba ('the dome'), near Sulṭān Muḥammad II.'s Mosque in Constantinople.
'Ālāja [4] Masjid Takia-sī', near the Lenkeh [Langa] Bey [Yenī Qapū] Gate at Marjamak.
'Sherbetdār [5] Takia-sī', in the quarter called Fāna'ī, at the Kassakī meadow.
''Alī Kuzī [6] Takia-sī', at Telurkluk in Qāsim Pāsha. *Saturdays.*
'Shaikh Kāmil Effendi Takia-sī', at Avret Bāzār, Stambūl.
'Birbir-lar [7] Shaikhī 'Ottoman [8] Effendi Takia-sī', at Bāyazīd Āghā Mahallasī Top Qapū.

Sundays.

'Sachlī Effendi Takia-sī', near the Chirāghjī ['candlestick-dealer's'] fountain, at Katchuk [? Kūchūk, 'Lesser'], Mustafā Pāsha.
'Kūkjī-zāda [9] Takia-sī', at the New (Yeni) Gate. It is the 'Tarsūs [10] Takia'.
'Toigar Tepesī [11] Takia-sī', Scutari. *Mondays.*
'Yāhyā Effendi Takia-sī', at Aiyūb: also known as the 'Hasīb Effendi Takia-sī'.

[1] Nabātī, 'Botanical'. An early poet with this title left mystical verses, but nothing seems known about his sect, but as he imitated the poems of Alahi he may have been a Naqshbandī. A descendant of the White Sheep dynasty, his death was a mystery (*GdOD.* i. p. 309).

[2] Mu'bir, *mu'abbir,* 'who explains, a soothsayer': a Mu'abbir Ibrāhīm is noted by Evliya as having a convent in Qāsim Pasha (*Travels,* i. 2 p. 45).

[3] Dibilī, ? *deble, duble,* 'abscess'.

[4] Ālāja, 'striped'.

[5] Sherbetdār, "a servant specially charged to prepare sweet beverages" (Redhouse, p. 1121).

[6] Kuzī, possibly from Pers. *kūz,* 'hunch-back' (cf. Qanbūr 'Alī, 'Alī the hunch-back: Evliya, i. pt. 2 p. 109). But cf. *qoz,* 'walnut' and Qozlī Bāba, a follower of Abū 'Isḥāq Kazerūnī, so named because he wore a chaplet of walnuts (*Der Islam,* ix. p. 224). *Qozi,* pron. *qozu,* = 'lamb'.

[7] Birbir-lar, from *berber,* 'barber', who was also a bone-setter, a dentist, and cupper.

[8] 'Ottoman = 'Usmān.

[9] Kūkjī, 'herbalist'.

[10] Ṭarsūs, in Cilicia.

[11] Toighār, which is on rising ground (*tepe*).

'Kara Sariklez [1] Takia-sī', near Muftī Hammām.
'Jindi Harem [2] Takia-sī', at Altī Mermer,

Wednesdays.

'Shaikh Halwāī [3] Takia-sī', at the Bozdāghān Kemeri [Aqueduct of Valen].
'Shaikh Nūrī [4] Takia-sī', in the Dabāgh-lar Maidān, Scutari.
'Khoja-zāda Takia-sī', near Top Khāna, at Firūz Āghā.

Thursdays.

'Al Yanāk 'Alī Effendi [5] Takia-sī', in the Mosque of Zehkerjī,[6] at Lalazar.
'Mehmed Shamsī Effendi Takia-sī', near Yenī Bāghcha.
'Rifā'ī Takia-sī', at the Eskī Manzil-khāna, at Scutari.

The Sa'dīas

Fridays.

'Convent of 'Qara Mustafā', near Āq Sarāī, Stambūl.
'Shaikh Ghanī [7] Takia-sī', near the Tabūtjī-lar,[8] Scutari.
'Chakir Agha [9] Takia-sī', near the Salma Tomruk,[10] Stambūl.

[1] Possibly for Qarā-ṣāriqlū, 'black-hatted', *i.e.* the civil functionaries.

[2] Jindī, = 'an expert horseman' in Turk. Ḥarm, the sacred territory of Makka or Madīna: *harm* = 'pyramid'.

[3] Shaikh Halwāī: 'Umr Halwāī is patron-saint of the pastry cooks, *ghūrābīa*, and is buried at Basra; while Halwāī 'Umr, whose tomb is unknown, is patron-saint of the bakers of *gūlāj* (in Bohemian, *kolatsh*) (Evliya, i. p. 2).

[4] Shaikh Nuri. At least five Turkish poets bore the title of Nuri, 'enlightened', and of these two earned that of Shaikh as well: (i) Shaikh 'Abd-ul-Ahmad, son of the judge Safayi Mustafa, grandson of Isma'il the *mufti* of Siwas, and sister's son to the Shaikh Siwasi Effendi, was born in 1594. In 1622 he succeeded to the Shaikhship of the convent of Muḥammad-Pasha (in Scutari), and was also appointed preacher in various mosques. Dying in 1647, he was buried at Aya Sofia near the mausoleum of Sh. Siwasi (*GdOD.* iii. p. 401). He must not be confused with the famous Shaikh 'Abd-ul-Ahad Nuri, or with Nuri Effendi, or with Nuri VII., the *darvish* Ahmad.

[5] Āl Yanāk, 'red cheek' (*yanāq*).

[6] Zehkerjī, probably for *zakhīrejī*, 'grain-merchant'.

[7] Sh. Ghanī may be Muḥammad 'Uṣmān al-Amīr Chanī, born in 1793 in the Hijāz, *d.* in 1853. He founded an order named after him, but also called by himself the Khatimia or 'the sealing'. Though not an off-shoot of the Sa'dias it may be under their protection at Constantinople (*E.R.E.* 10, p. 726). It affects white emblems (*Der Islam*, vi. p. 154).

[8] Tābūtjīlar, 'coffiin-makers'.

[9] Chākir, probably for *Chāqir*, 'falcon' (cf. Shāhbāz. *Chākir* would mean 'servant').

[10] Ṣalma Ṭomrūq, 'house of detention' or 'the stocks'.

'Kantārji [1] Takia-sī', at Dolma Bāghcha.[2]

Saturdays.

'Bālchik [3] Takia-sī', at Daftardār Eskele-sī ['landing-stage'], in Qāsim Pāsha.

Sundays and Wednesdays.

'Yagjī-zāda [4] Takia-sī', at the wharf of Bulban, Scutari.
'Kirpas-sī Mustafā Effendi [5] Takia-sī', at Aiyūb.

Sundays.

'Shaikh 'Alī Effendi Takia-sī', near the Otāgjī-lar [6] Badawī [7] Takia-sī, at Tatavala.
'Sanjāqdār [8] Khair-ud-Dīn [9] Takia-sī', near the Chinār ['Plane'] Mosque.
'Arab Hasan Effendi Takia-sī', near the 'Bāb ['Gate'] Maulavī-khāna'.
'Saif-ud-Dīn Effendi Takia-sī', in Chāūsh Dere, Scutari.

Mondays.

''Abd-ul-Salām [10] Takia-sī', near Hasan Pāsha Khān: also well known under the name of 'Koghajī Shaikh [11] Takia-sī'.
'Finduk-zāda [12] Takia-sī', at Yūksik Kalderim.[13]
'Jigerim Dede [14] Takia-sī', near the Marine Barracks.
''Abd-ul-Bāqī Takia-sī', at Qādī Kiūī.
'Badr-ud-Dīn-zāda-lar [15] Takia-sī', at Psamathia.

Tuesdays.

[1] Qantārjī, 'maker or seller of steelyards', 'a public weigh-master' (Redhouse, p. 1476).

[2] Ṭolma Bāghcha, 'the filled-in garden', a suburb on the European side of the Bosphorus, the site of a former harbour for galleys.

[3] Bālchiq, 'plaster'.

[4] Yaghji, 'a dealer in oil, butter, or the like'.

[5] ? Kirpasi, from *kirpas* or *kirbas*, 'linen cloth'.

[6] Otāgjī-lar, for Otāqjī-lar. Tatavala is one of the 'bad places' of Evliya (i. pt. 2 p. 109).

[7] Badawī, here again the sub-title suggests that the convent is really a Badawīa-Aḥmadīa foundation, protected by the Sa'dia.

[8] Sanjāqdār, 'standard-bearer'.

[9] Hyred Deen in original.

[10] A Sīdī 'Abd-us-Salām al-Asmār ('the dusky') is mentioned by the author of a treatise on the doctrines of the Aḥmadīa (*Der Islam*, vi. p. 152).

[11] Qoghajī, 'a bucket-maker or seller'.

[12] Funduq, Turk. *findiq*='nut' and *findiqjī* would mean 'nutseller'.

[13] Yūksek, 'high': Qāldirim, 'pavement'. The Yūsik Qāldirim is a main thoroughfare leading up the hill from the suburb of Galata to Pera.

[14] Jigerim could only mean apparently 'my heart' (lit. 'my liver').

[15] A Badr-ud-Dīn-zāda, named Maulāna Muḥammad Amīn, born in Shirwān, is buried near the convent of Qaraja Aḥmad Sulṭān (Evliya, i. pt. 2 p. 83). But the Egyptian affinities of the Sa'dīas suggest that the Badr-ud-Dīn alluded to is possibly the one described on p. 157 *supra*.

'Mehmed Effendi[1] Takia-sī', at Qara Gumruk; called also 'Ejder[2] Effendi Takia-sī'.
'Qapū Agha-sī Ismā'īl Āghā Takia-sī', near Āghā Hammām, Scutari.
'Shaikh Jauhar Takia-sī', at the Oq-Maidān.
'Kullami Takia-sī', in the Charsu,[3] and at the Yaila.
'Shaikh Amin Effendi Takia-sī', in the Pashmaqjī Chāyir.
'Hāzirī-zāda Takia-sī', at Sudluja. *Wednesdays.*
''Ābid Chelebī[4] Takia-sī', near Kazi Chashma. *Thursdays.*
'Tāshlī Burūn[5] Takia-sī', near Aiyūb.
'Āt Yamez Takia-sī', near Psamatia, Stambūl.
'Khalīl Pāsha Takia-sī', near the wharf of Dāūd Pāsha, Stambūl.
'Sultān 'Usmān Takia-sī', at Sīra Servi-lar,[6] in the Otāg jī-lar.

The Shāzilīs

'Shāzilī Takia-sī', near 'Alī Bey village. *Mondays.*
'Shāzilī Takia-sī', at the Kaban Dakīk, Stambūl. *Thursdays.*

The Sunbulīs

Fridays.
Convent at Kioja 'Mustafā Pāsha', Stambūl (cf. p. 85).
Convent of 'Sinān Erdebeli', near the Mosque of St. Sophia.
'Balāt Takia-sī', near the Balāt Mosque,[7] Stambūl.
'Kashfī Ja'far Effendi[8] Takia-sī', at Funduklī. *Saturday.*

[1] A Meḥmed Bābā has a *turba* at Stambūl. He was the Saqqā-bāshī of Sulṭān Muḥammad II., and accompanied his army as water-carrier, having an inexhaustible cup of copper. He fell at the taking of Stambūl, and was buried where he was slain. His shrine is visited by all in misfortune, and he is a revealer of fate. But his special function is to bring rain in times of drought in response to vows (F. Schrader, *Konstantinopel*, p. 98). This seems to account for his other name, 'the Dragon saint'.

[2] Ezhder, 'dragon'.

[3] Charshū, 'market-place'. Yaila, 'summer pasture'.

[4] Shaikh 'Ābid Chelebī, a *shaikh* of the time of Sulṭān Bāyazīd II., and a descendant of Jalāl-ud-Dīn Rūmī (Evliya, i. pt. 2 p. 103).

[5] Ṭāshlī Būrūn, 'rocky point'.

[6] Sīra Servī-lar, apparently for Ṣireh Selvī-lar, 'the row of cypresses'; *selvi*, Ṭurk. (vulg.) for Pers. *sarv*, 'cypress'. But von Hammer gives Serai selwleri, 'the Cypresses of the Serai', as one of the quarters of Eyub (*GdOR*. x. p. 648).

[7] Balāṭ, 'palatium'. The Balāṭ Qapū was so called after the palace of the Blachernae, which was situated there (*E.I.* i. p. 873).

[8] Kashfi, 'the holder of revealed truth', a title borne by five Turkish poets, none of whom are recorded as mystics. But the first and last holders of the title claimed to have been the first to hold the censer at the building of Bayazid's mosque. Hence Kashfi I. deemed that he scattered spiritual incense as others did actual incense (*GdOD*. i. p. 284, and ii. p. 515).

Sundays and Wednesdays.

'Bairām Pāsha Takia-sī', near the Khassakī Mosque, Stambūl.

'Mīr Akbar Takia-sī', near the Seven Towers. *Sundays.*

'Safwatī Takia-sī', at the Āghā Chāyir ['meadow'] near the Selivria Gate.

Mondays.

'Hājī Avhad [1] Takia-sī', near the Yadī Kuli or 'Seven Towers'.

Tuesdays.

'Shāh Sulṭān Takia-sī', at Baharīa, called also 'Nijātī [2] Effendi Takia-sī'.

'Ibrahīm Pāsha Takia-sī', at Qūm Qapū, in the Mosque Nishānji.

'Koruk [3] Takia-sī', near Mulla Korani.

'Isā-zāda Takia-sī', near Deragman. *Wednesdays.*

'Sirkajī [4] Talia-sī', at Jubbalī [Jubba 'Alī], Yenī Qapū-sū.

'Mimār Takia-sī', at Mimār Chārsū.

Thursdays.

'Merkez Effendi [5] Hazreteri Takia-sī', outside the Maulavī-khāna.

[1] Avḥad, 'unique'; Ar. awḥad. Sa'īd Ḥusain, the poet Auḥad Shaikhī, devoted himself to the service of Sa'īd 'Abd-ul-Ahad, Shaikh of the Khalwatīs at Constantinople, and was preacher in the convent of al-Ḥaj Auḥad near the Seven Towers in 1655. He died in 1693 (*GdOD.* iii. p. 563). The convent must thus be older. But the title al-Ḥaj or Ḥājī does not appear to have been borne by the eminent mystic poet of Persia, Auḥad-ud-Dīn of Kirmān, who actually associated with Sh. Muḥyī-ud-Dīn ibn ul-'Arabī, and was doubtless influenced by him (E. G. Browne, *Lit. Hist. of Persia*, ii. p. 500). A pupil of Shihāb-ud-Dīn Suhrawardī, he died in 536 H. = A.D. 1141 (Huart, *Saints des Dervishes tourneurs*, i. pp. 345-46).

[2] Najāti, 'the possessor of salvation', a title borne by three Turkish poets, including the great Isa, of Amasia, who died in A.D. 1508. He retired to a cloister, or rather a dwelling, which he built for himself near the tomb of Shaikh Wafa (*GdOD.* i. pp. 162 and 166). Though his adherence to the Sunbulīs is not there recorded, he may well have joined the order whose founder died in 1529.

[3] Koruk, kyūrek, 'oar'.

[4] Sirkajī, 'vinegar-merchant'. A Sirkejī *takia* is one of the most ancient in Constantinople, founded when 'Aiyūb besieged the city. It was afterwards turned into a nunnery, but made a convent again when Muḥammad took it. Its first Shaikh was Uwais (Evliya, i. pt. 1 p. 173).

[5] Merkez = 'centre'. Le Chatelier mentions the Khalwatīa Sunbulīa 'Merkasīa' (*Confréries Mus. du Hedjaz*, p. 50). Shaikh Muslāh-ud-Dīn Effendi, disciple and son-in-law of Muslāh-ud-Dīn Merkez, head of the Khalwatīs, is buried near his master outside the New Gate. For a tale concerning Merkez see Evliya, i. pt. 2 p. 20. Coffee made with water from a well dug at his instance is a cure for fever. He said, "I am a spring of reddish water . . ." and seems to have been a water-diviner. Markaz Effendi was, however, more than a mere miracle-monger, as he busied himself in the instruction of the poor (F. Schrader, *Konstantinopel*, p. 107),

THE 'USHSHĀQĪS

'Mahmūd Effendi Takia-sī', at Gechajī-lar.[1] *Tuesdays.*

Thursdays.

'Khussam-ud-Dīn[2] 'Ushshāqī Takia-sī', at Qāsim Pāsha.

To these must now be added the following Baqtāsh shrines, restored of recent years :

1. The *takia* at Merdiven Keui, said to contain the grave of Shāh Kulu Sulṭān, an ancient warrior-saint who is said to have fought against Constantine, whence it is called his *dargāhī*. It also contains the grave of Azbī Chāūsh. The *takia* possesses a library.
2. The Chamlīja *takia*, of Hājī Tāhir Bābā.

The above are on the Asiatic side of the Bosphorus. On the European side are :

3. The *takia* of Parushān Bābā at Kazlī Chashma, near Yedi Kūla. Destroyed by Maḥmūd II. it was refounded by Parushān Bābā, who died in 1273 H. (A.D. 1857).
4. The *takia* near Takiajī Mahallasī outside the Top Qapū, refounded by 'Abdullāh Bābā after the Revolution of 1908.
5. The *takia* of Ḥāsib Bābā in Kara Agāch.
6. The *takia* called Bādamlī Dargāh, in Sudlija, founded by al-Hajj Ibrāhīm Munīr Bābā at the close of the nineteenth century.
7. Ayūb.
8. Rumelī Hissār.

Besides these eight *takias* there is the Iranlaryñ *takia-sī* at the Saiyid Aḥmad *deresī*, in the great cemetery, only used at the Muḥarram.

NOTE.—The above list is from R. Tschudi's App. to Jacob's *Die Bektaschijje*. It agrees in all essentials with that given by Hasluck in *Annual*, B.S.A. xxi. pp. 99-100, but omits the *takia* at Kariadin (above Eyoub), probably the *takia* at Ayūb of Tschudi's list. Hasluck gives Shāh Kulu's name as

---

where a picturesque account of the shrine and the beliefs attached to it will be found. The Sunbulī monastery of Markaz ('centre') Effendi, founded by Shaikh Muṣliḥ-ud-Dīn Markaz Mūsā, who died in A.D. 1552, is one of the most important in the city (*E.I.* i. p. 872).

[1] Gechajī, 'a maker or seller of felt', from *keche*, 'felt'.

[2] Khussam-ud-Dīn may be for Husām-ud-Dīn, 'Sword of the faith', or for Khussān-ud-Dīn, 'Stars about the North Pole'. Khaṣm = 'antagonist' (Redhouse, *T.-E. Lex.* pp. 783, 846, and 850). In Evliya's day the convent of 'Ushshāqī Effendi, 'near the garden of Hājī Haidar', existed at Qāsim Pāsha (*Travels*, i. 2 p. 45). The roses of the vineyard of the Bosnians were "a blessing from Sh. Boshnāk, a disciple of the order" (p. 46).

Shahkouli. He says that the *takias* at Yedi Koule and Top Qapū are for celibates, and that in that at Rumelī Hissār the *shaikhs* are hereditary and of Albanian descent. It seems that when the *takias* were destroyed the graves were generally spared. Even that of Aḥmad Bābā Shahīd is shown at Scutari. He was *pōst-nashīn* of the *takia* at Merdiven Keui, and was put to death when the Janissaries were suppressed.

INDEX